The Great
Chicago-
Style
Pizza
Cookbook

The Great Chicago-Style Pizza Cookbook

Pasquale Bruno, Jr.

CONTEMPORARY
BOOKS, INC.
CHICAGO

Library of Congress Cataloging in Publication Data

Bruno, Pasquale.
  The great Chicago-style pizza cookbook.

  Includes index.
  1. Pizza.   I. Title.
TX770.B78   1983   641.8'24   83-1830
ISBN 0-8092-5730-0

Published by Contemporary Books, Inc.
180 North Michigan Avenue, Chicago, Illinois 60601
Manufactured in the United States of America
Library of Congress Catalog Card Number: 83-1830
International Standard Book Number: 0-8092-5730-0

To my wife Gale,
for her support and thoughtfulness.

Contents

BAKER'S ADVANTAGE®
BY ROSHCO

DEEP DISH
PIZZA
RECIPES

BASIC CRUST

   1 pkg. yeast
½ cup warm water
   4 cups plus 4 tbls. flour
1⅓ cups hot water
   4 tbls. oil
   4 tbls. sugar
   2 teas. salt

Dissolve yeast in warm water. Set aside. Mix remaining, ingredients together with fork. Add to yeast mixture. Let rise about 20 to 30 minutes. Grease fingers and work dough into pan, shaping up over pan sides. Prebake crust 10 to 12 minutes at 375 °F before filling.

PIZZA TOPPING

2 large cans "special" pizza sauce
1 12-oz. can tomato paste
1 chopped onion
   Pepperoni
   Grean olives
3 cups mozzarella cheese
1 cup Cheddar cheese
   Parmesan cheese

Combine pizza sauce, tomato paste and onion. Spoon over crust. Top with pepperoni, olives, mozzarella and Cheddar cheeses. Sprinkle with Parmesan cheese. Bake at 400 °F 12 to 15 minutes or until bubbly.

EASY DEEP DISH PIZZA

3½ cups Bisquick®
   1 cup water
1½ lbs. ground beef
   ½ cup chopped onion
   ½ tsp. salt
   2 cloves garlic, crushed
   22 oz. tomato sauce
1½ tsp. Italian seasoning
   6 oz. jar sliced mushrooms, drained
   ½ cup green pepper, chopped
2½ cups shredded mozzarella cheese

WO CRUST PIZZA PIE

2 16-oz. pkgs. frozen bread dough
2 tbls. cornmeal
1 cup Parmesan cheese
1½ lbs. hamburger, browned and
    drained
1 med. onion, browned with
    hamburger
1 6-oz. can mushrooms, drained
8 oz. sliced mozzarella cheese
1 15½-oz. can thick spaghetti sauce
    Milk

Shape each loaf into ball and let rise according to package directions until nearly double. Punch down; cover and let rise 10 to 15 minutes. On floured board roll 1 loaf dough into 15" circle. Fit dough into pan; sprinkle with ½ cup Parmesan cheese. Top with meat, onion, mushrooms and cheese slices. Spoon on spaghetti sauce and sprinkle Parmesan cheese on top. Roll remaining dough and place on top. Pinch and flute edges to seal. Cut slits in top. Bake 15 minutes at 400°F. Brush with milk and spinkle with cornmeal. Bake 15 more minutes or until brown. Let stand 10 minutes before cutting.

Chicago, Illinois 60641

Acknowledgments

I would like to thank the many people who helped make this book possible: Ike Sewell, Nick Perrino, Ed Jacobson, Joe Boglio, Sam Levine, Nick D'Amato, Bill Mailhot, the cooks in all the places I visited, and Donald Link, who did the photography. They are all nice people who do things the way they should be done—professionally.

Introduction

Chicago, without a doubt, has become the fertile crescent of the pizza business, and Chicago, not Naples, is the pizza capital of the world. I can make this bold (and somewhat heretical) statement based on the number of pizza restaurants in Chicago. Then there are Chicago's innovative pizza recipes and pizza supply houses; and, most assuredly, Chicago has more serious pizza eaters than any other city in the world. (The drive between pizza restaurants in Chicago is about as long as your car.)

Chicago deep-dish pizza (also known as pizza-in-the-pan) has made its way into all areas of the United States and countries abroad; it has had a resounding effect on the pizza business, as sales continue to increase.

Millions of people visiting this city each year consume hundreds of thousands of pizzas—a Mecca for pizza lovers. Chicago pizza has been flown out on private planes and carried onto commercial flights bound for everywhere. The rubbish cans behind Uno's have been raided by would-be pizza restaurant owners looking for "secrets"—labels from cans, flour bags, and so on. And Chicagoans do more than their share for the pizza business, making regular visits to the originals—Uno's, Due's, Home Run Inn, and Gino's East—and to successful newcomers such as Nancy's, Giordano's, and Edwardo's until their stomachs are awash in tomatoes, cheese, and all those savory toppings.

The unmistakable, mouth-watering aroma of pizza also fills the elevators of apartment buildings all over Chicago, every night of the week, and pizza delivery men are often challenged by offers of a higher price from people coming home from work—"scalped pizza"? While Chicago pizza is often thought of exclusively as the deep-dish type, and visitors to Chicago feel cheated if they get any other kind, every Chicagoan is fiercely loyal to his or her own favorite style of pizza, and favorite pizza restaurant, and will defend them to the last piece.

There are now well over 2,000 pizza restaurants in the Chicago area, serving all types of pizza: thin crust, medium crust, thick crust, stuffed, rolled, square, and stacked. They're yours for the choosing; one has to search hard to find a bad pizza in Chicago.

A Chicagoan, and a serious pizza eater who loves all types, I have included in this book recipes for many different styles of pizza for all pizza eaters, serious or not!

WHERE IT ALL BEGAN

The history of pizza stretches back to the ancient Pompeiians, who formed a coarse bread dough into a rectangular or round shape, topped it with olive oil, and baked it in crude but efficient ovens that were fired by wood.

There is little doubt that pizza is from Naples itself in origin. In the beginning it was a crude, primitive, inexpensive food that was eaten by the poor, but the poor were eating well. Naples is still the hard-core pizza center of Italy, and the stalls that sell pizza there have multiplied many times over. The *Lazzari,* or street urchins, who knew a good thing, are now being pushed aside by tourists from around the world who want to experience pizza at its birthplace. There is always a market for originals.

While Naples may boast of the original, all the regions of Italy now boast of some form of pizza. Each one takes on the identity of the area in which it is made, using ingredients that are abundant and fresh: sardines, anchovies, regional cheeses, salami, sausage, seafood, and so on.

Not even national borders can contain the ubiquitous pizza. Cross over the Italian border at Bordighera, and from there to Marseilles you will find direct descendants of the Neapolitan pizza. In Nice, tasty little black olives are an important part of the pizza topping; in Cannes, they add egg to the crust. Even in Paris, on the Boulevard des Italiens, there are many pizza restaurants, and they are as busy as the hundreds of other types of restaurants surrounding them.

Pizza, like pasta, is one of the oldest of foods; this is a documented fact. And, much like the evolution of many other foods, pizza has become a staple in many parts of the world. With time came the refinements and experimentation, the subtle changes and the not so subtle, the frozen and partially baked versions, the good pizza restaurants and the not so good. Through it all, pizza has managed to survive with such success that it is the single most popular food in the United States today. What makes it so popular? It's tasty, versatile, nutritious, affordable, convenient, and fun to eat. What more can you ask for?

The Great
Chicago-
Style
Pizza
Cookbook

1
Ingredients

FLOUR

Obviously, flour and yeast are the two most important ingredients in making a good pizza crust. I discussed flour and its characteristics with Bill Mailhot, a flour expert with General Mills Co. in Minneapolis. Mr. Mailhot offered the following advice and information.

General Mills' institutional division supplies a brand of flour called H&R (hotel and restaurant) to hotels and restaurants. (I saw this brand being used in the majority of pizza restaurants that I visited.) It is a bleached all-purpose flour with a protein level of 10½–11 percent. (Unbleached flour has about the same percentage, and bread flour has a protein level of 12–12½ percent.) Essentially, the higher the protein level, the higher the gluten level. Gluten makes the dough strong and elastic and able to expand with the growth of the yeast and the air bubbles it makes. Whole wheat flour, for example, is low in gluten; therefore, bread flour is added to increase the gluten when making a whole wheat pizza crust.

Here are a few tips on making the best possible pizza dough:

- *Sugar makes the dough rise faster and helps the crust brown, but too much sugar slows the action of the yeast. Salt also slows the yeast action.*

- *Shortening makes a dough more tender and adds to its keeping quality.*

- *For a more tender dough, use as little flour as you can while still being able to handle the dough. When using bread flour, you must knead it longer to develop the extra gluten.*

YEAST

The yeast used in the recipes in this book is active dry yeast because it has a longer shelf life than cake yeast, it is readily available, and it is easy to measure and use. As a precaution, always check the expiration date stamped on the package.

The modern technology used in processing yeast has practically eliminated the need for proofing yeast; however, the photos in Chapter 3 show you how to do so if you need this assurance.

Follow one basic rule when using active dry yeast to get your dough off to a good start: The water temperature for dissolving the yeast is important—use warm water (105° F.–115° F.). If the water is too cold or too hot, the yeast can be destroyed.

The action that takes place when yeast is combined with flour and liquids is simple: yeast loves to eat the sugars in flour, and this creates alcohol, which, in turn, produces carbon dioxide. This carbon dioxide gas gets trapped within the dough and causes it to rise.

During the kneading of the dough the gluten is formed, creating a framework that acts like a mesh to trap the gas. This is why bread doughs and doughs made of flour with a low gluten content are not as light as those made with a high-gluten flour like bread flour.

TOMATOES

Choosing tomatoes for your pizza is an important consideration; all tomatoes, fresh or canned, are not the same. Some canned tomatoes have a lot of water; some tomatoes are canned before they are fully ripened; some canned pizza sauces will result in a heavy, spicy taste. There is no set formula I can offer, but there is a simple solution—use the tomatoes or sauces that suit your taste. Since the purpose of a cookbook is to guide and advise the user, however, my advice on the tomato question follows.

Extensive testing has led me (and my select group of taste-testers) to a strong liking for a brand of canned tomatoes carrying the label 6 in 1. These are a combination of whole and crushed tomatoes. They are not herbed, the quality is consistent, and they are less acidic than other brands tested. They are a product of Escalon, California, and are available in Italian specialty food stores in three can sizes—16-ounce, 28-ounce, and the restaurant size, 6 pounds, 9 ounces. This brand is highly recommended for deep-dish and stuffed pizza; it is the brand used by many pizza restaurants.

Also recommended are canned Italian-style plum tomatoes. Lisanti, Pezzullo, and Contadina brands are good choices.

The rule to follow with canned tomatoes is simple; try different brands, and when you find one that you like best, stick with it.

When using canned tomato puree, avoid those that are already seasoned; otherwise you have no control over the seasonings that suit your taste. Also, many of the preseasoned types are heavy with preservatives. Some of the brands of canned tomato puree that I recommend are Roman Holiday, Contadina, Pastorelli, Progresso, and Suzy Bel. When using a canned puree, it sometimes helps to simmer it with a balance of seasonings—basil, oregano, parsley—for about 20 minutes. This will help develop the flavor of the tomatoes, which will enhance the taste of the pizza.

Do not add tomato paste to any type of tomatoes used. This will result in an uncharacteristically strong flavor that will impart a burned, heavy taste to the pizza after it is baked.

Fresh tomatoes—regular or plum—should be peeled, seeded, and passed through a food mill, chopped (lightly) in a food processor, or crushed with your hands (see photos in Chapter 3). If the tomatoes are not almost fully ripened (see details under Tomatoes in Chapter 3), don't use them at all; you will not like the results.

Watch the amount of liquid found inside the actual tomatoes, the canned plum variety particularly, to avoid soggy-top pizza.

CHEESE

What is true of tomatoes is also true of cheese: all cheese is not the same. In pizza making we are dealing with three basic types of cheese: mozzarella, Parmesan, and Romano. (There are however, two exceptions in this book.)

MOZZARELLA—This cheese in Italy is made from the milk of the water buffalo; the United States variety is made from cow's milk. Our mozzarella works better on pizza, but the Italian mozzarella is better for eating by itself.

Part-skim or low-moisture mozzarella is my choice for pizza making. One pizza restaurant that I visited combined three different brands of mozzarella—the owner's reasoning was that the milk delivered by the cow has a taste relative to what she ate; therefore, the cheese could be sweeter, milder, or blander. His secret was to blend the cheeses to develop a unique taste.

Mozzarella cheese may be sliced thin and placed directly on the dough or grated and sprinkled over the sauce (see photos in Chapter 3).

PARMESAN—Generally, in pizza making, Parmesan cheese is used sparingly, as the mozzarella plays the starring role. Used discreetly, though, Parmesan can add a nice flavor dimension to any pizza. Always use freshly grated Parmesan when it is available. Take caution if using bottled Parmesan; it can be very salty.

ROMANO—For simplification, Romano cheese is a pecorino cheese (made from sheep's milk). It is similar to Parmesan and used more often than Parmesan in Italy from Rome south to the tip of the boot. It has a sharper, more insistent, less sweet taste than Parmesan. Some pizza restaurants use a combination of Parmesan and Romano (usually more of the former).

SAUSAGE

Most pizza restaurants buy their sausage in bulk from meat purveyors. In Chicago Anichini Brothers seem to be the popular choice of many, as they will season the ground pork to the buyer's particular taste—pepper, fennel, salt, etc. For home use there are two basic choices.

1. Italian sausage in the casing is usually available three ways: sweet or mildly seasoned with pepper but without fennel; mild, which has a bit more pepper and fennel or not, depending on the maker; and hot, which contains black pepper and crushed red pepper.

2. Bulk ground pork is usually ground from pork butts and normally has no seasonings at all. There is an advantage here in that you can season it to your taste. Be careful that it doesn't have an excessive amount of fat.

TOPPINGS

What a series of groans, head shaking, and cries of *"that's strange,"* I could elicit if I listed all the toppings I have seen, eaten, waved away, or had suggested to me. I will leave toppings to you and your personal tastes; oblige me, though, by reading these few thoughts on the subject.

When using vegetables—green peppers and onions, for example—saute them in a bit of oil until slightly softened, drain off the excess oil, and use at once or reserve for later use.

Trendy raw vegetables, such as zucchini, carrots, and cauliflower, do not have a place on pizza.

Fruits of any shape, taste, or color do not belong on pizza.

Resist all those urges to make a Pizza Supremo Deluxe Special by topping your pizza with a week's worth of leftovers or Aisle C from the supermarket.

SEASONINGS

Pizza seasonings are pretty straightforward.

OREGANO—This is an herb with a sharp and heavy taste. It adds an excellent flavor to tomatoes, but it should be used judiciously. Marjoram, a cousin to oregano, is a bit milder and can be used as a substitute for oregano.

BASIL—This herb has a natural affinity for the tomato. Deliciously spicy and aromatic, it is a superb addition to any pizza sauce. If using fresh basil, tear a freshly washed leaf into small pieces and add directly to the sauce or topping. Dried basil does not have the same distinct flavor as fresh, but it is better than none at all. Use half the amount of dried as you would use fresh.

OTHER SEASONINGS—Used in combination or separately, thyme, bay leaf, fennel, and parsley can be added to pizza. Let your palate be your guide.

2
Equipment

PIZZA PANS

1.

This is the pan you will need for making deep-dish and stuffed pizza. It is made of steel, it is two inches deep, and the diameter you select is relative to the number you wish to serve. When you buy this pan it will have a shiny look. If you avoid scouring the pan after use, it will eventually turn black like those pictured in the restaurant photos. Once this happens the pan will be highly seasoned and will give you a better pizza crust. (See seasoning and cleaning instructions in this section.)

2.

This pan is similar to the one above in size and shape. The difference is the removable bottom, which makes it easier to cut and serve the pizza on the metal tray bottom after it is pushed up from the ring. It works the same as a removable-bottom quiche pan.

3.

The rectangular jelly roll pan pictured here is excellent for making what I call Italian bakery pizza. The size shown is 15″ × 10″ × 1″ deep. This size works perfectly with the Italian Bakery Pizza recipe in this book.

4.

Pictured here are four sizes of pizza pans for making thin and medium crust pizza. The sizes shown are 8-inch, 10-inch, 12-inch, and 14-inch. They are flat with an edged, rolled rim. These pans are made of aluminum and are heavyweight restaurant quality.

METHOD FOR SEASONING: All the metal pans shown must be seasoned before using the first time. Wash the pan in hot, sudsy water. Rinse well and dry thoroughly. Put about a tablespoon of cooking oil on a piece of paper towel. Rub the oil on the entire cooking surface of the pan, bottom and sides, lightly, leaving no puddles. Put the pan in the oven and "bake" for 45 minutes at 325° F. Remove the pan from the oven. After the pan has cooled, wipe off any excess oil with clean paper towels. The pan is now ready for use. Remember to avoid excessive scouring with abrasive scouring pads, as this will destroy the seasoning of the pan.

PIZZA SCREEN

5.

This is called a pizza screen, a little-known but excellent device for baking thin and medium crust pizza. It is also the only way (if you must) to bake a frozen pizza. The screen should be brushed lightly with oil (use a pastry brush) each time it is used. When using the screen, do not put the oven rack too close to the oven floor or the crust will brown too quickly.

BAKING STONES

6.

Shown are two styles of baking stones for baking pizza and bread. The stones that I recommend most highly are made by a company called Old Stone Oven. Suffice it to say that I invented these stones in 1970 and claim that they are the best on the market today. I am no longer involved with the company but can testify to their performance and durability. The point of these baking stones is that they are somewhat porous, which means that the stone will draw out the moisture from the crust. This results in a nicely browned non-soggy crust.

The stone is put into the oven during the preheat cycle. The pizza is slid onto the stone and baked directly on the hot stone. The hotter the stone, the crisper the crust. Complete instructions for care and use of the stone is included in the manufacturer's package.

PIZZA PEEL

7.

Pictured is a wooden pizza peel. You may have seen them used in pizza houses. The one shown here is 16″ × 18″ with a 6″ handle. This is an invaluable piece of equipment for use with the baking stones described earlier; it makes it easy to slide the pizza onto the preheated stone.

PIZZA CUTTER

8.

Pizza cutters come in a variety of sizes and styles. I prefer the larger style with a cutting wheel that is 4 inches in diameter (the large one pictured on top). Note that the size of the handle enables the user to get a good firm grip that ensures greater leverage and cutting power.

PAN GRIPPER

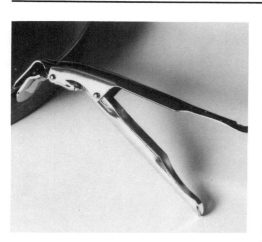

9.

This is called a pan gripper. You may have seen one used in pizza houses. It is an ingenious device for moving a deep dish pizza pan in and out of the oven. It can be used for other pans in your kitchen as well.

3
Basic Techniques

USING THE PIZZA SCREEN

The pizza screen, as noted earlier, is an excellent piece of equipment for obtaining a crisper crust on a pizza.

1.

Dip a pastry brush in some olive oil or vegetable oil and brush the surface of the screen.

2.

Roll out the dough or stretch it with your hands. Stretching is a good, optional method for shaping a pizza crust. Put both hands under the dough (make a fist with each hand— thumbs tucked away to avoid making holes) and move your hands apart as you rotate the dough.

3.

Gently pull the dough and continue to rotate it until the desired size is reached.

4.

Lay the dough on the oiled side of the screen.

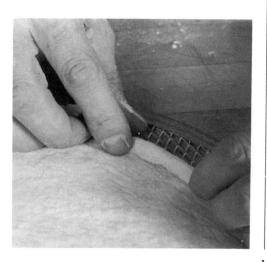

5.

Roll an edge around the entire perimeter of the crust. The dough is now ready for the topping.

6.

A finished pizza that was cooked on the screen.

To avoid oven mess, be careful of excess liquid in the tomatoes and avoid using too many tomatoes. If you make a thick, rolled edge and keep the topping about one-half inch from the edge, your pizza sauce shouldn't drip over the edge of the crust. Also remember to put the screen on the top rack of your oven—away from the heating element—to prevent the crust from becoming too crispy.

USING THE BAKING STONE

The baking stone is an excellent piece of equipment for baking pizza (see details in Chapter 2). Place the baking stone in the oven on the lower rack. Preheat the oven as directed in the recipe.

The process of getting the pizza on and off the stone is made easier if you use a pizza peel.

1.

Sprinkle the pizza peel quite liberally with cornmeal. This looks like a lot, but most of it will stay on the peel after the pizza has been slid onto the stone.

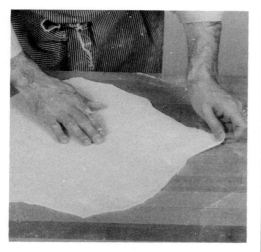

2.

Roll out the dough with a rolling pin or stretch it with your hands.

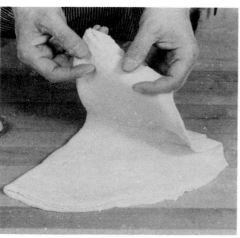

3.

Fold the dough in half, then in half again. Make sure the dough is not sticky.

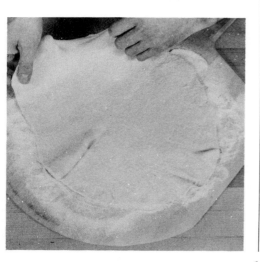

4.

Unfold the dough on the pizza peel and roll an edge as shown for using the pizza screen. Put the topping on the pizza.

5.

Slide the pizza onto the hot stone by using a swift, jerking motion with your hand.

Bake the pizza as directed in the recipe. Remember, the hotter the stone, the crisper the crust, and the baking time may be slightly reduced.

Take special care when handling the stone, especially when it is hot.

TOMATOES

Fresh vine-ripened plum tomatoes would always be my first choice for a first-class pizza topping. There is little chance that those purchased in a store will be ripe enough to use at once. Three to four days before they are to be used, put the tomatoes on a windowsill or countertop that receives plenty of light. When they have turned a dark, deep red, and the skin is not tight, they are ready to be used. The ideal, of course, is to grow your own plum tomatoes. Seasonal as homegrown tomatoes are, those moments of pleasure when eating a succulent vine-ripened plum tomato are hard to beat. The type I grow, and find the tastiest, are Roma VF and San Marzano.

HOW TO PEEL AND SEED PLUM TOMATOES

1.

Lower the tomatoes into a pot of boiling water.

2.

Retrieve them with a slotted strainer or spoon after just 10–15 seconds.

3.

Using a sharp knife, cut out the core end (the tapered end).

4.

Peel away the skin. It should come away easily, often in one piece.

5.

Cut the tomato in half lengthwise, which facilitates removing the seeds.

6.

Open up the tomato to expose the interior. Do all the work over a bowl to catch the juices, should they be needed.

7.

Run your thumb or finger down the length of the tomato to remove the seeds.

Chop the tomatoes coarsely with a knife or squeeze them with your hands. They are now ready for use. Drain off the excess liquid, especially if you are making a thin crust pizza.

Some people like the taste of the seeds in the tomatoes. In that case, after the tomatoes have been cored and peeled, simply crush them with your hand as shown in the photos. This method is recommended for canned plum tomatoes, too.

HOW TO MAKE THE DOUGH FOR A PIZZA CRUST

The photo sequence that follows shows the basic method for making pizza dough. Alternate methods will be detailed in selected recipes.

1.

The water temperature for dissolving the yeast should be between 105° F. and 115° F. (41° C.–45° C.). An instant read thermometer is an accurate method for testing the water. If you don't have one, test the water by holding the inside of your wrist under the faucet; it should feel very warm. It is better, if in doubt, to have the water a little too cool rather than too hot; water that is too hot will kill the yeast.

2.

Sprinkle the dry yeast into the water and stir well to dissolve the yeast. Set aside.

3.

It will take about five minutes for the yeast to start foaming (this is also known as "proofing"). Adding a small amount of sugar to the water and yeast will accelerate the foaming. Modern yeast processing methods, however, have practically eliminated this proofing step; dried yeast can be mixed with the warm water and flour right in the mixing bowl. Both methods will be used in the recipes.

4.

Measure the flour. Use the "dip and sweep" method—dip the measuring cup into the flour and sweep off the excess with a spatula or the back of a knife. Do not sift the flour.

5.

Put the flour into a mixing bowl. Add the salt, if used, and mix thoroughly.

6.

Make a well in the center of the flour; add the liquid ingredients—yeast mixture, additional water, and oil, if used.

7.

Stir the dough with a spatula or wooden spoon until a rough ball is formed. Now, use your hands and bring it all together into a tight ball of dough. Turn the dough out of the bowl onto the counter.

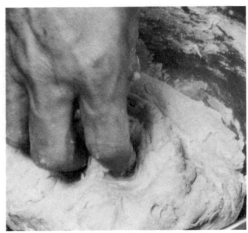

8.

Start the kneading process. Push down firmly on the dough with the heel of your hand, turn the dough, and repeat the process. Continue doing this until the dough is smooth and doesn't feel at all sticky. If the dough does stick to your hand during the kneading, dust it lightly with flour.

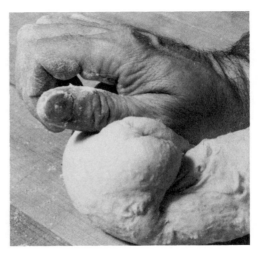

9.

The dough is now ready for rising. Dust both sides lightly with flour and put it into a large floured bowl.

10.

Cover the bowl completely with plastic wrap and then with a towel. Place the bowl in a warm, draft-free location.

11.

The dough will double in bulk in 60–90 minutes, depending on the recipe, the warmth of the kitchen, the liquids used, and so forth.

12.

After the dough has doubled in bulk, punch it down. Pull off any small pieces of dough that may have stuck to the sides of the bowl and knead them into the ball of dough.

13.

Turn the dough onto the counter and knead it for a minute or two. It is now ready for use.

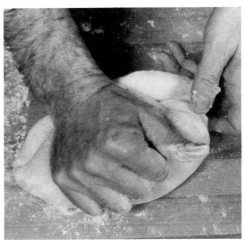

NOTE: Most pizza restaurants retard the dough. That is to say, the kneaded dough is refrigerated overnight. Early the next morning it is brought to room temperature. It is then ready to use. The same technique can be used at home. Don't retard the dough for more than 24 hours, however, as it starts to lose the strength needed during baking.

HOW TO MAKE PIZZA DOUGH IN A FOOD PROCESSOR

1.

Add the required amount of flour (dip and sweep method) to the workbowl, fitted with the steel blade.

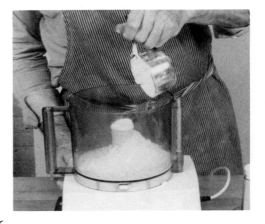

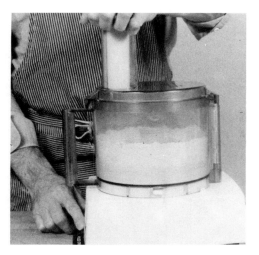

2.

Add the salt, if used, and turn on the machine for about 5 seconds to combine the salt and flour.

3.

Add the wet ingredients—yeast/water mixture, oil, and additional water.

4.

Turn on the machine and process until a ball of dough is formed. If the dough does not ball up, add warm water in small doses through the feed tube until it does. If the dough seems excessively sticky and wet, add a bit more flour.

5.

The dough should be soft and slightly sticky if done properly. Notice that there is very little dough left on the sides and bottom of the workbowl.

6.

Place the dough on the counter and knead it by hand for several minutes, until it is smooth. Dust with flour if it sticks to your hand at all.

7.

This is the dough when ready for use. Notice that it is smooth and satiny.

4
Preparing Various Types Of Pizza

HOW TO MAKE A CHICAGO DEEP-DISH PIZZA

This is the authentic, step-by-step method for making the original Chicago deep-dish pizza. It is the same method used at *Pizzeria Uno* and *Due* in Chicago.

1. This deep-dish pizza pan is 14 inches in diameter and 2 inches deep. Oil the bottom and sides of the pan with olive oil or vegetable oil, using just enough for a light coating.

2. Take a ball of once-risen dough; this piece of dough weighs 26 ounces (see recipe for specific ingredients). Spread the dough in the pan with your fingers. The dough will spread easier if you let it sit in the pan (as shown in the photo) for about 10 minutes.

3. Work the dough by pushing it with your fingers until it completely covers the bottom of the pan.

4. Pull the edge of the dough up to form a lip. Now cover the pan completely with a towel and let the dough rise in the pan, in a warm place, for 30 minutes. Preheat the oven to 475° F.

5.

After the dough has risen in the pan for 30 minutes, prick the entire crust with the tines of a fork. Parbake the crust (no topping at this point) in the preheated oven for exactly four minutes. This gives the dough its initial "spring." This is a necessary step as the weight of the cheese and the tomatoes will compact the dough and cause it to be heavy. After the four-minute parbake, brush the crust lightly with olive oil—use your fingers or a pastry brush.

6. Lay the thinly sliced mozzarella cheese over the crust. Do not put the cheese over all the dough—leave a ½-inch edge around the perimeter.

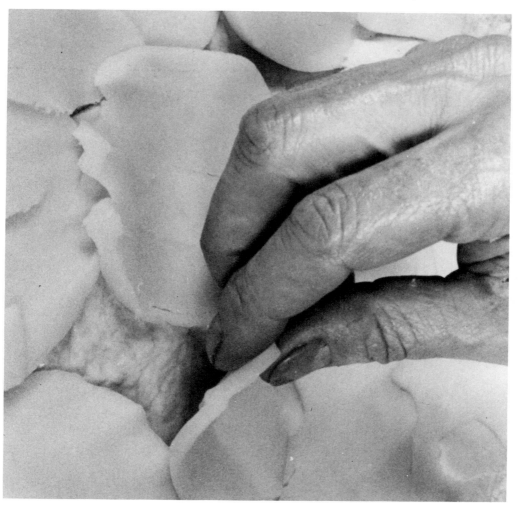

7. Add the tomatoes. Here I am using 6-1 tomatoes that have been seasoned with basil, oregano, and salt (see recipes for exact amount).

8. Sprinkle on freshly grated Parmesan cheese.

9. Drizzle olive oil on top. Notice that the topping stops about ½ inch from the edge of the dough. The pizza is now ready for the oven.

10. Your finished Chicago Deep-Dish Pizza. Buon appetito!

HOW TO MAKE A CHICAGO STUFFED PIZZA

1. For this particular stuffed pizza, we are using spinach. This is fresh spinach that has been washed, dried, and chopped lightly in a food processor.

2. To the spinach we add grated mozzarella cheese and mix thoroughly. Set aside. (These two steps can be done earlier in the day. Refrigerate the mixture in that case.)

3. You will need two pieces of once-risen dough. The bottom layer should be rolled out three inches larger than the diameter of the pan. The second piece, or top layer, should be the exact diameter of the pan.

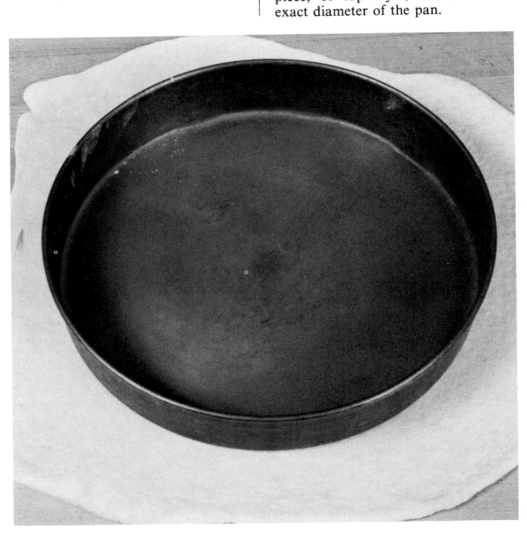

4. Oil the pan. Spread the oil over the bottom and sides—a light film.

5. Take the larger piece of dough and lay it in the pan.

6. Push the dough into the bottom and sides of the pan.

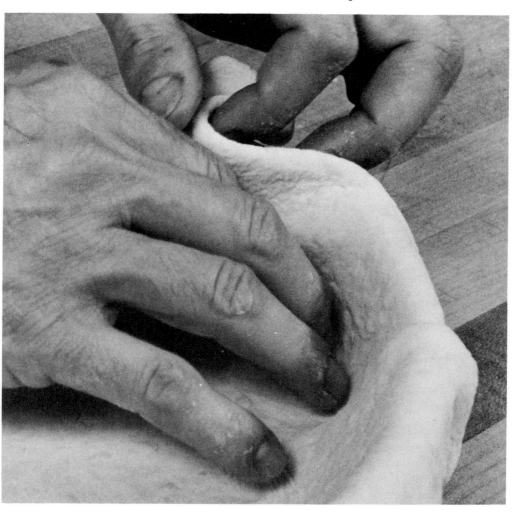

7. Work the dough around the pan. Notice the overlap.

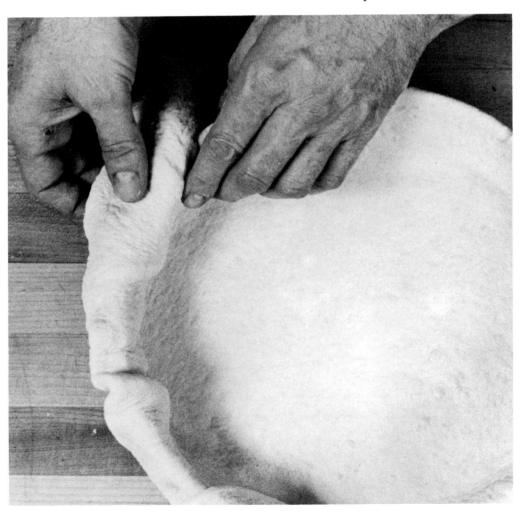

8. Trim off the excess dough, but leave about ¼ inch for the folding.

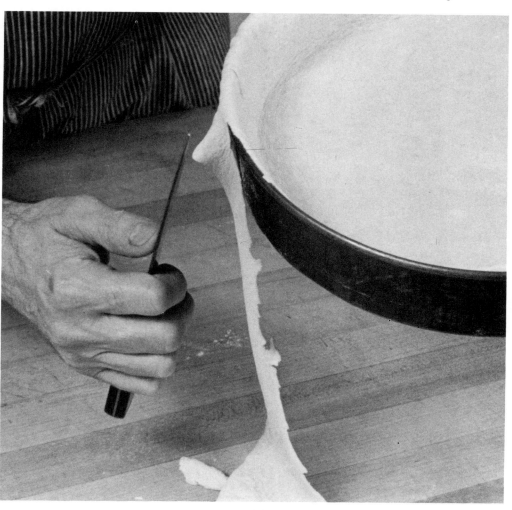

9. Add the spinach/cheese mixture to the pan.

10. Add the top layer of dough.

11. Roll the two edges of dough together to form a thick border.

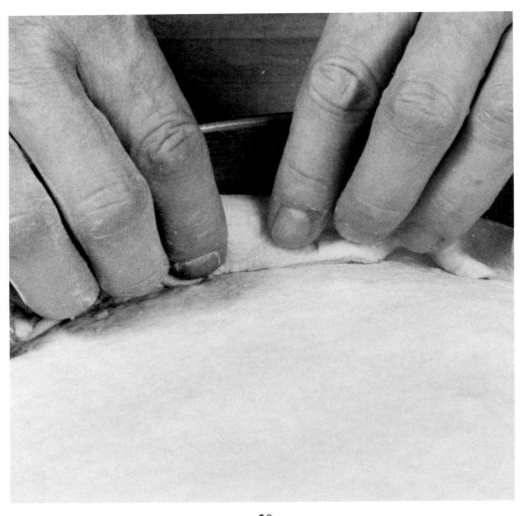

12. This photo shows how the edge is formed.

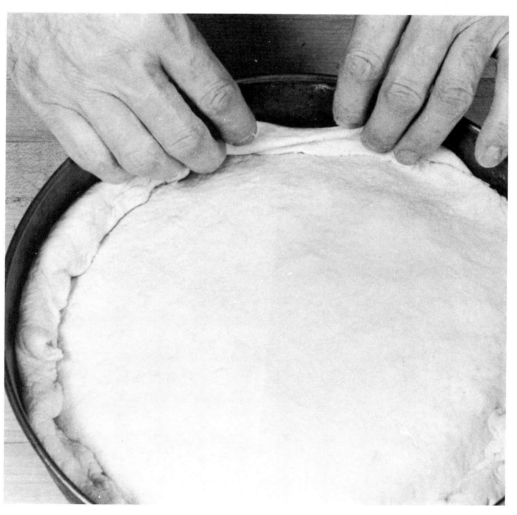

13. Make a slit in the center of the top crust to allow the steam to escape.

14. Add the tomatoes. (Those in the photo are canned plum tomatoes that have been crushed and drained. They were seasoned with basil, oregano, olive oil, and salt.) Freshly grated Parmesan cheese can be sprinkled on the tomatoes, if you wish. The pizza is now ready for baking.

15. A spinach stuffed pizza, ready to be enjoyed. It is easier to cut and serve if removed from the pan.

HOW TO MAKE A THIN CRUST PIZZA

Eliminate pizza-making problems by having everything ready to go when it is needed.

1. Grate the mozzarella cheese ahead of time. Notice the side of the grater used in the photo.

2. Grating the cheese, as shown, eliminates the excessive stringiness of the melted cheese.

3.

Also have the tomatoes ready. Here the tomatoes are seasoned in the bowl, ready to go.

4. Oil the pizza pan. Use your fingers or a pastry brush. Only a light film of oil is necessary.

5. Prior to rolling out, stretch the dough with your fingers. This will make rolling with the pin easier.

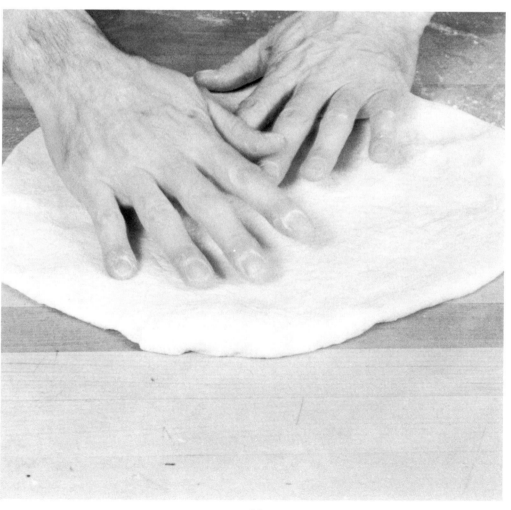

6. Roll out the dough, working it into a sort of circle. Flour it lightly should it stick to the rolling pin.

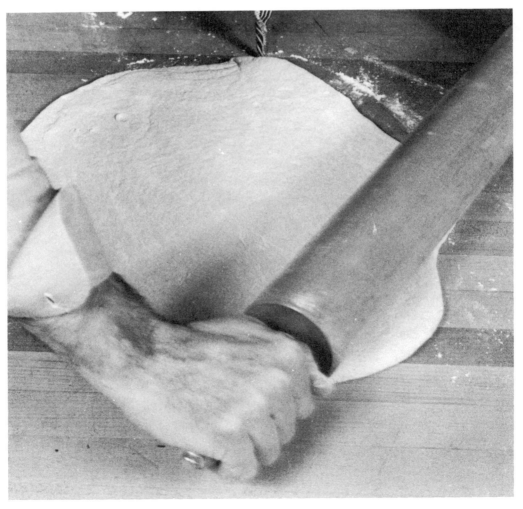

7. Lay the dough on the oiled pan.

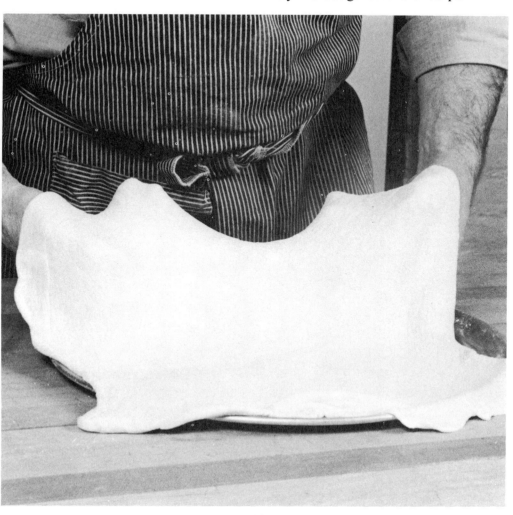

8. Roll the edges with your fingers to form a thick border around the pizza.

9. Here is a closer view of making the edge.

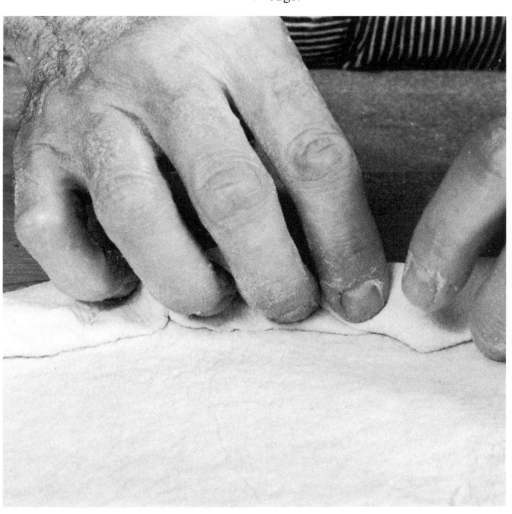

10. Push the dough toward the outside rim of the pan.

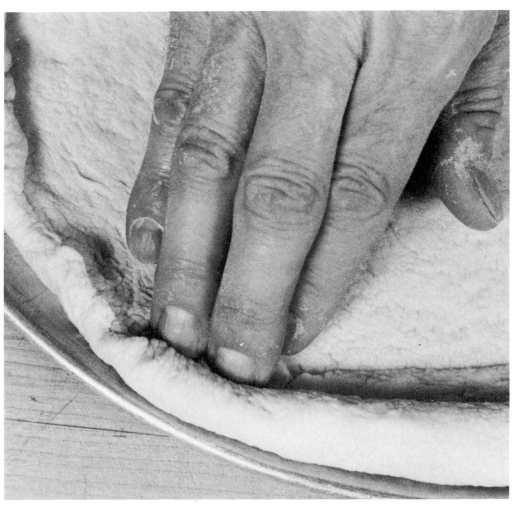

11. Using a pastry brush or your fingers, brush on some olive oil. This helps seal the dough to prevent a soggy crust.

12. Add the tomatoes, spreading them evenly.

EDWARDO'S

NANCY'S

Edwardo's on North Dearborn Street in Chicago features new ideas, like this thin crust, whole wheat pizza with fresh spinach.

Owner Ed Jacobson's innovative approach to pizza-making is reflected in his use of fresh herbs from the restaurant's on-location herb farm. Here he (right) and the author sample two favorite selections, thin crust and stuffed pizza.

Tom Cirrincione, owner of award-winning Nancy's pizza.

Nancy's pizza—a truly delicious creation, stuffed with cheese, mushrooms, onions, and green peppers.

GINO'S EAST

Started in 1966, Gino's East is a landmark for pizza lovers.

D'AMATO'S

HOME RUN INN

Nick D'Amato, owner of D'Amato's Bakery, shoveling a pizza into his 90-year-old stone hearth oven.

Joe Fiore loves his work, and the delectable foccaccia he bakes at D'Amato's.

Quality ingredients and know-how are the trademarks of Home Run Inn pizza.

Nick Perrino proudly displays the boxed pizza that he sells to a select number of stores in the Chicago area.

GIORDANO'S

UNO AND DUE

Joe Boglio, owner of Giordano's chain of pizza restaurants, prepares his famous double-crusted pizza.

A taste-bud-tingling slice of famous spinach stuffed pizza.

Aldean Stoudamire has been making pizzas at Uno's for 26 years. A lot of pizza has passed through her hands—"too many to count," she says.

A man who knows and likes the pizza business, the progenitor of Chicago Pizza, Ike Sewell, in his comfortable office.

13. Add the grated mozzarella cheese evenly over the tomatoes.

14. Here I am adding Italian sausage that was removed from the casing. The sausage will cook through better if you flatten it instead of using thick chunks.

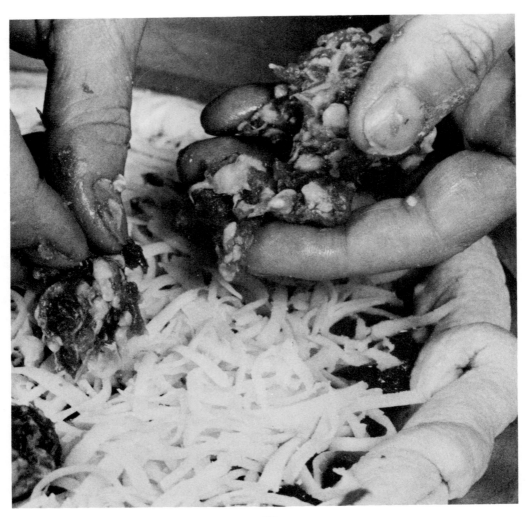

15. Drizzle olive oil over the pizza, and it is ready for baking.

The thickness of the crust is relative to the rising times used. After the first rising, if the dough is rolled out and the pizza assembled and baked, the crust will be thinner. If, after the first rising, the dough is rolled out and formed on the pan (no topping at this point), and allowed to rise for 30 minutes or so, the resulting crust will be thicker. The choice is yours.

Pizza shells of the thin crust type can be frozen for future use. Follow all the steps for making a thin crust pizza, up to brushing the dough with oil and adding the topping. Prick the crust with the tines of a fork and bake in a preheated 450° F. oven for 5 minutes. Put the crust on a cooling rack. When completely cool, wrap in plastic wrap and aluminum foil and freeze.

When ready to use, bring the frozen shell to room temperature, add your favorite topping, and bake.

16.

A thin crust pizza, ready to be enjoyed.

HOW TO MAKE AN ITALIAN BAKERY PIZZA

1. Italian bakery pizza is generally rectangular in shape. Roll out the dough with a pin, or stretch it by hand.

2. Place the dough in the oiled pan and stretch it into the sides and corners. This is easier to do if you let the dough rest in the pan for about 10 minutes.

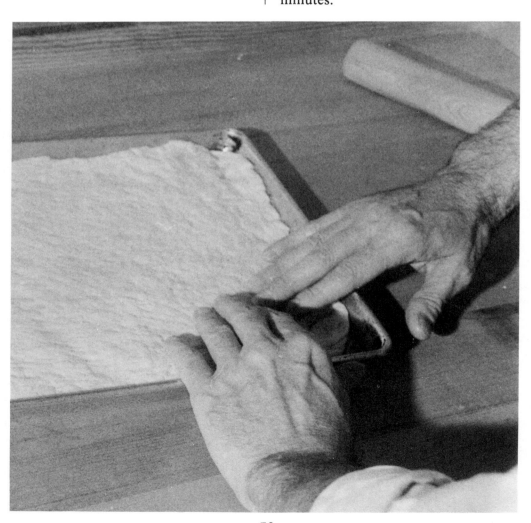

3. The tomatoes are spread over the dough. Use puree or fresh or canned Italian plum tomatoes with the seasonings you prefer.

4. The tradition, many years ago, for this type of pizza was to use only grated Parmesan cheese. Now most people prefer mozzarella cheese. Here I am using grated Parmesan, sprinkled evenly over the tomatoes.

5. Here is the Italian bakery pizza ready for the oven. I drizzled some good Italian olive oil over the tomatoes and added some torn fresh basil leaves.

6. Italian bakery pizza out of the oven, ready to eat.

5
Pizza Recipes

DEEP-DISH PIZZA NO. 1

This is as authentic a Chicago deep-dish pizza recipe as you will find. Using high-fired rotating ovens or stacked ovens, pans that have turned black from heavy use, and giant mixers that do a superb job of kneading the dough gives a slight edge to the restaurant pizza maker. In spite of that edge, you can do a great pizza at home with this recipe.

YIELD: 1 14-inch deep-dish pizza

EQUIPMENT

Liquid measuring cups
Dry measuring cups and spoons
4- to 5-quart mixing bowl
2- to 3-quart mixing bowl
Cheese grater
14-inch round pizza pan 2 inches deep

DOUGH

1½ packages active dry yeast
½ cup warm water (105° F.–115° F.)
1 tablespoon sugar
3½ cups unbleached flour
1 teaspoon salt
½ cup yellow cornmeal
¼ cup vegetable oil
½ cup warm water

TOPPING

1 28-ounce can 6–1 brand tomatoes
   or 1 28-ounce can Italian-style
   plum tomatoes (see note)
1 teaspoon dried basil or 2 teaspoons
   chopped fresh basil
1 teaspoon oregano
Salt to taste
10 ounces mozzarella cheese, sliced
   thin
¼ cup freshly grated Parmesan cheese
½ pound Italian sausage, casing
   removed
Olive oil

DOUGH: Dissolve the yeast in the ½ cup of warm water. Add the sugar and stir well. Set aside. In a large mixing bowl, combine 3½ cups of flour, salt, and cornmeal. Make a well in the center of the flour. Add the yeast mixture, the vegetable oil, and the ½ cup of water. Stir and mix thoroughly until the dough cleans the sides of the bowl and a rough mass is formed.

Turn the dough out of the bowl onto a well-floured work surface. Knead and pound the dough (dust with flour if the dough sticks to your hands) for 5–6 minutes until it is smooth and soft. Dust the dough and a large mixing bowl lightly with flour. Place the dough in the bowl and cover the bowl with plastic wrap and a kitchen towel. Let rise in a warm place until doubled in bulk, about 1½ hours.

After the dough has doubled in bulk, turn it out of the bowl and knead it for about 2 minutes. Oil the bottom and sides of the pizza pan. Spread the dough in the pan with your fingers and palm. (It will spread more easily if you let it sit in the pan for about 10 minutes.) Work the dough until it covers the bottom of the pan. Pull the edges of the dough up to form a lip or a pronounced border all around the pan. Preheat the oven to 475° F. Prick the dough bottom with a fork at ½-inch intervals and parbake the crust for exactly 4 minutes in the preheated oven. Brush the crust lightly with olive oil.

TOPPING: In a 2- to 3-quart mixing bowl, combine the tomatoes, basil, oregano, and salt. Set aside.

TO ASSEMBLE AND BAKE: Lay the slices of mozzarella cheese evenly over the crust (not the border). Spoon the tomatoes over the cheese. Sprinkle the grated Parmesan over the tomatoes. Next, add the Italian sausage—flatten the sausage pieces (about the size of a half-dollar) between your thumb and forefinger and distribute evenly over the tomatoes. Drizzle about 1 tablespoon olive oil on top.

Bake the pizza in a preheated 475° F. oven on the bottom oven rack for 5 minutes; move the pizza to an oven rack 2 slots above the lower rack and bake an additional 30 minutes, until crust is lightly browned and sausage is cooked through.

NOTES: If using the canned plum tomatoes, drain off all the liquid, put the tomatoes into a mixing bowl, crush them with your hand, and add the seasonings.

In pizza restaurants the raw sausage is put on top of the cheese, not the tomatoes. They can get away with this due to the high heat in their ovens.

Baking the pizza for 4 minutes on the lowest oven rack assures a better crust bottom. Parbaking the crust is necessary to give the dough its initial spring; otherwise, the weight of the cheese and tomatoes will compact the dough and cause it to be heavy.

Needless to say, other toppings of your choice—onions, peppers, anchovies, mushrooms, and so forth can be added.

DEEP-DISH PIZZA NO. 2

This is another version of the deep-dish pizza that Chicago is famous for. The addition of milk to the dough makes it softer and richer. The use of ricotta as the dominant cheese is a nice variation.

YIELD: 1 14-inch deep-dish pizza

EQUIPMENT

Liquid measuring cups
Dry measuring cups and spoons
3- to 4-quart mixing bowls
2- to 3-quart mixing bowls
14-inch round pizza pan, 2 inches
    deep

DOUGH

¾ cup warm water (105° F.–115° F.)
2 packages active dry yeast
3 cups unbleached flour
6 tablespoons milk

TOPPING

1 28-ounce can Italian-style plum
    tomatoes
4 ounces mozzarella cheese, grated
10 ounces ricotta cheese
1 large egg
1 teaspoon salt

DOUGH: Dissolve yeast in warm water, stir well, and set aside. Put the flour in a 3- to 4-quart mixing bowl. Make a well in the flour. Add the yeast mixture and the milk. Stir and mix until the dough cleans the sides of the bowl.

Turn the dough out of the bowl onto a floured work surface. Knead the dough for 5–6 minutes (dust lightly with flour if the dough sticks to your hands) until it is soft and smooth. Lightly flour a 3- to 4-quart mixing bowl and the dough. Place the dough in the bowl. Cover the bowl with plastic wrap and a kitchen towel. Set the bowl in a warm place for the dough to rise (1–1½ hours).

Take the dough out of the mixing bowl; knead for about 2 minutes. Oil the bottom and sides of the pizza pan. Stretch the dough gently with your hands to about ½ the size of the pizza pan. Put the dough in the pan and stretch it with your fingers and palm until it completely covers the bottom of the pan. Pull the dough up the sides of the pan to form a pronounced border. Cover the pan with a kitchen towel. Let the dough rise in a warm place for 30 minutes.

TOPPING: Drain off ½ the liquid from the can of tomatoes, put them into a bowl, and crush them by hand. Set aside.

In a 2- to 3-quart mixing bowl, combine the mozzarella, ricotta, egg, and salt. Refrigerate the mixture if not using at once.

TO ASSEMBLE AND BAKE: Preheat oven to 450° F.

After the dough has risen the second time, lay in the ricotta cheese mixture to cover the crust (not the border). Spoon on the half-drained tomatoes.

Bake the pizza in the preheated oven, on the lowest oven rack, for 5 minutes. Move the pan 2 slots above the lower rack and bake an additional 20–25 minutes, until the crust is brown.

NOTES: The dough can be made a day ahead and refrigerated: flour the kneaded dough and a mixing bowl; cover the bowl with plastic wrap; put the bowl into the refrigerator. The dough will rise (slower, of course).

Take the dough out of the refrigerator at least 1 hour before using. Dust with flour and knead for 2–3 minutes. Proceed with the stretching in the pan.

STUFFED PIZZA WITH SPINACH

Stuffed pizza has become something of a sensation in Chicago in the past few years. The combination of flavors is expansive; the end result becomes an exciting taste treat.

YIELD: 1 12-inch round stuffed pizza

EQUIPMENT

Liquid measuring cups
Dry measuring cups and spoons
4- to 5- quart mixing bowl
2- to 3-quart mixing bowl
Cheese grater
Rolling pin
12-inch pizza pan, 2 inches deep

DOUGH

3 teaspoons sugar
2 packages active dry yeast
1¼ cups warm water
  (105° F.–115° F.)
3¼ cups (more or less) bread flour
3 teaspoons salt
4 tablespoons vegetable oil

SAUCE

1 28-ounce can 6–1 brand tomatoes
  and 1 16-ounce can 6–1 brand
  tomatoes or 1 28-ounce can plum
  tomatoes and 1 14-ounce can plum
  tomatoes
2 tablespoons olive oil
1 teaspoon oregano
2 teaspoons chopped fresh basil or 1
  teaspoon dried basil
1 teaspoon salt
1 clove garlic, crushed
¼ cup freshly grated Parmesan cheese

STUFFING

¼ pound fresh spinach
8 ounces mozzarella cheese, grated

DOUGH: Dissolve sugar and yeast in water. Set aside.

Mix flour and salt in a large 4- to 5-quart mixing bowl. Make a well in the flour; add the yeast mixture and vegetable oil. Mix and knead thoroughly until a rough mass of dough is formed that cleans the sides of the bowl. Turn the dough out onto a floured work surface; knead for 5–6 minutes until the dough is smooth and soft. Dust with flour if the dough sticks to your hands. Dust the dough lightly with flour; place it in a lightly floured mixing bowl. Cover the bowl with plastic wrap and a kitchen towel. Set it in a warm place to rise for 1–1½ hours, until doubled in bulk.

Punch down the dough; turn it out onto a work surface and knead for about 1 minute. Divide the dough into pieces—1 slightly larger. Roll out the larger piece (this will be the bottom layer of dough) until it is about 3 inches larger than the pan and ⅛ inch thick. Oil the bottom and sides of the pan. Place the dough in the pan; push it into the bottom and sides. The dough should overlap the pan by about 1 inch. Trim off the excess overlap with a knife. Set the pan aside. Roll out the second piece of dough until it is about the same size as the pan.

SAUCE: If using the canned plum tomatoes, drain off all the liquid from each can and crush the tomatoes with your hands and then add the remaining ingredients (do not cook).

STUFFING: Wash the spinach thoroughly and dry it completely. Remove the stems. Finely chop the leaves (food processor works nicely). In a 2- to 3-quart mixing bowl, combine the spinach and mozzarella.

TO ASSEMBLE AND BAKE: Preheat the oven to 475° F. Put the spinach and cheese mixture into the pan. Lay the second piece of dough over the spinach-cheese mixture. Crimp the 2 edges of dough together with your fingers to form a thick border. Press down on the filling with your hand. Cut a 1-inch slit in the center of the top crust to allow steam to escape.

Spread the tomato mixture evenly over the top crust.

Bake the pizza in the preheated oven, on the lowest rack, for 10 minutes. Move the pizza to an oven rack 2 slots above the lower rack and bake an additional 25–30 minutes, until the crust is lightly browned.

VARIATIONS: 1. Substitute blanched (3–4 minutes) chopped broccoli for the spinach. You will need about 1 pound.

2. Leave out the spinach entirely and add 1 pound of Italian sausage (casing removed, cooked, and drained) to the grated mozzarella cheese.

3. Instead of the sausage, use chopped salami, cubed ham, or chopped mortadella.

VEGETARIAN STUFFED PIZZA

The sauce and dough in this pizza are quite similar to those in the preceding recipe. The difference is in the vegetables.

YIELD: 1 12-inch round stuffed pizza

EQUIPMENT

Liquid measuring cups
Dry measuring cups and spoons
4- to 5-quart mixing bowl
2- to 3-quart mixing bowl
Cheese grater
10-inch skillet or sauté pan
Rolling pin
12-inch pizza pan, 2 inches deep

DOUGH

3 teaspoons sugar
2 packages active dry yeast
1¼ cups warm water
   (105° F.–115° F.)
3¼ cups (more or less) bread flour
3 teaspoons salt
4 tablespoons vegetable oil

SAUCE

1 28-ounce can 6-1 brand tomatoes
   and 1 16-ounce can 6-1 brand
   tomatoes or 1 28-ounce can plum
   tomatoes and 1 14-ounce can plum
   tomatoes
2 tablespoons olive oil
1 teaspoon oregano
2 teaspoons chopped fresh basil or 1
   teaspoon dried basil
1 teaspoon salt
1 clove garlic, crushed
¼ cup freshly grated Parmesan cheese

STUFFING

1 small zucchini, sliced
1 green pepper, chopped
1 medium yellow onion, chopped
1 small eggplant, peeled and chopped
8 ounces mozzarella cheese, grated

DOUGH: Dissolve the sugar and yeast in the water. Set aside.

Mix the flour and salt in a large 4- to 5-quart mixing bowl. Make a well in the flour; add the yeast mixture and vegetable oil. Mix and knead thoroughly until a rough mass of dough is formed that cleans the sides of the bowl. Turn the dough out onto a floured work surface; knead for about 5 minutes, until the dough is soft and smooth. Dust as needed with flour if the dough sticks to your hands. Dust the dough lightly with flour; place it in a lightly floured mixing bowl. Cover the bowl with plastic wrap and a kitchen towel. Set the bowl in a warm place to rise for 1–1½ hours, until doubled in bulk.

SAUCE: If using the canned plum tomatoes, drain off all the liquid from each can and crush the tomatoes by hand, then add the seasonings and combine thoroughly (do not cook).

STUFFING: In a skillet or sauté pan, cook the vegetables in about 2 tablespoons of olive oil in this order: pepper, zucchini, eggplant, onion. Cook each separately, in the same pan, until slightly softened; do not overcook. In a mixing bowl, combine the vegetables with the grated cheese.

TO ASSEMBLE AND BAKE: Use the same method as in the preceding recipe.

THIN CRUST PIZZA WITH FONTINA AND MOZZARELLA

YIELD: 1 12-inch pizza

EQUIPMENT

Liquid measuring cups
Dry measuring cups and spoons
3- to 4-quart mixing bowls
2- to 3-quart mixing bowls
Rolling pin
Cheese grater
14-inch flat pizza pan or pizza screen

DOUGH

1 teaspoon active dry yeast
**½ cup plus 1 tablespoon warm water
  (105° F.–115° F.)**
1½ cups bread flour
½ teaspoon salt
1 tablespoon olive oil

TOPPING

**1 28-ounce can Italian-style plum
  tomatoes or 1½ pounds fresh plum
  tomatoes, peeled, seeded, and
  chopped**
1 teaspoon basil
1 teaspoon oregano
Salt to taste
3 ounces mozzarella cheese, grated
3 ounces fontina cheese, grated
**8 ounces Italian sausage, casing
  removed**
Olive oil

DOUGH: Dissolve yeast in warm water and stir well. Set aside.

Combine flour and salt in a mixing bowl. Make a well in the center of the flour. Add the yeast mixture and the oil. Stir and mix with a wooden spoon until a rough ball of dough is formed and the dough cleans the sides of the bowl. Turn the dough out of the bowl onto a lightly floured work surface. Knead the dough for 7–8 minutes (dust with flour if the dough feels sticky) until it is smooth and soft. Dust the dough and a 3- to 4-quart mixing bowl lightly with flour. Put the dough in the bowl; cover with plastic wrap and a kitchen towel. Put the dough in a warm place to rise for 1½ hours, until doubled in bulk.

After the dough has doubled in bulk, punch it down and turn it out of the bowl onto a lightly floured work surface. Knead it lightly for about 2 minutes. Roll out the dough into a circle approximately 13 inches in diameter and ⅛ inch thick. Fold the dough in ½ and then in ½ again and transfer to a 14-inch flat pizza pan or pizza screen that has been lightly oiled. Roll the edge of the dough to form a thick border all around. Cover the dough with a kitchen towel and let rise in a warm place for 30 minutes. Preheat the oven to 425° F.

TOPPING: While the dough is rising the second time, combine the tomatoes with the seasonings in a mixing bowl. If using the canned tomatoes, drain off all the liquid, put them into a small bowl, and crush them by hand. Grate the cheeses and combine them. Prepare the sausage.

TO ASSEMBLE AND BAKE: Brush the dough with a thin film of olive oil. Sprinkle the cheese evenly over the dough. Spoon on the tomatoes. Flatten small pieces of sausage between your thumb and index finger (about the size of a half-dollar) and place evenly over the tomatoes. Drizzle a small amount of olive oil over the pizza.

Bake the pizza in the preheated 425° F. oven for 15–20 minutes, until the crust is nicely browned.

VARIATIONS: Other possible cheese combinations are fontina and Gruyère or fontina and muenster, or muenster alone. (Real fontina is difficult to find in some parts of the country. A facsimile, fontinella, will do in a real pinch.)

SARDINIAN PIZZA

This pizza combines the classic elements of pizza made in Sardinia—a rich, eggy crust, olives, and anchovies.

YIELD: 1 10-inch pizza

EQUIPMENT

Liquid measuring cups
Dry measuring cups and spoons
2-'to 3-quart mixing bowls
10-inch sauté pan or skillet
Garlic press
Rolling pin
Cheese grater
14-inch pizza screen, flat pizza pan,
  or baking stone

DOUGH

½ package active dry yeast
¼ cup warm water (105° F.–115° F.)
1½–2 cups unbleached flour
4 tablespoons butter, softened
½ teaspoon salt
1 large egg

TOPPING

1 clove garlic, put through garlic
  press
2 tablespoons olive oil
1 medium onion, sliced thin
1 28-ounce can Italian-style plum
  tomatoes, well drained and
  chopped or 1¼ pounds fresh plum
  tomatoes, peeled, seeded, and
  chopped
1 tablespoon chopped fresh basil or 1
  teaspoon dried
Salt to taste
¼ cup freshly grated Parmesan cheese
1 dozen small pitted black olives
6–8 anchovy fillets, washed free of
  salt
Olive oil

DOUGH: Dissolve yeast in warm water and stir well. Set aside.

In a mixing bowl, combine 1½ cups flour with the softened butter and the salt. Make a well in the center of the flour and add the yeast mixture and the egg. Stir and mix well with a wooden spoon until a rough ball of dough is formed. If the dough is excessively sticky, add flour ¼ cup at a time until the dough cleans the sides of the bowl. Turn the dough out onto a floured work surface. Knead the dough (dust with flour if the dough sticks to your hand) until soft and smooth. Dust a 2- to 3-quart mixing bowl and the dough lightly with flour. Place the dough in the bowl; cover the bowl with plastic wrap and a kitchen towel. Set the bowl in a warm place and let the dough rise for 1½–2 hours, until doubled in bulk.

After the dough has doubled in bulk, punch it down and turn it out of the bowl onto a floured work surface. Knead the dough lightly for about 2 minutes. Roll out the dough to get a circle approximately 11 inches in diameter. Fold the dough in ½ and then in ½ again. Transfer it to an oiled flat pizza pan, pizza screen, or baking sheet. Roll the edge of the dough to form a thick border. Cover the dough with a kitchen towel and let it rise in a warm place for 30 minutes.

TOPPING: While the dough is rising the second time, lightly brown the garlic in the oil in a sauté pan or skillet over medium heat. Add the onion; cook and stir until lightly softened. Add the tomatoes and cook until most of the moisture has evaporated. Add the basil. Salt to taste.

TO ASSEMBLE AND BAKE: Preheat oven to 425° F. Spoon the tomatoes over the crust. Sprinkle the Parmesan over the tomatoes. Arrange the olives on the tomatoes. Lay on the anchovies between the olives. Drizzle a small amount of olive oil over the topping.

Bake in the preheated 425° F. oven (middle rack) for 15 minutes. Lower the temperature to 350° F. and bake an additional 10 minutes (4–5 minutes with a stone), until the crust is a light brown.

If using a baking stone, put the stone on the lowest oven rack. Slide the assembled pizza off the pizza peel onto the hot stone. Bake for 20 minutes at 375° F.

PIZZA RICOTTA

When I was very young one of my favorite snacks was a slice of freshly baked Italian bread smeared with homemade ricotta cheese. This recipe delivers a bready thick crust pizza that is an adaptation of that snack.

YIELD: 1 9-inch pizza

EQUIPMENT

Liquid measuring cups
Dry measuring cups and spoons
2- to 3-quart mixing bowls
Cheese grater
9-inch round quiche, tart, or cake
  pan, ¾–1 inch deep

DOUGH

¼ cup warm water (105° F.–115° F.)
2 teaspoons active dry yeast
2 cups all-purpose bleached flour
1 teaspoon salt
½ cup milk

TOPPING

1 14½-ounce can Italian-style plum
  tomatoes or 5–6 fresh plum
  tomatoes, peeled, seeded, and
  chopped
¾ cup ricotta cheese
¼ cup grated Parmesan cheese
1 teaspoon salt

DOUGH: Dissolve yeast in warm water and stir well. Set aside.

In a 2- to 3- quart mixing bowl, combine the flour and salt. Make a well in the center of the flour. Add the yeast mixture and the milk. Stir and mix with a wooden spoon until a rough mass of dough is formed and the dough cleans the sides of the bowl. Turn the dough out of the bowl onto a lightly floured work surface. Knead the dough for 5–6 minutes (dust lightly with flour if the dough sticks to your hand) until smooth and soft. Dust the dough and a mixing bowl lightly with flour. Place the dough in the bowl; cover the bowl with plastic wrap and a kitchen towel. Set the bowl in a warm place for the dough to rise, about 1½ hours, until doubled in bulk.

After the dough has doubled in bulk, punch it down and turn it out of the bowl onto a lightly floured work surface. Knead the dough lightly for about 2 minutes. Oil the pan. Spread the dough into the pan, using your fingers and the palm of your hand.

Cover the pan with a kitchen towel; let rise for 45 minutes in a warm place.

TOPPING: If using the canned tomatoes, drain off ½ the liquid. Put the tomatoes into a small bowl and crush them by hand.

Combine the tomatoes with the ricotta, Parmesan, and salt. (Some ricotta cheese can be very bland, so you may wish to increase the amount of salt. Also, some ricotta cheese is watery. If this is the case, put it into a strainer to drain for 10–15 minutes.)

Refrigerate the mixture if not using within 15 minutes.

TO ASSEMBLE AND BAKE: Preheat the oven to 400° F. After the dough has risen the second time, spoon the topping onto the crust, leaving a ¼-inch border of dough uncovered.

Bake in the preheated oven at 400° F. for 40–45 minutes, until the crust is brown and the pizza is cooked through.

WHOLE WHEAT PIZZA WITH BROCCOLI

YIELD: 1 12-inch pizza

EQUIPMENT

Liquid measuring cups
Dry measuring cups and spoons
3- to 4-quart mixing bowls
1-quart saucepan
2-quart saucepan
Cheese grater
Rolling pin
14-inch flat pizza pan or pizza screen

DOUGH

1 package active dry yeast
¼ cup warm water (105° F.–115° F.)
1 cup bread flour
1¼ cups whole wheat flour
1 teaspoon salt
⅔ cup milk

TOPPING

10 ounces tomato puree
½ teaspoon oregano
½ teaspoon basil
¼ teaspoon salt
⅛ teaspoon pepper
1 10-ounce package frozen chopped broccoli
8 ounces mozzarella cheese, grated
Olive oil

DOUGH: Dissolve the yeast in the ¼ cup of warm water. Set aside.

In a 3- to 4-quart mixing bowl, combine the bread flour, whole wheat flour, and salt. Stir and mix thoroughly.

Make a well in the center of the flour. Add the yeast mixture and the milk. Stir and mix with a wooden spoon until a rough ball of dough is formed. Turn the dough out of the bowl onto a floured work surface. Knead the dough for 6–8 minutes, until it is soft and smooth. Dust a 3- to 4-quart mixing bowl and the dough lightly with flour. Put the dough into the bowl; cover with plastic wrap and a kitchen towel. Put the dough in a warm place to rise for 1½ hours, until doubled in bulk.

After the dough has doubled in bulk, punch it down, turn it out of the bowl onto a lightly floured work surface; knead for 2 minutes. Roll out the dough into a circle about 13 inches in diameter and ⅛ inch thick. Fold the dough in ½ and then in ½ again; transfer it to an oiled flat pizza pan or pizza screen. Fold the edges of the dough all around to form a thick border. Cover the dough with a kitchen towel and set the pan in a warm place for the dough to rise for 30 minutes.

TOPPING: While the dough is rising the second time, combine the tomato puree and the seasonings in a small saucepan. Simmer over low heat for 10–15 minutes.

Cook the broccoli according to package directions. Drain well. Put the pan back on low heat and cook and stir for 2 minutes to dry out the broccoli. Set aside.

TO ASSEMBLE AND BAKE: Preheat the oven to 450° F. Lightly brush the top of the crust with olive oil. Spoon the sauce on the crust. Spread the broccoli evenly over the sauce. Sprinkle on the grated mozzarella. Drizzle a small amount of oil over the cheese.

Bake in the preheated oven for 15–20 minutes, until the crust is nicely brown. If using the pizza screen, place it towards the upper part of the oven to avoid overcooking the crust.

VARIATION: Fresh broccoli can also be used. Wash, break into flowerets, chop the stalk, and then blanch it for 3–4 minutes. Do the stalks first as they will take slightly longer to cook.

THIN CRUST PIZZA WITH PEPPERS, ONIONS, AND PEPPERONI

YIELD: 1 12-inch pizza

EQUIPMENT

Liquid measuring cups
Dry measuring cups and spoons
2- to 3-quart mixing bowls
10-inch fry pan or sauté pan
Cheese grater
Rolling pin
14-inch flat pizza pan or pizza screen

DOUGH

1 package active dry yeast
¾ cup warm water (105° F.–115° F.)
2 cups unbleached flour
Pinch of salt
1 tablespoon olive oil

TOPPING

10 ounces tomato puree
1 teaspoon oregano
1 teaspoon basil
Salt to taste
1 tablespoon olive oil
1 medium-sized green pepper,
   chopped
1 medium-sized yellow onion,
   chopped
6 ounces mozzarella cheese, grated
8–10 slices pepperoni

DOUGH: Dissolve yeast in warm water, stir well, and set aside.

Combine flour and salt in a 2- to 3-quart mixing bowl. Make a well in the flour. Add the yeast mixture and the olive oil. Mix and stir the dough until a rough ball is formed and the dough cleans the sides of the bowl. Turn the dough out of the bowl onto a floured work surface. Knead the dough for 5–6 minutes (dust lightly with flour if the dough sticks to your hands) until it is smooth and soft. Lightly flour the ball of dough. Place the dough in a lightly floured mixing bowl; cover the bowl with plastic wrap and a kitchen towel. Let rise in a warm place for 1½ hours, until doubled in bulk.

Take the risen dough out of the bowl and knead lightly for 2 minutes, dusting with flour as necessary. Roll out the dough to approximately 13 inches in diameter and ⅛ inch thick. Fold the dough in ½ and then in ½ again; transfer it to an oiled flat pizza pan or pizza screen. Roll a thick border edge around the dough. Cover the pan with a kitchen towel and set it in a warm place to rise for 20 minutes.

TOPPING: While the dough in rising the second time, combine the tomato puree, oregano, basil and salt to taste in a small mixing bowl.

In a fry pan or sauté pan, over medium heat, sauté the onions and the peppers until just cooked through. Sweating the onions and peppers under a cover or a round of wax paper over low heat will help maintain the identity of the vegetables without burning them. It is best to cover the pan after the first 2 minutes of cooking (turn down the heat a bit). Stir occasionally.

TO ASSEMBLE AND BAKE: Preheat the oven to 450° F. Distribute the tomato puree evenly over the crust; add the onions and peppers and the grated mozzarella. Arrange the pepperoni slices on top of the cheese.

If using a baking stone, transfer the folded dough onto a pizza peel that is liberally covered with cornmeal. Unfold the dough, add the toppings, and slide the pizza onto the baking stone in the preheated oven. Bake the pizza in the middle of the preheated oven for 20–25 minutes, until the crust is brown.

ITALIAN BAKERY PIZZA NO. 1

This is one version of a thick, bready pizza that is usually a sideline product for Italian bakeries. It is simple in appearance but delectable in taste. The dough is given a light-in-texture head start by making a sponge.

YIELD: 1 15-by-10-inch pizza

EQUIPMENT

Liquid measuring cups
Dry measuring cups and spoons
4- to 5-quart mixing bowls
Cheese grater
2- to 3-quart bowl
15-by-10-inch baking pan, 1 inch deep

DOUGH

For the sponge:
½ cup warm water (105° F.–115° F.)
1 package active dry yeast
¾ cup unbleached flour

For the dough:
¾ cup (more or less) warm water
2 tablespoons vegetable oil
Pinch of salt
3½ cups unbleached flour

TOPPING

3 cups 6-1 brand tomatoes or tomato
  puree
2 teaspoons oregano
Salt to taste
2 tablespoons olive oil
10 ounces mozzarella cheese, grated

DOUGH: First, make the sponge: Put the ½ cup of warm water into a 4- to 5-quart mixing bowl. Sprinkle the yeast on the water and stir to dissolve. Add the flour and mix well with a wooden spoon. Cover the bowl with plastic wrap and a kitchen towel. Set aside in a warm place to rise for 1 hour.

After the initial sponge rise, add most of the ¾ cup of water, vegetable oil, salt, and the rest of the flour to the sponge. Stir and mix thoroughly. If the dough seems at all stiff, add more warm water.

Turn the dough out of the bowl onto a floured work surface. Knead the dough for about 8 minutes until it is smooth and soft. If the dough feels sticky, dust with flour. Place the dough in a lightly floured, 4- to 5-quart mixing bowl; cover the bowl with plastic wrap and a kitchen towel. Set the bowl in a warm place and let the dough rise for 1½ hours, until doubled in bulk.

After the dough has doubled in bulk, punch it down and turn it out of the bowl onto a lightly floured work surface. Knead the dough for about 2 minutes. Lightly oil the bottom and sides of the pan. Stretch the dough with your hands until it is about the size of the pan. Place the dough in the pan and press and stretch until it fits the pan. (The dough will stretch into the pan much easier if it rests in the pan for about 5 minutes or more.) Try to make the dough an even thickness. Set the pan in a warm place, covered with a kitchen towel. Let the dough rise in the pan for 40 minutes.

If you experience difficulty in stretching the dough in the pan with your hands, use a rolling pin to stretch the dough to the size of the pan.

TOPPING: In a bowl, combine the tomato puree and the oregano. Taste for salt.

TO ASSEMBLE AND BAKE: Preheat the oven to 425° F. After the dough has risen in the pan, spread the tomato puree evenly over the surface of the dough. Leave about a ½-inch border. Drizzle the oil over the tomatoes. Sprinkle on the grated mozzarella.

Bake the pizza in the preheated oven for 30–35 minutes, until the crust is brown and the dough cooked through.

VARIATIONS: Needless to say, any additional toppings such as sausage, onions, pepperoni, etc., can be added.

ITALIAN BAKERY PIZZA NO. 2

The addition of olive oil makes the crust on this pizza slightly coarser and richer in taste. The tomatoes are used sparingly; Parmesan cheese adds to the tomato bread flavor.

YIELD: 1 18-by-13-inch pizza

EQUIPMENT

Liquid measuring cups
Dry measuring cups and spoons
4- to 5-quart mixing bowl
2- to 3-quart mixing bowl
Cheese grater
18-by-13-inch baking pan, 1 inch deep
   (also known as a half sheet pan)

DOUGH

1 package active dry yeast
¼ cup warm water (105° F.–115° F.)
4 cups unbleached flour
2 teaspoons salt
¼ cup olive oil
1¼ cups (more or less) warm water

TOPPING

1 28-ounce can Italian-style plum
   tomatoes, drained and crushed by
   hand, or 1½ pounds fresh plum
   tomatoes, peeled, seeded, and
   crushed
1 teaspoon oregano
1 teaspoon basil
Salt to taste
2 tablespoons olive oil
½ cup freshly grated Parmesan cheese

DOUGH: Dissolve the yeast in ¼ cup of warm water and stir well. Set aside.

In a 4- to 5-quart mixing bowl, combine the flour and salt. Make a well in the center of the flour. Add the yeast mixture, olive oil, and 1 cup of water. Stir and mix the dough until it forms a rough mass. Add the other ¼ cup of water if the dough is stiff. Turn the dough out onto a floured work surface and knead vigorously (slap the dough down on the counter occasionally) until the dough is soft and smooth.

Lightly flour a 4- to 5-quart mixing bowl and the ball of dough. Place the dough in the bowl. Cover the bowl with plastic wrap and a kitchen towel. Set the bowl in a warm place and let the dough rise for 1½ hours, until doubled in bulk.

After the dough has doubled in bulk, punch it down and turn it out of the bowl onto a lightly floured work surface. Knead the dough for about 2 minutes. Lightly oil the bottom and sides of the pan. Place the dough in the pan; stretch and press the dough with your fingers and the palm of your hand as much as possible. Let the dough rest for 5–10 minutes, then finish stretching the dough until it covers the bottom of the pan. Cover the pan with a kitchen towel; let the dough rise in a warm place for 45 minutes.

TOPPING: *The canned tomatoes must be completely drained of all liquid for this recipe to work properly.* In a mixing bowl, combine the tomatoes, oregano, basil, and salt to taste.

TO ASSEMBLE AND BAKE: Preheat the oven to 450° F. After the second rise in the pan, spread the tomatoes evenly over the dough, leaving a ¼-inch border all around. Drizzle the olive oil over the tomatoes. Sprinkle the Parmesan cheese over the tomatoes.

Bake the pizza in the preheated oven for 30–35 minutes until the crust is golden brown and the dough is cooked through.

VARIATIONS: 1. Using fresh basil leaves, washed and chopped, in place of the dried, adds a lot of extra flavor.

2. If you don't have a baking pan of the size required, use one that is 15 by 10 by 1 inch deep. Cut off about 6 ounces of the once-risen dough and freeze for later use or give it a second rise and bake a small loaf of bread.

BREAD LOAF PIZZA

This recipe will deliver a pizza that is quite thick—almost bread loaf size. The interaction of the honey with the yeast gives this dough extra lightness and makes it subtly sweet.

YIELD: 1 8-inch round pizza

EQUIPMENT

Liquid measuring cups
Dry measuring cups and spoons
2- to 3-quart mixing bowl
1-quart mixing bowl
Cheese grater
8-inch round cake or pizza pan, 1½–2
    inches deep (a 9-inch pan can also
    be used; the dough will not be as
    thick)

DOUGH

¾ teaspoon honey
⅔ cup warm water (105° F.–115° F.)
1 teaspoon vegetable oil
2–2¼ cups bread flour
¼ teaspon salt
1 teaspoon active dry yeast

TOPPING

½ cup tomato puree
3–4 fresh basil leaves, washed and
    torn into bits, or ½ teaspoon dried
    basil
½ teaspoon oregano
Salt to taste
1 teaspoon olive oil for the pan
2 teaspoons olive oil for the topping
½ cup grated mozzarella cheese

DOUGH: In a 2- to 3-quart mixing bowl, dissolve the honey in the warm water. Add the vegetable oil and stir thoroughly. Add 1½ cups of the flour, the salt, and the yeast. Stir and mix thoroughly. Add another ½ cup of flour and mix until the dough comes clean from the sides of the bowl.

Drop the dough onto a floured work surface; knead for 5–6 minutes, until smooth and soft. Add more flour as you knead; the dough will be sticky at first. Lightly flour the ball of dough and a mixing bowl. Cover the bowl with plastic wrap and a kitchen towel. Let the dough rise in a warm place for about 1 hour, until doubled in bulk.

After the dough has doubled in bulk, punch it down and turn it out of the bowl onto a lightly floured work surface. Knead the dough lightly for about 2 minutes.

Oil the bottom and sides of the pan. Press the dough into the pan with your fingers until it covers the bottom. Cover the pan with a kitchen towel. Set the pan in a warm place. Let the dough rise in the pan for a minimum of 45 minutes.

TOPPING: While the dough is rising the second time, combine the tomato puree, basil, and oregano. Salt to taste.

TO ASSEMBLE AND BAKE: Preheat the oven to 400° F. Spread the tomato mixture evenly over the dough, leaving a ¼-inch border. Drizzle 2 teaspoons of oil over the tomatoes and top it off with the grated mozzarella.

Bake the pizza in the preheated oven for 20 minutes at 400° F. and 5–10 minutes at 425° F. until the crust is light brown and cooked through.

VARIATIONS: As with any pizza, additional toppings are a matter of choice and taste.

PIZZA BREAD SANDWICH

This is a totally unique creation that will serve nicely as a party appetizer or a main course.

YIELD: 1 8-inch round pizza

EQUIPMENT

Liquid measuring cups
Dry measuring cups and spoons
2- to 3-quart mixing bowls
1-quart saucepan
8-inch skillet or fry pan
Cookie sheet or flat pizza pan
Cheese grater
8-inch cake or pizza pan, 1½–2 inches
   deep

DOUGH

¾ teaspoon honey
⅔ cup warm water (105° F.–115° F.)
1 teaspoon vegetable oil
2–2¼ cups bread flour
¼ teaspoon salt
1 teaspoon active dry yeast

TOPPING

½ cup tomato puree
1 teaspoon oregano
2 tablespoons grated Parmesan cheese
Salt to taste
¼ pound Italian sausage, casing
   removed
½ teaspoon fennel
2 teaspoons olive oil
6–7 thin slices mozzarella cheeese

DOUGH: In a 2- to 3-quart mixing bowl, dissolve the honey in the warm water. Add the vegetable oil and stir thoroughly. Add 1½ cups of flour, the salt, and the yeast. Stir and mix thoroughly. Add another ½ cup of flour and mix until the dough comes clean from the sides of the bowl. Drop the dough onto a floured work surface; knead for 5–6 minutes, until smooth and soft. Add more flour as you knead; the dough will be sticky at first. Lightly flour the ball of dough and a mixing bowl. Cover the bowl with plastic wrap and a kitchen towel. Let the dough rise in a warm place for about 1 hour, until doubled in bulk.

After the dough has doubled in bulk, punch it down; turn it out onto a lightly floured work surface. Knead the dough lightly for about 2 minutes.

Oil the bottom and sides of a pan with about 1 teaspoon olive oil. Stretch the dough into the pan with your fingers until it covers the bottom. Cover the pan with a kitchen towel. Set the pan in a warm place. Let the dough rise in the pan for 45 minutes.

TOPPING: While the dough is rising the second time, combine the tomato puree, oregano, Parmesan cheese, and salt, in a small saucepan. Simmer over low heat for 6–7 minutes.

In a small skillet, cook the sausage with the fennel in the oil until cooked through, breaking up the larger chunks with a fork. Drain off all fat. Add the sausage to the pan with the tomatoes. Keep the sauce warm.

TO ASSEMBLE AND BAKE: Preheat the oven to 400° F. After the second rise, bake the pizza bread in the preheated oven for 35–40 minutes, until light brown and cooked through. Turn the bread out of the pan onto a cooling rack. When the bread is cool enough to handle, slice off the top ½ inch horizontally with a serrated or very sharp knife. Distribute the tomato mixture evenly over the top of the bottom piece of bread. Spread the cooked sausage evenly over the tomatoes. Replace the top lid of the bread; press down lightly. Lay the sliced mozzarella on top, letting it drape down a bit over the sides.

Put the pizza on a flat pan or cookie sheet. Bake in a preheated 400° F. oven for 5–6 minutes, until the cheese melts down over the sides and is starting to brown. Cut into wedges and serve.

NOTE: This entire recipe can be made a day ahead. Let the dough rise in the refrigerator overnight (take it out 2 hours before the second rise in the pan). The sauce and sausage can be made ahead and refrigerated.

CALZONE

Calzone is a type of pizza that varies from region to region in Italy. This is my version—stuffed with salami and mozzarella and baked in the oven. To serve the calzone as an appetizer or for a party buffet, roll smaller circles (4 to 5 inches in diameter) and divide the filling evenly, or, slice the larger calzone into individual serving pieces.

YIELD: 6 servings

EQUIPMENT

Liquid measuring cup
Dry measuring cups and spoons
4- to 5-quart mixing bowl
Rolling pin
Cheese grater
Cookie or baking sheets
Pastry brush

DOUGH

1 package active dry yeast
½ cup warm water (105° F.–115° F.)
4 cups unbleached flour
1 teaspoon salt
Warm water as needed

FILLING

6 ounces Italian hard salami, diced
12 ounces mozzarella cheese, grated
Olive oil
1 egg beaten with a little water

DOUGH: Dissolve yeast in warm water, stir well, set aside. Put the flour in a 4- to 5-quart mixing bowl with the salt. Stir to combine. Make a well in the flour. Add the yeast mixture. Work the flour into the liquid in the center. Add the warm water ¼ cup at a time until you have a soft dough that cleans the sides of the mixing bowl. Turn the dough out onto a lightly floured work surface. Knead the dough for 5–6 minutes until it is smooth. Lightly flour a 4- to 5-quart mixing bowl and the ball of dough. Place the dough in the bowl. Cover the bowl with plastic wrap and a kitchen towel. Set the bowl in a warm place for the dough to rise for 1–1½ hours until doubled in bulk.

Take the risen dough out of the mixing bowl; knead for about 2 minutes. Divide the dough into 6 equal pieces. On a lightly floured work surface, roll each piece into a circle that is 8–9 inches in diameter and about ⅛ inch thick. Brush the surface lightly with olive oil. In the center of each circle put an even amount of salami and cheese. Moisten the edges of each circle with the beaten egg. Fold the dough over onto itself to form a half-circle. Press the edges together firmly using the tines of a fork. Brush the outside of each calzone with a small amount of olive oil. Set them on a baking sheet, cover with a towel and set them in a warm place for 1 hour. Bake the calzone in a preheated oven at 375° F. for about 30 minutes until they are golden brown.

NOTE: Prosciutto can be substituted for salami. The baked calzone can be kept in a warm oven for 15–20 minutes before serving, if necessary.

BRUNCH PIZZA

This pizza leans a bit into the omelette family and falls smack into the apple pancake clan. Whatever its relationships, it's a nice departure from the traditional pizza crust, yet with all the dominant pizza flavors.

YIELD: 3–4 servings

EQUIPMENT

Liquid measuring cups
Dry measuring cups and spoons
1-quart mixing bowl
Small bowl for beating the eggs
Whisk
Cheese grater
8-inch skillet or fry pan
12-inch omelette or fry pan

TOPPING

¼ pound Italian sausage, casings
   removed
2 teaspoons olive oil
¾ cup tomato puree
¼ cup grated fontina, Gruyère, or Bel
   Paese cheese
1 teaspoon oil for the omelette pan

BATTER

½ cup milk
½ cup flour
Pinch of salt
3 large eggs
1 teaspoon oregano

TO MIX BATTER: In a small mixing bowl, add the milk to the flour gradually to avoid lumps. Beat vigorously until smooth. Mix in the salt. In a smaller, separate bowl, beat the eggs lightly. Add the eggs to the milk and flour batter. Mix thoroughly. Add the oregano and stir to blend. Refrigerate the batter until ready to use.

TOPPING: In a small skillet over medium heat, cook the sausage in the oil until all the red is gone from the meat. Break up large pieces with a fork. Drain off all the oil and set aside.

TO COOK BATTER: Preheat oven to 500° F. Brush a 12-inch omelette pan or skillet (nonstick or well seasoned) with 1 teaspoon olive oil. Set the pan over medium-high heat for 1 minute. When the pan is hot, add the batter all at once. Cook until the bottom is set (2–3 minutes). Do not stir.

TO ASSEMBLE AND BAKE: Off the heat, add the cooked sausage and puree evenly over the batter.

Bake the pizza in the preheated oven for 10 minutes, or until it starts to rise. Turn oven down to 450° F. and bake 10 minutes more. Five minutes before the pizza is done, sprinkle on the grated cheese. The finished pizza will be puffed and golden brown. Cut into wedges and serve at once.

NOTE: When I make this pizza, I use a nonstick pan with the brand name T-FAL. It works like a charm, and the batter never sticks. The plastic handle needs to be wrapped with two layers of aluminum foil for protection in the oven.

PESTO PIZZA

Fresh basil, if the trend continues, will be cropping up in more and more recipes, Italian or not. It seems to have a natural compatibility with many foods, and urban and suburban gardeners are growing basil with a consuming passion. My kitchen windows always harbor fresh basil plants, and by rooting cuttings from the mother plant I have a continuous supply ready for a pasta, pizza, or sauce.

YIELD: 1 12-inch deep-dish pizza

EQUIPMENT

Liquid measuring cups
Dry measuring cups and spoons
4- to 5-quart mixing bowls
2- to 3-quart mixing bowls
Cheese grater
Food processor with steel blade, or
    blender, or mortar and pestle
12-inch pizza pan, 2 inches deep

DOUGH

1½ teaspoons honey
2 teaspoons vegetable oil
1½ cups warm water
    (105° F.–115° F.)
4–4½ cups unbleached flour
½ teaspoon salt
2 teaspoons active dry yeast

TOPPING:

2 cups fresh basil leaves, washed and
    dried
2 tablespoons pine nuts (pignola)
1 garlic clove, crushed
¼ cup olive oil
½ cup grated Parmesan cheese
½ teaspoon salt
1 teaspoon pepper
1 28-ounce can Italian-style plum
    tomatoes, well drained and crushed
6 ounces mozzarella cheese, grated

DOUGH: In a large mixing bowl, combine the honey and the vegetable oil with the warm water. Add 3 cups of the flour, the salt, and the yeast to the bowl. Stir with a wooden spoon until the dough forms a sticky ball. Add an additional ½ cup of flour and knead this into the ball of dough with your hands. Turn the dough out of the bowl onto a well-floured work surface. Knead and pound the dough, adding more flour if the dough sticks to your hand. You should use at least 4 cups of flour but not more than 4½. Knead the dough for 5–6 minutes until smooth and soft.

Dust the dough and a large mixing bowl with flour; cover with plastic wrap and a kitchen towel. Let rise in a warm place until doubled in bulk, about 1½ hours.

After the dough has doubled in bulk, turn it out of the bowl (it will be slightly sticky), and knead for 2–3 minutes, dusting lightly with flour if it feels too sticky. Oil the pizza pan, bottom and sides, with olive or vegetable oil. Press the dough into the pan with your fingers and the palm of the hand. (It will spread easier if it sits in the pan for 10 minutes.) Work the dough until it covers the bottom of the pan. Pull the edges of the dough up the sides of the pan to form a lip or pronounced border all around the pan. Cover the pan with a kitchen towel and set it in a warm place to rise for 30 minutes.

PESTO SAUCE:

The pesto sauce can be made several hours ahead and refrigerated.

1. Food processor method. Put the basil leaves, pine nuts, garlic, and oil in the work bowl fitted with the steel blade. Turn on the machine and process until a smooth puree is formed (scrape down the sides of the bowl once or twice). Transfer the pesto to a small bowl. Stir in the grated cheese, salt, and pepper.

2. Blender method. (see food processor method, above).

3. Mortar and pestle method. Pound the basil leaves in a mortar with the pine nuts and garlic. Slowly add the oil, continuing to mix thoroughly with the pestle to form a smooth paste. Add the cheese, salt, and pepper. Combine thoroughly.

Combine the pesto sauce with the drained tomatoes. Mix thoroughly.

TO ASSEMBLE AND BAKE: Preheat the oven to 425° F. After the dough has completed the second rising in the pan, spoon the topping onto the crust. Spread the grated mozzarella evenly over the sauce.

Bake the pizza in the preheated oven at 425° F. for 30–35 minutes, until the crust is brown and the pizza cooked through.

VARIATION: This pizza takes on added flavor with the use of fresh plum tomatoes instead of canned. You will need about 8—skinned, seeded, chopped.

PIZZA ON A BUN

These are better than any hamburger—at home or out. The freshly made buns, the tangy sausage sauce, and the cheese all come together in a flavorsome melange of taste. They're great for parties and snacks.

YIELD: 8 pizza buns; 16 open-faced pizza sandwiches

EQUIPMENT

Liquid measuring cups
Dry measuring cups and spoons
3- to 4-quart mixing bowls
2- to 3-quart saucepan
Cooling rack
4-inch English muffin rings or a
    biscuit plaque with 4-inch diameter
    wells

DOUGH

2 packages active dry yeast
½ cup warm water (105° F.–115° F.)
4–4½ cups unbleached flour or bread
    flour
1 teaspoon salt
1 cup milk

SAUCE

10–12 ounces Italian sausage, casing
    removed
1 tablespoon olive oil
2 16-ounce cans tomato puree
2 teaspoons dried basil
2 tablespoons finely chopped parsley
2 teaspoons oregano
3 tablespoons grated Parmesan cheese
Salt and pepper to taste
1 slice mozzarella cheese for each
    sandwich

DOUGH: Dissolve yeast in warm water and stir well. Set aside.

In a 3- to 4-quart mixing bowl, mix 4 cups of flour and the salt. Combine well. Make a well in the center of the flour. Add the yeast mixture and the milk. Stir and mix with a wooden spoon until a rough mass of dough is formed and the dough cleans the sides of the bowl. Turn the dough out of the bowl onto a well-floured work surface. Knead and pound the dough, dusting frequently with flour when the dough sticks to your hands. Knead the dough for 5–6 minutes, until smooth and soft.

Dust the dough completely with flour. Place the ball of dough in a large mixing bowl; cover the bowl with plastic wrap and a kitchen towel. Set the bowl in a warm place for the dough to rise, about 2 hours, until doubled in bulk.

After the dough has doubled in bulk, punch it down and turn it out of the bowl onto a lightly floured work surface. Knead the dough gently for about 2 minutes.

Lightly oil the rings or plaques. If using the rings, place them on a cookie sheet that has been lightly oiled. (A good alternative is 7-ounce tins from tuna fish, minced clams, pineapple, and so forth. Remove the bottom and top of the can and the label. Scrub thoroughly and make sure there are no sharp edges.)

Divide the dough into 8 equal pieces. Each piece should weigh a little more than 3 ounces. Press the dough into the rings or plaques and cover with a kitchen towel. Put the buns in a warm place to rise for 30–40 minutes.

Preheat the oven to 425° F. After the second rising, bake the buns in the preheated oven for 20–25 minutes at 425° F. until they are nicely browned and cooked through. After the buns have been baked, place them on a cooling rack.

SAUCE: Over medium-high heat, cook the sausage in the oil, breaking up the larger chunks with a fork or wooden spatula, until the sausage is cooked through. Drain off excess fat. Add the tomato and seasonings, stir in the cheese, and add the salt and pepper. Stir well. Turn the heat to low and simmer the sauce for 30–40 minutes, stirring occasionally.

TO ASSEMBLE AND BAKE: When the buns are cool enough to handle, slice them in 2, like hamburger buns. Place the sliced buns on an ovenproof plate, a flat platter, flat pizza pan, or the like. Spoon a portion of the hot sausage sauce on top of each half-bun; place a slice of mozzarella cheese on top of the sauce. Place them under a broiler until the cheese melts and begins to brown. Serve at once.

The buns take nicely to freezing, so they can be made ahead, frozen, and reheated just before adding the sauce and the cheese. The sauce can also be made ahead (refrigerate after it has cooled a bit).

VARIATIONS: 1. Add sautéed onions or mushrooms to the basic sauce. 2. Add some crushed garlic. 3. Sauté chunks of pepperoni in place of the sausage, and then—for the hearty ones in the crowd—add some crushed red pepper flakes.

FAMILY-SIZE PIZZA RECIPES

Keeping the big families and the big eaters in mind, the following recipes will make *two 13- to 14-inch thin crust pizzas*. Eat one and freeze one, or eat them both. The recipe for the dough is below, followed by a variety of toppings.

PIZZA DOUGH

YIELD: 2 13- to 14-inch pizza shells

EQUIPMENT

Liquid measuring cups
Dry measuring cups and spoons
3- to 4- quart mixing bowl
Rolling pin

DOUGH

1 package active dry yeast
1 cup warm water (105° F.–115° F.)
3½ cups unbleached flour
1 teaspoon salt
2 tablespoons olive oil

PIZZA DOUGH: Dissolve yeast in warm water and stir well. Set aside. Combine flour and salt in a 3- to 4-quart mixing bowl. Make a well in the center of the flour. Add the yeast mixture and the olive oil. Stir and mix well until a rough mass of dough is formed and the dough cleans the sides of the bowl. If the dough seems dry and stiff, add 1–2 tablespoons of warm water.

Turn the dough out of the bowl onto a work surface. Knead the dough for 6–8 minutes, slapping it down hard on the counter occasionally, until smooth and soft. Lightly flour a large mixing bowl and the dough. Place the dough in the bowl. Cover the bowl with plastic wrap and a kitchen towel. Set the bowl in a warm place for the dough to rise until doubled in bulk, about 1½ hours.

After the dough has doubled in bulk, punch it down, turn it out of the bowl, and knead lightly for about 2 minutes.

Divide the dough in ½. Roll each piece into a 13- to 14-inch circle about ⅛ inch thick. Transfer the dough to an oiled flat pizza pan or pizza screen of 14- to 15-inch diameter (or to a pizza peel, if using the baking stone). Roll the edge of the dough to form a thick border all around. Rub the top of the crust with a little olive oil, and add 1 of the classic toppings that follow.

NOTE: For a thicker crust, let the dough rise on the pan or screen for 30–45 minutes before adding the topping.

CLASSICO SUPREME

YIELD: topping for 2 13- to 14-inch shells

EQUIPMENT

Liquid measuring cups
Dry measuring cups and spoons
12-inch frying pan or sauté pan or 4-
   to 4½-quart saucepan
Cheese grater
2 14-inch flat pizza pans or pizza
   screens

TOPPING

1 clove garlic, sliced thin
1 tablespoon olive oil
1 large onion, chopped
1½ pounds Italian sausage
2 large (28-ounce) cans Italian plum
   tomatoes, drained and crushed
¼ cup grated Parmesan cheese
1½ teaspoons oregano
1½ teaspoons basil
1 tablespoon salt
1 pound mozzarella cheese, grated

TOPPING: In a large, deep fry pan, lightly brown garlic in oil. Discard garlic. Remove sausage from casing and add sausage and onion to the oil in the fry pan. Sauté over medium-high heat until the sausage is cooked through. Drain all liquid from the pan. Add well-drained tomatoes, Parmesan cheese, oregano, basil, and salt. Simmer over low heat for 20 minutes.

Spoon ½ the topping onto each pizza shell, using a slotted spoon. Sprinkle mozzarella cheese (8 ounces for each shell) on top.

Bake the pizza in a preheated 450° F. oven for 20–25 minutes, until crust is crisp and brown.

MUSHROOM DELIGHT

YIELD: topping for 2 13- to 14-inch shells

EQUIPMENT

Liquid measuring cups
Dry measuring cups and spoons
2- to 3-quart saucepan
10-inch fry pan or skillet
Cheese grater
2 14-inch flat pizza pans or pizza
    screens

TOPPING

2 16-ounce cans tomato puree
2 tablespoons grated Parmesan cheese
1 pound fresh mushrooms
2 tablespoons unsalted butter
1 pound mozzarella cheese, grated
2 tablespoons olive oil

TOPPING: Simmer the tomato puree and cheese in a saucepan for 20 minutes over low heat. Wash the mushrooms, slice off the stem bottoms, and slice thin. Sauté mushrooms in the butter over medium heat for 5–6 minutes. Spoon ½ the tomato sauce on each pizza shell, followed by ½ the mushrooms and ½ the cheese. Drizzle 1 tablespoon of olive oil over each pizza.

Bake the pizza in a preheated 450° F. oven for 20–25 minutes, until crust is crisp and brown.

ALL-ITALIAN

YIELD: topping for 2 13- to 14-inch shells

EQUIPMENT

Liquid measuring cups
Dry measuring cups and spoons
10-inch sauté or frying pan or 2- to 3-
    quart saucepan
Cheese grater
2 14-inch flat pizza pans or pizza
    screens

TOPPING

2 16-ounce cans tomato puree
1 teaspoon salt
1 teaspoon basil
1 teaspoon oregano
2 tablespoons chopped parsley
2 tablespoons grated Parmesan cheese
1 pound mozzarella cheese, grated
½ pound pepperoni sausage, sliced

TOPPING: In a large, deep sauté pan or saucepan, simmer the first 6 ingredients over low heat for 20 minutes.

Spoon ½ the sauce on top of each pizza shell. Divide the mozzarella and sprinkle on each pizza. Divide the pepperoni and arrange the slices over the cheese.

Bake the pizza in a preheated 450° F. oven for 20–25 minutes, until crust is crisp and brown.

VEGETABLE AND BEEF

YIELD: topping for 2 13- to 14-inch shells

EQUIPMENT

Liquid measuring cup
Dry measuring cups and spoons
12- to 12-inch sauté pan or frying pan
8- to 10-inch frying pan
Cheese grater
2 14-inch flat pizza pans or pizza
    screens

TOPPING

2 16-ounce cans tomato puree
1 teaspoon basil
1 teaspoon oregano
2 tablespoons grated Parmesan cheese
¾ pound ground beef
1 tablespoon olive oil
2 medium-sized onions, chopped
2 medium-sized green peppers,
    chopped
1 pound mozzarella cheese, grated

TOPPING: Simmer the first 4 ingredients in a sauté pan or skillet for 20 minutes. In a separate skillet, cook the ground beef until just cooked through; remove the beef from the pan and reserve. To the same pan, add olive oil; sauté the onions and peppers until just softened.

Spoon ½ the tomato sauce on top of each pizza shell, followed by ½ the pepper and onion mixture. Do the same with the beef and then the mozzarella.

Bake the pizza in a preheated 450° F. oven for 20–25 minutes, until the crust is crisp and brown.

6
The Great Pizza Restaurants

EDWARDO'S

How did a nice young man, a former accountant, get into the pizza business? Accountants, after all, are well known to keep pretty much within themselves and their numbers. Who told this accountant that he could just waltz into this highly competitive business and in four years carve out a strong niche in the consuming Chicago pizza market? Like all accountants, Ed Jacobson, the owner of Edwardo's Pizza Restaurants (there are three, and more on the way), was savvy about net profit. Now he's savvy about making pizza *and* making a profit—not a bad combination.

"Why the pizza business?" I asked. "Were you keeping the books for a pizza operation and saw some good figures dropping down to the bottom line?" Ed's answer showed him to be part accountant, part entrepreneur, and part lover of good food and the restaurant business: "It's the fastest growing segment of the food business; it's an established part of the American diet; it's recession-proof; it takes a small investment; it's fun and I really enjoy what I do." These were just a few of Ed's rapid-fire answers.

The first Edwardo's opened at 1937 Howard Street in June 1979. The January 1980 issue of *Chicago* magazine rated Jacobson's pizza the most innovative in the city. His creation—spinach soufflé pizza—is certainly that. Fresh chopped spinach is mixed with mozzarella cheese and loaded onto the first layer of dough. Another layer of dough follows, and this is topped with a rich, flavorful tomato sauce. The bonanza that comes out of the oven is a real pulse-racing pizza. Ed frankly admits that it took a while to get the proper combinations and balance of ingredients and that in the beginning the spinach soufflé pizza did not sell all that well.

Like other pizza restaurant owners who take pride in what they make and serve, Ed is always watching, always learning. For example, he took a course at the American Baking Institute, where research is done on flour, baking, dough, etc.

Another common bond that unites the better pizza restaurants is the use of quality ingredients. Edwardo's uses quality ingredients from quality purveyors—sausage, cheese, and mushrooms—but goes one step further by getting fresh herbs year-round from an on-location, multitiered herb farm. The sweet, fragrant smell of the fresh basil is, by itself, a heady experience; when you know it's being used in the pizza it's staggering. Ed Jacobson's newest Edwardo's, on Dearborn Street, is a modern affair, marked by brass, chrome, and good lighting, and it's spanking clean. But it's more than a pizza restaurant. Ed describes it as an "Italian market." "We're selling bakery goods, salads, caponata. This separates us from the rest of the crowd," he said. And the latest addition is a wine bar. It seems like Ed is on the move again.

NANCY'S

Nancy's specialty is a type of pizza called *stuffed*—a feeling that serious pizza eaters have a close acquaintance with. At Nancy's they do stuff the pizza—with cheese, mushrooms, onions, peppers—almost anything you crave. Nancy's has two locations: the original at 7309 West Lawerence in Harwood Heights and a cavernous affair at 4258 North Central. My interview with Tom Cirrincione, the owner and operator, was at the Central Avenue location. "Nice to meet you, Tom," I said. My next question was, "How old are you?" I wasn't surprised when he said, "Twenty-three." I was surprised to see someone so young operating one of the top-rated pizza restaurants around. (Are the young Turks taking over the pizza business in Chicago?) It seems that Tom has been making pizza since he was 12—"My father started the business, but I think I've always known what my line of work would be," he said.

Nancy's is a real sleeper. It doesn't get as much ink as some of the other pizza places, but it always comes out on top in magazine or television polls on favorite pizza restaurants. What makes this even more unusual is that Nancy's serves a full menu selection of Italian food. This causes little problem as there is a separate kitchen just for the pizza operation; the pizza kitchen seems to get the most action. One fact remains hard and true; customers come to Nancy's in a fairly steady stream to put away the award-winning pizza.

What makes the pizza so good? Once again, it's the use of top-quality ingredients, in the proper combinations and in the correct balance—plus attention to detail. The ingredients, for example, are the best: Anichini Brothers bulk pork sausage, 6-1 tomatoes, low-moisture mozzarella, freshly made dough. Add to this *consistency*. Tom Cirrincione will tell you, "We are consistent. . . . We do it the same way all the time. That's why people rave about our pizza; nobody makes it like we do."

Like many of his fellow restaurateurs, Tom works six days a week and most often 10–12 hours a day. In spite of all this hard work, I'll bet that Tom Cirrincione will look 23 when the new century rolls in. It seems like the pizza business keeps people looking young—or is it something in the pizza?

GINO'S EAST

Gino's East, like Uno's and Due's, is a landmark for pizza lovers. Started in 1966 by two former cab drivers, Sam Levine and Fred Bartoli, it ranks right up there with the let's-take-one-back-on-the-plane crowd. And salespeople at the prestigious Water Tower Place shopping complex two blocks north of Gino's are frequently asked by out-of-towners, "How do we get to Gino's?" You can't ask for stronger endorsements than those. (The word gets around fast when there's good pizza to be had.)

Gino's is somewhat reminiscent of the restaurant-bars that are often found in college towns: built for heavy use and abuse, dark, initials and names carved into the wood tables and walls, and young perky waitresses. The decor is certainly "early college bar," but the pizza is definitely Chicago. Whichever you choose to call it, deep-dish or pizza-in-the-pan, there is no mistaking its authenticity and its goodness—a delightful melange of tomatoes, cheese, sausage, and whatever else suits your taste.

Gino's never advertises. "No need to," said Sam Levine. And Sam Levine doesn't talk to writers. "Bad luck," he says. "Who needs bad luck?" After a number of phone calls Sam finally agreed to sit down with me and discuss the pizza business. It was not a private meeting. In a booth on the upper floor of the restaurant Sam was holding forth with his banker from up the street (bankers like pizza restaurant owners), a friend from his cab driving days, and Alex Oppolus, a food purveyor. Sam greeted me warmly and said, "I hope you don't bring me any bad luck."

Sam Levine is 72 years old, is in his restaurant six days a week, and the word *retire* is not one that he recognizes.

"Why do people like your pizza so much?" I asked. "It's good" was Sam's lengthy reply.

The owners of Gino's East would not allow me to visit their kitchen— "it could bring bad luck."

So, the secrets of how pizza is made at Gino's East is still a secret. Maybe that's what luck is all about.

D'AMATO'S

When I entered D'Amato's Bakery on West Grand Street it was like stepping back in time. The dough mixer, the proofing boxes, the scales, the dough cutters, were the same as I remembered from the Italian bakery that I grew up next to. What really made my pulse race, however, was the old brick oven—a brick hearth oven, fired by coal! A brick hearth oven more than 70 years old! A brick hearth oven loaded wth loaves of golden Italian bread! And Italian bakery pizza!

Bakers who use brick ovens agree that no other kind can make as good a loaf of bread. And once you taste D'Amato's bread and D'Amato's pizza, you'll understand why I'm in love with brick hearth ovens.

Nick D'Amato, the owner, was a wreath of smiles as we watched his relatives and employees mix, knead, pound, roll, slash, load, shovel, and poudly display his breads and pizzas. Nick is from the small Italian town of Adelfia, which is close to Bari. For 20 years Nick has been baking his bread and pizza in Chicago—with a little help from his family and friends. The small storefront retail part is usually run by his wife Rosa. The general baking work is done by assorted relatives: Joe Fiore, Vito La-Salva, Joe and John Pugliese, Tony Virgilio, Mike Marinelli. Authentic Italian bread? You bet it is! Authentic Italian pizza? Ditto! This is the kind of pizza I cut my teeth on. The crust is thick and bready yet light. The tomatoes are not loaded on heavily. The cheese is used sparingly (quite often a combination of Parmesan and Romano is used in place of mozzarella). And it's rectangular in shape, not round. You might ask if this changes the taste; probably not, but old taste habits are hard to break.

HOME RUN INN

At the Home Run Inn pizza restaurant the tables are loaded every day, and the action under the kitchen lights is even better. Nick Perrino, the owner, and his son Joe, the general manager, run an operation that allows little chance for errors. And Nick's team—the pizza assemblers, cooks, and waitresses—all proudly wear baseball hats with patches across the front that say Home Run Inn. There's no lack of team spirit at this restaurant. Sound crazy? Wait until you taste the pizza—it's a grand slam, every bite, every time. The clientele is as varied as the pizza is consistent—from shoulder-to-shoulder uniformed softball teams clustered around huge tables to suit and tie and silk dress couples at tables for two. Social status aside, they are all here for the same thing—great pizza.

Nick Perrino arrived in Chicago from Italy when he was 16 years old. He is a bit past 70 now, works six days a week, and, with his son Joe, supervises a one-restaurant operation that makes and sells more than 2,000 pizzas a day. I first met Nick in 1967. The Home Run Inn was a favorite lunch stop for me and a lot of my business friends. Nick was serving the best medium crust pizza in Chicago, and we drove for 20 minutes to get some—twice a week on the average. There were only about 12 tables and a 40-foot bar in 1967. Today there are more than 100 tables and things have been spruced up a bit. One thing hasn't changed—the pizza.

It's top quality because Nick uses quality ingredients. He makes his own pork sausage, keeping three butchers busy boning pork butts; he blends three different types of mozzarella cheese, he makes his own dough for the crusts; and he uses choice tomatoes. And what a staff of people. Large companies could get a lesson in employee morale from this place. Several employees have been there since the late '40s—that's pretty steady stuff in the restaurant business.

Nick is like an actor who, having worked the road and the joints for years learning his craft, has suddenly been "discovered," an overnight sensation. Nick has worked at making pizza for 36 years and in his own way has always been a sensation at making pizza—it's a good story. Nick worked in his uncle's gas station for nearly 15 years. When he was 31 he was drafted into the U.S. Army. The Army in its divine wisdom made Nick a cook—but only after he had passed a test (with flying colors) on engines, brakes, spark plugs, and drive shafts. To this day, Nick has trouble rationalizing their thinking but laughs thunderously when he relates the story. "I tried to talk them out of it, but who was I to argue with an officer in the U.S. Army," he says.

Nick cooked his way through the war, rising to the rank of company mess sergeant, all the while studying his eighth-grade spelling book to improve his writing ability. After the war Nick put his cooking skills to work. He opened his small restaurant just two blocks from the gas station. Several expansions later he is still there, in the same neighborhood, doing what he knows best—making great pizza! Nick always seems to find time for charity work and to greet his steady customers, who unequivocally defend Home Run Inn as the best pizza restaurant in Chicago.

It's been a dream come true for a man who asked, "What kind of fig is that?" when he first came to America and saw a banana. This nice thing is that success has not changed Nick Perrino. He has said to me, and many others, many times: "I'd like to stand on every street corner and shout over and over again, 'God Bless America.' "

There are many people in Chicago who stand on the corner of West 31st Street and shout, "God bless Home Run Inn pizza!"

GIORDANO'S

The shape of Chicago pizza took on a new look in 1973, the year that Joe Boglio, the owner of Giordano's chain of pizza restaurants, unveiled his spinach stuffed pizza. It became, in a short time, the star of the show and still is, every day and every night at the 10 Giordano's restaurants in and around Chicago. In 1967 Joe Boglio came to Chicago from Torino, Italy, by way of Buenos Aires and took a job in a pizza restaurant. Since then a sequence of events has taken place that has made Chicago pizza lovers very happy.

"We were serving a good pizza at the place I worked. I also tried the pizza in other places around the city. They weren't nearly as good as that which my mother made," he said. "So, my brother Efren and I set out on our own. We opened our own pizza restaurant, and our specialty was a variation of a pizza that our mother made. A double-crusted pizza that she made on Easter, which was stuffed with ricotta cheese. We took our mother's pizza a few steps further. We added spinach, cheese, and tomatoes, along with compatible seasonings—a double deep-dish pizza of sorts. The spinach stuffed pizza is our most popular," he added. "But it didn't happen overnight; we worked on getting the proper combination for a long time."

This unassuming approach to creating a new type of pizza soon grabbed Chicago pizza fanatics by their mozzarellas, and Giordano's (the name comes from Mother Giordano) was on the way to success.

Joe explained a few things about the pizza business to me one afternoon over coffee in one of his newest restaurants. "We don't have any secrets," he said. "Our philosophy about the business is simple—pay attention to the quality of the ingredients, to the simple obvious details, to making customers feel comfortable. And serve only the best. We know what we must do, and we always try to do it well." Joe does it so well that every day thousands of customers make a calculated assault on his restaurants, and they come away satisfied and content that they did a good job of consuming Joe's creations.

Giordano's pizzas are not eaten only in Chicago. Many travelers from around the country have been seen arriving at Chicago's O'Hare Airport with one or more of Joe's pizzas carefully cradled in their arms.

This is all pretty exciting stuff for the handsome, slim Italian, who lights up like a Neapolitan street when he talks about making pizza. "Would you like me to make a pizza for you?" he asked, as we concluded our table talk about the pizza business. My swift movement toward the kitchen was my obvious answer to the question—I wasn't about to miss this.

So Joe Boglio, the creator of spinach stuffed pizza, whose favorite foods are chicken sautéed in oil and veal (any which way) and whose wife admits to eating frozen pizza on occasion, continues to build his pizzas and his business. The best part of it all is that he is having fun doing it.

UNO'S

Pizza was not considered serious food back in the early '40s. In Chicago the only place you could get pizza was in the Italian neighborhood on and around Taylor Street, and it was served as a snack—it was purchased by the piece and usually eaten while standing. Pizza came out of the storefront, stand-up bakeries and moved into the restaurant-with-table-service phase in June of 1943, when Pizzeria Uno opened on the corner of Ohio and Wabash streets on the near north side of Chicago.

This bold and daring step of serving pizza as a meal was the brainchild of two young men—Ike Sewell and Ric Riccardo. Ric had come to Chicago from New Orleans in 1935 and was the proprietor of Riccardo's, a popular Italian restaurant. Ike had come to Chicago from Texas as head of the midwestern division for a large distiller. Mutual interest pulled them together as friends, and they talked about starting a Mexican restaurant.

The Mexican restaurant idea was temporarily shelved as Ric went off to World War II. When Ric got back to Chicago he convinced Ike to open a pizzeria instead—millions of GIs were coming home from Italy where they had consumed a lot of pizza. Ric knew pizza would be a winner anywhere.

It took only four months for Pizzeria Uno to become a success. In 1955 Uno's sister, Pizzeria Due, was opened one block North at Wabash and Ontario streets. Some 10 million pizzas later Uno's and Due's are still going strong. They are now places of worship for pizza aficionados from around the world, not just in Chicago or the Midwest. For example, Uno's was the first eating stop for the string section of the Israeli Symphony Orchestra on a recent visit to Chicago.

What makes these two pizzerias the most popular in Chicago? I spent several hours in the kitchen at Uno's, and I think I have the answer: choice, quality ingredients—tomatoes, cheese, sausage, freshly made dough, fresh (not canned) mushrooms—and dedicated, loyal people in the kitchen, people who know what they're doing, pizza after pizza. I was dazzled by their expertise: the high-fired ovens were at the proper temperature by 10:00 a.m., at 11:00 a.m. the first orders started to come in, and the kitchen crew, like a well-drilled team, went to work.

Several days later I had the opportunity to visit Ike Sewell in his office one floor above Pizzeria Due. Ike Sewell has certainly done his part to elevate the stature of pizzeria owners. His office is an oasis of quiet luxury—marble fireplaces, highly polished wood floors with thick Orientals here and there, beautiful wood walls. "The pizza business has been good to me," Ike said. It seems like it's getting even better, as there are now restaurants called Ike Sewell's Pizzeria Uno in major cities across the country. These are franchised operations, but they are carefully watched and visited often by Ike. "I resisted many offers, many times, to franchise. When the people came to me that I knew could maintain the quality, and not damage my reputation of 35 years, I agreed to do business," he said.

Index

Patterns of
World History

Patterns of World History

VOLUME ONE to 1600

Brief Third Edition

Peter von Sivers
University of Utah

Charles A. Desnoyers
La Salle University

George B. Stow
La Salle University

New York   Oxford
OXFORD UNIVERSITY PRESS

Oxford University Press is a department of the University of Oxford.
It furthers the University's objective of excellence in research,
scholarship, and education by publishing worldwide. Oxford is a
registered trade mark of Oxford University Press in the UK and
certain other countries.

Published in the United States of America by Oxford University Press
198 Madison Avenue, New York, NY 10016, United States of America.

© 2018, 2015, 2012 by Oxford University Press

Library of Congress Cataloging-in-Publication Data
Names: Von Sivers, Peter, author. | Desnoyers, Charles, 1952– author. | Stow,
  George B., author.
Title: Patterns of world history / Peter von Sivers, University of Utah;
  Charles A. Desnoyers, La Salle University; George B. Stow, La Salle
  University.
Description: Third brief edition. | New York : Oxford University Press,
  2017. | Includes bibliographical references and index.
Identifiers: LCCN 2017013736| ISBN 9780190697310 (pbk. : alk. paper) | ISBN
  9780190697327 (pbk. : alk. paper)
Subjects: LCSH: World history—Textbooks.
Classification: LCC D21 .V66 2017 | DDC 909—dc23 LC record available at https:
//lccn.loc.gov/2017013736

9 8 7 6
Printed by Webcom, Canada.

Coniugi Judithae dilectissimae

—PETER VON SIVERS

To all my students over the years,
who have taught me at least as much as I've taught them;
and most of all to my wife, Jacki, beloved in all things,
but especially in her infinite patience and fortitude
in seeing me through the writing of this book.

—CHARLES A. DESNOYERS

For Susan and our children, Meredith and Jonathan.

—GEORGE B. STOW

—I hear and I forget; I see and I remember; I do and I understand
(Chinese proverb) 我听见我忘记;我看见我记住;我做我了解

Brief Contents

PART 1:

From Human Origins to Early Agricultural Centers

PART 2:

The Age of Empires and Visionaries

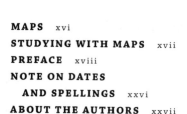

Contents

PART ONE

From Human Origins to Early Agricultural Centers

PREHISTORY–600 BCE   2

Features:

Patterns Up Close:
The Disappearance of
Neanderthals   20

Against the Grain:
The Hobbits of
Flores Island   25

Features:

Patterns Up Close:
Babylonian Law Codes   36

Against the Grain:
Akhenaten the
Transgressor   51

Features:

Patterns Up Close:
Against the Grain:

Chapter 4
5000–481 BCE

Agrarian Centers and the Mandate of Heaven in Ancient China

Features:

Patterns Up Close:
Against the Grain:

Chapter 5
16,000–600 BCE

Origins Apart: The Americas and Oceania

The Age of Empires and Visionaries

Chiefdoms and Early States in Africa and the Americas

Chapter 8
600 BCE–600 CE

Empires and Visionaries in India   169

Features:

Patterns Up Close:

Against the Grain:

Chapter 9
722 BCE–618 CE

China: Imperial Unification and Perfecting the Moral Order   190

Features:

Patterns Up Close:

Against the Grain:

Chapter 18
1500–1800

Features:

Patterns Up Close:
The Columbian
Exchange   420
Against the Grain:
Juana Inés de la Cruz   430

Maps

Studying with Maps

MAPS

World history cannot be fully understood without a clear comprehension of the chronologies and parameters within which different empires, states, and peoples have changed over time. Maps facilitate this understanding by illuminating the significance of time, space, and geography in shaping the patterns of world history.

Global Locator

Many of the maps in *Patterns of World History* include *global locators* that show the area being depicted in a larger context.

Projection

A map *projection* portrays all or part of the earth, which is spherical, on a flat surface. All maps, therefore, include some distortion. The projections in *Patterns of World History* show the earth at global, continental, regional, and local scales.

Topography

Many maps in *Patterns of World History* show *relief*—the contours of the land. Topography is an important element in studying maps, because the physical terrain has played a critical role in shaping human history.

Scale Bar

Every map in *Patterns of World History* includes a *scale* that shows distances in both miles and kilometers, and in some instances, in feet as well.

Map Key

Maps use symbols to show the location of features and to convey information. Each symbol is explained in the map's *key*.

One map in each chapter is accompanied by an icon that indicates that the map can be analyzed in an interactive fashion (see pages xxiii–xxiv).

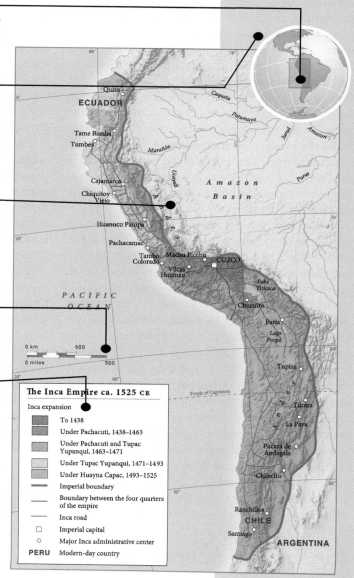

The Inca Empire ca. 1525 CE

Inca expansion

To 1438
Under Pachacuti, 1438–1463
Under Pachacuti and Tupac Yupanqui, 1463–1471
Under Tupac Yupanqui, 1471–1493
Under Huayna Capac, 1493–1525
Imperial boundary
Boundary between the four quarters of the empire
Inca road
☐ Imperial capital
○ Major Inca administrative center
PERU Modern-day country

Preface

The response to the first two editions of *Patterns of World History* has been extraordinarily gratifying to those of us involved in its development. The diversity of schools that have adopted the book—community colleges as well as state universities; small liberal arts schools as well as large private universities—suggests to us that its central premise of exploring *patterns* in world history is both adaptable to a variety of pedagogical environments and congenial to a wide body of instructors. Indeed, from the responses to the book we have received thus far, we expect that the level of writing, timeliness and completeness of the material, and analytical approach will serve it well as the discipline of world history continues to mature. These key strengths are enhanced in the third edition of *Patterns* by constructive, dynamic suggestions from the broad range of students and instructors who are using the book.

It is widely agreed that world history is more than simply the sum of all national histories. Likewise, *Patterns of World History*, Third Edition, is more than an unbroken sequence of dates, battles, rulers, and their activities, and it is more than the study of isolated stories of change over time. Rather, in this textbook we endeavor to present in a clear and engaging way how world history "works." Instead of merely offering a narrative history of the appearance of this or that innovation, we present an analysis of the process by which an innovation in one part of the world is diffused and carried to the rest of the globe. Instead of focusing on the memorization of people, places, and events, we strive to present important facts in context and draw meaningful connections, analyzing whatever patterns we find and drawing conclusions where we can. In short, we seek to examine the interlocking mechanisms and animating forces of world history, without neglecting the human agency behind them.

The *Patterns* Approach

Our approach in this book is, as the title suggests, to look for patterns in world history. We should say at the outset that we do not mean to select certain categories into which we attempt to stuff the historical events we choose to emphasize, nor do we claim that all world history is reducible to such patterns, nor do we mean to suggest that the nature of the patterns determines the outcome of historical events. We see them instead as broad, flexible organizational frameworks around which to build the structure of a world history in such a way that the enormous sweep and content of the past can be viewed in a comprehensible narrative, with sound analysis and ample scope for debate and discussion. In this sense, we view them much like the armatures in clay sculptures, giving support and structure to the final figure but not necessarily preordaining its ultimate shape.

From its origins, human culture grew through interactions and adaptations on all the continents except Antarctica. A voluminous scholarship on all regions of the world has thus been accumulated, which those working in the field have to attempt to master if their explanations and arguments are to sound even remotely persuasive. The sheer volume and complexity of the sources, however, mean that even the knowledge and expertise of the best scholars are going to be incomplete. Moreover, the humility with which all historians must approach their material contains within it the realization that no historical explanation is ever fully satisfactory or final: As a driving force in the historical process, creative human agency moves events in directions that are never fully predictable, even if they follow broad patterns. Learning to discern patterns in this process not only helps novice historians to appreciate the complex challenges (and rewards) of historical inquiry; it also develops critical thinking abilities in all students.

As we move through the second decade of the twenty-first century, world historians have long since left behind the "West plus the rest" approach that marked the field's early years, together with economic and geographical reductionism, in the search for a new balance between comprehensive cultural and institutional examinations on the one hand and those highlighting human agency on the other. All too often, however, this is reflected in texts that seek broad coverage at the expense of analysis, thus resulting in a kind of "world history lite." Our aim is therefore to simplify the study of the world—to make it accessible to the student—without making world history itself simplistic.

Patterns of World History proposes the teaching of world history from the perspective of the relationship between continuity and change. What we advocate in this book is a distinct intellectual framework for this relationship and the role of innovation and historical change through patterns of origins, interactions, and adaptations. Each small or large technical or cultural innovation originated in one geographical center or independently in several different centers. As people in the centers interacted with their neighbors, the neighbors adapted to, and in many cases were transformed by, the innovations. By "adaptation" we include the entire spectrum of human responses, ranging from outright rejection to creative borrowing and, at times, forced acceptance.

Small technical innovations often went through the pattern of origin, interaction, and adaptation across the world without arousing much attention, even though they had major consequences. For example, the horse collar, which originated in the last centuries BCE in China and allowed for the replacement of oxen with stronger horses, gradually improved the productivity of agriculture in eleventh-century western Europe. More sweeping intellectual–cultural innovations, by contrast, such as the spread of universal religions like Buddhism, Christianity, and Islam and the rise of science, have often had profound consequences—in some cases leading to conflicts lasting centuries—and affect us even today.

Sometimes change was effected by commodities that to us seem rather ordinary. Take sugar, for example: It originated in Southeast Asia and was traded and grown in the Mediterranean, where its cultivation on plantations created the model for expansion into the vast slave system of the Atlantic basin from the fifteenth through the nineteenth centuries, forever altering the histories of four continents. What would our diets look like today without sugar? Its history continues to unfold as we debate its merits and health risks and it supports huge multinational agribusinesses.

Or take a more obscure commodity: opium. Opium had been used medicinally for centuries in regions all over the world. But the advent of tobacco traded from the Americas to the Philippines to China, and the encouragement of Dutch traders in the region, created an environment in which the drug was smoked for the first time. Enterprising rogue British merchants, eager to find a way to crack closed Chinese markets for other goods, began to smuggle it in from India. The market grew, the price went down, addiction spread, and Britain and China ultimately went to war over China's attempts to eliminate the traffic. Here, we have an example of an item generating interactions on a world-wide scale, with impacts on everything from politics to economics, culture, and even the environment. The legacies of the trade still weigh heavily on two of the rising powers of the recent decades: China and India. And opium and its derivatives, like morphine and heroin, continue to bring relief as well as suffering on a colossal scale to hundreds of millions of people.

What, then, do we gain by studying world history through the use of such patterns? First, if we consider innovation to be a driving force of history, it helps to satisfy an intrinsic human curiosity about origins—our own and others. Perhaps more importantly, seeing patterns of various kinds in historical development brings to light connections and linkages among peoples, cultures, and regions—as in the aforementioned examples—that might not otherwise present themselves.

Second, such patterns can also reveal differences among cultures that other approaches to world history tend to neglect. For example, the differences between the civilizations of the Eastern and Western Hemispheres are generally highlighted in world history texts, but the broad commonalities of human groups creating agriculturally based cities and states in widely separated areas also show deep parallels in their patterns of origins, interactions, and adaptations. Such comparisons are at the center of our approach.

Third, this kind of analysis offers insights into how an individual innovation was subsequently developed and diffused across space and time—that is, the patterns by which the new eventually becomes a necessity in our daily lives. Through all of this we gain a deeper appreciation of the unfolding of global history from its origins in small, isolated areas to the vast networks of global interconnectedness in our present world.

Finally, our use of a broad-based understanding of continuity, change, and innovation allows us to restore culture in all its individual and institutionalized aspects—spiritual, artistic, intellectual, scientific—to its rightful place alongside technology, environment, politics, and socioeconomic conditions. That is, understanding innovation in this way allows this text to help illuminate the full range of human ingenuity over time and space in a comprehensive, evenhanded, and open-ended fashion.

Options for Teaching with *Patterns of World History*

For the sake of continuity and to accommodate the many different ways schools divide the midpoint of their world history sequence, Chapters 15–18 overlap in both volumes; in Volume 2, Chapter 15 is given as a "prelude" to Part Four. Those using a trimester system will also find divisions made in convenient places, with Chapter 10 coming at the beginning of Part Two and Chapter 22 at the beginning of Part Five.

Patterns of Change and Six Periods of World History

Similarly, *Patterns* is adaptable to both chronological and thematic styles of instruction. We divide the history of the world into six major time periods and recognize for each period one or two main patterns of innovation, their spread through interaction, and their adoption by others. Obviously, lesser patterns are identified as well, many of which are of more limited regional interactive and adaptive impact. We wish to stress again that these are broad categories of analysis and that there is nothing reductive or deterministic in our aims or choices. Nevertheless, we believe the patterns we have chosen help to make the historical process more intelligible, providing a series of lenses that can help to focus the otherwise confusing facts and disparate details that comprise world history.

> *Part One (Prehistory–600 BCE):* Origins of human civilization—tool making and symbol creating—in Africa as well as the origins of agriculture, urbanism, and state formation in the three agrarian centers of the Middle East, India, and China.

> *Part Two (600 BCE–600 CE):* Emergence of the axial-age thinkers and their visions of a transcendent god or first principle in Eurasia; elevation of these visions to the status of state religions in

empires and kingdoms, in the process forming multiethnic and multilinguistic polities.

> *Part Three (600–1450):* Disintegration of classical empires and formation of religious civilizations in Eurasia, with the emergence of religiously unified regions divided by commonwealths of multiple states.

> *Part Four (1450–1750):* Rise of new empires; interaction, both hostile and peaceful, among the religious civilizations and new empires across all continents of the world. Origins of the New Science in Europe, based on the use of mathematics for the investigation of nature.

> *Part Five (1750–1900):* Origins of scientific–industrial "modernity," simultaneous with the emergence of constitutional and ethnic nation-states, in the West (Europe and North America); interaction of the West with Asia and Africa, resulting in complex adaptations, both coerced as well as voluntary, on the part of the latter.

> *Part Six (1900–Present):* Division of early Western modernity into the three competing visions: communism, supremacist nationalism, and capitalism. After two horrific world wars and the triumph of nation-state formation across the world, capitalism remains as the last surviving version of modernity. Capitalism is then reinvigorated by the increasing use of social networking tools, which popularizes both "traditional" religious and cultural ideas and constitutionalism in authoritarian states.

Chapter Organization and Structure

Each part of the book addresses the role of change and innovation on a broad scale in a particular time and/or region, and each chapter contains different levels of exploration to examine the principal features of particular cultural or national areas and how each affects, and is affected by, the patterns of origins, interactions, and adaptations:

> • *Geography and the Environment:* The relationship between human beings and the geography and environment of the places they inhabit is among

the most basic factors in understanding human societies. In this chapter segment, therefore, the topics under investigation involve the natural environment of a particular region and the general conditions affecting change and innovation. Climatic conditions, earthquakes, tsunamis, volcanic eruptions, outbreaks of disease, and so forth all have obvious effects on how humans react to the challenge of survival. The initial portions of chapters introducing new regions for study therefore include environmental and geographical overviews, which are revisited and expanded in later chapters as necessary. The larger issues of how decisive the impact of geography on the development of human societies is—as in the commonly asked question "Is geography destiny?"—are also examined here.

- *Political Developments:* In this segment, we ponder such questions as how rulers and their supporters wield political and military power. How do different political traditions develop in different areas? How do states expand, and why? How do different political arrangements attempt to strike a balance between the rulers and the ruled? How and why are political innovations transmitted to other societies? Why do societies accept or reject such innovations from the outside? Are there discernible patterns in the development of kingdoms or empires or nation-states?

- *Economic and Social Developments:* The relationship between economics and the structures and workings of societies has long been regarded as crucial by historians and social scientists. But what patterns, if any, emerge in how these relationships develop and function among different cultures? This segment explores such questions as the following: What role does economics play in the dynamics of change and continuity? What, for example, happens in agrarian societies when merchant classes develop? How does the accumulation of wealth lead to social hierarchy? What forms do these hierarchies take? How do societies formally and informally try to regulate wealth and poverty? How are economic conditions reflected in family life and gender relations? Are there patterns that reflect the varying social positions of men and women that are characteristic

of certain economic and social institutions? How are these in turn affected by different cultural practices?

- *Intellectual, Religious, and Cultural Aspects:* Finally, we consider it vital to include an examination dealing in some depth with the way people understood their existence and life during each period. Clearly, intellectual innovation—the generation of new ideas—lies at the heart of the changes we have singled out as pivotal in the patterns of origins, interactions, and adaptations that form the heart of this text. Beyond this, those areas concerned with the search for and construction of meaning—particularly religion, the arts, philosophy, and science—not only reflect shifting perspectives but also, in many cases, play a leading role in determining the course of events within each form of society. All of these facets of intellectual life are in turn manifested in new perspectives and representations in the cultural life of a society.

Features

- **Seeing Patterns/Thinking Through Patterns:** "Seeing Patterns" and "Thinking Through Patterns" use a question–discussion format in each chapter to pose several broad questions ("Seeing Patterns") as advance organizers for key themes, which are then matched up with short essays at the end ("Thinking Through Patterns") that examine these same questions in a sophisticated yet student-friendly fashion.

- **Patterns Up Close:** Since students frequently apprehend macro-level patterns better when they see their contours brought into sharper relief, "Patterns Up Close" essays in each chapter highlight a particular innovation that demonstrates origins, interactions, and adaptations in action. Spanning technological, social, political, intellectual, economic, and environmental developments, the "Patterns Up Close" essays combine text, visuals, and graphics to consider everything from the pepper trade to the guillotine.

- **Against the Grain:** These brief essays consider counterpoints to the main patterns examined in each chapter. Topics range from visionaries who challenged dominant religious patterns, to women who resisted various forms of patriarchy, to agitators who fought for social and economic justice.

- **Marginal Glossary:** To avoid the necessity of having to flip pages back and forth, definitions of key terms are set directly in the margin at the point where they are first introduced.

Today, more than ever, students and instructors are confronted by a vast welter of information on every conceivable subject. Beyond the ever-expanding print media, the Internet and the Web have opened hitherto unimaginable amounts of data to us. Despite such unprecedented access, however, all of us are too frequently overwhelmed by this undifferentiated—and all too often indigestible—mass. Nowhere is this more true than in world history, by definition the field within the historical profession with the broadest scope. Therefore, we think that an effort at synthesis—of narrative and analysis structured around a clear, accessible, widely applicable theme—is needed, an effort that seeks to explain critical patterns of the world's past behind the billions of bits of information accessible at the stroke of a key on a computer keyboard. We hope this text, in tracing the lines of transformative ideas and things that left their patterns deeply imprinted into the canvas of world history, will provide such a synthesis.

Changes to the New Edition

Streamlined narrative To facilitate accessibility, we have shortened the text by approximately 25 percent for this Brief Edition. This reduction has not come at the expense of discarding essential topics. Instead, we have tightened the narrative, focusing even more on key concepts and (with the guidance of reviewers) discarding extraneous examples. We are profoundly grateful to the reviewers who pointed out errors and conceptual shortcomings. Factual accuracy and terminological precision are extremely important to us.

Updated scholarship All chapters were revised and updated, in accordance with recent developments and new scholarship. Here is a chapter-by-chapter overview that highlights the changes we made in the third edition:

- **Part One** Chapter 1 includes three major changes: a discussion of the new stone tool finds in Kenya, dated to 3.3 million years ago; revisions to our understanding of the Neanderthals, on the basis of the new Bruniquel Cave finds; and revisions to our understanding of the human settlement of the Americas, resulting from new genetic studies (2015–2016). Chapter 2 clarifies the conceptual transition from nature spirituality to what is commonly called polytheism. Chapter 3 updates the material on ancient India and Harappans, and the "Patterns Up Close" in Chapter 5 adds the results of a new 2016 genetic study on corn.
- **Part Two** The title of Chapter 7 has been changed to "Interaction and Adaptation in Western Eurasia: Persia, Greece, and Rome" to more emphatically show the interactions among these cultural zones. Chapter 8 contains a revised section on Jainism, and Chapter 9 adds a survey of the contemporary debate about the "Han Synthesis."
- **Part Three** Chapter 10 offers clearer discussions of the Arab conquests of the Middle East, North Africa, and Iberia during the 600s and early 700s as well as of the composition of Islamic salvation history in the 800s, including the biography of the Prophet Muhammad. The coverage of Byzantium has been improved with a discussion of iconoclasm and the split between Catholicism and Greek Orthodoxy in 1054. Chapter 12 focuses more strongly on the Mongol interval and adds specificity to the discussion of Neo-Confucian philosophy. The new chapter subtitle, "Contrasting Patterns in India and China," reflects these changes.
- **Part Four** In Chapter 17 we eliminated considerable detail from the presentation of the European religious wars and broadened the focus in the English case to include the War of the Three Kingdoms. Chapter 21 updates the discussion of the Chinese rural economy and the debate about the High Level Equilibrium Trap. It also improves the discussion of Qing concepts of multicultural empire.
- **Part Five** In Chapter 22 the basic concepts of modern nationalism are reformulated: We now distinguish between the patterns of constitutionalism and ethnic nationalism as keys for the

understanding of political modernity. In addition, the process of Italian ethnic nationalist unification is presented more clearly. Chapter 23 is completely reorganized, emphasizing in addition the significance of the Paraguayan War of 1864–1870. In Chapter 24, the role of the Hakkas in the Taiping movement is described more clearly. Chapter 26 emphasizes the importance of the steam engine in the Industrial Revolution more strongly and reconceptualizes the nineteenth-century class structure in the emerging industrial societies. Chapter 27 defines more sharply the pattern of the New Imperialism during the nineteenth century.

- **Part Six** Chapter 29 updates the "Patterns Up Close" feature on the Non-Aligned Movement. In Chapter 30 we shortened the text so as to create room for an improved coverage of the Lebanese civil war, the Iranian Islamic Revolution, the US Vietnam War, and the Brazilian economic miracle. In Chapter 31, we similarly removed text and replaced it with paragraphs on the travails of the Arab Spring, the new military regime in Egypt, the "Islamic State" of Iraq and Syria, the failed coup d'état in Turkey, as well as the new populist anti-globalism, complete with "Brexit" in Europe and Donald J. Trump's electoral victory in the United States. The "Patterns Up Close" essay on information technology was updated to include IT's misuse by terrorists.

Ensuring Student Success

Oxford University Press offers instructors and students a comprehensive ancillary package for qualified adopters.

- **Dashboard:** Simple, informative, and mobile, Dashboard is an online learning and assessment platform tailored to your textbook that delivers a simple, informative, and mobile experience for professors and students. It offers quality content and tools to track student progress in an intuitive, web-based learning environment; features a streamlined interface that connects students and instructors with the most important course functions; and simplifies the learning experience

to save time and put student progress first. Dashboard for *Patterns of World History*, Third Edition, includes:

- An embedded e-book that integrates multimedia content, providing a dynamic learning space for both students and instructors. Each chapter in *Patterns of World History* includes:

image analysis

document analysis

map analysis, interactive timelines, and interactive concept maps

Many chapters also include video analysis

audio flashcards

- Three sets of quizzes per chapter for both low stakes and high stakes testing. The quizzes are aligned according to Bloom's Taxonomy: quiz 1 tests basic concepts and terminologies; quiz 2 provides questions that test both basic facts and ability to apply concepts; quiz 3 tests ability to evaluate and analyze key concepts.
- The complete set of questions from the testbank (1,500 questions), that provide for each chapter, approximately 40 multiple-choice, short-answer, true-or-false, and fill-in-the-blank as well as approximately 10 essay questions.
- **Ancillary Resource Center (ARC):** This online resource center, available to adopters of *Patterns of World History*, includes:
- **Instructor's Resource Manual:** Includes, for each chapter, a detailed chapter outline, suggested lecture topics, learning objectives, map quizzes, geography exercises, classroom activities, "Patterns Up Close" activities, "Seeing Patterns

and Making Connections" activities, "Against the Grain" exercises, biographical sketches, and suggested Web resources and digital media files. Also includes for each chapter approximately 40 multiple-choice, short-answer, true-or-false, and fill-in-the-blank as well as approximately 10 essay questions.

- **Oxford World History Video Library:** Includes short, two- to three-minute videos that offer overviews of such key topics as the the Golden Age of Islam, Genghis Khan, the steam engine, and the atomic age.
- **PowerPoints:** Includes PowerPoint slides and JPEG and PDF files for all the maps and photos in the text, an additional 400 map files from *The Oxford Atlas of World History*, and approximately 1,000 additional PowerPoint-based slides from OUP's Image Bank Library, organized by themes and topics in world history.
- **Computerized testbank:** Includes approximately 1,500 questions that can be customized by the instructor.
- **Course cartridges:** containing student and instructor resources are available for the most commonly used course management systems.

Additional Learning

- *Sources in Patterns of World History:* **Volume 1: To 1600:** Includes approximately 75 text and visual sources in world history, organized by the chapter organization of *Patterns of World History*. Each source is accompanied by a headnote and reading questions.
- *Sources in Patterns of World History:* **Volume 2: Since 1400:** Includes approximately 90 text and visual sources in world history, organized by the chapter organization of *Patterns of World History*. Each source is accompanied by a headnote and reading questions.
- *Mapping Patterns of World History,* **Volume 1: To 1600:** Includes approximately 50 full-color maps, each accompanied by a brief headnote, as well as blank outline maps and Concept Map exercises.
- *Mapping Patterns of World History,* **Volume 2: Since 1400:** Includes approximately 50 full-color

maps, each accompanied by a brief headnote, as well as blank outline maps and Concept Map exercises.
- *Now Playing: Learning World History Through Film:* Designed specifically to accompany *Patterns of World History*, this free supplement examines thirty-two films to show how key themes in world history play out in a variety of time periods and contexts.
- **Open Access Companion Website (www.oup .com/us/vonsivers):** Includes quizzes, note-taking guides, and flashcards.
- **E-book for Patterns of World History:** E-books of all the volumes, at a significant discount, are available for purchase at www.redshelf.com or www.vitalsource.com.

Bundling Options

Patterns of World History can be bundled at a significant discount with any of the titles in the popular Very Short Introductions, World in a Life, or Oxford World's Classics series, as well as other titles from the Higher Education division world history catalog (www.oup.com/us/catalog/he). Please contact your OUP representative for details.

Acknowledgments

Throughout the course of writing, revising, and preparing *Patterns of World History* for publication we have benefited from the guidance and professionalism accorded us by all levels of the staff at Oxford University Press. John Challice, vice president and publisher, had faith in the inherent worth of our project from the outset and provided the initial impetus to move forward. Meg Botteon guided us through the revisions and added a final polish, often helping us with substantive suggestions. Katherine Schnakenberg carried out the thankless task of assembling the manuscript and did so with generosity and good cheer, helping us with many details in the final manuscript. Carrie Crompton copyedited the manuscript with meticulous attention to detail, and Keith Faivre steered us through the intricacies of production with the stoicism of a saint.

Most of all, we owe a special debt of gratitude to Charles Cavaliere, our editor. Charles took on the daunting task of directing the literary enterprise at a critical point in the book's career. He pushed this project to its successful completion, accelerated its schedule, and used a combination of flattery and hard-nosed tactics to make sure we stayed the course. His greatest contribution, however, is in the way he refined our original vision for the book with several important adjustments that clarified its latent possibilities. From the maps to the photos to the special features, Charles's high standards and concern for detail are evident on every page.

Developing a book like *Patterns of World History* is an ambitious project, a collaborative venture in which authors and editors benefit from the feedback provided by a team of outside readers and consultants. We gratefully acknowledge the advice that the many reviewers, focus group participants, and class testers (including their students) shared with us along the way. We tried to implement all of the excellent suggestions. We owe a special debt of thanks to Evan R. Ward, who provided invaluable guidance for the revision of the coverage of Latin America and the Caribbean in Part 5, and to Jonathan S. Perry, who deftly assembled the documents. Of course, any errors of fact or interpretation that remain are solely our own.

Reviewers of the New Edition
Kevin Eoff, Palo Verde College

Christina Firpo, CalPoly University

Aaron Hagler, Troy University

Ephraim Harel, Montgomery College, Rockville

Michael Markus, Alabama State University

Scott Merriman, Troy University

Curtis Morgan, Lord Fairfax Community College

Joanna Neilson, Lincoln Memorial University

Jahan Salehi, Central Piedmont Community College

William Skiles, California State University, San Marcos

Marika Snider, Miami University

Daniel Stephen, Colorado State University

Jason Tatlock, Armstrong State University

Michael Thensted, Mississippi Gulf Coast Community College

Walter Ward, University of Alabama at Birmingham

Paul Tenkotte, Northern Kentucky University

Daniel R. Pavese, Wor-Wic Community College

and one anonymous reviewer.

Please let us know your experiences with *Patterns of World History* so that we may improve it in future editions. We welcome your comments and suggestions.

Peter von Sivers
pv4910@xmission.com

Charles A. Desnoyers
desnoyer@lasalle.edu

George B. Stow
gbsgeorge@aol.com

Note on Dates and Spellings

In keeping with widespread practice among world historians, we use "BCE" and "CE" to date events and the phrase "years ago" to describe developments from the remote past.

The transliteration of Middle Eastern words has been adjusted as much as possible to the English alphabet. Therefore, long vowels are not emphasized. The consonants specific to Arabic (alif, dhal, ha, sad, dad, ta, za, `ayn, ghayn, and qaf) are either not indicated or rendered with common English letters. A similar procedure is followed for Farsi. Turkish words follow the alphabet reform of 1929, which adds the following letters to the Western alphabet or modifies their pronunciation: c (pronounced "j"), ç (pronounced "tsh"), ğ (not pronounced but lengthening of preceding vowel), ı ("i" without dot, pronunciation close to short e), i/İ ("i" with dot, including in caps), ö (no English equivalent), ş ("sh"), and ü (no English equivalent). The spelling of common contemporary Middle Eastern and Islamic terms follows daily press usage (which, however, is not completely uniform). Examples are "al-Qaeda," "Quran," and "Sharia."

The system used in rendering the sounds of Mandarin Chinese—the northern Chinese dialect that has become in effect the national spoken language in China and Taiwan—into English in this book is *hanyu pinyin*, usually given as simply pinyin. This is the official romanization system of the People's Republic of China and has also become the standard outside of Taiwan, Republic of China. Most syllables are pronounced as they would be in English, with the exception of the letter q, which has an aspirated "ch" sound; ch itself has a less aspirated "ch" sound. *Zh* carries a hard "j" and j a soft, English-style "j." Some syllables also are pronounced—particularly in the regions around Beijing—with a retroflex r so that the syllable *shi*, for example, carries a pronunciation closer to "shir." Finally, the letter r in the *pinyin* system has no direct English equivalent, but an approximation may be had by combining the sounds of "r" and "j."

Japanese terms have been romanized according to a modification of the Hepburn system. The letter g is always hard; vowels are handled as they are in Italian—e, for example, carries a sound like "ay." We have not, however, included diacritical markings to indicate long vowel sounds for u or o. Where necessary, these have been indicated in the pronunciation guides.

For Korean terms, we have used a variation of the McCune-Reischauer system, which remains the standard romanization scheme for Korean words used in English academic writing, but eliminated any diacritical markings. Here again, the vowel sounds are pronounced more or less like those of Italian and the consonants, like those of English.

For Vietnamese words, we have used standard renditions based on the modern Quoc Ngu ("national language") system in use in Vietnam today. The system was developed by Jesuit missionaries and is based on the Portuguese alphabet. Once more, we have avoided diacritical marks, and the reader should follow the pronunciation guides for approximations of Vietnamese terms.

Latin American terms (Spanish, Nahua, or Quechua) generally follow local usage, including accents, except where they are Anglicized, per the *Oxford English Dictionary*. Thus, the Spanish-Quechua word "Tiahuanacu" becomes the Anglicized word "Tiwanaku."

We use the terms "Native American" and "Indian" interchangeably to refer to the peoples of the Americas in the pre-Columbian period and "Amerindian" in our coverage of Latin America since independence.

In keeping with widely recognized practice among paleontologists and other scholars of the deep past, we use the term "hominins" in Chapter 1 to emphasize their greater remoteness from apes and proximity to modern humans.

Phonetic spellings often follow the first appearance of a non-English word whose pronunciation may be unclear to the reader. We have followed the rules for capitalization per *The Chicago Manual of Style*.

About the Authors

Peter von Sivers is associate professor of Middle Eastern history at the University of Utah. He has previously taught at UCLA, Northwestern University, the University of Paris VII (Vincennes), and the University of Munich. He has also served as chair of the Joint Committee of the Near and Middle East, Social Science Research Council, New York, 1982–1985; editor of the *International Journal of Middle East Studies*, 1985–1989; member of the board of directors of the Middle East Studies Association of North America, 1987–1990; and chair of the SAT II World History Test Development Community of the Educational Testing Service, Princeton, NJ, 1991–1994. His publications include *Caliphate, Kingdom, and Decline: The Political Theory of Ibn Khaldun* (1968), several edited books, and three dozen peer-reviewed chapters and articles on Middle Eastern and North African history, as well as world history. He received his Dr. phil. from the University of Munich.

Charles A. Desnoyers is professor of history and director of Asian Studies at La Salle University in Philadelphia. He has previously taught at Temple University, Villanova University, and Pennsylvania State University. In addition to serving as History Department chair from 1999–2007, he was a founder and long-time director of the Greater Philadelphia Asian Studies Consortium and president (2011–2012) of the Mid-Atlantic Region Association for Asian Studies. He has served as a reader, table leader, and question writer for the AP European and World History exams. He served as editor of the organization's *Bulletin* from 1995–2001. In addition to numerous articles in peer-reviewed and general publications, his work includes *Patterns of Modern Chinese History* (2016, Oxford University Press) and *A Journey to the East: Li Gui's "A New Account of a Trip Around the Globe"* (2004, University of Michigan Press). He received his PhD from Temple University.

George B. Stow is professor of ancient and medieval history and director of the graduate program in history at La Salle University, Philadelphia. His teaching experience embraces a variety of undergraduate and graduate courses in ancient Greece and Rome, medieval England, and world history, and he has been awarded the Lindback Distinguished Teaching Award. Professor Stow is a member of the Medieval Academy of America and a Fellow of the Royal Historical Society. He is the recipient of a National Defense Education Act Title IV Fellowship, a Woodrow Wilson Foundation Fellowship, and research grants from the American Philosophical Society and La Salle University. His publications include a critical edition of a fourteenth-century monastic chronicle, *Historia Vitae et Regni Ricardi Secundi* (University of Pennsylvania Press, 1977), as well as numerous articles and reviews in scholarly journals including *Speculum*, *The English Historical Review*, the *Journal of Medieval History*, the *American Historical Review*, and several others. He received his PhD from the University of Illinois.

Patterns of
World History

PART ONE

From Human Origins to Early Agricultural Centers

PREHISTORY–600 BCE

World history is the discipline that tells us what humans had in common as they evolved both materially and mentally from prehistory to the present. The first period of world history (prehistory–600 BCE) can be subdivided into three wide-ranging phases.

The Origins of Modern Humanity

The first phase (6.5 million years ago–8500 BCE) began with the origins and evolution of humanity in Africa. After about 5.5 million years, around 80,000–50,000 BCE, groups of modern humans left Africa and began carrying their civilization across the entire world.

Technologically, the modern humans who left Africa had the skills to make tools from stone, bone, and wood. Mentally, they were also creating artifacts to which they attributed symbolic meaning, such as seashell necklaces and stone surfaces incised with geometric figures. This fully human civilization spread across the globe until the last ice age (32,000–12,000 years ago). Separated by impenetrable ice or desert barriers, modern human groups developed their own distinct regional technologies and cultures.

These groups organized themselves into larger lineage societies with shared initiation rites. Even the stone tools, jewelry, figurines, and rock images displayed remarkable similarities across their respective regions. In short, African-originated material technology and mental culture dominated the world.

Origins, Interactions, and Adaptations

7 million years ago
Toumaï, oldest possibly hominin fossil to date

15,500 years ago
Earliest archaeological evidence of humans in the Americas

300,000 years ago
Homo sapiens, or Modern Human, emerges in East Africa

9500 BCE
End of last ice age

The Origins of Agricultural Centers

The second phase (8500–3300 BCE) began once the global climate normalized. In the Middle East, foragers resumed their migratory patterns. Between 8500 and 7000 BCE, these foragers settled in permanent villages situated below mountain ranges, where seasonal runoff water supported forests and meadows. They collected plant seeds, which they developed into domesticated wheat, barley, rice, millet, and corn. They also captured and domesticated animals for their meat, milk, and hair.

Some of the early hill farmers moved into river valleys and deltas, where they expanded irrigation systems, supporting the rise of cities and kingdoms. The first agrarian-urban centers of the Middle East, India, China, and the Americas originated in irrigated river valleys between 3500 and 2500 BCE. Structured societies emerged in which kings and administrative and military ruling classes governed craftspeople and farmers.

The Origins of Empires

In the third phase, people outside the original Eurasian agrarian centers adapted to agriculture through interaction with these centers (3300–600 BCE). Steppe peoples, who controlled the mines containing the materials for making bronze, used their horses and bronze weapons to migrate to, conquer, or establish new kingdoms. These nomadic steppe peoples of Europe and central Asia connected the three agrarian centers of the Middle East, India, and China. A pattern was established whereby the three centers continuously adapted to each other's technological and cultural achievements, with steppe nomads functioning as their intermediaries.

From 1100 BCE onward the three Asian agrarian centers replaced bronze with iron for weapons and tools. Political and military competitiveness among kingdoms escalated. The first empires, such as the Neo-Assyrian Empire in the Middle East, appeared. Meanwhile, in Africa and the Americas, agrarian centers grew more slowly.

Thinking Like a World Historian

≫ What is the best way to describe the three early phases of world history?

≫ Why and how do we differentiate "modern" humans from earlier ancestors?

≫ What adaptations were necessary to improve agriculture? How did improvements in agriculture affect the development of society?

≫ What adaptations changed the methods of early warfare? How did developments in warfare affect regional interactions among civilizations?

≫ How did regional interactions with agricultural centers give rise to early kingdoms?

interactive timeline

8500 BCE
Beginnings of agriculture in Fertile Crescent

3000 BCE–200 CE
Lapita cultural complex in western Pacific

2500–1700 BCE
Flourishing of Harappan culture in Indus River valley, India

1650 BCE
Hittite Empire

750–600 BCE
Greek city-states: from aristocrats to citizen assemblies

ca. 7000 BCE
First evidence of rice cultivation in Yangzi valley

ca. 2700 BCE
First American city at Caral-Supe in Peru

1766–1122 BCE
Traditional dates for the Shang dynasty

1200 BCE
Beginning of Iron Age

>> Chapter 1   **PREHISTORY–10,000 BCE**

The African Origins of Humanity

O n November 30, 1974, Donald Johanson and Tom Gray left their
campsite in the Afar desert of Ethiopia in northeastern Africa to
search for fossils of human predecessors. Members of the expedition had
so far found only animal bones.

After two hours, Johanson glimpsed something out of place and called
out, "That's a bit of a [hominin] arm." He and Gray began to locate other
bones nearby. "An unbelievable, impermissible thought flickered through
my mind," Johanson remembered. "Suppose all these fitted together?
Could they be parts of a single, extremely primitive skeleton? No such skeleton had ever been found—anywhere." The two raced back to the camp,
sharing their excitement with the other scientists and local Afar workers.
That night, a tape recorder was playing the Beatles' song "Lucy in the Sky
with Diamonds"; so fossil Hadar AL 288-1, dated to 3.2 million years ago,
became known ever after as "Lucy."

Today, while Lucy is neither the oldest nor the most significant skeleton
ever found, she remains the most famous. For many people Lucy—the
petite female buried for 3.2 million years—is all they know about human
origins.

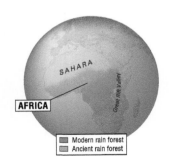

SAHARA

AFRICA

Great Rift Valley

◻ Modern rain forest
◻ Ancient rain forest

ABOVE: **Satellite view southward across the African Rift Valley.**

The story of Lucy introduces our study of the origins and evolution of humankind. In the course of millions of years, splits among hominin lineages produced lines of early humans who could fashion stone tools. From among other African lineages, the line of anatomically and intellectually modern humans evolved who fashioned cultural artifacts such as jewelry, geometric figures cut into stone, and rock drawings. Once more, humans left Africa and spread to Eurasia, Australia, and the Americas. These first modern humans had become *cultural beings*, by means of which they had acquired a measure of freedom from evolution: Instead of nature writing their history, they could create their own human history.

The Origins of Humanity

Interactions between climate, environment, and genes led to the emergence of fully evolved modern humans in Africa about 100,000 years ago. As we will see, history depends both on human agency and its resulting actions. Thanks to the work of archaeologists and anthropologists, we are beginning to recognize the complexity of all that had to happen on our evolutionary path to make us fully human.

Hominins: No Longer Chimpanzees, but Not Yet Human

Modern humans are the descendants of early human-like primates called **hominins**, which in the distant past lived in East Africa. The line of hominins split from that of the other apes around 5 million years ago. The parentage among the 20 or so known species of hominins coming thereafter is unclear. The fog begins to lift only around 1.8 million years ago, with the emergence of *Homo erectus*, the first hominin that left Africa and was adaptable to many new environments in Eurasia.

Many historians view the *pre*history of humans as a field belonging to archaeologists and anthropologists. For these historians, *history* begins only with the rise of the first cities in Mesopotamia around 3500 BCE, in which scribes created written documents. This view is unfortunate, since historians routinely consider the findings of scholars in other disciplines, such as archaeology, anthropology, climatology, geography, medicine, and sociology, when they write histories on topics after about 3500 BCE. Since written records, furthermore, are unreliable, historians turn to the findings of other disciplines wherever they can. Indeed, in the twenty-first century some historians have argued for eliminating the artificial distinction between prehistory and history, speaking instead of the "deep history" of humanity.

Who Are Our Ancestors?   The specific environmental and genetic interactions favorable for the split between hominin and other ape lines are complex. Climate change, reflected in the African rain forest advancing and retreating, played a part. It took about 1 million years, from 5 to 4 million years ago according to the genetic clock, and a fairly large population of 50,000–70,000 animals for the split between the chimpanzees in the ape line and the first hominins to begin and be completed. The genetic clock, however, is not only not beyond controversy; it is also not synchronized with the three oldest known tropical African fossils, which seem to depart from the rest of the ape line. The Toumaï skull (7–6 million years old), Orrorin femurs (6.1–5.7 million years old), and Kaddaba teeth (5.8–5.4 million years) seem

Australopiths:
Prehuman species of the
genus *Australopithecus*
that existed before those
classed under the genus
Homo.

Bipedalism: The first
human characteristic of
hominins; specifically,
the ability to walk
for short periods or
distances on hind legs.

Human Origins. Donald Johanson with Lucy.

to indicate hominin features. But whether the three can be counted as having belonged to human ancestors is still debated.

Firmer ground is reached with Ardi (*Ardipithecus ramidus*, 4.5–4.3 million
years ago), a descendant of Kaddaba. If the genetic clock is correct, the members
of this lineage lived on the hominin side of the chimpanzee–hominin split. In
their home in the tropical rain forests and savannas of East Africa, their capabil-
ity for straight-limbed tree-walking allowed them to move easily back and forth
between these two environments. Ardis could step out of the rain forest and walk
upright in the savanna, thereby increasing their adaptability, especially during dry
periods when the rain forest shrank. Most other apes, by contrast, stayed in the
rain forest.

Ardis apparently were not able yet to venture very far into drier environments.
After only 200,000 years they were replaced by a different species, the **australopiths**
(scientific name *Australopithecus*). These hominins date to 3.9–1.8 million years ago
and were widespread (see Map 1.1). We are fairly certain of these date ranges and
regional distributions because of a couple of key paleoanthropological finds: (1) a
set of fossilized footprints uncovered in Kenya and (2) "Lucy," the almost complete
skeleton found in Ethiopia. The footprints reveal how much improved the australopiths were as walkers on the ground, but they were still also very much at home in
the rain forest.

Environmental Adaptability   Improved upright walking, or **bipedalism,**
became a key evolutionary advantage to hominins. Walking on two feet frees the
arms to do something else. Being upright exposes a smaller body surface to the
sun, a factor important for venturing out from the rain forest into the **savanna** and
steppe. The plant resources available in these environments made the diet of hominins more flexible than other apes, which were limited to their rain-forest habitat.
It was in the savanna environment, today the Kenyan Turkana steppe basin, that
hominins around 3.3 million years ago fashioned the first stone tools, that
is, rocks split in such a way that the broken pieces had sharp edges. The
discovery of these tools, made in 2011, dethrones the 2.5-million-years-
old Oldowan tools, also unearthed in the Turkana basin in 1936, from
their place as the oldest tools. It now appears that the first evidence of
awakening intelligence has to be located in the earliest hominins, rather
than their successors.

On the Threshold of Humanity   The making of tools became
more refined and widespread about 2.5 million years ago in the hands
of australopith successor lineages. These younger flaked stones are
called **Oldowan** tools (after the Olduvai region in the Tanzanian
Great Rift Valley) and enabled the hominins to broaden their diet
from vegetarian foods to more or less regular meals of meat. Hominins became omnivores, partaking of a broader range of nutrition
available in nature. The making of stone tools marks the beginning
of the **Paleolithic,** or Old Stone Age, in prehistory, which lasted until
about 11,500 years ago.

A cool, dry spell of the climate about 1.8 million years ago made mobility again very important. A new hominin line, *Homo erectus* (*Upright*

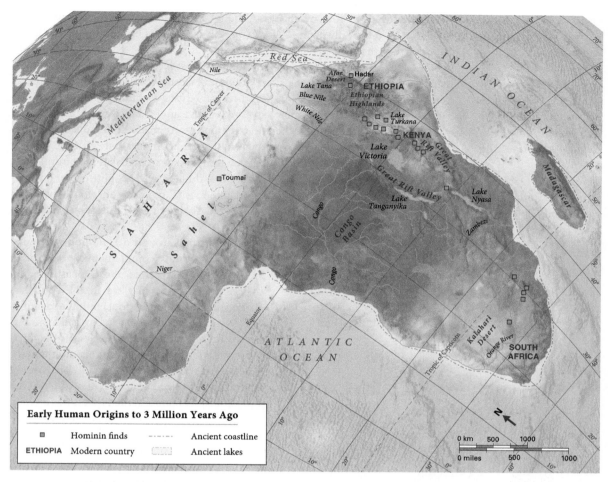

Early Human Origins to 3 Million Years Ago

- ◻ Hominin finds
- ETHIOPIA Modern country
- ------- Ancient coastline
- ▢ Ancient lakes

MAP 1.1 **Early Human Origins to 3 Million Years Ago.**

Human), evolved, which no longer climbed trees, was fully stabilized on its feet, and could walk long distances. It could deal equally with rain forest, savanna, grasslands, and now also steppe habitats, and it mastered the control of fire in caves one million years ago, as announced in 2004 on the basis of finds in South Africa. Small groups of hominins, so scholars assume, formed camp groups, huddling around fires at cave

interactive timeline

7–5.4 million years ago
Toumaï, Orrorin, and Kaddaba, possibly hominin fossils

4.5 million years ago
Ardi hominins, first assumed human ancestor line

1.8 million years ago
Homo erectus, present in Asia and Africa

5 million years ago
Split of the chimpanzee–hominin lines, as indicated by the genetic clock

4.2–1.8 million years ago
Multiple lines of australopith hominins

300,000 years ago
Homo sapiens, or Modern Human, emerges in East Africa

60,000–50,000 years ago
Modern humans migrate to Australia

13,500–13,000 years ago
Traditional assumption of human arrival in the Americas

80,000–60,000 years ago
Modern humans migrate from East Africa to Asia

35,000 years ago
Earliest evidence of modern humans in Europe and Siberia

9,400–9,300 years ago
"Spirit Cave Mummy" and "Kennewick Man" in the North American West

Oldowan toolmaking: Early stone-carving technique, which consisted of splitting a stone into two, thereby producing sharp edges on both fragments. See also **Acheulian** and **Levallois toolmaking**.

Paleolithic: Old Stone Age, 2.5–11,500 million years ago.

entrances or under rock overhangs. Although the brain size of *H. erectus* was about half of that of the fully evolved *H. sapiens,* this new line of hominins was the first to adopt habits that we can recognize as human.

H. erectus created improved stone tools in most places where the line lived. Instead of continuing to use the simple Oldowan stones with sharp edges, *H. erectus* created the new **Acheulian** [ah-SHOI-lee-yan] stone technology, around 1.8–1.6 million years ago. (This technology was named after Saint-Acheul, a suburb of Amiens in northern France where the first finds were made in the nineteenth century.) Acheulian tools were oval or pear-shaped hand axes cut with the help of hammer stones from larger cores, or they were one or more flakes split from cores. When the edges of these hand axes became dull, *H. erectus* split further, smaller flakes away to resharpen the edges. A simple visual comparison of Oldowan and Acheulian tools reveals how much the manual skills of early humans advanced in about a million years.

Fossils from around 1.8 million years ago indicate the almost simultaneous presence of *H. erectus* in East Africa, the Caucasus region in eastern Europe, and Java in the southeast Asian archipelago. Stone tools in India, dated to 1.8–1.6 million years ago, can be similarly interpreted as indicators of the presence of *H. erectus* in the subcontinent. Given this simultaneity, scholars are reconsidering the traditional "out of Africa" theory assumed for *H. erectus.* Until the early 2000s scholars assumed that it was a group of this line that led the first great wave of hominins leaving Africa for the Middle East and Asia. But now it seems possible that one or several of the predecessor lines accomplished this feat several hundred thousand years earlier.

The *H. erectus* fossils from the Dmanisi Cave in Georgia in the Caucasus, discovered in 2005, are important to this revision of the theory of *H. erectus* as the first hominin out of Africa. The cave contained five sets of fully preserved skulls and bones, the anatomies of which were very different from each other. Had they been found individually in caves distant from each other, researchers would have viewed them as belonging to five different lines of early *Homo.* Instead, researchers concluded not only that the five fossils belong to the same line but that numerous other fossils found in Africa as well as Asia and dated to around 1.8 million years ago are members of the same hominin line. The ancestor clearly came from Africa, but the line of *H. erectus* itself was perhaps of non-African origin.

Oldest Stone Tools to Date. These tools, discovered in Kenya at the Lomekwi 3 archaeological site in the Turkana Basin, are 3.3 million years old.

Human Adaptations: From Africa to Eurasia and Australia

H. erectus was the ancestor of *H. sapiens* (Wise Human, "Modern Human" in this chapter), the species of modern humans to which we belong. Scholars are far from agreed, however, as to how many intermediate lineages existed between then and now. When *H. sapiens* emerged in Africa about 300,000 years ago, two characteristics distinguished this human being from its forerunners: *technical skills* and *cultural creativity*. These two characteristics represent a fundamental transformation of hominins.

The African Origins of Human Culture

The oldest specimen of a *H. sapiens* found so far is a jawbone with teeth recovered from the site of Jebel Irhoud in Morocco. It was dated in 2017 to about 300,000 years ago. The archaeological record documenting modern humans in Africa is still spotty, but the 17 sites containing bone and skull remnants of *H. sapiens* as well as a half-dozen sites with human artifacts demonstrate that *H. sapiens*, in a process of gradual development in Africa, became physically and intellectually fully human and capable of culture. While humans remained subject to the interaction between environment and genes, requiring constant adaptation, culture gave them the freedom to accept and reject—a completely new dimension largely independent from nature.

Livelihood   Early hominins were scavengers, not hunters. They may have purposely followed predators and chased them away after the kill. Stone scrapers, once invented, facilitated the separation of meat from carcasses. An elusive post–*H. erectus* line introduced spears in the form of sharpened sticks some 400,000 years ago and thus allowed the transition from scavenging to hunting. Really effective spears had to await *H. sapiens* as the creator of the much-refined new stoneworking technique, the **Levallois** [le-val-WAH], derived from the name of a suburb of Paris, France, where in the nineteenth century the first spear points were found. With this technique, a craftsperson chipped off small flakes from the edges of a prepared stone core and then hammered a larger flake—flat on the bottom, domed on the top, and sharpened by the small flakes around the edge—from the center, leaving a deep indentation in the spent core. These center flakes could be as large as hand axes and meat cutters or as small as spear points. The appearance of spear points and increasingly large numbers of animal bones in the archaeological sites indicates that *H. sapiens* was emerging as an efficient hunter. The hunt tended to be the province of males and remained a prestige occupation for much of human history. But it provided no more than a supplement to *H. sapiens'* nutrition, which remained plant-based.

The combination of the male-dominated hunt with the communal gathering of plant foods defines "forager society." Foraging, sometimes called "hunting and gathering," was the dominant pattern of human history for several hundred thousand years. It is also the least documented period, requiring for its understanding a combination of archaeology with the anthropological insights gained from observation of surviving foraging societies. Thus, descriptions of such societies are unavoidably somewhat speculative.

Acheulian toolmaking: A technique which consisted of flaking a hard piece of rock (especially flint, chert, or obsidian) on both sides into a triangle-shaped hand axe, with cutting edges, a hand-held side, and a point.

Levallois toolmaking: A stone technique whereby stone workers first shaped a hard rock into a cylinder or cone.

H. sapiens continued to live in sheltered places provided by cave entrances and rock overhangs. But there were also campsites with hut-like shelters made from branches. Clothing consisted of skins and furs acquired through hunting. Hearths, in which *H. sapiens* could build fires, served as places for cooking and warmth. Anthropological studies suggest that extended families congregated around the hearths for comfort and companionship. In the vicinity of the campsite, a total of a dozen dispersed families formed a clan, among which sexual partners were chosen.

Around 120,000 years ago, food gathering and preparation appear to have become considerably more varied. *H. sapiens* began to include fish and shellfish in their diets, using tools carved from bone, such as hooks and barbed points mounted on spears. With the help of grindstones, men and women pulverized hard seeds for consumption or storage. Plaster-lined storage pits appeared in the camps, as did separate refuse dumps. As the settlements became more numerous, trade networks sprang up, providing toolmakers with obsidian mined as far as 200 miles away. Obsidian is a glass-like hard rock found near volcanoes and therefore relatively rare, so it was much sought after. This initial period of trade marks the beginning of increasing human *interaction*—a process vital to the transferring of cultural and technological innovation among human groups.

Gender Relations   A central element in human culture is the relationship between men and women. Unfortunately, archaeology is unable to reveal much about this relationship in Paleolithic forager society. Obviously, the roles of men and women were less specialized among foragers than in agrarian–urban society: males and females spent most of their time collecting and preparing plant foods together, and the male-dominated hunt was a supplemental occupation. But how much these occupations furthered a male–female balance or allowed for one of the two genders to become dominant is not easy to determine.

With the rise of feminism in academia scholars revived the idea, popular in the nineteenth century, of an early female-centered society. This society, it has been asserted, was egalitarian, peaceful, and goddess-oriented. It was agrarian, but assumed to have had deep roots in the preceding forager stage of human life. In this view, warlike male dominance came about only with the rise of horseback-riding herders from the Eurasian steppes.

Other anthropologists, instead, assumed that male dominance began at about the same time that warring kingdoms emerged in the Middle East. War captives became slaves, and hierarchies emerged in which women, in turn, found themselves relegated to inferior positions. However the origins of patriarchy are explained, there is little controversy over its connection with agrarian–urban life. What came before, however, and was prevalent during the Paleolithic forager period of human history is impossible to determine one way or the other.

Creation of Symbols   Activity in the camps of *H. sapiens* expanded from the craftsmanship of tools to that of nonutilitarian objects. This expansion was perhaps the decisive step with which *H. sapiens* became truly modern. Around 135,000 years ago, humans in what is today Morocco in northwest Africa perforated seashells and fragments of ostrich eggshell and strung them on leather strips as pendants and necklaces. The significance of this step cannot be overemphasized. By themselves, seashells and ostrich eggshells are natural objects of no particular distinction, but as jewelry they have the unique meaning of beauty for their wearer. They are *symbols*, which are mental concepts distinct from shells found as objects in nature.

H. sapiens was the first and only being that did not think only in the concrete, practical terms of toolmaking but also in *abstract* symbolic terms by using something to express something else, such as jewelry for the concept of beauty. This transformation may be seen as the foundation of art, religion, philosophy, science, and all other intellectual pursuits.

Archaeological examples for the emergence of abstract symbolic thinking in Africa are not yet very numerous. But taken together they powerfully suggest an intellectual modernity emerging to match the anatomical modernity of African *H. sapiens*. From about 90,000 years ago, for example, we begin to see gravesites—indicators of reflection on the significance of life, death, ancestral dignity, and generational continuity. Humans added jewelry as the preferred grave gift, suggesting the contemplation of an afterlife.

Even more recognizably abstract are the early symbols appearing on a 70,000-year-old small piece of ochre excavated in 1991 from Blombos Cave and on 60,000-year-old ostrich eggshell fragments excavated in 1996 from Diepkloof Rock Shelter, both in South Africa. They display geometrically arranged engravings, the meaning of which is unknown. Ochre is a soft, reddish form of rock easily ground into powder and as such often found as a gift in prehistoric graves, symbolizing blood with its power of life. Ostrich eggshells served as containers that could be adorned with engravings.

Finally, a small stone plaque from the Apollo 11 Cave in Namibia, discovered in 1969–1972, featuring the image of an animal is of particular importance for the appreciation of the African origin of *H. sapiens*. The plaque is estimated to be 25,000 years old. Collectively, the above examples can be taken as a confirmation of *H. sapiens* not only as a technically versatile toolmaker but also as the one animal capable of creating symbols that signify something beyond the materials from which they were made.

Migration from Africa Once the *H. sapiens* lineage was fully equipped with practical skills and the foundations of culture, it was adaptable to almost any environment. In 2016, three teams of genetic researchers working independently from each other came to the conclusion that all non-Africans in the world today descend from groups of Africans who left the continent between 80,000 and 50,000 years ago. Many scholars assume that these groups left Africa for Asia by crossing the straits between Ethiopia and Yemen and between Oman and Iran. The members of this group, it is thought, moved along the coast, arriving in India, Malaysia, and Indonesia about 77,000 years ago. Some of their descendants seem to have reached China about 70,000 years ago, sailing to Australia sometime after 60,000 years ago, and crossing from Korea over a then existing land bridge to Japan about 30,000 years ago. Eventually, modern humans from south Asia migrated northwestward to Europe and northeastward to Siberia, where they arrived around 44,000 years ago. The Siberian groups then made their way to Alaska in North America 23,000 years ago, completing the journey around the world in 60,000 years (see Map 1.2).

Apollo 11 Cave, Namibia. An animal depicted on a stone slab, from about 25,000 years ago. Together with the Blombos Cave ochre, this artwork is evidence of early humans' ability to create symbols.

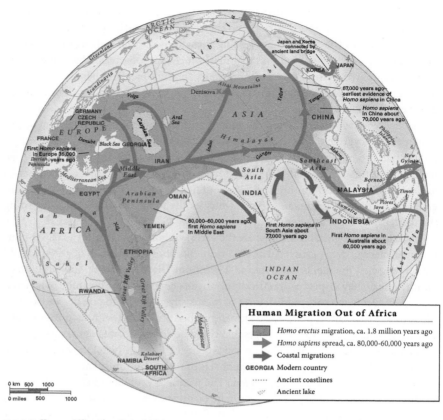

MAP **1.2 Human Migration Out of Africa.**

Migration from South Asia to Australia

Australia was the only large world region where foraging remained dominant until the modern scientific–industrial age and, therefore, could be studied almost until today. Largely isolated from the rest of the world until the eighteenth century, the Australian foragers developed a distinct culture of their own. But since they shared the same *H. sapiens* genes as their hunter-gatherer relatives on the Afro-Eurasian continent, the life patterns of both also remained fundamentally similar, in terms of foraging, social organization, and symbolical expression.

Geography and Migration   Although it is the smallest of the earth's continents, Australia extends across a variety of geographical zones. In the north, rain forest became dominant. In eastern Australia, various mixtures of forest, savanna, and steppe evolved. The center and most of the west of the continent developed a mixture of steppes, deserts, and lakes. The south (today's southeastern Australia and Tasmania) became temperate, with an almost South African or Mediterranean climate. Small pockets of mountain vegetation came into existence only in what are today the central parts of eastern Australia and southern Tasmania. These geographical environments became the homes to modern humans, who descended originally from Africa and had adapted to life in south Asia.

During an ice age 70,000–60,000 years ago, south Asia and most of the northern islands of Indonesia were connected by land bridges. Farther south, island chains where one could travel by raft without losing sight of land encouraged further travel. Inevitably, the mariners reached a point where land was no longer visible on the horizon. About 60,000 years ago, the distance from the island of Timor to Australia was 65 miles. Scholars have speculated that smoke rising from lightning-produced brush fires in the south could have suggested to some enterprising mariners that there was land beyond the horizon. Whatever motivated them to take to the sea, they evidently succeeded in crossing it.

Settlement of the Continent *H. sapiens* groups arrived on the Australian continent and slowly fanned out. The descendants of the original settlers became known in our own time as **Aboriginals**. Bringing their African and south Asian foraging customs with them, the settlers hunted the Australian animals and gathered edible plants. Unlike in Africa and Eurasia, with their profusion of dangerous animals, there were few predator species to threaten these first humans. The Aboriginal peoples gradually hunted the largest species to extinction, and by about 16,000 years ago, only medium and small animals, such as kangaroos and wombats, were left to hunt.

As elsewhere in foraging societies, men were the hunters. They used spears and spear throwers—short sticks with a curve or hook on the end to extend the length of the thrower's arm and give additional power to the flight of the spear. Once the large animals were gone, hunting became a highly diversified set of activities for the Aboriginals.

Women, and secondarily men, were responsible for gathering plant foods. The basic staples were wild millet and rice. The main fruits and vegetables were the solanum [sow-LAH-num], a tomato-like fruit; the yam daisy, a sweet, milky tuber; and the quandong [KWAN-dong] fruit. Women used grindstones to prepare vegetables and hard seeds, such as pine nuts, flax, and acacia seeds, as well as bracken (a large fern) and bindweed (a family of vines).

Eucalyptus, a native of Australia found nearly everywhere on the continent, served for firewood in stone-built hearths. People also used fire as a hunting tool and to promote revegetation. Controlled fires drove animals to where strategically positioned hunting parties could slaughter them. Forest fires were used to synchronize more closely the production and collection of nuts and fruits on trees. Over time, the Aboriginals developed a keen sense of how to efficiently exploit as well as preserve nature.

Australia was less rich in grasses suitable for grain cultivation than southwest Asia. Australia had only two types of edible grass seeds; in southwest Asia, there were around 40 types. Thus, foraging remained the dominant mode of subsistence, even if people stayed in their camps for long periods of time before moving. Only in the south, where eel trapping was the main form of livelihood, did permanent villages appear, similar to their counterparts in late forager Africa, Europe, North America, and Japan. Aboriginals thus remained closely adapted to the basic patterns of forager livelihood until the first English settlers arrived at the end of the eighteenth century CE.

Social Structures and Cultural Expressions Since modern-day Aboriginals remained faithful to their traditional forms of life, a great deal about their social

Aboriginals: The original settlers of Australia, who arrived some 60,000–50,000 years before the arrival of European settlers at the end of the eighteenth century CE.

structures and organization is known. Australian anthropologists have collected a wealth of data, observing forager culture as it existed in the nineteenth and early twentieth centuries.

According to this literature, in the traditional Aboriginal society of the nineteenth century or earlier, marriages were predominantly *monogamous*. Some men who not only were successful hunters but also became wealthy through trade could acquire additional wives. Families that camped together formed *clans*, units in which all families considered themselves to be descendants of a common ancestor. Groups of clans formed lineages of between 500 and 1,500 members. Generally, lineages were too large to camp or move about together. They were, rather, loose associations of clans living miles apart from which individuals selected their marriage partners. Marriages took place among members of one group of clans and members of another group. Lineages met collectively once a year at one of the sacred places of their land for rituals and ceremonies.

The Dreamtime   Despite this loose social organization, lineage members considered themselves trustees of clearly marked parcels of ancestral land. Typical markers were identifiable features of the landscape, such as rocks, rivers, or trees. *Taboos*—things or practices that were forbidden—and myths surrounded both land and markers. People venerated them through myths and rituals presided over by respected elders. The most esteemed elders possessed a deep knowledge of the clan's past in the **Dreamtime**, the name given to the ancient period in which the lineage's past was embedded.

The Dreamtime consisted of the stories, customs, and laws that defined the lineage in its original, perfect state at the time of creation. Elders acquired access to this time through trance states, requiring many years of initiation, training, and practice. Their knowledge of the Dreamtime, it was believed, gave them access to creation's hidden powers. Elders, however, did not possess a monopoly on this knowledge. All members of the clan had access to its sacred heritage and could use it to practice magic.

Aboriginal elders never were able to wield political power through armed forces within their own lineages. Since there was no agriculture and, therefore, no agricultural surplus, and since trade did not evolve beyond the exchange of obsidian, tools, and weapons, elders could not acquire enough wealth to pay fighters. On the continent's northern coast there was a modest trade in local pearls for goods from Timor; but it was insufficient to support the rise of powerful chiefdoms. Aboriginal society thus remained "stateless" in the sense of possessing no administrative institutions.

Australian Rock Art   How much the Dreamtime involved rock paintings is unfortunately not known. Contemporary Aboriginals are unable to interpret the meaning of early rock paintings. Changing climatic conditions leading to different migration patterns are presumably responsible for modern Aboriginals losing their familiarity with the meanings of ancient Australian rock art.

The best-known Australian rock images are the so-called Bradshaw paintings in the Kimberley Region of northwest Australia, which probably date to a period of 30,000–20,000 years ago. Scholars divide the Bradshaw paintings into two major stylistic periods, beginning with (1) indentations, grooves, and animals and followed by (2) elongated human figures with tassels or sashes; fruits and vegetables

Dreamtime: In the Australian Dreamtime, the shaman constructs an imaginary reality of the lineage's origins and roots, going back to the time when the world was created and the creator devised all customs, rituals, and myths.

resembling human figures; and clothespin and stick figures.

The two periods are very difficult to date, since so far none of the places where they have been found have yielded any material that could be reliably carbon dated. So far, only one Bradshaw painting has been dated, to some 17,500 years ago. Scholars generally assume that the proliferation of Bradshaws was roughly contemporary with the flourishing of prehistoric rock art in Europe.

The striking parallelism between Australian and European rock art demonstrates that humans did not have to interact to express themselves culturally in similar ways. Similar forager patterns could evolve without mutual contact. The fact that a proliferation of rock paintings occurred more or less simultaneously in Australia and Europe suggests that none of the human groups migrating away from Africa was privileged over any other. This cultural parity among foragers needs to be kept in mind as we turn to African *H. sapiens* migrating to Europe.

Australian Shamans in a Trance. These "Bradshaw" figures are usually interpreted as showing movements and communication with the spirits of animated cosmic nature.

Migration from Asia to Europe

There was a gap of at least 30,000 years between groups of modern humans leaving Africa (80,000–60,000 years ago) and migrating to Europe (44,000 years ago). Scholars assume that these humans settled first in central Asia before their descendants fanned out to East Asia and Europe. By that time, *H. sapiens* was well adapted to the climate of the savannas and steppes. Little is known about the migratory path these descendants chose as they walked across the Asian interior to Europe (see Map 1.2).

Neanderthals and Other Lines   When *H. sapiens* arrived in Europe around 44,000–35,000 years ago, this region was already settled by another human line, that of the **Neanderthals** [nay-AN-der-tall, after a valley in northwest Germany where the first specimen was found in the nineteenth century]. This line is assumed to have descended from a successor to *H. erectus* 300,000 years ago, although the exact descent is unclear. In fact, on the basis of fossil finds in Spain (Sima de los Huesos) and Siberia (Denisova), as well as subsequent DNA analyses of these finds during 2010–2013, scholars now speak of several successor lineages, coexisting and interbreeding with *H. erectus* in Europe and Asia.

Neanderthals are the best-documented Paleolithic fossil humans in Europe and western Asia, with over 600 finds. The fossils range in age from 230,000 to 24,000 years old and are distributed between western Europe, the Altai Mountains in eastern Asia, and the Middle East. Early European *H. sapiens*—or **Crô-Magnon** [crow-MAG-non, after the name of the cave in southwestern France where, in the nineteenth century, European *H. sapiens* bones were first found]—was clearly an intruder in an inhabited, if still sparsely settled, human landscape.

In their forager livelihood, the two species were very similar. The former, however, were smaller and more heavily boned than modern humans. Neanderthals were probably able to talk, albeit in a rudimentary way, since they did not possess the throat structures of *H. sapiens*. Unlike modern humans, they buried their dead without gifts.

The stone and bone toolkits of the two were alike, but whether Neanderthals created paintings is at present not certain, in spite of some claims that they might be responsible for a few controversial images (for example, the image of two seals in a cave near Málaga, Spain, dated in 2012 to 43,000 years ago; hand stencils and disks in the cave of El Castillo, Spain, redated in 2012 to 40,800 years ago; and a cross in Gorham's Cave, Gibraltar, dated in 2014 to 39,000 years ago). Most intriguing is the discovery, publicized in 2016, of the cave of Bruniquel in southwestern France. At a distance of 1,100 feet from the entrance, some 176,000 years ago Neanderthals broke off stalagmites from the floor and arranged them in one large and one incomplete small circle. Burned bones testify to the use of fire (for lighting?) in the cave. Slowly, we are beginning to receive a more detailed idea of the depth of Neanderthal life and culture in Europe and Asia.

Rock Paintings and Figurines *H. sapiens'* cultural creativity continued after the migration into Asia and Europe. On the latter continent, there are some 700 caves with rock paintings and engravings, as well as aboveground sites with small figurines. Currently, the oldest known artifacts are the paintings of El Castillo and a small ivory figurine of a mammoth dating to 35,000 years ago and found in 2007 in southwestern Germany.

Several thousand years later, an entire class of female figurines called "Venuses" appeared all over western Europe. These figurines were made of stone or bone, and one of them, unearthed in the Czech Republic, was formed of fired clay ca. 26,000 years ago. The creation of the first ceramic pieces was thus a Paleolithic invention, even though the regular production of pottery appeared only some 17,000 years later, in agrarian society. All figurines were small and transportable. Some Venuses have been interpreted as fertility goddesses, indicating an early matriarchy, but this interpretation is questionable, given the variety of female and male figurines of the Venus type. Other scholars view these figurines as dolls for children in the camps or as representatives of relatives or ancestors in camp rituals.

The great majority of rock paintings in Europe show animals, either alone or in herds, at rest or in motion, chasing or fleeing other beasts, or locked in conflict with each other. The oldest paintings found so far are of steppe animals—reindeer, horses, cattle, aurochs, bison, mammoths, or rhinoceroses—with which modern humans, migrating from the Russian steppes into central and western Europe, were familiar. Dating to 30,000 years ago, they were discovered in 1994 in Chauvet [show-VAY] Cave in southern France.

Depictions of humans are comparatively rare. The best-known image, at Lascaux [las-COE] in southwestern France and dated to 17,000 years ago, is that of a prostrate human figure with an erect penis. In front of him is a bison that may have been hit by a spear. Nearby is a spear with a bird on top. A rhinoceros faces away from the man.

Modern chemical analyses have shown that the rock painters knew how to grind and mix minerals to make different colors. They used protrusions in the rock walls to enhance three-dimensionality. In a number of images, frontal and lateral views are combined. One image depicts a bison with six legs, evidently simulating its swift motion. Thus, the thematic diversity of images had its complement in technical versatility.

The main places with rock art are halls and domes deep inside often miles-long caves. The complete darkness inside was illuminated with torches and grease-filled

image analysis

25,000-Year-Old Venus Figurine. This is the oldest known figurine made of fired clay. It was excavated at Dolní Věstonice, Czech Republic, in 1925. Many more broken figurines were found near the kiln. They perhaps represented family members during rituals and, as bearers of their spirits, had to be destroyed at the end of the rituals so as to end their influence.

Lascaux Cave. This 17,000-year-old image could be interpreted as depicting the scene of a mortally wounded, angry bison attacking a defenseless human. Alternatively, it might also depict a human in deep sleep or trance (hence the erect penis) in the presence of one of the most common steppe animals, also with an enlarged sexual organ. The interest in sexuality, also reflected in the Venus figures, might represent a growing awareness not only of a common spirituality in humans, animals, and plants, but also of a common vitality animating the world.

bowls with wicks. Flutes, made of swan bones, and stalagmites, tapped as percussion instruments, testify to the presence not only of painters but also of musicians. To judge by the extant footprints, teenagers as well as adults, men as well as women assembled inside the caves. Modern scholars speculate that the caves were places for rituals, perhaps even shamanic assemblies, in which elders, in trance, entered a spiritual world shared with other living beings. It is possible to recognize in the Paleolithic artifacts the beginnings of religious thought, specifically the idea of a spiritual nature connecting humans, animals, and plants with each other.

The Ice Age Crisis and Human Migration to the Americas

Modern humans experienced two ice ages. The first one, 70,000–60,000 years ago, created land bridges that enabled humans to cross much of the Indonesian archipelago on foot and travel the rest of the distance by boat to Australia. This ice age was comparatively mild and brief, in contrast to the last ice age of the world's history, 30,000–13,500 years ago, which severely altered the flora and fauna on all continents. Humans, although suffering through it, exploited it for one major achievement: their migration from Siberia to the Americas.

The Ice Age
The end of the Paleolithic era occurred during one of the climatically most inhospitable periods in world history. Large parts of the world either descended into a

deep freeze or became bone dry. The northern zone of Eurasia, from England to Siberia, became a desolate wasteland, partially covered with gigantic ice sheets. The central zone, from southern France to Mongolia, consisted of semiarid steppe lands. The southern zone, from Iberia to southern China, was temperate but semidry, with grasslands and pockets of woodlands.

In Africa and Australia, the rain forest was reduced to a few areas in central Africa and the northern tip of Australia, leaving the rest of those continents largely exposed to drought. The northern Sahara and southern Kalahari in Africa as well as the interior of Australia transformed what were once rich savannas and rain forests into deserts. Life for modern humans in Eurasia, Africa, and Australia during this ice age was an arduous struggle for daily survival (see Map 1.3).

Difficult Living Conditions   Signs of stress testify to the harsh conditions of the Ice Age. Because of the difficult conditions, humans abandoned the northern European and Russian plains, which remained uninhabited for 15 millennia. Central European settlements were hemmed in between Scandinavian and Alpine glaciers. Many animal species, adapted to warmer weather (including Neanderthals; see

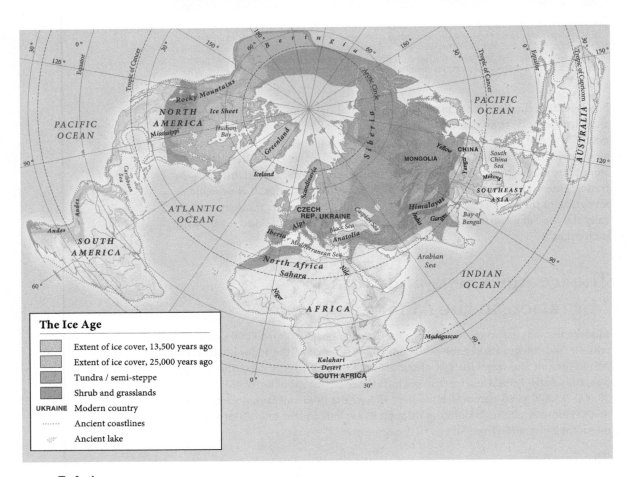

MAP 1.3 **The Ice Age.**

Patterns Up Close) did not take the Ice Age well, and died out. Species that thrived in colder weather (such as woolly mammoths, mastodons, woolly rhinoceroses, and giant deer) failed to adjust after the end of the Ice Age when the weather became warm again. Whether humans hastened the disappearance of the latter animals through overhunting is a matter of dispute. Ultimately, most of these huge beasts died out around 6,000–4,000 years ago.

Although life was not easy, *H. sapiens* possessed the technological and mental resources to survive. The modern humans had a variety of implements for catching fish, snaring birds, and hunting animals, including harpoons, fishhooks, and darts made of bone; fishnets; and bird traps. Boomerangs, invented independently in Europe and Australia, were used for hunting larger fowl. Wooden handles attached to large stone axe heads increased the efficiency of cutting meat or wood. In a situation of increasingly scarce large animals, *H. sapiens* became efficient at hunting small animals.

Human mobility increased substantially. Canoes took the form of dugouts or were constructed of bone and wood frames covered with skins. As a result of innovations like the canoe, the range for trading expanded. Baltic *amber* (fossilized tree resin prized for making jewelry) has been found 600 miles away from its origin in southern Europe, and Mediterranean shells in Ukraine, 800 miles to the northeast.

Ice Age humans dressed themselves warmly, wearing hooded fur coats stitched together with bone needles, using thin leather strips, as evidenced by figurines discovered in Siberia. An imprint left on kiln-fired clay, found in the Czech Republic, indicates that humans also began to weave woolen cloth on looms. No doubt, *H. sapiens* groups were decimated by the impact of the Ice Age, but survivors were still hanging on when the world finally warmed up again around 14,500 years ago.

The Beringia Land Bridge   During the coldest period of the Ice Age, around 19,000 years ago, global sea levels dropped by some 450 feet, increasing the land mass of the continents by about 100 miles in all directions and exposing land bridges connecting Indonesia to Malaysia, Japan to Korea, and Asia to North America. The land bridge connecting Asia and North America to Siberia and the Americas was Beringia, a large landmass of some half-a-million square miles, which today has been reduced to the area of what is Alaska and northwestern Canada.

Northern Beringia was covered with ice and **tundra**, but the southern rim was apparently ice-free. Sediment cores taken from the seabed off Alaska contain pollen as well as plant and insect fossils, suggesting the existence of shrublands and forests. Therefore, it was possible for humans and animals to survive along the southern rim of Beringia. A few stone tool and spear point finds in Alaska lend weight to the human survival theory.

But, as research published in 2014 argues, survival would have been at the cost of isolation, with humans cut off from both Siberia and the lower Americas for some 10,000 years. Indeed, genetics points to such an isolation, since the mitochondrial DNA (genetic information passed on by mothers) taken from present-day Native Americans indicates that their genome emerged in Siberia about 25,000 years ago, but did not spread within the Americas until about 15,000 years ago. Thus, Beringia

Tundra: Landscape in which the topsoil unfreezes during the summer and supports dwarf shrubs, sedges and grasses, mosses, and lichens.

The Disappearance of Neanderthals

The lineage *Homo neanderthalensis* flourished in Eurasia between 300,000 and 110,000 years ago, when a generally warm and wet climate supported dense woodlands and savanna. Neanderthals frequently camped near wetlands, lakes, and rivers. As hunters, they stalked and ambushed animals from behind trees with thrusting spears. They were therefore not well adapted to the colder and drier steppe lands, which during this time were limited to the eastern reaches of central Asia and which they generally avoided.

Beginning about 110,000 years ago the climate gradually changed from warm and wet to cold and dry, bringing about an increase in steppe and open grasslands. This change, however, often reversed for periods of varying length. During times of greater fluctuation, sometimes within three or four generations, Neanderthals had to adjust their hunting style to open landscapes where larger hunting parties and throwing spears were required. During a time of respite about 75,000–44,000 years ago, when the climate and environment stabilized at a relatively warm and wet level, Neanderthals happily returned to their accustomed forms of livelihood.

Donaña National Park in southwestern Spain.

Unfortunately, the subsequent period, when the climate resumed its shift from warm and wet to cold and dry, brought havoc to Neanderthal populations in Europe. As open grassland, and eventually steppe, replaced forest and savanna, Neanderthals retreated from north to south. At the same time, *H. sapiens* advanced together with grassland and steppe from southern central Asia and Russia westward into Europe. Scholars assume that the migration of *H. sapiens*, fully adapted to life in open landscapes, into central and western Europe occurred along the Danube valley, around 35,000 years ago.

would have been the only refuge for early humans in a mostly uninhabitable, northern hemisphere stretching from Scandinavia and Siberia to Canada and Greenland.

Migration to the Americas   Around 13,500 years ago, it is thought that the ice sheet in what is today the Canadian province of Alberta split, creating a narrow passageway that made a human pathway from Alaska possible. If there was indeed a migration, it must have occurred soon after the passageway opened. Since many of the thousands of spear points that have been found all over North America south of the ice sheet—the so-called Clovis points (see Chapter 5)—go as far back as 13,000 years ago, there were about 500 years for humans to migrate from Alaska to North America. Traditionally, scholars have thought it plausible that it was at this time that humans settled the Americas.

The bone record of *H. sapiens*, however, is still extremely poor, and at present there is only one *H. sapiens* fossil from Romania that has been securely dated to 34,000 years ago. The earliest western European fossils of *H. sapiens* date to 30,000 years ago, and at present it is impossible to determine who created the figurines and cave paintings during a critical period of about 4,000 years. *H. neanderthalensis* and *H. sapiens* clearly coexisted, but the fossil record is entirely that of Neanderthals. In fact, in 2010, the Swedish-born paleogeneticist Svante Pääbo and his team based in Leipzig, Germany, completed an analysis of Neanderthal DNA (from bones from Croatian Neanderthals) and found that there was interbreeding with modern humans: The genome of modern humans contains some 1–4 percent of Neanderthal genes. What the nature of this coexistence was—peaceful or hostile— became a major point of contention toward the end of the twentieth century.

More refined carbon measurements, published in 2014, suggest that earlier dating methods tended to systematically underestimate the age of Neanderthal fossils. As a result, a number of scholars now believe that Neanderthals had already disappeared around 40,000 years ago. Their interbreeding with *H. sapiens* must have occurred in western Asia, where their coexistence lasted the longest. In southern Spain, where *H. sapiens* appeared the latest, the extended survival of Neanderthals to 28,000–24,000 years ago is now in doubt, although for the time being no new dates have been offered.

Ultimately, it was the environment, not defeat by more resourceful modern humans, that did the Neanderthals in. It just so happened that when climate change resulted in a cold and dry steppe environment, and during the Ice Age that dominated world history from 30,000 to 13,000 years ago, the more versatile *H. sapiens* was poised to master the challenge.

Questions

- Before reading this essay, what misconceptions did you have about Neanderthals?
- Is it important for world historians to study the history of Neanderthals? If yes, for which reasons?

In the 1990s and early 2000s, however, a number of spear points and human settlements older than 13,000 years ago were discovered. Sites as far from each other as Chile, Pennsylvania, Venezuela, and South Carolina have been reliably dated to 14,000–16,000 years ago. The effect of the new research has been that the arrival of humans prior to 13,500 years ago is no longer mere speculation but is fast becoming the scientific consensus (see Map 1.4).

Long-distance ocean travel in ancient times was perhaps less difficult than has been previously assumed. After all, *H. sapiens* had already traveled by raft or boat from Indonesia to Australia 60,000 years ago. Could modern humans have sailed along the Pacific coastline from Beringia to what is today the state of Washington about 16,000 years ago? Unfortunately, since the coastline was some 50 miles farther out in the Pacific than it is today, any settlement traces would now be submerged

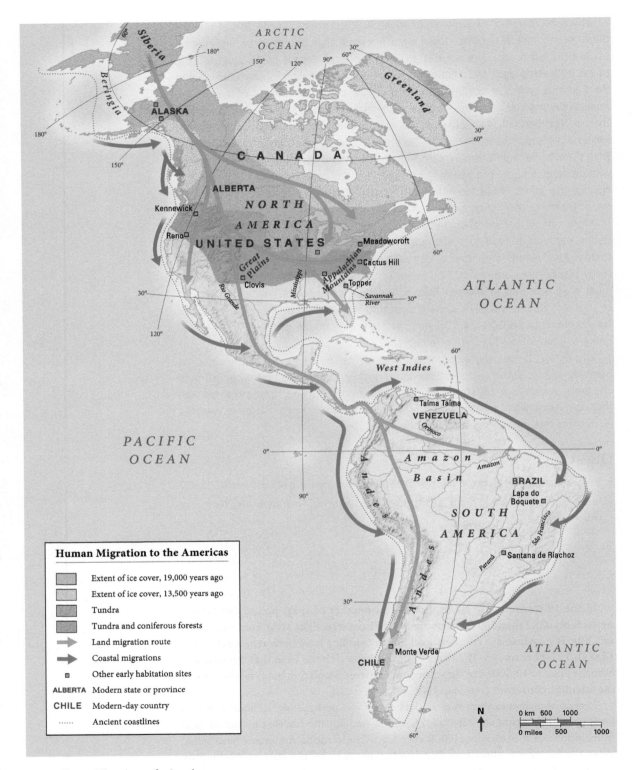

MAP **1.4** **Human Migration to the Americas.**

below sea level. In the absence of underwater archaeology so far, nothing is known about such settlements.

An American Water Nymph   A possible answer to the question of migrations prior to that of the Clovis spear-point people ca. 13,500 years ago can be gleaned from the genetic study of two human teeth recovered in 2007 from a sinkhole on the Yucatán peninsula. The teeth were from an almost perfectly preserved skeleton of a 15- or 16-year-old girl named Naia (from Gr., *naias*, water nymph) who had fallen into the sinkhole. According to the study, published in 2014, Naia's skeleton dates to 13,000–12,000 years ago. Her mitochondrial DNA—as well as that of the "Anzick-1" fossil of the same age found in Montana also published in 2014—is closely related to that of the groups of Siberian *H. sapiens* that had migrated to Beringia during the Ice Age.

It appears, therefore, that members from one single, genetically uniform population in Beringia have populated the Americas from at least ca. 16,000 years ago, that is, if one accepts the pre-Clovis archaeological record. Two papers published in 2016 confirm the assumption of a genetically uniform population of first settlers coming from Beringia. This population is related to Siberians but has small DNA admixtures (1–2 percent) pointing to people from the Andaman islands (west of Malaysia), New Guinea, and Australia. The two papers agree that these admixtures happened prior to the arrival of the above population in the Americas but differ on how early and directly these admixtures took place. Prior to 13,500 years ago these Beringians must have traveled by boat along the Pacific coast. Then, around 13,500 years ago they likely walked through the Alberta split in the North American ice shield.

Native Americans or Amerindians   In 1996 a skull was discovered on the banks of the Columbia River near Kennewick, Washington. Subsequently, the archaeologist James Chatters found most of the bones belonging to the skull nearby and dubbed the fossil "Kennewick Man." A California lab dated them to about 9,000 years ago.

According to US law, ancient remains found on federal land (which is the case in Kennewick) belong to the Native American tribe that can prove parentage. An Oregon tribe claimed the bones, and a lengthy lawsuit ensued between several tribes, backed by the US government, and a number of archaeologists concerned to have scientific access to the fossil. The lawsuit was settled in 2004 in favor of the archaeologists who claimed that the cranial features of Kennewick Man pointed more to a person of Ainu descent in Japan than to Native American parentage. New DNA tests in 2015, however, determined that Kennewick Man is definitely Native American, even if his skull seems to be different. Therefore, the US Army Corps of Engineers in 2016 began procedures to determine which Native American group may rebury Kennewick Man's remains.

It is thus clear today the original settlers of the Americas are descendants of a single population that had moved from Siberia to Beringia some 23,000 years ago. During various stages of the thaw after the Ice Age (16,000–13,500 years ago), groups from among this population traveled by boat or on foot to the Americas, where they dispersed rapidly and also diversified genetically. We call these settlers today Native Americans or Amerindians.

⟫ Putting It All Together

The time it took from Ardi to the first modern humans in East Africa was slightly less than 7 million years. Another 100,000 years elapsed before modern humans peopled the earth, down to Clovis and the transition to agriculture in the Fertile Crescent of the Middle East. From there, in another 10,000 years we reached our own time. The time proportions are staggering: The history from Clovis and the Fertile Crescent to the present is a mere 0.02 percent of the time from Ardi to the present and 4 percent of that from the first *H. sapiens* fossil to the present. Practically the entire time we needed to become genetically human is buried in the "deep history" mentioned at the beginning of this chapter.

Nearly as deeply buried is the process during which we began to carve out the space for culture. Realizing how long these genetic and cultural time spans of prehistory are is what matters for us today: The 10,000 years of history from the shift of forager to agrarian–urban and eventually scientific–industrial society represent a breathtakingly short, yet overwhelmingly complex, time of development. When we consider the much slower deep history of humanity, we become aware that, had it not been for this slow incubation, we would never have been able to sustain the speed of the later history of which we are the current product.

The principal reason for the slow pace of deep history was the conscious effort of foragers to limit population growth. Women as well as men, constantly on the move in search for food, had a strong interest in having few children. Of course, Paleolithic populations grew over the course of the millennia; otherwise, there would not have been a pattern shift from foraging to agrarian–urban life. Thus, even though the culture of foraging sought to inhibit population growth, this culture was not so rigid that people under climatologically and environmentally benign circumstances were not open to material and cultural change. It was under these circumstances at the end of the Ice Age, 13,500 years ago, that humans in some parts of the world gradually abandoned foraging and began adapting to agriculture.

Review and Relate

Thinking Through Patterns

Examine the ways historians approach the big questions of this chapter.

⟫ **What made it possible for *H. sapiens* to survive in a dangerous environment? Why is it difficult to imagine life as a prehistoric forager?**

We are twice removed from the world of foragers: After foraging came farming, which is also difficult to understand, because today's pattern of life is part of scientific–industrial civilization. *H. sapiens* foragers in prehistory relied on their stone tools, bows and arrows, rock shelters, clan members, and unsurpassed knowledge of animals, berry bushes, fruit and nut trees, mushroom patches, and grass fields to guide them through their daily lives. Collecting vegetables, catching fish, and killing the occasional animal did not take as much of an effort as farming later did, and foragers had more leisure time than farmers engaged in the annual agricultural cycle.

After modern humans left East Africa, probably in several waves between 80,000 and 60,000 years ago, in all likelihood they first went to northern India, before fanning out in all directions to Australia, Siberia, and Europe. They encountered *H. erectus* and successors, such as Neanderthals, and interbred with the latter. The modern humans who settled in Australia remained foragers because the Australian flora did not include grasses that could be cultivated through selective breeding into grains. From the complex lineage societies into which they evolved, we can see that forager life could acquire a differentiated culture, expressed in the so-called Dreamtime. However, when the Ice Age hit, forager clans and lineages had to adapt to harsh environmental conditions and retreat southward. Foremost among the adaptations were the abilities to make protective woolen clothing and build boats with which to travel to more favorable places.

The existence of tens of thousands of prehistoric cave paintings and figurines found on all continents attests to the great importance *H. sapiens* gave to the representation of humans, animals, plants, and hybrid figures with which they shared the natural world. The attention they paid to these beings—be they at rest or in motion, alone or in groups, in outline or full detail—shows how important it was to them to identify the inhabitants of their world accurately and to teach the young how to recognize them in nature. Yet, as important as it was to have an accurate knowledge of visible things, these early humans also conceived of an invisible world in which identities could be exchanged, shared, or merged. In this sense, prehistoric art can be seen as the first expression of spiritual experience, in which humans expressed awareness not only of the visible world in all its diversity but also of an invisible world of other identities.

> ❯❯ **Where did humans go when they left Africa, and how did they establish themselves in the areas where they settled? How did they adapt to the worsening Ice Age?**

> ❯❯ **Why did early humans create cave paintings and figurines? Do they show patterns that can be interpreted?**

| **Against the Grain**

Consider this as a counterpoint to the main patterns examined in this chapter.

The Hobbits of Flores Island

In 2003, an Australian–Indonesian team unearthed the partial fossils of 13 hominins in a cave on the island of Flores in the southern archipelago of Indonesia. The fossils were of beings that measured only 3–4 feet high and had brains no larger than those of chimpanzees or some australopiths. Layers of earth in which the fossils were discovered seemed to date to fairly recent times and, accordingly, their owners were declared to have lived as late as 18,000 years ago. Their closest relatives seemed to be members of the species *H. erectus*; and to the astonishment of the scholarly world, this diminutive new type of hominin, dubbed *H. floresiensis*, appeared to have survived well into the period of modern humans, even if isolated from mainland Asia.

- The story of *H. floresiensis* is a story of overlapping species. Which other examples of species overlapping each other are there?

- Improved measurement technologies require constant revisions. Which cases of revision, in addition to that of *H. floresiensis*, come to mind?

The hominins of the island entered popular imagination as the "hobbits of Flores," on account of their seeming similarities with the diminutive characters in J. R. R. Tolkien's *Lord of the Rings* novels. Did these hobbits perhaps survive even later than 18,000 years ago? Researchers cited oral history among the modern inhabitants of Flores, recorded by ethnologists, which included stories about small creatures in remote parts of the island stealing food and snatching children around the time of the Portuguese arrival in the sixteenth century. It looked like evolution had reversed itself.

In 2016, however, new and improved measurements of the layers of soil surrounding the fossils revealed that the hobbit finds were much older than originally calculated: The hominins lived actually on the island between 100,000 and 60,000 years ago. Nevertheless, even if—disappointingly—hobbit islanders and *H. sapiens* on the way to Australia did not meet, the long survival of *H. erectus* still remains remarkable indeed.

Key Terms

audio flashcards

Aboriginals   13
Acheulian toolmaking   8
Australopiths   6
Bipedalism   6

Dreamtime   14
Hominins   5
Levallois toolmaking   9
Oldowan toolmaking   8

Paleolithic   8
Savanna   6
Tundra   19

For additional resources, please go to
www.oup.com/us/vonsivers.
Please see the Further Resources section at the back of the book for additional readings and suggested websites.

Agrarian–Urban Centers of the Middle East and Eastern Mediterranean

The high priestess Enheduanna [en-hay-doo-AN-nah] lived at the end of the third millennium BCE and was a daughter of Sargon of Akkad, ruler of Mesopotamia's first recorded kingdom. She is the first writer in world history we know by name. Her best-known poem, "The Exaltation of Inanna," was written after a rebel leader had deposed Enheduanna as high priestess. In the poem Enheduanna sadly wonders why Inanna (also later known as Ishtar), the goddess of love, fertility, and war, has abandoned her, and she pleads to the goddess to take her back into her favor.

After reciting prayerful poems night and day, Enheduanna finally succeeded: Inanna accepted her priestess's appeals and the rightful ruler returned Enheduanna to her temple position.

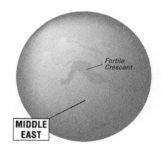

By the end of the third millennium BCE, **agrarian–urban society** had become well established in several different areas. Foragers had pioneered agriculture and village settlements during a long period of 5,000 years in the Fertile Crescent of the Middle East. Once these early inhabitants had become farmers, they began interacting with foragers in the marshes of the Mesopotamian river delta. This combined population founded cities in which

ABOVE: Standard of Ur (ca. 2500 BCE) in Mesopotamia, showing the so-called Peace/Banquet Scene, with the king (first row, third from left) observing a variety of urban and rural activities.

Seeing Patterns

> What are the main factors that enabled the transition from foraging to farming?

> Where did the pattern of agricultural life first emerge and why?

> How did the creation of agrarian–urban society—what we commonly call "civilization"—make for an entirely new pattern in world history?

Agrarian–urban society: A type of society characterized by intensive agriculture and people living in cities, towns, and villages.

craftspeople, priests and priestesses, merchants, kings, and rebels mingled, creating the fundamentals of the urban amenities of contemporary civilization. This chapter will trace the origins of farming, villages, cities, kingdoms, and empires in the Middle East, the first of the agrarian–urban centers in world history.

Agrarian Origins in the Fertile Crescent, ca. 11,500–1500 BCE

The movement from foraging to agriculture took several millennia. During this time, farmers built villages, in which they worked small garden-like plots and depended on annual rains for the growth of their crops. Farming gathered momentum as people mastered methods of irrigation. Farmers began to settle in the two great river valleys of the Tigris–Euphrates [you-FRAY-teez], in present-day Turkey, Syria, and Iraq, and of the Nile in Egypt. In these valleys, irrigation using river water allowed for larger plots and bigger harvests. Nutrient-rich river silt from the regular floods made the fields more fertile and provided for surpluses of grain. These surpluses allowed populations to build cities and states with ruling institutions composed of kings, advisors, armies, and bureaucracies.

Sedentary Foragers and Foraging Farmers

The Middle East and the eastern Mediterranean region stretches over portions of three continents—eastern Europe, southwestern Asia, and northeastern Africa. This region has always formed a single geographical unit within which there was circulation of goods and ideas, although it did not constitute a single cultural zone. After the rise of the political institution of the empire, from about 1100 BCE, areas in the Middle East and the eastern Mediterranean were often also in competition with each other.

Geography and Environment   The western half of the region includes Thrace and Greece in the north, together with numerous islands in the Aegean Sea. The terrain on the mainland as well as the islands is mostly mountainous and forested. To the east lies Anatolia, which comprises most of modern Turkey. Anatolia is a peninsula consisting of a central high plain ringed by mountain chains and traversed by rivers.

South of Anatolia and lying on the eastern shore of the Mediterranean Sea is the Levant, encompassing modern Syria, Lebanon, Israel, and Palestine. Along the coastline is a mountain chain reaching from Mount Lebanon in the north to the hill country of Palestine in the south. The Levant, the Taurus Mountains of southeastern Anatolia, and the Zagros Mountains of southwestern Iran are often referred to collectively as the "Fertile Crescent —the birthplace of agriculture (Map 2.1).

To the east of the mountain chain extends the Syrian steppe, which gives way on the south to the Arabian Desert. South of the Levant on the African continent are Egypt and Nubia (today's northern Sudan) on both sides of the Nile River. Both are largely covered by desert but bisected by the fertile Nile valley. Also in the Middle East are three smaller regions:

- Persia (modern-day Iran), stretching from the Caspian Sea southward to the Persian Gulf
- Mesopotamia, "the land between the rivers," namely, the Euphrates and Tigris in present-day Iraq and Kuwait
- the Arabian Peninsula, consisting of modern Saudi Arabia, the United Arab Emirates, Qatar, Oman, and Yemen.

Recent historical climate research has established that between the end of the Ice Age (around 11,500 BCE) and 4000 BCE, monsoon rain patterns extended farther west than they do today. When the monsoon still covered the Middle East, from the Mediterranean coast to the Persian Gulf, vegetation covered land that is desert today. At present, only the highlands of Yemen and mountain rings around the central salt desert of Iran receive enough rain to sustain agriculture. At the eastern end of the Middle East is Afghanistan, a country with steppe plains and high mountains bordering on India. It was also a center of early **agrarian society**.

Agriculture first appeared in the Fertile Crescent for several reasons: its moderate climate, its fertile soil, and its access to abundant water sources for irrigation. Other advantages of this region included large areas of wild grains as well as a variety of domesticated animals. Finally, because of its location, agricultural advances were easily transmitted from the Fertile Crescent to Egypt in the West and to India and China in the East.

Agrarian society:
At a minimum, people engaged in farming cereal grains on rain-fed or irrigated fields and breeding sheep and cattle.

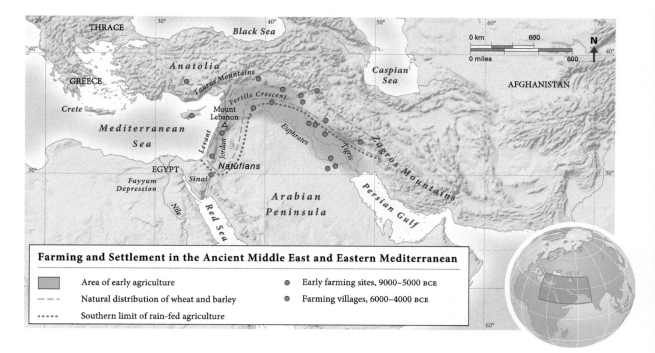

Farming and Settlement in the Ancient Middle East and Eastern Mediterranean

	Area of early agriculture		Early farming sites, 9000–5000 BCE
– – –	Natural distribution of wheat and barley		Farming villages, 6000–4000 BCE
· · · · ·	Southern limit of rain-fed agriculture		

MAP 2.1 **Farming and Settlement in the Ancient Middle East and Eastern Mediterranean.**

The Natufians   The richness of the Fertile Crescent in plants and animals during the early centuries after the end of the Ice Age seems to have encouraged settlement. Semipermanent hamlets, forming the Natufian culture (11,500–9500 BCE), arose in the Jordan and upper Euphrates valleys.

Each hamlet of the Natufians, consisting of about 60 inhabitants, contained a few semicircular pit houses. The Natufians buried their dead underneath the floors of abandoned houses or along the edges of settlements. Some graves contained ornaments, and at least two persons have been found buried with their dogs. Later Natufians often removed the skulls of their ancestors—whether before or after the burial of the body is unknown—and venerated them in altar niches in their houses. Thus began an important ancestral cult that spread across the Middle East and lasted for several millennia.

The Natufians went out into the woods with baskets and obsidian-bladed sickles to gather wild cereal grains. Back in the hamlets, the grain was ground with pestles on grindstones. Storage seems to have been minimal, limited to portable containers, such as baskets. The abundant food supply, however, did not last. A near-glacial cold and dry period from 10,900 to 9600 BCE, called the "Younger Dryas," caused wild cereal stands to wither and game animals to leave. Most of the sedentary foragers deserted their hamlets and returned to a fully migratory life of foraging. The short-lived, semisettled culture of the Natufians collapsed.

In the few hamlets that survived, people turned to storing grain in plastered pits or stone silos to get through the harsher winters. In spring, they planted some of their stored grain. When warmer and more humid weather returned, a new era began: the **Neolithic**, or New Stone Age. Scholars use this designation for the period from about 9600 to 4500 BCE in the Middle East because it was characterized by innovations such as polished stone implements (spades and sickles); the introduction of agriculture; animal domestication; and sun-dried bricks, plaster, and pottery.

Neolithic Age: Period from ca. 9600 to 4500 BCE when stone tools were adapted to the requirements of agriculture, through the making of sickles and spades.

Selective Breeding of Grain and Domestic Animals   In the early Neolithic Age, summer temperatures increased by an extraordinary 7 degrees in just a few generations. For another 2,000 years, temperatures continued to rise at a more modest rate. In this balmy climate, hamlets expanded into villages of around 300–500 inhabitants. People continued to collect grain but also began to plant fields. Through selective breeding, they gradually weeded out early-ripening varieties and began

interactive timeline

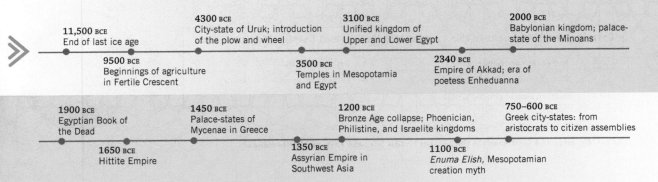

11,500 BCE
End of last ice age

4300 BCE
City-state of Uruk; introduction of the plow and wheel

3100 BCE
Unified kingdom of Upper and Lower Egypt

2000 BCE
Babylonian kingdom; palace-state of the Minoans

9500 BCE
Beginnings of agriculture in Fertile Crescent

3500 BCE
Temples in Mesopotamia and Egypt

2340 BCE
Empire of Akkad; era of poetess Enheduanna

1900 BCE
Egyptian Book of the Dead

1450 BCE
Palace-states of Mycenae in Greece

1200 BCE
Bronze Age collapse; Phoenician, Philistine, and Israelite kingdoms

750–600 BCE
Greek city-states: from aristocrats to citizen assemblies

1650 BCE
Hittite Empire

1350 BCE
Assyrian Empire in Southwest Asia

1100 BCE
Enuma Elish, Mesopotamian creation myth

harvesting fields in which all grain ripened at the same time. It was not until about 7000 BCE that farmers in the Middle East had bred the large-grained wheat and barley of today.

Parallel to the selective breeding of grain, farmers also domesticated *pulses*— the edible seeds of pod-bearing plants—beginning with chickpeas and lentils. Pulses helped to refertilize grain fields, as the pods, stalks, and roots contain nitrogen needed by all plants to grow. Farmers continued to hunt, but they also captured young wild goats and sheep and through selective breeding accustomed them to live with humans in their houses and in pens—the first domestication of livestock.

The original agriculture—the cultivation of grain and pulses and the domestication of goats and sheep—relied on annual rains in the Fertile Crescent and became more widespread when farmers tapped creeks for irrigation during dry months. Inhabitants of this region discovered the benefits of rotating their crops and driving goats and sheep over the stubble of harvested grain fields, using the animals' droppings for refertilization and leaving the fields fallow for a year. Around 6500 BCE, these peoples added cattle, pigs, donkeys, and pottery to their farms. The epic transition from foraging to farming had been completed.

The Origin of Urban Centers in Mesopotamia and Egypt

FIRST AGRARIAN-URBAN CENTERS

During the fifth millennium BCE, the climate of the Middle East and eastern Mediterranean changed from one with monsoon rains falling during the summer to one with wet winters and dry summers prevailing in the west and north and general dryness in the east and south. Most of the Arabian Peninsula began to dry up. In lower Mesopotamia, drier conditions forced settlers to pay closer attention to irrigation. All of these changes would contribute to the rise of the first agrarian–urban centers founded along rivers—in the Middle East, Egypt, the Indus valley in the Indian subcontinent, and later the Yellow River valley in China.

Euphrates and Nile Floods   The swift Tigris River in eastern Mesopotamia did not lend itself to the construction of irrigation canals. The slower Euphrates River in western Mesopotamia, however, provided favorable conditions for irrigated farming. At its lower end, in present-day Iraq, the Euphrates united with the Tigris and dispersed out into swampland, lagoons, and marshes, which supported a rich plant and animal life. It was here that the first farmers of the Fertile Crescent settled, establishing the Ubaid culture (6000–4000 BCE).

The annual snowmelt in the mountains of northeastern Anatolia caused the Euphrates and Tigris to flood the plains below. The floods arrived in early spring just as the first grain was ready for harvest, forcing the farmers into heroic efforts to keep the ripening grain fields from being inundated by water. And yet the spring floods helped prepare the fields for the growing of smaller crops. The floods also softened hardened soils and sometimes leached them of salt deposits. Thus, in spite of some drawbacks, irrigated farming in lower Mesopotamia, with its more predictable water supplies, was more productive than the more irregular rain-fed agriculture to the north.

The Egyptian Nile originates in East Africa, where the rains hit during the early summer. Much of this rain is collected in Lake Victoria, from which the White Nile flows northward. In the Sudan it unites with the Blue Nile from Ethiopia, which carries water and fertile silt. The Nile usually begins to swell in July, crests in August–September, and recedes during October. For the Neolithic inhabitants of Egypt, these late-summer and fall floods created conditions quite different from those of lower Mesopotamia, which depended on the spring floods.

In Egypt, the floods coincided with the growing season of winter barley and wheat. Silt carried by the Nile fertilized the fields every year prior to planting. The first agricultural settlements appeared in the Fayyum [fay-YOOM], a swampy depression off the Nile southwest of modern Cairo, around 5200 BCE. By about 3500 BCE, agriculture had spread south along the Nile and north into the delta.

Early Towns   Between 5500 and 3500 BCE, villages in lower Mesopotamia and Upper Egypt developed into towns. They were composed of a few thousand inhabitants, with markets where farmers exchanged surplus food staples and traders offered goods not produced locally. The Mesopotamian towns administered themselves through local **assemblies**, in which male adults decided on communal matters. For nearly two millennia towns in this region regulated their irrigated agriculture through communal cooperation (see Map 2.2).

Irrigation made it possible for townspeople in Mesopotamia and Egypt to accumulate agricultural surpluses to protect themselves against famine and allowed for population increases. Some people accumulated more grain than others, and the first social distinctions along the lines of wealth appeared. Gradually, wealthy families became owners of land beyond their family properties. **Sharecroppers** who

Assembly: Gathering of either all inhabitants or the most influential persons in a town; later, in cities, assemblies and kings made communal decisions on important fiscal or juridical matters.

Sharecroppers: Farmers who received seed, animals, and tools from landowners in exchange for up to two-thirds of their harvest and access to land.

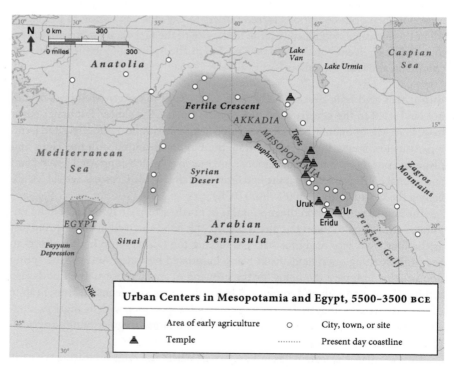

MAP **2.2** **Urban Centers in Mesopotamia and Egypt, 5500–3500 BCE.**

map analysis

worked these lands paid rent (in the form of grain) to the new landowners. Other landless farmers left agriculture altogether and became **nomads**, breeding *onagers* (ancestors of donkeys), sheep, and goats on steppe lands. Wealthy landowners appropriated the places of ritual and sacrifice in the villages and towns and constructed temples, mansions, workshops, and granaries.

Eventually, the landowning priestly families turned the production of such goods as tools, pottery, cloth, and leather goods over to specialized craftspeople, paying them with grain rations. The landowners employed traders who traveled to other areas with crafts (pottery, cloth, leather goods), trading them for raw materials. Mesopotamian merchants traveled with cloth and tools to villages and towns in the Zagros Mountains and returned with timber, stone, obsidian, and copper. Egyptian villagers traded textiles with villagers in the Sinai Peninsula in return for copper and with Nubian villagers in return for gold.

Around 4300 BCE, some mountain people in the region had mastered the crafts of mining and smelting copper. This metal was too soft to replace obsidian, but the many other uses to which it was put have led scholars to mark the middle of the fifth millennium BCE as the moment when the Neolithic, or New Stone Age, of polished stone tools came to an end and the *Chalcolithic*, or Copper Age, began.

Temples In the course of the fifth millennium BCE, wealthy landowners gained control over the communal grain stores and clan shrines and enlarged these into town shrines. Adjacent to the early temples were kilns, granaries, workshops, breweries, and administrative buildings. The wealthy landowners, presiding over the temples as priests, were responsible for the administration of all aspects of cult ritual in the temples, as well as the provision of labor in the temple fields.

In Upper Egypt, landowner-priests presided over the construction of the first temples around 3500 BCE, together with elegantly embellished tombs for themselves. One such tomb painting shows a leader carrying out an expedition on the Nile upstream to Nubia, returning with gold and ebony to create ornaments for his temple and tomb. Unfortunately, the sparse archaeological record in Egypt at this point presents few details concerning the transition from village to town.

The World's First Cities In contrast to a town, a **city** (or **city-state**, if the surrounding villages are included) is defined as a place of more than 5,000 inhabitants, with a number of nonfarming inhabitants, such as craftspeople, merchants, and administrators. The latter lived on the food they received in exchange for their own handiwork. To keep order, the dominant landowner-priest created a personal entourage of armed men. The first place in Mesopotamia to fit the definition of a city was Uruk, founded near Eridu around 4300 BCE. Within a millennium, it was a city of 50,000–80,000 inhabitants with a mixture of palaces, multistory administrative buildings, workshops, residences, palace estates, and villages clustered around the city with both large and small individual farms.

The people of Uruk were pioneers of technical and intellectual innovations. It was here that the first known plow was found. Plowing and controlled sowing allowed for much larger harvests. Uruk craftspeople introduced the potter's wheel, which accelerated and made more precise the manufacture of earthenware and ceramics. The sizes of jars, pots, and bowls gradually became standardized, simplifying the storage of grain and its distribution in the cities.

Nomads: People whose livelihood was based on the herding of animals, such as sheep, goats, cattle, horses, and camels; moving with their animals from pasture to pasture according to the seasons, living in tent camps.

City, city-state: A place of more than 5,000 inhabitants with nonfarming inhabitants (craftspeople, merchants, administrators), markets, and a city leader capable of compelling obedience to his decisions by force.

Cuneiform Script. Scribes impressed the syllables on the wet clay with a wedge-shaped reed stylus.

At the same time, two- and four-wheeled carts pulled by oxen expedited the transportation of large quantities of grain from the fields to the city. The grain was made into bread and beer. By some estimates, more than 40 percent of Mesopotamia's grain was committed to beer production.

Another important invention was bronze. Bronze is an alloy of copper and arsenic or tin; its strength makes it useful for tools and weapons. During the following centuries, bronze replaced stone and copper implements for all but a few purposes in the Middle East and eastern Mediterranean, leading historians to refer to this as the *Bronze Age* (in the Middle East, from 3300 to 1200 BCE).

Cuneiform Writing   The administrators in the bureaucracy, who were responsible for the accounting and distribution of grain, animals, ceramics, textiles, and imported raw materials, greatly simplified their tasks around 3450 BCE by inventing a form of writing. Scribes wrote in cuneiform [kyoo-NEE-uh-form] (from the Latin, meaning "wedge-shaped") script on clay tablets, using signs denoting objects and sounds from the spoken language. For the first time, scribes could not only write down the languages they spoke but also clarify for future generations the meaning of the sculpted and painted artifacts that would otherwise have been mute witnesses of history. With the advent of writing, record-keeping, communication, increasingly abstract thought, and, for the first time, history could all be recorded.

Kingdoms in Mesopotamia, Egypt, and Crete   With the introduction of the plow, city leaders greatly expanded their landholdings. They employed large groups of laborers to cut canals through riverbanks, making vast new areas of lowlands available for farming. Portions of this land served as overflow basins for floodwaters, to protect the ripening grain fields. Craftspeople invented devices to channel water from the canals into small fields or gardens. As a result of this field and irrigation expansion, the grain surpluses of both temples and villages increased enormously.

Kingship in Mesopotamia   A consequence of the expansion of agriculture was the rise of nearly two dozen cities in lower and central Mesopotamia. As cities expanded and multiplied, the uncultivated buffer lands that had formerly separated them disappeared. People drew borders and both negotiated and fought over access to water and the ownership of wandering livestock.

When wars broke out, city dwellers built walls and recruited military forces from among their young population. The commanders, often of modest origins, used their military positions to acquire wealth and demanded to be recognized as leaders. They challenged the authority of the priests, who had been the traditional heads of villages and towns. Depending on circumstances, the Mesopotamian city assemblies chose their leaders from either the self-made or the priestly leaders, calling the former "great man" (*lugal*) and the latter "king" (*en*).

Once in power, a royal leader sought to impose dynastic or family rule on the city. To set himself apart from his assembly colleagues, he claimed divine or sacred sanction for his kingship. The King List of 2125 BCE, in which the reigns of all early kings in lower Mesopotamia were coordinated, begins: "After the kingship descended from heaven, the kingship was in Eridu." In other words, the kings argued that as divinely ordained rulers, neither they nor their sons and grandsons needed the consensus of the assemblies for their power. The earliest king known by name and attested in the archaeological record was Enmebaragesi [en-me-ba-ra-GAY-see] of Kish, who reigned around 2500 BCE.

Akkadia and Babylonia   During the 2000s BCE, Mesopotamian cities began competing for military supremacy. The first royal dynasty to bring them together in a unified territorial state or polity was that of Akkadia (ca. 2340–2150 BCE). Sargon ("The Great"), the first major king (r. 2334–2279 BCE), commanded several thousand foot soldiers. At its height, Sargon's Akkadian empire—the world's first—stretched from Mesopotamia into Asia Minor and Syria. Sargon's grandson, Naram-Sin, added the Zagros Mountains and Syria to the Akkadian kingdom and claimed to be the "king of the four (world) shores." He was the first king to conceive of the unification of the ethnically, linguistically, and religiously diverse peoples of the Middle East, with or without their consent. However, he did not yet possess the military means to embark on large-scale conquests and **empire** building (see Map 2.3).

> **Empire:** Large multiethnic, multilinguistic, multireligious state consisting of a conquering kingdom and several defeated kingdoms.

A later major Mesopotamian kingdom was Babylonia. Its best-known king was Hammurabi (r. 1792–1750 BCE), who ordered the engraving of the entire code of Babylonian law onto a 7-foot slab of basalt. Hammurabi saw himself as the executor of a divinely sanctioned law that punished evildoers and rewarded the righteous. By today's standards, Hammurabi's laws were harsh, threatening severe punishments for crimes against property, land, and commerce. The law of Mesopotamia was no longer the customary law of villages and towns but the royal writ, divinely ordained and backed by military force (see "Patterns Up Close").

Patriarchy and Gender   The development of society in the Middle East and beyond gave rise to another pattern: the patriarchal structure of society. The wars among the city-states and kingdoms were important events in the creation of new patterns of gender relations. War captives provided cheap labor as slaves in temple households and wealthy residences, giving the priestly and self-made kings an edge in the restructuring of agrarian–urban society. A ruling class emerged, composed of dynastic families who collaborated with other landowning and priestly families. One rank below the ruling class were the merchants and craftspeople, who formed a hierarchy among themselves. At the bottom of this increasingly hierarchical society were slaves and other marginal urban groups, such as day laborers and prostitutes.

The transition from agrarian societies to urban civilizations had several implications for gender roles. In more

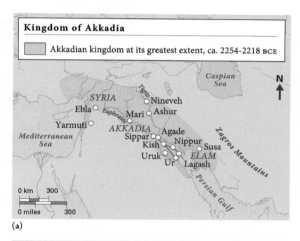

Kingdom of Akkadia

▨ Akkadian kingdom at its greatest extent, ca. 2254-2218 BCE

(a)

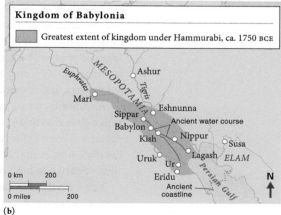

Kingdom of Babylonia

▨ Greatest extent of kingdom under Hammurabi, ca. 1750 BCE

(b)

MAP 2.3   **(a) The Akkadian Kingdom. (b) Kingdom of Babylonia.**

Babylonian Law Codes

Babylonians in lower Mesopotamia produced the earliest known collections of written laws. Because of their formal, written nature, these law codes differed from earlier oral and customary law common to all early cultures. When did these laws originate, how did they develop across time, and what was their influence on later ages?

The origin and evolution of the legal tradition are intertwined with developments associated with the complexity of urban life. Intricate systems of irrigation and drainage canals, along with dikes and dams, necessitated not only extensive planning and maintenance but also the allotment of plots of land. The emergence of complex political, economic, and social relationships called for the establishment of a set of centrally administered rules and regulations in order to provide for conflict resolution as well as retribution for wrongdoing.

Across a span of nearly 500 years, from the earliest codification of King Urukagina of Lagash in ca. 2350 BCE to the monumental code of Hammurabi in 1750 BCE, law developed through a successive series of increasingly comprehensive and refined legal codes consistent with the developing complexities of urban expansion. Consequently, evolving law codes address correspondingly wider audiences, they cover a broader spectrum of social classes, and they present more complex examples of potential infractions as well as more nuanced resolutions. Most of these legal codes open with a prologue, which is followed by a body of laws, and close with an epilogue. In terms of format, Sumerian laws follow the format of "if this, then that" regarding violations and ensuing punishments, and punishments are meted out with reference to social status. Finally, they pay growing attention to the importance of irrigation, with more and more references to the maintenance of river dikes and irrigation canals, along with harsh consequences for neglecting this.

The law code of Hammurabi, king of Babylon (r. 1792–1750 BCE), represents the first complete written and well-organized code of law. Like earlier models, the

egalitarian agricultural societies there was little room for gender distinctions. This changed with the growth of urban centers. New arrangements were required to accommodate the political, economic, military, and religious changes brought about by urban life. Each of these spheres was dominated by males. Men developed and administered military affairs, and fighting forces were restricted to males. Men also emerged as rulers and high-ranking administrators, regulated commercial and trading matters, and formed the ranks of scribes, priests, and other functionaries.

Another factor of urban life was the emergence of wealth and property rights, which gave rise to the need to ensure inheritance of private property through male descent. Because this required both establishing and maintaining the legitimacy of the male line, sexual activities of women were restricted. As a result, women's roles were confined to household functions, thereby subordinating their social status.

The formation of hierarchical social structures did not stop with the rise of social classes. As we shall see in later chapters, men assumed legal power over women on all levels of society in nearly every agrarian–urban culture. As attested in the law code of Hammurabi, married women enjoyed some legal rights, including the right

code acknowledges distinctions in social categories along with inequalities among them but goes beyond them in addressing more social classes and grouping the classes according to relative wealth and social standing. Also, like previous collections, the code is broken down into several categories, including issues related to property and family law; but here again, it covers many more possible scenarios in an effort to close previous loopholes.

Unlike its Sumerian predecessors, however, the code departs significantly when it comes to retribution in that it calls for more extreme punishments according to the principle of *lex talionis* ("an eye for an eye"). Thus, "If a man put out the eye of another man, his eye shall be put out." Further, the importance of maintaining irrigation systems is consistent with earlier themes but expressed in more nuanced terms: "If anyone open his ditches to water his crop, but is careless, and the water flood the field of his neighbor, then he shall pay his neighbor [grain] for his loss."

The long-term influence of Sumerian and Babylonian legal codes—particularly Hammurabi's code—extends far beyond ancient Mesopotamia. Instances of its influence appear in the development of biblical law, and striking similarities to the notion of *lex talionis* are found in Jewish law. And many of its principles found their way into Roman law, especially the organized codification of civil cases.

Questions

- What do the first law codes tell us about ancient Sumerian and Babylonian societies?

- Are the legacies of these first law codes still evident in modern Western legal practice today?

Stele with Hammurabi's Code.

to sue for divorce if they could prove mistreatment. In general, however, wives were in many ways considered the property of their husbands, who could divorce their wives in cases of neglect of the household without returning dowries, and who could engage in sexual relations with mistresses and prostitutes—while wives caught in adultery were thrown in the river along with their lovers.

Women in Egyptian society fared better in some ways than their Mesopotamian counterparts. Although they existed in a male-dominated society, women were accorded more respect in marriage, and they had more legal rights; they could own and transfer property, and they could sue for divorce. A few women in Egyptian royalty were considered nearly equal to men. In New Kingdom Egypt (1550–1070 BCE), princesses had the same rights of divine descent as princes. Sisters and brothers or half-brothers sometimes married each other, reinforcing the concept that their lineage was divine and pure.

In later millennia, after empires formed, noble women disappeared from their male-dependent public positions and lived in secluded areas of the palaces. Men tightened the law, relegating women to inferior family positions. Patriarchy was thus a product not of agrarian but of urban society in city-states and kingdoms of Mesopotamia and, a little later, Egypt.

Egyptian Kingdoms   In Egypt, the first city was Hierankopolis [hee-ran-KO-po-lis], founded around 3000 BCE in Upper Egypt. As in Mesopotamia, the rulers of cities began to develop into small-scale kings. Whoever among these was the first king, he unified all Egyptian lands and established the first dynasty of Egypt's Early Dynastic Period (ca. 3100–2613 BCE), choosing Memphis, near modern Cairo, as his capital. At first, lesser rulers continued their reigns in the other cities. They even rebelled against the king from time to time. Therefore, the early policies of the Egyptian kings were focused almost exclusively on the unification of Egypt.

The first king claimed divine birth from Egypt's founder god, Horus, the falcon-headed deity. As god on earth, the king upheld the divine order. Inhabitants of his kingdom were no more than humble servants whose duty was to pay the king taxes and construct a palace and tomb for him. Of course, in practice, this royal supremacy was far from complete. Even during times of strong centralization there were always some powerful figures, such as provincial landowners and governors, who held title to their properties and collected rents from the farmers working on these properties. As in Mesopotamia, the claim of the kings to divinity did not keep rivals from bidding for supreme power.

Hieroglyphs, Bureaucracy, and Pyramids   As with cuneiform in Mesopotamia, the Egyptian kings were greatly aided in the process of unification by the introduction of a system of accounting and writing. Around 3500–3200 BCE, administrators and scribes developed *hieroglyphic* writing in Egypt. In this system, formalized pictures symbolizing objects and syllables were used to represent words; hieroglyphic writing was limited to royal inscriptions. The writing material used in Egypt was papyrus, which was more expensive but less cumbersome than the Mesopotamian clay tablets.

In addition to aiding in communication, writing lent itself to a larger and more efficient bureaucracy in Egypt. At the beginning of the Old Kingdom (ca. 2613–2181 BCE), the royal palace and temple became hierarchical organizations in which everything was minutely regulated. Using arithmetic manuals, scribes calculated the quantities of bread, beer, and meat rations to be distributed; of timber for the shipyards; and of flax for the linen-weaving workshops. In its complexity, the Egyptian bureaucratic system of the Old Kingdom easily surpassed that of lower Mesopotamia during the contemporaneous Akkadian period (see Map 2.4).

The most astounding bureaucratic achievement of the Old Kingdom was the construction by Khufu (r. 2589–2566 BCE) of a pyramid near modern Cairo as a funerary monument for himself. Along with two other pyramids, Khufu's Great Pyramid makes up the famous Giza pyramids, which served as tombs for the bodies of later kings. By the orders of Khufu, stone workers quarried local limestone from cliffs along the Nile for the central portion of each of the pyramids. Finer, less brittle casing stones came from quarries upstream on the Nile. Ramparts of chipped

Egyptian Hieroglyphs. These hieroglyphs found in Luxor, Valley of the Kings, were carved into the wall and colored.

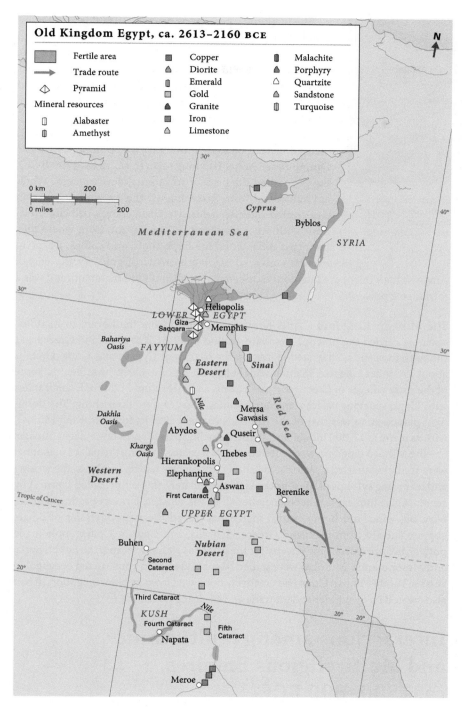

Old Kingdom Egypt, ca. 2613–2160 BCE

Legend:
- Fertile area
- Trade route
- Pyramid

Mineral resources
- Alabaster
- Amethyst
- Copper
- Diorite
- Emerald
- Gold
- Granite
- Iron
- Limestone
- Malachite
- Porphyry
- Quartzite
- Sandstone
- Turquoise

MAP **2.4 Old Kingdom Egypt, ca. 2613–2160 BCE.**

stone and other debris, as well as sledges, rollers, and heavy levers made of timber, helped laborers move the stone blocks into place, as much as 479 feet high. After the completion of the pyramid, the construction machinery was dismantled, and today sand covers what were once the workers' camps.

Great Pyramid of Giza and Sphinx. The pyramid of Khafre, one of the three pyramids at Giza, was constructed during the Old Kingdom (ca. 2500 BCE). The Sphinx, shown in the foreground, has the body of a lion and the face of a man, perhaps that of Khafre.

The workforce, perhaps as many as 10,000 laborers, consisted of farmers who were working off their annual 1-month labor service owed to the king. A special labor office made sure that regular field labor was disrupted as little as possible. Although the workers were strictly supervised, we know that they also occasionally went on strike. Labor unrest, however, could easily be suppressed by the Egyptian army.

The kings of the Middle Kingdom (ca. 2040–1750 BCE) focused instead on agricultural projects, mining, and trade. During Amenemhet III's long reign (r. ca. 1843–1796 BCE), Egypt reached the peak of its internal development. Workers transferred from Syria drained the Fayyum Depression and created irrigated fields. Merchants developed close relations with other merchants in the Levant, from where they imported cedar wood for ships, roofs, and coffins. Egyptian exports consisted of objects made of gold. By the end of Amenemhet's reign, the kingdom numbered about 1 million inhabitants and was a formidable power.

The Minoan Kingdom   After farming had spread from the Levant to Anatolia, seafarers carried the practice westward around 6500 BCE to mainland Greece and the Aegean islands. They settled first on the islands of Cyprus and Crete. Crete is about 170 miles long and 35 miles wide at its widest point. Over the millennia, some of the early villages of Crete grew into towns, and by around 2000 BCE small states with kings, spacious palaces, and surrounding villages were flourishing. The dominant **palace-state** was that of the Minoans (named after its founder, King Minos), with as many as 12,000 inhabitants in the sprawling palace and a few villages outside.

Palace-state: A city or fortified palace with surrounding villages.

The Minoan kingdom was centered on a vast palace. Among the palace personnel were scribes who used a pictorial-syllabic script on clay tablets similar to the writing and recording systems of Mesopotamia. Unfortunately, this script, called *Linear A* by scholars, has thus far not been deciphered. In the villages, farmers produced grain, olive oil, wine, and honey. Royal merchants traded these products for obsidian, copper, and tin from mainland Greece, Anatolia, and Cyprus. Craftspeople made pottery, bronze vessels, and jewelry for the palace as well as for export to Egypt, Syria, and Mesopotamia. Minoans were skilled boat builders who constructed oceangoing vessels. While Minoan Crete had creatively borrowed from its older neighbors, it had also created its own independent trade and seafaring traditions.

Interactions among Multiethnic and Multireligious Empires, ca. 1500–600 BCE

From around 1700 to 1000 BCE, society in the Middle East and the Mediterranean changed in important ways. Chariot warfare, iron tools, and iron weapons were developed and refined. Agriculture spread from the original core of Syria, Mesopotamia, and Egypt to the periphery in Greece, central Anatolia, central Asia, and Arabia. Conquerors built large empires in which a small, ethnically defined ruling class ruled over collections of other ethnic groups, speaking a multiplicity of languages and sacrificing to a multiplicity of gods.

The Hittite and Assyrian Empires, 1600–600 BCE

Agriculture spread from the Middle East to foragers in western Europe and central Asia. Villagers in central Asia, known as "Proto-Indo-Europeans," domesticated the horse and used it for pulling chariots. Later, Indo-Europeans migrated with their horses and chariots to the Middle East, India, and western Europe, where they settled as ruling classes among the indigenous villagers.

Horses and Chariots from Central Asia   The spread of agriculture into Europe and central Asia had major consequences for the Middle East and the eastern Mediterranean. Shortly after 3000 BCE, in the region around the Ural Mountains, Proto-Indo-European villagers domesticated the horse. Around 2000 BCE, town leaders in the southern Ural Mountains emerged who were equipped with horse-drawn chariots as well as with composite bows made of a combination of grooved wood and horn carefully glued together. This bow was much more powerful than the simpler bows dating back to the Paleolithic. A chariot could accommodate two or three warriors, one to guide the horses and the others to shoot arrows. Around 1700 BCE, both the chariot and the composite bow made their entry into the Middle East and eastern Mediterranean. They contributed to a major transformation of the kingdoms that had hitherto relied solely on foot soldiers.

The Hittite Empire   The first rulers in the Middle East to make use of chariots and composite bows for their military were the Hittites (1650–1182 BCE), Indo-Europeans settling in central Anatolia. This area, one of the richest mining regions in the Middle East, had large iron deposits. By around 1500 BCE, smiths in Anatolia had fully mastered the art of ironmaking. The Hittites incorporated iron into the equipment of their chariot armies, in the form of swords, helmets, and protective armor. The combination of these military elements gave the Hittites an early advantage, which they used to become the pioneers of a new type of conquering polity— an empire consisting of many different peoples, languages, and temple religions. At its peak, the Hittite Empire stretched from Anatolia to northern Syria, comprising peoples of many languages and religions.

To distinguish themselves from ordinary kings, the Hittite kings called themselves "great kings." When they conquered rival kingdoms, they left the lesser, conquered kings in place as provincial rulers. The core of Hittite armies consisted of a nobility of highly trained, disciplined, and mobile chariot warriors. In the conquered lands, the "great kings" placed nobles in strategic garrisons to keep the local, non-Hittite rulers in check. Since the imperial warehouses held limited amounts of foodstuffs, the nobility received land grants, using the rents they extracted from the towns and villages for their livelihood. This Hittite system of employing both its nobility and local rulers was to become the model of organization for all subsequent Middle Eastern and eastern Mediterranean empires.

Imperial Egypt   During the New Kingdom (ca. 1550–1070 BCE), the Egyptians vigorously pushed their border with the Hittites as far north as possible. The Egyptians eventually clashed with the Hittites at Qadesh [KAH-desh] in northern Syria

(1274 BCE), where they engaged in the largest chariot battle ever fought in the Middle East. Neither side prevailed, and in the earliest known peace treaty—the Treaty of Kadesh—the two empires decided to curb their imperialism and coexist diplomatically with each other, with Syria divided between them.

A short time later, this coexistence was shattered by invasions of the "Sea Peoples" from the Aegean Sea. Originally a mixture of former foot soldiers, mountaineers, and herders from northern Greece had raided the Mycenaean [my-sen-EE-yan] kingdoms of southern Greece, as we discuss later in this chapter. These people, joined by survivors of the collapsing kingdoms, took to the sea (hence their name "Sea Peoples") and sailed to the wealthy kingdoms of the Levant. One group of Sea Peoples, presumably remnants of one of the Mycenaean kingdoms, destroyed the Hittite Empire in 1207 BCE. The Egyptian Empire lost southern Syria to another set of seafaring invaders, the Pelesets [PE-le-sets, Philistines] and retreated to Sinai, abandoning its imperial ambitions.

The invasions by Sea People triggered the so-called **Bronze Age collapse** of ca. 1200 BCE with which the **Iron Age** in the Middle East and eastern Mediterranean began. The collapse is explained as a crisis in which the overextended early empires of the Hittites and Egyptians were unable to sustain the enormous expenses required for chariot warfare.

The Assyrians Emerging after the Bronze Age collapse, the Assyrians (ca. 1350–607 BCE) founded a new empire, which, like the Hittite Empire, was based on rain-fed agriculture. Its capital was Assur, a city founded in upper Mesopotamia around 2000 BCE on an island in the Tigris River. Originally, Assur's farming base was too limited to support territorial conquests. Instead, its inhabitants enriched themselves through trade. They built trading outposts as far away as central Anatolia and exchanged textiles for timber, copper, tin, and silver, much of which they sold to the Babylonians in the south. In the fourteenth century BCE, the Assyrian kings began to use Assur's commercial riches to finance their first large-scale conquests.

The Assyrians expanded into both the Zagros Mountains and Syria, reaching the borders of the Hittite Empire and claiming equal status with them. Stopped at the Hittite borders, Assyrian troops turned southeastward and expanded into lower Mesopotamia. Here, they occupied Babylon for a short period, humiliating their wealthy neighbors by carrying away the statue of the city god.

After some severe military setbacks, during which Assyria was reduced to its upper Mesopotamian center, ambitious kings renewed Assyrian expansion, creating Neo-Assyria (New Assyria), which lasted from 934 to 607 BCE. They systematically and ruthlessly conquered the lands around them. In fact, the Assyrians were among the most ruthless campaigners in recorded history. They destroyed temples, razed cities, and forcibly deported the defeated inhabitants of entire provinces to other parts of the empire. Scholars have estimated that hundreds of thousands of deportees had to walk hundreds of miles through the countryside before being settled in new villages. At the peak of their conquests (745–609 BCE), the Assyrian rulers became the first to unify all of the Middle East, a dream first expressed by King Naram-Sin of Akkad centuries earlier. This same accomplishment would be repeated many more times in years to come.

Bronze Age collapse: Around 1200 BCE, this was the result of the collapse of the Hittite Empire and the weakening of the Egyptian New Kingdom; chariot warfare had become unsustainable in these early kingdoms.

Iron Age: Around 1500–1200 BCE, smiths were able to produce sufficiently high temperatures to smelt iron bloom, a mixture of iron and a variety of impurities.

image analysis

Tutankhamen Hunting. Detail from a painted chest found in the king's tomb, Thebes, ca. 1340 BCE.

Small Kingdoms on the Imperial Margins, 1600–600 BCE

Syria was a region between the Hittite (or, later, Assyrian) Empire in the north and the Egyptian Empire in the south. The dominant form of political organization in these regions was the city-state under a royal dynasty. In northern Syria, the city-states were those of the Phoenicians; in southern Syria, they were those of the Pelesets on the coast and the Israelites in the hills. In the eastern Mediterranean, outside the military reach of the Hittite and Assyrian Empires but in commercial contact with them, were the Mycenaean palace-states and early Greek city-states.

The Phoenicians   The people known in Greek as "Phoenicians" and by the Egyptians as "Canaanites" held the city-states of Byblos, Sidon, and Tyre (ca. 1600–300 BCE), each with a population of several tens of thousands. The Phoenicians also controlled the slopes of Mount Lebanon with its famous cedars, which were much sought after in the Middle East and eastern Mediterranean as construction material. No less important was a species of sea snail collected on the beaches, from which a highly valued purple textile dye was extracted. Urban craftspeople made ceramics, textiles, leather goods, jewelry, and metalware with distinctive Phoenician designs, destined for sale abroad. More than any other territorial states in the Middle East, the Phoenician city-states were engaged in trade.

Phoenicians as traders appear in the historical record from 2500 BCE onward. During ca. 1600–1200 BCE, the Phoenicians and Mycenaeans shared the sea trade of the eastern Mediterranean. On land, they preferred paying tribute to, and occasionally putting their fleets at the service of, Hittite or Egyptian imperial overlords. When the Mycenaean kingdoms and Hittite Empire collapsed and the Egyptians withdrew around 1200 BCE under the onslaught of the Sea Peoples, the

ᛉ᛭ᛊᛝ᚛᛫ᛈᚱᛉᛝᛟ᛫ᛇᛁᛜᛁᛚᛉᛝᛁᚦᛁᚤᛇᚨᛁᛝᛉ

1. Phoenician alphabet

ΑΒΓΔΕΖΗΘΙΚΛΜΝΞΟΠΡΣΤΥΦΧΨΩ

2. Greek alphabet

ABCDEFGHIKLMNOPQRSTVXYZ

3. Roman alphabet

Phoenician, Greek, and Roman Alphabets. This illustration reveals similarities among the Phoenician, Greek, and Roman alphabets. Phoenician traders carried the alphabet across the Mediterranean, where it was adopted by Greeks. Subsequent interactions among Greeks, Etruscans, and Romans resulted in the transition to Roman letter forms, which in turn ultimately provided the foundation for English characters.

Phoenicians seized their chance. Systematically expanding their reach in the Mediterranean, they established trade outposts on islands and along the Mediterranean coast as far west as modern Morocco and Spain.

In addition to founding numerous ports and outposts around the Mediterranean, the Phoenicians introduced the letter alphabet. From rock inscriptions discovered in 1998 in Egypt, it appears that Phoenician (or Syrian) merchants began experimenting around 1900–1800 BCE with a writing system in which letters replaced the traditional signs and syllables, with each letter standing for a spoken consonant. The Phoenician alphabet of ca. 1200 BCE was the most widely used, becoming the ancestor of all alphabetical scripts.

The Pelesets and Israelites   During its imperial phase (ca. 1550–1200 BCE), Egypt controlled the Palestinian towns of Gaza, Ashkelon, Ashdod, Gath, and Ekron. Occasionally, the Egyptian kings aided their governors in these towns by carrying out punitive campaigns. After one such campaign, a defeated people in southern Syria was "stripped bare, wholly lacking seed," as an Egyptian inscription of 1207 BCE recorded. The name used in the inscription for this people was "Israel," the first time this name appeared in the records. "Israel" seems to refer to some sort of tribal alliance among Canaanite villagers and herders in the hills.

A short time after the Pelesets, or Philistines, took over southern Syria and Egypt withdrew, agriculture and trade recovered from Egyptian taxation. The coastal Philistines established garrisons among the Israelites in order to secure trade routes. In response, as is recorded in the Hebrew Bible (the Old Testament in Christian usage), a military leader named Saul and a number of tribal leaders recruited a military force that began a war of liberation against the Philistines. According to this scripture, Saul was killed during the early stages of the war, and his successor, David, completed the liberation, establishing himself as king in Jerusalem shortly after 1000 BCE.

According to the Hebrew Bible, Jerusalem was a town on top of a mountain spur in southern Syria. To date, archaeologists have found few traces of the early city. Moreover, they have not even been able to confirm the rise of Jerusalem from village to city level. For historians, therefore, the biblical account, like that of many ancient texts, is perhaps best understood not as history but as a religious foundation story.

According to the Hebrew Bible, the two states that emerged after Solomon, Israel in the north (930–722 BCE) and Judah in the south (930–587 BCE), enjoyed only short periods of independence after being liberated from the coastal Philistines. The empire of Assyria and its successor, Neo-Babylonia (626–539 BCE), conquered the two kingdoms in the eighth to seventh centuries BCE. Thousands of people had to resettle in other parts of Syria or in Mesopotamia. The Philistines, together with people in the Syrian steppes (collectively called "Arabs"), suffered similar defeat. In their place, Anatolian and Iranian populations settled in Syria. The final wave of Israelite deportations, under the Neo-Babylonians in 597–582 BCE, became the "Babylonian captivity" mourned by prophets in the Hebrew Bible.

The Mycenaeans and Early Greeks   Parallel to the Phoenicians, Pelesets, and Israelites in Syria, the Mycenaeans arose in Greece and the eastern Mediterranean during the middle of the second millennium BCE. After the adaptation to farming, demand for agricultural products among the villages had advanced sufficiently to result in the emergence of towns and cities which traded in these goods as well as in copper and bronze wares. Around 1700 BCE, in Attica and the Peloponnesus, leaders built forts as refuges in times of war. The best known among these forts were Mycenae, Tiryns, Pylos, Sparta, and Athens.

Two centuries later, the forts evolved into palaces with warrior lords and kings, as well as administrative offices, surrounded by clusters of villages. In these palace-states, scribes introduced a new, cuneiform-derived script, which has been identified as Greek, and unlike the Linear A of the Minoans, has been deciphered. This *Linear B* script provides us with invaluable information for understanding early Greek culture. About 1450 BCE, chariot and bronze weapon–equipped Mycenaean warriors sailed to Minoan Crete and conquered the island. The Mycenaeans were a major seafaring power in the eastern Mediterranean, establishing trading outposts in competition with the Phoenicians.

The Mycenaean palace-states were short-lived. When an earthquake hit, around 1250 BCE, the walls of many palaces collapsed. Former mercenaries (skirmishers in the chariot armies of the Hittites) joined by herders from northern Greece raided the weakened Mycenaean palace-states. The descendants of the kings, however, managed to salvage some wealth, as evidenced by their tombs. Iron swords and jewelry found in these tombs were of Phoenician origin and indicate that some sea trade continued even after the destruction of the Mycenaean states.

A general recovery in Greece began during the eighth century BCE. Trade in agricultural goods was revived. The Anatolian craft of ironworking spread to Greece. Literacy returned as the Greeks adapted the Phoenician alphabet for their own language. The population increased rapidly. After 750 BCE, many Greeks emigrated to the Anatolian west coast and as far as Italy and the Black Sea to colonize the land and establish new cities. As they developed into city-states of their own, the settlements on the Anatolian coast became known collectively as "Ionia."

Instead of a palace, a sacred precinct in a city's center served as an open space for general assemblies. Contained within this space were a temple and administrative buildings. Farmers in villages outside the city walls produced foodstuffs for the urban dwellers. A city with surrounding villages formed a city-state, or *polis*. Each of these new city-states administered its own internal and external affairs, although they also formed alliances or pursued hostilities with each other.

Initially, kings from among the landowning families (the aristocracy) were responsible for the administration of the city-states. During the period 750–600 BCE, conflict often broke out between the aristocracy and the common folk over the distribution of wealth. Some aristocrats exploited these tensions and allied themselves with groups of commoners. Once allied, these aristocrats assumed power as tyrants, who attempted to create family dynasties.

Other aristocrats opposed the tyrants and agreed to power sharing with the commoners. Through trade, many commoners were becoming wealthier than the aristocrats. Both aristocrats and commoners served as foot soldiers in the city-states' defense forces. These armies relied not on charioteers but on foot soldiers, who were heavily armed with shields, lances, and swords.

In the narrow valleys and defiles of Greece and Ionia, these disciplined regiments were nearly impossible to break if each man held his position and the men in the

Republicanism:
A system of government in which, in the place of kings, the people are sovereign, electing representatives to executive and legislative offices.

Democracy: A system of government in which most or all of the people elect representatives and in some cases decide on important issues themselves.

back moved up to take the place of those who fell. It was not individual aristocratic valor that counted but the courageous willingness of each citizen-soldier to support and protect another. Thus, as many ordinary city dwellers became the military equals of the aristocracy in the crucible of battle, they began to demand an equal share of political power in times of peace.

Political reformers in the sixth century BCE gave commoners their first political rights. The best-known reforms were those introduced in Athens and Sparta. In Athens, aristocratic rule was replaced with political rights distributed according to levels of property ownership. The poorest class had the right to participate in the citizen assembly, cast votes, and sit on juries; members of the wealthier classes could run for a variety of leadership and temple offices. In Greece, and later Rome, these traditions would evolve into the ancestral forms of many of the political institutions we live under today, particularly **republican** and **democratic** offices.

In Sparta, the traditional rule by two coequal kings was held in check through a board of five officers elected annually from among the popular assembly. These officers were responsible for the administration of day-to-day affairs in Sparta. The assembly was made up of all landowners wealthy enough to live in town because of the revenue they collected from their legally indentured (unfree) tenant farmers in the surrounding villages. These political reforms, however, did not prevent new tyrants from rising up in periodic takeover attempts. Thus, in the middle of the first millennium BCE, Greeks were still struggling to find a consistent direction for their political development.

Religious Experience and Cultural Achievements

By around 5500 BCE, when agriculture had replaced foraging, many human groups began to move from naturalism to polytheism as their new form of religion. In *naturalism*, people revere the forces of the natural world. However, there is no indication in the available archaeological record that people identified these creatures and forces with particular deities. With the rise of cities and the development of writing, these forces received names. *Polytheism* is the general term used to denote religions of personified forces in nature. Since many of the religious and cultural achievements were expressed in writing, we can evaluate them today with far better understanding than we can the culture of the foragers and early farmers.

Toward Polytheism   The creators of the Paleolithic rock paintings in Africa, Europe, and Australia (discussed in Chapter 1) have left us few hints of their spiritual preoccupations in their world full of dangerous animals. In the Neolithic transition period from foraging to agriculture, the principal change was the transfer of ritual from caves to aboveground sanctuaries and towns.

An example of the transfer to a sanctuary was Göbekli Tepe in southern Anatolia, a place where foragers came together for rituals during 9000–6000 BCE. Images of animals, mostly in the form of reliefs, have been unearthed. These images show that naturalism was still in force, even if the venue was no longer a cave. The oldest place documenting the transfer of ritual from the cave to the town is Çatal Hüyük [Tsha-TAL Hoo-YOOK] (7500–5700 BCE) in southern Anatolia. At its height, the town had 5,000 inhabitants, who lived in densely packed houses accessible only from the top with ladders. The inhabitants farmed outside of town, and hunted extensively. Large rooms in town, probably communal, contained a concentration of artifacts, among which Venus-type figurines and reliefs and wall paintings of animals are prominent. The imagery is reminiscent of that of the Paleolithic foragers, but the emergence of urban places of ritual indicates that humans were far along in the transition from nature to civilization.

In Ubaid Mesopotamia (6000–4000 BCE), urban places of ritual evolved into temples. Urban dwellers then took the decisive steps of transition from naturalism to polytheism in the period 3500–2500 BCE, when forces of nature began to lose influence in daily life. With the advent of a partnership with nature in the production of food supplies instead of hunting and gathering, as well as kings ruling cities and the appearance of writing, the transition from natural sprituality to polytheism was begun. This connection between writing, kingship, and gods is crucial for an understanding of polytheism and religion in general: Prior to 3500 BCE, religion tended to be an impersonal and nameless naturalism; thereafter, it was the polytheism of kings, often with colorful personalities, told in myths and epics.

In polytheistic empires, rulers were very tolerant toward the phenomenon of multiple gods, even though they had a personal relationship with only one god, their patron deity, and the priesthood of their deity's temple. Even strong rulers never had the power to force the many temple priesthoods of their empire to give up their gods. Egyptian kings, however, unified Egypt more thoroughly than their Mesopotamian counterparts, who never overcame the long city-state tradition of their region. Under royal influence, therefore, Egyptian priesthoods devised a hierarchically organized pantheon of all gods, along with elaborate stories about these gods.

During the New Kingdom period (ca. 1550–1070 BCE), kings and priests came into close contact with other empires of the Middle East. They developed an understanding that all gods taken together were really only a few deities, or even only one, with many different manifestations. One king, Akhenaten (1353–1336 BCE), went even further, conceiving of the Sun as the only god, to whom all Egyptians were henceforth to pray. The new Sun religion—not yet true monotheism, in which God the One would have to be invisible—was too radical to survive Akhenaten. But its brief appearance demonstrates the full range of meaning which polytheism as a religion could acquire. (See "Against the Grain.")

Akhenaten and His Family. This wall painting shows Akhenaten, the 18th-Dynasty (New Kingdom) Egyptian pharaoh, and his family worshiping Aten. Images like these were designed to broadcast Akhenaten's devotion to the solar disc among his subjects.

Mesopotamian and Egyptian Literature   Among the earliest writings in the world exploring religious themes are the *Epic of Gilgamesh* and the myth of *Enuma Elish*, which had their origins in third-millennium BCE Mesopotamia. The first is

perhaps Akhenaten was determined to replace the former polytheism with a mono-theistic religion devoted to *his* power, and not to the solar disc. A third theory suggests that Akhenaten was interested in opening up religion to wider participation by all Egyptians. Perhaps the most provocative of speculations concerns whether Akhenaten was the forebearer of later monotheistic worship in the ancient Near East.

Key Terms

Agrarian society   29

Agrarian–urban society   27

Assembly   32

Bronze Age collapse   42

City, city-state   33

Democracy   46

Empire   35

Iron Age   42

Neolithic Age   30

Nomads   33

Palace-state   40

Republicanism   46

Sharecroppers   32

audio flashcards

For additional resources, please go to
www.oup.com/us/vonsivers.
Please see the Further Resources section at the back of the book
for additional readings and suggested websites.

Shifting Agrarian Centers in India

The inscriptions on the ancient seals were unlike anything General Alexander Cunningham had seen before in India. Some years previously, in 1856, British engineers working on an extension of the East India Railway had found ancient mounds stuffed with fire-baked bricks. They looted the bricks to use as support for the railroad tracks. Fortunately, the men noticed that some of the bricks contained these puzzling signs and sent them to Cunningham, who was known for his archaeological work at Indian Buddhist sites. Intrigued by their antiquity, Cunningham had the sites placed under protection. The tracks of the railroad, it turned out, were being supported by the remains of one of the world's most ancient cities! Identifying the civilization that created it, however, would prove to be one of archaeology's greatest challenges.

The railroad workers had stumbled upon the "lost city" of Harappa—the center of one of the world's oldest societies. Although archaeologists have been working at Harappa since the 1920s, basic questions about this society remain to be answered. For example, how did their writing system—composed of the symbols carved on the seals first brought to Cunningham—work? Why did Harappan society vanish almost entirely after just 600 years? And while scholars believe that Harappan village life set

ABOVE: The animal depicted in this Harrappan "unicorn seal" is still elusive and remains the subject of considerable debate.

≫ Who were the
Harappans? Where did
they come from? What
evidence exists for their
origins?

≫ What explanations
have been offered for
the collapse of Harappan
society?

≫ How well do the
rival theories hold up,
given what scholars
and archaeologists have
discovered?

≫ How can we know
about the newcomers
to northern India?
What sources exist for
historians to examine?

≫ What patterns can
we see evolving in the
Ganges River states that
will mark the subsequent
development of Indian
civilization?

many of the patterns for later Indian rural society, what were the fundamental patterns that marked these founding cultures, and how did these patterns change the lives of the peoples in the region and come to be adopted and adapted by them?

One important pattern marking the history of northern India, like that of Mesopotamia, lies in regular migration and invasion. Although all of India did not experience rule by a single regime until the nineteenth century CE, cultural and religious unity had already been created thousands of years earlier under the influence of newly emerging states along the Ganges River. Maintaining this cultural continuity while managing innovation from outside has marked India to the present day. Among their most significant achievements, these early Ganges states gave rise to some of the world's most important religions: Hinduism, Jainism, and Buddhism.

The Vanished Origins of Harappa, 3000–1500 BCE

Unlike Egypt or Mesopotamia, the cities of the Indus valley flourished for less than 1,000 years—from about 2500–1700 BCE—before vanishing. Anchored by two major cities—Harappa [hah-RAP-uh] in the north and Mohenjo-Daro [moe-hen-joe DAH-roe] in the southwest—and extending from the upper Ganges River to the Arabian Sea, a network of small cities, towns, and villages marked by a consistency of architecture and artifact occupied the largest cultural area of the third millennium BCE. Trade with southwest Asia and Egypt extended Harappan influence even farther.

Although the sophistication of this "Harappan" or "Indus valley" culture's urban planning, the standardization of weights and measures, and the attention to cleanliness and comfort all suggest social organization, we know virtually nothing of its arrangement. Scholars have not yet deciphered most of the Harappan pictographic symbols. The fundamental question remains: Why, as the new mode of urban society gathered momentum elsewhere, did the inhabitants of the Indus Valley abandon their cities and disappear from the historical record? To look at what we can and do know about these mysterious people, we must start with the geography of the Indus and its region.

The Region and People

The subcontinent that includes the modern states of India, Pakistan, and Bangladesh is attached to the Eurasian landmass, but is almost completely cut off from it by forbidding physical barriers. The lower two-thirds of India form a peninsula surrounded on three sides by the Arabian Sea, the Indian Ocean, and the Bay of Bengal. To the north of the bay, extending from Bangladesh through the Indian province of Assam to the north and east and deep into Myanmar (formerly Burma), are continuous ranges of forested mountains. Some of the world's highest annual rainfall totals—over 100 inches—are recorded here.

Forming the northeastern border of the subcontinent above the rain belt is the Himalayan Mountains. These meet another range, the Hindu Kush, which extends into Pakistan and, with the Sulaiman and Kirthar ranges, marks the northwestern border of the region. Access to the Indian peninsula by land is thus limited to a handful of mountain passes through the Himalayas and the more substantial Khyber and Bolan Passes of the northwest. Historically, these have been avenues of trade, migration, and invasion (see Map 3.1).

The Monsoon System   Surrounded by water and framed by high mountains, India's internal **topography** also influences its climate. The Deccan Plateau, Vindhya Range, and other internal highland areas tend to both trap tropical moisture against the west coast and funnel it toward the region drained by the Ganges River in the northeast. The moisture itself comes from the summer winds of the monsoon system. The winds, which carry moisture generated from the heat of central and southern Africa as they flow southwest to northeast over the Indian Ocean from June through October, govern the climatic cycles of southeastern Asia, Indonesia, and southern China, as well as India. In the winter months the winds reverse direction and pull hot, dry air down from central Asia. During this dry season, rainfall is scant or nonexistent over large areas of south Asia.

Topography: The physical features—mountains, rivers, deserts, swamps, etc.—of a region.

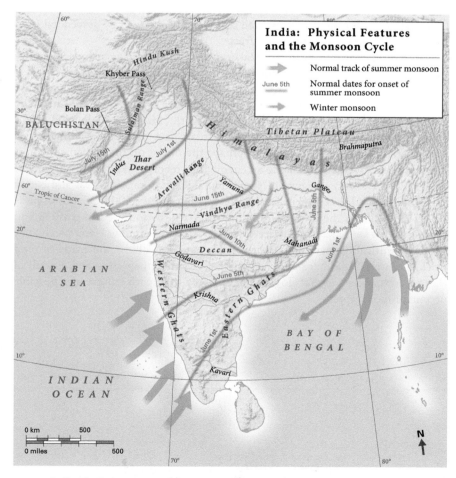

MAP 3.1   **India: Physical Features and the Monsoon Cycle.**

The monsoon cycle exerts a powerful influence on Asian agriculture. In India, where the monsoon rainfall amounts differ widely from region to region, even minor variations in the timing of the cycle or the volume of rain may spell potential flood or famine. Generally speaking, the subcontinent becomes drier as one moves farther north and west until one reaches the Thar, or Great Indian, Desert and the plain of Sind. It is this arid region bordered by mountains and watered by the Indus River system that saw the rise of the first Indian cities.

Harappan civilization depended on the Indus. This vast river system has a slow, meandering course that for millennia has left behind rich deposits of fertile soil. Moreover, like the Yellow River in China, the constant buildup of silt in the riverbed periodically caused the water to overflow its banks and change course—dangerous for those living close by but an effective means of spreading soil over a wide area.

Mehrgarh Culture The peopling of the Indian subcontinent has been the subject of intense research over the last several decades. The advent of advanced dating techniques and the refinement of DNA analysis and genetic testing have yielded a complex picture of the region's historical demography. Groups of people in India's extreme south still chant prayers so ancient that the meaning of the words has long been lost. Recent testing has suggested that they may be directly descended from some of the earliest migrants out of Africa.

More recent peoples, perhaps speakers of a parent language termed "Elamite-Dravidian," are believed to have moved into the region near the Indus. They may have been part of a wave of early agriculturalists emerging from the area of the Fertile Crescent. Researchers have found a number of Neolithic sites near the river, one of the most productive being Mehrgarh [MARE-gar], located near a strategic mountain pass in Baluchistan. Scholars have dated the Mehrgarh culture to about 6000 BCE, making it perhaps the oldest on the Indian subcontinent for which we have a reliable archaeological record. Like the inhabitants of the Fertile Crescent, villagers in Neolithic Baluchistan raised wheat and barley and domesticated sheep, goats, and cattle. As long ago as 5500 BCE, pottery was being produced in the area. Also dating from this period are the crafting and trading of fine *lapis lazuli* beadware, later a coveted item among Harappan luxury goods. Significantly, even the earliest Baluchistani dwellings are made of mud brick, a material that became a hallmark of the Harappan cityscape. For all of these reasons, some archaeologists have viewed Mehrgarh culture as a possible precursor to Harappa.

interactive timeline

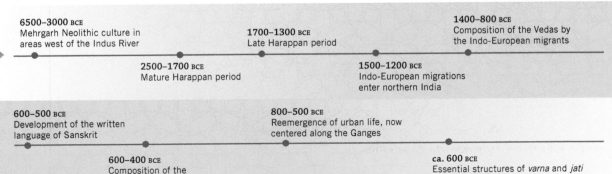

6500–3000 BCE
Mehrgarh Neolithic culture in areas west of the Indus River

1700–1300 BCE
Late Harappan period

1400–800 BCE
Composition of the Vedas by the Indo-European migrants

2500–1700 BCE
Mature Harappan period

1500–1200 BCE
Indo-European migrations enter northern India

600–500 BCE
Development of the written language of Sanskrit

800–500 BCE
Reemergence of urban life, now centered along the Ganges

600–400 BCE
Composition of the Upanishads

ca. 600 BCE
Essential structures of *varna* and *jati* (caste) social systems in place

Scholars agree that by about 3000 BCE a culture of villages and towns with trade networks, pottery, and domesticated plants and animals had long been established in the hills of Baluchistan adjacent to the Indus and its western tributaries. Attracted by the ease of growing crops in the fertile river valleys, the inhabitants of these hill sites extended their settlements eastward sometime before 2600 BCE, culminating in the region's first cities.

Adapting to Urban Life in the Indus Valley

By about 2300 BCE the two major cities of Harappa and Mohenjo-Daro anchored a system of small cities, towns, and villages encompassing between 650,000 and 850,000 square miles (see Map 3.2). At its height, the city of Harappa had a population of over 40,000—comparable to that of the largest Mesopotamian cities of the period. Located on a floodplain, these cities were built on artificial hills to protect them from flood damage. Mohenjo-Daro, for example, was built on two 40-foot mounds separated by a channel 200 yards wide for easy access to the Indus.

Harappan Uniformity   While the cities of Mesopotamia and Egypt contained culturally specific architectural features, Harappan cities seem almost to have

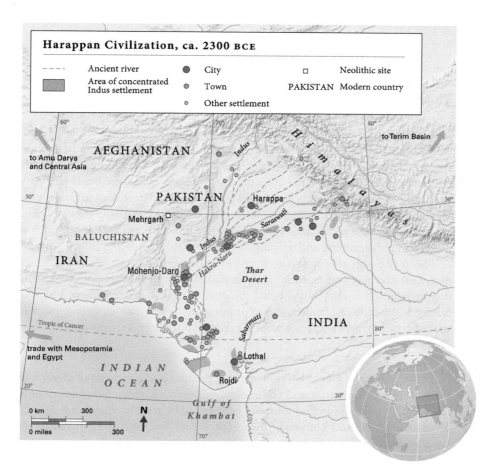

MAP 3.2 **Harappan Civilization, ca. 2300 BCE.**

map analysis

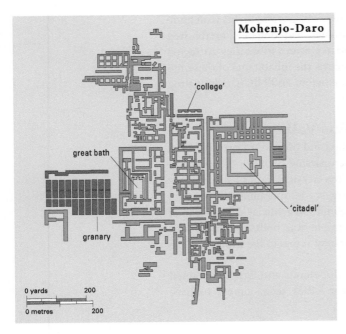

MAP **3.3 Mohenjo-Daro.**

Cesspits: Deep holes or trenches used to deposit human waste and refuse; in the case of Harappa, they were flushed with water into city sewers and drains, ultimately leading to the adjacent river.

been designed by the same hand. Harappa and Mohenjo-Daro, as well as several smaller cities and numerous towns, are laid out according to a planned grid, with squares, public buildings, and markets at regular locations. The larger streets are straight and paved with brick. They are laid out according to standard widths, with drains and gutters connected to a sewer system (see Map 3.3). The bricks themselves were produced according to a uniform ratio. Moreover, the Harappans developed perhaps the world's first decimal system and used it in designing highly refined scales of weights and measures.

This uniformity extended to individual buildings. Houses of several stories were made of brick and plastered with gypsum, their floor plans similar even at widely spaced sites. Many had brick-lined indoor wells and primitive toilets emptying into terra-cotta **cesspits** whose overflow connected to the city's drains and sewers. Nearly all dwellings had a bathing room with a waterproof floor and drain system to direct the water into channels in the street. Wheel-turned, mass-produced clay pots, jars, cooking vessels, copper- and bronzeware, and even toys have been found at various sites.

The Harappan Diet The rich soil of the region supported the staple crops of wheat and barley as well as peas, melons, figs, and sesame. Recent work has uncovered sophisticated irrigation systems designed to conserve water during dry periods. Cattle appear to have been the chief domestic animals, and large herds may have been signs of wealth. It is not clear, however, whether they were used principally for food and milk or as work animals, as were water buffaloes. Whatever the case, some scholars see in their importance at this early time the origins of the later centrality of the cow in Indian culture and religion.

Sheep and pigs also appear to have been an important part of the Harappan diet. Seal carvings and figurines suggest that the Harappans were sophisticated dog breeders. It is also thought that the chicken was first domesticated here in Neolithic times. Rice, which figures so prominently in later Indian agriculture, may have also been grown but, because of the relatively arid climate, does not appear to have been a staple.

Harappan Identity and Government   Evidence concerning the identity of the Harappans is obscure and contradictory. Everyday items and statuary offer few clues. Symbols found on what are believed to be merchant seals are seen by some to hold tenuous links to a "Proto-Dravidian" language group distantly related to that of most modern south Indian peoples. Scholars have also suggested that the Harappans may have been an eastern branch of a people called "Proto-Mediterraneans," who ranged across southwest Asia. More recently, as noted above, their predecessors in the region may have been the Elamite-Dravidian speakers from the area around the Fertile Crescent/Zagros Mountains. Complicating the matter further, archaeologists have identified an urban society designated as the "Bactria-Margiana Archaeological Complex" (BMAC) to the northwest of the Indus valley culture that shares some technological features with the Harappans. However, the uniqueness of Harappan urban life argues against any theory of simple cultural diffusion.

As with other early urban cultures, there appears to have been a close relationship among the religious, political, and social spheres of Harappan society. Nevertheless, the clues again yield little that is definitive. For example, the replication of city plans and architecture throughout such a wide area might indicate the kind of strong central authority and bureaucratic control typically found in a kingdom or empire. Yet we know virtually nothing of how it might have been organized. Indeed, there seems to be an absence of the kind of monumental architecture of palaces and temples so characteristic of other wealthy, centralized states. Moreover, some departures from the uniformity of previous sites found in recent work at Rojdi [ROEJ-dee] have led scholars to amend this picture in favor of one of overall unity marked by discernible regional styles. This modified view, along with findings that suggest that remnants of Harappan culture survived the collapse of the cities, would seem to work against theories of highly centralized control.

Harappan Trade The ability to mass-produce a vast array of articles and the existence of elaborate port facilities imply an occupation-based class system as well as a merchant class with overseas connections. Mesopotamian records from about 2300 BCE tell of a people called "Meluha," now believed to be the Harappans, who carried on seaborne trade and maintained colonies of merchants in several of their cities. There is evidence of Harappan merchandise being traded as far away as Egypt and central Asia.

Because of the apparent occupational specialization of the Harappans, some scholars have theorized that they may have belonged to *guilds*, organizations whose members all pursue the same trade or craft. However, the uniformity of Harappan dwellings, in contrast to their amenities—generous living quarters, indoor plumbing, and so forth—defy any easy generalizations about class structure.

The Harappans appear to have maintained complex trade networks both within their cultural sphere and outside of it. Fortified border settlements, evidently trading posts, extended their influence to the borders of modern Iran and as far north as the Amu Darya, or Oxus, River, the region of the BMAC. Curiously, however, we see virtually no evidence of foreign trade goods such as handicrafts in the Indus cities, suggesting perhaps tight government control over outside influences.

The Horned God. The figure on this seal found at Mohenjo-Daro may be a depiction of a Harappan deity. Its cross-legged "lotus" position and multiple faces prompted archaeologist Sir John Marshall to theorize in the 1930s that it was an early version of the Hindu god Shiva. More recently, some scholars have moved away from this claim, noting that mention of Shiva does not occur for another 1,000 years during the Vedic period. Above the figure is a typically short sample of the pictographic Harappan script.

In addition to bulk foodstuffs, the Mesopotamian records of the Meluha note that their merchants dealt in beadwork, lapis lazuli, pearls, rare woods, cotton cloth, and dog and cat figurines. Due in part to our inability to decipher the Harappan symbols, we know much less about their imports. The network of cities along the Indus also seems to have been pivotal in the long-distance trade of copper from Baluchistan and in the exchange of gold, silver, semiprecious stones, shells, and timber throughout an extensive area north and west into Afghanistan and east to central Asia.

Lothal   Located several miles up the Sabarmati River from the Gulf of Khambat (Cambay), Lothal [LOW-tall] was a large Harappan seaport. Recent work has shown it to be not only a vital link in Harappan maritime trade in the Arabian Sea and points west but an important manufacturing center, as well.

Lothal's central structure is an enormous basin that was once connected to an inlet of the river. Most researchers believe that this was a dock for oceangoing ships, though some contend instead that it was a reservoir for water storage. Nearby are a number of structures believed to have been warehouses, each marked with what appear to be the stamps and seals of merchants.

Lothal was also a regional craft center, with microbeads used for decorative craft items and jewelry as its chief product for internal trade and export. The city's site may have been chosen because of its proximity to sources of stones for bead making. The site, with the city planning and water systems typical of Harappan cities, is also notable for its pottery kilns and bead "factories," complete with worker housing. Yet, for all this wealth of artifacts, answers to such questions as who the merchants or workers were, how they were organized and governed, what levels of mobility there might have been among different classes, and even precisely what those classes might have been, remain elusive.

Harappan Religion   Clues about Harappan religion are equally tantalizing. The swastika, a symbol associated with the cyclical nature of life in Indian and Buddhist art long before its appropriation by the Nazis in the twentieth century, is first found in the cities of the Indus. Scholarship suggests that the Harappan system of symbols, always assumed to be a form of writing, may instead be understood as a form of religious shorthand for use in the multiethnic and multilingual Indus society. Figurines depicting real as well as mythical animals have been found, which, along with female figurines and **phallic stones**, may connote a type of fertility religion. Like many Neolithic and agrarian–urban cultures, the Harappans interred their dead with ornaments, pottery, and perhaps food, and may have believed in an afterlife. Such finds suggest continuities with later Hindu practices. However, for the moment, the nature of Harappan religion remains an open question.

Phallic stones: Stones in the shape of or meant to evoke the male sex organ; Indian religions use a host of phallic images, or *lingams*, in shrines, rituals, and festivals to symbolize the male, or active, forces of both natural and supernatural creation.

The Collapse of the Cities

Around 1900 BCE the major cities of Harappan society appear to have been in decline. By 1700 BCE the great cities appear to have been abandoned; their people moved out to smaller outlying towns and villages, many returning to farming or becoming herders.

Dockyard at Lothal. While some scholars maintain that this structure was a holding tank or reservoir for the local irrigation system, the current consensus is that it was in fact a technologically advanced area for loading and unloading oceangoing ships. A sophisticated system of channels kept it flooded to the proper level, prevented overflow, and, with locks and gates, allowed access to the river and sea.

Some recent interpretations of Harappan urban decline attribute it to ecological collapse. The surrounding land had reached the limits of its capacity to support large cities. Weather-related problems may have stretched these limits even further. One theory holds that a prolonged regional drought occurred around 2200 BCE, resulting in a drying up of vital branches of the Indus watershed. Increasing salt levels in the Indus may have played a role, perhaps as the result of diverting too much of its water for irrigation and supplying the cities; another study places part of the blame on earthquakes, which may have partially diverted the river's flow around 1800 BCE. We do know that the Hakra-Nara River was abruptly shunted into the Indus by the early eighteenth century BCE, resulting in a progressive drying up of its old watershed and increased flooding on the lower Indus.

By about 1500 BCE remnants of Indus civilization were found only within isolated regional cultures that blended Harappan influences with those of neighboring peoples. The expansion of Harappan village agriculture to the east and south, however, continued. Indeed, the hallmarks of Harappan urban life—the cultivation of regionally appropriate staple crops and domesticated animals by people organized in villages—might justly be called the foundation of Indian social history. It would be centuries, however, before India again saw the rise of cities.

Interactions in Northern India, 1500–600 BCE

The "villains" of the Harappan collapse were long considered to be Indo-European-language-speaking migrants from the north who called themselves "Aryans" (Sanskrit, "the noble ones")—a term which, through a series of twisted associations and garbled history, Adolf Hitler and the Nazis later identified with Germans. The identification of the Indo-European family of languages with the peoples of northern Europe in the nineteenth century prompted the Nazi appropriation of the term "Aryan" for those of Germanic ethnicity in the 1930s and 1940s. The tales associated with them recount their movement south and east through the Khyber Pass and across the Punjab between 1700 and 1400 BCE. Their accounts of epic battles were formerly assumed to refer to their conquest of the Harappans. The earliest of their religious texts, the *Rig-Veda* [rig VAY-duh], refers to a short, dark-skinned people whom the Aryans contemptuously called *dasas*, or "the others." It also mentions conflicts with sedentary phallus-worshipping people who lived in cities, which would seem to describe the Harappans.

These works, however, were not written down until centuries after the events may have occurred, and whether their references date from the mid-second millennium BCE or were added later on is still not resolved. Moreover, while battles undoubtedly did occur, periods of peaceful migration and settlement also appear to have taken place. Perhaps the most significant problem, however, is that the Harappan cities appear to have been largely abandoned by the time the newcomers arrived.

In addition, the relative lack of Aryan artifacts; conflicts of interpretation among archaeologists, classical scholars, and linguists; and a growing body of scholarship by Indian researchers have challenged the role of Aryan migration. Indeed, some scholars have suggested that long-held assumptions about the Aryans grew out of nineteenth-century beliefs of European superiority supported by the British occupation of India. Their contention is that the roots of Vedic society came not with invaders from the north but from peoples—perhaps the remnant of the Harappans themselves—already long established in Punjab and, later, along the Ganges River. One problem with this interpretation, however, is that the society depicted in the Vedas—male-centered, aristocratic, centralized—appears to bear little resemblance to the urban, egalitarian-appearing, Harappans. The importance of the horse to later Vedic society also suggests a close connection to the Indo-Europeans, the people who appear to have domesticated the horse. Some scholars feel that the cultural discrepancy can at least be explained by the necessity of a societal shift as the Harappan remnant migrated east, ultimately settling around the Ganges. The debate will most likely remain unresolved for some time.

The Vedic World, 1750–800 BCE

Most scholars assign a prominent role to the Indo-European migrants. While, as we have seen, their exact homeland is unknown, scholars believe it to be in the area around the Caspian Sea. Nomadic peoples speaking a set of languages called "Proto-Indo-European" appear to have migrated into Asia Minor, the eastern Mediterranean, Iran, and deep into central Asia. They spread such technologies as ironworking and the use of the horse and chariot.

Indo-European Origins   Their ancestors had already introduced items and ideas throughout Eurasia long before the Aryans arrived in India; their presence may have even predated the Neolithic settlement of the continent. More recently, branches are believed to have migrated east and west across the continent from perhaps 4000 to 2500 BCE. They are believed to have introduced the domestication of the wild horses of the central Asian steppes, along with such items as bridles and weapons for use on horseback. Similarly, it seems likely that they spread the technology of the chariot from the Mediterranean to China.

Scholars believe that a Proto-Indo-European language these groups spoke is the parent tongue of a family of languages that includes Latin, German, Greek, the Slavic and Celtic languages, and what became the Indian literary language, Sanskrit. A number of words with common roots for certain basic objects or concepts may be found among these languages. Examples include *pater* (Latin), *Vater* (German), and *pitar* (Sanskrit) for "father"; *septem* (Latin) and *sapta* (Sanskrit) for "seven"; and the place name "Iran" (from "Aryan"). However, a new group of scholars has argued for a "Paleolithic continuity theory," in which these groups had already begun to differentiate linguistically by the beginning of the Neolithic period and were not involved in massive "invasions" on the continent from the fifth to the third millennium BCE.

The Vedas   Around 2000 BCE a linguistic group designated "Indo-Aryans" had already split off from the Indo-Iranian subgroup and began moving toward northern India. However, this history is extraordinarily difficult to unravel. Some scholars see the Indo-Aryans as emerging from the BMAC culture; others see them as engaging in wars within the BMAC against the indigenous settled inhabitants; still others see them as migrating into the Punjab long after the Harappan cites declined. In this context, they view their accounts of great "battles" and storming "citadels" as in reality cattle raids and attacks on village corrals.

In any case, the migrants had an oral tradition of epic poetry, hymns, prayers, and allegorical myth and history that would be preserved until it was committed to writing after 600 BCE. The core works, composed from around 1400 to 800 BCE, are the religious hymns known as the Vedas ("knowledge" or "truths").

The *Rig-Veda*, the earliest of the Vedas, is currently believed to have been composed between about 1400 and 900 BCE. Its verses were memorized and passed down orally from generation to generation by priests and their successors until written down ca. 300 BCE. The oldest recorded poetry in any Indo-European language, the *Rig-Veda* provides an allegorical vision of a society led by warrior chieftains and priests, and composed of herders, cultivators, artisans, and servants. These groups became the prototypes of the four early social divisions, or *varnas*—priests, warriors, merchants, and commoners (see Patterns Up Close). Material wealth and skill in battle were the most valued attributes of Vedic culture. This emphasis on struggle and daring is seen as evidence of a strongly *patriarchal*, hierarchical society based on kinship and prowess.

Early North Indian Society and Economy   The Indo-Europeans benefited from the diffusion of earlier Bronze Age crafts and distributed these crafts throughout Eurasia. Their bronze spear tips, arrowheads, and blades, in addition to their chariots and horse-borne warriors, gave them an advantage over the village communities they encountered. After the beginning of the first millennium BCE, they also helped spread the use of iron.

The Vedic peoples made extensive use of horse-drawn wagons and chariots in battle. The earliest migrants may have introduced the horse to northern India, and it is likely that they first brought the chariot to late Xia or early Shang China. Bridles, yokes, harnesses and other items related to the use of horses have been found at a number of sites. The horse was so potent a symbol of power in Vedic culture and religion that its sacrifice became the most sacred of all ceremonies.

Ranging across vast stretches of grassland, the early Vedic peoples carried much of their food supply with them in the form of domestic animals. As with the Harappans, cattle were the chief measure of wealth, thus continuing the centrality of the "sacred cow" to the Indian religious experience. Sheep and goats were also mainstays of their livestock, while milk and butter, particularly the clarified butter called "ghee" [gee, with a hard "g"], occupied a prominent place in their religious symbolism.

The Settlement of Northern India   While the Vedas provide a literary account of Indo-European society and religion, the history of the settlement of northern India is more obscure. Evidence suggests a prolonged period of migration and settlement in the northwest of the subcontinent marked by a gradual transition of the Vedic peoples from a nomadic and pastoral life to a settled and agricultural one. Evidence of large towns in the area around present-day Delhi dates to as early as 1000 BCE. An important catalyst in the reemergence of large cities was the beginning of widespread rice cultivation in the newly opened lands to the east.

First domesticated in Neolithic southeast Asia and south-central China, rice proved well suited to the climate of the Ganges basin once the forests had been cleared. The introduction of iron tools such as plows and axes was instrumental in preparing the land. High yields and a climate warm enough to permit two crops per year helped ensure the surpluses necessary to support a network of villages, towns, and cities, sometimes called by archaeologists India's "second urbanization."

However, the labor required at every stage of the rice plant's growth cycle needed many hands for its successful cultivation. Hence, the infrastructure of rice culture—the dikes, drainage ditches, terraces, raised paths, and other items related to water control—demanded sophisticated social organization. From roughly 800 BCE, strong agrarian-based states called *janapadas* [jah-nah-PAH-duhs] ("populated territories" or "clan [*jana*] territories") emerged in northern and northeastern India.

Statecraft and the Ideology of Power, 800–600 BCE

By the sixth century BCE the *janapadas* were close to a cultural, if not a military, conquest of the subcontinent. Supported by the agricultural wealth and trade of the region, their religion spread steadily east and south. Sixteen large states, or *mahajanapadas* [MAH-hah-jah-nah-PAH-duhs], now dominated northern India from the Bay of Bengal to the foothills of the Himalayas. The largest of these, along the Ganges, grew increasingly contentious. Buoyed by large revenues and supported by belief in kingship as almost divine, their respective quests for domination grew as they absorbed their weaker neighbors. In this respect, as we shall see in Chapter 4, these states shared much in common with their contemporaries, the states of Zhou China.

Centralization and Power among the Ganges States The growing power and prosperity of the larger states led to increasing centralization. The two wealthiest *mahajanapadas*, Magadha and Kosala, found the route to consolidation through centralized kingdoms supported by the Brahmans, or priests. By the sixth century BCE this combination of state power and religion had produced kings, or *maharajas* [mah-hah-RAH-juhs], who wielded power that was seen as both secular and divine.

Other large states retained systems of government in which power was more diffuse. Ruled by councils as opposed to kings, scholars sometimes refer to these states as "republics." The most powerful of the republics, the Vajjian Confederacy, was ruled by a chief whose authority was derived from a council of representatives of the principal clans. The council members were in turn responsible to local assemblies of clan elders and notables.

Growing economic prosperity coupled with fierce competition among all the states required ever greater efficiency in collecting revenue and spending for defense, and pushed them toward either monarchy or absorption. The Vajjian Confederacy, for example, was eventually absorbed by Magadha during its drive for empire in northern India.

Thus, by the sixth century BCE, these states, like the Greek *poleis* and the states of late Zhou China, were in continual political crisis. Attempts to create a balance of power repeatedly failed as the largest states relentlessly vied for control. Increasing sophistication in strategy, tactics, and military technology put a premium on manpower and revenue, thus giving the larger states further advantages. By the late fourth century BCE, when these armies faced the threat of invasion by the forces of Alexander the Great and his successor Seleucus, they would number in the hundreds of thousands of men.

The Ideology of Rulership Warfare conducted by kings with god-like status raised ethical and practical questions about the nature of kingship, the responsibilities of rulers to their subjects, and their role as agents of a universal order. How should the ideal ruler comport himself for the good of his kingdom, subjects, and himself in accordance with his divine mission?

The growing size, wealth, and power of the Ganges states made such questions increasingly important. By 600 BCE, all the Gangetic rulers were in the situation later described by the political strategist Kautilya [kaw-TEEL-yuh] of Magadha in his political treatise, the *Arthashastra* [ar-tah-SHAS-truh]. In this constant war of all against all, says Kautilya, the wise ruler understands that those who encircle him on all sides and "prevail in the territory adjacent to his are . . . known as the enemy." On the other hand, those who control the territory "that is separated from the conqueror's territory by one [namely, the enemy's territory] is the constituent known as friend." Hence, one's policy toward neighboring states should be opportunistic: Attack the weak, seek allies against the strong, bide one's time with equals, and practice duplicity wherever and whenever necessary. As we shall see, there are many parallels with late Zhou Chinese treatises such as Sun Zi's *Art of War*. The prime purpose of such action,

Illustration from the Mahabharata. The stories of the Mahabharata continue to be among the most popular forms of entertainment in India today. In this 1598 CE painting, Arjuna confronts his relatives on the battlefield.

however, must always be the welfare of one's subjects by means of the survival and prosperity of the state.

This grim vision of statecraft was tempered by the themes of the epics, composed during the Vedic period. Though committed to writing only in the third century BCE, the two most famous epics are the Mahabharata [Mah-hah-BAH-rah-tuh] and the Ramayana [Rah-muh-YAH-nuh]. The Mahabharata describes the struggles among the descendants of the king Bharat, and the conflicting obligations imposed on the individual by state, society, and religion. The sixth book, the Bhagavad Gita [BAH-guh-vahd GEE-tuh] (Song of the Lord), has been called the "Indian gospel" because of its concentration on the balance of ethics and action.

On the eve of a battle in which the enemy includes his relatives and former companions, Arjuna, the protagonist, agonizes over fighting against his family and friends. His charioteer—the god Krishna in disguise—reminds him of the need to fulfill his duty according to *dharma* [DAR-mah] (literally "that which is firm"). Krishna tells Arjuna that the higher law of dharma demands that he put aside his personal reservations and fulfill his larger obligation to fight and win. If Arjuna forces himself to do his duty because it must be done, abandoning his attachment to the result—whatever it may be—then, according to Krishna, he is acting wisely and advancing the course of the universe.

By about 600 BCE, the largest of the northern Indian states were attempting both to expand southward and to absorb their neighbors along the Ganges. In this volatile political environment, they developed ideologies of kingship and power based on a common understanding of the Vedas and a realistic appraisal of their respective political environments. At once supported and trapped by the idea of dharma as it relates to kingship, they would struggle for the next several centuries until the state of Magadha incorporated the northern third of the subcontinent into an empire (see Map 3.4).

Indian Society, Culture, and Religion, 1500–600 BCE

The first chronicles of Indian history do not make their appearance until well after the beginning of the Common Era. The documentary evidence we have about social history is found in religious and literary texts, law codes, and the collections of folktales and genealogies called the *Puranas* [poor-AH-nuhs] ("legends"), which date from about 500 BCE.

Society and Family in Ancient India

While part of Indian religious thought was increasingly concerned with the nature of the absolute and ways to connect with it (see Chapter 8), much of the rest dealt

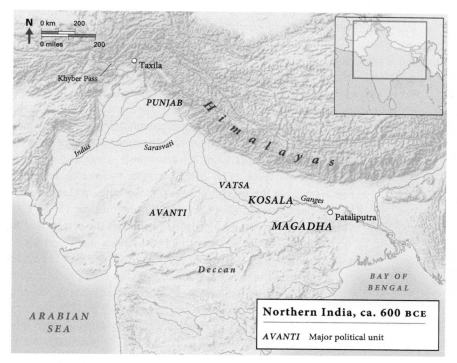

N
0 km   200
0 miles   200

Taxila

Khyber Pass

PUNJAB

Indus

Sarasvati

H i m a l a y a s

VATSA

KOSALA *Ganges*

AVANTI

Pataliputra

MAGADHA

Deccan

BAY OF
BENGAL

ARABIAN
SEA

Northern India, ca. 600 BCE
AVANTI   Major political unit

MAP 3.4 **Northern India, ca. 600 BCE.**

with the arrangement of society, law, and duty; the role of the family and its individual members; and relationships between men and women.

Dharma and Social Class   The Bhagavad Gita illustrates the dilemmas of following one's dharma: duty in accordance with one's capabilities and the requirements of one's place in society. Krishna outlines these duties quite succinctly to Arjuna in the Bhagavad Gita passages that closely echo the *varnas*: "Tranquility, control, penance, purity, patience, and honesty, knowledge, judgment, and piety are intrinsic to the action of a priest," he notes, while "heroism, fiery energy, resolve, skill, refusal to retreat in battle, charity, and majesty in conduct are intrinsic to the action of the warrior." The activities that support the subsistence of society such as farming, herding cattle, and commerce "are intrinsic to the action of a commoner," while "action that is essentially service is intrinsic to the servant."

The great majority of Indians followed Krishna's last two sets of injunctions. Although one of the distinctive developments in the rise of the Gangetic states had been the rebirth of urban life in India, the village remained the center of the social world for most of the subcontinent's inhabitants. Villagers were organized by clan and *jati*, or **caste** (see Patterns Up Close).

Rigidly hierarchical, the social system based on *jati* ("to be born into") functioned as a kind of extended family, each with its own clans, villages, local dialects, gods, laws, advisory councils, and craft and work specializations.

Caste: A system in which people's places in society—how they live, the work they do, and whom they marry—are determined by heredity.

The Caste System

The *janapadas* developed an interlocking social order based on ethnicity and occupation. As the Vedic peoples settled into northern India, their nomadic society became firmly defined by ritual position and occupational status. There were four *varnas* ("form; shape"; though it is also sometimes interpreted as "color"): the first three for priests, warriors, and commoners, respectively, and a fourth that included both servants and laborers. The origin of the *varnas*, according to the *Rig-Veda*, lay in the seminal sacrifice of the cosmic being Purusha, which gave form to the universe: His mouth became the Brahmans, or priests; his arms became the *kshatriyas* [kuh-SHA-tree-yahs]—kings and warriors; his two thighs the *vaishyas* [vy-SHEE-yahs], or merchants; and from his two feet came the *shudra*, or peasants, servants, and laborers.

Brahman

Kshatriya

Vaishya

Shudra

The newcomers' task of establishing themselves as an elite class over the indigenous peoples meant that the system had to accommodate all, but with tight restrictions placed on social mobility. Thus, it appears that intermarriage was forbidden between the new elites and *dasas*, the term used for non-Aryans, and the latter were incorporated into the peasant/laborer/servant *varna*. By the sixth century BCE divisions between Aryans and non-Aryans originally based on ethnicity or locale were giving way to ones based on occupation. An elaborate *jati*, or caste, system was already developing.

Based on the original divisions of the four *varnas*, each caste included an infinite number of subcastes according to hereditary occupations. A new category of "excluded" castes—the so-called untouchables (today called Dalits)—was added, comprising people whose occupations were considered ritually unclean. The

Thus, as the organization of society became more complex, the ritual importance of the four *varnas* of the Vedas was giving way to the occupational emphasis of *jati*.

As the system expanded south, it incorporated local leaders, clan elders, and other notables into the higher castes. Sometimes entire villages were accorded their own castes on the basis of lineage or occupational specialty. At its peak, the number of castes and subcastes may have exceeded 3,000. As the various peoples of the subcontinent were brought into the structure, the older ritual divisions of the early Vedic era were broken down even further, though their traces remain even to the present.

The force of dharma extended into the personal realm as well. Behavior in village society and the family, and even the possibilities for religious fulfillment, hinged upon carrying out the demands of dharma. These demands varied according to an individual's social standing, gender, and place in the family.

Gender Roles: Men and Women in Society   The importance of family life in India is evident in religious scriptures and the law codes, or *smriti* [SMER-tee]. By

excluded castes also came to include "outcasts," people who for various offenses had "lost caste" and were therefore placed on the fringes of society. In what was perhaps a lingering vestige of early Vedic attempts at ethnic separation, stringent prohibitions were imposed on sexual relations between *shudras* and members of the castes within the first three *varnas*.

The evolving *jati* system expanded southward as the Ganges River states pushed farther into these areas. Eventually, it incorporated villages, clans, and sometimes even entire tribal groups into their own *jatis*. Though highly restrictive in terms of social mobility, these arrangements guaranteed a prescribed place for everyone in society. Moreover, the idea of movement between castes became part of Indian religious traditions through the doctrines of continual rebirth and the transmigration of souls. Thus, the Indian response to the problem of incorporating a multiplicity of ethnic, linguistic, and religious groups into its expanding culture was to create a space in society for each, while ensuring stability by restricting social mobility and encouraging good behavior through the hope of a higher place in the next life. The fact that the system continues today despite its dissolution by the Indian government is testimony to its tenacious cultural roots and long-standing social utility.

1805 French Lithograph of Indian Funeral (*top*) and Upper-Caste Dress (*bottom*).

Questions

- How is the caste system a cultural adaptation?
- How does the persistence of the caste system today demonstrate its social utility?

600 BCE, *artha* [AHR-tah], the pursuit of subsistence and prosperity, was recognized as a moral course of action necessary to sustain family position and harmony. For example, the male householder of the upper caste was expected to habitually sacrifice his own needs for those of his family and dependents.

The position of women in the Indian family and in Indian society is more difficult to determine. Unswerving loyalty and devotion on the part of wives and daughters was demanded and highly prized. In household matters a wife should be engaged "in the collection and expenditure of . . . (the husband's) wealth, in cleanliness, in dharma, in cooking food for the family, and in looking after the necessities of the household." The position of women in this context, the code says, is "deserving of worship." The reciprocal aspect of the demand for loyalty and devotion, as the Code of Manu advises, is that, "regarding this as the highest dharma of all four classes, husbands . . . must strive to protect their wives."

Women's sexuality was seen as simultaneously compelling and threatening. The idea of *kama*, as encapsulated in the later *Kama Sutra*, included the enjoyment of sex by men and women as part of a balanced social and religious life. In contrast, the material world in general, and sexuality in particular as its most enticing aspect, was also understood to divert a person from fulfilling his or her dharma and to pose a threat to the social and natural order if not properly controlled. The close relationship between society and religion in this regard allowed men to explore ways of going "beyond" the material and sexual world by engaging in solitary, often celibate, religious practices. On the other hand, it also bolstered the idea that a woman without the protection of a husband or family was a danger to herself and a source of temptation to others. For both men and women, independence from the social system of family, clan, or caste—unless channeled into an approved religious or social practice—was subject to severe sanction. But due to the concept that the family was the foundation of society as a whole and the place of women was at the center of family life, the burdens of supporting the system and the penalties for failing to do so fell far more heavily on women than on men.

Cultural Interactions to 600 BCE

The social system of *varna* and *jati* held together as the religion of the Vedas expanded into the diverse body of beliefs, practices, and philosophy that would later be referred to by outsiders as "Hinduism." The term is derived from the Persian word *hindu*, taken from the Sanskrit *sindhu*, or "rivers," in reference to the inhabitants of the Indus valley.

Priests   As the members of the most important *varna*, the prestige of the Brahmans (priests) grew as they monopolized the performance of rituals and sacrifices. The priests maintained the oral tradition of the Vedas, preserving the exact formulas of the old rituals while also creating new ones centered on the needs of a more sedentary, agrarian people. The growing emphasis on the precise details of various rituals spurred the development of education among the men of the upper castes. By the sixth century BCE, the major works of the Vedic and Brahmanic oral tradition were being committed to writing in Sanskrit, from this time forward the sacred language of Indian scriptures.

Toward New Religious Directions   At the same time, this trend contributed to an increasing *belief* within the Vedic-Brahmanic tradition that only the precise observance of all the proper forms of ritual behavior could ensure their effectiveness. Since the formulas for these rituals were for the most part accessible only to the upper *varnas* and considered the special province of the Brahmans, there was considerable social and religious exclusiveness attached to the tradition as well. Indeed, the punishment prescribed for those in lower *varnas* caught overhearing the inner secrets of Brahmanic ritual was to have molten lead poured into their ears.

A movement away from this restrictive view was already apparent by 600 BCE. Instead of appeasing the gods through the precise performance of ritual, some in the upper *varnas* began seeking the forces behind that order and trying to achieve communion with them. Two paths within the Vedic-Brahmanic tradition emerged.

One path was *asceticism*, full or partial renunciation of the material world. The Vedic tradition revered hermits and those who fled society in order to purify themselves. The many schools of ascetic practice held that the distractions of making a living, raising a family, and even the body itself hindered the quest for one's spiritual essence. These schools developed strategies for uncovering the unchanging, and thus real, "self" removed from a world where everything is impermanent and illusory.

The practices of certain schools of *yoga* ("discipline"), for example, were based on the belief that mastery of the body allowed the adept to achieve communion with this inner self. Since the body, as part of the physical world, is subject to constant change, the discipline of postures, breathing, and meditation allows the practitioner to go beyond its limitations and find that which is unchanging within.

The other emerging path to a deeper spiritual reality was scriptural. Between the seventh and fifth centuries—though perhaps from as early as 800 BCE—a group of writings called the Upanishads [uh-PAHN-ee-shahds] ("secret knowledge") marked a new direction within the Vedic tradition. The Upanishads represented the Vedanta, the "fulfillment" of the Vedas, in which the hidden symbolism was revealed and inconsistencies were reconciled.

The material world was increasingly regarded as extraneous as well. The individual "self" (*atman*) was ultimately to become identified with the cosmic "essence" (*brahman*—note that this usage is different from the same term used to describe the priestly *varna*).

Karma-Samsara   Such speculation about the nature of individual and universal "essence" was beginning to be reflected in culture and society. Caste, and its accompanying obligations, led to the idea of *karma-samsara*, the transmigration of souls and reincarnation. By the sixth century BCE the two ideas appear to have been widely accepted. The concept of a nonmaterial essence or "soul" carrying with it the residue of one's deeds—*karma*—is coupled with the idea of the rebirth of the soul into a new body—*samsara*. Successful pursuit of dharma within the context of the caste system ensures an advance in caste in the next life. Ultimately, one achieves *moksha*—release from the karmic cycle—when one is fully able to grasp the principles of *atman: brahman* and *dharma*.

Asceticism. For millennia great respect has been accorded those who withdraw from the lure of the material world and seek the unchanging within. Here, a modern "world renouncer," or *sannyasi*, is shown.

image analysis

Bathing in the Ganges at Varanasi. The sacred character of rivers in the Indian religious experience may go back all the way to the Harappans. As the multiple religious traditions we know as Hinduism developed in the Ganges valley, that river assumed a position of central importance in terms of ritual purification. Here, bathers are shown on the ghats—steps built on the riverbank—of the city of Varanasi, also known as Benares, site of some of Hinduism's holiest shrines.

≫ Putting It All Together

In the Indus valley, as in Egypt and Mesopotamia, the factors required for the transition to agrarian-based cities emerged around 2500 BCE. Yet many questions remain unanswered about how Harappan society worked and why it fell.

Invasion by nomads was formerly seen as the cause. The pattern of struggle between the settled and the nomadic did indeed play out in various parts of the world for thousands of years. However, recent scholarship suggests that for the Harappans, the coming of the nomadic Indo-Europeans may not have had much of an impact, making the questions of interaction and adaptation that much more intriguing.

In India, the interruption in urban life lasted nearly 1,000 years. When cities again arose, they were centered hundreds of miles from the old, now forgotten Harappan sites. Instead of the apparent uniformity of the earlier society, the new one was to be marked by the struggle of individual states for supremacy. Yet, although these Gangetic states lacked political unity, their cultural and religious similarity remained an important factor throughout Indian history. The *jati* system allowed Indian society to adapt to increasing complexity.

Not surprisingly, this unsettled period of interaction and adaptation within the Gangetic societies was marked by widespread questioning of social, political, and religious arrangements. In the India of 600 BCE, the Vedic tradition was steered in new directions through the speculations of the earliest Upanishads. Moreover, amid the diversity of ascetic religious experience, some visionaries were shortly to map the direction of entirely new religious paths. One of these, Buddhism, may be seen as the beginning of a vitally important new pattern of world history.

interactive concept map

Review and Relate

|Thinking Through Patterns

Examine the ways historians approach the big questions of this chapter.

≫ **Who were the Harappans? Where did they come from? What evidence exists for their origins?**

The mystery of the origins of the Harappans remains unsolved. Most scholars believe their ancestors had been in the Indus region or nearby Baluchistan for millennia. Some also see them as perhaps related to extremely ancient peoples inhabiting the region around modern Kerala. While carbon-14 dating, linguistic tracking, DNA surveys, and sedimentary analysis of ruins have all enhanced our understanding, our inability to decipher the Harappan script means that a key tool for understanding any civilization, the literary record, remains elusive.

≫ **What explanations have been offered for the collapse of Harappan society? How well do the rival**

Collapse can come from predictable causes—war, famine, ecological degradation— or random ones like earthquakes or volcanic eruptions. The literary record of the Indo-Europeans long suggested that they had conquered the Harappans, but this record seems in conflict with more recent discoveries about the flooding patterns of the Indus, the sedimentary analysis of built and rebuilt structures, and salinization levels at various points in the river. As is most often the case, historians generally expect to find no single *sufficient cause*—one that by itself led to the collapse—but rather a number of *necessary causes*—ones that contributed but were not capable of causing the collapse all by themselves.

Another ongoing debate revolves around the identity and nature of the newcomers into northern India. Here, as noted in the previous discussion, the literary record of the Vedas, particularly the oldest, the *Rig-Veda*, appears in conflict with much of the archaeological evidence. While the Vedas are clear about where the newcomers ended up, they are vague about where they originated. Indo-European-speaking peoples ranged across Eurasia, which we can tell from the spread of their languages and the technologies associated with them. But because they left little in the way of archaeological sites, piecing together their story from their material culture is extremely challenging.

Not all of the early north Indian states were monarchies, but the religious aura of the monarchs and its relationship to the first stirrings of what will become Hinduism is striking. The permeation of society by religion is a pattern that continues to this day, as is the desire for transcending the bounds of the material world through ascetic or scholarly methods. The most pervasive pattern lies in the development of the caste system as the basic social structure of society, which endures even today in the face of a constitutional ban.

theories hold up, given what scholars and archaeologists have discovered?

≫ How can we know about the newcomers to northern India? What sources exist for historians to examine?

≫ What patterns can we see evolving in the Ganges River states that will mark the subsequent development of Indian civilization?

| Against the Grain

Consider this as a counterpoint to the main patterns examined in this chapter.

A Merchants' Empire?

Patterns of development among the land-based agrarian–urban civilizations of the Mesopotamians, the Egyptians, the Gangetic states, and (as we will see in Chapter 4) the states arising in ancient China depended on rivers for the fertility of their soil, for irrigation, and for transport. Such riverine societies, which need large-scale public works projects to control the rivers on which they depend, develop powerful central governments capable of directing their enormous undertakings. Such governments control vast labor resources, and tend to display their power by means of monumental architecture and other visible signs of state and religious unity and harmony.

The exception to this pattern appears to be the Harappan system of cities in the Indus valley. Although the Indus cities were at least as reliant on the river as the cities of these other agrarian–urban civilizations, we see practically no evidence of a central government of any kind, aside from the striking uniformity of buildings and materials.

- What similarities and differences do you see among the Harappans and other river-based agrarian–urban societies?

- Based on your reading of this chapter, is there evidence that works against the theory of a "merchants' empire" to explain the apparent differences between the Indus valley and other early river civilizations?

We see no monumental palaces or tombs. Apart from what may be modest temples and baths, we see little in the way of any kind of state religion or cult, though religious objects themselves are quite numerous. There is little to suggest a large state presence of any kind as reflected in the categories of artifacts found in, say, Egypt or Mesopotamia.

So how did things function? One intriguing (if still unproven) theory suggests that, rather than having a powerful central government and bureaucracy to marshal the resources of the state, the Harappan cities were part of a well-integrated merchants' empire. This possibility is supported in part by the vast amount of trade articles recovered in the Indus region; the many apparent craft factories and warehouses; the harbor and docking facilities; and by the theory that Harappan writing may in fact be a sophisticated shorthand script used principally by merchants.

If this is indeed the case, it goes "against the grain" not only of the early patterns of riverine civilization but of the trends of world history in general. One thinks of the Republic of Venice, three thousand years later, as another trading empire, run by a merchant aristocracy for the benefit of its traders. It may well have been that the Harappan system was organized and run along similar lines. If so, its size and influence make it unique in its mode of operation—as it appears to have been in so many other ways.

Key Terms

Caste 67

Cesspits 58

Phallic stones 60

Topography 55

audio flashcards

For additional resources, please go to
www.oup.com/us/vonsivers.
Please see the Further Resources section at the back of the book
for additional readings and suggested websites.

Agrarian Centers and the Mandate of Heaven in Ancient China

The twenty-first Shang king, Wu Ding, prepared to commune with his ancestors about his wife's pregnancy. Fu (Lady) Hao was his favorite (and most powerful) wife. Well educated and highly capable as an administrator, Fu Hao had even on occasion led Shang armies in the field. Now she was entrusted with what Wu Ding and his court considered to be the most important duty of all: continuing the line of Shang kings. These kings believed that the past, present, and future rulers of their line formed an unbroken continuum, with the deceased existing in a spirit realm accessible to the living by ritual divination. Therefore, Wu Ding, whose concern for Fu Hao and her unborn child was paramount, sought the advice of the ancestors about her condition and that of her child to come. Wu Ding and his chief diviner, Que [chway], intoned their questions and held a cleaned and dried shoulder blade of an ox over heat. The diviner then tapped it carefully with a bronze rod and attempted to read the meaning of the cracks as they appeared in the hot bone. As a final step, they incised Que's name as diviner, the date, the question, and the ancestors' response into the bone as a permanent record of the inquiry.

Que's reading of the cracks was: "It is bad; it will be a girl." Although this was considered disappointing because of the desire for a male heir, Fu Hao remained Wu Ding's most beloved wife until her death, after which

ABOVE: **Skeleton and Shang War Chariot, Anyang, China.**

❯ How did the interplay of environment and climate help to influence the earliest patterns of Chinese civilization? How do historians address the question of whether "geography is destiny" in this case?

❯ What can the remains of Neolithic Chinese settlements tell us about the continuities and disruptions of Chinese history?

❯ How did the Zhou concept of the Mandate of Heaven operate?

the king continued to seek her advice through oracle bones. Her tomb, one of the most completely preserved from the Shang era, tells us a great deal about society and gender, economics and trade, and the origins and interactions of Chinese states among themselves and with neighboring peoples.

Like Harappa along the Indus, the Shang state also developed along a river, China's Yellow River. But while Harappa and the other cities of the Indus all but disappeared, the Shang and subsequent dynasties developing in China's Yellow River valley have profoundly influenced East and Southeast Asia to the present day. Unlike the history of India, the political and cultural experience of China was marked by relatively little outside influence and thousands of years of centralized rule. Moreover, for the great majority of its history, China would be perhaps the world's greatest exporter of ideas and goods.

The Origins of Yellow River Cultures, 5000–1766 BCE

Over the centuries, the origins and development of some of China's first Neolithic cultures took place along the Yellow River and the Wei River. China's most famous Neolithic village lies at Banpo on the Wei, and the area where the Yellow and Wei converge features burial mounds from China's early village and town cultures. Nearby is the modern city of Xi'an [SHE-ahn], the capital of no fewer than 13 Chinese regimes during its long history. Here, too, is the famous tomb complex of China's first emperor, Qin Shi Huangdi [chin SHUHR hwang-DEE], packed with thousands of life-sized terra-cotta soldiers.

Geography and Climate

China's natural boundaries have had a profound effect on its history and society. As with India, the Himalayas and Pamirs along the southern border of Tibet mark one natural barrier. River systems have also represented past borders, though not impermeable ones. The northern and western deserts—the Gobi, Ordos, and Taklamakan—have also served as natural boundaries.

These geographical features have limited the principal avenues of outside interaction to the narrow corridor running west of Xi'an, south of Mongolia, and north of the modern province of Qinghai, spanning the route of the famous Silk Road. Like the Khyber Pass in India, this route has historically been the main avenue into China; unlike the Khyber, however, it has seldom been an invasion route for outsiders. While the origins and early development of ancient China were more isolated than those of the other Eurasian centers of civilization, the relative absence of interaction with outside competitors facilitated both cultural and political unification.

China's climate is more varied than that of India. The area south of the Qin [chin] Mountains marks the northern boundary of the region regulated by the monsoon, with warm temperatures and abundant summer rainfall. The suitability of the southern regions for rice cultivation resulted in rapid growth and high population density there, as in the Gangetic societies of India. Above the monsoon line, temperatures and rainfall amounts are influenced more by the weather systems of the Eurasian interior. Thus, northern China is subject to blistering summers and frigid winters with low precipitation.

As a result, China's population has historically been concentrated in the plains along the major river valleys and the coast. Three main river systems—the Pearl River (Zhujiang) in the south; the Yangzi [YAHNG-zuh] River (at 3,988 miles, the third longest in the world); and the Yellow River (Huanghe)—where the most influential early Chinese societies developed, have remained the primary avenues of agriculture and commerce (see Map 4.1).

The Yellow River   Rising in the highlands of Gansu and flowing north to the Ordos Desert, the Yellow River then turns south and east out of Inner Mongolia for 500 miles before making its bend to the east and the sea, a total distance of about 3,000 miles. The mineral-rich soil it picks up as it flows gives it a yellowish tint, and hence its name. As with the Nile in Egypt, the rich soil carried by the river has brought abundantly productive agriculture to arid northern China, but like the Indus, the constant buildup of silt in the riverbed also causes it to overflow its banks and devastate fields and villages in its path.

This building up and bursting of natural levees, along with earthquakes and occasional human actions, have caused the Yellow River to change course 26 times over the last 3,000 years. Efforts to control the river have a prominent place in the mythology, history, and political and social organization of the region. For example, Yu, the supposed founder of the Xia dynasty, was said to have labored for decades to control the river's rampages. Thus, despite its gift of fertility over the course of thousands of years, the Yellow River's unpredictable nature has prompted writers to sometimes refer to it as "China's sorrow."

The Origins of Neolithic Cultures

Between 70,000 and 20,000 years ago, modern *Homo sapiens* became established in eastern Eurasia. Human communities ranged across north and central China from about 30,000 years ago, marking an extensive foraging culture. Within a few millennia of the last glacial retreat, settlements began to appear in northern China containing the first traces in the region of the transition from forager to agrarian society.

Agriculture developed quickly in China. Sites of rice cultivation in central China, dating to 7000 BCE, are among the earliest in the world. Even earlier, **millet** was being grown in the north. Recent work suggests that early strains of wheat and barley, perhaps spreading from areas around the Fertile Crescent, may also have been grown. Chickens, pigs, sheep, cattle, and dogs were also widely raised. Areas along the Yellow River contain some of the earliest agricultural villages in China, and several *prototypical cultures* emerged here and along the North China Plain over the next several thousand years.

Banpo Village   Perhaps the most studied of the thousands of Neolithic sites across China is Banpo [BAN-paw] Village, located on the outskirts of Xi'an. Banpo Village is representative of Yangshao [YAHNG-shaow], or "painted pottery," culture, which flourished from 5000 to 3500 BCE. Although the potter's wheel had not yet been introduced from western Eurasia, Yangshao communities like Banpo had sophisticated kilns that fired a variety of clay vessels painted with animal and

Chapter Outline

- The Origins of Yellow River Cultures, 5000–1766 BCE

- The Interactions of Shang and Zhou History and Politics, 1766–481 BCE

- Economy, Society, and Family Adaptation in Ancient China

- Interactions of Religion, Culture, and Intellectual Life in Ancient China

- Putting It All Together

Millet: A species of grass cultivated for its edible white seeds and as hay for animal feed.

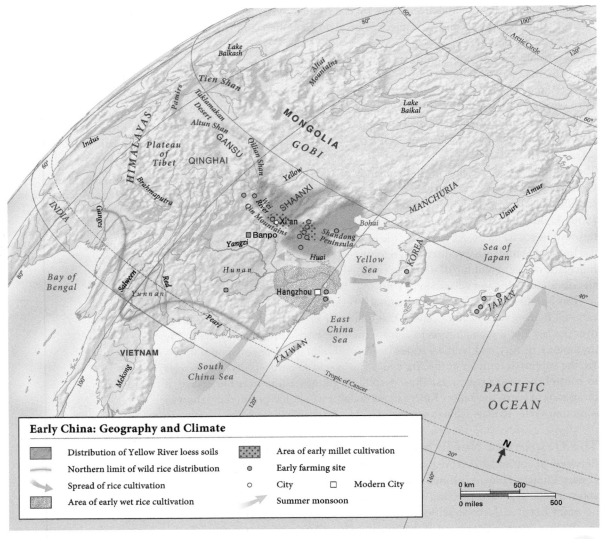

Early China: Geography and Climate

▨	Distribution of Yellow River loess soils	▨	Area of early millet cultivation
⌒	Northern limit of wild rice distribution	◉	Early farming site
➤	Spread of rice cultivation	○	City ☐ Modern City
▨	Area of early wet rice cultivation	➤	Summer monsoon

MAP 4.1 **Early China: Geography and Climate.**

map analysis

interactive timeline

10,000–8000 BCE	5000–3500 BCE	2852–2205 BCE	ca. 2000 BCE
First Neolithic settlements in Yellow River valley	Yangshao culture develops along upper Yellow River	Traditional era of "culture heroes" and "sage kings"	Flourishing of Erlitou, believed to be a city and palace complex of Xia dynasty

ca. 7000 BCE	4500–1500 BCE	2205–1766 BCE
First evidence of rice cultivation in Yangzi valley	Longshan culture develops along lower Yellow River	Traditional dates for Xia dynasty

1766–1122 BCE	ca. 1300 BCE	770–256 BCE
Traditional dates for Shang dynasty	Introduction of chariot to northern China	Eastern Zhou dynasty: capital moved to Luoyang

ca. 1400 BCE	1122–771 BCE	722–481 BCE
Earliest "oracle bone" caches with archaic Chinese writing	Western Zhou dynasty: capital located at Xi'an	Spring and Autumn period

geometric designs. The inhabitants of Yangshao villages also produced stone implements to support hunting, farming, and fishing.

The perimeter of Banpo is surrounded by a defensive ditch, rather than the walls characteristic of later towns and cities, with 40 thatched-roof homes of mud and straw arranged around a rectangular central structure believed to be a clan meeting house or religious site. The village contains features believed to be early forms of long-standing patterns of rural life in northern China, such as raised clay beds with flues laid through them—an early version of the *kang* [kahng], the heated bed still found in older northern Chinese farming homes today. Silkworm cocoons and crude needles suggest the early development of silk weaving. Especially interesting are the pot shards bearing stylized pictures of animals and geometric markings that some Chinese scholars have speculated may be ancestral forms of the Chinese written language.

Longshan Culture   Settled life in villages and towns appears to have expanded during the Longshan period from about 4000 to 2000 BCE. The earliest distinct Longshan artifacts have now been dated from as far back as 4500 BCE. A later branch of Longshan culture based in what is now Henan [HEH-nahn] Province is also believed to have arisen around 2000 BCE, lasting until about 1500 BCE, when it was absorbed by the Shang dynasty.

Like their Yangshao counterparts, Longshan potters were highly skilled. The black-colored pottery associated with Longshan culture is particularly refined. The introduction of the potter's wheel from the west in the mid-third millennium BCE—one of the earliest indications of late Neolithic Chinese interactions with other peoples—permitted unprecedented precision, while improved kilns and experimentation with kaolin clays began a process of ceramic innovation that ultimately resulted in the first porcelain thousands of years later.

After 2000 BCE, the Longshan and other late Neolithic cultures began a transition to a society marked by large towns and small cities supported by agriculture. Towns of several thousand inhabitants have been uncovered, and a number of sites contain elaborate altars. The use of gold, copper, bronze, and jade in jewelry is also increasingly evident. Craft specialization and emerging social classes are detectable.

Beyond the North China Plain   In the regions below the Yangzi River basin in central China, the most extensive distinctive culture is that of Dapenkeng [DAH-pen-keng], which flourished from 5000 to 2500 BCE. Artifacts including pot shards, arrowheads, and polished tools and axes indicate a sophisticated coastal and riverine society along a corridor from the borders of modern Vietnam along the south China coast to Fujian Province and across the Taiwan Strait to the western coast of that island.

The extent of Dapenkeng culture and the similarity of its artifacts over a wide area suggest interaction with peoples throughout the region. The origins of this culture appear to be quite different from those of the north. Linguists have

Painted Pottery, or Yangshao, Earthenware Basin Found at Banpo Site. Contrast and compare this piece with the one from Longshan (p. 80). What similarities and differences can you spot?

Longshan (Black Pottery)
Culture Stemmed Beaker (bei),
Shandong, ca. 2000 BCE.

image analysis

established this area as part of a Proto-Austronesian-speaking region, one whose parent language is distinct from the Sino-Tibetan language group that contains the various Chinese dialects and that has strong links to the Austronesian speakers on modern Taiwan. Scholars studying the origins of the Polynesian language family—which is part of the Austronesian group—are searching for links with these people on Taiwan and along the China coast.

Origins of Rice Cultivation   The most far-reaching innovation in the regions south of the North China Plain was the development of widespread rice cultivation, which likely originated in Southeast Asia and the area extending from China's modern province of Hunan to the coastal reaches of the Yangzi River. Southeast Asia remained an important source of new rice strains that allowed China's food production to keep pace with its population until well into the nineteenth century. Other food sources domesticated elsewhere making their appearance in Neolithic south China include chickens and cattle, especially the water buffalo. Cattle were raised primarily for farmwork, rather than consumption.

Toward a Chinese Culture   While it was long believed that Chinese civilization originated in and expanded outward from the Yellow River valley cultures, scholars now suggest that around 3000 BCE the area approximating modern China consisted of a collection of agrarian communities that remained distinct in their own right but whose interactions with each other resulted in cultural elements that ultimately became identified as "Chinese." Though scholars have filled in much of the picture of these ancient cultures, the precise time and duration of their transition to one marked by cities is still debated. Chinese chroniclers, however, drawing upon the world's largest and longest literary record, have long given pride of place in this regard to their first three dynasties: the Xia, Shang, and Zhou.

The Age of Myth and the Xia Dynasty, 2852–1766 BCE

The Chinese are a historically minded people. For thousands of years, the use of writing for purposes of record keeping has been of paramount importance, and the written word itself was considered to have a kind of inner power. For millennia, the careful study and writing of history have been vital elements of individual self-cultivation as well as key mechanisms for political and social control (see "Patterns Up Close").

Among the earliest collections of Chinese writings we have are those of the *Shujing* [SHOO-jeeng]. Also known as the *Book of History* or *Classic of Documents*, the *Shujing*, a compilation of material purportedly from 2357 to 631 BCE, is a principal documentary source for information about China's first three dynasties: the Xia [she-AH], Shang [shahng], and Zhou [joe].

Culture Heroes and Sage Kings   According to Chinese legend, mythical culture heroes and sage kings reigned from 2852 to 2205 BCE and introduced many of China's basic elements and institutions. Among the contributions attributed to the first culture heroes were medicine, divination, writing, agriculture, fire, and silkworm cultivation. The three sage kings—Yao, Shun, and Yu—whose reigns followed the culture heroes, set the example for strong moral leadership. They are credited with passing the role of leadership on to the land's most worthy men instead of to their own family members.

Between Myth and History   The *Shujing* acclaims Yu, the last sage king, as the tamer of the Yellow River. He is also traditionally considered to be the founder of the Xia dynasty in 2205 BCE. Because of the difficulty in establishing a clear archaeological record, however, Yu and his successors have largely remained suspended between myth and history.

Moreover, as the sole literary account we have of the period, the *Shujing* has assumed a dominant and, most likely, misleading role as the master narrative of ancient Chinese history. Some scholars have even argued that the Xia were an invention of the Zhou. More recently, some have suggested that their rule was in fact a kind of Shang mythology. On the other hand, some, notably a group of Chinese archaeologists, have noted that the relative accuracy of the dates given in the *Shujing* for events in the Shang dynasty suggests a similar level of reliability for its accounts of the earlier Xia.

Recent archaeological work has moved closer to confirming the historical existence of a widespread culture, if not yet a state, corresponding to the literary accounts of the Xia. Artifacts, particularly early bronze ritual vessels, appear throughout regions described in the *Shujing* as belonging to the Xia and, in some cases, considerably beyond it.

Xia Society   Much of what is known about the Xia is based on the premise that the Xia was a transitional society, building on the material culture of the late Longshan and Yangshao cultural periods. Of particular note in this transition are the growing importance of bronze casting, the increasingly complex symbols on pottery, and the widespread evidence of large-scale efforts at flood control.

As we have seen, the Yangshao and Longshan cultures stretched across a continuum from small hunting, fishing, and farming villages to substantial agriculturally supported towns. The Xia, however, appear to have reached the tipping point at which most of the hallmarks of urban society began to appear. For example, excavation at the Erlitou [AR-lee-toe] site in southern Shaanxi Province, dated to perhaps 2000 BCE, reveals a walled city of moderate size containing what is believed to be the foundation of China's first palace.

Literary evidence suggests that Xia leaders exercised a strong family- or clan-based rule, and the archaeological evidence seems to support this. Evidence indicating the role of the elites as mediators with the spirit world, and particularly with the ancestors of Xia rulers, is also found at Erlitou. China's first bronze ritual vessels, as well as jade figurines, turquoise jewelry, the world's earliest lacquered wood items, and cowry shells (a medium of exchange monopolized by the Xia rulers) all testify to their leaders' religious and social roles. As with a number of Longshan sites, cemeteries outside the city suggest the development of social classes in the number and kind of burial artifacts and the position and richness of elite plots.

Though the boundaries of Chinese history have been pushed back considerably by such work, the Xia remain, like their contemporaries the Harappans, an elusive—if perhaps not a "lost"—civilization. For at least one leading scholar, however, the findings at Erlitou represent not merely a regional variation among many ancient cultures, but "an early form of Chinese civilization" (Sarah Allen, "Erlitou and the Formation of Chinese Civilization," *Journal of Asian Studies*, 66:2 [May, 2007]: 490).

The Interactions of Shang and Zhou History and Politics, 1766–481 BCE

The Shang dynasty represents the first genuine flowering of urban society in East Asia, featuring the attributes of such cultures elsewhere: metallurgy, a varied agricultural base, an increasingly centralized political and religious system, growing **social stratification**, a written language, and cities. In all of these areas the Shang made considerable contributions.

Social stratification: A hierarchical arrangement of groups or classes within a society—for example, peasants, merchants, officials, ministers, rulers.

The Shang Dynasty, 1766–1122 BCE

Unlike the idealized rule of the sage kings depicted in the *Shujing*, Shang social and political organization was kinship-based, with an emphasis on military power and efficiency of command. As in Mesopotamia, the advent of cities required rulers to wield greater power for defense and internal regulation, while appealing to an authority beyond human power for legitimacy. Thus, loyalty was pledged to the Shang king and his family. Members of the king's extended family controlled political and religious power, with more distant relatives acting as court officials.

Among the Shang kings mentioned in literary records, rulership often passed from uncle to nephew, though sometimes it went from elder brother to younger. Unlike in the Aryan system of *varna*, there was no rigidly defined priestly class, though spirit mediums and diviners were widely used by Shang rulers. Local leaders who controlled walled cities and towns and their surrounding lands were employed by the ruling families as regional officials, as were specially designated Shang allies. Though small compared to the forces commanded by their successors, the armies fielded by Shang rulers were the most powerful of East Asia in their day (see Map 4.2).

The Introduction of the Chariot The chariot was possibly introduced to China through interaction with Indo-Europeans, around 1300 to 1200 BCE. Chariots were shortly preceded by the introduction of the horse from the west, an innovation that had already revolutionized transport and warfare through much of Eurasia. The small Mongolian ponies native to the northern reaches of Shang lands were not useful as transport or draft animals, but the larger and faster steeds of central Asia and western Eurasia were to remain important items of trade for the Chinese for thousands of years.

Shang chariots were pulled by two horses and generally held three men. Detachable wheels held by linchpins permitted easy storage and repair. Both charioteers and infantry wielded large composite bows that curved away from the archer in their unstrung state for additional power. As with other ancient peoples, the combination of archers with the chariot gave Shang forces considerable striking power, especially when employed against infantry formations.

Shang Weapon. A bronze ceremonial axe head with intricate decorative markings, from the thirteenth to the eleventh century BCE.

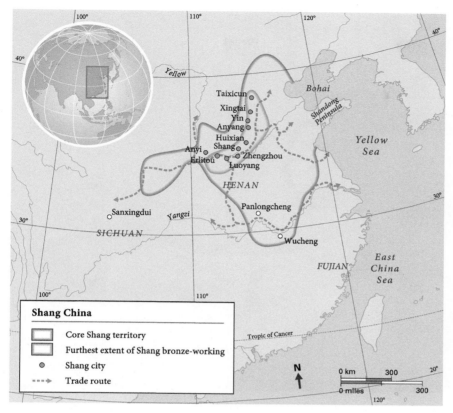

MAP 4.2 **Shang China.**

Shang Politics and Foreign Relations Because their prestige depended on their military power and harmony with their ancestors, the Shang rulers constantly mounted campaigns for sacrificial victims—both material and human. Archaeological evidence and oracle bone inscriptions suggest that the greater part of Shang foreign relations with **client states** and allies consisted of enforcing tribute and labor service. Shang kings, especially Wu Ding, led expeditions against settled peoples to the west, the most prominent of whom, the Zhou, based around modern Xi'an, were ultimately enlisted as allies and clients. Wu Ding's successors met with less success, however, and over time shifting coalitions of former allies and client states began to encroach on Shang lands.

Client states: States that are dependent on or partially controlled by more powerful ones.

Shang Interactions From the beginnings of the Xia to the end of the Shang, ties between the northern Chinese states and the other Eurasian civilizations seems to have been tenuous. The most direct links appear to have been through the trade and migrations of an ethnically and culturally diverse group of nomadic–pastoral peoples who ranged along northern Eurasia from modern Ukraine to modern Manchuria in the east. Though they left few traces, scholars have theorized that these nomads included both speakers of Altaic languages—the distant ancestors of the Mongols, Manchus, Turks, and perhaps the Huns—and the Indo-European peoples.

A number of objects in Shang tombs carry clear signs of their foreign origins. For example, Fu Hao's tomb contains a number of bronze and jade objects that only later

Shang Chariot. Whether used for battle or state functions, Shang-era chariots were distinctive in their wide stance, roominess, and portability. The photograph shows a careful reconstruction of a Shang chariot with authentic bronze decorations and lacquered finish. Note the linchpins holding the wheels to the axles. These could be quickly removed for ease in changing wheels or breaking down the chariot in order to carry its parts separately.

would come into widespread use in China. The Shang circulated local and foreign items such as bronze vessels, weapons, and jade throughout the region and beyond. Many of these foreign items have been found as far south as northern Vietnam, and the peoples of surrounding areas acknowledged Shang predominance in wealth and culture. Widespread recognition of Shang sophistication marks, with the ascendancy of the Zhou, an example of a recurring pattern of world history: conquerors on the cultural periphery interacting with and adapting to the culture of the conquered.

The Mandate of Heaven: The Zhou Dynasty to 481 BCE

Unlike the Xia and Shang dynasties, the nearly nine centuries of Zhou rule are extensively documented in literary works. Like the *Shujing*, these other Zhou records contain much of uncertain origin. Nevertheless, they suggest both an ongoing quest for social, political, and moral order and institutional and intellectual experimentation. They also provide us, in the closing date of the *Spring and Autumn Chronicles* (481 BCE), with an important transition point with which to end this chapter. As we will see in Chapter 9, out of the increasingly fierce competition among the Zhou states for expansion and survival in the succeeding Warring States period came China's ultimate unification into an empire that would last, with brief interruptions, for over 2,000 years.

The Mandate of Heaven By the twelfth century BCE, the size of the Shang state had shrunk considerably due to encroachment by peoples to the north and west. Oracle bones also suggest an increased concentration of power in the hands of the last Shang kings, a situation coinciding with their dissolution and corruption. Against this backdrop, the state of Zhou to the west—which had become a Shang dependency—took military action. The *Shujing* tells of the Zhou kings pushing their holdings eastward from 1122 BCE, taking much of the Shang territory under their control. Sometime around 1045 BCE, Zhou forces captured and burned the last Shang capital and stronghold near Anyang. The Zhou sought to portray their conquest as morally justified by Shang decadence (see Map 4.3).

Conquest by one of the three earliest Zhou dynasties, as depicted in the literary record, did not mean exile, extinction, or enslavement for those defeated. On the contrary, the conquerors were shown as presenting their victories as acts of moral renewal by ridding the conquered of oppressive or degenerate rulers and restoring leadership to the worthy. The idealized speeches of the new rulers in the *Shujing* attempt to justify their actions and seek the cooperation of all classes in the new order.

As the compilers of this literary record, the Zhou sought to place themselves firmly within it. While it is unknown whether the practices they recorded had been widespread or were newly invented by the conquerors, they provided the backdrop for one of China's most enduring historical and philosophical concepts: the Mandate of Heaven.

According to this idea, a dynasty's right to rule depends on the moral correctness of its rulers. Over time, dynasties grow weaker and tend to become corrupt. Under such conditions, rebellion from within or conquest by outside forces becomes morally justified. The success of such actions is then seen as proof that heaven's approval or "mandate" has been taken from the old rulers and bestowed on the insurgents, who may then legitimately found a new dynasty. Ultimately, however, the new dynasty, too, will decline. The idea of such a "dynastic cycle" operating as the driving force of history was later codified by court historians during the Han dynasty (202 BCE–220 CE).

Throughout Chinese history, these concepts not only allowed political renewal to take place internally but framed a remarkably durable system within which the Chinese and outside conquerors could maintain governmental and societal continuity.

Western Zhou and Eastern Zhou By the end of the eleventh century BCE, nearly all of northern China had come under Zhou rule, marking the beginning of the Western Zhou era, which lasted until 771 BCE. Zhou rulers placed

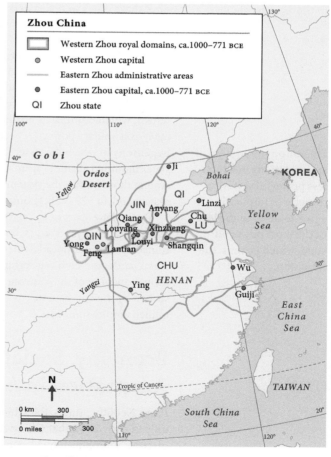

MAP **4.3** **Zhou China.**

family, distinguished subjects, allies, and even some defeated Shang notables in leadership positions of these territories. By the eighth century BCE, however, the more powerful of these territories had begun to consolidate their holdings into states of their own. Though the states would continue to pledge their loyalty to the Zhou court, this resulted in a weakening of Zhou political power. A half century of war among court factions for ultimate rule, border struggles with nomadic peoples to the west and north, and a devastating earthquake further weakened Zhou power, resulting in the court being driven from its capital at Xi'an in 771 BCE and relocating to the east in Luoyang. This forced move began the Eastern Zhou period (770–256 BCE).

The Zhou in Decline   The Zhou system of decentralized government called *fengjian* [FUNG-jien], usually rendered as "**feudalism**," gave autonomy to its local rulers and thus contributed to the weakening of the Zhou central government and the strengthening of its dependent states. As these dependent states grew in power, local rulers became less loyal to the Zhou leadership.

The prestige of the Zhou court was further weakened after its flight to Luoyang in 770 BCE. Continuing border problems with nomadic–pastoral peoples to the north and west around the Zhou home state and the isolation of its new capital drastically cut the flow of revenue from the dependent domains. This isolation was important, since these states were in a period of economic expansion. Within a few generations of the inauguration of the Eastern Zhou in 770 BCE, Zhou power had significantly weakened.

From 722 to 481 BCE, there were repeated attempts at creating a stable political and social order among the 15 major Zhou states. These attempts were frustrated by shifting power dynamics and the rise of dominant states on the Zhou periphery.

During the mid-seventh century, the most important of these states was Qi [chee], which dominated northeast China and much of Shandong. Through diplomacy and military power, Qi became the first "senior," or *ba* [bah], state in a system of **hegemony** in which the lesser Zhou states deferred to the *ba* state. The successive *ba* states mounted alliances against non-Zhou states and attempted to regulate relations among those within the system. Qi was succeeded by Jin, which reorganized the *ba* system and, in 579 BCE, sponsored a truce and disarmament among the Zhou states.

By the latter part of the sixth century, a rough balance of power among the four leading states of Jin, Chu [Choo], Qi, and Qin held sway. While this system functioned for several decades, new powers on the peripheries, expansion into non-Zhou lands, and civil war in Jin led to the partition of Jin in 403 BCE, marking the formal opening of the Warring States period. By its close, Zhou itself had been absorbed by the combatants (in 256 BCE), and Qin would emerge as the creator of a unified empire in 221 BCE.

Feudalism: A system of decentralized government in which rule is held by landowners who owe obligations of loyalty and military service to their superiors and protection to those under them.

Hegemony: A system of state relations in which less powerful states directly or implicitly agree to defer to the lead of the most powerful state, which is, thus, the hegemon.

Economy, Society, and Family Adaptation in Ancient China

From Neolithic times, the Chinese economy has been based on agriculture. It was only in early 2012 that China's urban population outstripped its rural one. Still, as of 2015 approximately 44 percent of China's people were involved in agricultural pursuits. Both the Yellow River states and those in the south of China outside of the control of the Shang and Zhou dynasties relied on a peasant subsistence economy based on family and clan landownership, with much of the local political power diffused to the villages. While the problems of land-centered social relationships long occupied Chinese rulers, China, unlike some other agriculturally based societies, never developed an extensive system of slave labor.

Family life played a dominant role among all members of ancient Chinese society. Here, as in other agrarian kingdoms, the position of women in power among the elite eroded over time. By the late Zhou period, the hierarchy of patriarchy and the growing influence of notions of *filial piety*—a behavioral model based on relationships among members of a family headed by the father—were becoming established.

Shang Society

Though Shang leaders frequently moved their headquarters, nearly all of their newly established capitals were comparable in scale to those developing in India and the Mediterranean.

Erligang   The capital city at Erligang [AR-lee-gahng] was characteristic of the late Xia or early Shang period. It had a defensive wall enclosing an urban center. The area within the walls was the province of the rulers, related families, diviners, and craftspeople who served the elites. Merchants and craftspeople involved in the manufacture of non-elite items lived outside the city walls, as did peasants and slaves.

Life in Erligang for the non-elite centered on communal agriculture. They tilled the soil with small plows, stone-tipped hoes, and assorted wooden implements. They grew millet and vegetables and raised water buffalo, sheep, chickens, and pigs. The pig had been domesticated since at least Yangshao times. Even today, the written character for "family" or "household" (家, *jia*) is represented by a stylized depiction of a pig under a roof.

Social Class and Labor   Outside the larger cities, a more differentiated social structure, with artisans of various trades organized according to lineage, emerged. Craft guilds and other organizations came to be dominated by family groups, as was the case later in imperial China. The constant warfare of Shang rulers and their increasing interest in monumental projects, such as flood control along the Yellow River and its tributaries, all boosted the need for labor. Professional soldiers and local militia satisfied Shang military needs. Conscript labor, however, constituted an increasingly important part of the workforce.

Interactions of Zhou Economy and Society

The large size of the territory claimed by the Zhou dynasty, and the enhanced trade that this expansion entailed, added to the wealth and power of all the rulers of its dependencies. The expansion of these dependencies to the Yangzi River basin brought much of East Asia's most productive farmland under some form of Zhou control and increased interaction with the region's inhabitants.

Innovation and Adaptation in Agriculture   In the north, the introduction of the soybean from Manchuria boosted crop yields and pushed growers to cultivate more marginal lands. The rotation of wheat and millet allowed for more intensive farming. The use of more efficient ox-drawn plows and, from the fourth century

BCE, iron-tipped tools, as well as irrigation and water-conservancy efforts, pushed yields even further. In the south, the Zhou dependencies developed as rice cultivation facilitated population growth, and the economic and demographic center of China moved steadily southward. By the middle of the sixth century BCE, the Zhou kingdoms taken together constituted the world's most populous, and perhaps richest, agriculturally based urban society.

Zhou Rural Society   The Zhou rulers devised a system of ranks for governing their dependencies based on the size of landholdings.

Members of the aristocracy were responsible for collecting taxes from their dependents, and the commoners were required to provide military service to those of higher rank in return for protection. Peasants worked their own lands, with the lands of the aristocracy often scattered in plots among those of the commoners.

The Well-Field System   The Zhou were the first to attempt a uniform system of land tenure in China. This method of land division, called the *well-field system,* was said to have been devised by the Duke of Zhou. In this arrangement, each square *li* (one *li* is about one-third of a mile), consisting of 900 *mou* (each *mou* is approximately one-sixth of an acre), was divided into a grid of nine plots. Individual families would each work one of the eight outside plots while the middle one would be farmed in common for the taxes and rents owed the landowner or local officials. The term "well-field" comes from the Chinese character for "[water] well" (井, *jing*), which resembles a grid. Whether the system was ever widely practiced is a matter of debate, yet it remained the benchmark against which all subsequent attempts at land reform were measured.

By the late 500s BCE, the needs of individual Zhou governments to use the wealth of their states to support their militaries and bureaucracies prompted them to institute land taxes based on crop yields and, in some cases, to commute labor obligations to direct taxes payable in kind to the state. Then, as now, the taxes tended to affect the poor the most.

The New Classes: Merchants and *Shi*   Further evidence for the decline of the Zhou feudal system is the rise of new classes. The growing power of the new merchant class began a struggle with governments for control of vital commodities. It also introduced the perception of merchants as *usurpers,* whose drive for profit from trafficking in the goods of others endangered the stability of Zhou social institutions. Accompanying the rise of a merchant class was the advance of a cash economy and the coining of money.

Though viewed with distaste by the landed aristocracy, merchants were increasingly seen as useful resources. Their rise to economic prominence, however, meant that their social position lay outside the traditional structures of agrarian life. Their independence and mobility, along with the growth of cities as centers of trade, helped spur centralization as Zhou rulers attempted to create more inclusive systems of administration. Direct taxation by the state, uniform law codes, and administrative restructuring altered the old arrangement of mutual obligation between aristocratic landowners and dependent peasant farmers. Here, members of the new *shi* class, drawn from the lower aristocracy and wealthier commoners, took on the role of bureaucrats and advisors. From the ranks of the *shi* would rise many of China's most famous thinkers, starting with Confucius.

Central Asian Interactions   The growing wealth of north and central China spurred an increase in trade outside of the Zhou realm as well as among its constituent states, particularly in the south and along well-established routes into central Asia. In this interchange, Zhou traders were increasingly helped by the carriers of the central Asian exchange.

By the sixth century BCE, a series of loosely related cultures along this northern front can be discerned. These peoples appear to have taken Zhou goods much farther than originally thought, and scholars are only now beginning to realize the extent of their trade relations. What goods may have been involved in such exchanges remains unknown, however, until a period of better-recorded trade along the Silk Road began in the second century BCE.

Gender and the Family

Serious study of gender roles in ancient China is difficult because of the scarcity of records from earlier times. However, the development of women's instructional literature from roughly the first century BCE to the first century CE allows scholars to chart a shift in perspectives of female "virtue" and proper behavior in the home and in public.

Elite Women of the Shang   In marked contrast to later Chinese court life, with its seclusion of wives and concubines, elite women of the Shang often participated in political, and even military, affairs. As we saw in the opening of this chapter, one of the most complete Shang burial sites is that of Fu Hao, who was buried with hundreds of artifacts— as well as the sacrificial skeletons of sixteen people and six dogs. The 1975 discovery of her tomb helped bring to life a woman whose existence, though well established in written records, has otherwise been elusive.

The artifacts also shed light on Shang technology and material culture, court life, and especially the position of women among the aristocracy. For example, inscriptions on oracle bones in Fu Hao's tomb indicate that she wielded considerable power and influence even before becoming Wu Ding's principal wife. Prior to coming to court at the Shang capital of Yin sometime in the late thirteenth century BCE, she owned and managed a family estate and was apparently well educated. She both supervised and conducted religious rituals at court and during military expeditions. As Wu Ding's chief confidant she advised him on political and military strategy and diplomacy. She even conducted her own military campaigns against Shang adversaries.

Women's Status in Transition   Elite women like Fu Hao appear to have shared a comparatively equal status with male rulers, even to the point of leading armies and practicing divination, though it should also be mentioned that their tombs tend to be smaller and less elaborate than males of comparable rank. In the literature of the early Zhou era, women were depicted as occupying important positions as mentors and advisors. Women's crafts such as spinning and weaving were highly regarded. The *Poetry Classic* (Book of Odes), in depicting the lives of ordinary people, suggests a far more egalitarian relationship between men and women than would be the case during the imperial period.

The wives and concubines of rulers in many instances had their own sets of records and genealogies as well, an important asset among the powerful in this family-conscious society. Even by the late Zhou period, a woman like Lady Ji of the state of Lu was able to instruct her son, the high official Wen Bo (Earl Wen), in the arts of government. In this role of advisor, she was much praised for her virtue by subsequent thinkers.

Although late Zhou women might be well educated and highly capable, they seldom ruled in their own right. In fact, during the Spring and Autumn period (722–481 BCE), women were frequently barred from involvement in state affairs. The same general trend may be glimpsed at other levels of society as well. The web of family, clan, village, and class associations of the Zhou era reflects considerable respect for the wisdom and work of women, but these skills were increasingly seen as best exercised in the home instead of in the public sphere. The later development of state-sponsored Confucianism, with its emphasis on filial piety, ushered in a markedly secondary role for women.

Interactions of Religion, Culture, and Intellectual Life in Ancient China

Like the gods of the early Mesopotamians, the first Chinese gods were local deities that inhabited a spirit world presided over by a ruling god. In China, the rulers' ancestors occupied the highest rungs of the spirit world, and worship largely consisted of communication with them. Religion was not separate from everyday life, but permeated all aspects of it.

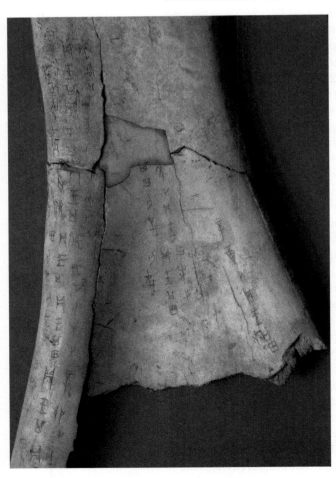

Shang Oracle Bone Inscription on Shoulder Blade of an Ox.

While it creatively adapted and adopted many other aspects of Shang culture, the Zhou era marked a turn toward a more abstract concept of religion. As an illustration of this, Shangdi [SHANG-dee], the chief Shang deity, and other beings with superhuman powers but human-like personalities, began to give way to the more distant Zhou concept of "heaven" (*tian* [tien]) as the animating force of the universe. By the late Zhou era, this concept of heaven as the guiding cosmic force had become central to nearly every major Chinese religious and philosophical tradition.

Oracle Bones and Early Chinese Writing

As we saw earlier with Wu Ding, seekers of guidance would consult the diviner, who would ask questions of the ancestors. The bones were then heated, tapped with a rod, the resulting cracks interpreted as answers, and the information incised in the bone. Several thousand distinct symbols have been identified, and many are clearly ancient versions of modern Chinese characters. Chinese characters became increasingly stylized and, after the Qin era (221–202 BCE), put into standard forms. But in most cases, these retained enough of their earlier character to be recognizable to later readers. Moreover, the political and religious significance of Shang and Zhou ritual vessels, which, in many cases, contained inscriptions in archaic characters, ensured that some knowledge of them would be preserved.

Shang Bronzes   Although some of the early bronze articles and weapons found at late Longshan sites may have come by way of trade routes from western Asia, bronze-casting techniques used in China quite likely diffused northward from Southeast Asia at about the same time. The best evidence for this is that the technique favored by Shang and Zhou casters is unique to China and radically different from the method of the peoples of western Eurasia. Shang and early Zhou ritual vessels themselves, with their richly stylized reliefs of real and mythical animals incorporated into the design, are unlike anything outside of East Asia.

Shang Religion   The use of elaborately decorated bronze vessels was important to elite Shang religious ceremonies, where offerings of meats, grains, and wine were made. Although we know little about the religious practices of Shang commoners, the number of artifacts and oracle bones found at the gravesites of elites and at the remains of royal palaces has clarified the belief system of the rulers.

The principal deity, Di or Shangdi, presided over the spirit world and governed both natural and human affairs. Shangdi was joined by the major ancestors of the dynastic line, deities believed to influence or control natural phenomena, and local gods appropriated from various Shang territories. The religious function of the Shang ruler, as it appears to have been for the Xia and would be for subsequent Chinese dynasties, was to act as the intermediary between the world of the spirits and that of humanity. Hence, rituals appear to have consisted largely of sacrifices to ancestors to ensure their benevolence toward the living. As we have seen, the Shang sought the guidance of their ancestral spirits through divination on a wide variety of human affairs as well as on natural phenomena.

As the Shang state grew more powerful, the size of the sacrifices also increased. Like the Xia, the Shang practiced human sacrifice. Excavations at both Erligang and later capitals have yielded numerous sites containing headless skeletons. The evidence suggests that the death of a ruler was accompanied by the slaughter of hundreds of slaves, servants, and war captives, perhaps to serve the deceased in the spirit world.

Adaptations of Zhou Religion, Technology, and Culture

The Zhou sought to legitimize their reign by adopting many of the forms of art and ritual practiced by the defeated Shang. As before, the ruler maintained his place as mediator between the human and divine worlds. But the Zhou also appear to have followed the trend toward more abstract religious ideas we have observed in other early civilizations.

Ritual Vessel with *Taotie* Design Pattern.

Heaven   The Zhou introduced the concept of *tian*, "heaven," as an impersonal controlling force of the universe. It replaced the more human-like Shangdi. It was this more abstract heaven whose mandate gave the right to rule to all

Patterns Up Close | The Chinese Writing System

Of all the innovations associated with China, perhaps the one with the longest-lasting impact is its writing system. Like those of the Egyptians, the Harappans, and the Mayans, it was originally a system based on pictures. As with these other systems, the pictures became simplified and standardized for ease of interpretation.

The association of the written language with early Chinese religious practices, court ceremonial functions, and self-cultivation and character development imbued it over the centuries with a spiritual dimension. The discipline demanded by learning the thousands of characters necessary for advanced literacy and the artistic possibilities embodied in the brush and ink traditionally used to write them placed calligraphy at the top of Chinese aesthetic values. Thus, wherever written Chinese is used, skill in the three interrelated "excellences" of painting, poetry, and calligraphy is esteemed.

The Chinese written language had a tremendous impact on the course of Asian history. While it requires extensive memorization, it is remarkably adaptable as a writing system

Three Excellences. Chinese children learn at an early age to combine painting, poetry, and calligraphy as the highest form of self-expression.

subsequent Chinese dynasties. Thus, throughout the history of imperial China, the emperor retained the title of *Tianzi*, "son of heaven," as a symbol of his obligation to fulfill heaven's mandate as a son serves his father.

Iron Casting   The use of iron was introduced during the Zhou period. Some late Shang and western Zhou tombs contained iron objects of foreign origin, probably obtained from Indo-European peoples. By the seventh century BCE, technologies for mining and working iron are in evidence in western China. Significantly, it appears that the casting techniques of bronze production were adapted to this purpose. By combining these techniques with the high-temperature technologies employed by Zhou potters, the Chinese produced the world's earliest cast iron. By the sixth century BCE, cast- and wrought-iron weapons, tools, and farm implements were instrumental in opening up new lands for cultivation and multiplying the deadliness of warfare.

Folk Culture: *The Book of Songs*   Although little is known about the lives of the common people during the Xia, Shang, and Zhou dynasties, one of the few sources that do provide some clues is the *Shijing*, the *Poetry Classic*, sometimes called *The Book of Odes* or *The Book of Songs*. The subject matter ranges from homely observations on the cycles of rural life to protests and cleverly veiled satire. It appears that, in most cases, the verses were meant to be sung. Though we do not know the

Ancestor Worship and Human Sacrifice from the *Shijing*

because the meaning of the characters is independent of their pronunciation. Thus, speakers of non-Chinese languages could attach their own pronunciations to the characters and, as long as they understood their structure and grammar, could use them to communicate. This versatility enabled Chinese to serve as the first written language not only for speakers of the Chinese family of dialects and languages on the Asian mainland but also for the Koreans, Japanese, and Vietnamese, whose spoken languages are totally unrelated to Chinese. The pattern of interaction and adaptation prompted by the acquisition of the written language allowed the vast body of Chinese literature, philosophy, religion, history, and political theory to tie the literate elites of these states together within a common cultural sphere. In this respect, it functioned in much the same way as Latin among the educated of Europe. Even today, in all these countries, the ability to read classical Chinese is still considered to be a mark of superior education. Moreover, the cultural heritage transmitted by Chinese characters continues to inform the worldviews of these societies.

Questions

- How did the pattern of interaction and adaptation that characterized the development of the Chinese writing system bring people together into a common cultural sphere?

- How does the impact of the Chinese writing system compare to the impact other writing systems have had in other parts of the world?

names of the authors of these works, it is believed that a number of them were written by women.

As historical source material as well as art, the *Shijing*'s songs and poems of the lives and loves, burdens and laments of peasants and soldiers, young wives and old men are still striking in their immediacy today. One of the most famous of these is a kind of concealed lament about taxes containing the lines:

"Big rat, big rat,
Don't eat my millet!
Three years I've served you
But you won't care for me."

—ODE 113: "BIG RAT," FROM *THE BOOK OF SONGS*

≫ Putting It All Together

The period from the first Neolithic settlements in the Yellow River valley to the birth of Confucius in 551 BCE witnessed the foundations of the cultures of China and East and Southeast Asia. Like the other agricultural–urban cores in Mesopotamia, along the Nile, and in the Indus valley, the society that emerged in northern China was a product of its major river system. As early as 10,000 BCE, the Yellow River basin saw the rise of self-sufficient agricultural villages, marking the transition from

interactive concept map

forager to agrarian society. The early states that developed here dominated the Chinese historical record. The Xia dynasty late in the third millennium BCE saw the first evidence of Chinese cities and people, places, and events traceable through later literary sources.

The Shang conquest of the Xia, traditionally held to be in 1766 BCE, marks the emergence of China's bronze age. The centering of political, military, and religious authority in one ruler; the development of a unique form of writing; the growth of cities; and the use of bronze run parallel to developments in other early centers of civilization. In their casting techniques and design motifs of bronze ritual vessels and their system of writing, however, Shang contributions were original and long-lasting.

The theme of moral renewal came with the rise of the Zhou after 1122 BCE. Nearly all of China from the Yangzi River basin north was incorporated into a decentralized governmental system centered on the Zhou court at Xi'an. But the growing power of the largest Zhou territories eventually eclipsed that of the court; this began an era of struggle between the states. The increased wealth and power of rulers and the emergence of new social classes such as merchants and the *shi* contributed to the breakdown of feudal social patterns during the Spring and Autumn period, from 722 to 481 BCE. Continual warfare stimulated both a drive for political consolidation and a questioning of the foundations of society. The radical ideas of Confucius (Chapter 9) about the nature and aims of society would soon be adopted by a Chinese imperial system that would last over 2,000 years.

Review and Relate

Thinking Through Patterns

Examine the ways historians approach the big questions of this chapter.

> How did the interplay of environment and climate help to influence the earliest patterns of Chinese civilization? How do historians address the question of whether "geography is destiny" in this case?

In northern China, the river both allows a large, reliably fertile area for cultivation to be maintained and restricts the ability to live close to it because of flooding. The efforts of the early Chinese states to control the river proved central to the character of these states. But what kinds of larger conclusions can we draw? Some scholars in the past theorized that early civilizations based around rivers developed many similarities in their patterns of governing, such as centralization, bureaucracy, and elaborate labor regulations. But here the key is in the details: How similar can we say Egypt is to Shang-dynasty China? As for the larger question of geography and destiny, most historians would say that geography is an important *conditional* factor, among many others, in determining how a civilization develops.

> What can the remains of Neolithic Chinese settlements tell us about the

These remains can suggest the kinds of plants and animals that were domesticated, the kinds of shelters that housed people, how gender roles were assigned, how people defended themselves, and how the dead were handled. Many of these things are open to debate, however. Scholars in the People's Republic of China, for example, argued that such Neolithic villages were matriarchal and matrilineal; those from outside are less sure of the evidence for this. If true, the later switch to the strong patriarchal tradition represents an important change in the structure of Chinese families.

The Mandate of Heaven was a way for the Zhou to retrospectively legitimize their conquests and to create a precedent for future moral renewal. As part of a dynastic cycle, it set the pattern for the Chinese view of history. The rule of a particular dynasty was expected to advance in reform and expansion in its early stages, reach a comfortable point of harmony in its middle stages, and go into moral and material decline in its final stages. From that point, revolt breaks out and heaven transfers its mandate to a new dynasty—*if that revolt succeeds*. This pattern of dynastic cycle and heavenly mandate made China's historical experience—conveniently fitted to the theory—not only comprehensible but also predictable. Alert rulers searched for signs that the mandate was in danger; the people speculated about portents presaging dynastic change. Even China's modern rulers are heirs to this pattern: During human-made and natural disasters, the Communist Party is even more alert to possible signs that the people are expecting a "dynastic" change.

continuities and disruptions of Chinese history?

> **How did the Zhou concept of the Mandate of Heaven operate?**

| Against the Grain

Consider this as a counterpoint to the main patterns examined in this chapter.

Women's Voices

Although scholars debate whether Neolithic villages like Banpo may have been matrilineal or matriarchal, there is agreement that by the time of the first three dynasties, the northern Chinese states and their successors were a rigorously patriarchal society and culture. As we shall see in Chapter 9, this would be reinforced by Confucian values. Yet women were not without influence in ancient China; indeed, male Confucian writers noted the exploits of outstanding women of the past, even those who went beyond what came to be seen as the filial, domestic ideals celebrated in manuals of female deportment.

Long before this period, however, the *Shijing* (Book of Songs), in its collections of sung poems from the common people, contained a number of compositions that, although the individual authors are unknown, show strong evidence of having been either composed by women or perhaps in the persona of women. In them we have one of the few glimpses of the authentic voices of ancient Chinese women. Consider this lament from a young woman facing the challenges of family expectations for marriage:

My mind is not a mirror;
It cannot [equally] receive [all impressions]

- It often seems as if women had somewhat greater freedom among the earliest civilizations we have encountered than they would in the period after 600 BCE. Do you think this is a fair observation? If so, which of these societies seemed to offer the most agency to women?

- Why did China become increasingly patriarchal over time? Does the development of urban–agrarian society necessarily lead to patriarchy?

> I, indeed, have brothers,
> But I cannot depend on them.
> I meet with their anger . . .
> Silently I think of my case,
> And, starting as from sleep, I beat my breast. (Number 26; "Cypress Boat")

In an almost visceral way, she gives voice to the frustration of the independent mind and heart in conflict with family and social convention. Her song was to be a familiar one over the intervening centuries.

Key Terms

audio flashcards

Client states 83	Hegemony 86	Social stratification 82
Feudalism 86	Millet 77	

For additional resources, please go to
www.oup.com/us/vonsivers.
Please see the Further Resources section at the back of the book
for additional readings and suggested websites.

Origins Apart:
The Americas and Oceania

In 2001, anthropological archaeologists announced a stunning discovery in the archaeology of the Americas. The scientists had conducted **radiocarbon dating** tests on plant fibers taken from site excavations of Caral, in the Supe valley in Peru. The site had stirred interest because of its immense size, monumental pyramids, and evidence of early urban living. The test results, however, now demanded a complete retelling of the history of civilization in the Americas.

Because earlier evidence suggested a relatively late arrival for modern humans in the Americas, and given the difficulty of domesticating staple grain plants, the earliest known American civilizations had been assumed to be much more recent than their earliest Eurasian and African counterparts— until now, that is.

But the Caral-Supe [KAH-rahl SOO-pay] results put the date of the materials tested at 2627 BCE, making the city as old as the pyramids of Egypt and the most ancient Mesopotamian cities. Indeed, work at nearby sites showed that they had been occupied by substantial villages for far longer, that the entire area was supported by irrigation works, and that Caral-Supe is just one of 18 similar urban sites in the Supe valley.

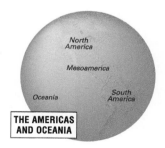

ABOVE: **Cut from copper, this bird was made by villagers of the early American Hopewell culture (c. 200 BCE–500 CE).**

≫ What do historians see as the advantages and disadvantages of the separation of the Americas from the societies of Eurasia and Africa?

≫ The wheel is often cited as the most basic human invention, yet large and sophisticated civilizations were able to flourish without this signal innovation. Why do you think it did not develop in the Americas?

≫ Why did no cities develop on the larger Pacific Islands?

Quipu: Spanish for Quechua *khipu;* the knots in the strings and the varying distances from each other have supposedly numerical or symbolical meanings.

The Americas present a counterpoint to the development of agrarian-based cities and states in Eurasia and Africa. There are some similarities: food surplus accumulation; the development of urban centers; and the kinds of buildings (such as pyramids).

Yet there are enticing differences. For example, Caral-Supe appears to have been thriving long before ceramics turn up in Peru, whereas in Eurasia and Africa, the appearance of ceramics *predated* cities. In addition, although there is some evidence of record keeping by *quipu,* the much later system of knotted ropes used by the Incas, there is no writing—again, something the major Eurasian civilizations developed. Finally, as with later American civilizations, there is no evidence of the use of the wheel. Thus, in our search for patterns of world history, the Americas provide an independent test case for analysis.

In Chapter 5, we will explore these similarities and differences appearing in societies separated by thousands of miles of ocean and with no evidence of contact. How did interactions and adaptations take place across thousands of miles, in the Americas and the islands of the Pacific? (See "Against the Grain.") How do the elements of environment and culture play out in societies separated from direct contact with societies in Eurasia and Africa? How much bearing do environment and culture have on the human societies on the islands of Oceania? How did the peoples interact with each other and adopt or reject certain innovations? Indeed, how "isolated" were the occupants of these islands from each other and the societies of Asia, Australia, and the Americas? Finally, given the importance that we place on interaction and adaptation among peoples, what advantages and disadvantages did such separateness bring?

The Americas: Hunters and Foragers, 16,000–600 BCE

The remoteness of human beings on the American continents from the peoples of Eurasia and Africa raises a key question of world history: What would people do in places far removed from other human communities over long periods of time? The initial great migration out of Africa had equipped human beings with tools, practices, and habits for an effective *foraging* society. These foragers spread out to Eurasia and Australia, and the coming of humans to the Americas represented the final stage of their great migration from Africa.

The advances and retreats of the great ice sheets of the polar region over the last 70,000 years allowed humans to migrate from the Eurasian landmass. Studies published in 2016 confirmed that the first inhabitants of the Americas appear to have migrated from Siberia to the southern tier of Beringia—the land bridge between Eurasia and North America exposed by the drop in sea levels during the last Ice Age—perhaps 23,000 years ago. Because of a 10,000-year gap in the genetic trail, it is believed that these Beringians stayed in place for millennia, blocked by the ice sheets in Eurasia and North America. Some may have sailed to ice-free areas down the North American coast. With the Alberta split in the North American ice shield, however, the way was open for land migration into the Americas about 13,500 years ago. After this date, the number and range of humans grew rapidly on the two continents.

These migrants had already begun to adapt the technology of spears, bows, and other hunting equipment to the big game of the new continent. As the success of their hunting began to reduce the populations of their favored game, a question arises for world historians: Would they now follow the same patterns by undergoing a Neolithic revolution similar to those of humans in Eurasia and Africa?

It appears that they did. During the period from about 6000 to 4000 BCE, in what is today Mesoamerica and the Andes Mountains in Ecuador and Peru, people began to settle in villages, domesticated crops, and founded the first forms of agrarian society in the Americas. Separated by thousands of miles from the peoples of Eurasia and Africa, they were nevertheless following the same early pattern of world history: moving from foraging to farming and to settled life. However, there were also some important differences.

The Environment

Next to Eurasia, the two continents comprising the Americas encompass the largest landmass on earth and form the Western Hemisphere. Located north and south of the equator, the Americas share somewhat similar types of landscape and climate (see Map 5.1).

The Americas' most prominent geographical feature is a contiguous spine of mountain ranges, or **cordilleras** [cor-dee-YEH-ras], near or along the entire western coast. Known as the Rocky Mountains in the north, these ranges become the Sierra Madre in the center and the Andes in the south. Water from these mountains feeds nearly all river systems on the continents. Both continents also share low mountain systems along their eastern coasts. North and South America meet in Mesoamerica near the equator, with North America then reaching northward to the North Pole and South America extending southward almost to Antarctica. Thus, the climatic zones of both South and North America range from extreme cold to subtropical and tropical warmth.

Geographical Regions   North America consists of four main geographical regions:

- The Mountain West
- The Canadian Shield, which stretches from today's Canada to Greenland
- The Great Plains and central lowlands in the center of today's United States
- The Appalachian Mountains in the east and the broad coastal plain along the Atlantic Ocean.

The four regions vary considerably in precipitation and temperature. Historically, they have produced widely differing modes of subsistence and society among their inhabitants.

Mesoamerica and South America form six distinct geographical regions:

- The Central American mainland and the Caribbean islands
- The Andes Mountain region along the west coast
- The Guyana Shield, a rocky plateau that separates the Amazon River and basin in the south from the Orinoco River
- The Brazilian Shield, a rocky crust in the east jutting into the South Atlantic Ocean
- The *Gran Chaco* in the east between the Andes and Paraguay River
- The Patagonian Shield, in the center of the continent's southern tip.

Here, the size of the mountains and the extent of the rain forests dictated even greater regional separation than in North America until recent times.

Chapter Outline

- The Americas: Hunters and Foragers, 16,000–600 BCE
- Agriculture, Villages, and Urban Life
- The Origins of Pacific Island Migrations
- Putting It All Together

Radiocarbon Dating: Sometimes referred to as "carbon dating" or "carbon-14 dating." Carbon 14 is a weak radioactive isotope of the element carbon formed by the interaction of cosmic rays and atmosperhic nitrogen. Plants absorb small doses of it during photosynthesis and animals acquire it by eating plants or plant-eating animals. When the organism containing carbon 14 dies, the isotope begins to decay at a regular rate. Scientists can use the proportion of carbon 14 in a sample to determine the age of the plant or animal in question. Because of carbon 14's relatively short half-life, its dating accuracy is only good to about 50,000 years.

Cordilleras: A continuous spine of mountain ranges near or along the entire western coast of the Americas.

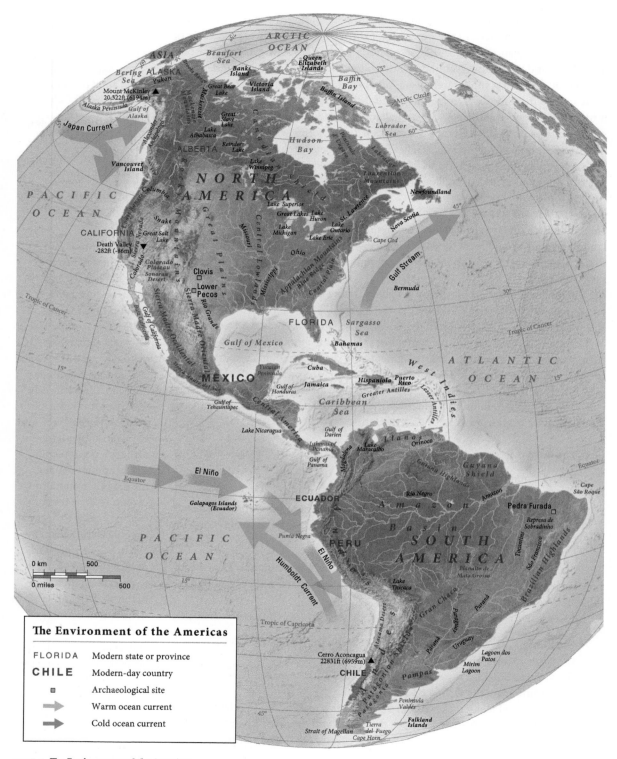

The Environment of the Americas

FLORIDA   Modern state or province

CHILE   Modern-day country

☐   Archaeological site

➡   Warm ocean current

➡   Cold ocean current

MAP 5.1 **The Environment of the Americas.**

During winters in North America, freezing winds from the Arctic blow south across the Canadian Shield into the central plains, or American Midwest. By contrast, at the southern tip of South America, air currents are predominantly westerly and more moderate and do not push winter frost very far northward. Thus, apart from the southern tip at Cape Horn and Tierra del Fuego, snow and frost are mostly limited to the Andes. In North America, winter and summer temperatures vary greatly, as do precipitation levels. Generally, the eastern and midwestern regions of North America receive regular rainfall throughout the year, while the western regions and lower Pacific coast tend to be drier.

In Mesoamerica, the Caribbean, and the northern two-thirds of South America, temperatures and humidity levels tend to be high. Large steppe and desert areas cover the western third of North America, while in South America deserts and steppes are mostly found along the northwestern coast and in the interior of the south. Prior to modern times, large forests covered the eastern two-thirds of North America and the northern half of South America.

Ocean Currents, Hurricanes, and El Niño   Like the monsoon system that influences the agriculture of India, China, the Indian Ocean, and western Pacific regions, large-scale weather events governed at least in part by the actions of ocean currents and continental weather systems have played historical roles in the Americas. Their cycles have only recently been understood.

Running roughly parallel to the eastern coasts of northern South America and nearly all of North America, the Gulf Stream current of the Atlantic Ocean moves warm water from the south Atlantic along the Eastern Seaboard of the United States before heading northeast toward the European coast. In the Americas, the Gulf Stream's interactions with wind patterns in fall and winter in eastern North America frequently result in large storms called "nor'easters."

More destructive is the frequency with which the Gulf Stream guides hurricanes into the Caribbean Sea and along the North American coast. The immense "heat pump" of the African interior and Sahara Desert spawns tropical disturbances in the eastern Atlantic, which gain strength over the warm waters there and the Caribbean as they move westward. Historically, the east–west winds that drive the tropical disturbances played a vital role in fostering the first European voyages to the Western Hemisphere as well as the trans-Atlantic slave trade by making navigation swift and predictable (Chapters 16 and 19). In the case of hurricanes, however, the storms are often picked up by the Gulf Stream, fed by its warm waters, and directed north from

interactive timeline

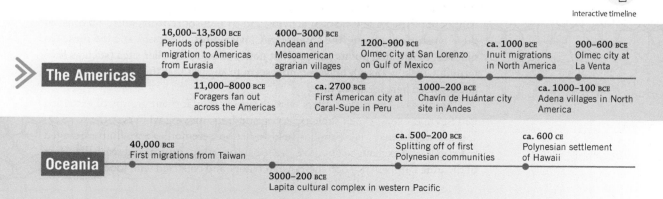

The Americas

16,000–13,500 BCE
Periods of possible migration to Americas from Eurasia

11,000–8000 BCE
Foragers fan out across the Americas

4000–3000 BCE
Andean and Mesoamerican agrarian villages

ca. 2700 BCE
First American city at Caral-Supe in Peru

1200–900 BCE
Olmec city at San Lorenzo on Gulf of Mexico

1000–200 BCE
Chavín de Huántar city site in Andes

ca. 1000 BCE
Inuit migrations in North America

ca. 1000–100 BCE
Adena villages in North America

900–600 BCE
Olmec city at La Venta

Oceania

40,000 BCE
First migrations from Taiwan

3000–200 BCE
Lapita cultural complex in western Pacific

ca. 500–200 BCE
Splitting off of first Polynesian communities

ca. 600 CE
Polynesian settlement of Hawaii

Cuba along the North American coast, where, in modern times, they have caused immense destruction.

In the Pacific, the Humboldt and Japan currents work in a similar fashion. Warm waters of the western Pacific and along the Japanese Pacific coast move northward toward the Aleutian Islands and then down the west coast of the Americas. This has a moderating effect on climate, particularly from the coast of southern Alaska to northern California. From northern California to Chile, the currents are generally cooler than the surrounding ocean and provide important fish and marine mammal habitats. For millennia, these supplied the peoples of the west coast with sustenance and allowed settled life with a minimum of agriculture.

El Niño: A periodic reversal of the normal flow of currents in the Pacific, greatly altering weather patterns.

The Pacific region is also home to the **El Niño** phenomenon, which plays an immense role in global climatology. In cycles that vary from 3 to 8 years, large areas of abnormally warm water appear off the coasts of Peru and Chile. The results can alter the jet stream patterns and cause abnormal rainfall and storm levels over large areas of the globe, particularly in the Americas. The reverse phenomenon, La Niña, occurs when the oceans in the region have large areas of abnormally cold water.

Human Migrations

One of the most contested debates in modern archaeology is who the first people to appear in the Americas were, and where they came from. As we saw in Chapter 1 and above, however, the genetic record now suggests that the first Americans came in one migration from Beringia; all are now classified as *Native Americans* (also often called *Amerindians*).

Clovis points image analysis

Early Foragers   Scientists have attempted to track and date the migrations of early Americans through their hunting technology. The earliest arrivals hunted with *stabbing spears* meant to be thrust into an animal's body or thrown from a very short distance. During the period from 11,000 to 8000 BCE, such spears were equipped with a stone point that was fluted on both sides. These fluted sides allowed the spearhead to be inserted into a groove cut into one end of the spear and fastened there with a leather strip. As in Eurasia and Africa, the size and shape of spearheads and arrowheads provide valuable clues to regional variations in technology and to migration patterns. In North America, where the spearhead flutes were oval, they are known as "Clovis points," from the town in New Mexico near where scholars first identified them.

The pervasiveness of Clovis points in the north and a fishtail style of spear flutes in South America had suggested to scholars until very recently that their users were indeed the first migrants to the continents. It was also widely thought that their close dating and use in big-game hunting indicated that these people had settled both continents within a few years of arriving and had, in short order, killed off most of the prehistoric big game. The absence of Clovis points in Eurasia, and the presence of less sophisticated points and tools at newly examined earlier sites (such as Buttermilk Creek in Texas), however, now seem to suggest that the Clovis people had already been here for some time.

These early American settlers were foragers. They formed groups of extended families and lived in rock shelters, caves, and huts, moving whenever the food resources were exhausted. Families held initiation ceremonies for adults, arranged marriages, and exchanged goods such as obsidian, copper, mica, and seashells. Most of the time families stayed in their own territory and collected wild foods.

The fluted spear points were designed for hunting big game, such as mammoths, moose, and bison. The warming climate, however, favored the expansion of forests and was detrimental to big mammals. As big game became scarce, hunters shifted to smaller spear points and smaller game. By about 8000 BCE most big mammal species were gone from the Americas.

Toward Settlements   As larger game became scarce, people in coastal areas began relying more on fish and shellfish, and those in inland regions increased their collection of seeds and nuts. Hunters developed the spear thrower, a device for hurling smaller spears from a greater distance at small animals. Obsidian, traded over long distances, became the preferred material for spear points. Following a pattern similar to humans in Eurasia and Africa, humans in the Americas learned to work stone to make axes, mortars, pestles, and grindstones. Bone was used for spears, fishhooks, awls, needles, combs, and spatulas. Humans continued to live in rock shelters and caves, but also constructed huts covered with skins.
More permanent wooden structures appeared along the seacoasts, the Great Lakes, and large rivers, where there were plentiful resources of fish, shellfish, and waterfowl. The first domesticated animal, the dog, appeared. As bands of hunters and gatherers acquired more goods, they became less inclined to move large distances. As in Eurasia and Africa, they increasingly tended to stay close to long-term food sources and centers of ceremonial life.

Early Ceremonial Life   Sedentary foragers began to bury their dead in cemeteries, which soon became territorial centers. Hunter–gatherers in the Americas buried their dead with gifts to help them in the life after death. Leaders of hunter–gatherer bands were often *shamans*, elders with spiritual powers. These shamans fell into trances, during which they experienced merging with powerful animals or other people, charming animals into submission, exorcising evils from humans, or healing afflictions. Leaders and elders formed councils for the administration of their settlements and hunting grounds.

Shaman-led ceremonies often took place in caves or under overhangs, where people painted animals and humans on the rock walls. Probably the oldest paintings are those of Pedra Furada [PAY-drah Foo-RAH-dah] in northeastern Brazil, dating to about 8000 BCE. One of the most distinctive ceremonial paintings is the "white shaman" at Lower Pecos in Texas, dating to 2000 BCE. He is depicted in a trance; his feet are feline, his arms are feathered, and he is surrounded by animals and humans, both dead (upside down) and alive (upright).

The White Shaman, Lower Pecos, Texas, ca. 2000 BCE. The practice of *shamanism*—the belief in the ability of certain individuals to communicate with spirits or inhabit the spirits of people or animals—appears to be a common feature of many widely diverse peoples, including peoples in Siberia and other areas in northern Eurasia. Many scholars believe that migrants from Asia carried these religious forms with them to the Americas.

Agriculture, Villages, and Urban Life

One major change associated with the pattern of transition from foraging to agriculture is the ability to maintain large populations. Another change is the creation of the potential for conflict and destruction on an unprecedented scale. In the Americas, this pattern of world history appears to have begun somewhat later than in many areas of Eurasia and Africa.

The Neolithic Revolution in the New World

The first steps toward agriculture took place in central and southern Mexico in Mesoamerica and in Ecuador and Peru in the Andes. Temperatures in these regions turned warmer after about 4000 BCE. Foragers shortened their annual migrations and extended existing patches of wild bean and **teosinte,** [tay-oh-SIN-tay] (a wild grass precursor of maize [corn]). Careful harvesting and replanting led to early domesticated varieties of these plants. Beans were domesticated first in Peru, and maize followed later in southern Mexico. By about 3000 BCE, foragers in these regions had completed their transformation into farmers (see "Patterns Up Close").

Teosinte: a wild grass native to Mesoamerica, believed to be ancestral to maize (corn).

Early Domestication of Plants and Animals   Humans in Mesoamerica and the Andes exchanged beans, corn, and other domesticated staples. In Mesoamerica these included squash, manioc, avocado, and chili pepper; in the Andes, quinoa, amaranth, potatoes, tomatoes, and cotton. In time, these plants spread via trade throughout both regions.

The domestication of animals in the Americas was more modest. As most large mammals had died out after the last Ice Age, there were few animals left of the right size for use as draft, pack, or riding animals (see Figure 5.1). The Americas had no horses or cattle until they were brought by the Spanish in the sixteenth century CE. The development of the wheel, so intimately connected with draft animals, never took place in the Americas, though some of the world's best roads were built through the Andes. The llama was the only animal in pre-Columbian America to provide even modest transportation services as a pack animal. The wool of the alpaca became an important textile fiber in the Andes. In the relative absence of domesticated animals raised for meat, hunting and fishing remained important methods of obtaining food (see Figure 5.1).

Midden: A refuse pile. Archaeologists treasure such piles because a great deal can be learned about the material culture of a society by what people threw out over long periods of time.

Early Settlements   Early agricultural settlements ranged in size from a few extended families to as many as 1,000 inhabitants. As in Neolithic China, the typical dwelling was a round wooden house with a sunken floor, stone foundation, and thatched roof. Some early American agrarian peoples mummified their dead, while others buried their dead in **midden** piles on the outskirts of their villages or in the sand dunes along the beaches. Funerary gifts were modest. In contrast to more transient hunter–gatherer settlements, agrarian villages became settled communities of the living and the dead.

Between 3000 and 2000 BCE, villagers in the lowlands along the Andes coast of Peru built rafts of balsa wood, which enabled them to fish farther from shore. They

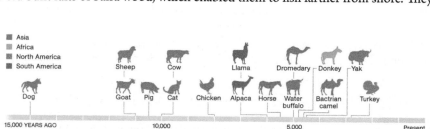

Figure 5.1 Comparative Timeline for Domestication of Animals.

also pioneered the use of irrigation in the dozens of river deltas along the coast. With crop yields boosted by irrigation, the population of the villages increased, and the first signs of social stratification appeared. Scholars have speculated that upstream families had more water and thus accumulated greater food reserves than downstream families. Under the leadership of upstream elders, inhabitants of several villages pooled their labor and built monumental plazas, platforms, and terraces.

As had other societies making the agrarian transition, Mesoamerican and Andean societies also began producing pottery. The earliest known pottery dates to about 3300–3200 BCE on the northern Andean coast; by 1800 BCE pottery making had spread throughout central and southern Mexico. Cotton textiles dating to about 3000 BCE have been found along the coasts of Ecuador and Peru. Condors, double-headed snakes, felines, and human figures were typical motifs on the textiles.

The Origins of Urban Life

Caral-Supe is one of at least 18 sites of a culture that flourished in the valleys descending from the Andes to the coast. It features monumental stone architecture, including pyramid-shaped temples, plazas, dwellings of different sizes, and a large amphitheater. In 2001, carbon dating revealed the artifacts at the site to be from 2627 BCE, making this by far the oldest city in the Americas and contemporary with the early Mesopotamian cities and the Great Pyramid of Egypt.

Caral-Supe   Scholars now theorize that this city, like the similarly mysterious sites along the Indus, was part of a civilization supported by agriculture and fishing, with trading networks and a class system. They have linked the Caral-Supe culture to that of Áspero nearby, of the same age. The varied climate, ranging from the coast through lowland plains and river valleys up to mountain highlands, produced pumpkins, squash, sweet potatoes, corn, chilies, beans, and cotton, while the rivers and sea yielded a variety of edible aquatic life. The agriculture of the valley was supported by a sophisticated irrigation system (see Map 5.2).

Farmers were the largest social class, with merchants, administrators, and priests also in evidence, although class hierarchy remains unclear. Varying sizes of houses suggest disparities of wealth, and the proximity of some of the houses to pyramids seems to indicate a religious or bureaucratic connection. The uses to which the amphitheater was put can only be guessed.

Perhaps the most intriguing artifact of all is an intact quipu, a device of knotted ropes tied together in patterns that form a system of communication. Since the quipu was also used by the Incas over 4,000 years later, it represents not only a direct connection between these two societies but one of the world's first, and oldest, systems of record-keeping in continuous use.

Other Andean Cultures   Of smaller scale and a somewhat later period are the structures at El Paraíso, Peru, which date from about 2000 BCE. Villagers built large rectangles of locally quarried rock and mud mortar. They filled the interior of the rectangle with rock rubble encased in large mesh bags, which may have been used to measure the amount of labor each villager contributed. Multichambered and multistoried buildings made of stone occupied some of the platforms. Steep staircases led from the lower plazas up to these buildings, which were plastered and painted. Wooden beams supported the roofs.

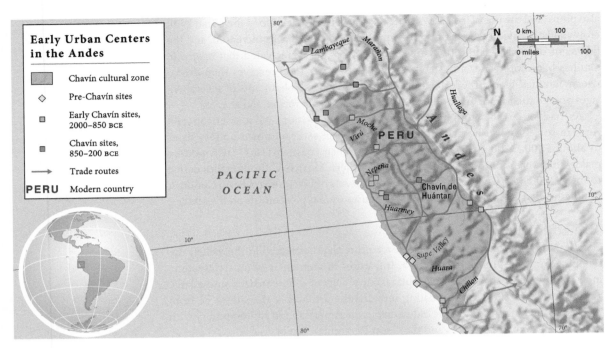

MAP 5.2 **Early Urban Centers in the Andes.**

Charcoal-filled pits in the building chambers indicate that some form of sacrifice took place there. The chambers were small, allowing access to no more than a few prominent villagers or shamans. The rest of the villagers assembled on upper and lower platforms, according to their social status, to participate in religious functions and share communal feasts. Early sculptures dating to 1519 BCE suggest that villagers might also have assembled for military displays.

Farmers in the Andean highlands also built ceremonial centers in their villages. As in the lowlands, these centers contained firepits for sacrificial offerings. Highlanders, in addition to farming, engaged in trade, exchanging obsidian and cotton for lowland pottery. Sometime around 1500 BCE, highlanders developed skills in metallurgy, laying the foundation for the development of exquisitely crafted metalwork.

Chavín de Huántar   Work on the small highland city of Chavín de Huántar [Cha-VIN de Oo-WAN-tar] (ca. 1000–200 BCE) has yielded important insights into Andean cultural patterns. Situated in a valley high in the Andes Mountains on both banks of a tributary to the Marañón River, Chavín carried on long-distance trade, built and graded roads protected with retaining walls, and cleared mountain paths. Residents of Chavín imported obsidian and metals and exported textiles, pottery, and gold and silver artifacts.

Early Chavín was a small place of some 300 inhabitants, most of whom—including priest-rulers and craftspeople—were detached from agriculture. Another 700 full-time farmers and herders lived in outlying hamlets. Farmers grew potatoes, quinoa, and some corn on the slopes and valley floor, supplementing the rainfall with irrigation. Corn was used for bread and also for brewing a type of beer called *chicha*. On the higher grasslands, herders bred llamas and alpacas for dried meat and wool. Llamas also served as pack animals.

Chavín's ceremonial center consisted of U-shaped ramparts built on a plaza and lined with cut and polished stone. The walls enclosed partially interconnected underground complexes. Within the U was a round, sunken court accessible via staircase. A cross-shaped, centrally located chamber contained a stone sculpture of what is assumed to have been the center's main deity: a fanged, snarling feline creature, standing upright like a human, with one clawed paw extended upward and the other hanging down. The sculpture might have had a shamanic significance, symbolizing the priest's ability to assume the powers of a wild animal.

Other underground chambers were used for sacrificial offerings, possibly human as well as animal. Canals guided water through the underground chambers. Priest-rulers and the assembled villagers used the temple complex to offer sacrifices, observe open-air rituals, celebrate feasts, dance, and perform music.

By around 500 BCE, the population had grown to about 3,000 inhabitants. Artisans living in the town began to specialize in particular crafts. Whether these craftspeople had given up agricultural labor completely is not known. Homes for the wealthy were built of stone, while those of the less-well-off were made of adobe. The rich dined on the meat of young llamas; poorer residents subsisted on the meat of decommissioned pack animals. Around the town, there must have been a number of villages with farmers producing enough food to feed the urban dwellers.

The increased population meant larger assemblies, which in turn required bigger platforms and a larger temple for more sacrifices. By 400 BCE, Chavín had become the culturally dominant center of the region. Travelers, traders, and pilgrims visited the temple, offering seashells, coca leaves, and textiles to the priests in return for receiving temple blessings. Residents of Chavín provided services for the visitors, such as lodging and meals. Craftspeople produced clothing, wall hangings, banners, and pottery in what were identifiable Chavín patterns, motifs, and styles.

Inhabitants of Chavín pioneered new techniques in the making of textiles and in metallurgy. Goldsmiths devised new methods of soldering and alloying gold and silver to make large ornamental objects. Small objects, such as golden headbands, ear spools, beads, and pins, signified prestige and wealth. Gold artifacts found in the graves of the wealthy attest to the high value residents of Chavín appear to have placed on gold.

Chavín came to a gradual end, perhaps declining as other centers began producing equivalent goods and competing in trade. In any event, sometime after 500 BCE, archaeologists note a decisive trend toward militarization, with the emergence of fortified villages and forts. Chavín may have succumbed to military attack. Sometime around 200 BCE, it appears that squatters invaded the largely deserted city, which subsequently fell into ruin.

Chavín de Huántar, New Temple. Chavín is one of the best-studied sites and over the years has yielded considerable information about town and small-city life in the ancient Americas.

The Origin of Corn

The *teosinte* grass does not seem to be a likely productive food crop, or even edible. Yet when some bold people first began to cultivate it, they unknowingly launched one of the most momentous revolutions in world history: a completely independent chapter in the transition from foraging to agriculture and, ultimately, to agrarian-based urban civilization. The ultimate result of their work—maize, or corn—ultimately became the world's most versatile and widely grown food crop (see Map 5.3). Indeed, ancient Mayans believed that humans themselves were made from corn.

Various Types of Corn.

The origin of corn is believed to be in what is now southern Mexico, which may have been inhabited by humans for as few as 7,000 or 8,000 years. Perhaps 6,000–7,000 years ago, they began the process of cultivating this unpromising grass into the grain that would eventually sustain vast numbers of people. Yet plant geneticists are not in agreement as to how this transition took place. Recently, however, a number of enticing clues about the process have emerged.

In a 2016 study by researchers from the Natural History Museum of Denmark, a 5310-year-old maize cob from the Teotihuacán Valley was subjected to DNA testing. The analysis established that this was maize in an intermediate stage of domestication. That is, a number of key genes had already been altered by the process of humans selecting the seeds of promising plants. Among the most significant of these are the elimination of a hard seed coat—for softer, more edible kernels—and changes in the plants' flowering time. Changes still to come included raising the sugar content in the kernels, multiplying their number, and controlling the plants' seed dispersal time to make harvesting easier and more uniform. Thus, the researchers theorize that this intermediate maize was not yet a staple, but rather a supplement in the diets of small, mobile, seasonally foraging clans.

The First Mesoamerican Settlements

In Mesoamerica, the first permanent villages appear to date from around 1800 BCE. The first ceremonial centers appeared along the Pacific coast of southern Mexico and Guatemala around 1500 BCE. As in the Andes, the ceremonial centers consisted of plazas, platforms, and terraces. Metallurgy, however, did not develop here for another millennium; instead of metals, craftspeople used jade for ornaments. By around 1200 BCE, agrarian society throughout the Andes and Mesoamerica was characterized by ceremonial centers centrally located among several villages, monumental structures of plazas and platforms, and the production of sacred ornaments.

The Olmec   The first important Mesoamerican center was that of the Olmecs at San Lorenzo (1200–900 BCE), located on the Gulf of Mexico in forested coastal lowlands. Farmers in these lowlands had to cut down and burn the dense tropical

Regarding the other changes leading to staple maize, promising results were presented by plant geneticist Mary Eubanks in 2004, who attempted to experimentally trace the origins of corn. Her experiments showed convincingly that *teosinte* was, in fact, an ancestor plant of modern corn but that it had at some point been bred with *gamagrass*, which contains key genes for multiplying and enlarging the kernels on each ear. Moreover, her work supported other recent research that suggested that the plant had developed very rapidly into a usable staple, though it would seem that it spent a considerable time in its intermediate stage as a supplemental crop.

We have to assume that this momentous feat was accomplished by plan and experimentation, given its complexity. The result was one that permanently altered the agricultural patterns of world history, particularly over the last 300 years. Corn's versatility allows it to be cultivated on every habitable continent, often on land too marginal to support any other staple crop. It is widely used as human and animal food and helped to sustain population expansions in North America, Asia, and Europe. It spawned huge industries in such modern foodstuffs as corn syrup and oil and older ones like whiskey and beer. Most recently, and controversially, it has been touted as a biofuel. In short, this American innovation's uses are still unfolding.

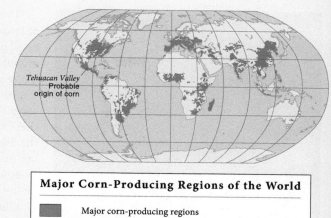

Major Corn-Producing Regions of the World

▨ Major corn-producing regions

MAP 5.3 **Major Corn-Producing Regions of the World.**

Questions

- Why is the innovation of corn a "momentous revolution in world history"?

- How does the fact that this example of bioengineering occurred 6,000–7,000 years ago put today's debate on genetically modified foods into a new perspective?

rain forest before they could plant corn. Once the riverbanks had been cleared, the silt deposited by floods during the rainy season and the rich soil created favorable agricultural conditions. As in Mesopotamia, Egypt, India, and China, the rivers here proved productive. The high yield from corn harvests allowed for the rise of wealthy ruling families, who assumed a dominant position over small farmers.

The ceremonial center of San Lorenzo was located on a plateau, on which archaeologists have unearthed some 60 terraced platforms, 20 ponds, countless basalt-lined drainage troughs, and the foundations of dwellings for 1,000 inhabitants. The dense concentration of dwellings suggests that San Lorenzo was an urban center inhabited by priests, administrators, and craftspeople. Based on estimates of crop yields in the area and the number of dwellings at the site, scholars believe that some 10,000 small farmers lived around the center, producing the surplus food needed by the urban center.

Olmec Jade Mask. Like the Chinese, Mesoamerican peoples appear to have worked jade from very ancient times.

The priest-rulers of San Lorenzo engaged thousands of farmers as laborers to construct the plateau and its terraced platforms. Laborers quarried blocks of basalt from a mountain range 70 miles to the northwest of San Lorenzo. Large groups of workers shouldered beams from which the basalt blocks, weighing 18 tons on average, hung in slings. They carried these blocks to the coast and shipped them to San Lorenzo on rafts. There, sculptors fashioned the blocks into fierce-looking, helmeted heads, kneeling or sitting figures, and animal statues. It is unknown whether these figures represented priest-rulers, gods, or divine beings.

Olmec priest-rulers also commissioned sculptors to craft figurines and masks from jade and serpentine. Since jade and serpentine could be obtained only from areas some 200 miles away, San Lorenzo appears to have been not an isolated urban center but a place with far-reaching trade connections.

La Venta   Around 900 BCE, a mysterious event took place that destroyed San Lorenzo. Whatever occurred, the event left San Lorenzo's large stone sculptures mutilated and buried in carefully prepared graves, along with the sculptors' tools used in creating the images.

Following the fall of San Lorenzo, La Venta, 50 miles to the northeast, became the leading Olmec center. The first settlers at La Venta cleared the rain forest from a ridge on a swampy river island in the lowlands and then graded the ridge to create a plateau. On the plateau they erected terraced platforms and a 100-foot-high earthen mound to establish an urban center. Burial sites at La Venta contained axes and figurines made of serpentine and jade as well as mirrors ground from iron-bearing ores. Rulers' regalia included mirrors, but what significance these might have had is unknown.

About 600 BCE La Venta ended under circumstances as mysterious as those that destroyed San Lorenzo. The next Olmec center was at Tres Zapotes, a more modest complex 70 miles to the northwest. Tres Zapotes endured from about 500 to 1 BCE, when it was eclipsed by new ceremonial centers in the highlands west of the Olmec lowlands.

Through their long-distance trade, the Olmecs left a cultural imprint throughout Mesoamerica. Olmec traders obtained obsidian in Guatemala and jade from mines south of the Mexican Basin and in Guatemala and Costa Rica. In exchange for these raw materials, the Olmecs exported cacao beans, pottery, textiles, and jewelry. Along their trade routes, the Olmecs maintained settler outposts to supply the traders.

Olmec Writing   In 2006 scientists at Cascajal (kahs-ka-HAHL) in Veracruz, Mexico, found a large stone with what is currently believed to be Olmec writing on it. Dating to somewhere between 1100 and 900 BCE, it appears to be the oldest writing in the Americas. Moreover, it is unlike any of the later scripts of the Mayas or Aztecs and thus seems to have died out as a system with the decline of the Olmecs.

Like Egyptian hieroglyphics and Chinese Shang-era scripts, the Olmec characters contain stylized representations of objects like fish, insects, and plants, but there are also some that seem to have a phonetic component. Unfortunately, the number of symbols contained on the Cascajal stone and a stone roller-stamp dating from a few centuries later is simply too small to be deciphered. It is hoped that with the accumulation of other samples in the future, the fragments of an Olmec literature may ultimately come to light. In the meantime, like the Linear A script of the Minoans and the seal figures of the Harappans, the Olmec figures present scholars with an important challenge in decoding the past.

Foraging and Farming Societies Outside the Andes and Mesoamerica

After 2000 BCE, many foragers in North and South America had adopted agriculture as a full or partial mode of subsistence. While most societies in the Andes and Mesoamerica had become fully agrarian by around 2000 BCE, foraging groups continued to persist—in some places down to the present. Using stone tools, they hunted in the extreme north, slowly cleared some of the forests of east and midwest North America, irrigated and farmed arid areas of the southwest, and foraged and farmed in the Amazon basin of South America.

The Inuit   The Inuit [INN-ooh-it] from Siberia arrived in the far northern tundra of North America around 2000 BCE. For a long period the Inuit remained traditional hunter–gatherers. Much later, during the first millennium CE, they began hunting whales. As many as 20 sailors with paddles manned a boat built of walrus ribs and skin. In the summer, boats sailed the coastal seas for weeks at a time. A whale carcass could feed a hamlet for an entire winter.

The Inuit lived in pit houses framed by whale ribs, covered with walrus skin, and piled over with sod. The entrances were long, dipped tunnels that trapped the cold air below the floor of the house. On winter hunts, people built snow houses, or *igloos*, from ice blocks. During the summer, the Inuit moved from the pit houses to tents. Women used caribou sinew and seal and caribou pelts to make warm and watertight clothing. For transportation on snow and ice, the Inuit used dog teams to pull sleds. They traded mammal teeth and carved bone artifacts for timber and earthenware from the south. By 1000 CE the Inuit had expanded from the North American Arctic eastward to Greenland.

Adena and Hopewell   Agricultural villages appeared in the cleared forest areas of North America by the first millennium BCE. The villagers of the Adena (1000–100 BCE) and Hopewell cultures (200 BCE–500 CE) pooled their labor to build ridges and mounds used in ceremonies and rituals. The phenomenon of mound building seems to have been widespread among peoples living in the east and midwest of North America. A small mound covering a child's grave in Labrador is estimated to be some 7,500 years old. Others, much larger and more recent (about 4,500 years old), have been found in the lower Mississippi valley. At Hopewell, large square and circular enclosures contained multiple mounds encompassing dozens of acres of land. Research suggests that some of the Hopewell settlements were connected by roads up to 60 miles long, perhaps serving communal purposes such as official visits and gift exchanges (see Map 5.4).

Amazonian Peoples   In the floodplains of the Amazonian rain forest in South America, agricultural villages also date to the first millennium BCE. The best-explored culture is that of Marajó (Mah-rah-HO), on a large island in the mouth

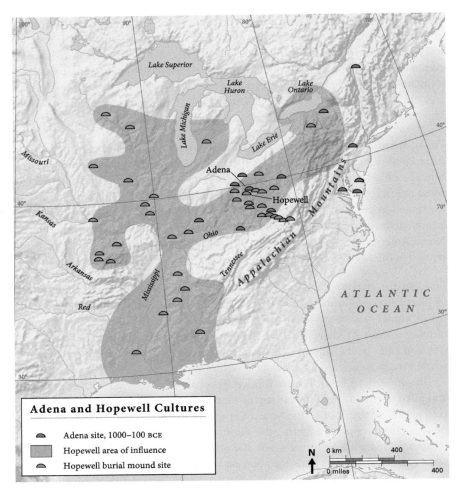

MAP 5.4 **Adena and Hopewell Cultures.**

of the Amazon. At its height in ca. 500 BCE, the Marajó built large funeral mounds. The cultures of the floodplains in the upper Amazon drainage are still largely unexplored. For example, at an unknown date, the Baures culture in today's Bolivia established a complex of canals, raised fields, moat-enclosed villages, and causeways connecting the villages. The complexity of this culture left a strong impression on the Spanish missionaries who visited the area in the sixteenth century CE.

The Islands of the Caribbean   The earliest hunter–gatherer settlements in the rain forests of the Caribbean islands date to the fourth millennium BCE, but from where on the mainland these first settlers came is unknown. The first agricultural settlements appeared between 500 BCE and 500 CE, when migrants from the Orinoco River region in the northeast of South America colonized the eastern Caribbean as far west as today's Dominican Republic and Haiti. These people built villages and terraces, and their ceramics suggest a shamanic religion. Beginning in eastern Hispaniola around 500 CE, villagers supported the emergence of the Taíno [Ta-EE-no] chieftain society that by ca. 1500 comprised nearly the entire Caribbean. Influenced by Mayan culture (see Chapter 6), some Taíno chiefs built ball courts and causeways. In their villages, the chiefs employed specialized craftspeople. Sailors using canoes traveled extensively to the mainland and among the islands in search of salt, jade, and metals. These travels connected the Taíno chiefdom society with Mesoamerican societies on the mainland.

The Origins of Pacific Island Migrations

The peopling of the islands of Oceania may be seen as an extreme case of one of the great patterns of world history—interactions between cultures separated by great expanses of ocean. In prehistoric times, Asians traveled not only to the Americas but also to the islands of the Pacific and Indian Oceans (see Map 5.5).

The populating of Oceania must rank as one of humankind's greatest feats. Vast amounts of open ocean had to be crossed between many of the island groups in the Pacific in order to settle them. Nevertheless, early seafaring people settled island after island, traveling until they had discovered nearly every island of Oceania.

map analysis

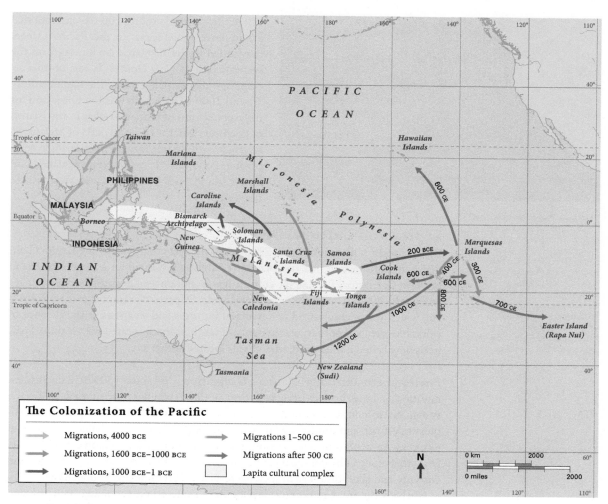

MAP 5.5 **The Colonization of the Pacific.**

Bwaimas, Papua New Guinea.
Some of the earliest known human attempts at agriculture took place in the highlands of Papua New Guinea perhaps 9,000–7,000 years ago. The introduction of yams several millennia later created an enduring staple crop, and their portability allowed their spread as they sustained seafarers throughout the Pacific. Bwaimas are storehouses for yams.

Tupaia, the great
Polynesian navigator

As we saw in Chapter 4, their homeland appears to have been Taiwan and the Indonesian-Philippine archipelagos. Using linguistic analysis, scholars theorize that the people of Oceania are at least partially related to Taiwan's aboriginal population. About 6,000 years ago, the first seafaring people left Taiwan and, together with subsequent waves of emigrants, spread out in westerly and easterly directions. They settled in the Philippines, Indonesia, and the Malay Peninsula, bestowing their languages and ethnic identities on the aboriginal peoples of these lands.

Descendants of these settlers later spread farther into the Indian and Pacific Oceans. In the Indian Ocean, they sailed as far west as Madagascar, an island off the east coast of Africa, where they arrived around 200 CE and founded a number of chiefdoms. In the Pacific Ocean, they sailed to the Bismarck Archipelago, off the eastern coast of New Guinea. It was on this archipelago that settlers created the Lapita culture around 1600 BCE, which was the homeland for the colonization of Oceania—that is, the islands of Polynesia, Micronesia, and parts of Melanesia. On the map, Oceania forms a huge triangle comprising Polynesia, Hawaii, New Zealand, and Easter Island, with Micronesia and Melanesia to the west.

Lapita and Cultural Origins

By the fourth millennium BCE, a sophisticated system known as the Lapita (Lah-PEE-tah) cultural complex had become established. Named for a site on the island of New Caledonia, the Lapita culture was a system of kinship-based exchanges among the inhabitants of thousands of islands. Of particular importance was obsidian, which was highly prized as a material for tools and weapons in the absence of workable metals. Another item in demand was pottery decorated with stamped patterns now called Lapita ware, after shards located at that site.

Environment and Long-Distance Navigation   By about 1600 BCE decisive innovations in long-distance navigation over hundreds of miles of open sea as well as the systematic colonization of otherwise uninhabitable islands had emerged. Large, sophisticated sail- and paddle-driven oceangoing canoes provided reliable craft for such journeys. An orally transmitted storehouse of navigational information enabled sailors to set their courses by the sun and stars, retain mental maps of islands, read winds and currents, and take advantage of seasonal reverses in prevailing wind directions.

Perhaps the most important development centered on supplying such voyages. The cultivation of storable root crops, especially yams and taro, proved invaluable in sustaining long voyages. Among other staples circulated among the colonized islands were breadfruit, coconuts, and bananas, as well as such domesticated animals as pigs, chickens, and dogs. From 1600 to 100 BCE, Lapita sailors moved eastward and settled the islands of Vanuatu, Tonga, Fiji, and Samoa. Archaeologists believe that Fiji may be the source of the culture that sparked the next outward migration: that of the Polynesians.

Creating Polynesia

As populations grew, the primary mode of governmental and economic organization, the kinship-based chiefdom, became increasingly elaborated. On Tonga, the Society Islands, the Marquesas, and later the Hawaiian Islands, the power of local chiefs extended to nearby island systems. The inclination of human societies toward centralization, as well as tension with smaller regional societies that we discussed in Chapter 4, is apparent.

Conflict, Interaction, and Expansion   The effect of centralization and intensified agriculture in the more productive islands on their inhabitants is uncertain. Up to a point, it may have made

Early Pacific Seafaring Rafts. During the first millennium CE, Polynesian navigators benefited from advances in ship design as they colonized far-flung island chains. The Norwegian adventurer Thor Heyerdahl demonstrated the seaworthiness of similar designs when he constructed a replica of the type of raft utilized by aboriginal seafaring Peruvians. The raft measured approximately 45 feet by 18 feet and consisted of several large balsa tree trunks arranged in a crisscross design. The craft was outfitted with a 29-foot mast and a huge sail, along with a sizable cabin to provide shelter for the six-man crew. For sustenance, large quantities of drinking water and food supplies—mostly coconuts, sweet potatoes, and other Peruvian staples—were carried on board.

these societies more efficient as food producers. But the difficulties we have seen in other societies of sustaining large populations on limited amounts of land were undoubtedly intensified in an island society. Environmental problems related to overpopulation may have developed in the Cook Islands and the Marquesas around 500 BCE and again in 200 BCE. Political disputes arising from the struggles between centralizing and decentralizing factions may have played a role as well. In any case, there seems to have been a break around 500 CE that resulted in the longest period of migration yet: to Hawaii around 600, Easter Island (Rapa Nui) about 700, and New Zealand by 1200.

Later Interactions   By the time of the first European contact in the early sixteenth century, nearly every habitable island had been settled, and some had populations of many hundreds of thousands. As we shall see in subsequent chapters, however, this vast achievement of exploration and colonization would soon be threatened by disease and a new breed of conquerors and colonists. The next three and a half centuries of European exploration of the Pacific would carry with them disastrously unforeseen consequences.

Putting It All Together

Though separated from each other by thousands of miles of ocean, the Americas and Oceania share common patterns with each other as well as with the cultures

interactive concept map

of Eurasia and Africa. The first pattern is that even in such widely separated areas, human foraging communities at roughly the same time *independently began a process toward the development of agriculture and animal domestication.* While domestication of the first plants and animals and gathering into more settled village life began shortly after the last retreat of the glaciers in Eurasia, it came somewhat later in the Americas, perhaps because human groups were still few in number and could be sustained by large-game hunting. The many different types of plants available as food were relatively high in protein, an important feature as large game became increasingly scarce. It is also the case that the plant that ultimately became a chief staple of the American societies, corn, required extensive experimentation before becoming domesticated. Thus, it is only around 4000 BCE that we see the beginning of its extensive cultivation.

The second pattern is *growth and sophistication of social structures and the development of the city and of monumental architecture for religious and political purposes.* In some cases, the types of structures—pyramids, terraces, and obelisks, for example—seem to follow an almost "universal" pattern, so much so that scholars still struggle to find evidence of contact among widely separated cultures where none appears to have existed.

Recent finds at the Caral-Supe sites show how rapidly the development of large cities took place once the threshold of plant and animal domestication was crossed. Like those of the Indus valley, the accomplishments of the society that created Caral survived in the local practices of Andean peoples long after the cities themselves were abandoned. The settlements of the Olmecs, though coming somewhat later, were equally imposing in their architecture, the efficacy of their farming and irrigation, the sophistication of their social structures, and their development of writing. Yet it is also the case that people will not create all the aspects of "civilization" in the same ways and by the same means. One striking example of this is the use of the wheel. Despite the widespread use of ball courts employing spheres of rubber put through circular hoops as a central political and religious ceremony among Mesoamerican peoples and the enormous cyclical mathematical and timekeeping achievements of later peoples like the Mayas, the need for heavy-wheeled vehicles never arose, and thus the wheel never developed in the Americas as it did in Eurasia and Africa.

In the case of Oceania, the peopling of the islands of the Pacific was inseparable from trade and cultural connections. Colonizing uninhabited islands could take place only when the plants and animals required could be brought along and provision could be made to trade for unavailable items. Thus, in terms of square mileage, the Lapita system was one of the world's largest trading spheres, including thousands of islands. Yet, for a variety of reasons—the necessities traded, the remoteness of the islands from other trade centers, the lack of connections to mainland Asia and the Americas, the unique seafaring skills of the island navigators—the peoples of Oceania remained separated from other such systems. Even here, as in the Americas, Eurasia, and Africa, we see yet another pattern emerging within the political behavior of human societies: *centralization and resistance to it.* As with other fundamental patterns of world history, we will see this one emerge in a variety of guises as our story proceeds.

Review and Relate

Thinking Through Patterns

Examine the ways historians approach the big questions of this chapter.

This question is often debated. For one thing, we can ask instead why we should consider the Americas as "isolated," rather than Eurasia and Africa. But it is also true that the societies were not as large or diverse as their Eurasian counterparts. Historically, too, scholars still often view the two sets of continents as "old" and "new," and from that perspective view the Americas as "isolated." How one interprets the question also revolves around how one sees the roles of invasion, infusion of innovation, and cultural competition. Some scholars have argued that the very shape of Eurasia allowed for the dissemination of innovation along areas similarly situated in latitude and therefore climate. The Americas, however, were more longitudinally oriented, making such diffusion more difficult. Some argue that the separateness of the Americas allowed them to cultivate distinctive cultural traits among their populations. Yet others argue that constant mixing of peoples and ideas accelerates innovation and, hence, "progress." One distinct disadvantage of isolation is that peoples become susceptible to diseases suddenly inflicted on them. Thus, from the sixteenth to the early eighteenth centuries, virulent epidemics of Eurasian and African diseases like smallpox devastated the peoples of the Americas when introduced.

>> **What do historians see as the advantages and disadvantages of the separate evolution of the Americas?**

While the Pacific Islanders had abundant access to food, the islands themselves were generally too small to allow the accumulation of enough surplus food to free up the numbers of nonfarmers necessary to build and maintain a city. In addition, the islands themselves contained limited amounts of building materials and fresh water, while their isolation helped guard them against attack. Culturally, the islanders also had grown to *expect* that if their numbers outran the food supply, they could simply find another island to which the excess population could migrate.

>> **Why did no cities develop on the larger Pacific Islands?**

Historians look at this question in one of two ways: culturally or practically. Some cultural scholars see a lack of deep-seated affinities for circular motion in the belief systems of the American peoples as helping to prevent them from relating to the motion of the wheel in the way that Eurasian and African peoples did. Yet American societies were not unaware of the concept of circular motion. Scholars favoring a practical approach argue that the environment of the mountains close by seacoasts, rain forests, and dry, hilly regions was not conducive to bulk transport by wheeled vehicles and that the peoples there simply were never forced to look for more efficient means of transport.

>> **The wheel is often cited as the most basic human invention, yet large and sophisticated civilizations were able to flourish without this signal innovation. Why do you think it did not develop in the Americas?**

| Against the Grain

Consider this as a counterpoint to the main patterns examined in this chapter.

Thor Heyerdahl

- In what ways do Heyerdahl's theories represent a good example of thinking "against the grain"?

- How do the sorts of evidence Heyerdahl and others have used to question the isolationist theory of early Oceanic and American history provide a different perspective on the types of sources most commonly associated with historical research?

The early Americas and Oceania present an interesting exception to the principal theme of this book. Because they were separated by thousands of miles of ocean from Eurasian and African developments, the peoples of the early Americas and Oceania were denied the benefits of cultural innovations resulting from interactions and adaptations. One might assume, therefore, that these isolated cultures were entirely dependent on indigenous cultural and environmental factors in the development of their emerging civilization.

The isolationist theory has not gone entirely unchallenged. Over the last few decades a few unorthodox archaeologists and historians have presented arguments that oppose these traditional views. One such challenger was Thor Heyerdahl, an amateur Norwegian archaeologist. Heyerdahl set out to demonstrate that South American sailors could have established east-to-west contacts by traversing the Pacific solely by relying on trade winds and ocean currents. In 1947 Heyerdahl successfully sailed across the Pacific from Peru to Polynesia aboard a large balsa raft named the *Kon-Tiki* (after a mythical Peruvian god), similar to those used by ancient Incans. The 5,000-mile voyage took 101 days to complete. This startling achievement convinced Heyerdahl that the original settlers of Polynesia were ancient Peruvians. (See photo of Heyerdahl's journey on p. 115.)

Heyerdahl's theory has met with mixed reception. His assumption that some of the early Polynesians were of Peruvian descent has been generally discredited by the academic establishment. By relying on mitochondrial DNA analyses, archaeologists have argued that in fact the first settlers of Polynesia were indeed of Asian—not Peruvian—descent. And yet more sophisticated genomic HLA (human leukocyte antigen) typing as well as DNA analysis of a select group of Easter Islanders indicates the presence of genetic traits found among Amerindians, most likely Peruvians. In addition, recent archaeological investigation has produced linguistic and material evidence in support of the diffusion of agrarian advances carried from Peru westward across the Pacific. For example, the sweet potato, indigenous to Peru, was present in Polynesia centuries before European expeditions across the Pacific. Therefore, despite its controversial approach and results, Heyerdahl's courageous adventure and radical suppositions suggest at the very least the possibility of transoceanic cultural diffusion by prehistoric Peruvian seafarers.

Key Terms

Cordilleras 99	Midden 104	Radiocarbon Dating 97
El Niño 102	Quipu 98	Teosinte 104

audio flashcards

For additional resources, please go to
www.oup.com/us/vonsivers.
Please see the Further Resources section at the back of the book
for additional readings and suggested websites.

PART TWO

The Age of Empires and Visionaries

600 BCE–600 CE

By the middle of the first millennium BCE, two major transformations changed the course of world history: kingdom formation became a near-universal pattern; and the foundations of religious civilizations were laid in the Middle East, India, China, and adjacent regions.

Kingdoms and Empires

Sub-Saharan Africa and the Americas.   Around 600 BCE, agricultural productivity allowed some chiefdoms to expand into kingdoms. In sub-Saharan Africa, the kingdoms were Meroë and Aksum, and in Mesoamerica, the kingdoms were those of the Maya.

The Middle East and the Mediterranean.   After the Hittites and Neo-Assyrians, around 600 BCE the Persian Achaemenids continued the pattern of empire building. The Macedonian Greek Alexander the Great, his Hellenist successors, and the republican Romans in the western Mediterranean adopted the imperial pattern, expanding into the Middle East. The Roman Empire competed with the Persian empires of the Parthians and Sasanids for dominance. The characteristic pattern of the Middle East and Mediterranean was competitive imperialism.

India and China.   Competition among small states led to the elimination of the weakest and the consolidation of larger kingdoms in both India and China around

ca. 800 BCE
Earliest evidence of iron smelting in sub-Saharan Africa

551–479 BCE
Traditional dates for life of Confucius

550–331 BCE
Achaemenid Persia

ca. 427–347 BCE
Plato, founder of the first philosophical school, the Academy

600 BCE. In contrast to the Middle East and Mediterranean, the pattern of India and China was one of rising and falling single empires, followed by periods of decentralization before the rise of unifying new imperial dynasties.

Interactions in Eurasia and with Africa.

Merchants in Eurasia and sub-Saharan Africa began to interact during the period 600 BCE–600 CE. They pioneered the sea routes to southern India, China, and eastern Africa and the land routes of the Silk Road through central Asia and across the Sahara from northern to western Africa. The trade in luxury goods stimulated the rise of merchant classes.

Visionaries and the Adoption of State Religions

Visionaries.

Around 700–500 BCE, individuals arose in Eurasia to proclaim a transcendent God or "first principle" in the place of the polytheistic universe in which gods and humans mingled. Their messages were not bound to particular kingdoms or empires, but were addressed to anyone who would listen. For the first time in world history, individuals claimed to have discovered standards of truth and justice that were beyond kingdoms and empires and their polytheistic pantheons. Not all agreed, however, that this measure could be translated into concrete doctrines, laws, and regulations.

Empires and the Adoption of State Religions.

The followers of visionaries popularized monotheism and monism and formed priestly classes, churches, and/or schools. Interaction among groups of followers led to the adaptation of some monotheisms and monisms to each other. As one might expect, kings and emperors sought to capitalize on these unifying forces. By 600 CE, monotheism or monism had become dominant in the empires and kingdoms in Eurasia and parts of sub-Saharan Africa.

Previous chapters focused on the patterns of social and political formation. Now—after the adoption of state religions—kings, emperors, and religious officials laid the foundations for the formation of religious civilizations.

Thinking Like a World Historian

≫ What is the connection between food, population density, and patterns of social–political formation in world history? Why did these patterns develop later in sub-Saharan Africa and the Americas?

≫ What elements did the visionaries of ca. 700–500 BCE share in common, and what made their visions so decisive in the course of world history?

≫ What is the difference between kingdoms and empires, and how did empires change as a result of the adoption of state religions?

322–185 BCE
Most of India united for the first time under Mauryan Empire

196 BCE–284 CE
Early Roman Empire (including imperial republic)

700 BCE–900 CE
Maya kingdoms in southeastern Mexico and Central America

322–550 CE
Much of India reunited under Gupta Empire

 interactive timeline

221–206 BCE
First Chinese Empire under Qin

100–750 CE
Moche chiefdom in northern Peru

300–600 CE
Kingdom of Aksum in northeastern sub-Saharan Africa

476 CE
End of western Roman Empire

Chiefdoms and Early States in Africa and the Americas

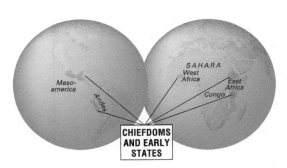

A humble stone carving in Oaxaca, in southern Mexico, carbon-dated to about 600 BCE, is the earliest documentation for the existence of a 260-day divinatory calendar in Mesoamerica, which later played a central part in Mayan time reckoning and divination. This calendar system is still in use by people in southern Mexico, making it among the world's longest-lived methods of reckoning time. Similarly, an astronomical observatory in Kenya, carbon-dated to 300 BCE, is the earliest example of the so-called Borana lunar calendar of 354 days. It is still in use today among the Kushite herders of East Africa. The two calendars are reminders of the diversity and relativity of all calendar systems.

During the period 600 BCE–600 CE, the Americas and sub-Saharan Africa shared patterns of agricultural development, spread of villages, emergence of chiefdoms, and early rise of kingdoms. These institutions evolved more slowly than in the more populated Eurasia. Since there was little contact between Eurasia on one hand and the Americas and much of

ABOVE: The ruins of Meroitic pyramids at Jebel Barkal in modern Sudan.

sub-Saharan Africa on the other, it is remarkable that the patterns of agriculture and life in villages, chiefdoms, and kingdoms were fairly consistent *within* world regions as much as *across* world regions. Nevertheless, as we saw in Chapter 5, the isolated world regions, through their own internal interactions, adapted to a transition from foraging to agriculture.

Through internal interactions, sub-Saharan Africans and Americans blazed indigenous trails in pattern formation, from villages to **chiefdoms** and **kingdoms**. The calendars of these two regions, while similar to Eurasian models, also illustrate the adaptation of the concept to local needs.

Agriculture and Early African Kingdoms

Sub-Saharan Africa transitioned from forager to agrarian–urban society less rapidly and less completely than Eurasia. However, north of the Sahara, Africans interacted with the Middle East and adapted to its agrarian patterns early on. They adopted village life, built cities, and created kingdoms (such as Kush and Nubia along the Nile) well before the period of 600 BCE–600 CE. After 600 CE, the kingdoms of Meroë [ME-ro-way] in the Nile valley and Aksum in the Ethiopian highlands flourished, while Africans farther south shifted from foraging to agriculture, villages, and chiefdoms. By 600 CE, urbanism had spread to West Africa and foraging had shrunk across the continent.

Saharan Villages, Towns, and Kingdoms

For many millennia, the Sahara was hospitable, furthering the pattern shift from foraging to agriculture. But around 5000–3000 BCE, the desert expanded, and savannas and steppes retreated southward. Agrarian life relocated to oases and the Nile River valley. In the northeast, the kingdom of Meroë established a capital of the same name in the middle Nile basin, supported by an agricultural surplus produced with the help of annual Nile floods and irrigation.

Saharan Chiefdoms and Kingdoms   The earliest evidence of Africans shifting from foraging to agriculture comes from around Khartoum, the capital of modern Sudan. Archaeological sites reveal a culture of raising cattle, cultivating sorghum, and shaping distinctive pottery. By the period between 4000 BCE and the first written records in Egypt in 3100 BCE, a substantial chiefdom had emerged in northern Sudan, then called "Nubia." This chiefdom was based on farming, livestock raising, and trading of gold as well as rain-forest ivory and timber from farther south. Archaeologists have noted that tombs in Nubia contained objects rivaling those of the Egyptians, including objects from southwest Asia and beyond. Nubian military prowess emerged in Egyptian records, with archers especially sought after as mercenaries.

After 2500 BCE, the growing kingdom in Nubia built a palace, large tombs, temples, and a wall around its capital city of Kerma, the first African city outside Egypt. During 1850–1400 BCE Kerma and Egypt were rivals for the control of Nile trade, until Egypt eventually destroyed Kerma and colonized Nubia for about half a

>> How does comparing and contrasting sub-Saharan Africa with the Americas during 600 BCE–600 CE help in understanding the agrarian–urban patterns of social and political development across the world?

>> Where did chiefdoms, cities, and kingdoms arise in sub-Saharan Africa and why? On which forms of agriculture, urbanization, and trade were they based?

>> Which areas in the Americas saw the development of a corn- and potato-based agriculture that did not depend on the plow, the wheel, and ironmaking?

Chiefdom: An agricultural village or town of up to 1,000 inhabitants, in which people know each other, requiring a person of authority (an elder or the head of a large family) to keep order as a respected chief.

Kingdom: A city-state or territorial state of at least several thousand inhabitants in which a ruler, claiming a divine mandate and supported by a military force, keeps order and provides for the defense against outside attacks.

AFRICA, SHOWING SITES IN MAURETANIA 2000 BCE–600 BCE

millennium. Nubia regained autonomy early in the first millennium BCE, in a state centered around the city of Napata. Later, the Napatan kings liberated themselves from Egyptian control and even assumed the throne of their northern neighbor as the twenty-fifth dynasty (ca. 780–686 BCE). But when Assyria, the first empire to unify all of the Middle East, conquered Egypt, the defeated king relocated himself farther upstream at Meroë.

The Villages of Tichitt-Oualata   Contemporaneously with the Nubian kingdoms, villages emerged in today's Mauretania. As in Nubia, the climate in the western Sahara had changed during 5000–3000 BCE. As the monsoon patterns moved eastward, foragers retreated to shallow lakes and oases. During 3000–2000 BCE, these foragers domesticated pearl millet, which required less water to grow.

Archaeological evidence points to the emergence of sizable villages at Dhar Tichitt [dar tee-SHEET] and Dhar Oualata [dar wah-LAH-tah] in Mauretania around 2000 BCE, which flourished until 600 BCE. There were corrals for cattle and granaries for millet, as well as evidence of craftspeople smelting copper. Tomb mounds, perhaps for the chiefs in the villages, held beads and copper jewelry. The social structure may have been based on wealth in livestock, but how society was regulated, its religion, and the form of chiefly authority are unclear. One theory holds that as these people eventually retreated farther south as the Sahara dried out, they may have been the founders of the kingdom of ancient Ghana (see Chapter 14).

Meroë on the Middle Nile   The kings of Meroë were successors of the twenty-fifth Nubia-descended dynasty of Egypt, who, under Assyrian pressure, withdrew to the steppes of the middle Nile. Here they built their capital, Meroë. At that time, the floodplain to the south of the capital still received sufficient monsoon rainfall to support agriculture. In addition, the kings built large water reservoirs to supply the farmers. Presumably, the kingdom financed itself with the agricultural surplus.

At its height, from the sixth through fourth centuries BCE, the city of Meroë encompassed 20,000 inhabitants. The kingdom was largely decentralized. The provinces downstream and upstream along the Nile were autonomous, ruled by their own town chiefs. Outside the agricultural area, cattle nomads grazed their herds.

The difference in power between the kings and the chiefs was defined by the royal control over trade. Miners in the desert north of the capital produced iron ore and farmers south of the capital grew cotton. Smiths and weavers in Meroë produced weapons, hoes, utensils, and cloth, both for local consumption and for trade beyond the kingdom. Hunters in the south acquired ivory from elephants and feathers from ostriches. Traders carried these down the Nile to Egypt or across the Red Sea to Yemen by boat, returning with olive oil and wine from Egypt and frankincense and myrrh from Yemen (see Map 6.1).

From the seventh century BCE, people in Meroë mined, smelted, and forged iron—perhaps the first to do so in sub-Saharan Africa. However, the origin of smelting and forging iron in sub-Saharan Africa is disputed. It is generally agreed that the craft of iron smelting evolved in Hittite Anatolia during several centuries after 1500 BCE (see Chapter 2). While the possible spread of ironworking from the Middle East to Africa has not been proven, the independent origin of ironworking in Africa has not been demonstrated conclusively either.

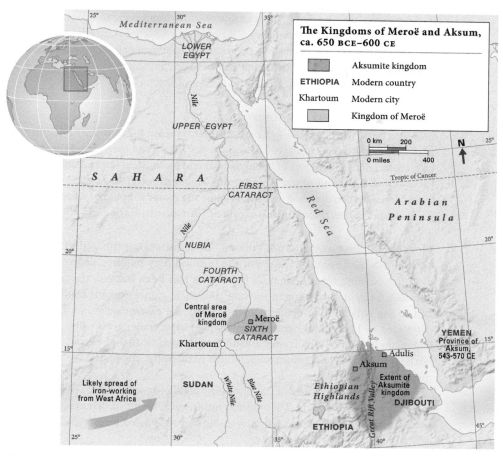

MAP **6.1** **The Kingdoms of Meroë and Aksum, ca. 650 BCE–600 CE.**

Meroë's Cultural Achievements   In Meroë, the kings adapted their Nubian–Egyptian heritage to the steppe and savanna south of the Sahara. Their monuments acquired a distinct style. Although the main temple was devoted mainly to the Egyptian pantheon, the priests also added native deities, such as the lion god Apedemek. The inherited Egyptian hieroglyphics seem to have "evolved" into an alphabetic script, although it is still undeciphered.

interactive timeline

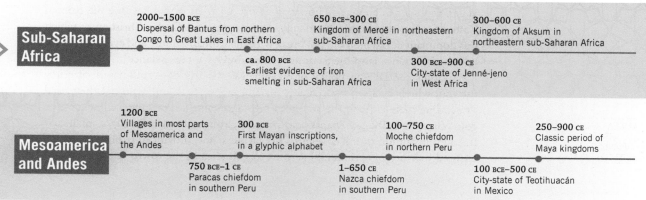

Sub-Saharan Africa

2000–1500 BCE
Dispersal of Bantus from northern Congo to Great Lakes in East Africa

ca. 800 BCE
Earliest evidence of iron smelting in sub-Saharan Africa

650 BCE–300 CE
Kingdom of Meroë in northeastern sub-Saharan Africa

300 BCE–900 CE
City-state of Jenné-jeno in West Africa

300–600 CE
Kingdom of Aksum in northeastern sub-Saharan Africa

Mesoamerica and Andes

1200 BCE
Villages in most parts of Mesoamerica and the Andes

750 BCE–1 CE
Paracas chiefdom in southern Peru

300 BCE
First Mayan inscriptions, in a glyphic alphabet

1–650 CE
Nazca chiefdom in southern Peru

100–750 CE
Moche chiefdom in northern Peru

100 BCE–500 CE
City-state of Teotihuacán in Mexico

250–900 CE
Classic period of Maya kingdoms

Meroë was well known to the outside world. Mediterranean travelers visited it frequently. In the early first century CE the kings of Meroë skirmished with Rome over border issues. As much as Meroë provided a physical network for regional travelers, it also provided an intellectual link between Eurasia and Africa—a link the people of Meroë facilitated through their adaptations.

The Kingdom of Aksum

Meroitic trade with the Red Sea crossed the Ethiopian highlands, and highlanders gradually acculturated to Meroë as well as Yemen. In the early first century CE, a king replaced the chiefdoms of the highlands and established the kingdom of Aksum (300–600 CE). Based on agriculture, this kingdom assumed control of the trade from Meroë, which declined. Aksum became the major supplier of African goods to the Roman Empire, from where it accepted Christianity in the early 300s.

Meroë's Decline and Aksum's Rise   Three factors contributed to Meroë's decline in the third century CE. First, the iron industry required charcoal, which is made by burning wood; when all the forests had been burned, the industry was doomed. Second, beginning in the late 200s BCE, camel nomads from the deserts east of the Nile raided northern Meroë. Third, the eastern neighbor, Ethiopia, acculturated to Meroë and became a participant in its trade; eventually, chiefs in the high plain of Aksum took it over. Aksum was located close to the coast and Red Sea ports. Agricultural and commercial wealth enabled the chiefs of Aksum to assume the succession of Meroë.

The agricultural bounty of the Ethiopian highlands southeast of Meroë was due to its location and climate. The summer monsoon brought sufficient and, in places, abundant rain to the plains and mountains and supported forests and subtropical agriculture in the lower elevations.

As in the Nile valley, agriculture in the Ethiopian highlands was of considerable age. In higher elevations, farmers grew teff, a high-yielding grain. Abundant grasslands supported cattle breeding. The Red Sea coast supported only a few ports dependent on their hinterland. Because of its elevation, Ethiopia was a largely self-contained region in Africa, remaining outside the large population movements and cultural assimilation characteristic of West and East Africa.

Aksum's Splendor   Aksum, founded around 100 CE, came into its own around 300 CE. Its king, Ezana (ca. 303–350 CE), adopted Christianity as the state religion in 333 CE. Like his counterpart, the Roman emperor, Ezana replaced tolerance for polytheistic religions with the requirement of conversion to a single faith (see Chapter 7). When the Roman emperors, however, embraced what would become the Roman Catholic interpretation of Christianity, Aksum opted for Coptic Christianity, which was dominant in Egypt. It did not break with the Roman Empire and even sided with it in the 500s CE against the Sasanid Persians, but it kept its distance.

Another centralizing policy of Aksum was the use of a gold-based currency through which taxation was facilitated. The kings of Aksum acquired their gold by sending merchants to the southern highlands outside the kingdom, where the gold was mined. The merchants paid with salt, iron, and cattle. Finally, a small central administration of tax collectors, tax farmers, and provincial tribute collectors ensured delivery of agricultural surplus to granaries in the towns and the capital.

Even though more centralized than Meroë, Aksum was well below the level of administrative coherence of a typical Middle Eastern or Mediterranean kingdom or empire.

Imperialism and Crisis   In the 500s CE, Aksum briefly engaged in imperialism. This century was a time of crisis in the Roman and Sasanid Persian empires, both of which were threatened by nomadic invaders from the central Asian and Russian steppes (see Chapter 7). The kingdom of Himyar in Yemen increasingly relied on camel caravan trade along the west coast of Arabia. A Yemeni usurper who had converted to Judaism seized the throne and persecuted the Christians in his land. In response, and encouraged by Rome, the Aksumite king invaded Yemen and defeated the usurper. After a period of political instability, Aksum made Yemen a regular province (543–570 CE).

But Aksum eventually lost this province when the Sasanid Persians invaded in 570 CE. The Sasanids had recovered earlier than the Romans from nomadic invasions and were determined to turn the long competition between the two empires to their favor. Seizing control over the India and East Africa trade was part of the Sasanid strategy to defeat Rome in the Middle East.

As a kingdom dependent on transcontinental luxury trade, Aksum became a victim of this new Persian ascendancy. After 570 CE, Aksumite trade in the Red Sea declined precipitously. The capital city shrank, and over time provincial rulers in the highlands farther south rose to prominence. Although Ethiopia did not disintegrate, as Meroë had done, after 600 CE its regional role was modest.

Aksumite Stela, pre-400s CE. This is the largest of hundreds of stone monoliths, some with tombs and altars, attesting to the architectural sophistication of the kingdom. Workmen transported them from quarries 3 miles away, where they had cut the stelae with iron tools. Some of the stelae, like the one above, have false windows and doors, looking like modern Art Deco buildings.

The Spread of Villages in Sub-Saharan Africa

By about 600 BCE, agriculture and pastoralism were common in East Africa and West Africa. Both emerged when people retreated from the increasingly dry Sahara, following the gradual southward shift of West Africa's three ecological zones. The first and northernmost zone was the steppe, or **Sahel** (Arabic *sahil*, or "coast" of the "sea" of the Sahara Desert). The second zone was the *savanna*. The third zone was a belt of rain forest along the coast from Guinea to Cameroon. By 600 BCE villages were most numerous in the savanna, where farming was most productive.

Sahel: An area of steppe or semidesert bordering the Sahara.

West African Savanna and Rain-Forest Agriculture

The village of Jenné-jeno [JEN-nay JEN-no] in the inland delta of the Niger and middle Senegal Rivers developed into a major urban center during 300–900 CE. It was a chiefdom with a regional trade for raw materials and luxury goods. In the rain forest, the so-called Bantu dispersal, with its combination of yam, taro, banana, and oil palm village agriculture, was well established.

Inland Delta Urbanism   The river Niger originates in the far west of the West African rain forest. Midway along its northeastern leg, it forms the 250-mile-long and 50-mile-wide inland delta. In the first millennium BCE, the delta was located entirely

Seated Figure, Jenné-jeno, Terra-Cotta, Thirteenth Century; New York, Metropolitan Museum. This convoluted figure, sculpted with exquisite refinement, shows a person in an apparently intense meditative pose.

Phytoliths: Many plants pick up silica from the soil. After these plants decay, the silica returns to the soil in the form of phytoliths, which can be analyzed microscopically. Carbon dating of soil layers provides approximate dates.

in the savanna, forming a huge area of canals, islands, and swamps. Over time, a dense network of villages developed. After 300 BCE some villages, increasing to town size, became the center of satellite villages. This is how Jenné-jeno, at the southern end of the delta, originated. By 900 CE Jenné-jeno was a *city* of between 5,000 and 13,000 inhabitants. A prominent craft was pottery, with some potters specializing in the creation of small terra-cotta figurines, such as horsemen, archers, and humans in convoluted poses. The city was surrounded by 25 villages. Other towns with satellite villages developed farther downstream, making the delta the most populated area in West Africa.

Little is known about the social stratification and power structures of Jenné-jeno. It is clear that this urban–rural center had a line of chiefs, some basic administrative offices, and craftspeople. A gold ring and objects made of copper and bronze dated to 850–900 CE have been found. Copper and iron ore had to be carried in from mines in the desert and savanna to be smelted and manufactured into weapons and implements. Two glass beads, dated to the pre-600 CE period, seem to have come from overseas. Thus, trans-Saharan trade seems to have been in existence, supporting an urban demand for luxuries.

Rain-Forest Settlements   Evidence for rain-forest agriculture comes from the Kintampo complex of 2250–750 BCE, located in today's Ghana. Archaeologists have found traces of wood and mud huts, domesticated livestock, pottery, terra-cotta figurines, and polished stone implements. The assumption is that the villagers practiced slash-and-burn farming, growing yams and oil palms.

Early Plant Domestication?   In 1996 at Nkang in the Cameroons, archaeologists were able to date banana **phytoliths** to about 500 BCE. Phytoliths are silica from soil sediments deposited in bananas. Their dating caused unrest among many Africanists who believed that the banana had arrived with Indonesian sailors on the East African coast sometime between 200 and 500 CE. It is becoming evident that Indian Ocean connections between Southeast Asia and East Africa are of greater antiquity than hitherto assumed. Did bananas, yams, sugarcane stalks, and rice travel westward with intrepid Polynesian sailors thousands of years ago?

Village Farming   West African slash-and-burn farming consisted of clearing small areas of rain forest for villages of up to 500 inhabitants. Virgin rain forest was relatively easy to cut, even with stone tools, prior to the arrival of iron axes in the 800s BCE. Each clearing was large enough for a village of a few hundred farmers, family fields, communal fallow land, and cattle and goats.

If a village grew beyond its population capacity, a group had to depart and select a new site in the rain forest for clearing. Yam fields had to lie fallow for 10–15 years, during which the rain forest grew back. This secondary rain forest had few tall trees and a proliferation of medium vegetation. After millennia of slash-and-burn cultivation, nearly all virgin African rain forests were replaced by secondary forest. As in so many other places in the world, what many might perceive as pristine "jungle" was in fact the creation of human hands.

The Spread of Village Life to East and South Africa

Groups of yam, banana, and oil palm farmers of southeast Nigeria, at the eastern end of the West African rain-forest belt, calling themselves "Bantu," exhausted their area for clearings around 2000 BCE. They were fortunate in their search for new spaces to clear, because they had the equatorial rain forest of the Congo at their disposal. Once there, a northerly group began to disperse around 1500 BCE eastward into the savanna of the Great Lakes in East Africa. On their way, they adapted to the cereal agriculture and iron crafting of the savanna villagers. Under Bantu impact, from 600 BCE–600 CE, nearly all foragers in the southern cone of Africa became either villagers or cattle nomads and adopted Bantu languages and culture (see Map 6.2).

Inland Villagers and Nomads   When the northern Bantu arrived around 600 BCE, much of the land around the Great Lakes was forested savanna. As villagers cleared the forest, the threat of the **tsetse fly** diminished, and nomads from the north were able to expand southward. As in the Middle East, these nomads had a symbiotic relationship with the villagers, from whom they acquired grain. In the meantime, the southern migrants of the original Bantu dispersal of 2000 BCE had

Tsetse Fly: This insect can carry the virus that causes sleeping sickness, causing extreme fatigue and eventual death in humans and domesticated animals. Some animal species were able to adapt as dwarf variations, notably horses, cattle, and goats. The fly thrives in low elevations in rain forests, along rivers, and around lakes.

map analysis

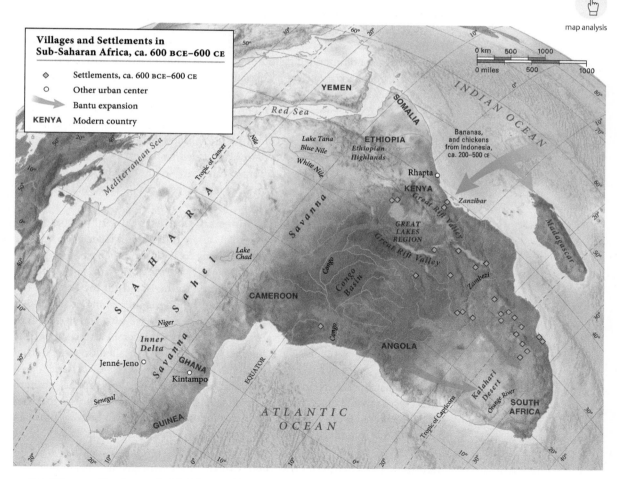

MAP 6.2 **Villages and Settlements in Sub-Saharan Africa, 600 BCE–600 CE.**

African spirituality: Perception of reality based on the concept of nature in all its manifestations (planets and stars, landscapes, trees and plants, animals and humans), pervaded by spirits and influencing each other.

Witchcraft: A belief in which an evil person (male or female) can harm an innocent victim at a distance and cause the victim to become possessed, with attendant illnesses.

settled the Congo equatorial rain forest and, under the impact of their northern and eastern cousins, had complemented their yam and oil palm agriculture with millet and sorghum, as well as ironworking. Only small pockets of the original Paleolithic foragers of the virgin rain forest, the pygmies, continued their traditional lifestyle, although they adopted Bantu languages.

The conversion of the foragers to farming was the work of both eastern Great Lakes and western Congo branches of Bantu descendants. The foragers either retreated before the farmers or adapted voluntarily to farming and speaking a Bantu language. Some savanna foragers, speaking Khoisan-family languages, retreated into the Kalahari Desert and steppe in western and central South Africa, and remained hunter–gatherers. The process from Bantu origins and Bantu interaction with the nomads and foragers of East and South Africa to the mutual adaptations was still incomplete in 600 CE.

African Traditional Rituals   An analysis of Bantu linguistic roots and of early Iron Age (350–900 CE) sites in South Africa provides a glimpse into traditional **African spirituality**. Bantus distinguished between the daily cycles of renewal and disintegration in village households and the fields on one hand, and the calendar movements of heaven on the other. Rituals and observance of taboos and omens kept the village and field cycles on their regular paths.

Ancestor and nature spirits had to be given their due respect through sacrifices, lest they disrupt the cycles of renewal and disintegration. Charms, mixed from herbs, protected against unintended insults of the spirits. Male or female witches in the villages could, out of envy, vengeance, or malice, severely harm or even kill their victims. Village diviners or healers were able to enter the spirit world, recognize bewitchment, and stop it through **witchcraft**. In the early African Iron Age, the adoption of rituals involving the human and field cycles—and, in some places, the calendar cycle, as evidenced by the Borana calendar—represented the main changes in African patterns of reality conceptualizations.

Indonesian Contacts   In 200–500 CE, Indonesian sailors brought new species of bananas and chickens to East Africa. These sailors were descendants from Austronesian farmers, who had dispersed to the islands of the Pacific, Philippines, and Indonesia, beginning around 4000 BCE, and who may have also traveled to East Africa, as discussed earlier in the chapter. The mariners of 200–500 CE sailed on large outriggers with canted square sails, which made it pos-

Stone Relief of a Large Outrigger Merchant Ship, Buddhist Temple of Borobudur, on the Indonesian Island of Java, ca. 800 CE. This type of ship traveled regularly from Java to East Africa on the cinnamon trade route, with its merchants exchanging spices for ivory, wild animal skins, and slaves during the early centuries of the first millennium.

sible to sail at an angle from the headwind. Prevailing wind patterns in the southern Indian Ocean would otherwise have made sailing westward from Indonesia to Africa difficult. Where on the African coast the Indonesians landed is unknown, although they definitely settled the still-uninhabited tropical island of Madagascar.

Incipient Urbanism on the East Coast   East Africans also benefited from trade with the Middle East. Archaeological evidence points to the inclusion of the northern East African coast into the Yemeni commercial network in the last centuries BCE, which connected Meroë, Egypt, Persia, India, Sri Lanka, and (indirectly) Indonesia and China.

By the mid-first century CE, a Greek-Hellenistic source mentions Yemenis intermarrying with locals in the town of Rhapta along the Kenyan coast. Although no archaeological remnants of Rhapta have been located, Roman glass beads and shards found on Zanzibar and the Tanzanian coast suggest regular journeys beginning around 200 CE. The beads and ceramics were presumably exchanged for ivory, rock crystal, ostrich feathers, and hardwood. If true, the later Swahili cities antedated the spread of Islam by several centuries—just as in the case of Jenné-jeno in West Africa before the rise of Islamic Saharan kingdoms.

Patterns of African History, 600 BCE–600 CE

Sub-Saharan Africa evolved along two basic patterns in the period 600 BCE–600 CE. First, in the northeast Meroë and Aksum adapted themselves to Middle Eastern agriculture, and both African-domesticated sorghum and millet—and in Aksum teff—were grown. Irrigated farming and long-distance trade allowed chiefs to build kingdoms, which lasted as long as the urban infrastructure could be supported. The exhaustion of timber ended the royal pattern of social and political evolution in the sub-Saharan northeast.

Second, in the northwest of sub-Saharan Africa, inhabitants pioneered the agricultures of the steppe, savanna, and rain forest. Millet was productive enough to support the rise of villages. In the inland delta of the Niger, the irrigated farming of millet and rice allowed for the rise of a city, Jenné-jeno. With its long-distance trade, this city foreshadowed the post-600 CE rise of Saharan kingdoms. Farther south, in the rain forest, the farming of yam, banana, and oil palm supported the emergence of small and widely dispersed villages. The expansion of the Bantus and their agriculture brought village life as well as iron smelting to all parts of sub-Saharan Africa.

Africa and the Americas   The Americas displayed similarities to the internal sub-Saharan interactions and adaptations. The latter, as we have seen, were responsible for patterns of village, city, and kingdom formation. In Mesoamerica as well as in the Peruvian Andes Mountains, internal processes of interaction and adaptation also supported a pattern of village, city-state, and kingdom development from 600 BCE to 600 CE.

The principal difference, however, was that in sub-Saharan Africa this evolution gradually expanded also to the central and southern regions, whereas in the Americas no such expansion took place until after 600 CE. Social and political formation patterns spread to North America only after 600 CE, as represented by the Pueblo and Cahokia cultures.

Early States in Mesoamerica: Maya Kingdoms and Teotihuacán

In Chapter 5 we saw that the chiefdoms of Caral-Supe (2600–2000 BCE) and Chavín de Huántar (1000–200 BCE) in the Andes as well as of the Olmecs (1200–600 BCE) in Mesoamerica represent the development from agriculture and villages to urbanization, chiefdoms, and kingdoms. In the period of 600 BCE–600 CE, in the southern Yucatán Peninsula of Mexico and the Mexican Basin in south-central Mexico, chiefdoms evolved into kingdoms. In the Andes, urban centers formed under chiefly rule, although in Teotihuacán and Moche the urban culture was nearly as diversified as in the Mesoamerican kingdoms.

The Maya Kingdoms in Southern Mesoamerica

By creating clear-cuts, elevated fields, and terraces on hill slopes, Mayan villagers in the Yucatán Peninsula established agriculture based on squash, beans, and corn. Around 600 BCE towns evolved into cities, where chieftains transformed themselves into kings. By organizing the farmers during the winter, they created city-states with temple pyramids and palaces, surrounded by outlying villages. Among these city-states, the most powerful during the period 600 BCE–600 CE were Tikal and Kalakmul (see Map 6.3).

Mayaland on the Yucatán Peninsula   The climate of the Yucatán Peninsula is subtropical, with a rainy season from May to September. The base of the Yucatán Peninsula consisted of rain-forest lowlands and swamps, traversed by rivers. To the south were rain-forest highlands, sloping from mountains that descended toward the lowlands in the north and the Pacific coast in the south. The northern region consisted of dry and riverless lowlands. Maya culture began in the center and south and later radiated into the southern mountains and northern lowlands. Limestone quarries in the northern lowland areas provided stone for construction. The volcanic south was quarried for its lava stone and was also rich in obsidian and jade.

The people in the Yucatán spoke a variety of Mayan dialects. The early Mayas cut down the rain forest in order to clear fields, drain swamps, and build villages on low

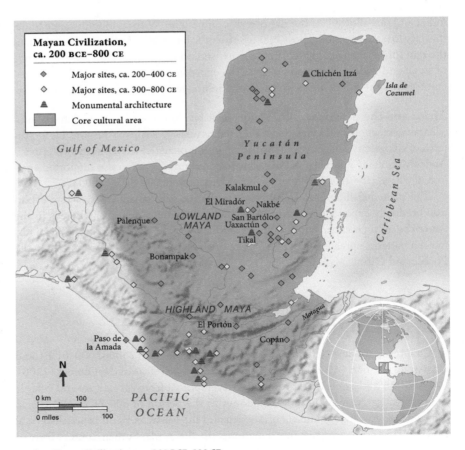

MAP 6.3 **Mayan Civilization, ca. 200 BCE–800 CE.**

stone platforms near water sources. By around 1000 BCE, some villages evolved into towns. Elite lineages under chieftains resided in the towns and controlled the best lands, while more humble lineages in the surrounding villages were on less productive soils. Although society was organized by familial descent, social stratification by wealth began to differentiate the lineages.

Early Kingdoms   As in the agrarian centers of Eurasia, debt dependence was probably the earliest lever of power in the hands of the Mayan chieftains. Rich farmers had larger families, built bigger homes, and had more domestic workers producing pottery and textiles. Thus, in the period 1000–600 BCE, these wealthy farmers transformed themselves into chieftains, exerting family rule for extended periods over a central town surrounded by satellite villages.

Beginning in the seventh century BCE, chieftains in some agriculturally rich areas increased their wealth so that they could claim to be kings. Kings surrounded themselves with military forces. They began to collect taxes, enlarge their towns into cities, and conquer other villages. During slack times in the agricultural cycle, these kings commanded farmers to construct ceremonial monuments. Nakbé (700 BCE–150 CE), a city in the north of the central lowlands, was the site of the first temple pyramids on ceremonial platforms. These pyramids were stepped stone structures, as high as 200 feet, with staircases to the temples on top where kings conducted sacrifices to the gods of the emerging divine pantheon.

A nearby town, El Miradór (600 BCE–150 CE), became a city with surrounding villages about a century after Nakbé. With about 100,000 inhabitants, hundreds of ceremonial and palatial structures on its platforms, and a 236-foot pyramid built around 300 BCE, this Mayan city was the largest early center of what ultimately were more than 4,400 Mayan urban and rural sites. Only the later Tikal (200–600 CE) reached a similar size. To the surprise of archaeologists, the El Miradór site has turned out to be as fully Mayan, with its temple pyramids, elite structures, stelae, ball courts, sweat houses, and commoner quarters, as the later and better-known centers. Maya culture at its peak has to be considered—as it is in this chapter—within a much longer time horizon than previously assumed.

Progress made in deciphering the Maya glyphic script has revealed that "Mayaland" consisted of some 15–17 dominant kingdoms in the central lowlands during the Early Classic Period, each with a capital and one or more secondary cities. Marriage alliances among the royal lineages of the capitals and secondary cities maintained the cohesion of the kingdom. Frequent wars in Mayaland were either intrakingdom rebellions or wars among secondary cities in different kingdoms. Direct military competition between the kingdoms of Tikal and Kalakmul, however, endured for many centuries.

El Miradór, La Danta Temple, 600 BCE–150 CE. By height (236 feet), volume, and footprint, this pyramid was the largest of all Maya sacred structures and one of the largest buildings of the premodern world. At present, the site is only partially excavated, and archaeological work is still ongoing. The temple visible atop the pyramid is surmounted by a rooster-like roof comb, once covered by stucco figurines of Maya deities.

Spirituality and Polytheism   Kings and their households lived in palaces adjacent to the temple pyramids. Kings often assumed the names of animals combined with human-made objects—for example, "Spearthrower Owl," "Shield Jaguar," and

The Mayan Ball Game

Although it shares its ancient age with similar games in China, the Persian Middle East, and the Greek and Roman Mediterranean, only in Mesoamerica was the team ball game played according to formal rules in stadiums constructed specifically for this purpose. In Mesoamerica, the oldest stadium to date, from 1400 BCE, was found in the ruins of Paso de la Amadain in the far southeast of today's Mexico. Adjacent to the palace of the chief, this ball court measures 260 by 23 feet, with two 7-foot-high spectator platforms on both long sides. Later on, during the Maya period, these platforms usually rose theater-style on both sides, for better viewing from farther away. Given the proximity of the ball court to the chief's residence, it is possible that other chiefdoms in the area engaged in what we would call today "league tournaments."

The solid-rubber ball was around 2 feet in diameter and weighed 8 pounds. Given these dimensions, players often wore protective gear around their hips and helmets on their heads, as shown in murals and on ceramics.

The Mayan Ball Game. Note the strong body protection around the midsection of the players as well as the elaborate headdresses, symbolizing animals.

"Smoke Squirrel." On wall paintings, earthenware vessels, and stelae, kings were recognizable by their richly decorated headdresses and clothing. When sons of kings were still minors, their mothers assumed the roles of regents. Occasionally, women ruled as queens. After death, kings were buried in pyramids or in separate tombs and were assumed to have taken their places among the gods.

Polytheism:
Personification of the forces of nature and the performance of rituals and sacrifices to ensure the benevolence of the gods and goddesses.

Polytheism emerged alongside traditional spirituality around 2500 BCE. Traditional spirituality was shared by all, commoners and chiefs. The gods of polytheism were more powerful than the spirits of ancestors. They were the embodiments of forces of nature whose favor the kings—more powerful than chiefs—had to curry if rich harvests were to occur and the kingdom was to flourish.

Mayan kings considered themselves servants of the gods that populated the divine pantheon by the time of the Olmecs in the eleventh century BCE and continued to grow during the Maya period. They made daily sacrifices to these gods in rituals in the temples atop the pyramids. The main sacrifice was the gift of blood—a heritage from traditional spirituality: blood as the force of life—which Mayan kings drew from their ear lobes, tongues, and penises. During times of war, captured enemies were also sacrificed. Through their blood, the kings nourished nature and supported the human and divine worlds.

The Ruling Classes   Kings and officials assembled for the administration of justice, the collection of rents and tributes, commercial exchanges, and diplomatic relations. Many of these functions required expert knowledge of the annual calendar. Other functions, such as military action, required divination to discover the most

Under the Maya, who called the game *pitz* and built about 1,500 courts, the rules became more formalized. Teams had from one to seven players. A basic rule was that the ball had to be hit with the hip, but in variations, players struck the ball with forearms, bats, or hand stones. The team that dropped the ball most often lost.

The significance of the Mayan ball game fits into the larger pattern of agrarian–urban society with its chiefdoms and kingdoms whose polytheism required elaborate rituals and sacrificial practices. Although the archaeological record is debatable, it appears that ball games took place during chiefly or royal festivities and fertility rituals, and perhaps also human sacrifices. The apparent but also disputed role of some players as human sacrifices on a number of murals was a late Mayan phenomenon. Today, these religious roots of "games" are largely forgotten. Instead, modern sports have rituals such as flag-waving, parading, tailgating, and hooliganism. Whether religious or secular, rituals are permanent fixtures that follow their own patterns, parallel to those of society at large.

Questions

- How did the ball game serve as a microcosm for larger patterns in Mayan society?
- What function could the ball game have played in relations among the various Mayan chiefdoms?

favorable star constellations under which to proceed. The tracking of these units of times fell to calendar specialists, mathematicians, and astronomers.

The Mayans used four calendars. One calendar was the 260-day, or 9-month, divinatory calendar, which scholars interpret as being related to the human gestation period. A second calendar, based on the solar year of 365 days and important for agriculture, was nearly as old. A third calendar, the Mayan Calendar Round, commenced every 52 years when the divinatory and solar calendars began on the same day. The Mayas believed that this calendar inaugurated cycles of calamitous as well as fortuitous times. The fourth calendar in use among the Mayas was the Long Count Calendar, which counted the days elapsed since the mythical origin of the universe. Sophisticated mathematics were required to coordinate these four calendars.

Other activities of the royal family and court consisted of daily processions, feasts, and ball games played in stadiums on the temple-palace grounds. These ritualized, refined pastimes were far beyond the reach of common farmers and craftspeople. A stratified social hierarchy typified the Maya kingdoms (see "Patterns Up Close").

The Commoners   The commoners, whose taxes supported the royal courts, lived in compounds of thatched huts around courtyards on stone platforms, safe from the floodwaters of the rainy season from May to September. In these houses, women were in charge of cooking, weaving, pottery making, the growing of garden vegetables and fruits, and the rearing of domestic animals. Women and men fabricated tools from chert, bone, and wood. In larger Maya kingdoms some households seem to have specialized in tool manufacturing and weaving, with both women and men participating.

Men grew corn in fields that were cut into the rain forest through slash-and-burn techniques. Fields near rivers and in swamps were raised, rectangular islands on which the mud from adjacent canals had been heaped. Slopes along river valleys were terraced in order to retain rain or irrigation water. Cotton, cacao, and tobacco fields formed special plantations requiring intensive labor. Hunting and fishing were important occupations among both royals and commoners.

The hard agricultural labor of the commoners produced an agricultural surplus, which supported ruling dynastic families as well as craftspeople in the cities. Craftspeople worked for the construction and maintenance of royal palaces, creating monuments, wall paintings, pottery, and inscriptions on stone pillars.

Glyphic script: The Maya developed a script of some 800 images. Some are pictograms standing for words; others are syllables to be combined with other syllables to form words.

Mayan Writing   Mayan writing is a **glyphic** as well as a syllabic script, numbering some 800 signs. It is structurally similar to Sumerian cuneiform and Egyptian hieroglyphics. In their basic form, glyphs are *pictograms*, one-word images of the most essential features of what is to be depicted. But gyphs were also used as syllables, consisting of one, two, or three signs combining consonants and vowels. Combinations of multiple syllabic glyphs, or *syllabaries*, are pronounced as a series of syllables. Given the immense number of possible combinations of pictograms and syllabaries, the complexity of Mayan writing long resisted all efforts to decipher it.

A breakthrough came when scholars interpreted stelae monuments as records of royal births, accessions to the throne, and deaths. First, scholars realized that Mayan writing had the above-mentioned syllabic component; then, the architect and Maya specialist Tatiana Proskouriakoff discovered that the inscriptions on many royal stelae contained information on dynastic dates and events. The final breakthrough came at the Maya site of Palenque in 1973 when scholars recognized the syllables *k'inchi* as referring to the Mayan sun god as well as to individual kings. Since then, scholars have assembled a dictionary of as many as 1,000 words, and it has become possible to chronicle the dynasties of Maya kingdoms.

The Crisis of the Kingdoms   Spectacular building activities characterized Mayaland during ca. 400–600 CE. Ruling classes must have grown considerably, and farmers in some kingdoms may have no longer been willing to produce food as well as provide labor for temples and palaces. Destruction identified in some archaeological sites could be the result of revolts. In other places, overexploitation of the soil, loss of topsoil on terraces, or salinization of lowland fields as the result of neglected drainage might have increased the imbalance between the peasants and ruling classes. Frequent wars among the kings might have reduced the size of the ruling class, with negative consequences for the farmers.

The destructive interplay among the ruling class, farmers, and the environment produced a crisis from the late 500s CE through the mid-600s CE. It led to the collapse of many older Mayan kingdoms and endangered the survival of the strongest newer ones in the southern lowlands. When the crisis ended, the political weight of Maya power shifted to the northern lowlands of the Yucatán Peninsula.

The Kingdom of Teotihuacán in the Mexican Basin

The subtropical climate of Yucatán extended northward into the highlands, in which the Mexican Basin was the largest agricultural region. The region supported the growing of beans, squash, and corn. The northern part of the basin developed village life later than the south, but its closeness to obsidian quarries gave these villages commercial advantages. Militarily and economically, the town of Teotihuacán in the north developed into a city-state that became politically and culturally dominant across all of what is today Mexico.

image analysis

The Mexican Basin The Mexican Basin is a large, 7,400-foot-high bowl without river outlets in southern Mexico. In the center of the bowl was Lake Texcoco [tes-CO-co], nourished by rivers flowing down from mountains chains on the eastern and western sides. As in Mayaland, the basin enjoyed a rainy season during the summer. River water, channeled through irrigation canals to terraces and the flatlands around the central lake, as well as numerous bays, supported a moderately productive agriculture.

During the period of village expansion (1200–600 BCE), many of the slopes surrounding this bowl were forested, providing firewood, timber, and game. Fish in the lake were another food source. Clay deposits in the flatlands and obsidian quarries on the slopes of the northeastern mountains provided resources for the manufacture of ceramics, tools, and weapons. However, the high elevation and temperature differences between winter and summer did not allow for cultivation of cotton, cacao, vanilla, and other tropical products of lowland Maya agriculture. These latter products had to be acquired by trade.

The principal plant fiber for the weaving of clothes came from the *maguey* [ma-GAY] plant, a cactus that grows in poor soil and does not need much water. The juice of this plant was fermented and consumed as an alcoholic drink called *pulque* [Spanish, PULL-kay; Nahuatl, *octli*]. If people wished to manufacture clothes from cotton or acquire cacao, vanilla, jade, or quetzal feathers, they had to trade their obsidian. Commercial exchange was necessary for village expansion and the subsequent pattern of kingdom formation.

Teotihuacán In a valley to the northeast of Lake Texcoco, villagers in the early centuries of the Common Era dug a large canal system with raised fields similar to those of the Maya. Villages around this canal network eventually formed the city of Teotihuacán. We do not know when the transition from chieftains to kings and chiefly dynasties occurred. The iconic writing system, less developed than that of the Mayas, does not allow for identification of any rulers or lineages. Teotihuacán was a city-state with an anonymous dynasty. In its physical appearance it was even more imposing than most of the Maya kingdoms (see Map 6.4).

In the first century CE, the rulers of Teotihuacán laid out an urban grid along a north–south axis that included two densely constructed city quarters of some 2,200 housing units. Near the central avenue, adobe houses lined both sides of the alleyways. Some 600 houses had the appearance of workshops, primarily for the making of tools. The workshops indicate a degree of nonagricultural crafts specialization, which one would expect from a city. Farther away, houses and fields were interspersed. Canals, reservoirs, and a drainage system facilitated the transportation of food, the provision of drinking water, and the elimination of waste. By around 300 CE, Teotihuacán had grown to as many as 100,000 inhabitants.

Mayan Glyphs. Beginning in the fourth century BCE, scribes in the Maya kingdoms developed a written language composed of pictograms and syllables, eventually numbering about 800 signs. This language allowed communication among educated people in the different Maya kingdoms, who spoke often mutually unintelligible local languages. Because of the double meaning of each glyph as pictogram and syllable, it took most of the twentieth century for scholars to decipher the Mayan language. The example shown here is from the Dresden Codex.

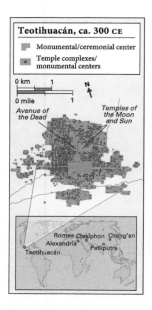

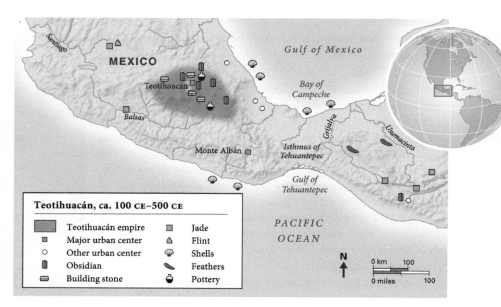

MAP 6.4 **Teotihuacán, ca. 100 CE–500 CE.**

Teotihuacán's temple pyramids, palaces, markets, and city quarters were built on a vast scale. The Temples of the Moon and the Sun, built at the northern end of the city, were ceremonial centers that attracted pilgrims from the Mexican Basin and beyond. Archaeologists interpret the Temple of the Sun as a construction on top of a cave symbolizing the entrance to the nether world. In the third century CE, the temple of the god of the feathered serpent (Nahuatl *Quetzalcoatl* [ket-sal-COA]) was built, probably in honor of the then reigning dynasty. The founding king sacrificed some 260 humans, probably war captives, to garner the good will of the god. After what appears to have been an internal uprising in the 400s CE, new rulers destroyed the temple's façade. Wall paintings and pottery, depicting rulers, priests, gods, and mythical figures in processions, rituals, and dances, attest to a highly developed aesthetic culture.

The Decline of the City   As in the case of the Maya kingdoms, the balance among the peasantry, urban inhabitants, dynasties, and construction programs was not always easy to maintain. Hints at an internal upheaval point to the balance being lost for the first time around 400 CE. Another such upheaval occurred in the late 500s CE. Thereafter, the population of the central city quarters declined. The outlying quarters reverted back to the village level as farming communities for centuries to come. The mid-500s CE saw prolonged periods of cooler weather and droughts and were generally a more difficult time for farming in the Americas. In contrast to the agriculturally richer Maya kingdoms, the Mexican Basin found a return to urbanism and dynastic states more difficult.

At its height, Teotihuacán exerted an influence considerably greater than the Maya kingdoms. Its trade reached deep into Mayaland and beyond, to the Isthmus of Panama. Teotihuacán exchanged its obsidian for cotton, rubber, cacao, jade, and quetzal feathers from the subtropical lowlands. Its gods, especially the deity of the feathered serpent, were sacrificed to everywhere in Mesoamerica. Similarly,

Teotihuacán was instrumental in spreading its architectural style (inward-sloping platforms, surmounted by temples) from the Basin of Mexico to the Yucatán Peninsula. In the later 300s CE and throughout the 400s CE, Maya rulers of Tikal, Uaxactún [wa-shac-TOON], and other kingdoms claimed descent from rulers of Teotihuacán, evidently seeking to benefit from the city's prestige as a ceremonial center.

The Andes: Moche and Nazca

In Andean South America, a pattern of chiefdom formation evolved between 3000 and 2000 BCE, a millennium earlier than in Mesoamerica. Given the absence of large plains and the enormous differences in elevation within short distances, however, relatively small chiefdoms remained the dominant social formation in the Andes

The Moche in Northern Peru

The Moche Valley was the place of the two largest ceremonial centers in the Andes, the Temple Pyramids of the Sun and the Moon. The power of its main chiefdom must have been impressive, since large numbers of farmers had to be mobilized for the construction of these pyramids. But it remained a federation of village chiefdoms clustered around an urbanized temple center with a dominant chiefly lineage.

Moche Origins   The Moche Valley was at the center of nine coastal valleys in what is today northern Peru. It had a subtropical climate with moderately wet winters and dry summers. It supported an irrigated agriculture of corn, pulses, cotton, and potatoes; llamas and alpacas from the highlands were domesticated for wool and light transportation. Here, the earliest evidence of the emergence of the Moche chiefdoms (100–750 CE) is the tomb of the "Lord of Sipán," dated to 50 CE. The tomb contained the chief's mummy, clad in warrior clothing and richly decorated with gold and silver jewelry. Eight people, including his wife, and a dog were buried with him. This chieftain was wealthy and powerful indeed.

Teotihuacán, Temple of the Feathered Serpent God Quetzalcóatl. This sculpture of a serpent's head with its exposed, menacing fangs and the collar made of feathers is one of many along the front wall of this temple. The hybrid deity [quetzal bird and snake (*cóatl*)], bringer of rain in the summer, bridged the fertile Earth and the planet Venus.

A Federated Chiefdom   Half a century later, Moche chieftains began the construction of the two Temple Pyramids of the Sun and the Moon. About 100 village teams participated in the construction, which lasted intermittently for centuries. At the feet of the two temples was a city that included administrative offices and workshops. Lesser chieftain lineages ruled in the more remote valleys.

None of the participating villages appears to have grown beyond the moderately large spaces at the mouth of valleys, and it seems that they coexisted peacefully. When the generally cooler and drier climate of the sixth century CE arrived, it had a greater negative impact on the agriculture of the central chiefdom in Moche, closer to the coast and at the end of the river streams, than on the chiefdoms upstream in the valleys. In the Moche Valley, with its two huge temples, the balance between chiefly elites and farmers was more difficult to maintain than in the farther valleys with smaller elites and comparatively larger peasantries. Eventually, in the early 600s CE, the Moche elite dissolved, while smaller elites in nearby valleys carried on and eventually disappeared also, sometime around 750 CE (see Map 6.5).

Paracas and the Nazca in Southern Peru

Southern Peru was much drier, and its agrarian population density lagged behind that of the north. Nevertheless, Paracas [pah-RAH-cas] and Nazca possess considerable cultural significance.

Paracas Chiefs   Desert conditions on the southern Peruvian coast and dependence on runoff water from Andean snowmelt required more elaborate irrigation works than on the northern coast. The patterns of social formation from foraging to villages and chiefdoms were correspondingly slower and more modest. Shamans and chiefs on the Paracas peninsula and the Ica valley set the pattern in motion when they unified a number of hamlets. Subsequently, other Paracas chiefdoms appeared in neighboring valleys, forming a loose confederation (750 BCE–1 CE).

MAP **6.5 Andean Centers, 600 BCE–600 CE.**

A necropolis on the peninsula contained hundreds of mummies of chieftains, wrapped in the colorful wool and cotton mantles still characteristic of southern Peru today. The icons woven into the mantles and painted on pottery allowed scholars to identify the Paracas chiefs. These icons included figures holding weapons, plants, or skulls; other icons were felines, birds, or whales, often with human-like features. Although contemporary with the Maya kingdoms in Mesoamerica, the Paracas chiefdoms in the Andes were culturally compact.

The Nazca Ceremonial Center   The transition from pottery painted after firing to predecorated (slipware) ceramics defines the shift from the Paracas to the Nazca chiefdoms (1–650 CE). Nazca chiefs built ceremonial centers, modest adobe structures that covered preexisting mounds. Cahuachi [ca-wooh-WAH-chee], the main pilgrimage center, contained 40 such structures, assumed to represent the contributing chiefdoms.

During the extended cold weather and drought periods of the sixth century CE, Nazca chiefs mobilized villagers for the construction of a tunnel network for irrigation. Workers tapped underground water in the mountains and guided it onto the slopes of the valleys and into reservoirs. These sophisticated constructions, with intermittent shafts and manholes for cleaning and repair, were built so sturdily that many of them are still in operation today.

The Nazca Geoglyphs   Another Nazca innovation was the so-called Nazca **geoglyphs**, large geometric and animal figures laid out in the dry highlands and on the valley slopes of the chiefdoms. Villagers constructed lines, triangles and trapezoids, as well as images of animals by removing dark-colored rocks and exposing the lighter sand underneath. These geoglyphs are unique to the Andes, and the closest parallel was not created until nearly a millennium later when the Incas arranged sacred objects outside their capital, Cuzco, in straight lines.

Geoglyphs: Long geometric lines and figures as well as outlines of animals formed in the desert by removing darker stones and exposing the lighter sand underneath.

Eventually, the Nazca came under the influence of the highland state of Wari, a later city-state in the Andes (see Chapter 15). This state expanded its political and cultural influence toward the southern Peruvian coast in the first half of the 700s CE and gradually transformed the identity of the Nazca chiefdoms.

>> Putting It All Together

In the period 600 BCE–600 CE, agriculture and life in villages became nearly universal. Only Australia remained outside this development from foraging to agrarian settlement. While remnants of foraging societies survived, notably in sub-Saharan Africa and in the Americas, humans in those two places developed in the same direction as those in Eurasia—toward cities, kingdoms, and long-distance luxury trade.

Agrarian-based urban culture, however, was a fragile achievement in Eurasia, sub-Saharan Africa, Mesoamerica, and the Andes. Irregularities of the weather and the slow improvement of food plant productivity meant that agriculture was a tenuous enterprise. Corncobs, especially, evolved only slowly toward greater length and were still quite short during the Maya period. Not until the time of the Aztecs did selective breeding produce corn of modern proportions. Dynastic cities regularly outstripped the natural resources of their local environments, as was the case in

interactive concept map

Meroë, Aksum, the Maya cities, and Teotihuacán. However, sooner or later, new city-based states arose.

The primary dynastic urban achievements were monumental architecture, sophisticated metal and textile craftsmanship, and forms of intellectual expression. In cities these crafts became the refined products of specialized workers who did not participate in farming.

Similarly, precocious intellectual achievements appeared both in nomadic contexts, as witnessed by the Borana calendar of the Kushite nomads in Kenya, and in small-town agricultural chiefdoms, as seen in the geoglyphs created in the desert landscape by the Nazca of Peru. By comparison, the intellectual pursuits in royal cities were much more sophisticated, such as the Mayan calendars and scripts.

Altogether, evolving largely on their own, both sub-Saharan Africa and the Americas made long strides in the period 600 BCE–600 CE toward expressing the same depth of humanity that was already on display in Eurasia. They did not yet have empires or possess the literary breadth that favored the rise of the visionaries of transcendence, hallmarks of the Middle East, India, and China during 600 BCE–600 CE. But their more compact cultures were not lacking in any of the overall patterns that characterized Eurasia.

Review and Relate

Thinking Through Patterns

Examine the ways historians approach the big questions of this chapter.

> **How does comparing and contrasting sub-Saharan Africa with the Americas during 600 BCE–600 CE help in understanding the agrarian–urban patterns of social and political development across the world?**

Innovations in world history usually originated in one specific place and then radiated outward to new populations through interactions among different peoples. Through adaptation, the new populations incorporated innovations into their own cultures. Given their isolation from Eurasia, sub-Saharan Africa and the Americas were partially or entirely limited to their own internal patterns of innovation. Encountering the same experiences and challenges as humans in Eurasia, their responses were remarkably comparable. Thus, the history of the world was not merely the history of peoples coming into more and more intensive contact with each other. It was also the history of peoples experiencing similar challenges without transcontinental interaction.

> **Where did chiefdoms, cities, and kingdoms arise in sub-Saharan Africa and why? On which forms of agriculture,**

Agrarian sub-Saharan Africa during 600 BCE–600 CE is an example where interaction with the Middle East—as well as, in some periods, the absence of interaction—formed the background for comparable processes of economic, social, and political developments. The middle Nile valley and the highlands of Ethiopia gave rise to the plow-based agrarian kingdoms of Meroë and Aksum, both receiving their original plows and grain from the Middle East and maintaining a lively trade for luxury goods with that region. By contrast, the West African inland Niger delta grew into the urbanized chiefdom of Jenné-jeno, with limited external interactions. Through interaction and adaptation, forms of farming as well as iron smelting (the latter perhaps received from the Middle East) traveled south in sub-Saharan Africa, together with the Bantu expansion.

Three regions in the Americas were favorable for the development of densely settled villages, some of which subsequently evolved into cities and kingdoms: Yucatán, with its Maya kingdoms; the Mexican Basin, with the city-state of Teotihuacán; and Peru, with the Moche and Nazca chiefdoms.

urbanization, and trade were they based?

≫ **Which areas in the Americas saw the development of a corn- and potato-based agriculture that did not depend on the plow, the wheel, and ironmaking?**

| Against the Grain

Consider this as a counterpoint to the main patterns examined in this chapter.

Nazca Lines and Speculation

Peruvian archaeologist Toribio Mejia Xesspe was the first scholar to describe the Nazca geoglyphs, which he viewed in 1927 from adjacent hills. The true extent of the glyphs, however, became known only once seen from the air. The pioneer of the aerial mapping of the site was Paul Kosok, an American historian who crisscrossed the area by plane during the 1940s. Further mapping was carried out by his assistant, Maria Reiche, a trained mathematician from Germany who devoted her life to recording and protecting the Nazca lines.

Based on the discovery that a number of lines converged at the winter and summer solstices, Reiche published her theory that the Nazca geoglyphs were elements of a complex astronomical calendar and observatory. Her theory did not find much support among later scholars, who demonstrated that only 20 percent of the glyphs had an astronomical significance. Reiche's theory, however, inspired popular writers to engage in frequently outlandish speculation about the site. For example, some have proposed that the Nazca lines were a version of GPS coordinates with which ancient civilizations encoded the locations of their sacred sites (Carl Munck, 2005); energy beams locating the earth in space (Alla Belocon, 2007); magnetic strips that in the distant past allowed a group of "Gliptolitic" earthlings to lift off to a space voyage (Kathleen Doore, 2008); or elements of an "exploded planet cult" among the Nazca (Allan Alford, 2000). Like many seemingly impossible large-scale works of engineering or art, the Nazca lines have proven particularly attractive to those who prefer outlandish speculation to evidence-based inquiry.

- Is it important to be aware of purely speculative theories of world history? For what reasons?

- What are some other feats of ancient engineering, architecture, or craft that seem to inspire speculative (or even fantastic) theories? Do historians have a particular responsibility to engage with or dispute "fringe" theories?

Key Terms

African spirituality 130
Chiefdom 123
Geoglyphs 141
Glyphic script 136

Kingdom 123
Phytoliths 128
Polytheism 134
Sahel 127

Tsetse Fly 129
Witchcraft 130

audio flashcards

For additional resources, please go to
www.oup.com/us/vonsivers.
Please see the Further Resources section at the back of the book
for additional readings and suggested websites.

Interaction and Adaptation in Western Eurasia

PERSIA, GREECE, AND ROME

At a banquet after vanquishing the Achaemenid [a-KEE-ma-nid] Persian Empire in 330 BCE, the world conqueror Alexander the Great (r. 336–323 BCE) had a violent confrontation with one of his leading commanders, Cleitus. Flatterers compared Alexander to the gods, and Alexander himself boasted that his conquests were far superior to those of his father, Philip. Cleitus, who had been an officer in Philip's army, angrily objected that it was the army that was the true victor. He further noted that he himself had saved Alexander's life in at least one of the battles against the Persians.

The exchange became heated, fueled by copious amounts of wine. Cleitus loudly complained about the way Alexander demanded that everyone, Greek and Persian, fall on their knees when entering his presence. As the shouting match continued, Alexander first threw an apple at Cleitus, then reached for his sword—which guards had prudently removed—and finally grabbed a javelin, killing Cleitus with a single thrust. Almost before the

ABOVE: **Detail from the Ara Pacis Augustae (Altar of Augustan Peace), commissioned by the Roman Senate in 13 BCE and consecrated in 9 BCE, to celebrate the end of the civil war after the triumphal return of Augustus (27 BCE–14 CE) from Spain and Gaul.**

≫ Why should the Middle East and Mediterranean Europe during the period 600 BCE–600 CE be studied as a single unit?

≫ What is transcendence, and why is it important to understand its importance in world history?

≫ Which elements characterize the institutions that grew out of the Middle Eastern monotheisms of Judaism and Christianity and the monism of Greek philosophy and science?

blow had been struck, Alexander regained his senses. Deeply remorseful, he grieved over the death of his companion.

Sources agree that the quarrel was about the question of Alexander remaining true to his Macedonian/Greek heritage or becoming a Persian "king of kings." Was he still a first among equals who would bring liberty to the Greeks of Asia? Or was he becoming a divinely mandated monarch who could command Persians and Greeks alike to obey him on bended knee? These questions arose as Alexander was on his way to becoming the exalted single ruler of the then known world.

The Middle East and Mediterranean during 600 BCE–600 CE was a culturally diverse area of intense military rivalry. However, already in the sixth century BCE, Greek, Jewish, and Iranian visionaries introduced very similar *monotheistic* (single personal god) and *monist* (single impersonal principle) forms of thought. This chapter focuses on one single region that had evolved from its Mesopotamian and Egyptian agrarian–urban origins and shared such basic patterns as imperialism, monotheism, and monism but was also torn apart by political and cultural differences. Intense internal interaction and adaptation characterized the Middle East and Mediterranean in the period of 600 BCE–600 CE.

Interactions between Persia and Greece

The Achaemenid Persian conquest of the Middle East, from Anatolia and Egypt in the west to northwestern India in the east, was relatively easy compared to the conquest of Greece, whose inhabitants resisted fiercely. Although Persia subjugated the Greek city-states of the Anatolian coast, it did not conquer the Greek mainland. A century and a half later, Alexander the Great unified Greece and led it to victory over Persia, establishing a short-lived Macedonian–Greek Empire. Alexander's generals divided the empire into three successor kingdoms under which politics stabilized until the Persians, under the Parthians and Sasanids, renewed the Persian imperial tradition.

The Origins of the Achaemenid Persian Empire

The Persians originated as agrarian villagers and nomadic horse and sheep breeders during the Bronze Age in central Asia south of the Ural Mountains. Toward the end of the third millennium BCE, groups of nomads migrated from the Urals southward to the Aral Sea region. The Persians were a branch that migrated sometime before the 800s BCE farther into the southwestern Iranian province of Fars, from which the name "Persia" is derived.

Persian Conquests   The first to appear in the historical record were the Medes, who had arrived from central Asia in southwest Iran at the end of the Bronze Age. They presided over a kingdom with provincial vassals adjacent to the Assyrian Empire in Fars. The head of one vassal family, Cyrus II the Great (r. ca. 550–530 BCE) of the Achaemenids, assumed the crown of the Persians in 550 BCE and Medes, and embarked on a series of imperial conquests. Outlined in a text on a clay cylinder, Cyrus describes himself as the representative of the high god Marduk on earth and his rule as that of peace and justice everywhere. He first expanded into Anatolia (modern-day Turkey), where he conquered the kingdom of Lydia [LIH-dee-ya]. Next, Cyrus turned to the neighboring Greek city-states of Ionia on the southwestern Anatolian coast. His generals besieged these cities until their inhabitants either surrendered or returned to the Greek mainland.

Cyrus himself was busy with the conquest of the Iranian interior and north, as far as Afghanistan. In 540 BCE he began his campaign against Neo-Babylonia in Mesopotamia, capturing the capital of Babylon a year later. The Phoenician city-states in Syria submitted voluntarily in the following years. Within a little more than a decade, Cyrus unified all of the Middle East except Egypt, which Persia conquered in 525 BCE (see Map 7.1). In Jerusalem, Cyrus permitted the rebuilding of the Temple by Jews returning from Mesopotamia in 538, where their ancestors had been deported a century and a half earlier (see Chapter 2).

Persian Arms   The Achaemenids achieved their conquests with the help of armed, mobile mounted archers as well as **cataphracts**—horsemen with heavy armor. The archers fought with composite bows, and the cataphracts with lances. Infantry soldiers armed with bows, arrows, shields, and javelins provided support for the cavalry.

Persian kings supplemented their armies with heavily armored infantry recruited from among the Anatolian Greeks. These foot soldiers, called **hoplites**, fought in ranks, called "phalanxes." They were equipped with spears, iron swords, shields, helmets, and protective armor. In close quarters, hoplite phalanxes were nearly invincible.

The Persian navy comprised as many as 1,200 galleys during its peak in the fifth century BCE. Apart from fighting naval battles against the Greeks, the navy also explored the western Mediterranean and the coast of Africa. Altogether, the Persian military was a formidable fighting machine.

Persian Administration   The Achaemenid Persian Empire encompassed Mesopotamia and Egypt as well as the Indus valley and had an estimated 15

Cataphracts: Heavily armed and protected cavalry soldiers.

Hoplites: Greek foot soldiers who fought in closed ranks, called "phalanxes."

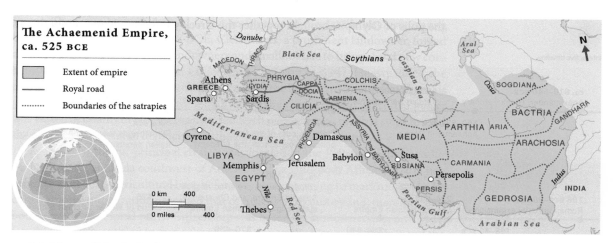

MAP **7.1 Achaemenid Persian Empire.**

Tyrtaeus, "Praise for the Virtuosity of the Citizen Soldier"

kings. Army service was of crucial importance in Sparta, and even women received vigorous physical training.

The village farmers in Sparta and the other Greek city-states were noncitizens of unfree status, in contrast to the free farmers in the Middle East. In Athens, small free farmers were at the center of early reform efforts. In Sparta, however, the farmers, called *helots*, were the descendants of surrounding peoples conquered by Sparta during its years of expansion.

Since, in addition to villagers, women were excluded from political participation, constitutional rule benefited only some in the Greek city-states. This was true even in the mid-fifth century BCE, when the final round of Athenian reforms under Pericles extended voting and office rights to all male citizens. Athens' "golden age" of democracy was in fact restricted to no more than one-third of the population at its height. In retrospect, Greece was not the only pioneer of constitutional rule: It shared this role with other early societies in Mesopotamia and India, although each adopted rule by assemblies independently and not as a result of interaction.

Greece and Persia Their maritime commercial wealth made the Greek city-states irresistible targets of Persian imperialism. When Athens supported the Ionian revolt of the Greek city-states in 499–494 BCE, the Persian monarchy found its justification to wage war against the Greeks. They suppressed the revolt and organized two invasions of the Greek mainland (492–490 and 480–479 BCE). To meet the invasion, the Greek city-states on the mainland united under the joint leadership of Athens and Sparta. In two battles, on land at Marathon (490 BCE) and on the sea at Salamis (480 BCE), the united Greeks repelled both Persian invasions. Greece managed to preserve its liberty and escape Persian imperial dominance. Soon, however, the Greek world was plunged into devastating internal conflict.

After the repulsion of the Persian invasions, Athenian–Spartan unity fell apart. As a substitute, Athens formed a league with as many as 200 poleis around the Aegean and Black Seas. When Athens diverted a portion of the league's membership contributions to the reconstruction of its Persian War–damaged citadel, the Acropolis, anger against this perceived self-service erupted into the Peloponnesian War (431–404 BCE). During this war, Sparta made itself the champion of liberation from what many Greek cities viewed as an Athenian empire. After depleting Athens' land forces, Sparta—with Persian financial support—built a navy, which won a brilliant victory over Athens, forcing the latter to sue for peace in 404 BCE.

Once involved again in Greek politics, the Achaemenid Persians stoked fears of Spartan dominance. During yet another round of hostilities, a coalition of city-states led by Athens and backed by Persia defeated Sparta. In the King's Peace of 386 BCE, the Persians granted the Greeks in Anatolia autonomy, provided they recognized Persia's dominance. Persian imperial hegemony over Anatolian Greece would last for about half a century.

Alexander's Empire and Its Successor Kingdoms

The one Greek area that remained outside Persian control was Macedonia, on the northern periphery of the Greek city-states. In the middle of the 300s BCE, a king, Philip II (359–336 BCE), unified Macedonia. He conquered the Greek city-states to the south, and his son Alexander continued the expansion with the conquest of Persia.

Alexander and His Successors In 337 BCE, Philip declared war on the Persian Empire. Just as Philip was getting ready to invade Anatolia, he was assassinated in a court intrigue. Philip's son Alexander took over both throne and campaign, setting off for Persia in 334 BCE. In three battles (334–330 BCE), Alexander defeated the Persian defenders. The Persian forces retreated into what is today Afghanistan. Alexander occupied the Persian royal towns and confiscated the Persian treasury. During a drunken revelry in the palace town of Persepolis, Alexander had the imperial palace burned down, as a final act of vengeance for the destruction of the Acropolis by the Persians.

East Meets West. A turbaned man stands next to a Corinthian capital in the Hellenistic city of Ai-Khanoum, founded in what is today northern Afghanistan—ancient Bactria—in the fourth century BCE, after Alexander's conquests. Ai-Khanoum was one of the focal points of Hellenism in the East. Archaeological excavations in the 1970s revealed a flourishing city, with a Greek-style theater, a huge palace, a citadel, a gymnasium, and various temples.

Alexander next invaded India, but monsoon rains and exhausted troops forced him to retreat. As he left, he appointed governors over northwest India. Under these governors, Greek culture entered the subcontinent (see Chapter 8). Alexander returned to the Middle East, where he died of a fever at the age of 33 (323 BCE). In just 11 years, he had turned the mighty Persian Empire into a Macedonian–Greek one (see Map 7.3).

Alexander's generals divided the empire among themselves, founding kingdoms, among which Antigonid Greece (276–167 BCE), Ptolemaic Egypt (305–30 BCE), and Seleucid southwest Asia (305–64 BCE) were the most important.

About 1 million Greeks emigrated during the 200s BCE to the Middle East, imprinting their **Hellenistic** (Greek-influenced) culture on urban life. Thus, even though the Macedonian–Greek Empire failed politically, its cultural legacy lasted for centuries.

Hellenism: Greek culture during the period from 323 BCE to 31 BCE.

Interactions between the Persian and Roman Empires

A century after Alexander's conquests, a resurgent Persia—in the shape of Parthia—emerged in the Seleucid kingdom. This coincided with Rome's expansion after the unification of Italy. On the periphery of the successor kingdoms of Alexander's Macedonian–Greek Empire, both Parthia and Rome pressed against the Antigonids, Seleucids, and Ptolemies. After conquering these kingdoms, Rome and Parthia eventually met in Anatolia and Syria in the early second century BCE. Neither, however, succeeded in eliminating the other. As a result, the Middle East and the Mediterranean remained politically divided.

Parthian Persia and Rome

Parthia was originally part of the Seleucid kingdom. In the 240s BCE distant relatives of the Achaemenid Persians migrated from central Asia to Parthia, where they defeated the Seleucid governor. The Parthians expanded their power and in 141 BCE conquered Iran and Mesopotamia. In 109 BCE, Mithridates II, "the Great"

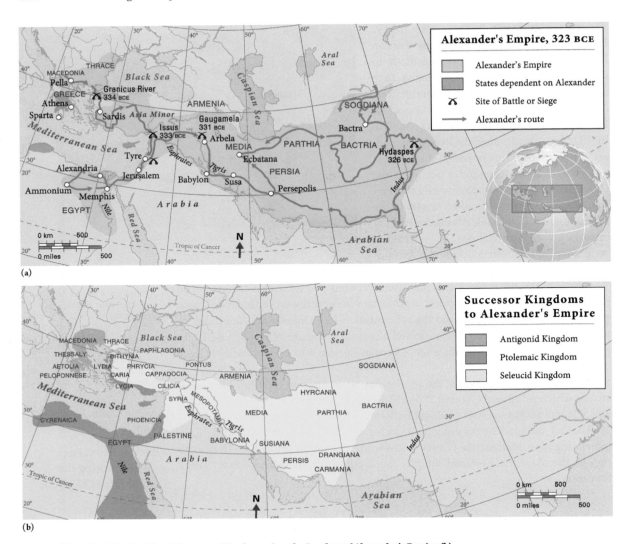

MAP **7.3** Alexander's Empire (a) and Successor Kingdoms after the Breakup of Alexander's Empire (b).

map analysis

(r. ca. 123–88 BCE), formally renewed the Persian Empire in his capital Ctesiphon (near modern Baghdad) by assuming the title "king of kings" and taking over the traditional Iranian pantheon of gods.

Parthian Diplomacy   Parthian Persia was a major diplomatic power. In 115, Wudi [woo-DEE] (r. ca. 140–87 BCE), the emperor of Han China, sent a diplomatic mission to Mithridates II, part of Wudi's ongoing efforts to secure his northern border against Turkic nomadic invaders and find allies among the nomads in Bactria. Although no alliance between Persia and China came to be, this first diplomatic contact opened up the Silk Road, which, for many centuries to come, was the main central Asian trade route.

At the other end of this empire, on the upper Euphrates River, the Parthian Persians established first contacts with Rome. Early efforts at diplomacy failed, however, and Rome and Persia soon came to blows.

Roman Republican Origins The western Mediterranean became part of the Middle Eastern and eastern Mediterranean agrarian centers in the course of the first millennium BCE. Phoenicians from the eastern Mediterranean established ports, the most important of which was Carthage, in today's Tunisia. Later on, Greeks established city-states in southern Italy and Sicily. In north-central Italy was the kingdom of the Etruscans, a local people who originally came from Anatolia and the Levant and settled in Italy ca. 2000 BCE. The kingdom included Rome, founded around 1000 BCE.

Around 500 BCE, the Romans overthrew their kings and created a **republic** (from Latin *res publica*, "public matter"), electing leaders and forming a constitutional government. Around 450 BCE, the Romans adopted the Twelve Tablets, a set of laws. A chief priest was responsible for administering the cult of the patron god, Jupiter, and fixing the calendar. The later polytheistic religious practices of the Romans resembled those of the Greeks and Persians.

Republic: State without a royal dynasty and with an elected executive.

Expansion of the Republic In the 300s BCE, when Rome began to unify the peninsula, it organized its citizen army into legions. The infantry of **legionaries** consisted of landed citizens able to pay for their weapons and armor. Wealthy Romans also manned the cavalry, including cataphracts, while small landholders made up the light infantry of skirmishers. With the help of these legionaries, Rome completed the unification of Italy and in three wars (246–146 BCE) conquered its strongest rival, Carthage.

Legionaries: Roman foot soldiers who fought in semiclosed ranks.

Around 200 BCE, Carthage sought to protect itself against Rome through an alliance with the kingdom of Antigonid Greece. In a first expansion east, the Romans defeated the Antigonids and, in 196 BCE, issued the Isthmus Declaration, according to which the Greeks of Greece, Anatolia, and farther east were to be "free" of Antigonid overlordship and governed by their own laws. When the Greeks rebelled in the middle of the second century BCE, they were ruthlessly repressed by the Romans, who eventually reduced Greece to provincial status.

With the Isthmus Declaration, Rome became an empire, in fact if not in name. (Historians usually date the official beginning of the Roman Empire to 27 BCE, when the Senate bestowed the title "Augustus" on Octavian.) In the wake of Rome's expansion into North Africa, Greece, and Anatolia during the second and first centuries BCE, a new ruling class of wealthy landowners emerged. These consisted of Italian aristocrats who had appropriated the land of smallholders absent for extended periods during their service as legionaries, turning these lands into large estates worked by tenant farmers or slaves. Ruling-class members also acquired conquered lands overseas, where they established estates worked by enslaved war captives.

Discharged legionaries and dispossessed farmers crowded Rome, while rebellious slaves on estates in southern Italy and Sicily rebelled. The most dangerous revolt was that of Spartacus in 73–71 BCE. Spartacus was an army deserter from Thrace in Greece who had been recaptured, enslaved, and trained as a gladiator. Spartacus devastated estates throughout Italy and held the Roman army in check for 3 years before it succeeded in defeating him.

Efforts by social reformers at improving the lot of the poor failed against the fierce resistance of the landowners. One reform that succeeded was that of Marius, who was senator from 107 to 85 BCE. He opened the army ranks to the landless and enlisted them for up to 20 years of service. Upon retirement, soldiers received

Augustus. The famous Augustus of Prima Porta, dated to 15 CE, is probably a copy of a bronze original commissioned by Augustus at some date after he was honored with the title "Augustus" in 27 BCE. Intended as a representation of the power and authority of Rome's first emperor, the statue depicts Augustus as barefooted, a symbolic image of gods and heroes.

Selections from "The Achievements of the Divine Augustus"

plots of land in conquered provinces. This reform benefited imperial expansion, but it also encouraged generals to use the army for their own ambitions.

In the middle of the first century BCE, three ambitious generals were vying for control of the empire. Julius Caesar (100–44 BCE), a magistrate, was from a prominent family and a successful conqueror of northwestern Europe. After his return from his conquests, in 48 BCE he defeated his last remaining rival, Pompey (106–48 BCE), also a consul and leader of the empire's strongest military forces. When Caesar then in addition to his consulate assumed several titles traditionally held by other magistrates, including that of "dictator for life," he provoked much opposition. In the Senate, several assassins killed Caesar, and a "triumvirate" of generals assumed power.

The triumvirate did not last. Civil war broke out, and the ultimate victor was Octavian (r. 31 BCE–14 CE). Octavian created a new constitutional order with himself as leader, always maintaining the pretense of being merely the first of the citizenry. In practice he possessed unlimited powers under the title of Augustus ("the Revered One"), bestowed on him in 27 BCE.

The Augustan Age   To consolidate his power, Augustus limited imperial expansion in the north to France, England, and Germany, west of the Rhine and Danube Rivers. He ordered the construction of a wall linking the two rivers to keep the Germanic tribes on the other side at bay. In the east, a series of wars (56 BCE–1 CE) with the Persian Parthian Empire ended inconclusively. Egypt, Syria, and Judea came under direct Roman rule; Armenia became a Roman client state; Upper Mesopotamia east of the Euphrates remained Parthian; and peace reigned between Rome and Parthia for two generations.

All 44 Roman provinces outside Italy had to pay poll and agricultural taxes, primarily to support a standing army, which Augustus reduced by half to the size of the earlier civil war armies. Tax money also supported the building and upkeep of roads and ports, as well as wheat subsidies and circuses for the inhabitants of Rome and other large cities. In contrast to the huge military, the number of civilian Roman administrators in the provinces was small. The Roman Peace (*pax romana*) rested more on the projection of military might than on a civilian administration, as in Han China.

The Sasanid Persian and Late Roman Empires

Parthia challenged Rome twice more (161–166 CE and 193–198 CE). It lost both times and had to give up the province of Upper Mesopotamia and much of its economic wealth. Divisions in the ruling class of the Parthians began to appear. In the early 200s, a priestly family in Fars assumed provincial leadership functions in opposition to the dynasty. Ardashir, a descendant of this priestly family, finally ended Parthian rule in 224 CE and declared himself king of kings, establishing the Sasanid Persian Empire (224–642 CE).

Roman Crisis   Just when Persian imperial power was rejuvenated through a new dynasty, the Roman Empire fell into a political and economic crisis that lasted half a century (234–285 CE). Some two dozen emperors followed each other in rapid succession on the throne, and for a while the empire even fragmented into three pieces.

In addition to the internal conflicts, Germanic tribes broke through the northern defenses and during 260–276 CE pillaged as far east as northern Italy. At the same time, both Rome and Persia were afflicted by an outbreak of mass disease in 251–266 CE, foreshadowing the plague of 541 (see "Patterns Up Close"). At the end of the 200s, it appeared that Rome was at its end.

Emperor Diocletian (r. 285–305 CE), however, salvaged the empire. He divided it into an eastern and a western half, doubled the number of provinces and civil administrators, and created military districts. He regularized tax collection, increased the number of legions, and created a mobile field army. Civil peace returned to the empire, albeit at the price of increased militarization.

Adoption of Monotheism   The early Sasanids were too busy consolidating their enormous territory to exploit the Roman crisis to the fullest. Although they invaded Roman territories in Syria and Anatolia, the Romans always regained control. Diocletian, after his reforms, was even able to push the border eastward to the Tigris River.

In the first half of the 300s, while Rome and Persia continued their inconclusive wars, both empires underwent religious transformation. They began to shift away from polytheism and toward the elevation of monotheism to the status of state religion. During the previous polytheist millennia in the Middle East and the Mediterranean, kings and emperors had supported imperial temple priesthoods in their capitals in return for the justification of their rule. But when the Romans and Persians suffered internal crises, rulers became aware of the need for a unifying single religious bond.

At the beginning of the reign of Emperor Constantine I, "the Great" (r. 306–337 CE), Christianity's adherents numbered about 10 percent of the Roman population. Christianity had begun three centuries earlier with the preaching of Jesus of Nazareth. Since Christians refused to recognize the pantheon of Roman gods, however, they were periodically persecuted. But their numbers recovered and by the early 300s, their existence in the Empire had become visible enough for contenders to the imperial throne to take Christianity seriously as a potential source for support.

General Constantine appealed to this support when he fought his way in 312 to power in Rome. A year later, as emperor, he issued an edict of toleration, and in 325 he presided over the Council of Nicaea, which issued the **Nicene Creed** as the common doctrinal platform among Christians. Baptized shortly before his death, Constantine can be considered the first Christian Roman emperor. Several pagan emperors succeeded Constantine before Christianity became the sole state religion, with the closing of the Temple of Jupiter in Rome in 380.

In Persia, under the sponsorship of Shapur II (r. ca. 307–379), Zoroastrian priests began to write down the Yasht, the oldest holy scripture of Zoroastrianism. The shahinshahs, with large Jewish and Christian minorities in Mesopotamia, made Zoroastrianism the preferential religion in ca. 350, with Christianity and Judaism accorded a protected status. Thus, both empires sought to strengthen internal unity through the adoption of a single monotheistic faith in the course of the fourth century.

Nicene Creed: Basic Christian doctrine defining faith as belief in God, the Father; Jesus Christ, his son of the same substance; and the Holy Ghost.

Nomadic Invasions   The Roman and Sasanid Empires experienced severe disruptions from the migrations of peoples across Eurasia. The migrations began in the

The Plague of Justinian

At the end of the 500s, neither the Roman nor the Sasanid Empire was as populous and wealthy as before the nomadic invasions from the north. In addition, for the first time (in 541 CE), a mass epidemic, the bubonic plague, hit the world, breaking out first in the Roman Empire and traveling thereafter to Persia and, in cycles of 15 years, by the 600s CE as far as China and England. This plague, recorded as the "Plague of Justinian"—it sickened the emperor himself for several weeks—dramatically reduced population levels everywhere. The Plague of Justinian originated either in East Africa or in Burma. It reached the Mediterranean through black rats infested with fleas traveling in ships on the Indian Ocean and the Red Sea.

Historians know now that for the plague to become a pandemic, average temperatures must have declined. Fleas are most likely to jump from rats to humans at 59–68 degrees Fahrenheit. Such a temperature decline might have occurred a few years prior to 541 CE, with the eruption of the volcano Krakatau in Indonesia in 535 CE, the ashes of which obscured the sun for years. Although the climate returned to normal a few years later, recurrent cycles of the plague every decade or two until well into the 700s CE prevented population levels from recovering.

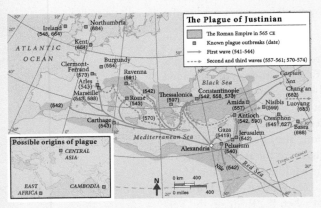

MAP 7.4 **The Plague of Justinian.**

mid-300s CE when the western branch of the Huns—nomads in the steppes of central Asia east of the Ural Mountains—moved westward and southward on the Silk Road. During their journey westward, the Huns grew into a federation of nomads, farmers, and town dwellers of mixed ethnic and linguistic composition.

As the Huns entered the Russian plains, they encountered local Germanic farming populations, whom they defeated. Other Germanic peoples, such as the Visigoths, fled from the Huns and negotiated their entry into the Roman Empire. In the early 400s CE, both Hunnish and Germanic peoples overcame the defenses of the Romans, poured into the western half of the Roman Empire, and eventually ended the western line of emperors, an event remembered as the fall of Rome in 476 CE (see Map 7.5).

The emperors in the eastern half of the empire withstood the migrants' threat, in part because of Constantinople's strategic location. The Sasanids succumbed to invasions in 483–485 and were forced to pay tribute for a number of years. A third branch of Huns invaded the Gupta Empire of India toward the end of the 400s CE. In the mid-500s the Sasanids eventually recovered from the invasions, but the Guptas did not. Further compounding matters, plague struck the Middle East and Europe in 541 CE (see "Patterns Up Close").

Roman and Persian Recovery The architect of the reconstruction of the Roman Empire was Justinian I, "the Great" (r. 527–565 CE). Justinian's generals

Observers in various cities of the Roman Empire have left vivid accounts. People infected by the plague bacillus developed a high fever, followed by swelling of the lymph nodes in the groin, the armpits, and the neck. Most people died within days. Although quarantine was practiced, there was no known medicine against the plague. Many clerical observers at the time were convinced that sinfulness was what had attracted God's wrath. For us modern observers, the most important lesson of the Plague of Justinian is the evidence it provides of how interconnected the various parts of Eurasia and Africa were toward the middle of the 500s CE (see Map 7.4).

The Plague of Justinian shows us also how climate and disease followed their own natural patterns in world history. By killing up to one-third of the population and keeping population levels low for at least a century, the Plague of Justinian severely impacted city-state, kingdom, and empire patterns. The reduced population levels led to increased labor costs and food shortages; it also made survivors wealthier. Plagues hit states and societies with impartial ferocity. Justinian's plague favored neither Rome nor Persia and thus had a more quantitative than lasting qualitative effect on the process of world history.

Questions

- What does Justinian's plague tell us about the interconnectedness of Afro-Eurasia at this time?

- How does understanding the impact of disease and climate on human societies add a new dimension to the patterns of world history?

reconquered most of the western Mediterranean and Italy from the Germanic invaders. As the empire stabilized, prosperity returned. With improved tax revenues, Justinian was able to finance reform measures, including a reorganization of the legal system. Justinian's *Codex Justinianus* later became the legal foundation for the Roman Empire's successor, the Byzantine Empire (610–1453 CE), as well as the Islamic empire of the Abbasids (750–1258 CE), together with Persian law.

Justinian also oversaw the construction of Hagia Sophia ("Holy Wisdom"), until the construction of Saint Peter's in Rome, the largest Christian church. Begun in 532, Hagia Sophia combines Roman features with new elements. It was designed to provide for a large open space, capped by a huge dome surrounded by windows.

In Persia, Khosrow I (r. 531–579) rebuilt the Sasanid Empire. He began his rule in the aftermath of a civil war that pitted Mazdak, a renegade Zoroastrian priest and social reformer, and the dynasty against the Zoroastrian priesthood and the ruling class. In this war, the dynasty confiscated landed estates from the ruling class and distributed its lands to small military landowners (*dihqans*). Khosrow, scion of the dynasty but siding with the ruling class, seized power and had Mazdak executed, ending the social reforms. But he maintained the military reforms in favor of the *dihqans*, thereby distancing himself from the traditional ruling class.

Like Justinian, Khosrow also pursued military expansion. In 530 CE, Khosrow reopened hostilities against the Romans. In the north, Khosrow defeated European and Turkic tribes, expanding the border eastward to Turkistan. A plea from the

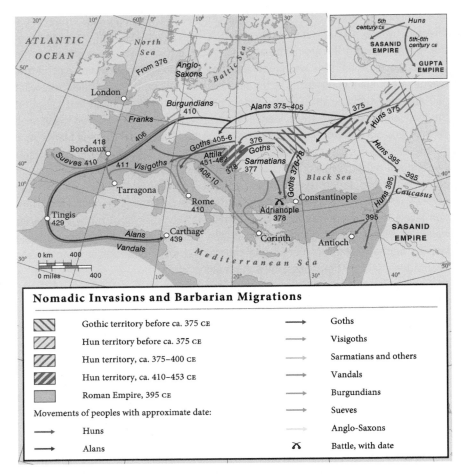

MAP **7.5** **Nomadic Invasions and Barbarian Migrations into the Roman Empire, 375–450 CE.**

king of Yemen in southwestern Arabia to aid him in his efforts to repel a Roman-backed Ethiopian invasion brought Khosrow's fleet to southern Arabia in 575–577 CE, and Arab vassal kings established Persian control over much of the rest of Arabia. In contrast to Rome, the reach of Persia was much expanded at the end of the sixth century.

Adaptations to Monotheism and Monism in the Middle East

Rome and Sasanid Persia were strong unitary empires at the end of the 500s CE. Both were religiously unified through the adoption of the monotheisms of Christianity and Zoroastrianism. The adoption of these religions came at the end of a lengthy process that originated at the beginning of the Achaemenid Persian Empire (550–330 BCE). Visionaries of religious monotheism and philosophical monism emerged at that time, but had only small numbers of followers. It took many centuries before followers of each faith achieved imperial sanction as the preferred or obligatory state religion.

Challenge to Polytheism: The Origins of Judaism, Zoroastrianism, and Greek Philosophy

Religious visionaries of the sixth century BCE arose in a polytheistic environment. All polytheisms had one basic characteristic in common: The gods all descended from something unnamable that existed prior to creation. Unity preceded multiplicity, and even though perceived reality consisted of both, in thought they could be separated from each other. Unity **transcended** multiplicity.

Transcendence: Realm of reality above and beyond the limits of sensory experience.

Judaism   The concept of transcendence occurred more or less simultaneously during the 600s BCE in Mesopotamia, Iran, and Anatolia. The historically most influential case was that of an anonymous Jewish visionary, whom scholars dubbed "Deutero-Isaiah" or "Second Isaiah" (fl. ca. 560 BCE) in Mesopotamia. After their deportation by the Neo-Babylonians from Palestine (597–582 BCE), as we saw in Chapter 2, a majority of Israelites lived in Babylonian exile. After the establishment of the Achaemenid Persian Empire and its subsequent conquest of Babylonia and Syria, including Palestine, Israelite scribes began to compile their religious traditions from Palestine. They became the founders of what is called today "Judaism," and one of them, Deutero-Isaiah, was the first to declare Yahweh [YAH-way], or God, to be the only god of the Jews. In Deutero-Isaiah's words, there are no gods but Yahweh, who is the single, invisible creator and sustainer of the world. He is transcendent—a conceptual reality beyond the sensory or empirical reality of this world.

Some of Deutero-Isaiah's followers petitioned the Persian king to allow them to leave for Jerusalem and restore the temple destroyed by the Neo-Babylonians. The Persian king issued the permit in 538 BCE, and a group of monotheists returned to Jerusalem to construct the Second Temple (completed in 515 BCE). A new priesthood took up residence in the Temple and administered the emerging monotheistic faith of Judaism.

Zoroastrianism   Zoroastrians attribute their origin to Zoroaster (also called Zarathustra), who is supposed to have lived around 1200 BCE, long before the rise of monotheism. The earliest recorded references to Zoroaster's teachings, however, date only to the rise of the Achaemenid Persian Empire in 550 BCE. These teachings were handed down orally by a priestly class, the magi. The main oral text is the Avesta.

The earliest text forms the section called "Yasht" in the Avesta. It speaks of the glories of Ahuramazda (God), the last of which, bestowed on humankind at the end of history, is that of the savior who will restore the world. Other sections of the Avesta describe a time of trial and tribulation just prior to the arrival of the savior. This period of devastation was later called the "apocalypse" (Greek *apocalypsis*, revelation). These themes—Savior or Messiah and apocalypse—are trademarks of Zoroastrian monotheism. In later centuries they became central in Judaism, Christianity, and Islam. They replaced the polytheistic notion of a shadowy afterlife in the underworld with salvation of the righteous in God's transcendent kingdom.

Zoroastrian Fire Temple. Consisting of a cube with a superimposed dome, this Zoroastrian temple, one of the best preserved, is located outside Baku in present-day Azerbaijan. Zoroastrianism was prevalent in the Caucasus region until the arrival of Christianity, and then, Islam.

It appears that under the Parthians the magi introduced traditional Iranian and Anatolian cults of fire, maintained in fire temples, into Zoroastrianism. How far the fire temples evolved into congregational places for priests and laity, however, is still a matter of conjecture.

Greek Philosophy   The first Greek philosophers are known to us: Thales, Heraclitus, and Thales' pupil Anaximander, who lived during the first half of the 500s in the city of Miletus on the Anatolian coast. Of these, Thales of Miletus is usually credited with beginning the Greek philosophical tradition of divorcing scientific explanations of natural phenomena from mythical forces. In contrast to Judaism and Zoroastrianism, Anaximander formulated the impersonal, or *monist*, "principle of the infinite" as the invisible cause underlying the world (*kosmos*). A debate over principles ensued after Anaximander and his successors proposed several other cosmic principles. This debate became the basis for the rise of the mathematical and physical sciences.

The Athenian Plato (ca. 427–347 BCE) extended the debate from principles in nature to a principle common to all areas of reality, calling it Being. In his thinking, called "philosophy" (love of wisdom), Being is embodied in the transcendent forms of Truth, Justice, and Beauty. These forms, so Plato argued, represent objective standards against which all earthly assertions about truth, justice, and beauty in daily life are to be measured. Anaximander's monism thus led to science and philosophy.

The Break from Polytheism to Monotheism   The common thread linking the three visions of transcendence is that they all involve transcendent symbols, such as God or Being, which can only be thought by the mind, not experienced by the senses. Polytheist reality, however, is undivided, with gods and humans sharing a world in which everything is felt by the senses. Given this contrast, it is not surprising that monotheism was incompatible with polytheism. Over time, polytheism disappeared from the Middle East and Mediterranean.

Toward Religious Communities and Philosophical Schools

The small Jewish community that built the Second Temple in Jerusalem grew more rapidly than the Zoroastrian fire temple communities and Greek philosophical schools and led the way to monotheism. It spawned a Jewish reform movement, Christianity, which in turn changed the Roman Empire from polytheism to monotheism.

Judaism in Palestine   The Achaemenid Persian kings allowed the Jews, who had moved from Mesopotamia to Palestine and had founded the Second Temple in Jerusalem, a large degree of autonomy. Under their successors, the Ptolemaic and Seleucid kings in the states after Alexander the Great, this autonomy declined. These kings introduced Greek-Hellenistic institutions and culture into Palestine, forcing the Jews to allow polytheism and philosophy in their midst. The Jews successfully rebelled, establishing the autonomous Hasmonean (also called "Maccabean") kingdom (140–37 BCE), which sought to limit the Hellenization of society.

However, educated Jews learned Greek and read the writings of the Greek philosophers. Scribes translated Jewish scriptures into Greek, and in the second half of the 200s BCE, prayer houses, called "**synagogues**," emerged in cities and towns. The monotheism of Yahweh continued to be exclusively administered by priests. But preachers in the synagogues, called "Pharisees," made this monotheism increasingly popular among ordinary Jews.

Synagogues: Jewish meeting places for prayer and legal consultation.

In the first century BCE, the Romans and Persian Parthians replaced the Seleucids and the Herodians replaced the Hasmoneans in Palestine. The Jews interacted not only with the culture of Hellenism but also with the culture of the Romans, their new overlords, and the Parthian Persians, their new neighbors to the east. Many Jews adapted to the Roman philosophical school of the Stoics (who advocated an ethics in harmony with the laws of nature) and to the Persian Zoroastrian-inspired apocalypse. Elements of philosophy and the apocalypse, coming together in the teachings of the Pharisees in the synagogues, found widespread followers in the Jewish population. Palestine was a cauldron of cultural influences—some monotheistic, others monist, many clashing with polytheism.

The Origins of Christianity   It was from this cauldron that the Jewish reform movement of Christianity arose in the first century CE. The earliest scriptures of the Christians, contained in the New Testament, describe the founding figure, Jesus of Nazareth, as a preacher in Galilee in northern Palestine. After he was baptized by John, Jesus is reported to have left the Mosaic as well as the Pharisaic law aside, and to have preached instead what he expressed as the "law of love" (Mark 12:29–30). Only if one loved God and one's neighbor as one loved oneself would one acquire the proper understanding of law and be prepared for the apocalypse and salvation in the heavenly kingdom soon to come.

When Jesus is reported to have gone to Jerusalem during Passover, he provoked the Temple priests by overturning the tables of the money changers and sellers of sacrificial birds to Jews performing the required animal sacrifices. According to the New Testament, his actions initiated the chain of events which ended with the priests turning Jesus over to the Roman governor, Pontius Pilate. The governor understood Jesus as having declared himself king of the Jews, an act of treason in the Roman Empire punishable by death on the cross.

Again according to the New Testament, shortly after Jesus's death, miraculous resurrection, and ascension to the right side of God, the Pharisee Paul of Tarsus converted to Jesus's law of love. Paul retained the concept of the apocalypse but also argued that salvation had already begun and would soon be completed with Jesus's return at the head of the heavenly kingdom. Paul traveled and preached to Christian communities which formed in the Roman Empire during the middle of the first century CE.

The Christian Church   Missionaries preached Christianity in the Roman Empire from scriptures that evolved in the first three centuries CE. During this time, the first canon of accepted writings, the New Testament, was assembled. A hierarchy of bishops and priests preached from these scriptures to laypeople. From early on, however, Christians were divided on how to understand the New Testament. The philosophically educated tended to interpret it figuratively—that is, by reading their philosophical concepts into scripture. Others, opposed to Greek philosophy, preferred a literal interpretation. A struggle over the integration of scripture and philosophy into a single Christian civilization ensued.

Principal figures in the struggle were theologians, called "Church Fathers." One of the most important was Augustine (354–430 CE). His two main works are the *Confessions*, in which he describes his conversion to Christianity and reflections on spirituality, and *The City of God*, in which he defends Christianity against the accusation by many Romans that its adoption as the state religion in 380 contributed to the decline of the empire. Thanks to the Church Fathers, the church was set on a path of merging monotheism and philosophy, as the basis for a Christian civilization.

As a result of the Church Fathers' theological works and debates in church councils during the period of ca. 400–600, three main Christian denominations evolved. The Orthodox Catholic Church, supported by the Roman emperors, patriarchs of Constantinople, and the pope in Rome adopted a Christology that defined Jesus Christ as being simultaneously fully human and fully divine. The Eastern Syriac Church, under the Catholicos (Patriarch), adhered to nearly the same Christology but was subject to the Sasanid shahinshahs. The Coptic Church in Egypt and Jacobite Church in Syria, by contrast, defined Christ as possessing only a single, divine nature from birth. Both Copts and Jacobites, subject to the Roman emperors but bitterly opposed to the two-nature Christology of the Orthodox-Catholic and Eastern Syriac Churches, represented a general tendency in early Christianity toward the divinization of Jesus. This tendency was cut short, however, in the 600s with the emergence of Islam, in which Jesus is viewed as entirely human (see Chapter 10).

Mural from Dura-Europos on the Euphrates. The city, founded in 303 BCE, was home to a sizable Jewish community whose synagogue was adorned with murals in the Parthian-Hellenistic style. Shown here is a depiction of the infant Moses being rescued from the Nile.

The Beginnings of Science and the Cultures of Kings and Citizens

Monotheism and philosophy entered society early on during the Jewish Second Temple kingdom in Palestine. In the Persian and Roman Empires this incorporation, in the form of preferred or state religions, took longer. Greek science became important in Ptolemaic Egypt (305–30 BCE). The Ptolemies provided state support for the development of mathematics, physics, astronomy, and the applied science of mechanics. The other, inherited forms of cultural expression—painting, sculpture, architecture, and literature—remained within traditional polytheistic confines. Nevertheless, in Greece and Rome these latter cultural forms underwent substantial innovation, influenced by Hellenism as well as Parthian and Sasanid Persia.

The Sciences at the Library of Alexandria

The Ptolemies and their Roman successors sponsored a new type of institution of Greek learning, the institute for advanced study. Centers of research, principally libraries and museums, flourished at Pergamon, Alexandria, and elsewhere. The Library of Alexandria (280 BCE–ca. 400 CE) was devoted primarily to research in the mathematical and natural sciences. The Library featured holdings of half a million scrolls, laboratories for anatomical dissection, an astronomical observatory, and botanical gardens.

The most developed branch of the sciences at the Library was geometry. Euclid (fl. ca. 300 BCE), one of the founders of the Library, provided geometry with its basic definitions and proofs in his *Elements*. In addition to geometry, mathematicians laid the foundations for algebra. In the absence of a practical Greek number system, however, algebra had to await the Muslims and the Arabic numeral system (originally devised in India)—to evolve fully.

Alexandrian geographers and astronomers calculated the earth's circumference and tilt and formulated the first heliocentric astronomical theory, according to which the earth spins around the sun. Unfortunately, this theory was rejected, and the opposite theory, which placed the earth at the center of the planetary system, became dominant. Claudius Ptolemy (ca. 87–170 CE) devised such a precise geometric system of the planets' movements that his geocentric view dominated until the work of Copernicus in the sixteenth century. In addition to astronomy, physics also flourished at the Library, exemplified by the work of Archimedes (287–212 BCE), who investigated the behavior of floating bodies in the new science of hydrostatics.

Star lists from Ptolemy's *Almagest*

The Library came to its end under unknown circumstances at the beginning of the 400s CE. Its legacy, however, was such that later Islamic rulers resumed the tradition of sponsoring institutes for advanced study.

Royal Persian Culture and Arts

As heirs of both Achaemenid Persian and Greek traditions, the Parthians forged a new synthesis between inherited styles and Greek-Hellenistic elements, while maintaining a palace culture of their own. For example, courtiers listened to bards who recited the exploits of Greek heroes. Other bards and minstrels traveled among aristocratic families, composing stories of their masters' courtly loves and intrigues or their exploits in battles against nomadic invaders from central Asia. After the end of the Parthians, these stories grew in both length and complexity. They exist today in a modern Persian version, called the *Book of Kings* (*Shahname* [Sha-ha-na-MAY]), compiled by the poet Firdosi [Feer-dow-SEE] in the eleventh century CE.

The Sasanids were major transmitters of Indian texts to the Middle East and Mediterranean. Examples include collections of animal fables, instruction manuals on chess, and medical texts complete with discussions of anatomy, diseases, and herbs. All these texts, which were both useful and entertaining, played important roles at the Sasanid court.

In architecture, the characteristic features of Sasanid palaces were the monumental dome and the barrel vault. The central audience hall of the palace in the capital, Ctesiphon, built ca. 250 CE, had a barrel vault 118 feet high. Other palaces had "squinched" domes of up to 45 feet across, covering square audience and banquet halls. *Squinches* were curved triangular transition spaces between the dome and the corners of the halls. In order to counter the outward thrust of the dome's weight, buttresses supported the walls on the outside. The techniques of both barrel vaulting and the dome were transmitted from Sasanid Persia to Christian Armenia, Rome, and ultimately western Europe, where they appeared in church architecture.

Greek and Roman Civic Culture and Arts

With the disappearance of kings and aristocracies in the Greek city-states during the sixth century BCE, wealthy citizens began to patronize artists and even created works of literature, sculpture, painting, and architecture themselves. Greeks began to experiment with individual shapes, types, and models, seeking realistic representation in their art.

As in Mesopotamia and Egypt, seasonal festivals were of great importance in Greece. In contrast to Mesopotamia and Egypt, however, Greek city culture encouraged personal artistic expression, and festivals became occasions for the composition of songs and poems whose authors were remembered by name.

Monumental Barrel Vault of the Sasanid Royal Reception Hall, Ctesiphon.

Greek Literature and Art   The earliest Greek literature dates to the eighth century BCE. The period 750–600 BCE was a time of close cultural contact between the rising Greek city-states and the Neo-Assyrian Empire, which dominated Syria and Anatolia. Assyrian versions of the Mesopotamian epic and creation myths, *Gilgamesh* and *Enuma Elish*, made their way to the Greeks, where they were incorporated into Greek culture.

This incorporation was the work of two writers, Homer (fl. ca. 730 BCE) and Hesiod (fl. ca. 700 BCE), both from Greek city-states in Anatolia, and both familiar with Mesopotamian literature. Homer composed two epics in the form of extended poems, the tragedy *Iliad* and the narrative legend *Odyssey*. Hesiod's *Theogony* begins with "Chaos, the Abyss," out of which the earth, or Gaia, came into being. The rest of the *Theogony* is devoted to telling the stories of some 300 divinities descended from Chaos and Gaia. Three of the first four generations of deities destroyed each other violently. The fourth, the Olympians, became the present pantheon of gods, with Zeus as the patriarch. The Greek theater emerged around 500–480 BCE out of the rituals of the Dionysiac cult. During the annual Dionysiac processions, groups of citizens competed for the presentation of the best tragedy or comedy. These competing groups, or *choruses*, performed through declamation and dance. Tragedy developed out of Dionysiac myths and comedy from the Dionysiac processions.

Among the most important writers who composed for the early Greek stage were the tragedians Aeschylus, Sophocles, and Euripides, as well as the comedian Aristophanes. In *The Persians*, Aeschylus developed the theme of the Greeks defending their freedom from Persian tyranny, a theme which in the course of time changed into the Europeans defining their culture as superior to that of the Other, the inferior Orient. In this chapter, which focuses on Persia, Geece, and Rome as equal partners in a single, undivided region of the Middle East and the Mediterranean Sea, we seek to overcome the otherization of the Orient. In other respects as well, all four authors of tragedies, and many of their successors, continue to exercise a profound influence on the evolution of culture today.

In the fifth century BCE, Greek sculptors abandoned the traditional Middle Eastern symbolic royal style that required figures to project dignity and solemnity. Instead, sculptors began to explore physical movement and emotion. In terms of themes, poses, and individuality, Greek vase paintings and sculptures achieved a remarkably wide range, from athletes exerting themselves to serene models of human beauty. Faithful to their democratic polis culture, Greek sculptors and painters turned from a symbolic to a realistic style of representation.

Greek Realism. The Greeks used decorated stelae to mark the burial places of the dead in much the same way we use tombstones today. This intimate relief, from about 450 BCE, memorializes a young girl. The treatment of the child's body is realistic—note the chubby arms—and the way the girl tenderly holds her pet doves transforms the little scene into a touching story.

Roman Literature and Art   Greece influenced Roman culture early on. By the middle of the third century BCE, Romans had translated Greek plays and poetry into Latin, and prose writings on political and historical themes, also modeled on Greek precursors, appeared. In his epic poem *The Aeneid*, Virgil (70–19 BCE) played down the influence of Greece by positing the origins of Rome in Troy, the rival of Greece. In his Odes, Horace (65–8 BCE) glorified courage, patriotism, piety, justice, and a respect for tradition, which he regarded as uniquely Roman virtues. These writers viewed Rome as the culmination of civilization.

to the prevailing view of Athenian democracy?

- In what ways does this image of women in Athens compare and contrast with women's status in other ancient civilizations?

Several indicators point to policies of marked gender inequality. Athenian women could neither vote nor own property. Their marriages were often arranged, primarily for monetary gain; once married, women could not sue for divorce. A married woman was under the constant control of guardian, either her husband or her nearest male relatives. Women were required to bring dowries into the marriage, which were immediately assigned to the husband's control.

For the most part, women's roles consisted of bearing and raising children, inculcating in them the values of the polis, and managing the household. Because women were believed to be more emotional and driven by sexual passion than men, they were seen to pose a threat to stability. Thus, Athenian women were largely confined to the home, although they frequented the marketplace and civic center and occasionally attended festivals. Women also participated in funerals, weddings, and religious rituals, and some were priestesses. Educated women routinely accompanied men as companions to plays and dinner parties. At the bottom of the social ladder were slave women and prostitutes.

Why were Athenian women relegated to second-class citizenship? In a patriarchal society like Athens, men determined cultural norms, which reflected negative views of women. For example, in Euripides' *Medea* the protagonist laments "If only children could be got by some other way without the female sex.... If women didn't exist, human life would be rid of all its miseries." And in his *Politics* Aristotle observes that "the male is by nature superior, and the female inferior; and the one rules, and the other is ruled; this principle, of necessity, extends to all mankind."

Key Terms

Cataphracts 147	Nicene Creed 155	Synagogues 161
Hellenism 151	Oracles 148	Transcendence 159
Hoplites 147	Republic 153	
Legionaries 153	Shahinshah 148	

audio flashcards

For additional resources, please go to
www.oup.com/us/vonsivers.
Please see the Further Resources section at the back of the book for additional readings and suggested websites.

Empires and Visionaries in India

I
t was one of the most intriguing meetings of the ancient world, though
no one could have foreseen its significance. By the age of 30, Alexander
the Great had already become the most successful military leader the
world had ever seen. However, the conquest of northern India had so far
eluded him. As Alexander prepared to invade the most powerful Indian
state, Magadha, he retreated to the northern city of Taxila, near the modern
capital of Islamabad in Pakistan, to replenish his forces and rethink his
situation.

While in Taxila, Alexander met with a man identified by his biographers
simply as "Sandrokoptros," who had recently fled the Magadhan court after
a failed attempt to overthrow its government. Though we can only speculate
about their meeting, Alexander's use of local politics in his past military campaigns suggests that he sought to take advantage of Sandrokoptros's knowledge of Magadha in planning his attack. The intelligence Alexander obtained
must have been discouraging, for he soon abandoned his plans to invade
India and, facing the possibility of mutiny among his men, withdrew to the
safer confines of Persia, where he died in 323 BCE. Following Alexander's
death, one of his commanders, Seleucus Nikator [si-LOO-kus Ni-KAY-tor],
gained control of the eastern reaches of his empire. By 321 BCE, however,
Seleucus Nikator found his territory around the Indus River threatened
by a powerful new Indian state created by none other than Alexander's

INDIA, 800 BCE–800 CE

ABOVE: **Buddhism in its many forms remains one of the world's most widespread religions. The detail on the Sanchi Stupa shown here
depicts motifs typical of this early form of sacred structure found throughout the Buddhist world.**

Seeing Patterns

≫ Think about the reasons for the spread of Buddhism inside and outside of India. How have historians seen the decline of Buddhism in India?

≫ What do you consider to be the most influential patterns in Indian history to this point? Why?

≫ Do you think some of Ashoka's ideas could be implemented by governments today? Why or why not?

former ally, Sandrokoptros. It was not until the end of the eighteenth century CE, however, that the shadowy "Sandrokoptros" was identified by English Sanskrit scholars as Chandragupta Maurya [chahn-drah-GUP-tah MOR-y-ah], the founder of India's first and largest indigenous empire.

The meeting between Alexander and Chandragupta symbolized a key future pattern of Indian history: intensifying exchanges of ideas and goods between peoples of vastly different cultures and beliefs.

Indian visionaries and innovators have made profound contributions to patterns of world history. In turn, India's place as a crossroads of trade and invasion continually brought innovation from outside. Many centuries later, the lore of India's wealth and culture would fire the imaginations of Europeans and drive them to seek out the connection first established by Alexander and Chandragupta.

Patterns of State Formation in India: Republics, Kingdoms, and Empires

By 1900 BCE, people were abandoning the agrarian–urban center of the Indus valley and migrated eastward to the Punjab and Ganges valley, where they drew on their past experience as they built the new agrarian–urban centers of northern India. State formation proceeded rapidly. The earliest traces of villages date to about 1200 BCE. Thereafter, polities emerged quickly, in the form of warrior republics and kingdoms. Both flourished in the early first millennium BCE.

A gradual consolidation process set in from about 800 BCE onward, with a few kingdoms emerging as the strongest states, while the warrior republics disappeared. The process of state formation reached a first peak with the Mauryan Empire, which united northern and central India and experimented with Buddhism. State and religion were firmly united in the Hindu Gupta Empire (320–550 CE), which, along with its contemporary, Christian Rome, became the first states in world history to lay the foundation for a religious civilization.

The Road to Empire: The Mauryas

In the early first millennium BCE, the emerging states along the Ganges River valley developed political systems ranging from republics to centralized monarchies whose rulers were accorded god-like status. The agricultural advances made in these areas, particularly the dikes, ponds, flooded fields, and drainage systems necessary for growing rice, resulted in the emergence of wealthy, centralized states led by Magadha and Kosala, along with the lesser kingdoms of Vatsya and Avanti farther west (see Map 8.1).

During the half century before Alexander attempted to expand his empire into northern India, Mahapadama Nanda [mah-hah-PAH-dah-mah NAHN-dah], a member of the *shudra* (or lowest) *varna*, seized power in Magadha and conquered Vatsya and Avanti. By the 330s BCE, the taxes imposed by the Nandas brought unprecedented wealth to the Magadhan capital of Pataliputra [pah-tah-lee-POO-trah]. The Nandas, however, were not alone in their aspirations for universal empire.

Chandragupta Maurya   Little is known of Chandragupta's early life. It is believed that he was taught by the philosopher Kautilya, whose *Arthashastra* became the most influential political treatise in Indian history (see Chapter 3). Kautilya was instrumental in the young Chandragupta's first attempt to seize power from the ruling Nandas. When the revolt was unsuccessful, the two fled to Taxila, a dominant trade crossroads strategically located near the Khyber Pass, where they encountered Alexander.

Alexander's role in building Chandragupta's empire is less obvious. The disruptions caused by Alexander's attempted invasions allowed Chandragupta to secure the most vulnerable of the Nandas' client states while methodically surrounding and, ultimately, conquering Magadha. By 321 BCE Chandragupta had secured the capital and embarked on a campaign to enlarge his empire. Following a series of battles with Alexander's successor, Seleucus Nikator, the Greeks surrendered their north Indian and Indus territories to Chandragupta. Seleucus and his successors maintained relations with the Mauryas through the Greek ambassador Megasthenes, posted to the Mauryan capital of Pataliputra. Megasthenes's accounts of the enormous wealth of the capital and the efficiency of Mauryan government formed the basis of classical and medieval European understanding of India.

Chandragupta stepped down from his throne around 297 BCE and joined an ascetic religious order, the Jains, formed on the basis of the teachings of the visionary Mahavira (see below). Chandragupta's son continued to expand the Mauryan domains to the west and south, but it was his grandson Ashoka [ah-SHO-kah]

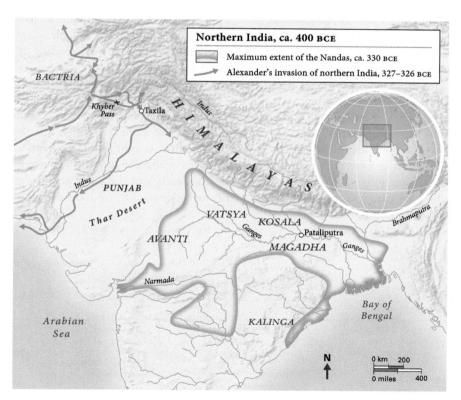

MAP 8.1 **Northern India, ca. 400 BCE.**

(r. ca. 273–231 BCE), who emerged as perhaps India's most dominant ruler until the nineteenth century CE.

Ashoka   Born around 304 BCE, Ashoka may have actually seized the throne from his father. Like his predecessors, he drove the Mauryan Empire deeper into the south (see Map 8.2). The climax of his efforts was a war he fought with the kingdom of Kalinga. By Ashoka's own admission, 100,000 people were killed in the conflict. At the height of his power but deeply moved by the carnage in Kalinga, around 260 BCE Ashoka abruptly converted to Buddhism and vowed to rule his kingdom by "right conduct" alone.

Ashoka told much of his own story and outlined his Buddhist-inspired ideas for proper behavior on inscriptions in caves and on rocks and pillars set up in strategic places throughout his empire. These inscriptions present a fascinating glimpse of the ruler and his personal vision of the idea of dharma (see Chapter 3).

One distinctive innovation of Ashoka's support of dharma was his taking up of the Buddhist concept of *ahimsa*, or nonviolence. Ashoka declared dozens of animal species to be under his protection, forbade the wholesale burning of forests, and even warned his people not to burn grain husks, in order to avoid injuring any creatures living within them. Ashoka's devotion to dharma even extended to sending his sons as Buddhist missionaries to Sri Lanka.

Although Ashoka advocated the peaceful principles of dharma, the records of his reign also indicate that his empire was a kind of police state. While allowing the practice of religions other than Buddhism, Ashoka kept a tight rein on his subjects through a network of spies and informers, a practice begun by his grandfather Chandragupta. All government officials were subject to periodic review of their adherence to dharma. Thus, the governmental apparatus was geared toward uplifting the people's morality and supervising their happiness.

Ashoka also encouraged a unified system of commercial law, standardization of weights and measures, and uniform coinage—innovations that facilitated commerce. A majority of state revenues came from taxes on harvests of grain plus those on internal and external trade. Under the Mauryans, India was the major crossroads in the exchange of gold and silver sought by the Hellenistic kingdoms and for the expanding maritime trade accompanying the advance of Buddhism into Southeast Asia. In the north, Taxila and the cities and towns along the caravan routes from China to the west grew wealthy from the exchange of luxury goods.

interactive timeline

800–600 BCE
Early patterns of state
formation in the
Ganges valley

700–600 BCE
Upanishad reformers
of Vedic tradition

322–550
Much of India
reunited under
Gupta Empire

340–370
Flourishing of Kalidasa,
poet and playwright

600–480 BCE
Mahavira, founder of
Jainism, and Buddha,
founder of Buddhism

324–323 BCE
Alexander the Great's
campaigns in northern India

510
Battle of Gwalior;
decline of Gupta power

450–520
Migrations of Huns into
northern India

321–185 BCE
Most of India united
for the first time under
Mauryan Empire

273–231 BCE
Reign of Ashoka,
Mauryan emperor

300–800
Rise of the Pallava and Chalukya
kingdoms in the south

ca. 90 BCE–300 CE
Movements of central
Asian peoples into
India's northwest

78 CE–101 CE
Reign of Kanishka of Kushan
Empire; Buddhist works among
Bactrian Greeks; flowering of
Gandharan art

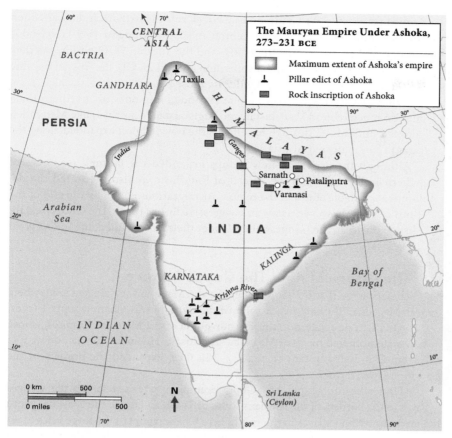

MAP 8.2 **The Mauryan Empire under Ashoka, 273–231 BCE.**

The immense wealth and power flowing into Ashoka's court in Pataliputra made that city of half a million perhaps the richest in the ancient world. The wealth at Ashoka's command and his devotion to dharma allowed the government to spend lavishly in sponsoring public works as well as temples and shrines for various religious groups.

Ashoka's regime represents an attempt to construct a moral order, a pattern of world history that emerged repeatedly as states seeking to become world empires turned to religious and philosophical systems that proclaimed universal truths. The ultimate end of this process, which we will explore in detail in Part 3, was the development of religious civilizations.

The Nomadic Kingdoms of the North   With the end of the Mauryan Empire, northern India was transformed into regional kingdoms run by local rulers. Greek-speaking peoples from Bactria—descendants of troops and colonists who had followed Alexander the Great—controlled some of these territories. Their most famous ruler, Menander, achieved immortality in Buddhist literature as "King Milinda."

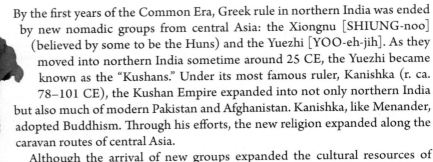

By the first years of the Common Era, Greek rule in northern India was ended by new nomadic groups from central Asia: the Xiongnu [SHIUNG-noo] (believed by some to be the Huns) and the Yuezhi [YOO-eh-jih]. As they moved into northern India sometime around 25 CE, the Yuezhi became known as the "Kushans." Under its most famous ruler, Kanishka (r. ca. 78–101 CE), the Kushan Empire expanded into not only northern India but also much of modern Pakistan and Afghanistan. Kanishka, like Menander, adopted Buddhism. Through his efforts, the new religion expanded along the caravan routes of central Asia.

Although the arrival of new groups expanded the cultural resources of northern India and aided the spread of Buddhism, it also prevented the development of stable states in the region. As migrations ebbed by the end of the third century, however, a new and aggressive line of rulers, the Guptas, established power in the Ganges valley. Under their rule would come India's great classical age.

The Classical Age: The Gupta Empire

Scholars agree that the Gupta line, like the Mauryans, originated somewhere near Magadha. The first major ruler of the dynasty was Chandragupta I (r. ca. 320–335 CE; no relation to the Chandragupta of the Mauryan Empire), whose new state occupied much of Magadha and Kosala. His successor, Samudragupta [sahm-OO-drah-gup-tah] (r. ca. 335–380 CE), expanded the borders of the empire even farther.

Under Samudragupta, the Gupta dominion extended far up the Ganges River to the borders of the Kushans south of Taxila and down the coast deep into the territory of the Pallavas in the south. Like Chandragupta I, he forged ties to regions outside of Gupta control, whose populations in turn pledged their loyalty to him. Samudragupta's son Chandragupta II (r. ca. 380–413 CE) continued to expand the empire, adding the southern and western Gujarati territories of the Shakas. The cumulative effect of these conquests was that, once again, the Indian subcontinent stood on the threshold of unity (see Map 8.3).

Court and Culture   During the reign of the Guptas, the collection of religious traditions called **"Hinduism"** flourished. Indeed, the Guptas actively used the gods and practices of Hinduism, particularly in their devotion to Vishnu and Shiva, to extend their legitimacy not just as kings but as universal rulers.

Although the Guptas made Hinduism the privileged religion in the state, they permitted the practice of other faiths, including both Jainism and Buddhism. Under their influence, the first distinctly "Hindu" art included a staggering profusion of temples and shrines built to honor a variety of deities. Literary culture flourished, from classical treatises on political and social behavior to poetry and plays.

The Waning of Gupta Power   Gupta power began to fade under the reigns of Chandragupta II's son and grandson. A new wave of central Asian nomads, the Hunas, defeated the Guptas in 510 CE and established themselves as the dominant force in northwest India. By 515 CE, the eastern tributary states of the Guptas had

Capital of Ashoka Pillar of Sarnath. The lion motif atop the chakravartin wheel, symbolizing universal kingship, tops one of Ashoka's famous pillars. The one from which this capital was taken had been set up to commemorate the Buddha's first sermon in Sarnath's deer park.

image analysis

MOVEMENT OF NOMADIC PEOPLES, 300 BCE–100 CE

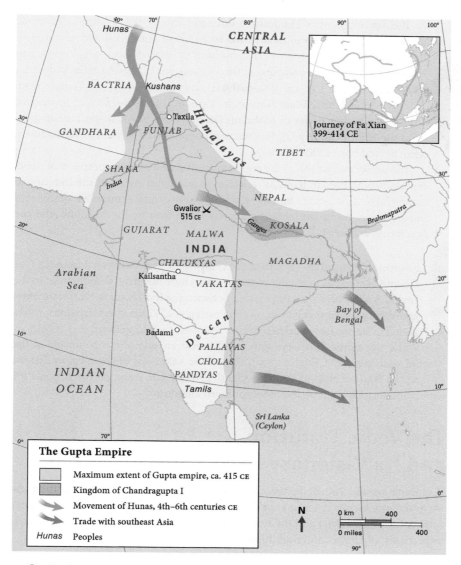

MAP **8.3 The Gupta Empire.**

broken away, while in the west the kingdom of the Rajputanas emerged in Gujarat by mid-century.

The Southern Kingdoms, ca. 300–600 CE

The southern regimes of the Pallavas, Pandyas, Cholas, and Chalukyas of peninsular India were comparatively stable from the decline of the Guptas until the installation of the Muslim sultanates of the north. One reason was the absence of a powerful empire pushing south. Freed from the need to defend themselves, the southern kingdoms could pursue the pacification of their own realms. In addition, their ruling classes shared to some degree a common culture.

Hinduism: A convenient shorthand term for the vast multiplicity of religious practices derived from the Vedic, Brahmanic, Upanishadic, and later traditions in India and those places influenced by Indian culture.

Coins of the Northwest Kingdoms, Second Century BCE and Late First Century CE. The complex history of the area encompassed by modern Afghanistan and Pakistan has been understood principally through the coins minted by the many rulers of frequently shifting territories. The silver coin (above) was minted by a Bactrian Greek king, probably in the second century BCE. The gold coin (below) with the Greek inscription was the product of the reign of the famous Buddhist king Kanishka (78–101 CE) of the Kushans, and depicts the king himself.

Devotional: In the context of this chapter, belonging to a branch of Hinduism in which one dedicates oneself to practices that venerate, honor, or adore a particular god or divinity. The largest of these branches are dedicated to Vishnu and Shiva.

The development of Hinduism among the Tamils, the region's chief ethnic group, included the rise of **devotional** branches of Hinduism and an outpouring of spectacular religious art. The southern kingdoms' most tangible remains are the Hindu temple complexes. The Pallavas, for example, under Mahendra Vikruma Varman I (r. ca. 590–630 CE), carved the Mandapa Temple from solid rock. His descendant Narasimha Varman II (r. 695–728 CE) sponsored the seven rock pagodas of Mahabali Purana. Perhaps most spectacular of all was the eighth-century CE Rashtakutra complex of Krishna I at Kailasantha, again carved from solid rock.

The power and wealth of the region was enhanced by the promotion of trade, especially with the "Indianized" enclaves of southeast Asia and the Indonesian archipelago. As a result, Indian religions, culture, and economics dominated Indian Ocean trade until it was gradually taken over by the Muslims after the fourteenth century CE.

Regional Struggles   South of the Ganges, the systems of *varna* and *jati* (see Chapter 3) tended to revolve more around where one lived than they did in the north. A major division also existed between the local leaders, who were often members of the upper *varnas,* and their subjects. Within these divisions, rulers tended to be predatory in their efforts to enrich their kingdoms.

The rise of the Chalukya state on the western side of the peninsula in the mid-sixth century CE, along with that of the Vakatakas of the Deccan Plateau and the Rashtakutras in the early eighth century CE, resumed the struggle for wealth and territory among the older southern kingdoms.

The Vedic Tradition and Its Visionary Reformers

Beginning around 700 BCE, visionaries sought to reform the Vedic tradition. As we noted in Chapter 3, the first of these men created the Upanishads. In the next two centuries, Mahavira and the Buddha followed, becoming the founding figures, respectively, of Jainism and Buddhism.

Reforming the Vedic Tradition

The Vedas consisted of hymns to the Hindu gods and and described the rituals these deities required. They thus framed the culture of the period 1200–600 BCE, a time when warrior republics and kingdoms competed against each other for wealth and power in the Punjab and Ganges valley. It was against the backdrop of this competition that the authors of the Upanishads (ca. 700–300 BCE), Mahavira (trad. 599–527 BCE), and Gautama, the Buddha, sought to reform the polytheistic Vedic heritage through the formulation of a single first principle.

The Upanishad Visionaries   Many authors of the more than 100 Upanishads were Brahmanic priests whose principal objective was a vision of cosmic unity. This Upanishadic vision, with its proclamation of monism, was similar to those propounded in the Middle East and China during the same time: They insisted on a transcendent first principle as universal truth.

The Kailasantha Temple. Hewn from a single, solid rock, the Kailasantha Temple, part of an elaborate complex in east-central India, is considered the world's most monumental sculpture. Strongly influenced by south Indian architectural traditions, the temple complex dazzles the visitor with carvings of innumerable deities, mythic figures, and erotic imagery.

The Indian visionaries were hermit teachers whose disciples sought to merge their personal selves (*atman*) into the universal self (*brahman*) and thereby achieve salvation. These teachers led their disciples through brief aphorisms, paradoxes, and negations into deep meditation, through which they considered salvation could be achieved. In the highest state of understanding of atman–brahman, one could attain release from the cycles of death and rebirth and thus enter into transcendence, or *moksha*.

Criticism of the Vedic Rituals and Sacrifices   Although they were advocates of monism, the authors of the Upanishads remained faithful to the Vedic rituals, sacrifices, and doctrines. However, as strong kingdoms emerged in the 500s BCE, criticism of religious ritual grew. Urbanization and trade created new classes to whom rituals and sacrifices meant less than they did to the kings and the priestly class. These new classes viewed the rituals and sacrifices as formalistic and wasteful. For the kings and priests, these religious practices were essential to legitimize their power. The Vedic doctrine that eventually divided the priests and their strongest critics, however, was that of the cycle of karma–samsara (see Chapter 3), death and rebirth.

The Ascetic Break: Jainism   The founder of the Jains, Nigantha Nataputta [nee-GAN-tah nah-tah-POO-tah], was born around 540 BCE. At the age of 30 he left home and gave up all his worldly possessions to become an ascetic, and after 12 years he found meditative enlightenment. He was given the title of *jina*, or "conqueror," and his followers became known as Jains. For the next 40 years, he wandered throughout India without clothes or possessions, spreading the new sect's principles and practices. Finally, demonstrating the movement's ideal of not taking the life of any being, Mahavira refused all food and died in Pava, near Pataliputra.

Jain world map

Statue of the Jain Saint Gomateshwara at Karnataka. The world's largest statue cut from a single stone, this figure was built at the site of the famous Jain monastery where, it was said, Chandragupta Maurya entered the order and fasted to death, following the example of the sect's founder, Mahavira.

Schism: A division; when used in a religious context it usually refers to the splitting of members of a certain religion into two or more camps over matters of doctrine, ritual, etc.

Atheistic: Not believing in a god or supreme being.

The Buddha

Jain doctrine begins with a universe in which all things possess *jiva*, a kind of "soul" that yearns to be free from the material world. Jains believe that even inanimate objects possess *jiva*, though at different levels or "senses." These "souls" are governed by the degree to which a thing's past karma stands between it and its release from material bondage. For humans, karma builds up according to the injuries one does to others, intentionally or not. The way to enlightenment is to act so that one acquires as little karma as possible, while performing actions of suffering and self-sacrifice to reduce the karma one already has. As karma dissipates, the soul becomes free.

Ahimsa   Jain monks try to prevent injury to any object, especially living things. There has been a **schism** between those who insist on complete nakedness—to avoid injuring creatures that might be trapped in one's clothing—and those who wear a simple white robe. Some wear gauze masks to prevent breathing in invisible organisms; others carry brooms to sweep small creatures out of one's path. Monks live by begging food from others. The most dedicated ritually fasted to death in resolute refusal to harm living things; this was seen as the ultimate act of ahimsa, or nonviolence.

The strict practices of the Jains did not appeal to most people. As a result, a laity grew to support the Jains. The patronage of kings, including Chandragupta Maurya, helped ensure the sect's vitality. Modern Jains practice a modified form of the earlier traditions, engaging in vegetarianism or veganism, though often wearing clothes indistinguishable from those of other traditions. Some also still participate in certain ceremonies in the nude or with their traditional white garments. The religion's most distinctive element, however, is that it is rigorously **atheistic**, choosing not to worship any god but insisting instead on meditatively merging into a unity that is both universal and transcendent.

The Middle Way: Buddhism   Buddhism began in part as a reaction against such extreme ascetic practices. Siddhartha Gautama, whose title of "Buddha" means "the Enlightened One," is believed to have been born a prince in the Shakya republic in the Himalayan foothills. His traditional birth date is given as 563 BCE, though recent accounts have moved it to at least the mid-400s BCE. At the age of 29, Gautama left his world of privilege and followed various Vedic paths. At one point, following a discipline of extreme asceticism, his path of self-deprivation led him to fast nearly to death.

During his travels, Gautama was exposed to human suffering. His shock and compassion drove him to try to understand the round of death and rebirth. According to Buddhist accounts, after deep meditation he achieved enlightenment. Shortly afterward, Gautama went to a deer park in Sarnath, near the city of Varanasi (Benares), where he found five former disciples and preached to them what became known as the Middle Way.

The Four Noble Truths, the Eightfold Path, and Nirvana   Gautama believed that the nature of the universe is change. All beings suffer because they attach themselves to what they will ultimately lose. Although they crave permanence, they rely only on their senses, which provide the illusion of stability but actually obscure the true nature of things. In pursuit of their desires, they commit evil deeds and accumulate karma. Over many lifetimes, the karma stays with them, building up with each life and keeping them from breaking free of the cycle of death and rebirth. Gautama distilled these insights into the Four Noble Truths:

1. All life is suffering.
2. Suffering arises from craving.
3. To stop suffering, one must stop craving.
4. One stops craving by following the Eightfold Path of right views, right resolve, right speech, right conduct, right livelihood, right effort, right mindfulness, and right concentration.

Later sermons and commentaries further described the Eightfold Path. The path represents a course of life in which one avoids extreme behaviors, adheres to a code of conduct that favors **altruism** and respects the life of all living beings, and through meditation and "right mindfulness" reaches a state of calm nonattachment with an uncluttered mind able to grasp the universal truth. This final stage is known by the Sanskrit word *nirvana*, or nothingness. In Buddhism, this nothingness is a version of the *moksha*—transcendence—first explored in the Upanishads.

Altruism: The practice of acting in an unselfish manner for the good of others.

After the Buddha's death, disputes arose about the correct interpretations of his teachings and questions about how followers should conduct themselves. Over the following two centuries, several Buddhist councils were held, and during one of these meetings, one group separated from the main body of adherents. The now-separate group became known as Theravada [ter-rah-VAH-dah], "the teachings of the elders." Under Ashoka's influence, Theravada Buddhism became the approved sect, with the first complete surviving texts dating from this time.

Buddhist Texts The *Pali Canon*, written in Pali, the sacred language of Buddhism, is a collection of texts that forms the foundation of Theravada Buddhism and nearly all Buddhist schools. The collection consists of the *Tripitaka* [tree-pee-TAH-kuh], or "Three Baskets"; the *Vinaya* [vee-NAI-yah], treatises on conduct and rules of discipline for monks; the *Sutras* [SOO-truhs], or "discourses," most of them believed to have originated with the Buddha; and the *Abhidhamma* [ah-bee-DAH-mah], doctrines of philosophy and metaphysics.

As Theravada Buddhism spread, it became more accessible. Stories of the Buddha's last days implied that he would save everyone who followed his path. Coupled with this was a developing tradition of the Buddha as one in a long line of past and future buddhas, suggesting the potential for a devotional component. Finally, the concept of the *bodhisattva* [boh-dee-SAHT-vuh] described one who, having achieved enlightenment, does not proceed to nirvana but instead helps the suffering achieve their own enlightenment.

Theravada and Mahayana During the first century CE, the largest branch of Buddhism, Mahayana [mah-hah-YAH-nah], the "greater vehicle," emerged. Mahayana spread along the trade routes into central Asia, into the borderlands of the Parthians, and ultimately to China, Korea, Japan, and Tibet (see Map 8.4). As it spread, its schools divided into *esoteric* branches—those seeking enlightenment through scriptural or other kinds of deep knowledge—and devotional branches. Of the devotional schools, that of Amitabha [ah-mee-TAH-bah], the Heavenly Buddha of the Western Paradise, is today the most popular Buddhist sect in both China and Japan (see Chapters 9 and 13).

Great Buddhist Stupa at Sanchi. The need for commemorative burial mounds and reliquaries for the Buddha's relics spawned a characteristic structure called a stupa, meaning "gathered" or "heap." Brimming with symbolic motifs representing the stages of enlightenment, the structures changed considerably from this example—built in the first century BCE over an earlier one from the Mauryan period—as they spread through East Asia, where they assumed the shape of the pagoda.

As Buddhism spread across Asia, its decline had already begun in India. With the revitalization and consolidation of the older Vedic and Brahmanic traditions into Hinduism, Buddhism faced competition for converts and noble patronage.

The Maturity of Hinduism: From the Abstract to the Devotional

During the period from the Mauryans to the rise of the Guptas, the continuing push of state formation to the south meant that local deities were incorporated into the older Vedic and Upanishadic traditions. From these southern areas emerged devotional cults, especially those of Vishnu and Shiva, culminating in the *bhakti* movements beginning in the seventh century CE.

On the other hand, the growth of new religions like Buddhism and Jainism challenged such cultural mainstays as the caste system, the inevitability of the karmic cycle, and the domination of society and salvation by the traditional ruling classes. As a result of these challenges and through the popularity of the grand epics of the Mahabharata and Ramayana, the spreading of the classical texts of the first and

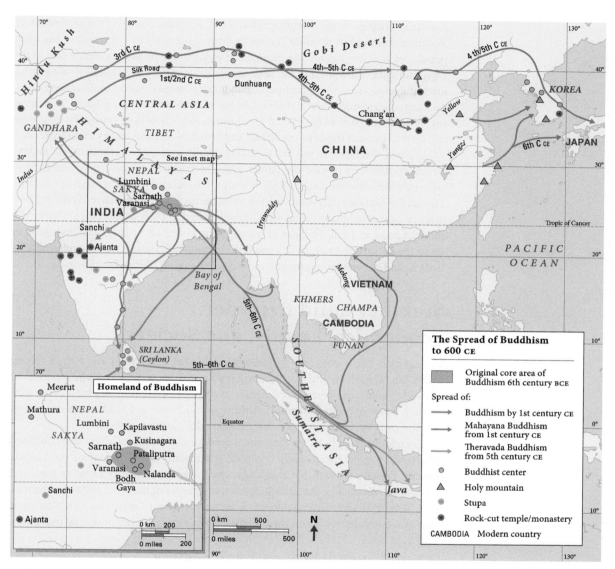

MAP **8.4** **The Spread of Buddhism to 600 CE.**

map analysis

second centuries, and Gupta patronage, a rejuvenated brand of religious experience, Hinduism, is distinctly recognizable by the fourth century CE.

Avatars, Shakti, and Tantra   Hindu beliefs hold that the subcontinent was a single land united by faith—*Bharat*—from the name of a legendary king said to have achieved this unification. Another belief is a full continuum of religious experience, ranging from the highly abstract to the emotional and mystical, springing from devotion to a particular god. Perhaps due to the influence of Buddhism and Jainism, salvation was increasingly seen as accessible to all.

The most important Hindu gods were Brahma, Vishnu, and Shiva. Of these, the main divisions of devotion emerged between Vishnu, the beneficent preserver, and Shiva, the powerful, fertile giver and destroyer of life, the "Lord of the Dance" of the universe. Both Vishnu and Shiva can manifest themselves through avatars or incarnations, the most popular of which is Krishna, an incarnation of Vishnu, who plays a central role in the Bhagavad Gita. The appeal of the new devotional traditions of Hinduism to all castes made the religion increasingly popular. Hinduism allowed that one could achieve salvation according to one's caste and ability. By the seventh century CE, religious poets were carrying the message of devotional Hinduism to all believers in vernacular languages and created some of the most passionate and beautiful religious poetry ever recorded.

A related development was that of Shakti, literally "power," sometimes called "tantra." Shakti practitioners probed the darker edges of the multiple natures of the gods—especially Shiva and his consort Kali, or Durga—associated with death and destruction. Toward this end they purposely violated social norms, with the objective of proving their mastery over attachment to the acts themselves and to push beyond the ordinary dualities of good and evil. The idea of transcending norms also passed into Buddhism at about the same time, in the fourth and fifth centuries CE. Here, it was also referred to as "tantra," and its mysticism formed important elements of Tibetan Buddhism.

Stability amid Disorder: Economics, Family, and Society

The agrarian-based economy of India remained for 2,000 years the richest (along with China's) in the world. As the economy flourished, society as a whole remained relatively stable. The hierarchical nature of the caste system maintained continuity through times of political turmoil. Although Buddhism and Jainism did not recognize the caste system, they did not fundamentally alter that system.

The relationships between men and women and among family members outlined in Chapter 3 grew increasingly complex, particularly from the age of the Guptas onward. Despite the trend in Buddhism toward greater equality between men and women, beliefs such as the strictly delineated spheres of husband and wife, the idea of the female as a fundamental force of the universe, and a male vision of women as simultaneously desirable and threatening became more prevalent during this time.

Tax and Spend: Economy and Society

By 600 BCE, the inhabitants of the emerging Gangetic states had long since made the transition to being settled agriculturalists. With the vast majority of inhabitants of the new states being peasants from the lowest *shudra varna*, the chief form of revenue was harvest taxes. The average tax levied on the people of these early states appears to have been around one-sixth of their annual harvest.

Accelerating Taxes   With the expansion of Magadha in the fifth and fourth centuries BCE, the agricultural tax increased dramatically. The accelerating pace of urban life, the explosion of trade, and the increasingly differentiated castes allowed whole new classes of items to be taxed. Moreover, the increase in trade had led to a growing commercial class expanding beyond the traditional *vaisya* (merchant) *varna*, while the growing need for capital and credit was met by guilds of bankers and traders in precious metals.

Agricultural taxes of about one-quarter to one-third of the harvest continued under the Guptas. As under the Mauryans, bankers and merchants were frequently tapped by rulers for ready cash. Despite low **tariffs**, the Guptas enjoyed a favorable balance of trade. Indeed, the empire's self-sufficiency in nearly all commercial items meant that foreign traders had to pay for their goods in gold or silver.

Tariffs: Taxes levied on imports.

Trade and Expansion   By the time of Persia's invasion in the late sixth century BCE, the reputation of the wealth of northern India was already well established among the Greeks. Interactions with the expanding Hellenistic world extended the reach of Indian trade through the eastern Mediterranean and the expanding Roman domains.

With the decline of the Mauryans and the adoption of Buddhism by peoples of the northwest, the region around Taxila became the hub of a caravan trade that from the third century BCE to the third century CE linked nearly all of Eurasia from Roman Britain to Han China and beyond through the Silk Road (see Chapter 9). In addition, Buddhist, Jain, and Brahmanic religious elements all spread westward to enrich the intellectual climate of the Parthians, Greeks, and Romans.

Indians also dominated the region's maritime trade until they were gradually displaced by the Arabs from the ninth to the fifteenth centuries CE and by the Europeans shortly thereafter. Colonies of Greek, Roman, Persian, and Arab traders clustered in the western port cities of Broach and Kalliena. A testament to the importance of trade in the Greco-Roman world was the first-century guide to the Indian Ocean, the *Periplus* (marine atlas) *of the Erythrean Sea* (see "Patterns Up Close: The Global Trade of Indian Pepper").

Indian Influence beyond India   By the first century CE, this expanding trade region had established outposts in southeast Asia and the Indonesian archipelago. In the second century CE, small settlements of Indians on the Malay Peninsula led to the first Indianized kingdom in the area, that of Funan in the Mekong delta of Southeast Asia, ruled by the brahmin Kaudinya. The spread of both Buddhism and the Indian system of "god-kings" soon reached the nearby Khmers [ke-MARES] and the state of Champa [KAM-puh] in modern Cambodia and Vietnam. By the seventh and eighth centuries CE, these areas became important trade centers connecting the Indian states with Tang China and Heian Japan.

These countries formed important way stations in the expanding traffic of Buddhist pilgrims. The appeal of Buddhism enhanced the Indian economy by both increasing the volume of trade on the subcontinent and providing a uniform structure for its expansion abroad. Pilgrims and monks were natural candidates to assist in the circulation of goods and ideas. Monasteries served as way stations along well-traveled routes; commercial centers grew up around larger complexes along branches of the Silk Road. The international character of Buddhism linked India to an emerging cultural sphere that soon spanned Eurasia. By the fourth century CE, trade ties had been established with the Romans, the Sasanids, the remnant states of Han China, and the Buddhist and Indianizing territories of southeast Asia (see Map 8.5).

Caste, Family Life, and Gender

The basic patterns of Indian society were already being forged by the seventh century BCE. Thereafter, the fusion of Vedic traditions into a distinct form of Hindu culture, drawn heavily from the Brahmanic religious and social practices, proceeded apace. In the Gupta Empire, Hinduism evolved into a religious civilization.

Maturation of the Caste System   Perhaps the most distinctive marker of Hinduism as a religious civilization is the caste (*jati*) system. One of the caste

The Global Trade of Indian Pepper

Pepper was perhaps the world's most sought-after commodity for thousands of years. Indeed, its importance ultimately drove European adventurers to the Americas as they sought a direct all-water route to its source in India.

The black pepper plant (*Piper nigrum*) is a vine native to the Malabar Coast of India in the modern state of Kerala. As far back as the thirteenth century BCE, Egyptian records show black pepper being used in mummifications.

By the third century BCE, pepper had become a mainstay of south India's burgeoning Indian Ocean trade, with annual cargoes going to China, Southeast Asia, and Egypt. The Hellenistic cultural exchange conducted through Ptolemaic Egypt spread the use of pepper throughout the Mediterranean world. By the first century BCE, traders from Egypt, coastal Arabia, and northeast Africa made annual voyages to the Malabar ports for pepper. But it was after the Roman acquisition of Egypt that pepper became the subject of a kind of mania throughout their empire. Contemporary Romans like Pliny the Elder regularly complained of the amount of gold required to keep the empire adequately spiced, and the export of gold to India was ultimately curtailed.

How does one account for pepper's popularity? Initially, part of pepper's attraction may have been its exotic quality. But it had also long been used for medicinal purposes in India, and from Roman times through the European Middle Ages it was hailed in European and Arab treatises as healthful. Moreover, although pepper's

Pepper Pot. The earliest records of pepper being imported into Britain are from the first century. Discovered in 1992, this exquisite pepper pot—a special container intended to hold this expensive spice—is designed in the shape of an empress and dates to the fifth century CE. Made of gold and silver, it testifies to the high value placed on such a precious commodity, especially in a remote place like Britain.

system's chief functions was to absorb and acculturate peoples of divergent languages, ethnicities, and religious practices into an integrated social whole. Within the framework of caste, all people had reciprocal rights and responsibilities. Even those at the bottom levels had a necessary, if disagreeable, societal function.

During the Mauryan era, Ashoka's advocacy of dharma reinforced older notions of duty according to social position, while such treatises as the *Code of Manu* (written down by 200 CE) helped solidify concepts of model conduct among the various classes. By the Gupta period, renewed interest in societal stability after nearly five centuries of disorder prompted increased attention to stricter boundaries for acceptable behaviors within the different *jati*. Along with this, the idea of **ritual pollution** resulting from unsanctioned contact with lower castes becomes increasingly common.

Yet the caste system had strengths that contributed to its longevity. Like religious organizations and guilds in medieval Europe, *jati* membership gave each person a recognized and valued place in society. In some areas, especially in the south, entire villages or clans were incorporated into their own *jatis*; in others, ethnicity or occupation might be the determining criteria. Although the upper castes dominated the political structure of rural society, social power was in fact more diffuse. For example, the members of various caste and guild councils were customarily represented at state functions. Some castes became associated with special feasts and their sponsoring deities, giving them a degree of informal power.

Ritual pollution: The act of someone or something becoming "unclean" in terms of religious taboos or prohibitions.

effectiveness as a preservative is question-able, it was nonetheless useful as a flavor enhancer in a variety of preserved foods.

The Arab occupation of the prime trans-shipment areas of the eastern Mediterra-nean and the termini of the Silk Road and, by the fourteenth century, their domination of Indian Ocean trade caused the price of Indian commodities to soar in Europe. The urge to break the Islamic monopoly of the spice trade ultimately drove the Portuguese to sail around Africa, and Columbus to sail into the Atlantic, hoping to go directly to the Malabar Coast. The commercial net-work built on pepper and other spices was now positioned to drive what would grow into the world's first global trading system.

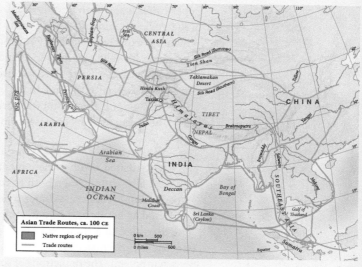

MAP 8.5 Asian Trade Routes, ca. 100 CE.

Questions

- How does the global trade in Indian pepper show the connectedness of Eurasia in this period in world history?

- What are the origins of the pepper trade? How did it change over time through interactions? What adaptations, if any, resulted from these interactions?

Jainism, Buddhism, and Caste   Jainism and Buddhism influenced the caste system as well, offering powerful alternative traditions to the acceptance of varna and *jati*. Moreover, their potential for anyone, regardless of social position, to break free of the cycle of death and rebirth undermined the hierarchical order of the caste system and made Jain and Buddhist practitioners equals in a society of believers. Their alterna-tive institutions, self-sufficiency, good works, and commercial expertise also gave them considerable material power, particularly when patronized by nobles or monarchs.

Family Life and Hindu Culture   As we saw in Chapter 3, the role of women in Indian society was perhaps more complex than in other agrarian-based cultures. On the one hand, the idea of female "dependence" was central to the Hindu conception of the family. Obedience and loyalty to senior female and male authority within the hierarchy of the family was a woman's dharma, her duty regardless of her position in the caste system.

Although in the Tamil areas of the south families remained matrilineal, prop-erty rights were limited. Yet wives customarily controlled the household accounts and supervised servants and hired help. Women of higher classes were expected to have knowledge of poetry, literature, and conversational skills. And the vast majority of men and women were united through marriages arranged by their families after careful negotiation and often betrothed before adolescence.

A number of texts described the "four stages of life" for men: student, householder, hermit, and wanderer. In the first stage, that of the student, boys of the "twice-born"

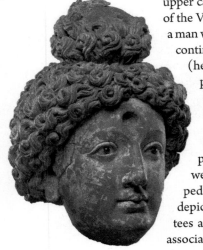

Gandharan Buddhas.
One of the most stunning syntheses of artistic and religious traditions occurred in the wake of the decline of the Seleucid states and the invasion of the Kushans. In the area centered around Gandhara (in modern northeast Afghanistan and northwest Pakistan), Hellenistic artistic techniques of realistic human representation fused with the developing practices of Mahayana Buddhism to create sculptures like the head pictured here, from the second or third century CE, believed to be that of a bodhisattva, or perhaps of Siddhartha Gautama.

upper castes were taken into the household of a *guru*, or teacher, to study the works of the Vedic–Brahmanic–Upanishadic tradition. At the second stage (householder), a man was expected to make a good marriage, establish a prosperous household, and continue his religious duties. As old age approached, he entered the third stage (hermit) and was expected to retreat to the forest and work to master the self in preparation for the end. In the final (wanderer) stage, he would move beyond desire for life or death, wandering without home or possessions and, ideally, attaining moksha (release from the cycle of death and rebirth).

Balancing Male and Female Roles   Although women were, for the most part, treated as subservient members of a patriarchal society, as in China, they were also seen by men both as complementary opposites and as potential impediments to moksha. Women in literature, like Sita in the Ramayana, were often depicted as heroic and resourceful. Moreover, from the Gupta period on, devotees appealed to a number of goddesses. Fertility, sexuality, and growth, largely associated with femaleness, were all celebrated in Hindu literature, statuary, and religious symbolism. The depictions of sexuality in Hindu temples are among the most erotic art in the world. In contrast with this celebration of sexuality, however, was the perception of women as temptresses who anchored men to the sensual world, potentially delaying their release from the karmic cycle.

These contradictions are illustrated in Vatsyayana's [vaht-see-ai-AH-nah] *Kama Sutra*, or *Aphorisms of Love*, written perhaps sometime in the first or second century CE. Although best known in the West for its descriptions of sexual practices, it is more properly understood as a guide to the everyday worship of living. The majority of the text deals not with sex but rather with how to become a person of culture. For women, the *Kama Sutra* details such activities as singing, dancing, and cooking—but also chemistry, metallurgy, and even driving horses and elephants.

Strength in Numbers: Art, Literature, and Science

The vast number of cultural contributions from India makes it impossible to do more than hint at their richness here. One area worth noting, however, is Gandharan art. During the time of the Kushan Empire, the influences of the old empire of Alexander the Great met the new religious movements within Buddhism to create this new style.

Early representations of the Buddha had been symbolic: the "wheel of dharma," an empty throne, or a footprint. Around the beginning of the Common Era, the tradition of depicting the Greek gods as realistically human merged with the new Buddhist sensibilities to create the first images of the Buddha, which looked remarkably like some Greek depictions of the god Apollo. This Gandharan approach spread across northern India. Over time, however, the style declined as less realistic, symbolic representations became standard throughout the Mahayana religious sphere.

The Classical Age   The Gupta period brought an explosion of art and literature from artists patronized by the court and the upper classes. The "perfection" of Sanskrit as the medium of the sacred texts of Hinduism caused it to be viewed and preserved as unchanging. As a classical language, Sanskrit was used in works of poetry, prose, and drama.

Science and Mathematics   In addition to Buddhism, the most profound intellectual influences from India on the surrounding regions were in science and mathematics. From the second century BCE until the second century CE, India was an importer of scientific and mathematical concepts from the Greco-Roman and Persian spheres. Greek geometry, for example, made its way into northern India during this time. In exchange, however, concepts of Indian health regimens—some involving yoga discipline—along with the vast body of Indian medicine, with its extensive knowledge of herbal remedies, also seem to have moved west. The second-century CE medical text *Charaka Samhita*, for example, like its counterparts in the Mediterranean and later European world, taught a health regimen based on the balance of humors.

In the area of mathematics and astronomy an important synthesis of ideas took place from the time of the Mauryans through the twelfth and thirteenth centuries CE. During the Hellenistic period, Indians adopted the calendar of the eastern Mediterranean and southwest Asia, which had a 7-day week, a 24-hour day, and a 365-day solar year—along with the 12 zodiacal signs of the Greco-Roman world. Indian thinkers refined these imported concepts to levels unsurpassed in the ancient world. The subtleties of some of the philosophical schools had already required intervals of time and numbers that still stagger the imagination today. For example, cycles of time marking eternity in some philosophical schools were measured in intervals larger than current estimates of the age of the universe. Philosophical discussion on the nature of matter in infinitesimal space among some schools anticipated key arguments of modern physicists regarding the principle of indeterminacy.

Like the Chinese, Indian mathematicians and astronomers during the Gupta period had already developed a decimal system; however, they now employed the first use of the zero, initially marked by a dot, as a placeholder, and developed a system of positive and negative numbers. Their work with the geometry of the Greeks enabled them to calculate pi to four decimal places as well as to develop methods for the solving of certain kinds of algebraic equations. By the eleventh and twelfth centuries CE, the acquisition of these techniques by the Arabs and their transmittal of them to the new universities of Christian Europe gave us the system we still use today, known by the somewhat erroneous name of "Arabic numerals."

❯ Putting It All Together

In roughly a millennium, a number of important patterns of world history emerged in India. The political, cultural, social, religious, and economic systems of the states along the Ganges River were diffused to all parts of the Indian subcontinent. With the maturing of these patterns came the tendency to see the subcontinent as a unified entity in nearly every way except in politics. Here, despite the accomplishments of the Mauryans and Guptas, unity would prove elusive—in some respects even to the present day. This would prove particularly true, as we will see in later chapters, with the coming of Islam.

In terms of its regional influence and beyond, India's impact was disproportionately large. By at least the time of Ashoka, the population of the subcontinent was second only to that of China. Within it was contained one of the world's most active sources of religious traditions. The influence of Hinduism spread to Indonesia and Southeast Asia; Buddhism through this period was the world's largest religious system, as well as the first "universal" one.

interactive concept map

Paradoxically, many of the factors that allowed for this tremendous richness of religious, cultural, and intellectual traditions also contributed to the subcontinent's political instability, particularly in the north. Here, continual migrations of outside peoples cross-fertilized the cultural resources of the region but also impeded political unification.

Review and Relate

Thinking Through Patterns

Examine the ways historians approach the big questions of this chapter.

> Think about the reasons for the spread of Buddhism inside and outside of India. How have historians seen the decline of Buddhism in India?

An important historical pattern is that of individuals we call "visionaries." In this chapter, we place the Buddha in this category as a man who sought to go beyond the Hindu bounds of death and rebirth. Like the other visionaries we examine, however, the Buddha's fundamental message of transcendence and enlightenment can be adapted to any belief system. As his message moved outward from India, it adapted to local customs by borrowing bits of indigenous religious mythology and belief while keeping the fundamental message intact. Local people in turn adapted it to their own beliefs and made it their own. In East Asia, it received a boost from the translation of Buddhist scriptures into literary Chinese and the circulation of Buddhist practitioners, monks, merchants, and pilgrims throughout the Buddhist cultural sphere. Its decline in the place of its birth appears to have been due in part to the shift of its cultural center to China and Japan and the official support of the Guptas for Hinduism.

> What do you consider to be the most influential patterns in Indian history to this point? Why?

How do historians establish criteria of "importance"? One measure of this is to assess the influence of certain patterns and practices on a culture or society over time. Change over time (or the lack of it) is an important indicator of the prevalence and kind of innovation taking place in a society. So some influential patterns in Indian history might include the permeation of religion into all aspects of Indian life, the search for transcendence of the material world, the caste system as the social fabric of the subcontinent, and the prominence of India as a crossroads astride the trade routes of the Indian Ocean and the great land routes across Eurasia.

> Do you think some of Ashoka's concepts could be implemented by governments today? Why or why not?

Ashoka's ideas seem quite modern in many ways, and his decrees regarding the protection of animals and ecological matters might certainly have some current application. Yet it must also be remembered that he is still far removed in time and culture from the modern world. His ideas of dharma as duty might not carry exactly the same import as today. Historians are routinely conscious of the pitfalls of identifying too closely with peoples in very different cultures in the remote past. "The past is a foreign country," it is often said. "They do things differently there."

|Against the Grain

Consider this as a counterpoint to the main patterns examined in this chapter.

India's Ancient Republics

In addition to kingdoms, the ancient Gangetic states also included republics (*ganas*). Accustomed as we are to thinking of such political institutions as exclusive to the Mediterranean world, representative forms of government have appeared in nearly all human societies. Yet until very recent times, as scientific-industrial society and the nation-state have come to dominate global politics and economics, republics had proved problematic to sustain. In Greece and Rome, for example, popular-based governments seemed inevitably to descend into factionalism, demanding a strong ruler to restore order.

The early Indian republics of the late Vedic period were also seen by contemporaries to be models of power sharing in some respects, but were as vulnerable to internal dissention and factionalism as their counterparts elsewhere. For states moving toward a unified conception of concentrated power and religious unity, the instability of power sharing seemed increasingly unattractive, even dangerous. Moreover, the requirements of economic stability in agrarian societies and the growing rigidity of caste also militated against the viability of republics.

And yet this form of social organization was discussed a number of times in the Mahabharata, in the accounts of Alexander's expeditions into India, and in a number of Buddhist accounts of northern Indian states as late as the second century CE. Detailed descriptions of their workings occur in the political treatises of Kautilya; and Arrian, the historian of Alexander, notes that republics such as Mallas offered the Greek armies some of the fiercest resistance they encountered. Perhaps here lies a clue to what contemporaries viewed as their true strengths and vulnerabilities: All commentators insist that no form of government works better when the people are unified and have a stake in the existing order; but factionalism and division are in the end fatal. As Indian society as a whole became more complex and differentiated, the drive for political unity, so it was believed, would become that much stronger. With the creation of empires by the Mauryans and Guptas, the age of the republics in India was to pass—until 1947. Today, with its constitution and representative government, India prides itself on being the world's largest democracy.

- What difficulties did all republics that sprang from agrarian–urban society face? Were they in the end insurmountable? Why?

- Do you think Indian republics were more vulnerable than those elsewhere to problems of disunity and factionalism? What role do you think religion played in sustaining or undermining them?

Key Terms

Altruism 179

Atheistic   178

Devotional   176

Hinduism   174

Ritual pollution   184

Schism   178

Tariffs   183

audio flashcards

For additional resources, please go to **www.oup.com/us/vonsivers.**
Please see the Further Resources section at the back of the book for additional readings and suggested websites.

China

IMPERIAL UNIFICATION AND PERFECTING THE MORAL ORDER

THE FIRST
CHINESE
EMPIRES

"**V**enerable sir, since you have not considered a thousand *li* too far to come, may I presume that you bring something that may profit my kingdom?" Even today one can sense the air of challenge, however polite, in the question. The speaker, King Hui of Liang, had seen his kingdom steadily eroded by the powerful surrounding states at the height of China's Warring States period (403–221 BCE).

The "venerable sir" to whom he addressed his question, however, was in no mood to banter. Warming to his topic, the Confucian sage Mencius laid out his rebuttal:

> If Your Majesty says, "How may I profit my kingdom," the great officers will say, "How may we profit our families"; and the lesser officers and common people will say, "[H]ow may we profit ourselves." Superiors and inferiors will try to snatch this profit from each other and the kingdom will be endangered . . . [but] there never has been a humane man who neglected his parents. There never has been a righteous man who made his ruler an afterthought.

—James Legge, trans., *The Works of Mencius* (New York: Dover Reprint, 1970, pp. 125–126)

ABOVE: One of the world's most recognizable structures, this section of the Great Wall near Beijing was upgraded in the early fifteenth century CE.

Chastened but intrigued, King Hui and his son and successor, Xiang, finally said to Mencius, "I wish quietly to receive your instructions."

This story from the opening pages of the fourth-century BCE *Book of Mencius*, illustrates the role of intellectual innovation, the ultimate direction of Chinese political thought, the way Chinese ideas would influence nearby peoples, and, more generally, the larger pattern of empires and states adopting the ideas of visionary thinkers. As we shall see, starting with Confucius—from whom Mencius drew his ideas—Chinese thinkers suggested ways of looking at the world, how to behave in it, and how to govern it that ranged from radically abstract to firmly practical, from collective to individualistic, and from an absence of active government to near totalitarianism.

From the Han dynasty (202 BCE–220 CE) until the twentieth century, Confucianism would be the governmental system of China. Moreover, as Chinese was adopted as the first written language by the Koreans, Japanese, and Vietnamese, Confucian concepts would take root in these lands as well. So in China, as in India, Persia, Rome, and eventually the Islamic world, the legacy of "visionaries" would be adopted by rulers as officially approved thought. An important pattern of world history emerges by the beginning of the Common Era: Large "world" empires utilize religions and systems of thought that have universal application and appeal.

Visionaries and Empire

The period from the eighth century BCE until the first unification of China under the Qin in 221 BCE is regarded as China's most fertile period of intellectual exploration. The foundations of nearly every important school of Chinese philosophy were laid during this era. Of these various systems, those that had the greatest impact were Confucianism, Legalism, and Daoism.

Confucianism, Legalism, and Daoism

The historical Confucius is an elusive figure. According to traditional accounts, he was born in 551 BCE to a family named Kong. In Confucian texts he is referred to as "the Master" (*zi* or *fuzi*) or "Master Kong" (*Kong fuzi*) [koong FOO-zuh]. European Roman Catholic missionaries in China during the seventeenth century rendered *Kong fuzi* into Latin, where it became "Confucius." As a member of the growing *shi* class (see Chapter 4), Confucius sought a position as political adviser to the courts of Zhou states in northern China. However, like the visionaries of India, he spent most of his life as an itinerant teacher, spreading his ideas about ethics and politics to a growing group of followers.

Confucian Doctrine Confucius has been called "China's first great moralist." His teachings—as presented in the *Lunyu*, or *Analects*, the central Confucian text—see human beings as inclined toward ethical behavior and human society as a perfectible

Seeing Patterns

≫ Was the First Emperor's ruthlessness justified by his accomplishments in his empire?

≫ How would you compare the values expressed by Confucius and Mencius to those of contemporary society?

≫ How have historians viewed the role of women in early imperial China?

selections from the *Analects*

Reciprocity: Mutual
exchange of things,
ideas, etc.

Junzi: According to
Confucius, the "superior
man" or "gentleman"
who behaves according
to an ethical and moral
ideal. A society run
by *junzi* will foster
social institutions
that encourage proper
behavior.

moral order. According to Confucius, there are certain fundamental patterns that are manifestations of the *Dao* ("the Way") of the universal order.

One of these fundamental patterns is the relationship between parent and offspring. People develop their moral character to reflect well upon their parents and serve those in higher social or political stations as they serve their own parents. This example of human society as a kind of extended family applies at every level; indeed, drawing on the idea of the Mandate of Heaven (see Chapter 4), Confucius makes the ruler himself responsible to heaven for his country. Emperors in later regimes would habitually refer to themselves as the "sons of heaven," to emphasize this filial duty.

For Confucius, mutual obligations serve as checks on the arbitrary exercise of power. Hence, when asked to sum up his thinking in one word, Confucius answered, "**Reciprocity**: Do not do unto others what you would not have them do to you." Confucius believed that individuals should strive for the qualities of *ren* (kindness or humaneness toward others) by practicing *li* (usually translated as "ritual": the observance of rules of decorum as guides to appropriate behavior toward others). People who did so would not only perfect their own character but also set an example for the rest of society.

Confucian Government   Confucius lived during a time of social and political disorder. His teachings center on ways to restore order and make government and society more humane. But because Confucian doctrine emphasizes personal responsibility, the structure of government is far less important than the ethical fitness of the ruler and the people. Good government, according to Confucius, begins with educated leaders and officials of strong moral character. To describe this ideal of behavior, Confucius introduced the concept of the **junzi** ("the superior man" or "gentleman"). Those who attain these ideals comprise a kind of aristocracy of merit, while rulers with these qualities set an example for their subjects.

Just as the *junzi* cultivated his personal ethics and morals, a state run by *junzi* would spread these values to society by fostering ritual and social institutions that encouraged proper behavior. The observance of *li* (ritual) would make appropriate behavior routine and help people to develop a sense of right and wrong, thus acquiring a stake in the social order.

Confucius died in 479 BCE. Two later students of Confucian doctrine, Mencius and Xunzi [SHWUN-zuh], continued to spread his teachings, with their own contributions. Despite challenges from competing philosophical schools, Confucian ideals became the standard for Chinese politics and scholarship.

Mencius   By Mencius's time, in the fourth century BCE, the continual warfare among the Zhou states had led many thinkers to question assumptions about the private and the social good. Their answers varied from radical individualism to universal love and altruism.

Mencius (*Mengzi*, or Master Meng; ca. 385–312 BCE), like Confucius, believed that people were fundamentally good and that individuals must continually work to refine this goodness in order to avoid being led astray by negative influences. He concluded that the way to proper behavior is through cultivating the Confucian virtues as a bulwark against negative forces.

The *Mengzi*, or *Book of Mencius*, is written in more of a narrative form than the *Analects*. Its most powerful sections deal with the obligations of rulers to their subjects. A ruler's primary duty for Mencius is to maintain the "people's livelihood" and uphold the "righteousness" of the state. A state ruled by righteousness and humanity ensured that the people would be prosperous and orderly. A ruler who abused or neglected his subjects upset the social order and the natural tendency of people toward good. In such a case, the people had the right and the obligation to invoke the Mandate of Heaven and depose him. In the end, said Mencius, the people, not the ruler, are the foundation of the state.

Xunzi   As states grew increasingly powerful and warfare more deadly, Mencius's optimistic view of human nature seemed less practical. Like Mencius, Xunzi (trad. ca. 310–219? BCE) was also a student of Confucian philosophy, but had a much darker view of human nature. During the Warring States period, Xunzi came to believe that individuals were self-involved creatures capable of regulating themselves only through immense effort. Only by enforcing the restraints of civilization could individuals approach the Confucian ideals of virtue and humanity. Thus, by the end of the third century BCE, Confucian thinkers had come to radically opposed conclusions about the nature of human beings. Xunzi's pessimism formed the basis of the Legalist school that finally restored order and created the first Chinese empire.

Legalism   For Legalists, building a strong state was of utmost importance. Out of Xunzi's view of humans as inclined toward evil, his students Han Fei (d. 233 BCE) and Li Si (d. 208 BCE) developed laws and practices based on the absolute will of the ruler. Order in a state, they claimed, could be implemented only through the institution of strict laws imposed on all subjects. Since Legalists believed that compliance on small matters led to compliance on larger ones, they imposed harsh punishments for even tiny infractions.

The Legalists argued that all subjects must serve the state through productive activities, especially agriculture and military service. Other occupations were discouraged, and idlers were put to work by force. Only government-approved history and literature were tolerated.

Although Legalism had many critics, it was its strict practices, not the more moderate ideals of Confucianism or Daoism that imposed order on China.

Daoism   While most Chinese philosophical schools accepted the Dao as the ordering principle of the universe, they varied as to the means of achieving harmony with it. For Confucians, study and self-cultivation put the individual in tune with the Dao. For followers of the Daoist tradition, attributed to Laozi (Lao Tzu), however, the

Han Fei, selections on Legalism

interactive timeline

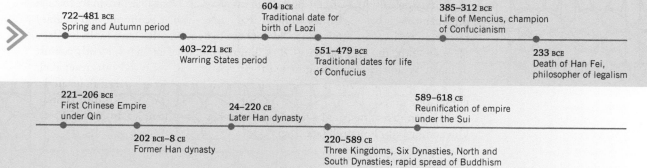

722–481 BCE
Spring and Autumn period

604 BCE
Traditional date for birth of Laozi

385–312 BCE
Life of Mencius, champion of Confucianism

403–221 BCE
Warring States period

551–479 BCE
Traditional dates for life of Confucius

233 BCE
Death of Han Fei, philosopher of legalism

221–206 BCE
First Chinese Empire under Qin

24–220 CE
Later Han dynasty

589–618 CE
Reunification of empire under the Sui

202 BCE–8 CE
Former Han dynasty

220–589 CE
Three Kingdoms, Six Dynasties, North and South Dynasties; rapid spread of Buddhism

Confucian path prevented genuine understanding of and harmony with the Dao. The historical Laozi is even more obscure than Confucius. In fact, many scholars believe Laozi to be a mythical figure. Chinese tradition cites his birth date as 604 BCE and gives his name as Li Er.

For Daoists, in contrast to the Confucians, the Dao was not the ordering force *within* the universe but the transcendent first principle *beyond* the universe. The Confucian Dao can be named; the Daoist Dao, like the relationship between atman and brahman, cannot be named. The Dao is beyond all dualities and unifies them in a great whole. In fact, the vocabulary Laozi used for this measure of all phenomena is similar to that of other Eurasian visionaries discussed previously: Deutero-Isaiah, the Zoroastrian reformers, Anaximander, and the Buddha, as well as the Upanishad writers.

Since the Dao transcended the world, including all such opposites as "good" and "evil," no single path of action would lead an individual to union with it. To choose the good, as the Confucians do, is therefore to follow only a limited part of the universal Dao. Instead, the Daoists taught that only through self-reflection and contemplation of paradoxes might an individual come to know the Dao.

Daoism and Government   Daoist political theory held that the best government was that which governed least. Here, the key idea is one from the most famous Daoist work, the *Daode Jing* (*The Classic of the Way and Virtue*, often spelled *Tao Te Ching*): "By non-action there is nothing that is not done." The ruler should not push specific policies but rather let all things take their natural course, for even as they run to extremes they will always reverse. The ruler's understanding of these universal cycles leads to union with the Dao and keeps the world in equilibrium.

These three schools of thought were all to play a role in the development of China's political and cultural life. Confucianism would provide the basis for the bureaucracy of China's empires and ideals of a perfectible moral order; Daoism would provide the mystical dimension of Chinese culture; finally, Legalism would unify the last of the warring states into a single structure under the Qin [chin].

The Qin Dynasty

The Qin state ultimately claimed victory over its opponents and established centralized rule throughout China. Qin had several powerful advantages over its competitors. Its position on the western fringe of the Zhou world meant that it was free to expand its economic base by promising land to peasant cultivators as the state seized territory on its western frontier.

Qin and Zhou   The agricultural surplus that resulted from these land grants led to increased prosperity for the state. Qin's location was also a benefit when it came to military preparedness. Many of the warring states were in close proximity to each other, and the constant battles among them depleted their economic and military resources. Qin, on the other hand, did not have to fight off other states at its borders. Consequently, the Qin participated in limited military campaigns, mostly against nomadic groups, which strengthened their fighting skills but did not upset their economy or weaken their army. By 350 BCE, Qin rulers reorganized the state by eliminating the last of the old Zhou institutions and replacing them with a centralized system that anticipated a number of later Legalist principles. In 256 BCE, the Qin conquered Zhou itself (see Map 9.1).

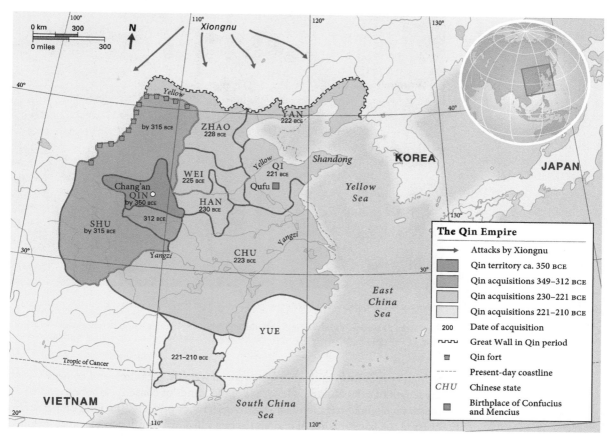

MAP **9.1** **The Qin Empire.**

With its strong economy, expert military, and the Legalist theorists Han Fei and Li Si advising the court, Qin rapidly conquered the other northern Chinese states. Qin armies, now swollen to hundreds of thousands of men, drove south and eliminated the opposition of the many tribal peoples below the state of Yue, continuing into the northern part of modern Vietnam.

In the north and west, Qin armies fought a series of campaigns to drive nomadic peoples, especially the Xiongnu, or Huns, from newly established borders and secure the trade routes into central Asia. By the end of the 220s BCE, the Qin had subdued all of the states that would constitute the first Chinese empire.

The First Emperor   In 221 BCE, the Qin ruler Cheng (r. 246–221 as Qin ruler; 221–209 BCE as First Emperor) proclaimed himself Qin Shi Huangdi, the First Emperor of the Qin, and with Li Si as his chief minister instituted the Legalist system throughout the new empire. As a safeguard against attacks by nomadic peoples in the north, the First Emperor deployed tens of thousands of forced laborers to join together the numerous defensive walls of the old Zhou states. This massive project stretching over 1,400 miles would become the first iteration of the Great Wall of China.

With virtually unlimited resources and the ruthless drive of the Legalists to expand and fortify the state, the First Emperor undertook ambitious projects. The Chinese

Terra-cotta Warriors at the First Emperor's Tomb. One of the most important archaeological finds of the twentieth century, the Qin burial complex, was discovered in 1974 by a local farmer digging a well. Over 5,000 figures have been unearthed so far, all with individualized features. The dig has been enclosed and a museum built on site. Along with the Great Wall, it is one of China's most popular tourist destinations.

image analysis

writing system was standardized, as were all weights, measures, and coinage—even the length of axles on carts. Hundreds of thousands of conscript laborers worked on roads, canals, and irrigation and water conservancy projects. The First Emperor also ordered the construction of a tomb for himself, a mammoth complex that included an army of thousands of life-sized terra-cotta warriors intended to protect Qin Shi Huangdi after his death.

From his palace in Chang'an, the site of modern Xi'an, the First Emperor tightened his control. Scholars, particularly Confucians, who objected to government policies were buried alive. Any literature not officially sanctioned by the government was destroyed. Writers of the following Han dynasty have left accounts of mass executions of dissenting scholars.

When Qin Shi Huangdi died, his exhausted subjects erupted in rebellion. Minister Li Si provoked additional discontent by conspiring to keep the First Emperor's death a secret in order to rule as regent for the monarch's son. He was captured attempting to flee the rebellion and executed in 208 BCE; his captors lashed him to a board and slowly sawed him in half in accordance with Qin law. After a brief civil war, a general named Liu Bang restored order to the region. He proclaimed himself emperor in 202 BCE and called his new dynasty the Han.

The Han Dynasty

If the Qin constructed the Chinese empire, the Han perfected it. Like the Roman Empire with which it is frequently compared, the Han developed a centralized political system of rule that blended the administrative structures of the Qin with more moderate Confucian ideals of government as a moral agent. This model of rule endured—with some interruptions and modifications—for over 2,000 years.

Unlike earlier rulers who came from aristocratic families, Liu Bang, who had taken the reign name Gaozu (r. 202–195 BCE), had been a peasant. Perhaps because of this background, he had little interest in restoring the decentralized system of the Zhou, which favored the aristocratic classes. Instead, he left intact the Qin structure of centralized ministries and regional **commanderies**. Han rulers reduced taxes and labor obligations and rescinded the most severe punishments imposed under the Qin. Han rulers altered the Qin system of leveling social classes by instituting uniform rules for different segments of society—aristocrats as well as commoners. Under the Han, the upper ranks of society were taxed at lighter rates and exempted from most forms of corporal punishment.

> **Commanderies:** Districts under the control of a military commander.

As the Han Empire expanded, so did its bureaucracy. Officials were divided into graded ranks ranging from the heads of imperial ministries to district magistrates. Below these officials were clan leaders and village **headmen**. Landowners were to collect and remit the taxes for themselves and their tenants, while the lower officials recorded the rates and amounts, kept track of the labor obligations of the district, and mobilized the people during emergencies.

> **Headmen:** Local leaders; these were usually chosen by the people of the village, clan, district, etc., rather than appointed by the government.

Wudi, the Martial Emperor   Like both his predecessors and successors, Wudi, whose reign name means "Martial Emperor" (r. ca. 140–87 BCE), faced the problem of defending the empire's northern and western boundaries from nomadic peoples, especially the Xiongnu. He extended the Great Wall begun by the Qin to provide greater protection. Hoping that a strong Chinese presence would discourage invaders, Wudi encouraged people to move to areas along the northern and western borders of the empire (see Map 9.2).

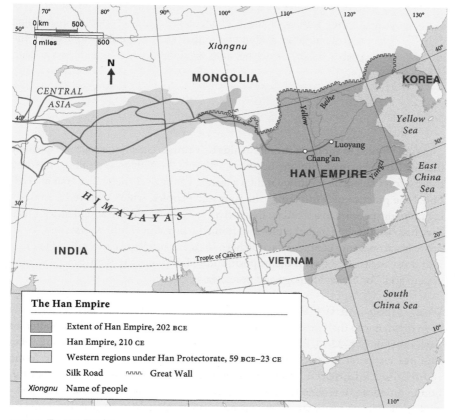

MAP **9.2** **The Han Empire.**

Patterns Up Close | The Stirrup

The stirrup joins the long list of familiar Chinese pathbreaking technologies such as paper, the compass, printing, the horse collar, and gunpowder. The stirrup has been recognized by historians as being of major importance. It not only completely changed the way humans used horses but ushered in a new type of warfare that altered the structure of societies and dominated military strategy for 1,000 years.

Although the horse had featured in Eurasian warfare for over 2,000 years, its utility had been limited to pulling chariots and supporting mounted archers and riders with light spears. The central problem of using horses in pitched battles was the difficulty of mounting a horse when one was weighed down with armor and weapons. In addition, it was easy to be knocked from horseback, especially in close combat.

Around the beginning of the Common Era the first attempts at saddles with straps for supporting a rider's feet began to appear in northern India. But these employed only a simple toe loop, and the saddle concentrated the rider's weight on a small area of the horse's back, tiring the animal. This idea for the stirrup appears to have spread via the Silk Road, and by the early 300s CE a recognizably modern iron stirrup with a flat bottom and semicircular top began to be used in north and central China; the earliest remains discovered so far date to 302 CE. At about the same time, saddles with a rigid frame to distribute the rider's weight more evenly and better padding to cushion its effects on the horse began to be employed.

The effects of these changes were soon apparent in a China now dominated by feuding states and marauding nomads in the post-Han era. With his legs secured to his mount and a high

Jin Dynasty Iron Stirrups. Widespread use of the stirrup not only brought the use of horses back to the forefront of warfare, it led to a resurgence in power of Eurasian mounted nomadic peoples. The ornate stirrups pictured here helped the nomadic Jurchen people displace the Northern Song dynasty (see Chapter 12) and set up their own Jin dynasty, which lasted from 1127 to 1234. Their downfall was brought about by another mounted nomadic people—the Mongols—who not only displaced the Jurchens but went on to conquer the Southern Song in 1279 and incorporate their new Yuan dynasty into the short-lived Mongol super-empire spanning Eurasia in the late thirteenth and early fourteenth centuries.

Wudi worked to suppress Xiongnu raids on central Asian trade routes, especially the Silk Road. He made diplomatic efforts, offering the Xiongnu supplies, but when those efforts failed, he mounted military campaigns against them. The Han also adopted the practice of "**sinicizing**" the nomadic peoples, which involved encouraging nomadic peoples to assimilate themselves to Chinese culture and identity. Once they had been assimilated, the threat of nomadic invasion would be lessened. Wudi drove his armies into central Asia, northern Vietnam and Korea, extending Han rule into those areas. Along with the imposition of Han rule came the Chinese writing system and Confucian ideology and practices.

Sinicizing: The pattern by which newcomers to areas dominated by Chinese culture were encouraged to adopt that culture for themselves.

Wang Mang and the Red Eyebrow Revolt The Han era has traditionally been divided into the Former, or Western, Han (202 BCE–8 CE) and the Latter, or Eastern, Han (24–220 CE). During the brief interval between 8 and 24 CE, Han rule was temporarily interrupted when a relative of the royal family, Wang Mang (45 BCE–23 CE), seized power. Wang Mang attempted to reform land distribution in an effort to reduce the huge disparity between rich landowners and peasants. Wang Mang's proposed reforms provoked a revolt led by a Daoist secret society

saddleback to cushion him in combat, a mounted warrior could use a long lance to charge directly into enemy formations without fear of being immediately un-horsed. Furthermore, both he and his horse could wear heavier armor than before. The stirrup proved so effective that by the fifth century CE the armies of all the states in China had adopted and refined the technology. In China, it helped pave the way for the Sui reunification in 589.

It was in western Eurasia, however, that the new technology saw its greatest impact after its arrival in the seventh century CE. The politically fractured eras of post-Roman and post-Carolingian Europe meant that local elites and regional strongmen had to mount their own defenses. The stirrup and related military inno-vations allowed them to do this without heavily equipped armies, while the expenses necessary to adopt the new technology ensured that it would remain a monopoly of the rich and powerful. Thus the relationships comprising feudalism matured as peasants placed themselves in the service of their mounted protectors. The rough parity and independence of this widely dispersed warrior elite proved a powerful ob-stacle to the patterns of centralized state formation and empire building. Ironically, it would be another Chinese invention that would ultimately end this way of warfare many centuries later: gunpowder.

Questions

- How does the stirrup show how a technological innovation can lead to broader cultural and societal adaptations?

- Which environmental and geographical conditions facilitated the impact of the stirrup across Eurasia in ways not possible in the Americas?

called the Red Eyebrows. The rebels killed Wang Mang and sacked the capital of Chang'an. An imperial relative restored the Han dynasty in 24 CE but moved the capital to Luoyang, where the empire continued in somewhat reduced size.

Wang Mang's attempts at land reform and the Red Eyebrow revolt hastened the collapse of the last of the old aristocratic landholdings. Together with the sense of renewal accompanying the restoration of the Han dynasty, these events temporarily masked the empire's growing weakness.

Han Decline   By the late second century CE the Han dynasty was showing signs of strain. Ambitious improvements ordered by Han emperors were carried out by peasant labor required by the government as a form of taxation. This made it difficult for peasants to farm, and agricultural productivity declined. Furthermore, the loss of some borderland territory reduced the tax base just when the empire required more revenue to maintain the Great Wall and military outposts protecting the empire from nomadic invasions. Battles within the royal family, aggravated by increasing re-gional power falling into the hands of Han generals and a Daoist revolt after 184 CE, finally brought the Han dynasty to an end in 220 CE.

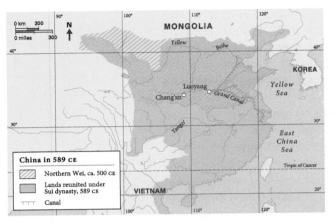

MAP **9.3 China in 589 CE.**

Between Empires   After the collapse of the Han, China experienced its most chaotic postimperial political period. This interlude of turmoil is traditionally divided into the era of the Three Kingdoms (220–280 CE), the overlapping Six Dynasties period (222–589 CE), and the also overlapping period of the North and South Dynasties (317–589 CE).

From the initial Three Kingdoms period through the numerous short-lived "dynasties" that followed, the aim of reconstituting the empire was always present. Parallels with the problems besetting the Roman Empire at the same time were striking: The growing power of landed elites, the increasing weakness of the bureaucracy, and defense problems of the north and west all persisted. In the absence of effective centralized administration, the infrastructure fell into disrepair, the internal economy grew more regionalized, external trade declined, and warfare, famine, and banditry haunted the land.

Unlike in the Roman Empire, however, by the fifth century CE the rebuilding process had begun, when an eastern Mongolian people known as the Toba established the state of Northern Wei in northern China. Taking advantage of the new military tactics growing from the development of the stirrup, Northern Wei established itself as a dominant power in the region. By the beginning of the sixth century, the Toba had a formal policy of assimilating into Chinese culture—taking Chinese names, marrying into leading families, reviving old imperial rites, and attempting land reform. In organizing land redistribution to the peasants, they helped pave the way for the return of centralized administration, military service, and tax collection. A Toba general named Yang Jian succeeded in uniting most of the old Han lands in 589 and called the reunified dynasty the Sui (see Map 9.3).

The Empire Reclaimed: The Sui   The Sui pursuit of empire building—particularly an ill-conceived invasion of the Korean peninsula after 589 CE—prompted unrest. The Sui used forced labor for construction projects, including palaces, roads, and the Grand Canal. Linking the Yangzi River with the Yellow River, the Grand Canal facilitated shipment of food crops from the south to the capital at Chang'an. The Grand canal, still in operation today, was important, as northern capitals increasingly depended on food supplies shipped from the south.

The outbreak of rebellion following the death of the second Sui emperor, Yangdi, brought the 16-year-old commander Li Shimin to power. Li had the Sui emperor killed, placed his own father on the throne, and announced the founding of the Tang dynasty in 618 CE. In less than a decade, he forced his father to abdicate and took power in his own right in 627 CE.

As we will see in the next part, the reconstitution of the Chinese empire under the Sui and its expansion and consolidation under the Tang placed China among the world's regions marked by the ascendancy of religious civilizations. Like Christianity in the late Roman Empire, Buddhism made inroads in China following the collapse of the Han. Indeed, through the work of Chinese monks it had also become established in Korea and Japan. The Tang would see the completion of this process.

Buddhism permeated Tang China to an extent never surpassed in later dynasties. For a period in the late seventh and early eighth centuries CE it even became the established Chinese state religion. In this regard, China became not only part of a regional religious and cultural sphere during the Tang but also an important part of a new world pattern that would encompass Islamic civilization, orthodox Christianity in the eastern Roman (Byzantine) Empire and much of eastern Europe, and the Christian civilizations of Roman Catholicism and Protestantism.

The Domestic Economy: Society, Family, and Gender

Throughout Chinese history, agriculture was the basis of the domestic economy. Yet from the Han dynasty on, China exported far more in luxury goods and technology than it imported. Unlike regimes in India, which actively fostered trade, the Confucian view of the pursuit of profit as corrupting meant that Chinese governments preferred to adopt a passive, but controlling, role in trade. Although merchants were held in low esteem, the state recognized that trade was indispensable to the financial health of the empire.

Industry and Commerce

By the first century CE, Chinese manufacturers were making paper using a method still considered to produce the highest-quality product for painting or literary work. Artists were also producing "proto-porcelain" that, with additional refinements, would one day be known as"china." Earthenware figurines produced in Tang China are among the most coveted in the world today. In other arts, the use of lacquer was also well established. By the second century CE, the Chinese had perfected silk production and had become world leaders in textile weaving. Both treadle- and water-powered looms were in widespread use, and silk with standardized designs was produced for export. Chinese silks were much in demand from Persia and Rome. But much of the most important domestic production centered on bulk strategic goods.

Iron and Salt   By the Han period, the Chinese were producing cast iron in huge foundries, and the mining industry may have employed as many as 100,000 people. The foundries produced ingots of standardized sizes and weights. Salt mines used complex gearing, bamboo piping, and evaporators fired by natural gas. Because of the enormous productivity of the iron-making and salt-mining industries, the government sought ways to regulate them.

The Han and succeeding dynasties viewed merchants as a parasitic class, and trade as a necessary evil. Nevertheless, government programs aimed at improving the empire's infrastructure facilitated commerce. The unpredictable flow of China's rivers required dikes, dredging, reservoirs, and canals to ease transportation (see Map 9.4).

Coal Mining. While the miners shore up a tunnel and gather coal into a basket lowered from above, a large bamboo pipe is thrust into the mine to draw off poisonous gases.

Land Reform   By the time of the late Han, the top of the social hierarchy was assumed by the *scholar-gentry*—the educated large landholders who constituted the Confucian bureaucracy. Since the upper ranks of the landowners and bureaucrats

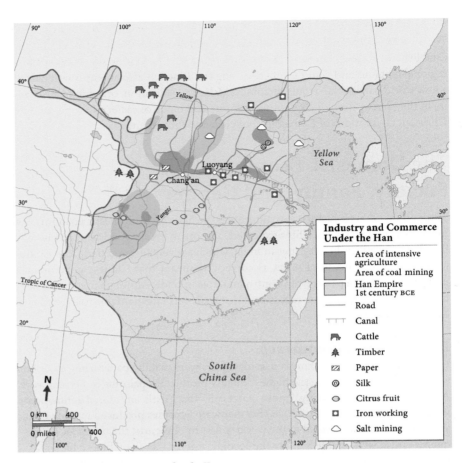

MAP **9.4** **Industry and Commerce under the Han.**

either were exempt from taxes or paid reduced amounts, the tax burden fell increasingly on tenants and owners of small parcels of land. Poor harvests made the situation even worse for those already heavily taxed. Because the north, despite its irrigation works, was more prone to crop failure than the south, it was also proportionally more heavily taxed.

Such problems made land reform and redistribution an ongoing concern. The Tang, for example, continued the policy of land redistribution begun during the brief Sui dynasty. Although the Tang land redistribution policy promoted prosperity, it also resulted in absentee landlordism, tenancy, and usury, particularly during times of economic stress. The continual problem of land tenure and attempts at reform and redistribution is even today a concern in China.

Agricultural Productivity Technical and systemic innovations increased agricultural productivity. In addition to such staples as wheat, millet, and barley in the north and rice in the south, a variety of semitropical fruits and vegetables were cultivated. New strains of rice resulted in larger harvests on more marginal land. Trade with central Asia had introduced wine grapes, and the production of fermented grain beverages had become a substantial industry. New techniques of crop rotation, fertilization, and plowing were introduced, as were the collar for draft animals and the wheelbarrow; oxen-drawn, iron-tipped plows; treadle hammers; undershot, overshot, and other types of waterwheels; the foot-powered "dragon" chain pump for irrigation; and the *fengche*—a hand-cranked winnowing machine with an internal fan to blow the chaff from the grain. With this technology, China led the world in agricultural productivity until the eighteenth century CE.

The Silk Road   The expansion of maritime and caravan trade from the seventh century CE on spread Chinese technology abroad and brought new products into the Chinese empire. Early examples of silk appear to have reached the Mediterranean and North Africa as early as the first millennium BCE. By the first century BCE, artifacts clearly identifiable as Chinese had turned up in Egypt; by the fourth and fifth centuries CE, Indian and Persian middlemen extended the Chinese trade to the African kingdoms of Kush and Aksum.

The principal route connecting the Chinese to the various trading centers of central Asia, and ultimately to the Mediterranean and Rome, was known as the **Silk Road** (see Map 9.5). Although the Chinese tried to guard the secrets of its

Silk Road: Overland trade routes that connected eastern and western Eurasia, beginning at the end of the fourth century BCE.

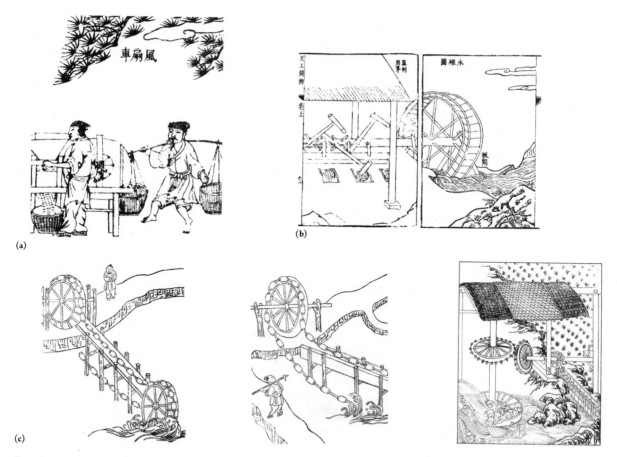

(a)

(b)

(c)

Han-Era Technology. By the first century CE, Chinese sophistication in crafts and labor-saving devices could be seen in a number of areas. While the illustrations here are from the famous seventeenth-century compendium of technology *Tiangong kaiwu* (The Works of Nature and Man), all of them illustrate techniques in use during the Han period: (*a*) *fengche* winnowing machine; (*b*) undershot waterwheel driving hammers in a pounding mill; (*c*) vertical and horizontal waterwheels driving chain-bucket "dragon pumps" for irrigation.

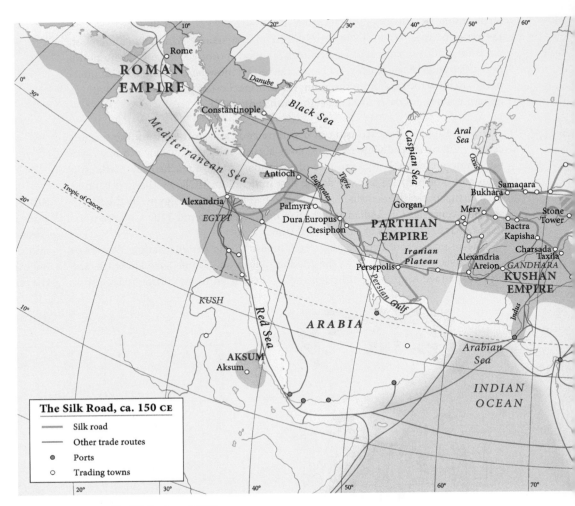

MAP **9.5** **The Silk Road, ca. 150 CE.**

production, the demand was so high that many peoples along the caravan routes were soon engaged in making silk themselves. Competition among producers and merchants in western Eurasia became so keen that the Roman emperor Justinian allied with the African kingdom of Aksum in the sixth century CE and contested the growing Persian dominance of the trade in fine silks. In the process, the Romans created their own silk monopoly to service the western trade.

Gender Roles

Women in imperial China were subordinate to men. Although early Confucian works were relatively flexible about the position of women, the Han period saw a more hierarchical, patriarchal model of women's behavior develop. At the same time, the emphasis on sons as carriers of the ancestral line and their potential to enter state service led to a devaluing of daughters. In times of severe economic stress on families, young girls were the first to suffer. Families, especially in rural areas, would sometimes sell their daughters into prostitution or kill female infants.

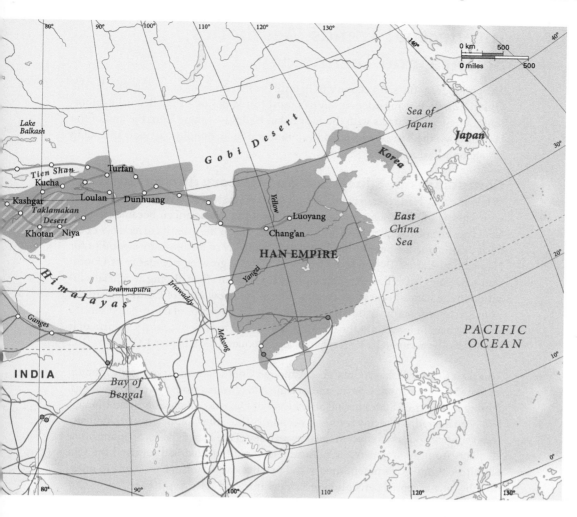

map analysis

Although some elite women achieved prominence in intellectual pursuits, like the historian Ban Zhao (48–116 CE), women's education centered on domestic virtues as well as spinning and weaving. Daughters were either married off or placed with another family through adoption or servitude. Yet, in theory at least, there was always supposed to be an element of complementarity and reciprocity between men and women, especially husband and wife.

From the fifth century CE on, the popularity of monastic Buddhism created attractive alternatives for those fleeing family pressures, especially women. Women enrolled in Buddhist schools could become highly educated, and the communities themselves, like Christian monasteries in Europe, often owned large tracts of land and wielded considerable local influence. At the same time, the strictness of regulations on sexual and family life varied, particularly among officials and the commercial classes. Foreign influences also affected behavior, particularly in places engaged in international trade. Tantric Buddhist (see Chapter 8) and Daoist sexual practices contributed to a more relaxed approach to relations between men and women during the Tang as well.

Intellectual Trends, Aesthetics, Science, and Technology

The period from the sixth century BCE until the first unification of China under the Qin in 221 BCE is regarded as China's most fertile period of intellectual exploration. Long-term contacts with the East Asian Buddhist sphere from the end of the Han through the Tang era resulted in a number of new Buddhist schools spreading throughout East Asia.

Confucianism, Education, and History during the Han

While the first Han rulers favored a philosophical system that combined Legalism with aspects of other schools, over time a form of Confucianism became the preferred governmental doctrine. Confucian emphasis on the ethical correctness of officials, caring for the people, filial piety, and the study of history were a good fit for Han administrators. By the second century CE, the growing popularity of Confucian academies led to their subsidization by the state, in effect placing all official education in the hands of these academies. This made knowledge of Confucianism the principal test for entrance into the bureaucracy. This practice of merit-based service would remain in force until the opening years of the twentieth century. A form of it would later be adopted by Korea, Japan, and Vietnam (see Chapter 13).

The Han Confucian Synthesis?   Although Confucianism served as the foundation for Han education, Confucian doctrine had changed from the early teachings. During the Warring States period and the era of Qin rule, much Confucian thought had been altered, and many texts had been lost. Thus, the Confucianism that finally received state approval reflected the new realities of the Han dynasty. So many other elements from the fragments of philosophical tradition that had survived the Qin period went into government theory and practice that scholars have come to question the long-accepted perception of a straightforward "Han Synthesis."

This diverse blending of political, ethical, and cosmological thought is evident in the era's chief treatise on government, the *Huainan zi*. In this document, the Confucian ideals of humane, righteous, and filial behavior by the powerful are linked with Daoist ideas of the ruler as divorced from day-to-day administration and Legalist notions on the role of officials. As the intermediary between heaven, humankind, and earth, the emperor occupied a position of cosmological significance. For continuity's sake, a dynasty had to be hereditary—in contradiction to Confucius's ideas. Hence, acceptance of a hereditary imperial line strengthened the emphasis on the notion of filial piety as a central virtue. Indeed, a short work that achieved widespread use as a first reader because of its basic ideas and limited vocabulary was the *Xiaojing*, the *Classic of Filial Piety*. At the same time, the idea of dynastic cycles and the Mandate of Heaven became even stronger during this period as they were elaborated by the great Han historians.

Han Historians   By the Han period, with the ideal of empire encouraging cultural unity, court historians collated historical materials that had survived the Qin purges in an attempt to systematize the writing of history.

For these men and women, the purpose of history writing was the accurate transmission of information and analysis of the events portrayed in terms of a larger vision of the direction and purpose of human history. For the Han historians, history was cyclical, and moral lessons learned from human events were to be tied to actions taken at various stages of these cycles.

The father-and-son team of Sima Tan (d. 110 BCE) and Sima Qian (145–86 BCE), whose *Shiji (The Records of the Grand Historian)* attempts the first complete history of the Chinese people, included a survey of non-Chinese peoples in that work. Hence, the Han records give us our first written accounts of Japan and other places on the Chinese periphery.

Several generations later, the Ban family comprised another dynasty of Han court historians. Writing after the Wang Mang interval, Ban Biao (3–54 CE) and his son Ban Gu (32–92 CE) pioneered the writing of dynastic history with their *Hanshu (The History of the Former Han)*, whose format was followed by all subsequent dynastic histories. Ban Gu's daughters were also scholars and writers, and his sister Ban Zhao (48–116 CE) carried on the family tradition of history writing as well as a treatise on women's behavior, *Admonitions for Women*.

Buddhism in China

By the mid-first century CE, when it is first mentioned in Chinese accounts, Buddhism had already split into the major divisions of Theravada (Hinayana), which had established itself in southern India and Sri Lanka, and Mahayana, which would be established in China.

The introduction of Mahayana Buddhism into China presents a number of interesting parallels with that of Christianity into Rome. Both religions emphasized personal enlightenment or salvation. Both were initially seen as "foreign" systems and subjected to periodic persecution before emerging triumphant. Finally, while both challenged existing hierarchies, the institutions of both were also adopted by rulers who wanted to expand their power.

Language and Scripture   The incompatibility of the Chinese written language with Sanskrit and Pali scriptures complicated the introduction of Buddhism to China. The earliest Buddhist missionaries had to borrow from Daoist terminology and invent a new vocabulary of Chinese terms. This eclecticism resulted in a proliferation of sects and a growing need on the part of Chinese converts to travel to India for study and guidance. The famous pilgrim Xuan Zang (596–664 CE) went to India in 623 CE and brought back the collection of scriptures still housed in the monastery he founded just outside Xi'an.

Buddhist Schools   The period between the dissolution of the Han and the ascendancy of the Tang saw the founding of many important schools of East Asian Buddhism. By the fifth century, the school of popular devotion to Amida, the Buddha of the Pure Land, was spreading rapidly in China. For Pure Land followers, merely invoking Amida's name is sufficient for salvation. Even today, it remains the most popular Buddhist sect in both China and Japan. Amida is often pictured with the bodhisattva Guanyin (*Kannon* in Japan), the Goddess of Mercy who is frequently invoked during times of peril.

Another influential Buddhist school was Tiantai, centered on the scripture of the *Lotus Sutra*. Tiantai emphasized contemplation of the sutras (Buddhist scriptures) as the vehicle to enlightenment and later inspired schools of esoteric (see Chapter 8) paths to enlightenment.

Bodhisattva Guanyin, Sixth Century CE. Originally incorporating aspects of both genders, Guanyin came to be depicted as female as Buddhism became firmly established in China. For Pure Land adherents, she was the bodhisattva invoked in times of extreme peril, and "the miracles of Guanyin" (*Kannon* in Japan) was a favorite theme of both Chinese and Japanese artists.

A third school was Chan Buddhism, better known by the name given it in Japan: Zen. As outlined in its central text, *The Platform of the Sixth Patriarch*, by Hui Neng (638–713 CE), the path to enlightenment is through meditation and the example of a master. While limited in its influence in China, the emphasis on discipline and obedience made Zen the preferred Buddhist school of Japan's warrior aristocracy after the twelfth century CE.

Intellectual Life

Aesthetics: The study of the beautiful; the branches of learning dealing with categorizing and analyzing beauty.

Chinese concepts of **aesthetics** that developed during the first millennium CE came to influence the arts throughout East Asia. The most important developments during this period were the maturation of poetry, painting, and calligraphy. Central to each is the idea of spontaneous creation as a reflection of the inner state of the artist. The artist in each of these media seeks to connect with the Dao by indirectly suggesting some aspect of it in the work itself.

The Sciences   Because the imperial establishment relied on the prediction of comets, eclipses, and other omens to monitor the will of heaven, astronomy and mathematics were especially important. Chinese mathematicians had worked out formulas and proofs to figure the areas of most standard geometric forms. They had also calculated pi to four places and were able to solve simultaneous algebraic equations. The astronomers Zhang Heng (78–139 CE) and Wang Chong (27–100) had each championed theories of a universe governed by natural forces. Zhang built a water-powered *armillary sphere*—a hollow globe surrounded by bronze bands, representing the paths of the sun, stars, and planets—and, in 134 CE, devised what was perhaps the world's first practical earthquake detector.

Earthquake Detector. One of the more ingenious pieces of high technology to come out of the Han period was a working earthquake detector created by Zhang Heng (78–139 CE) in 134 CE. In the model illustrated here, carefully balanced balls were placed inside the large vessel. A tremor coming from a particular direction would jar the ball closest to the direction of the quake and send it down a track where it would fly from the mouth of one of the dragons on the outside of the "vessel" and fall into the yawning mouth of the frog underneath. Thus, anyone checking the device could tell at a glance that a quake had occurred and from what direction by seeing which frog held a ball.

Printing and Proto-Porcelain   One of the signal innovations of Eurasia was printing. While woodblock prints of popular Buddhist works had become available in major Chinese cities by the eighth century CE, by the end of the Tang and the beginning of the Song dynasties, presses employing both carved block and movable copper type were in regular use in China, Korea, and Japan. The innovation of printing dramatically raised literacy rates, and by the beginning of the Song era, China had some of the highest preindustrial literacy rates achieved in human history.

Though there is debate about when the breakthroughs resulting in true porcelain first occurred, by the Tang period distinctive brown and green glazed figures, often depicting the peoples and animals of the caravan trade, were widely exchanged. By the Song, delicate white, crackled glaze and sea-green celadon ware were produced and sought by connoisseurs as the height of aesthetic refinement. Today, such pieces are considered to be among the world's great art treasures.

⟫ Putting It All Together

The political and social turmoil of the late Zhou era was also an innovative period in Chinese intellectual and cultural history. During this era the most important schools of Chinese thought and philosophy developed: Confucianism, Daoism, and Legalism. While Confucianism ultimately triumphed as the ideology of imperial China, it was the Legalist state of Qin that created the empire itself.

interactive concept map

When the Qin dynasty fell in 206 BCE, much of the infrastructure of the early empire, including the Great Wall, was in place. The Han dynasty, from 202 BCE to 220 CE, retained the administrative structure of the Qin but softened the harsh laws and punishments of the Legalists. Eventually, the form of Confucianism practiced by the empire's administrators became the imperial ideology. By the end of the Han, China had created a solid alliance between the state and this all-encompassing ethical and legal system.

The 400 years of unity under the Qin and the Han had conditioned the Chinese to believe that empire was the natural goal of the patterns of political formation in China and that any interruptions in these patterns would be brief. Thus, Chinese history has been marked by rhythms of inwardness and outwardness. Along with these rhythms came a belief, reinforced by dynastic historians, that human society and the cosmos were knit together in a moral order, made perfectible by the power of the empire and the dedication of a bureaucracy selected for its understanding of ethics in human affairs. Thus, throughout the imperial era—and even in our own time—Chinese students and scholars have both guided and remonstrated with those in power.

Review and Relate

| Thinking Through Patterns

Examine the ways historians approach the big questions of this chapter.

In ancient times, most people studied history for the moral lessons it offered and to avoid making the same mistakes their ancestors did. The Chinese studied it in hopes of grasping its basic patterns so as to understand the present and anticipate the future. For most of the twentieth century, historians have sought to avoid making moral judgments about the past, to see their job as being detectives rather than judges; to judge it by the standards of the present is to be "presentist." But how does one deal with such things as genocide, extreme cruelty, or slavery? Thus, one way out of this dilemma might be to weigh the actions of the First Emperor against the standards of morality current in *his* day. Yet here, too, we encounter a problem: There were so many new schools of thought emerging in China then that no single one dominated; moreover, the First Emperor himself created his own system of morality based on Legalism. Perhaps, then, the best that we can do is to note that he set the fundamental pattern for Chinese imperial government for the next 2,000 years—but at considerable cost.

⟫ **Was the First Emperor's ruthlessness justified by his accomplishments in his empire?**

≫ **How would you compare the values expressed by Confucius and Mencius to those of contemporary society?**

Perhaps the biggest difference between Confucian society and modern American society is in the way both see the ideal forms of societal relations. Americans see the individual, the rule of law, democracy, and equality as fundamental to a good society. The purpose of government is to allow people to do as they wish while stipulating the limits within which they can do so. Confucian concepts of government and society put a premium on hierarchy and harmony. People are not seen as mere individuals but as part of larger patterns: family, clan, village, society, state. These are seen as part of a hierarchy that stretches from the poorest peasant to the emperor himself. Reciprocal rights and responsibilities are present at every level for protection of the weak, but equality is not seen as important. The role of government itself is seen as providing a moral example to the people. If it teaches them well through regulations, customs, and ritual, then the people aspire to be good.

≫ **How have historians viewed the role of women in early imperial China?**

One of the most unattractive things about imperial China to the majority of us today is that it often appears that women were held in low regard, abused, denied basic human rights, and even tortured for fashion's sake, as with foot binding. The Confucian emphasis on hierarchy within society and the family tends to reinforce this impression. But scholars have in recent years shown the picture to be much more complex. While scholars agree that in some respects women's roles deteriorated, the evidence suggests that there were also times, such as during the Tang and early Song periods, when they exercised considerable freedom and influence. The pattern of "inner" and "outer" as it governed the traditional Chinese family is still discernible in many Chinese households today: While husbands go off to work, women definitely hold sway within the "inner" realm of the house.

| Against the Grain

Consider this as a counterpoint to the main patterns examined in this chapter.

Yang Zhu and Mo Di

- The appearance of visionary thinkers appears to have been an extraordinarily widespread phenomenon. Why were the times of great turmoil in these societies such fertile ones for new ideas?

- What ideas in other cultures seem to be like

The period of the "hundred schools" of thought range from the deceptively passive mysticism of the Daoists to the totalitarian ambitions of the Legalists. At its height, however, during the time of the Confucian thinker Mencius (385–312), the two schools of thought that he and his disciples considered most influential and dangerous were an exercise in extremes: the radical individualism of Yang Zhu and the advocacy of universal love of Mo Di (often spelled Mozi).

Yang Zhu taught that since life was short and death inevitable, people should take what enjoyment they can. After all, he said, the four great sages (including Confucius) "during their life had not a single day's joy. Since their death they have had grand fame that will last through the ages. . . . [but] their fame is no more to them than the trunk of a tree or a clod of earth." Moreover, the most infamous villains who enjoyed vast wealth and pleasures went smiling to their graves, caring not at all in death about their ill fame.

Mo Di, on the other hand, taught that the only truly humane way to approach the world was to love all people equally. To do otherwise is to be overly partisan in one's duties to society. The followers of Mo put these ideas into action during the Warring States period by volunteering to help the inhabitants of besieged cities defend themselves.

In the end, the extremes of both systems would undoubtedly have made them unworkable. That of Confucius, with its emphasis on family relationships and duties at the micro and macro levels, was ultimately more in harmony with Chinese society—so much so that it continues to shape that society even today.

those of Yang and Mo? How do they also differ? Do they spring from similar conditions?

Key Terms

Aesthetics   208
Commanderies   197
Headmen   197

Junzi   192
Reciprocity   192
Silk Road   203

Sinicizing   198

audio flashcards

For additional resources, please go to
www.oup.com/us/vonsivers.
Please see the Further Resources section at the back of the book for additional readings and suggested websites.

PART THREE

The Formation of Religious Civilizations

600–1450 CE

A vital pattern of world history during the period 600–1450 was the development of "religious civilizations." By this we mean religions and cultures shared by states and empires in entire world regions. In all cases, traditions based on monotheism or monism legitimized the polities that adopted them and helped unifiy individual states. Six religious civilizations emerged in Eurasia and Africa during the second half of the first millennium: Western Christianity (from 476), Eastern Christianity (640), Islam (750), Hinduism (550), Buddhism (Korea 550, Japan 594, Vietnam 971), and Neo-Confucianism (China 960, Vietnam 1010).

Uniqueness and Comparability

Uniqueness.   The rise of religious civilizations on the continents of Asia, Europe, and Africa unifies the period 600–1450. In this respect, it may be considered as a continuation of the intellectual and institutional transformations that began with the emphasis on transcendence by the visionaries of the mid-first millennium BCE.

Comparability.   Although the religious civilizations displayed many regional variations, they shared common characteristics:

- Religious civilizations formed in regions that were larger than any single state within them: They superseded empires as the largest units of human organization. They often consisted of commonwealths of competing states that shared characteristics and cultures.

633–651
Arab conquest of Syria, Iraq, Egypt, and Iran

794–1185
Heian period, Japan

918–1392
Koryo Kingdom, from which the name "Korea" is derived

ca. 1000
Tale of Genji, perhaps world's first novel, Japan

1204
Sack of Constantinople by Crusaders

618–907
Tang dynasty in China

850–1000
Kingdom of Chichén Itzá in northern Yucatán Peninsula

960–1127
Neo-Confucian synthesis in China

ca. 1000–1400
Kingdom of Ife in West African rain forest

1206–1310
Mongol Conquests of Asia, eastern Europe, and the eastern Middle East

- The civilizations were *scriptural*—that is, based on bodies of texts. In each religious civilization, followers merged the often conflicting texts into one coherent *canon:* a single, official interpretation adhered to by all.
- The guardians of the canon were educated elites who taught it to laypeople.
- Despite hostilities among religious civilizations, merchants, missionaries, pilgrims, and travelers visited each other's areas and exchanged innovations across Eurasia and Africa.

Origins, Interactions, and Adaptations

The era of religious civilizations illustrates key processes of origins, interactions, and adaptations.

Internal Forces.

The elements of religious civilizations came from the empires and kingdoms from the pre-600 period. These elements were found inside the territories of the evolving religious civilizations. Some exceptions include Korea, Japan, and Vietnam, which adopted Chinese Buddhist civilization from the outside.

In the majority of religious civilizations, the scriptural canons were completed within two or three centuries. Thereafter, refinement of the canons continued for centuries. Without outside challenges, however, these refinements slowed. Over time, scholars, thinkers, and artists exhausted the possibilities that their civilizations offered them.

External Challenges.

External intellectual challenges contributed to the reshaping of two religious civilizations during the period 600–1450: Neo-Confucian China and Western Christianity. China's intellectual foundation was based on Daoism and Confucianism. Buddhism, coming from India, presented an intellectual and institutional challenge by the 800s. In response, the Chinese reconfigured their canon from the mid-tenth century with the creation of Neo-Confucianism.

In Western Christianity, Latin Christians enlarged their canon twice: first around 1100–1250, after the arrival of Arabic and Greek texts, and second around 1400, after the arrival of another set of Greek and Hellenistic texts.

Thinking Like a World Historian

》 How was each religious civilization of the period 600–1450 unique? How were these civilizations comparable?

》 What impact did internal forces and external challenges have on the patterns of development in the religious civilizations of the period 600–1450?

》 Why do the civilizations of the Americas fall outside the patterns that characterize Eurasian and African civilizations during this period?

interactive timeline

1206–1526
Muslim Delhi Sultanate at height of power

1240–1645
Empire of Mali in West Africa (rain forest, Sahel, and savanna)

1257–1287
Vietnamese repel three attempted Mongol invasions

1336–1564
Dominance of Hindu state of Vijayanagar in southern India

1427–1521
Aztec Empire in Mesoamerica

1453
Constantinople falls to Ottoman Empire

1238–1492
Muslim kingdom of Granada

1250–1505
Kingdom of Great Zimbabwe in southern Africa

1268
St. Thomas Aquinas's *Summa Theologica*

1348–1352
Black Death in Middle East and Europe

1438–1533
Inca Empire in Andes

>> Chapter 10   600–1300 CE

Islamic Civilization and Byzantium

S afra, a wife whose husband left her for another woman in twelfth-century Cairo, describes her anguish in letters to her estranged husband Khidr. She is offended that Khidr denigrates her as unattractive and reveals secrets to his new lover, who is also married. In Safra's words, his "repulsive, shameless talk" causes her deep suffering. Were she not a good Muslim, she says, she would curse him both privately and in public.

The letters also reveal that she was independently wealthy, while her husband was not. Since he could not pay her the obligatory portion of the "bride wealth" at the time of the wedding, she let it stand as a loan. Not only did he not make payments; he did not even feed and clothe her or pay their rent. When he began his affair, she retreated to the countryside. But he insisted she return and promised to leave his mistress. As soon as she returned to Cairo, however, he went back to his lover. He slipped into Safra's house at night and stole most of the household furnishings, ultimately leaving her with an empty house.

Safra's story provides a glimpse into the legal side of Islamic civilization. Islamic law afforded women considerable protections. Safra was a woman of property, holding personal title to possessions as well as to debts payable to her. She could go to court, where she had standing as a complainant,

BYZANTIUM AND THE ISLAMIC WORLD, ca. 1000 CE

ABOVE: Detail of an early Quran (Surah 48: 27–28) written in Kufic script during the eighth or ninth century.

and could initiate divorce proceedings. Even though Islamic civilization was as patriarchal as the other religious civilizations of the time, women exercised considerably more rights than in the Persian and Roman Empires.

Seeing Patterns

≫ Why can the period 600–1450 be described as the age of religious civilizations? How do Eastern Christian and Islamic civilizations fit this description?

≫ Which cultural traditions combined to form Islamic religious civilization during its formative period? What were the most characteristic patterns?

≫ How did Eastern Christian or Byzantine civilization evolve over time? On which institutions was this civilization based, and how did it evolve, wedged between Islamic and Western Christian civilizations?

The central patterns of Islamic civilization flowed from an empire that conquering Arabs from northern Arabia built during 628–750. These patterns would then develop from the Iberian Peninsula to Turkestan. The empire evolved into a **commonwealth** of smaller states. From 750 to 950 its inhabitants adapted to inherited Greco-Roman and Persian cultures. By the mid-tenth century, the empire was fully developed, with few outside influences. After this time, Islamic civilization continued to be shaped by characteristic patterns of religious, political, and cultural traditions. These patterns remained largely unchallenged by outside influences until around 1850. In this respect, Islamic civilization was similar to Byzantine Eastern Christian, Hindu Indian, Neo-Confucian Chinese, and Confucian–Buddhist Japanese civilizations. All of these pursued a course more along their established internal patterns than as a result of innovation, interaction, and adaptation coming from the outside.

The Formation of Islamic Religious Civilization

Arab conquests and the rise of Islam were foundational events during the period 600–900. In the 600s, the Arabs carved out a kingdom by exploiting the preoccupation of the eastern Roman and Sasanid Persian Empires with their destructive wars of conquest in 602–628. Two Arab dynasties, the Umayyads and then the Abbasids, built an empire stretching thousands of miles. Given the enormous distances, the Abbasids granted autonomy to outlying provinces. In the process, their empire changed into a commonwealth of many states sharing a single Islamic religion. The pattern that Islamic religious civilization followed during its formative period was a variation of what happened in the other parts of Asia and Europe in the first millennium CE: regions of religious civilizations grew much larger than the political units within them, resulting in the appearance of commonwealths (Middle East, Europe, India) or periodic unity and disunity (China).

Commonwealth: An association of self-governing states sharing similar institutional and cultural traits.

The Beginnings of Islam

At the beginning of the 600s, the Sasanid Persian and Roman Empires battled each other in a lengthy war, which left their Arab subjects in Syria and Mesopotamia (Iraq) to their own devices. The Arabs had been nomadic inhabitants of the Syrian-Arabian desert since they began to use the camel as a pack animal around 1000 BCE (domesticated ca. 2500 BCE). They founded kingdoms and city-states on the Arabian Peninsula in the early centuries CE. By the early 600s, nearly all Arabs on the peninsula had been Christianized. In the mid-600s Arab leaders declared their rule over Roman Syria, conquered Sasanid Iraq, captured Egypt from the Romans, and destroyed the Sasanid Persian Empire. Through further conquests, the Arab realm became an empire, stretching by the mid-eighth century from Iberia in the west to the Indus River in the east.

Muslim: Initially:
believer in the
concordance among
all prophetic messages
from Abraham to
Muhammad. Later on:
believer who submits to
the will of God (*Allah*).

Caliph: Representative
of God, and later of
Muhammad, on earth.

Trinitarianism:
Christianity based
on the doctrine of God
the Father, Son, and
Holy Spirit.

The Final Roman–Persian War   The Roman–Persian rivalry reached a climax during the first three decades of the 600s. In 602, King of Kings Khosrow II (r. 590–628) invaded the Roman Empire. Within a little more than a decade, his generals had conquered Syria, Egypt, and Anatolia, and the Romans were hard pressed to defend themselves in their capital. The empire was saved by Heraclius (r. 610–641), the son of a governor from North Africa who seized power in Constantinople in 610. He reorganized the military and was able to drive the Sasanids back to Iraq. In 628 Khosrow was murdered by rivals, and the Sasanids were forced to make peace.

After his victory, Heraclius restored the prewar administrative structures in the province of Syria. He subsidized Arab leaders, reintroduced locally recruited garrisons and bishops in cities, and reduced the size of the army. To simplify the central administration, he replaced Latin with Greek as the language of the bureaucracy and the multiple Latin titles of the emperor (*imperator, caesar, augustus*) with the single Greek title of king (*basileus*), Christ's representative on earth. Thus it was under Heraclius that the Roman Empire became the Byzantine Empire, or Byzantium.

The Arab Empire of the Umayyads   The victory of Hercalius over the Sasanid Persians in 628 encouraged the Arabs to begin incursions from the north Arabian desert into Persian Iraq. After 602, when their viceroy was murdered by Khosrow II, they had retreated into the desert, where they allied themselves with the western Arabs. In a series of revenge raids 628–631, they invaded Persian Iraq. The Persians, racked by a dynastic war in the wake of Khosrow II's defeat by Heraclius and his murder by a family member, found it difficult to stop the Arabs. The success of the eastern Arabs against the Persians encouraged the Arabs in the west to begin raids in 632 againt the Byzantines in Palestine. Heraclius had reestablished Byzantine rule in Syria and Palestine after 628, but the exorbitant costs of the war against the Sasanid Persians had led him to concentrate his limited military forces in the north on the Persian frontier. His inability to defend the south with full force cost him dearly: In a series of battles 634-638 he lost Palestine and Syria to the Arabs and was forced to retreat to Anatolia. Subsequently, the Arabs conquered Byzantine Egypt (639-642) and ended the last resistance of the Sasanids in Persia in 651. An Arab empire rose in Palestine, Syria, Egypt, and Persia, which the strongman Muawiya (r. 661–680) consolidated under the dynastic rule of the Umayyads.

Umayyad Religious Developments   Under the third Umayyad ruler, Abd al-Malik (685–705), signs emerged of a religious orientation in the Arab Empire. Arabic inscriptions in and on the Dome of the Rock, dating to 691/692, refer to the prophet Muhammad and biblical predecessors, including Jesus the Messiah, as servants of God. Polemical verses oppose the Christian theology of Jesus as son of God, while other verses describe **Muslims** as believers in the "concordance" (*islam*) among all prophetic messages of the past. By implication this means that following God's commands in this concordance will bring salvation on the Day of Judgment.

The Dome of the Rock on Jerusalem's Temple Mount can be viewed as Abd al-Malik's counter-monument to the Church of the Holy Sepulcher on the other side of Jerusalem, built on the site of Jesus' tomb. Presumably he saw himself as the true "representative of God" (*khalifa*, or **caliph**) vis-à-vis the Byzantine emperor. Similarly, the emerging Islamic faith of the One God, Allah, which he was shaping as the state religion of the Umayyad Empire, was offered as a faith superior to **Trinitarian**

Byzantine Christianity. To buttress this anti-Trinitarian state religion, Abd al-Malik created a strong central administration and army, with Arabic as the bureaucratic language.

Umayyad Conquests in West and East Abd al-Malik's successors continued the Umayyad efforts to take over Byzantium. Armies composed of Arabs and Berbers conquered Byzantine North Africa in 686–698. Abd al-Malik's successors then became entangled in Western Christian politics. In 711, dissident Visigothic nobles called Berber and Arab troops into the Iberian Peninsula to help them oust the reigning Visigothic king. The Berbers, Arabs, and Visigothic allies then divided Iberia among themselves. In the same year, the Umayyads expanded their rule into central Asia and the Indus Valley.

Two decades later, the Iberian Berbers and Arabs pushed into France. One of these raids was commemorated in Western Christianity as the Battle of Tours in central France (732 or 733). Here, the founder of the Western Christian Carolingian Empire, Charles Martel (r. 714–741), beat back the invading raiders. Similarly, Arab campaigns in the Russian Caucasus failed around 740. It became evidently impossible to dispatch cavalry armies during summer campaigns from the capital of Damascus any farther than the Pyrenees, Hindu Kush, and Caucasus mountains (see Map 10.1).

From the Umayyads to the Abbasids The end of expansion and the need to shift from conquest to consolidation created a religio-political crisis in the empire. In Iran, the crisis exploded into revolution, as Persian military lords and Arab settlers expected a "rightly guided" leader (*Mahdi*, or Messiah) to arrive. This Mahdi would establish a realm of justice on earth at the end of time before God's Judgment. The revolutionaries overthrew the Umayyads in 750; but instead of the Mahdi and his realm of justice, the new dynasty of the Abbasids emerged. After moving the capital of the empire to Baghdad in Iraq, the Abbasids built the same kind of top-heavy central administration and army that had characterized the Umayyads.

Islamic Theology, Law, and Politics
In Iraq, the Abbasids completed what the Umayyads had begun in Syria. They enlarged and systematized the state religion of Islam, and sponsored the translation of scientific, philosophical, legal, and literary works from Syriac and Persian into Arabic. Schools and libraries spread from Baghdad to cities from Iberia to northwest

interactive timeline

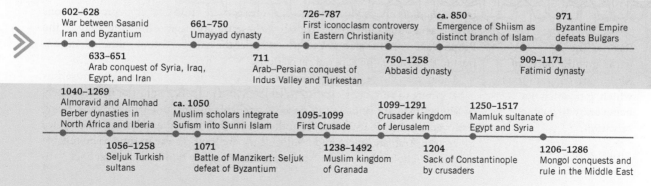

| 602–628 | 661–750 | 726–787 | ca. 850 | 971 |
| War between Sasanid Iran and Byzantium | Umayyad dynasty | First iconoclasm controversy in Eastern Christianity | Emergence of Shiism as distinct branch of Islam | Byzantine Empire defeats Bulgars |

| 633–651 | 711 | 750–1258 | 909–1171 |
| Arab conquest of Syria, Iraq, Egypt, and Iran | Arab–Persian conquest of Indus Valley and Turkestan | Abbasid dynasty | Fatimid dynasty |

| 1040–1269 | ca. 1050 | 1095–1099 | 1099–1291 | 1250–1517 |
| Almoravid and Almohad Berber dynasties in North Africa and Iberia | Muslim scholars integrate Sufism into Sunni Islam | First Crusade | Crusader kingdom of Jerusalem | Mamluk sultanate of Egypt and Syria |

| 1056–1258 | 1071 | 1238–1492 | 1204 | 1206–1286 |
| Seljuk Turkish sultans | Battle of Manzikert: Seljuk defeat of Byzantium | Muslim kingdom of Granada | Sack of Constantinople by crusaders | Mongol conquests and rule in the Middle East |

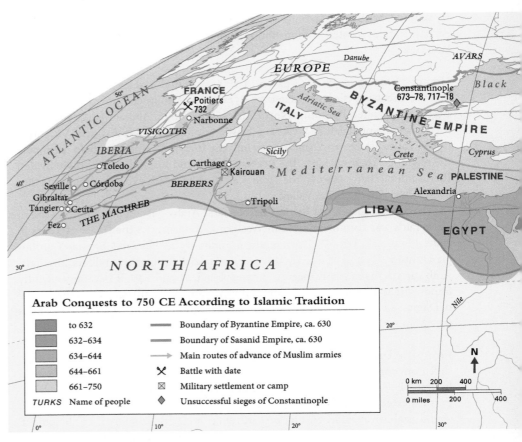

MAP **10.1** **Arab Conquests to 750.**

India. Many of these cities became cultural and political centers of their own, under autonomous dynasties that recognized the Abbasid caliphs in Baghdad but were basically independent. By around 950, an Islamic religious civilization organized into a commonwealth under ethnically diverse dynasties had emerged.

Shaping Islamic Theology In the 800s, scholars, judges, and bureaucrats in the Abbasid Empire completed the compilation of the Quran, the beginnings of which dated back to the mid 600s. Since it is God's word, Muhammad himself appears only a few times in the Quran. Therefore, parallel to the compilation of the Quran, traditions (*ahadith*) about Muhammad's life were gathered into encyclopedic collections as well as a biography (*sira*). Together, these traditions and the biography of the Prophet acquired the status of scripture, under the name of **Sunna**, although in contrast to the Quran, they are not revelations.

Sunna: The paradigmatic "path" of Muhammad's traditions, which, if trodden by believers, will lead to salvation.

Today, after more than a generation of extensive research, a scholarly consensus is beginning to emerge, according to which neither the traditions nor the biography of Muhammad are sufficient to serve as a reliable history of Islamic origins. Being removed by at least 150 years from the events they describe as having taken place in western Arabian Mecca and Medina, they are too far away in time to be reliable accounts. Scholars have so far been unable to trace any traditions further back than

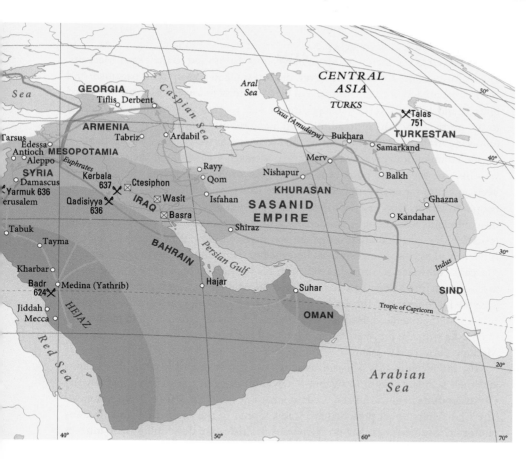

ca. 720, that is, roughly to the time of the sons of Abd al-Malik, who was discussed above as the ruler under whom the first signs of an emeriging Islam appeared. In other words, there is no Islamic documentation for the events of the early 600s; the only accounts we have date to the 800s and 900s.

This is not to say that the traditions and Prophet biography are devoid of kernels of historical truth. Present-day scholars of Islamic origins merely argue that it is not possible to identify any of these kernels clearly and unambiguously as historically true. They are embedded in the religious preoccupations of the Abbasids and their scholars, and are therefore theology more than history. Parallels to the gap between the literature on origins and the assumed earlier origins in Islam can be found also in Ancient Israel, Zoroastrianism, Christianity, Hinduism, Buddhism, Confucianism, and Daoism, as reflected in the corresponding chapters of this book.

According to the Abbasid theology of the 800s and 900s, Muhammad was born in 571 in Mecca, into a family that had once held the position of guardians of the pilgrimage sanctuary of the Kaaba. The sanctuary was founded by the biblical Abraham and his son Ismail (by Abraham's second wife Hagar), the founding ancestors of the Arabs. By the time of Muhammad, however, the Kaaba had deteriorated into a pagan temple. Muhammad himself grew up under the tutelage of one of his uncles, married the wealthy widow Khadija, and became a successful merchant buying and selling goods in Palestine and Syria. In the middle of his life (in ca. 610), during a meditative retreat, God sent his angel Gabriel and commanded Muhammad to preach the power as well as the mercy of the one invisible creator God to the pagan Meccans. The majority of the Meccans, however, did not want to give up their paganism and even threatened to kill Muhammad and his handful of followers. Muhammad saved himself and his followers by emigrating in 622 to Yathrib (renamed al-Madina) to the north. Here, Muhammad founded a community (**umma**) composed of his followers, Arab converts from among the Medinans, as well as Jewish inhabitants.

Umma: Community of all who believe in one God, with Muhammad as his prophet, and reject pagan idolatry (ignorance, *jahiliyya*) or associationism (*shirk*), such as the Christian doctrine of Trinity.

Muhammad now preached an enlarged message that assumed the size of what later became the divine book of the Quran. According to this message, there had been an entire series of prophets among the Israelites and Jews, all resisted by the people to whom God had sent them. They warned of the punishments of God if his commands would not be heeded. Muhammad was the final prophet, following Jesus the Messiah. God's Last Judgment was soon to follow. When the Jews rejected Muhammad as a prophet, however, he expelled them from Medina. And when the Meccans continued to resist his return to his birthplace, he battled against them, forcing them into a draw. In a final coup in 630, Muhammad arranged for a pilgrimage with his followers to the Kaaba, which he cleansed of all pagan divinities, rededicating it to the one God. He then returned to Medina and died in quiet meditation in 632. As with the prophets before him, God had finally granted him success: The Meccans converted to Islam.

The intention in this Abbasid theology of Islamic origins is clear: The caliphs and their scholars sought to further a new monotheistic religion that had left any Christian roots behind and centered on what one may call Islam's Triple Arabness: The Arab Muhammad preached an Arabic Quran to the Arabs of Arabia, thereby ending an assumed paganism on the peninsula. Instead of developing Islam into yet another soon-to-be-forgotten Christian sect in the Middle East, like others that had arisen in previous centuries, the Abbasids turned it into its own separate religion. For this religion they claimed superiority: Thanks to their zeal for holy war (**jihad**), the Muslims had conquered the Persians and had reduced the Byzantines to Anatolia and the Balkans.

Jihad: Literally "struggle (for the path of God—*fi sabil Allah*)." This can range from personal struggle for faith to war in the name of Islam.

Five religious duties identify a Muslim: the profession of faith, prayer, fasting, alms-giving, and pilgrimage to Mecca. The profession of faith is summed up in the formula "There is no God but God, and Muhammad is his messenger." Prayer occurs five times daily; on Fridays the noon prayer is performed in the congregational mosque. Fasting means a month-long abstinence during Ramadan from food, drink, and sex during the daylight hours. Alms-giving is a donation or tax to benefit the poor, and the pilgrimage is a journey made at least once in one's life to Mecca.

Creating Islamic Law   The five religious duties are part of the body of moral–legal duties, the **Sharia**. The Abbasids had inherited a judicial system from the Umayyads that was based on the legal traditions of Roman Syria and Sasanid Persia. In the late 700s, the dynasty sponsored the translations of digests of the Justinian Roman law codex in order to create a unified legal system. Since Muslims were at the same time compiling the Quran, it is not surprising that the creation of the Sharia became part of the same unification process. When it was completed in the mid-900s, the Sharia encompassed the legal verses of the Quran, the prophetic Sunna, and legal commentaries.

Sharia: The combined body of the legal verses of the Quran, the prophetic Sunna, and the legal commentaries of the 800s and 900s, covering law as well as morality.

The Separation of State and Religion   The shaping of Islamic theology and law became controversial toward the middle of the 800s. If all theology and law had to be based on the Quran and Sunna, sooner or later every possible moral or legal matter would be unchangeably grounded in God's authority. Nothing could be added to the Sharia or changed in it, and one could only interpret. To preserve their freedom to shape the Sharia, the caliphs instituted a loyalty oath from 833 to 849, which required all judges and jurists to support the policy of continued caliphal legislation.

A minority refused the oath and found support among the urban craftsmen and traders who believed that God's law should be above human manipulation. After riots the Abbasids enacted a compromise whereby the religious scholars (*ulama*) became the guardians of the Sharia and the caliphs its executers. This compromise resulted in a separation of religion and state, with the ulama responsible for the judicial system and the state executing the law according to its own interests.

Shiite Islam   From about 950 onward, Islam under the guardianship of the ulama is known as Sunni Islam. It expresses the Sunna of the Prophet and the consensus of the religious community represented by the ulama and laid down in the Sharia. Sunni Islam always encompassed the majority of Muslims (about 90 percent today). Followers of Shiite [SHEE-ite] Islam make up about 10 percent of Muslims worldwide, although they are the majority in contemporary Iran, Iraq, and Lebanon.

The origin of Shiite Islam dates to the end of the Umayyads, when revolutionaries proclaimed the imminent arrival of the Mahdi. Tradition places the Shiite beginnings in the period of the first four caliphs, when Caliph Ali lost his throne and Ali's grandson Husayn lost his bid for the caliphate against the Umayyads. According to tradition, Ali was a cousin of the Prophet; the husband of one of his daughters, Fatima; and the founder of the Alid family, where the eldest male in direct descent was entitled to the leadership of the Muslim community in place of the Umayyads.

The main differences between Sunnism and Shiism concern the roles of tradition and authority. The tradition of Husayn's martyrdom near Karbala in Iraq at the hands of the Sunni Umayyads is central for all Shiites and is commemorated during Ashura, the tenth day of the month Muharram. The authority of the Alid descendants in the past, and today of the leaders of the Shiite clergy, is absolute and infallible. Sunnis, by contrast, reject the Karbala tradition. For them the consensus of the community separate from rulers and the absence of a scholarly hierarchy among the ulama are supreme. Shiite–Sunni differences have flared up throughout history to the present day.

When the Abbasids squashed the apocalyptical expectation of God's kingdom at the end of time, apocalypticism went underground. It resurfaced in 874 when the twelfth-generation descendant of Ali was reported to have died without a visible successor. A radical group formed in Syria around the doctrine that a descendant of the seventh-generation leader would appear soon as the Mahdi. A dispute concerning the legitimate successor in the seventh generation divided the Shiites. Those who accepted the twelfth-generation descendant remained nonrevolutionary.

The radical group of "Seveners" fomented armed rebellions around 900 in outlying provinces of the Islamic commonwealth. The most successful rebellion was that of the Fatimids in 909 in eastern Algeria and Tunisia. The Fatimids were Shiites who founded a counter caliphate to that of the Abbasids, extending from North Africa

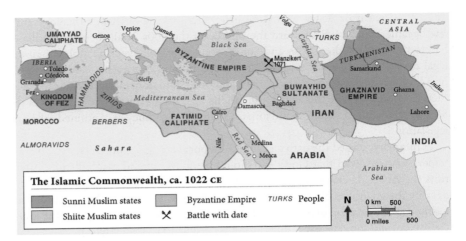

MAP 10.2 **The Islamic Commonwealth, ca. 1022 CE.**

to Egypt, western Arabia, and parts of Syria. Until their end in 1171 they claimed to represent God's kingdom on earth through a higher form of justice than that of the Abbasids.

The Abbasids in Crisis   In the second half of the 800s, the Abbasids were hit by severe financial problems. The Sasanid Persian expansion of agriculture between the Euphrates and Tigris Rivers, continued by the Abbasids, had reached the limits of its potential. Agricultural tax revenue shrank. As a result, the administration found it difficult to maintain its palace culture and bureaucracy. Palace guards, no longer paid, took over still-fertile tax districts directly as personal assignments in place of direct salaries.

By the early eleventh century, a majority of the soldiers in the guards were Turks, recruited as slaves and manumitted as adults. From 861 to 945, Turkic slave generals wielded power in Baghdad while retaining the caliphs as titular heads of the government. The main function of the generals was the control of political affairs in Iraq, but they also continued the Umayyad holy war against Byzantium. The only other active jihad activity was the Muslim conquest of Byzantine Sicily by an autonomous dynasty in Tunisia, completed by the Fatimids (827–902). For all practical purposes, the conquest period had ended.

Eastern Christian Civilization in Byzantium

Under siege by the Umayyads and Abbasids, the old eastern Roman Empire, now Byzantium, had retreated to Anatolia and parts of the Balkans. (In current scholarship, the transition from eastern Rome to Byzantium is usually dated to the loss of Palestine, Syria, and Egypt to the Arabs by ca. 640.) Byzantium survived because its emperors reconstituted the state on a military and religious basis: locally organized border defenses and redefinition of Christian doctrine. Similar to the Abbasid Empire, Byzantium evolved into the center of a commonwealth of Eastern Christian states.

Byzantium's Difficult Beginnings

The Roman transition to the Byzantine Eastern Christian civilization was gradual. Nevertheless, the switch in emphasized title from emperor to king (*basileus*), the Umayyad military pressure, the organization of the Anatolian defense, and iconoclasm amounted to a new civilizational identity. Once this new identity and the recovery from the Muslim (and, in the Balkans, Slavic) onslaughts were achieved, Byzantium followed a pattern similar to that of the Muslims. Eastern Christianity became a commonwealth, with autonomous Balkan and Ukrainian realms, and evolved into a top-heavy centralized state relying on palace guards.

Survival Strategies   Under constant Arab pressure in eastern Anatolia, northern Africa, and Sicily (636–863), the Byzantine Empire shrank to an Anatolian–Balkan realm. Between 653 and 833, both the Umayyad and Abbasid caliphs attacked Constantinople seven times. The empire survived the attacks only by withdrawing from much of the Balkans. Around 580, Slavs migrated southward to settle in the Balkans. Here, the Slavs gradually became the linguistically dominant population, assimilating speakers of other languages, such as Turkish-speaking groups of Bulgars from eastern Russia. These Bulgars migrated in the 500s to the Byzantine lower Danube, where they were influenced by Slavic culture and asserted their independence from Byzantium in 681. As the Byzantines were fighting for survival against the Arabs in Anatolia, the Bulgars became a major power in the Balkans.

Focusing initially almost entirely on Anatolia, the emperors created new, stationary troops known as "themes" (Greek *themata*) recruited from among volunteer foot soldiers in the interior Byzantine provinces. Themes were given small plots from imperial estates in the exposed provinces of Anatolia (and later also against the Slavs in the Balkans) as well as cash and food provisions, which were collected as taxes from large landowner estates and free farmers. The themes' main task was to harass the invading Arabs. Southern Anatolia suffered harshly from constant Arab raids. Provincial life in Anatolia became increasingly poor for its Christian inhabitants, and even Constantinople declined in wealth.

Iconoclasm   Throughout this period the Byzantine emperors actively shaped religious doctrine and law, similar to the caliphs in the Islamic empire. One religious dispute taken up by the emperors was **iconoclasm**, that is, the destruction of religious images in accordance with Exodus 20:40 in the Hebrew Bible (726–787 and 814–842). As the Christian church had evolved in the first six centuries CE, church fathers and theologians who stressed the divinity of Jesus and the role of his mother Mary as the "God bearer" gained prominence, especially in Egypt and Syria. Churchmen who, by contrast, sought to hold on to the human status of Jesus and Mary, became marginal or were declared heretical. The rise of Islam, of course, reversed this trend, with its radical emphasis on all prophets, including Jesus, being mere humans. In the 720s, when Byzantium was no longer burdened with the Churches of Egypt and Syria, the return to a more even-handed view of Jesus as both divine and human became attractive again in the eyes of bishops and emperors.

Under orders by emperors, the destruction or plastering over of images gathered speed in the 750s, although it was by no means uniform or intense in all parts of the empire. Since the production of art was expensive and the state was strapped for resources at a time of still-dangerous Muslim incursions, the emperors were relieved

Iconoclasm: Removal of all religious images from churches and monasteries during a period in the Byzantine Empire, under orders of the emperors.

The Byzantine Commonwealth. Characteristic of eastern Christianity are the many churches dedicated to Hagia Sophia, "Holy Wisdom," which can be found throughout the Byzantine commonwealth, from the Balkans to the Caucasus. Though each region developed its own architectural style, they all organized sacred space in similar ways. A masterpiece of design and engineering based in part on the theories of the third-century BCE mathematician Archimedes, the Hagia Sophia in Constantinople was dedicated in 537 by the emperor Justinian on the foundations of an earlier structure (a). Its massive dome was often compared to the great dome of heaven itself, and the church would become the prototype for many others throughout the commonwealth in subsequent centuries, including the Cathedral of Saint Sophia in Kiev, whose foundations were laid early in the eleventh century (b). While it exhibits a distinctly Kievan style of church architecture, including over a dozen cupolas, the cathedral nonetheless embodies an unmistakable Byzantine tradition whose roots extend deep into the past.

image analysis

to be able to reduce their patronage. But in the 800s, the Muslim danger abated; and resistance in the ordinary population, still deeply committed to the trend of the previous centuries, made it increasingly difficult for the emperors to remain committed to iconoclasm. Monks, who were much closer to the population than bishops, patriarchs, and emperors, had a particular interest in images: Many monasteries contained the tombs of saints and their images, and both functioned for pilgrims in the same way as Jesus and Mary did: they were intercessors to God. By 842 the emperors gave up their support of iconoclasm and thereafter withdrew from imposing doctrines on the Church. Like the caliphs in the Abbasid Empire, the Byzantine emperors left religion to the religious institution. As we will see in Chapter 11, a similar disengagement between politics and religion occurred in Western Christianity after the investiture controversy two centuries later. In this respect, the religious civilizations of Islam, Byzantium, and Western Christianity followed similar patterns of development.

Transformation into a Commonwealth   In the mid-800s, the strategy of using themes to defend Anatolia finally paid off. By exploiting the fiscal crisis of the Abbasids after ca. 850, theme commanders raided Muslim settlements in eastern Anatolia and northern Iraq with increasing frequency. By 965, Byzantium had regained all of Anatolia, and in 969 it retook the northern Syrian gateway of Antioch. The emperors now turned to the Balkans. Here, the Bulgars had converted to Eastern Christianity in 864 and, under their own emperors, had forced Byzantium to pay tributes in the early 900s. But in 971, the Byzantines crushed the Bulgars and reintegrated their realm into the empire. By the middle of the eleventh century, Byzantium's territory extended from Belgrade and the Balkans southeast to Antioch in northern Syria (see Map 10.3).

The reintegration of the Balkans into the empire formed the background for the transformation of Byzantium into a commonwealth of Eastern Christianity. In the late 700s, Kiev (in what is now the Ukraine) was an outpost of the mixed Jewish, Christian, and Muslim Khazar realm in southern Russia. The merchants in Kiev were "Rus" (from which the name "Russia" is derived), of Scandinavian origin. By the 800s, most Rus had intermarried with Slavs and had become culturally Slavic. In addition to trading, the Rus repeatedly raided Byzantium, thereby adding to the difficulties of the empire during the 800s and early 900s. By the mid-900s, Rus trading and raiding had made Kiev a regional power.

MAP 10.3 **The Byzantine Empire, ca. 1025 CE.**

In 988, Grand Prince Vladimir I of Kiev (r. 980–1015) decreed the conversion of his subjects to Christianity. With this conversion of the Ukraine, Eastern Christianity expanded beyond the Byzantine Empire into Russia. An Eastern Christian commonwealth of states emerged in this region similar to that of Islam in the Middle East and the Mediterranean.

Military Changes   The Kievan troops in the service of the Byzantine Empire, called the "Varangian Guard," formed the nucleus of foreign palace guards and fulfilled functions similar to those of the Turkic slave guards among the Abbasids. In Byzantium, they were added to balance older Armenian or indigenous regiments recruited from among the themes to protect the emperors from rivals for the throne. These rivals were often from provincial landowning families, which formed an aristocracy that remained prominent until the end of Byzantium in 1453.

In the later 900s, when the empire had recovered, the emperors embarked on a recentralization of the empire, reducing the themes in order to weaken the aristocracy. The effect of these changes in the military was a rising dependency of the emperors on palace guards and a weakening of the border defenses. The Byzantine

Byzantine Woman Defending Her Virtue. Conscious of their privileged status, the Varangian Guards often mistreated ordinary people in the population. Like the Turkish slave guards at the Abbasid court, they had the reputation of being thieves, murderers, and rapists. In this image, Ioannes Skylitzes (ca. 1040–1101), a historian and illustrator, delighted in depicting the story of a woman who not only defended her virtue successfully by killing her attacker but also had the stunned surviving Varangians turn over the clothes of their dead comrade to her.

Creed: "… [A]nd the Holy Spirit, the Lord, the giver of life, who proceeds from the Father and the Son [*filioque*], who with the Father and the Son is adored and glorified" (partial quote). The *filioque* was inserted into the Creed in Spain at the end of the 500s against Arianism, which denied the divinity of Jesus, but it was never ratified in the east.

Eucharist: The partaking of bread and wine in commemoration of Jesus Christ's last supper. Byzantium accused Rome of serving the flat Middle Eastern bread, which it denounced as "Jewish."

Celibacy: Abstinence from sexual relations and/or marriage. Eastern Christianity allows clerical marriage.

Empire experienced the same phenomenon of a top-heavy state and a power-hungry palace military that had already plagued the Abbasids for two centuries.

The first province where the beginning military weakness of Byzantium had consequences was southern Italy. In this restless place, the emperor had no choice in 1051 but to appoint a local lord to the governorship. Western Norsemen or Normans had entered the service of regional princes who combatted both the Byzantines and Muslim raiders from Sicily. Initially, Byzantium and the papacy in Rome cooperated against the Normans, even though the pope was at loggerheads with the patriarch of Constantinople over clerical jurisdiction in southern Italy. At one point, in 1053, the Normans achieved a military victory over the pope, but since they submitted to his authority soon thereafter, the latter was now free to pursue his jurisdictional claims more forcefully. Striving for jurisdictional supremacy over both Western and Eastern Christianities, the pope, Leo IX (in office 1049–1054), dispatched an embassy to Constantinople to assert his claim.

Unfortuantely for the lead ambassador, the patriarch of Constantinople, Michael I Cerularius (in office 1043-1059), was also a man of elevated views about his role. For him, the pope was at best a first among equals and he even viewed himself as the arbiter of the Byzantine imperial order, deciding among claimants to the imperial throne. He refused to meet with the ambassador for months, even though the emperor still favored continued cooperation with the pope. The two Churches had not been in communication for about half a century, disagreeing over a variety of liturgical and monastic practices (among others, the *filioque* in the **Creed**, the bread of the **Eucharist**, and **celibacy**). The central dispute was about the jusrisdictional authority of the pope as laid down in the *Donation of Constantine*, a document forged in Rome in the 700s that gave the pope supremacy over the patriarchs of Constantinople, Alexandria, Antioch, and Jerusalem. Although taken at face value in the eleventh century, the *Donation* was interpreted differently in west and east. Only in the Renaissance, as explained in Ch. 17, did scholars unmask the document as a fake.

Eventually, in July 1054, the ambassador placed a letter on the altar of the Hagia Sophia, excommunicating Michael from the Church. Michael responded with an excommunication of the embassy. In order to pacify the popular unrest that was forming in the streets, both patriarch and emperor blamed the events on a conspiracy by the governor of southern Italy, alleged to be a secret Catholic, who had sent a false embassy pretending to be from Rome. Thus, in 1054 the first formal step was taken to ratify what had been in existence already for several centuries, that is, the existence of two separate Christianities, an Eastern Orthodox Christianity and a Western Catholic Christianitiy.

The Seljuk Invasion and the Crusades

The decline of Byzantine power in Italy had an equally fatal parallel in the east of the Byzantine Empire, in Asia Minor or Anatolia. Islamized Seljuk [sel-JOOK] Turks had migrated in the early eleventh century southwestward from central Asia. They conquered the shrunken Abbasid realm and inflicted heavy land losses on the Byzantines in Anatolia. To beat back the Seljuks, the emperors called on the pope for help, the recent church split in 1054 notwithstanding. The pope responded by sending the First Crusaders, who conquered Jerusalem. The subsequent crusade kingdom of Jerusalem was of some help to Byzantium to regain land lost to the Seljuks in Anatolia, but it suffered a severe setback when Western Christians sacked Constantinople in the Fourth Crusade and established a Latin empire in Byzantium for nearly two generations (1204–1261). The crusader kingdom survived until 1291, when the Muslim Mamluks of Egypt and Syria captured Jerusalem.

The Seljuk Invasion   As discussed earlier, Turks formed part of the ethnic mix of Islamic civilization from the early 800s onward. Technically, they had the status of military slaves (pl. *mamalik*) in the service of Arab and Persian dynasties as elite troops. Once converted to Islam, however, they were free men, and as such, some Turks even founded dynasties. To replenish the ranks of Turkish elite troops, the rulers sent raiding parties into the grazing grounds of central Asia inhabited by pagan nomadic Turkish clans and federations. Gradually, however, nomadic Turkish leaders benefiting from trade developed an interest in urbanized Islamic civilization. This interest was similar to that of the Rus of Kiev seeking to adopt Eastern Christianity, as we saw above. It was in this context that the Seljuk Turks east of the Volga River converted and began their migration into the Islamic commonwealth.

Seljuk leaders believed that Muslims had grown lax with their holy war against the Byzantines. Furthermore, they considered Shiism a heresy. In Baghdad, free-born nonrevolutionary "Twelver" Shiites had partially replaced the Turkish slaves in the palace guards. In Egypt and parts of Syria the revolutionary "Sevener" Fatimids still sought to overthrow the Abbasids in Iraq. Assuming the exalted title "sultan" (from Arabic for power), the Seljuk leaders devoted themselves to jihad and began their first raids against the Byzantines in the 1040s. By 1059 they were in control of Baghdad, from which they conducted their holy war against Byzantium and the Fatimids.

The Defeat of Manzikert   Byzantine emperors did not have time to rebuild an army that could stop the Seljuk conquest. An effort in 1071 to drive the Seljuks from eastern Anatolia failed. The assortment of remaining theme soldiers and central regiments, as well as palace guards and other mercenaries, was unable to hold together at Manzikert in eastern Anatolia. In the end the emperor found himself a prisoner of the Seljuk sultan.

The consequences of the defeat were severe. In the following decade and a half, the Seljuks occupied most of Anatolia, leaving the Byzantines in command of only a few coastal cities and islands. In the mid-1000s, Normans carved out realms for themselves from Byzantine southern Italy and Greece. From here they invaded Greece and became a real threat for the empire in the second half of the eleventh century.

The situation improved only in 1092, when the reigning sultan died and the Seljuk Empire broke apart into competing successor states. By this time, a reform-minded emperor, Alexius I Comnenus (r. 1081–1118), had driven out the Normans from Greece. Alexius turned his attention to his most dangerous Muslim neighbor, the Rum Sultanate of the Seljuks in Nicaea, 60 miles from Constantinople. However, he needed more troops than he was able to pay for in the Varangian Guard,

Battle of Manzikert. The battle was not only a bitter defeat for the Byzantine army at the hands of the Seljuks; it was also a personal humiliation for Emperor Romanus IV, who had done his best to prepare for battle. This humiliation had such repercussions even in Western Christianity that Maître de Rohan, the artist of this miniature, in the early fifteenth century still found it worthy of commemoration. Rohan, in the service of members of the French aristocracy, was a major manuscript illustrator of his time.

his only reliable military force. Relations with Western Christianity had improved, and when Alexius sent an embassy in the spring of 1095 to Rome, he found a sympathetic ear.

The Crusades Alexius received more from the pope than he had bargained for. At the Council of Clermont in 1095, Pope Urban II (r. 1088–1099) called for an armed pilgrimage to aid Byzantium and liberate the church from the Seljuks. Well-equipped knights as well as poorer folk responded enthusiastically (for more on the Crusades, see Chapter 11). For Alexius, the crusade was an embarrassment. It included Normans who had battled him in Greece. Even if he were able to control them, how much land in Anatolia would the victorious crusaders turn over to him? And even if considerable territory were ceded, how would he be able to defend it by himself? At first, Alexius did indeed receive what he wanted: With the help of the Byzantine navy, the crusaders conquered Nicaea and grudgingly turned it over to him.

In the period thereafter, however, Alexius was under no illusion about the willingness of the crusaders to conquer Anatolia and Syria for him. Even though the emperor sent aid to the crusaders during their siege of Antioch (1097–1098), he did not receive the city after the crusaders' victory. Nor did he obtain Jerusalem, which the crusaders conquered from the Fatimids in 1099. Instead, in 1100 the crusaders made Jerusalem the capital of an independent crusader kingdom.

For Muslim historians in the early 1100s, the crusades were delayed Christian jihads in revenge for Arab expansion under the Umayyads. They dated the beginning of this revenge to the Norman invasion of Muslim Sicily in 1061 and the Castilian capture of Toledo in 1085. The fall of Jerusalem in 1099 exposed, they felt, an alarming laxness of Muslim religious zeal.

The loss of Sicily, Toledo, and Jerusalem was substantial. The Emirate of Sicily had flourished for a century and a half. The Emirate of Toledo had been part of a nearly three-century-old Islamic culture in Iberia whose power derived from its gold trade with West Africa and on palace guards manned by Slavic slave soldiers. The losses of Sicily and Toledo effectively ended Muslim dominance in the Mediterranean.

Muslim Recovery and Byzantine–Crusader Cooperation Imad al-Din Zenki (r. 1127–1146) was a Turkish-descended leader from Upper Iraq who took

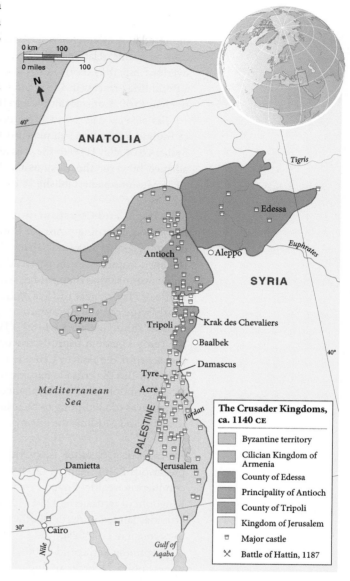

MAP 10.4 The Crusader Kingdoms, ca. 1140 CE.

The Crusader Kingdoms, ca. 1140 CE

- Byzantine territory
- Cilician Kingdom of Armenia
- County of Edessa
- Principality of Antioch
- County of Tripoli
- Kingdom of Jerusalem
- ⌂ Major castle
- ✕ Battle of Hattin, 1187

crusader Jerusalem

the admonitions of the historians to heart. He, and later his sons, made steady progress against the crusader kingdom. He weathered the Second Crusade of 1147–1149, mounted in response to Zanki's sack of Edessa, but could not prevent the crusaders from repairing relations with Byzantium. After submitting Antioch to Byzantine overlordship, they received naval support in return. The king of Jerusalem married a Byzantine princess in 1158, and the emperor himself married a princess from Antioch in 1160. Constantinople and Jerusalem forged a powerful alliance.

The alliance paid off in 1169: A Byzantine fleet carried crusaders to an invasion of Fatimid Egypt. The Fatimids had never recovered from the loss of the Palestinian–Syrian coast after 1099 to the crusaders. Unfortunately for the Byzantium–crusader alliance, however, the Muslims also coveted Egypt and drove out the Byzantines. By 1171 Muslims had established a formidable anticrusader realm.

Jerusalem and Constantinople Lost   The Sunni Muslim conquest of Shiite Egypt was a turning point for both the crusaders and Byzantium. The Kurdish-descended emir Saladin (Salah al-Din Yusuf ibn Ayyub, r. 1174–1193), leader of the anti-crusader realm, parlayed the agricultural wealth of Egypt into a formidable war machine that wore down the crusaders. In 1187, Saladin's victory in the Battle of Hattin, near the Sea of Galilee, enabled him to reconquer Jerusalem and nearly wipe out the kingdom.

The Third Crusade of 1189–1192, in response to the losses after Hattin, saved the rump kingdom from destruction. Its failure to regain Jerusalem, however, set the stage for the Fourth Crusade in 1204, planned as a mass campaign to take the holy city. But the crusade became instead a conquest of Byzantium with the sack of Constantinople in 1204. The concentrated urban wealth of Constantinople in Byzantium was too tempting to be resisted, even if Eastern Christians were brethren in the faith and Muslims the enemy.

Precarious Crusader Survival for Another Century   Having established a precarious Latin regime (1204–1257), western Europeans became obsessed with conquering wealthy Egypt. Five more crusades were launched for the benefit of the Kingdom of Jerusalem (1191–1291), whose capital was at Acre. Only one of these crusades landed in Acre; all others sailed to, or toward, Egypt without ever leading to permanent conquest.

Beginning in the mid-1200s, however, the crusader kingdom became the victim of new political forces arising in the Middle East. In 1250 the Mamluks—Turkish military slaves from the Russian steppes and dominant in the armies of Saladin's successors—established their own regime in Egypt (1250–1517). In 1260 the Mamluks had to face the pagan Mongols, who had emerged in the previous half-century under Genghis Khan (r. 1206–1227) and his descendants as a major power (see Chapter 13). The Mongols were tough competition for the Mamluks (see Chapter 12).

In 1255 the Mongols conquered Iran and Iraq, ended what remained of the Abbasid caliphate in Baghdad in 1258, and advanced into Syria. The Mamluks, however, defeated the Mongols in several battles between 1260 and 1303, and pushed them from Syria back into Iraq and Iran. Under the name of Ilkhanids, the Mongols converted to Islam and became linguistically Persian. Close to being free of the Mongol threat, the Mamluks terminated the crusader state in 1291 with the conquest of Acre.

Islamic and Eastern Christian Civilizations at Their Height

By 1300, the borders between Western and Eastern Christianity as well as Islam were again clearly drawn. The most important state was the Mamluk Sultanate in Egypt, Palestine, and Syria. Victorious against the crusaders and the Mongols, this rich and powerful state endured for nearly three centuries (1250–1517) and represented Middle Eastern Islamic civilization at its peak. Byzantium had been rebuilt as a small realm located mostly in the Balkans (1261–1453). Both the Mamluk Sultanate and Byzantium were eventually succeeded by the Turkish Ottoman Empire (Chapter 16), the origins of which date to 1300, and which shifted the center of Islamic civilization from Egypt northward to Anatolia and the Balkans.

THE MAMLUK EMPIRE, ca. 1300

State and Society in Mamluk Egypt

Few in the Mamluk ruling class spoke Arabic or intermarried with the indigenous population of their realm in Egypt and Syria. The indigenous population possessed its own autonomous institutions. Although the Mamluks provided military protection, especially during the time of the Mongol attacks, the indigenous population had to pay for it dearly.

The Mamluk Ruling Class   At the top of the ruling class was the sultan, who controlled the annual purchases of slaves and commanded the largest cavalry regiment. The Mamluk sultan governed with a council of emirs, each of whom commanded a cavalry regiment of his own. The lesser emirs in the council were stationed in the provincial cities of Egypt and Syria. Additional auxiliary troops consisted of sons of Mamluks, tribal nomadic contingents, and freeborn Turks. The sultans maintained a lavish court in Cairo. A civilian bureaucracy, composed of Muslims, Coptic Christians, and Jews, staffed the main ministries. Other officials oversaw the granaries, oil presses, the mint, hospitals, the postal service, water supplies, sanitation, horse stables, and the hippodrome (for polo games). The maintenance of a standing, well-supplied army was of utmost concern.

Mamluk power was based on a large, state-centered economy. At the center was a rich, irrigated agriculture. In the countryside, the top tier of Mamluk officers held tax assignments in the form of village districts. They used the revenues from these assignments to pay the lower officers and regular soldiers of their regiments. Bureaucrats and managers recruited from the indigenous Arab population aided them in the collection of the taxes.

In the cities, the same top officers owned buildings and collected rents. They hired large labor forces for the construction or repair of mosques, city walls, fortresses, and waterworks. Sultans and emirs usually paid regular wages to their workers but also used forced labor. Their military campaigns were occasions for large numbers of people to find additional employment. In short, nearly all economic activities in the villages as well as cities revolved around the demands of the sultans and emirs.

The Urban Working Population   Below the Mamluk ruling class and the intermediate urban elite were craftspeople, laborers, domestics, and farmers. Urban

Mamluk Cavalry. Mamluk horsemen, protected by chain-mail armor and wearing helmets with visors, wielded swords and lances similar to the crusaders. Stationed in barracks on Nile islands near Cairo, the Asian-born, originally pagan, Muslim-educated Mamluks formed a standing army of a dozen regiments that trained daily and could be mobilized within a short time. Their children were not slaves but freeborn Muslims, who were admitted only to auxiliary military units. The Mamluks were thus a one-generation ruling class replenished regularly through the purchase of military slaves from the outside.

working people lived in city quarters, which were organized according to religion, ethnicity, and, in the case of the Sunni majority, family and clan ties. The city quarters were not closed communities, however, and always contained minorities.

City quarters, crafts clusters, and neighborhood mosques and Sufi lodges were autonomous. Although overseen by appointees of the market inspectors, the residents often engaged in acts of resistance against the Mamluks in times of famine, overtaxation, or arbitrary rule. In addition, Syrian cities, such as Damascus and Aleppo, had a tradition of youth gangs fomenting unrest outside the city walls. During times of peace these gangs collected protection money from owners of workshops and market stalls, inevitably coming into conflict with the market inspectors. At times of economic or political distress they linked forces across city quarters and transformed themselves into formidable militias, holding back entire Mamluk regiments. The gangs provided a degree of protection for society from the state.

Byzantine Provincial and Central Organization

The one-generational system defining the Mamluk ruling class was a unique form of governmental organization in the history of Islamic religious civilization. Just as unique was the theme organization in the Byzantine Empire. The crucial difference, of course, was the time difference. The Mamluk Sultanate was a phenomenon at the height of Islamic civilization. The theme organization, which characterized the very beginning of the Byzantine Empire, was absent from the reconstituted Byzantine Empire in all but the name.

Divorce Court. Husband and wife arguing about a divorce before a judge; scene from al-Hariri, *Maqamat* (ms. dated 1222). Hariri's stories, among the most popular during the classical period, involve a poor but eloquent storyteller traveling from town to town in different disguises but being recognized each time by the fictional author. The stories include occurrences of everyday life, like this divorce.

The Rise of the Landed Aristocracy   In Egypt the requirements of irrigation favored administrative centralization. Byzantium, with its rain-fed agriculture, oscillated between free smallholder farms and big landlords on one hand and a large central administration on the other. This central administration flourished under conditions of relative external peace.

When the themes were introduced around 660 the empire still possessed a functional urban system and money economy. Granted, while the emperors settled foot soldiers and horsemen on plots of land, they also collected taxes in money and distributed them in the form of stipends among the soldiers. Furthermore, plenty of small freeholders and large landlords who owned property inherited from the late Roman period coexisted with the themes.

In the difficult years of defense, the emperor and his central administration were unable to prevent the rise of the landed aristocracy. From about the mid-700s, landlords acquired small farms and reserved the positions of theme generals for their families: they became a hereditary aristocracy. Free farmers turned increasingly into tenant farmers of the aristocracy. Like the Mamluk emirs a little later, the aristocratic landlords were the wealthiest segment of imperial society.

The Recentralization of the Empire   Generals from the aristocracy were the main competitors for the office of emperor in Constantinople. But when the empire recovered from the 900s onward, high officials of the bureaucracy developed their own ambitions hostile to those of the aristocracy. In the eleventh and twelfth centuries, the emperors were torn between the interests of the aristocracy and the central administration. In the eleventh century few emperors were up to the task of long-term reforms, such as ensuring regular theme training or exercises and prohibiting the acquisition of land by the aristocracy.

The easy way out was to hire mercenaries, beginning with the Varangian Guard. Competent emperors, as from the Komnenos dynasty (1081–1185), however, realized that the state could not finance more than small numbers of mercenaries. Instead, they made use of the land assignment institution (*pronoia*), which allowed an assignee to collect all taxes from a parcel of land in return for military service. This institution became the backbone of a patronage system in Constantinople.

Of course, after the hiatus of 1204–1261, the court and its top families were largely gone. What were left were the aristocratic families in the reconstituted provinces. Their reluctance to submit permanently to the new Paleolog imperial family of post-1261 eventually doomed Byzantium when the Ottomans decided to end it in 1453.

Commercial Relations from the Atlantic to the South China Sea

The Persians and Romans had pioneered the trade of gold and silver for luxuries during the period 600 BCE–600 CE. This trade expanded during the Fatimid and Mamluk periods in Egypt, facilitated by the cultural unity of Islamic civilization. In addition, Byzantium during its heyday (950–1050) and western Europe after the First Crusade (1099) were integrated in the luxury trade. An Afro-Eurasian commercial world system, extending from West Africa to China, linked the Islamic, Eastern Christian, and Western Christian civilizations to the Indian and Chinese civilizations (see Map 10.5).

Trade Routes and Commerce   To understand the West Africa–China world trade, we begin with West Africa. Villagers mined gold in the rain forest on the upper Niger and Senegal Rivers and traded with African merchants from kingdoms located along the middle Niger. The kings sent raiding parties to other regions in the rain forest to capture slaves. Merchants and kings then sold the gold and surplus of slaves to visiting Muslim merchants from North Africa and Iberia.

The visitors from the north paid with North African and Iberian manufactures and with salt from mines in the Sahara. In the Mediterranean basin, Muslims, Jews, and Western and Eastern Christians shared the trade of West African gold and

Anonymous, "The Farmer's Law" ca. 700 CE

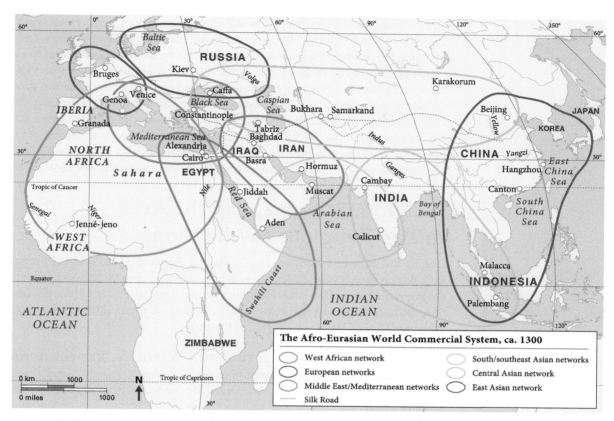

MAP **10.5** **The Afro-Eurasian World Commercial System, ca. 1300.**

European timber for Indian and Indonesian spices, dye stuffs, ointments, and cottons as well as Chinese silks, porcelain, and lacquerware. The Mamluks allowed only Muslims and Jews to travel beyond the Mediterranean, and thus Christians remained limited to the Mediterranean.

There were three secondary trade routes. First, there was the overland Silk Road with its gold-for-luxuries trade that connected Iran with China via central Asia, active particularly during the Mongol period. Second, there was the maritime East African trade route, where merchants exchanged manufactures for ivory, gold, and slaves. And third, there was the Volga route, where Rus merchants traded gold, silver, spices, ivory, silk, wine, and fur, connecting the Middle East with western Europe. Both primary and secondary trade routes yielded the Mamluks immense supplementary tax revenues.

Islamic and Jewish merchants in the Egyptian center of this network were for the most part wholesalers for whom the import and distribution of eastern luxuries formed only a part of their overall commercial activities. They also organized the regional production and distribution of raw materials and contracted with craftspeople for the production of various goods. Merchants who were also **tax farmers** maintained grain stores, with employees responsible for collecting, shipping, brokering, and marketing the grain. Others farmed the taxes from ports or public auction houses. Diversification was the preferred path to consistent profitability in the merchant class.

nautical chart of the eastern Mediterranean, ca. 1065 CE

Tax farming: A system for collecting taxes and rents from the population, where the state grants the right of collection to private individuals.

The Black Death Extensive travel, however, yielded unforeseen risks. The more densely people lived together and the more frequently they traveled, the more often they incurred the risk of spreading disease. The Black Death of 1346 was, scholars surmise, set off by the Mongol invasion of Vietnam. Southeast Asia was one of the permanent breeding grounds for the pandemic among rodent fleas. From here, the Mongols dispersed the bacillus via China and the Silk Road to the Black Sea area. Genoese merchants carried the virulent disease to the Mediterranean and northwest Europe (see Chapter 11). Egyptian sources indicate that the plague recurred for another century and a half. Not until the 1500s did Middle Eastern population levels recover to pre-1346 levels.

Religion, Sciences, and the Arts in Two Religious Civilizations

Despite the impact of the Black Death, Mamluk Egypt and reconstituted Byzantium during the 1300s and 1400s were active cultural centers. Scholars and artists developed their respective cultures within traditional boundaries. In Islamic civilization, the most important new cultural phenomenon was mystical (Sufi) Islam, and in Eastern Christianity it was a revival of Platonism.

Sufism: Meditative devotion to faith, expressed in the form of prayer, ecstasy, chanting, or dancing.

Islamic Culture: Intellectual and Scientific Expressions

Mystical Islam, or **Sufism**, developed from the Christian, Zoroastrian, and Greek philosophical heritages interacting within the Muslim world. Around 1050 Muslim scholars integrated Sufism into the Sunni-dominated Islamic civilization, and around 1200 Sunni mystics adapted Sufism to popular practice in the form of congregational brotherhoods in lodges. Educated Muslims were conversant in philosophy and the sciences, both of which flourished in the period 1050–1300.

Sunni–Sufi Islam Sufism involved a form of meditative practice in pursuit of a pure (and personal) experience of the internal and infinite divine. The practice went beyond the prayers prescribed in Islam. Since this experience took place within themselves, early Sufis in the 900s were often accused of violating the Islamic doctrine of God's transcendence. It was only in the second half of the eleventh century during the Seljuk-sponsored religious revival that a compromise was reached.

In the 1200s, teachers of Sufism founded lodges in which they provided training in meditative practice for Muslims. With time, these lodges branched out to urban centers as well as villages and even among nomadic tribes. Sunni Muslims of all walks of life joined. By around 1450, Islamic civilization was a commonwealth not only of competing states but also of competing Sufi brotherhoods. The Sunni–Sufi compromise dominated in Islamic civilization until ca. 1900.

Maritime Trade. This image, an illustration in Hariri's *Maqamat* (ms. dated 1236), depicts a stylized oceangoing sailing ship used in trade between Arabia and India.

Philosophy and Sciences As in the case of Sufism, philosophers also encountered opposition from among the proponents of Sunnism and did so for the same reason of violating the transcendence doctrine. Greek philosophical writings had attracted Muslim thinkers well before the emergence of mature Sunnism. A central concern of the Muslim philosophers was the reconciliation of Platonic-Aristotelian thought with Islam. Leading philosophers, such as Ibn Sina (Avicenna, ca. 980–1037) and Ibn Rushd (Averroës, 1126–1198), achieved this reconciliation by viewing philosophy as the discipline of logical concepts and religion its equivalent in images. Ibn Khaldun (1332–1406), a philosopher of history and political theorist, found philosophy and speculative theology incompatible with religion. As in Western Christianity, thinkers struggled with the question of compatibility between thought and faith.

As in philosophy, scientific texts were also available in translation. Islamic scientists made major contributions beyond the discoveries of the Greeks. The Greeks had developed geometry into a mathematical science, but they had left algebra undeveloped until the Alexandrian period of Hellenism. The Persian Muhammad ibn Musa al-Khwarizmi (ca. 780–850) laid the foundations for the conversion of algebra into a science.

The Golden Age of Islam

After Khwarizmi, mathematicians developed decimal fractions, raised numbers to high powers, extracted roots from large numbers, and investigated the properties of complex equations with roots and higher-degree powers. Persian and Arab astronomers refined the work of the Hellenistic astronomer Ptolemy (d. ca. 168 CE). Physicists elaborated on Archimedes' investigations into the physics of balances and weights and developed the impetus theory of motion.

Medicine was based on comprehensive handbooks, and specialized medical fields included ophthalmology, obstetrics and pediatrics, and pharmacology. The discovery in the 1200s of the pulmonary circulation system of the body anticipated similar European medical discoveries by several centuries. In general, prior to ca. 1500, the sciences in Islamic civilization were well ahead of those of the Western Christians. It was thanks to stimulation by the Muslims that the Christians eventually caught up.

Artistic Expressions in Islamic Civilization

During the formative period of Islamic civilization (800–950), secular poetry and prose flourished. As Sunni–Sufi Islam fully evolved (1050–1200), religion was interwoven with the telling of stories, the painting of miniatures, and the building of mosques and palaces. Persian artistic traditions reemerged from pre-Islamic times, and Turkish central Asian steppe traditions entered Islamic culture.

Islamic Literature   The first extant poems in Arabic celebrated the clan ethos of courage, trust, generosity, and hospitality in Arabia (800s). They follow the quest theme common to many folktales and myths. In the cosmopolitan culture of Baghdad, new forms of literature evolved, with urban themes such as the pleasures of sensual abandonment, seduction, and homosexual love. Essays expressing refined taste, elegance, and wit circulated widely. Popular collections of short stories included the *Maqamat,* about an impersonator telling tall stories to gullible listeners, and the *Arabian Nights,* first written down in Mamluk Damascus during the 1300s.

The story of Ali Cogia, a merchant of Baghdad, from *The Arabian Nights*

Persian and Turkish Muslims preserved their pre-Islamic pasts in epics celebrating the heroic deeds of their ancestral leaders in central Asia. The poet Firdosi (940–1020) collected the traditions of the Persians into the *Book of Kings* (*Shahnameh*). The anonymous epic *Dede Korkut* originated among the central Asian Turks at the

Byzantine Icons and Islamic Miniatures

One prominent result of the interactions between the Mediterranean and the Middle East in the early centuries CE was a merging of their respective realistic and hieratic artistic styles. Artists now focused on hieratic significance (that is, features essential for immediate recognition). While the main subject or object remained realistic, symbolical features highlighted its significance. Background features appeared in nonrealistic fashion, especially in miniature painting.

The halo is an example of the realistic–hieratic style. The halo, a traditional Mesopotamian motif, was associated with gods, heroes, and kings. The three Persian dynasties (Achaemenids, Parthians, and Sasanids) adopted this Mesopotamian tradition, as did the imperial Romans.

In the fourth century, the halo was transferred from the gods, heroes, and kings to depictions of Jesus. Thus, the pagan symbol of glory ultimately became the sign of holiness in Christianity. The halo similarly continued in Islamic miniatures where the Prophet Muhammad, prophets of the Hebrew Bible, and angels are surrounded by flaming halos. In contrast to Western art, both Byzantine Christians and Muslims retained the halo for rulers.

In Byzantium, icons became devotional paintings, predominantly on wooden panels, but also on other media, such as mosaics and textiles. They functioned as vehicles through which their owners transferred their veneration to the persons depicted. Icon painters also incorporated gold, silver, enamel, and gemstones on their icons. Portable or affixed to altars and walls, they became ubiquitous in Byzantium and later in Russia.

In the period of 900–1200, icons became not only increasingly important fixtures in churches and monasteries but also major elements in the church liturgy. Long rows of icons on church walls marked the days of the church year. Priests and monks carried double-sided icons during processions. Ironically, the largest production of icons for churches and monasteries occurred after the hiatus of the Latin Empire (1261–1453), during a time when Byzantium was a small and impoverished realm.

In contrast to the public role of church-commissioned icons in Byzantium, Islamic figurative art was private and entirely limited to the courts of rulers as

time of the Arab conquests and was written down in the 1300s. Both ethnic groups also produced outstanding poets, among whom the Afghanistan-born Jalal al-Din Rumi (1207–1273) acquired worldwide popularity. Although Arabic remained the basic literary language, Persian gained increasingly in popularity.

Painting and Architecture in Islam In the visual arts, Arabs and early Muslims followed the hybrid realistic-hieratic style that had become common in the Mediterranean and Middle East during the 300s. However, since Islamic law contains prohibitions against painting and sculpting, the visual arts disappeared

the only patrons of artists. Scholars assume that the Muslims developed their aniconism (opposition to figurative images) parallel to the Byzantine periods of iconoclasm. This attitude is represented in the Islamic tradition, where the Quranic warnings against idolatry (e.g., 21:57–59) are interpreted as prohibitions against figurative art. While the church hierarchy in Byzantium eventually overcame iconoclasm, however, there was no such hierarchy in Islam, and so aniconism remained in force.

The continuation of figurative art on palace walls or as miniatures in books attests to the power of the Mesopotamian hieratic traditions over which the Islamic religious scholars had no influence. This art became wide-ranging in its subjects, leaving the production of strictly hieratic representations of rulers in their glory far behind. It began with the Umayyad, Abbasid, and Fatimid palace frescoes, reliefs, sculptures, ceramics, and metalwares of ca. 700–1200. Illustrations in the medical literature dating to the 1110s show similarities with Byzantine icons. In the 1100s and early 1200s, courts in Iraq sponsored miniaturists for drawings of mechanical devices (al-Jazari, d. 1206) as well as urban and rural scenes in storybooks. After 1250, the Mamluk sultans commissioned miniaturists to illustrate their military exercise manuals and the kings of Granada hired painters to create frescoes. In later years miniature-painting proliferated under the Ottoman, Safavid, and Mughal rulers (see Chapters 16 and 20). Some miniaturists became famous for the illustration of Persian and Indian literary classics or the battles won by their benefactors. Similarly famous were the illustrated lives of the Prophet Muhammad and the prophets of the Muslim tradition, as if aniconism had never existed in Islamic civilization.

Christ Pantocrator. This is the oldest Christ icon, dating to the sixth century. It is kept together with a large collection of icons at the Monastery of Saint Catherine on the Sinai Peninsula in Egypt. Like most icons in this collection, it is encaustic—that is, painted with a mixture of heated beeswax and pigments. Later painters used egg yolk in the place of beeswax. The Greek word *pantocrator* means "Almighty" and refers to Jesus's majesty as the king of the kingdom to come. But Jesus was also the crucified human: The left side of his face is accordingly depicted—in a very subtle way—as more human than the right.

Questions

- Is it difficult to relate to the hieratic style in art, as exemplified by Byzantine icons, today? If yes, why?

- Why was representational art so important to Muslim rulers—so much so that they defied their religious scholars?

entirely from public spaces and retreated to the domestic sphere of the courts of rulers.

By contrast, the architecture of mosques and palaces was intended for public use. Mosques followed the architectural style of the Arab open courtyard and covered prayer hall or Persian open courtyard with surrounding half domes and galleries. Among the surviving palaces, the best preserved is the Alhambra of Granada (ca. 1350–1450), with its honeycomb-style decorations. Religious and palace architectures were perhaps the most direct forms in which the identity of Islamic culture was expressed.

Learning and the Arts in Byzantium

In contrast to Islamic civilization, the Eastern Christianity of Byzantium was a fully formed religious civilization from its beginning in 640. The principal institutions of higher learning were the secular Magnaura and the theological Hagia Sophia, which offered the study of the liberal arts and theology. During its difficult struggle for survival against the Arabs, Slavs, Bulgars, and Rus, Constantinople declined in both wealth and sponsorship of knowledge and the arts.

In the arts, Byzantine iconoclasm during the 700s and 800s caused the destruction of icons and mosaics. It also disrupted the transmission of artistic techniques. When the public display and veneration of images became the officially sanctioned doctrine again in the mid-800s, it took a while for the arts to recover.

Revival of Learning　The period of ca. 950–1200 saw an explosion in the production of icons, mosaics, and frescoes, as well as the building of new churches and monasteries. Byzantine mosaic craftspeople and painters were sought after by the caliphs in Córdoba, who avoided hiring artists from their Abbasid and Fatimid rivals. Byzantine craftspeople were also popular with the princes of Kiev, who, after their conversion, carried the Byzantine arts into the commonwealth of Eastern Christian states.

Higher learning also revived after 950. The state built public schools of law and philosophy in the middle of the 1000s, followed by a church school for theology at the end of the century. Philosophers revived the tradition of commenting on Plato, Aristotle, and the Neoplatonic synthesis inherited from Hellenistic antiquity. This revival aroused among churchmen the same suspicions as among the Muslim scholars and led to the condemnation of some philosophers.

Byzantine Renaissance　The disruption of 1204–1261 by the Fourth Crusade and Latin Empire saw a tremendous loss of Byzantine art as well as manuscripts, this time to Venetian pillage during the Fourth Crusade. When Byzantium was restored, Plato scholars initiated a recovery of philosophy, which resulted in a return of Western Christians, this time peacefully, to that city in search of Platonic writings. The Academy of Florence, a leading institution of the Italian Renaissance (see Chapter 17), invited Byzantine Plato scholars to help in the recovery of the texts of this philosopher. Further scholars emigrated to Italy after the fall of Constantinople to the Ottomans in 1453. Thus, Western Christianity renewed its adaptation to stimuli from a neighboring civilization, in contrast to Eastern Christianity and Islamic civilization, which continued within their existing traditions.

❯ Putting It All Together

interactive concept
map

Both Islamic civilization and Eastern Christian civilization were based on a synthesis of religious revelation and Greek philosophy and science. This synthesis had begun in the Roman and Sasanid Persian Empires. Muslims accomplished their cultural synthesis after the period of Arab conquest, roughly during 800–950. Eastern Christians completed their synthesis in the period 950–1050, after their recovery from the Arab, Slav, Bulgar, and Rus onslaughts. Both refined their internal civilizational achievements well into the 1400s. Thereafter, they did not absorb substantial new cultural stimuli from the outside until about 1700, when the Muslim Ottoman sultans invited western Europeans to reform their empire.

Islamic civilization was an outgrowth of the Arab conquests in the Middle East, central Asia, northern Africa, and Europe in the 600s and early 700s. It emerged as an adaptation of the Arabs to the heritages of the Jews, Christians, Greeks, Romans, and Persians. Its core was the monotheism of Allah, and its cultural adaptations were to Greek philosophy and science, Roman law, and Persian statecraft, as well as artistic and architectural traditions of the Middle East and Mediterranean. At its height, during 950–1450, a commonwealth of competing Islamic states represented Islamic civilization. This ethnically diverse commonwealth with Arab, Turkish, Persian, and Berber rulers and states shared a number of common characteristics, among which were the same canon of scriptures (the Quran and the Sunna), moral norms and laws (Sharia), and religious institutions (separate state and religious authorities as well as Sunni–Sufi brotherhoods). These characteristics endured to 1300.

The Byzantine Empire succeeded the Roman Empire around 640, when the emperors, under attack by the Arabs, reorganized their military forces and redefined the inherited Christian theology. Byzantium recovered politically and culturally in the mid-900s, and the empire changed into a commonwealth when Russian Kievan Rus converted to Eastern Christianity. The recovery lasted only a century. The Seljuk Muslim Turks conquered most Anatolian provinces of Byzantium (1071–1176), and the Venetians conquered Constantinople in the Fourth Crusade and established the Latin Empire (1204–1261). Byzantium recovered thereafter for another two and a half centuries, but after 1453 Eastern Christian civilization shifted to Russia.

Review and Relate

Thinking Through Patterns

Examine the ways historians approach the big questions of this chapter.

The adoption of Christianity and Zoroastrianism as state religions in the Roman and Sasanid Empires did not prevent these empires from eventual collapse. But both empires helped launch the period of religious civilizations. New empires arose in this period, beginning around 600. Byzantium was Christian from its inception. The Arab Empire adopted Islam early on, initially under the Umayyads and fully in the Abbasid-led commonwealth of states. Eastern Christian and Islamic civilizations were characteristic of religious civilizations because both embraced basic religious scriptures, upheld a form of separation of state and religion, and adapted to inherited cultural traditions.

The pattern of Islamic civilization included revealed scripture, a religiously interpreted history, the separation of state and religion, the fusion of revealed religion and Greek philosophy, and the adaptation to the scientific and artistic heritage from Rome and Persia. The pattern was completed early, by about 950, with the emergence

> Why can the period 600–1450 be described as the age of religious civilizations? How do Eastern Christian and Islamic civilizations fit this description?

> Which cultural traditions combined to form Islamic religious civilization? What were the most characteristic patterns?

of Sunni Islam, but continued to evolve internally through Sufi Islam. The result was an Islamic civilization around 1300 that was composed of many states and even more autonomous religious congregations existing alongside the mosques.

> ❯❯ **How did Eastern Christian or Byzantine civilization evolve over time? On which institutions was this civilization based, and how did it evolve, wedged between Islamic and Western Christian civilizations?**

The late Roman Empire achieved a close integration of Christianity, Greek-Hellenistic philosophy and science, and Roman law, but it was hard-pressed for survival by the conquering Arabs. When the eastern Roman, or Byzantine, Empire recovered, it elevated Eastern Greek Orthodox Christianity to a supreme position. A powerful recentralization effort strengthened the empire, especially in the Balkans. But in the wake of the Seljuk invasions and Western Christian Crusades, the empire weakened again, surviving in a much-diminished form until it was conquered by the Ottoman Muslims in 1453. Eastern Christianity survived as a state religion in Russia.

| **Against the Grain**

Consider this as a counterpoint to the main patterns examined in this chapter.

Did Ibn Taymiyya "Have a Screw Loose"?

- Was Ibn Taymiyya right in standing up against the Muslims of his time and in preaching jihad against Mongols who had converted to Islam? If yes, for which reasons?

- Are contemporary Islamists correct in claiming that their present situation in Islamic countries closely resembles that of Ibn Taymiyya facing the Mongols? If yes, are rulers in contemporary Islamic countries similar to the Mongols?

Born in Harran, northern Iraq, Taqi al-Din ibn Taymiyya (1263–1328) became a refugee as a child when his family fled from the pagan Mongols, fulfilling their Sharia duty to live in a Muslim-governed country. Ibn Taymiyya grew up in Damascus, then ruled by the Egyptian Mamluks, and became a prominent religious scholar in the Hanbali legal school.

Among the four legal schools, the Hanbali school was the one most devoted to the study of the Quran and prophetic traditions. Ibn Taymiyya invoked these traditions when he dedicated his scholarly career to combating the form of popular brotherhood and saintly Islam dominant in the Islamic world at the time. He did not condemn, however, Sunnis engaging in spiritual Sufi practices as individuals—a point often overlooked by modern reformist Muslims, for whom he is a hero.

Most of Ibn Taymiyya's contemporaries would have shrugged off his rantings against brotherhood members had he not shown exemplary courage during a time of continuing Mongol attacks. Since 1260 the Mongols had tried to conquer Mamluk Syria and Egypt, and in 1299–1303 they succeeded in occupying parts of Syria. At one point during the occupation, the Mamluks sent a mission of religious scholars, including Ibn Taymiyya, to the Mongols to implore their ruler Ghazan (r. 1295–1304) to end his attacks. Ghazan had officially converted to Islam in 1295 but continued to adhere to Mongol law rather than the Islamic Sharia. Only Ibn Taymiyya had the courage to stand before the Mongol ruler and accuse him of being an infidel. This feat of courage earned Ibn Taymiyya both admiration and resentment from scholars of the other religious schools.

Ibn Taymiyya apparently had both an aura of self-importance and a short temper—hence the unkind surmise by one contemporary scholar concerning his mental balance. (The rendering of this as "a screw loose" is by the Middle East scholar Donald P. Little.) It was this arrogance that Ibn Taymiyya's detractors confronted, attacking him on his own ground of legalism. They accused him of violating the Islamic unity doctrine himself in his teachings and misinterpreting the doctrine of fighting the infidels as a religious duty.

As a result of these accusations, the Mamluks imprisoned Ibn Taymiyya. In the end, Ibn Taymiyya died in jail, a lone dissenter during a time when the majority of Muslims adhered to the different form of saintly Islam. His teachings were revived, however, in the twentieth century when Islamists reclaimed him as the preacher of an Islamic revolution against their own "Mongol" rulers and Islamic laxity in general.

Key Terms

audio flashcards

Caliph 216	Iconoclasm 223	Sunna 218
Celibacy 226	Jihad 220	Tax farming 235
Commonwealth 215	Muslim 216	Trinitarianism 216
Creed 226	Sharia 220	Umma 220
Eucharist 226	Sufism 236	

For additional resources, please go to
www.oup.com/us/vonsivers.
Please see the Further Resources section at the back of the book for additional readings and suggested websites.

> Chapter 11   600–1450 CE

Innovation and Adaptation
in the Western Christian World

A round 575 a casual encounter took place in Rome that had enormous implications for the future of Western Europe. A monk from the Monastery of St. Andrew came upon several boys for sale in the slave market. Struck by their fair skin and light hair, he asked about their ethnic origin. He was informed that the youths were from the far-off island of Britain and were called "Angles." The monk replied that because of their angelic appearance they should instead be called "angels." He then asked whether the inhabitants of Britain were Christians. When told that they still clung to pagan beliefs, he remarked that it was a pity that such beautiful young persons were not blessed with Christian faith.

In the year 596 the monk, now elevated to the papacy as Pope Gregory I (r. 590–604), dispatched a group of monks to Britain, led by Augustine (later named the first archbishop of Canterbury), on a missionary campaign of conversion among the Anglo-Saxons of southern England. Throughout the seventh century, Roman Christianity spread into Anglo-Saxon England, eventually eclipsing the already established Celtic form of the faith brought over from Ireland in the fifth century. During the first half of the eighth century, English missionary monks, most notably St. Boniface (680–754), carried Christianity to the continent.

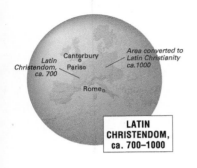

LATIN CHRISTENDOM, ca. 700–1000

ABOVE: **Detail of Bayeux Tapestry, an embroidered cloth dated ca. 1070 consisting of 75 scenes depicting events attending the Battle of Hastings, where William the Conqueror defeated Harold, Anglo-Saxon king of England. Here, the Latin title reads "King Harold is killed."**

The papal reign of Gregory I represents a new era in the history of Western Europe. By encouraging the conversion of Germanic kings to Christianity in return for the sanction of the church, Gregory advanced the role of the papacy throughout Europe and made the Roman papacy a significant power in the West. In the process, Gregory inaugurated new links between Rome and northwest Europe that contributed to a new civilization distant from the Mediterranean. In addition, Gregory's efforts led to the independence of **Latin Christendom** from the Eastern Greek Church at Constantinople. Moreover, Gregory established an institutional structure and organized a hierarchy that allowed for a unified Christian civilization in emerging Europe that would endure until around 1450, when the Renaissance ushered in a new phase in European history.

The Formation of Christian Europe, 600–1000

During the fifth century, Roman provincial rule in the west collapsed, and a new post-Roman period of cross-cultural interactions began, combining Greco-Roman and Germanic traditions, as well as Christian values. The Roman administrative practice of grouping provinces into dioceses formed the foundation of the diocesan system of the early church. A distinctively Christian European civilization gradually emerged. An important feature of this new civilization was the dominance of the church, whose alliance with Frankish kings—particularly Charlemagne—initiated a new church–state relationship in the West. This civilization nearly dissolved during the civil wars among Charlemagne's successors and the ninth-century invasions by non-Christians. During the later tenth century, however, the restoration of order was under way in post-Carolingian Europe. Despite the turbulence of the ninth and tenth centuries, a new cultural and religious cohesiveness provided a sense of optimism; Latin Christendom had survived.

Frankish Gaul and Latin Christianity

Amid the confusion caused by Germanic invasions and the breakdown of Roman rule during the fifth century, the first attempt to restore political order appeared in Frankish Gaul. Although Merovingian kings relied on force to unite the kingdom, they also recognized the importance of the church as a unifying force. After a period of political turmoil, a new line of Frankish kings, the Carolingians, emerged during the eighth century. At the same time, the Christian Church played a role in the shaping of Frankish Gaul and early medieval European civilization. The concept of *Christendom* as a common identity through the practice of Western Christianity began to take shape.

The Merovingians   The Franks were not invaders. Rather, they expanded within the borders of the western Roman Empire. Unlike most other Germans, they became Western Christians, and as a result were not rejected as heretics by native Gallo-Romans. For these reasons, Frankish Gaul was ideally suited to lay the foundation for a Christian state in post-Roman Europe.

The first Frankish dynasty, the Merovingians [mer-oh-VIN-gee-anz], was established by the Frankish king Clovis (r. 481–511). Clovis adopted Christianity, which gave him the backing of Christian bishops in Gaul. As a result, Clovis had powerful

Seeing Patterns

≫ How did the Merovingians and Carolingians construct a new Christian European civilization during the seventh and eighth centuries?

≫ What were key factors in the political, economic, and social recovery of Europe during the eleventh and twelfth centuries?

≫ What were some of the cultural and intellectual developments during the "twelfth-century renaissance," and how did they contribute to medieval civilization?

≫ How did the church influence political developments in Europe during the twelfth and thirteenth centuries?

≫ What events made fourteenth-century Europe so dismal? How did these combine to spell the gradual demise of medieval institutions and perspectives?

Latin Christendom: Those countries professing Christian beliefs under the primacy of the pope.

Chapter Outline

- The Formation of Christian Europe, 600–1000
- Recovery, Reform, and Innovation, 1000–1300
- Crisis and Creativity, 1300–1415
- Putting It All Together

Coronation: The act or ceremony of crowning a sovereign.

Unction: The act of anointing with oil as a rite of consecration.

The Rule of St. Benedict

allies in his attempt to control a unified Christian kingdom. However, because of the Merovingian practice of dividing inheritances among surviving heirs, soon after his death Clovis's kingdom was split up into Austrasia in the east, Neustria in the west, and Burgundy in the southeast.

The Carolingians   During the eighth century one aristocratic family, the Carolingians, rose to power in Austrasia and eventually took control of all of the Frankish lands. Carolingian leader Charles Martel ("the Hammer") (ca. 714–741) increased the authority of the Carolingians by promoting his ties with the church. His defeat of advancing Muslim armies at the Battle of Tours in 732 or 733 made him the leader of the most powerful force in Latin Christendom.

Martel's son, Pepin III ("the Short") (751–768), succeeded his father as mayor of the palace in 741, and enhanced ties with the church in two ways. First, in 751 he was crowned by the reigning pope as the king of the Franks, thereby replacing the former Merovingian line of kings with a new Carolingian dynasty. Second, the **coronation** established a new Franco-papal alliance. This affinity between Rome and Frankish Gaul allowed Europe to develop independently of the Byzantine Empire in the East. In addition, the pope included the ceremony of **unction** in the coronation ceremony, introducing into western European history the concept of sacred kingship "by the grace of God".

The Early Medieval Church   The church contributed to the development of a new era in Western history. The *secular clergy* included bishops—among them bishops of Rome, who later became popes—and urban priests. The *regular clergy* were monks who lived in rural monasteries. Each of these monasteries made distinctive contributions to early medieval culture.

The model for monastic life was established by St. Benedict (ca. 480–543) in his *Holy Rule*. The daily lives of Benedictine monks were devoted to prayer and manual labor and were regulated by a series of "offices," or times of the day given over to specific tasks.

In economic terms, Benedictine monasteries helped to revitalize rural agricultural production. Most monasteries had a watermill and a forge, and their large landholdings produced significant quantities of grain and wine. In addition, Benedictine monks expanded arable lands.

Monasteries also preserved classical and early Christian culture. The limited education available during the early medieval period took place mostly in monasteries. Monks copied and studied the works of the Church Fathers, along with texts from the Bible and papal decrees, thus laying the foundation for a new, Christian civilization for medieval Europe.

The Papacy   While monks lived in rural monasteries, bishops of the church resided in urban centers. Although major cities throughout the Roman Empire had bishops, the bishop of Rome emerged as spiritual head of the Christian Church in western Europe. The most important of the early medieval popes was Gregory I.

Gregory was responsible for making the Roman papacy a power in the West. His letters to Childebert II (r. 575–595), king of the Franks, laid the foundation for the Franco-papal alliance that came to fruition in the eighth century. Gregory also enhanced the prestige of the Roman papacy in Italy, which gave rise to the Papal States and the separation of the Roman and Eastern Roman Church. Finally, Gregory facilitated the conversion of pagans to Christianity.

The Age of Charlemagne Following the death of Pepin III in 768, his son Charlemagne ("Charles the Great") (r. 768–814) inherited the Frankish crown. Charlemagne represents the first full synthesis of Roman, Germanic, and Christian elements to forge a unified Christian empire. Because Charlemagne raised the status of western Europe to rival the civilizations of Byzantium and Islam, the Mediterranean was no longer the center of civilization in the West.

Through military campaigns and effective rule, Charlemagne administered the largest empire in Europe since the collapse of Roman rule in 476 (see Map 11.1). From a palace at Aachen, Charlemagne ruled over a centralized empire composed of different ethnic and linguistic groups. Charlemagne also reformed legal practices by instituting the Frankish inquest, a forerunner of the jury system, which was carried to England at the time of the Norman Conquest.

Charlemagne's reign also made intellectual contributions to medieval Europe, including educational reform. Monks were instructed to make copies of both Roman and Christian texts, including the Bible and the *Rule* of St. Benedict, preserving and disseminating many classical authors and texts.

Like his forebears, Charlemagne also took an active interest in affairs of the church. Not only did he promote the interests of Christianity throughout his kingdom, but he also intervened in papal affairs in Rome. In 774 Charlemagne journeyed to Rome to offer protection against the Lombards, and in 800 he gave assistance to Pope Leo III (r. 795–816), who was attacked by rivals. While attending Mass at St. Peter's on Christmas Day, Charlemagne was suddenly crowned "emperor of the Romans" by a grateful Leo III.

The creation of a new Roman emperor in the West announced the independence of western Europe from the Byzantine East, and it signaled a shift in the center of power away from the Mediterranean and toward Europe north of the Alps. Charlemagne's new imperial status was recognized (reluctantly) not only by the Byzantine court but also by the Abbasid caliph in Baghdad, Harun al-Rashid (r. 786–809).

Charlemagne's Throne. Charlemagne frequently traveled throughout his realm, and one place where he stopped several times was Ravenna on the Adriatic coast of Italy, where he would admire the magnificent sixth-century church of San Vitale. Inspired by its harmonious proportions and stunning mosaics, Charlemagne determined to build a replica at Aachen. The Palatine Chapel, the only surviving component of his palace, combines Byzantine and Carolingian architectural styles.

interactive timeline

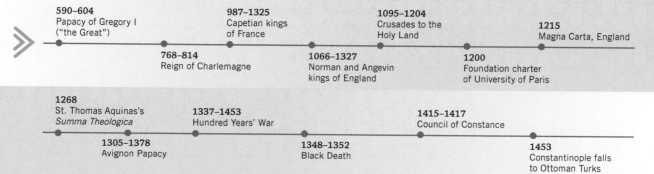

590–604
Papacy of Gregory I ("the Great")

768–814
Reign of Charlemagne

987–1325
Capetian kings of France

1066–1327
Norman and Angevin kings of England

1095–1204
Crusades to the Holy Land

1200
Foundation charter of University of Paris

1215
Magna Carta, England

1268
St. Thomas Aquinas's *Summa Theologica*

1305–1378
Avignon Papacy

1337–1453
Hundred Years' War

1348–1352
Black Death

1415–1417
Council of Constance

1453
Constantinople falls to Ottoman Turks

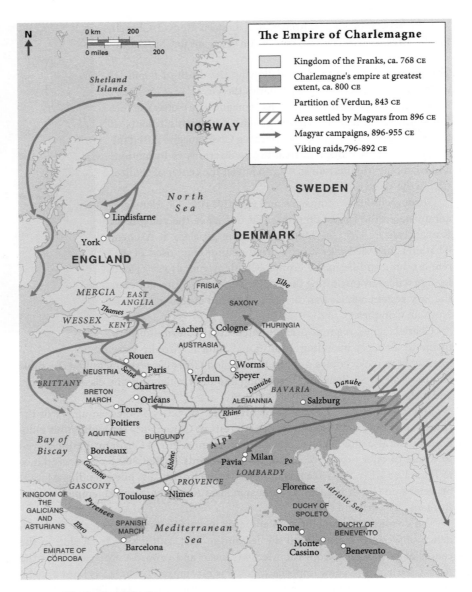

MAP 11.1 **The Empire of Charlemagne.**

Post-Carolingian Europe   Shortly after his death in 814, Charlemagne's empire was torn apart. Charlemagne's eldest son, Louis the Pious (r. 814–840), divided the empire among his three sons, who then squabbled over their respective shares. By the terms of the Treaty of Verdun in 843, the empire was divided into eastern, western, and central portions. At the same time, devastating raids by Vikings from the North and Muslim pirates from the south further disturbed the situation. Magyar horsemen from the plains of Hungary terrorized East Frankland in the same period, although they were more inclined to settle onto farmlands than to plunder (see Map 11.1).

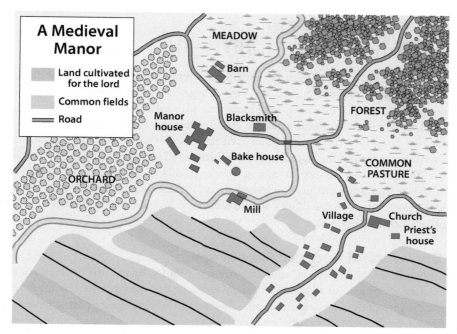

Figure 11.1 A Medieval Manor. This illustration shows the layout of a typical manor, with the manor and its satellite buildings next to a village surrounded by fields for planting and common (waste) land.

The Feudal Age   The name traditionally given to the form of governance that arose in West Frankland during the ninth through the eleventh centuries is **feudalism**. Historians have never fully agreed on a precise definition of the term. It is true that feudalism was based on no theory, and it was nowhere uniform or consistent. Yet, amid the turmoil of the ninth and tenth centuries, feudalism provided security at the local level in the absence of central government.

Feudalism consisted of powerful landed aristocrats (lords) who assembled small private armies consisting of dependents (vassals). Since wealth and power were now measured in terms of landholdings, vassals were rewarded for their services with grants of land, known as *fiefs*.

Lord–vassal relationships and institutions marked a turning point in European history that led to the later formation of centralized kingdoms. Most important was the concept of loyalty to someone higher in the feudal hierarchy. By using elements of feudal relationships to his advantage, a royal figure (such as a king) could convert the feudal relationships to royal control of his realm.

Whereas feudalism refers to the political and governmental aspects of life in the ninth and tenth centuries, **manorialism** refers to social and economic affairs of the time. Large manorial estates in rural areas constituted self-sustaining agricultural communities. The manorial estate consisted of several buildings: the castle or manor house, the church, the barn, and the mill (see Figure 11.1).

Peasants lived in small cottages in a confined area of the estate, surrounded by fields for crops, stands of timber for building and fuel, and a fishpond. Peasants had to provide free labor, called "boon work," on the lord's fields. The physical pattern of such manors may still be seen in many areas of France.

Feudalism: An arrangement in which vassals were protected and maintained by their lords, usually through the granting of fiefs, and required to serve under them in war.

Manorialism: The medieval European system of self-sustaining agricultural estates.

Recovery, Reform, and Innovation, 1000–1300

From about 1000 to 1300 Europe experienced revitalization, expansion, and cultural creativity and innovation. The period began with the appearance of competing, politically centralizing kingdoms and with advancements in agriculture, commerce, and trade. Reforms in the church provided a framework for a unified western European Christian religious civilization, culminating in papal supremacy over Europe around the beginning of the thirteenth century. During the so-called twelfth-century renaissance, extending from ca. 1050 to 1250, a cultural revolution in universities produced new philosophical and scientific perspectives that, along with interaction with the Islamic world, came to distinguish western Europe from other world civilizations.

The Political Recovery of Europe

Europe in the middle of the ninth century was plagued by internal civil wars and external invasions. All signs of central government had disappeared as a result of the collapse of the Carolingian Empire. By around 1300, however, most of western Europe was governed by centralized administrations headed by kings, who restored both political and fiscal health to their realms.

France and England The French nobility elected Hugh Capet (r. 987–996) as their king in 987 CE, establishing a new royal dynasty, the Capetians, in place of the former Carolingians. The king's court was where all disputes among his vassals were resolved, and the location of Hugh's royal **demesne** [deh-MAIN] in the lands around Paris meant that he was at the strategic and commercial center of France. Like the Carolingians, the Capetians enjoyed the support of the church. Not only did they have control over dozens of bishoprics and monasteries, they alone were anointed with holy oil (unction) as a part of the coronation ceremony.

Demesne: All territories within France controlled directly by the king.

Over the next 300 years, Capetian kings extended royal control in France through success in minor wars against the nobles and marriages between Capetian heirs and members of the nobility. Determined to make France the most powerful country in Europe, Philip IV (r. 1285–1314) established a representative assembly in France, the **Estates-General**, in order to raise revenues. Composed of the three social "estates"—the clergy, the nobility, and the townspeople—this body played an important role in later events leading up to the French Revolution.

Estates-General: The French representative assembly, composed of the three social "estates" in France, first convened by Philip IV.

Compared to the slow process of building a centralized monarchy in Capetian France, the establishment of centralized rule in England took a much shorter period of time. After the Norman duke William the Conqueror defeated an Anglo-Saxon army at the Battle of Hastings in 1066, he was proclaimed king of England as King William I (r. 1066–1087). William then seized control of all lands in the realm, distributing them to his followers. To secure his claim to the throne, he built castles throughout the country.

Baron: A term initiated by William I to designate feudal vassals who held lands in return for service and loyalty to the king.

William's successors continued his practice of centralizing authority. Henry II (r. 1154–1189), the first of the Plantagenet kings of England, reformed the judicial system by making royal courts the final courts of appeal, thereby overriding the authority of **baronial** courts. Moreover, Henry established a uniform code of justice (known as English common law), which replaced the complex jurisdictions of baronial and local courts. Even more effective was Henry's use of royal **writs** and the jury system, which provided justice for all disputants.

Henry's son John (r. 1199–1216), however, alienated the baronage of England, who forced John to sign Magna Carta ("the Great Charter") in 1215. Magna Carta established several important principles: the king must rule in accordance with established feudal practices; he must consult with the barons before levying taxes; and all free men have the right to trial by jury if charged with a crime. Many of these concepts also contributed to a new institution known as **Parliament**.

During the thirteenth century the English Parliament increased its power. In order to raise money for an anticipated French attack against England, Edward I (r. 1272–1307) convened in 1295 the so-called Model Parliament, composed of an upper house of nobles and a lower house of "knights of the shires and burgesses of the towns." This precedent established the origin of Parliament's House of Lords and House of Commons, which continues today.

Germany   Events in East Frankland, or Germany, took a different turn. One setback to centralized rule was the division of the eastern portion of Charlemagne's realm into five regional groupings, or *duchies*, each under the control of a powerful duke. This made it difficult for kings to centralize royal authority.

Imperial involvement in papal affairs in Italy also made centralization difficult. When Otto I of Saxony (r. 936–973) took power as king of the Germans, he extended Germanic influence in Italy in order to reestablish Charlemagne's protection of the papacy. In 962, Otto put down political disturbances and protests against the church. In gratitude, Pope John XII (r. 955–964) proclaimed Otto "emperor of the Romans," forming the basis of what has been termed the "Holy Roman Empire."

In ensuing years Otto's successors extended German control south of the Alps into Italy. Frederick I (1152–1190), the first to bear the title Holy Roman Emperor, greatly expanded German holdings in Italy in the north, and in 1155 he was named king of Italy. After his later defeat at the hands of a coalition of northern Italian cities in 1176, however, Frederick was forced to grant them quasi-independence, in return for their support against papal interests in the Italian peninsula. Frederick next turned his attention to Sicily. By marrying his son, the future Henry VI (r. 1190–1197), to Constance of Sicily, daughter of the Norman king of Sicily, Frederick added the Kingdom of Sicily to the lands controlled by the Holy Roman Empire.

The Economic and Social Recovery of Europe

Europe also recovered economically during this period. At the year 1000 agriculture was still the mainstay of the economy, there was little commerce, and the few cities were underpopulated. By 1300, however, trade and commerce were flourishing; urban life was expanding; and a new social class of merchants had emerged.

The Agricultural Revolution   Developments in agriculture contributed to Europe's economic revival. One important factor was the heavy-wheeled plow, fitted with an iron blade and a *moldboard* (a curved iron blade to cut through, lift and turn the newly dug soil). The use of fertilizers and the transition from a two-field to a three-field system also increased crop production. In the three-field

Writ: A written order issued by a court, commanding the party to whom it is addressed to perform or cease performing a specified act.

Parliament: A representative assembly in England that, by the fourteenth century, was composed of great lords (both lay and ecclesiastical) and representatives from two other groups: shire knights and town burgesses.

system, one field was planted in the spring for a fall harvest, another was planted in the winter for a spring harvest, and the third remained fallow to enable its soil to regenerate nutrients.

The agricultural revolution in Europe was largely due to innovations from elsewhere in Eurasia (perhaps from China), which were transmitted to Europe through cross-cultural interactions (mostly via the Silk Road trade network). Among these innovations were the use of horses with collar harnesses (instead of slower-moving oxen); the use of iron horseshoes; the use of the tandem harness, allowing horses to work in pairs; the vertical waterwheel; and the single-wheeled barrow.

Moreover, new forms of mechanical energy—also of Asian origin—were introduced to Europe through interactions with the Islamic world. As early as 1050, watermills were in wide use. Windmills, which were borrowed from Islamic Iran during the twelfth century, converted the power of water or wind into pounding and grinding motions used for the production of cloth goods, beer, and grain products. Even the first deep-drilled water well, introduced in the twelfth century, was of Chinese origin. Finally, through Muslim Spain the Europeans benefited from Islamic advances in agriculture.

These innovations meant an increase in both the quantity of agricultural production and in the quality and variety of food. Improvements to the European diet resulted in an increase in population: in 1000, the population stood at about 36 million; by 1100 it had jumped to 44 million, and by 1200 to 58 million. By 1300 the European population reached about 80 million.

Commerce and Trade   The revolution in agricultural production sparked a rejuvenation of commerce and trade. As Europe's population grew, so did the demand for consumer goods. The expansion of mercantile elites in urban centers also provoked a demand for luxury goods from beyond Europe.

One focal point of the revival of trade and commerce developed in northern Europe, where Flemish weavers began a flourishing exchange with wool-producing centers in England, particularly with monasteries in the north of the island, in the twelfth century. Another productive source of the commercial trade revival in northern Europe was the importation of French wines into England beginning in the later eleventh century, occasioned by the Norman Conquest in 1066.

Far more vital, however, was the revival of European commerce and trade across the Mediterranean. When Umayyad rulers were displaced by the Abbasids, maritime contacts between Islamic and Christian merchants resumed. In addition, the Norman conquest of southern Italy and Sicily (1046–1091) afforded the northern Italian maritime cities of Pisa, Genoa, and Venice the opportunity to collaborate with Islamic merchants in Alexandria and the Levant. By the end of the eleventh century, Italian traders had established commercial ties with Constantinople, Syria, and Cairo.

The most momentous change in European trade and commerce took place near the close of the thirteenth century. Around 1275, first Genoese and then Venetian maritime traders sailed westward across the Mediterranean, through the Strait of Gibraltar, and then out into the Atlantic. Then, Ferdinand IV (r. 1295–1312), king of Castile and León in Spain, claimed control of Gibraltar from the Muslims in 1309, ensuring full access to the Atlantic. Before these developments, trading patterns were primarily of a one-way nature: European merchants imported

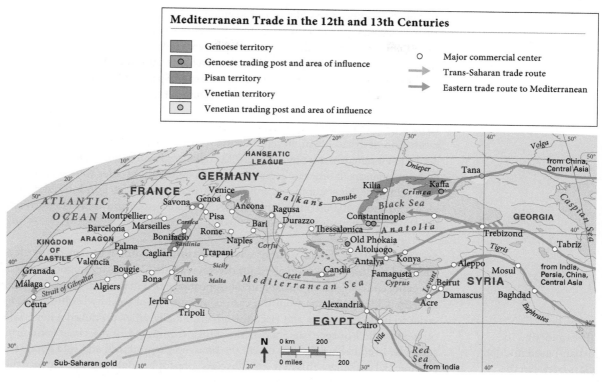

Mediterranean Trade in the 12th and 13th Centuries

- Genoese territory
- Genoese trading post and area of influence
- Pisan territory
- Venetian territory
- Venetian trading post and area of influence
- ○ Major commercial center
- → Trans-Saharan trade route
- → Eastern trade route to Mediterranean

MAP **11.2 Mediterranean Trade in the Twelfth and Thirteenth Centuries.**

modest quantities of goods from China and India. Thanks to economic advances in the West, however, European merchants now had products to export to the East (see Map 11.2).

Cross-Mediterranean trade and commerce were facilitated by navigational innovations, some of which were assimilated as a result of interactions with Islamic and Byzantine merchants. Navigation was improved by advances in European ship design, especially the incorporation of the sternpost rudder. The principal advantage of the stern-mounted rudder was that it allowed for the construction of larger ships, which in turn increased the volume of transported goods. Another improvement was the adoption from Muslim sailors of the *lateen sail*, a front-mounted triangular sail that allowed for tacking into the wind. It was largely owing to this navigational device that Italian ships were able to sail into the westerly winds that had previously prevented their sailing through the Strait of Gibraltar into the Atlantic. Most important was the introduction of the magnetic compass. Whether of independent invention or derived from China, where it was used on Chinese ships as early as around 1090, the magnetic compass first appeared in Europe in 1190. Use of the compass greatly facilitated maritime travel beyond the sight of land.

Early Capitalism and a Cash Economy   This renewed trans-Mediterranean commercial activity sparked innovations in commerce and monetary exchange that contributed to the development of European **capitalism**. Increasing commercial transactions prompted a need for coined money. Meanwhile, medieval fairs created

Capitalism: An economic system characterized by private or corporate ownership of capital goods, by investments that are determined by private decision, and by prices, production, and the distribution of goods that are determined mainly by competition in a free market.

new business procedures like record-keeping and accounting practices, along with bills of exchange (the forerunner of the modern bank check) to replace transport of large amounts of coins. These transactions were facilitated by the use of paper, invented in China, then adopted by Islamic merchants, and subsequently transmitted to Europe in the eleventh century through Muslim Spain. Other financial and legal instruments were devised to promote long-distance trade.

Urban Growth   The revitalization of trade and commerce contributed to the rejuvenation of urban life in eleventh-century Europe. Artisans and merchants were drawn to vibrant urban centers, along with craftspeople and laborers, many of whom fled rural manors in order to begin new lives in cities. These cities were small by today's standards. Most numbered around 5,000 people, although London and Bruges each held about 40,000 inhabitants, while cities like Venice and Genoa in northern Italy boasted populations of around 100,000.

Social Patterns   Social patterns within the revitalized urban centers of the eleventh and twelfth centuries evolved for several reasons. Of primary importance was the cash economy, which resulted in the appearance of a new social class: the hired military. Cities benefited from the cash contributions of wealthy businessmen in order to build cathedrals and large town halls. Finally, cities produced a new class of people, the **bourgeoisie** [boor-zhwa-ZEE]. Composed of merchants and artisans who lived in "burghs" (or cities) the bourgeoisie produced and sold goods for commercial exchange. This new "middle class" of people would greatly influence the development of medieval representative governments.

> **Bourgeoisie:** The urban-based middle class between the wealthy aristocracy and the working class.

Urban women were employed as butchers, candle makers, metal crafters, silk weavers, and bookbinders. However, women were rarely admitted as full members to craft **guilds**. For the majority of working women, better opportunities were available in what were known as "bye industries," or home-based enterprises, like spinning cloth and brewing ale. In some cases widows took over their late husband's trade and worked as single women.

> **Guilds:** Associations of artisans and merchants intended to protect and promote affairs of common interest.

Comprising a small but distinct minority of the European population in the eleventh century, Jews were spread in communities around the Mediterranean world. Through their travels, Jews developed both geographical knowledge and the command of multiple languages. They served as diplomats and engaged in moneylending and banking.

As the eleventh century unfolded, however, tolerance toward Jews began to wane. Jews were increasingly vilified as murderers of Christ, a sentiment fanned by the First Crusade in 1096. In many cases Jews were forced to live together in walled-off, gated ghettos in towns, which frequently held charters of liberty separate from those of the towns. Several countries expelled Jews—England in 1290, France in 1306, and a number of continental cities in the early 1400s—resulting in their dispersal throughout eastern Europe.

Religious Reform and Expansion

From 1000 to 1300 the clerical establishment of medieval Europe underwent dramatic reform. The reform movement in the church began in monasteries, then spread to the ecclesiastical hierarchy in cities, and eventually resulted in a new age of religious enthusiasm throughout Europe.

Monastic Reform   The effort at monastic reform began in France in a monastery founded at Cluny in 910 by Duke William I (875–918) of Aquitaine. Cluny was established as a monastery free of obligations to either feudal lords or local ecclesiastical control, and committed to the Benedictine rule. The number of reformed monasteries increased during the eleventh and twelfth centuries. The most successful of new monastic orders was the Cistercians, founded in 1098 in a remote area of France at Citeaux. The appeal of the Cistercian order lay in its austerity; Cistercians were enjoined to devote their total beings to "God's work" (*opus Dei*).

Papal Reform and the Investiture Controversy   The papacy underwent similar reform. The church sought independence from secular influence, particularly the practice by which lay rulers appointed clergy, including the pope, to their offices. Popes, however, believed it was the exclusive right of the clergy to make such appointments. The creation of the College of Cardinals in 1150, followed by the Papal Election Decree in 1059, ensured that only the College of Cardinals was empowered to elect the pontiff of the Holy Catholic Church. The result was the elimination of the role of the Holy Roman (German) emperor in the appointment of popes.

This conflict led to the "Investiture Controversy." Pope Gregory VII (r. 1073–1085) insisted that appointment of the clergy was to be controlled solely by the church. When the German emperor Henry IV (1056–1106) openly challenged Gregory's proclamation, the pope excommunicated him. The struggle between popes and emperors continued until 1122, when an agreement known as the Concordat of Worms was reached. This agreement stipulated that German bishops must be elected by church officials.

The investiture controversy produced mixed results. On the one hand, Gregory's actions proved that popes could force emperors to acknowledge papal authority. On the other hand, Henry IV's struggle with the church proved disastrous for his successors. Later German emperors never fully recovered from the distraction of attempting to control matters in both Germany and Italy. The five Germanic principalities reasserted their independence from royal control, and Germany remained disunited until the later nineteenth century.

The Virgin Mary Knitting. This fourteenth-century painting of the Virgin Mary knitting a garment for her unborn child is the earliest known representation of knitting, a medieval innovation. Knitwear was unknown in the ancient Mediterranean but was essential in the cold, damp climate of northern Europe.

Popular Piety and a Religious Society   As early as the eleventh century, ordinary Europeans took a more active interest in religion. This movement was caused by several factors. One was the reform movement in the church, which resulted in both higher standards of conduct among clergy and the increased authority of the pope. Another factor was the construction of shrines dedicated to Christian saints, whose relics were considered powerful aids in the quest for personal salvation.

(a)

(b)

Changing Views of Christ. The Crucifixion scene from the door of the basilica of Santa Sabina, Rome, ca. 430, is formal and stylized: Christ is remote (*a*). In contrast, the Crucifixion commissioned by the archbishop of Cologne, Germany, just before 1000, shows a suffering Christ—a human being in agony and sorrow, hanging from a cross (*b*).

Easter: Christian celebration of the Resurrection of Christ; celebrated on the Sunday following the first full moon after the vernal equinox.

Another factor was new ways of depicting Jesus and Mary, the mother of Jesus. Whereas in the earliest years of the church the crucifixion of Jesus was rarely represented, by the tenth century the Crucifixion was portrayed as a reminder of his sacrifice for the redemption of humanity's sins.

The popularization of Christian piety was further encouraged by new concepts of time. One concept derives from the biblical book of Genesis, where the creation of the earth took six days, leaving the seventh day as a day of rest. Another concept, the numbering of years in accordance with the Christian era, was introduced in 532 by Dionysius Exiguus (ca. 470–544), a Roman monk. For Dionysius historical time began with the birth of Christ, hence his designation of *Anno Domini* ("in the year of the Lord") to denote a new dating system.

These concepts of time had several implications for Europeans. Two Christian feast days now became standard: the birth of Christ was celebrated on December 25 (Christmas) and his resurrection on a movable date called **Easter**. Saints' days became major events. Finally, the ringing of church bells announced the hours of the day, which provided for regulation of daily routines.

One alarming aspect of popular piety was the appearance of heretical movements within the church (see "Against the Grain" below). In an effort to rechannel the devotion of the faithful, Pope Innocent III (r. 1198–1216) licensed two new religious orders, the Franciscans and the Dominicans. Founded by St. Francis of Assisi (1181/2–1226), the Franciscan order, by living simply and aiding the poor and the sick, inspired a new dedication to Christianity. The Dominicans, founded by St. Dominic (1170–1221) in 1216, believed that the best way to combat heresy was to teach the doctrines of the church. The Dominican order included many famous medieval theologians in its ranks, such as St. Thomas Aquinas (ca. 1225–1274).

The Crusades   Like the reform movement of the church, the Crusades were in part inspired by the new wave of religious enthusiasm sweeping Europe. But another factor was the so-called *Reconquista*, or reconquest, of formerly Christian lands that had been taken over by Muslims.

Spanish Christians had retreated into the far northwest of the Iberian Peninsula, while the Muslims controlled most of the lands from their capital in Córdoba. In 1031, however, squabbling among Muslim factions led to a loosening of Muslim control throughout Spain, which in turn prompted two kings of Christian territories to launch an offensive. The breakthrough occurred in 1085 when Toledo was liberated from Muslim control, resulting in almost half of Spain returning to Christian control.

A similar effort by Norman knights to retake Christian territory from Muslim control took place in southern Italy and Sicily between 1061 and 1090, resulting in a Norman kingdom in Sicily allied with the papacy. In return for their protection of the papacy, the kings were given total control over all the higher clergy in their realm.

These successes against the Muslims in the western Mediterranean occurred simultaneously with alarming developments in the eastern Mediterranean. As we have seen in Chapter 10, by the 1180s Seljuk Turks had seized control of substantial territories in the Middle East, prompting Pope Urban II to call for the launching of a crusade to the Holy Land in 1095 (see Map 11.3). Urban called on the barons of Europe to assemble their feudal armies and march to the east to liberate Jerusalem from Muslim control. Europe's feudal nobility most likely saw in this expedition the promise of new lands and a chance to use their military training for a good cause.

interactive map of the Crusades

In the summer of the following year, the main force crossed over into Asia Minor and in 1097 took Nicaea from the Turks. Two years later, in the summer of 1099, Jerusalem was finally freed from Muslim control—but at a horrific cost in human life.

Other crusades followed throughout the twelfth century. In 1144 the fall of the crusader state of Edessa (in present-day Turkey) to a resurgence of Islamic militancy caused renewed interest in a second crusade. Led by King Louis VII of France and Holy Roman Emperor Conrad III, this crusade failed to reach Jerusalem. The taking of Jerusalem by the Muslim leader Saladin in 1187 ignited the Third Crusade, led by kings Frederick I of Germany, Philip II of France, and Richard I of England. Although the crusaders captured Acre from the Muslims in 1191, dissension between Philip II and Richard I resulted in Philip's hasty return to France.

The Fourth Crusade was instigated by Pope Innocent III and launched in 1201. The crusading army contracted with the Venetians for passage by ship to the east. The Venetians, taking advantage of transporting a crusading army, attacked the Adriatic port city of Zara, their commercial rival. Outraged by an attack on a Christian city, Innocent III excommunicated the crusaders, most of whom ignored the papal ban. From Zara the Venetians transported the army to Constantinople in 1204, where they plundered the city, slaughtering innocent Christians in the process. In the long run, the Fourth Crusade not only weakened the authority of subsequent Byzantine rulers but also deepened animosities between the Roman and Eastern Orthodox Churches.

Although the crusading movement failed to keep Jerusalem out of Muslim hands and resulted in millions of casualties, the Crusades produced some positive achievements for Europeans. The ability of popes to organize European knights into armies enhanced their prestige in both the west and the east. The Crusades also helped to establish Western Christian dominance of sea traffic in the Mediterranean. In addition, the retaking of Christian territories in southern Italy, Sicily, and Spain gave European

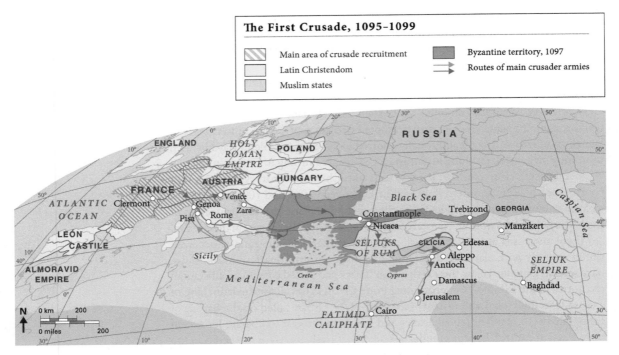

MAP 11.3 **The First Crusade, 1095–1099.**

scholars access to new sources of Greco-Arabic scientific advances, and it resulted in the transmission of Islamic architecture to western Europe (see "Patterns Up Close").

Intellectual and Cultural Developments

The High Middle Ages (ca. 1000–1300) saw new directions in the intellectual and cultural expressions of Western Christian religious civilization. Two symbols of this civilization—the Gothic cathedral and the university—were born during the "twelfth-century renaissance."

Universities   Monastic schools in rural areas gave way to cathedral schools in urban centers, which offered instruction in the skills required by the commercial world of the twelfth century. Creative thinkers and the students they attracted flocked to cathedral schools in the larger cities of Europe. In time, groups of students and teachers formed the first universities at Salerno, Bologna, and Paris.

Particularly in Paris, the university curriculum began to focus on the philosophy of Aristotle, whose rediscovery was owing to the efforts of Gerbert of Aurillac (ca. 946–1003), later named Pope Sylvester II (r. 999–1003). As a young man Gerbert had studied mathematics, astronomy, and Aristotelian logic in Islamic Spain. Later, as deacon of the cathedral school at Reims, Gerbert introduced both the sciences and Aristotelian logic to his students, many of whom in turn helped spread the new learning throughout cathedral schools in Europe.

Scholasticism: A medieval method of determining theological and philosophical truth by using Aristotelian logic.

During the eleventh and twelfth centuries, two important developments in universities resulted from the popularity of Aristotelian logic. One of these was a method of pursuing philosophical and theological truth by use of Aristotelian logic, known as **scholasticism**. The problem was that Aristotle posed a serious threat to church authority, since a better understanding of his ideas revealed just how incompatible his thinking was with religious doctrine.

What emerged was a fundamental disagreement between those who placed the truths of *faith* before the truths of *reason* in attempting to gain knowledge of God's existence and those who placed reason first. The most famous advocates of these opposing schools of thought were St. Anselm (ca. 1034–1109) and Peter Abelard (1079–1142). Anselm argued that faith must precede reason ("I believe in order that I might understand"). Abelard, the most popular teacher at the cathedral school of Notre Dame in Paris during these years, disagreed, arguing, "I understand in order that I might believe." Abelard's apparent favoring of reason over faith tipped the balance in favor of those who were inclined to question traditional Christian doctrine.

So popular was Aristotle by the middle of the thirteenth century that in addition to the earlier division between those who advocated either the truths of faith or reason, a third perspective was offered by those who took a middle path. It was to the latter camp that St. Thomas Aquinas (ca. 1224–1274) belonged. In his *Summa Theologica*, Aquinas argued that, instead of considering the truths of reason as being totally irreconcilable from the truths of faith, it was possible to consider a compromise, or a synthesis of the two, that would in the end lead to a knowledge of God's existence and, thus, to personal salvation.

Law and Medicine   In the twelfth century, universities began to offer training in law and medicine. Scholars at Bologna discovered the Roman legal tradition preserved in Justinian's *Corpus Iuris Civilis*. It was at Bologna around 1140 that the *Corpus* inspired a monk named Gratian to compile a compendium of ecclesiastical law known as the *Decretum*. Gratian's student Peter Lombard's *Book of Sentences*, produced in 1150, served along with the *Decretum* as the foundation for the development of **canon law**, utilized by the papacy in its struggles to contest secular power.

Canon law: The law of the church.

Medical studies were taught at Salerno in the late eleventh century. Located in Sicily, Salerno was able to assimilate Islamic and Byzantine medical advances. Serving as the nucleus of medical studies at Salerno were the works of the Roman physician Galen and the *Canon of Medicine* compiled by the Islamic scholar Ibn Sina (or Avicenna, 980–1037). These works formed the foundation of medical studies throughout medieval European universities.

Medieval Science   Medieval scholars were fascinated by scientific texts of the ancient Greeks. This interest was sparked not only by Gerbert of Aurillac but also by Christian advances into Spain and southern Italy in the late eleventh century. The Christian conquest of Toledo in 1085, followed by the retaking of Sicily in 1090, provided European scholars access to Islamic scientific learning. Adelard of Bath (ca. 1080–1152), who translated Greek scientific texts from Arabic into Latin, served as a bridge between the Islamic and Western Christian worlds.

Perhaps the most important of Adelard's successors in England was Robert Grosseteste (ca. 1175–1253), a bishop of Lincoln and a dabbler in the new scientific studies of natural phenomena. Grosseteste recognized the value of mathematics. He was also among the earliest scholastics to question the scientific authority of Aristotle. Grosseteste's arguments were developed by his student Roger Bacon (ca. 1214–1294), whose principal contribution to the development of Western science was to emphasize the role of induction and experimentation.

The Gothic Cathedral

Although the Gothic cathedral is the iconic symbol of medieval European Christianity, its origins can be traced back to late imperial Rome. Following Constantine's Edict of Milan in 313, Christians no longer had to worship in secret, and church leaders sought a public building that could accommodate larger congregations. The Roman *basilica*, a civic hall traditionally used for public functions, was ideal for early Christian worship. Its design was assimilated by the church and transformed from pagan to Christian usage. The basilica style featured a long central aisle (or nave), roofed over with timber, ending with an intersecting transept and an arched passage into a semicircular *apse* with a raised platform.

Nave of the Abbey Church of St. Denis.

During the post-Roman early medieval period, other earlier Roman and Christian architectural styles were adapted to European circumstances. The result was the Romanesque style of church architecture, which appeared from ca. 800 to 1000. A key feature of Romanesque architecture was the replacement of the basilica's low timber roofs with stone barrel vaults, which required massive stone piers and exterior walls to support the weight. In addition, the apse was expanded beyond the transept by the addition of a circular walkway (the ambulatory) to allow pilgrims to view Christian relics. Finally, the focal point of the exterior was now the western façade, flanked by two towers. During the tenth and eleventh centuries, further changes in Romanesque churches included the enlargement of interiors, the increased height of the nave, and the addition of a clerestory with rounded arches above the nave to admit more light into the interior.

The revitalization of urban life and lay piety in the eleventh and twelfth centuries led architects to assimilate some features of the Romanesque into a new design. The first attempt to open up gloomy Romanesque interiors—and an early expression of the new Gothic style—was made in 1144 at the abbey church of

During the early years of the fourteenth century another "school" of natural scientists, the so-called Oxford Calculators, advanced scientific studies. They challenged many of Aristotle's mistakes regarding natural science. Perhaps the best known of the Calculators' contributions is the mean speed theorem, which anticipates Galileo's law of falling bodies (objects of different weights fall with uniform rates of acceleration in a vacuum).

Crisis and Creativity, 1300–1415

The fourteenth century marks the final phase of European Christian civilization. The early part of the century witnessed a series of economic reversals. Near mid-century a devastating plague originating in Southeast Asia ravaged Europe. A long, drawn-out period of war between England and France began in 1337 and ended in 1453. In addition, the authority of the papacy was both challenged from without

St. Denis in Paris under the direction of Abbot Suger (1085–1151). To enlarge the space and provide more light, Suger turned to solutions already in practice in late Romanesque churches: the pointed arch, the ribbed vault, and flying buttresses.

Pointed arches allowed for higher vertical thrusts in weight distribution, resulting in soaring naves. The pointed arch, widely used as early as the eighth century in Islamic architecture, was most likely transmitted to Europe from Sicily.

Ribbed vaults were improvements over earlier Romanesque groin vaults in that they provided for elevated vaults while at the same time directing the vertical thrust downward through more slender columns, thus providing greater interior space. Ribbed vaults also allowed for thinner outer walls, which could accommodate large glass windows that allowed in more light. There is considerable conjecture over whether the technique of ribbed vaults may have originated in earlier Islamic architecture. It has been argued, however, that the earlier Islamic models were of a different sort than those of Christian Europe in that they were primarily used in domes instead of the nave, and in any event were designed for symbolic and decorative purposes, rather than for structural design.

Flying buttresses—perhaps the most innovative feature of the Gothic style—were then used to support the thinner outer walls, distributing the thrust of the ribbed vaults and pointed arches away from the outer wall and down toward the ground. Another innovation at St. Denis was the incorporation of stained-glass panels (frequently depicting stories from the Bible) in the outer walls, which provided dazzling arrays of color and light in the interior.

Questions

- How does the Gothic cathedral demonstrate the origins–interactions–adaptations process in action?

- What types of cultural adaptations are evident in houses of worship built in modern times?

and weakened from within. As bleak as things were, however, signs of new creative forces appeared as early as the middle of the century.

The Calamitous Fourteenth Century

Fourteenth-century Europeans suffered deeply. Reversals in the economic and social realms, a prolonged period of poor harvests followed by famine, and a disastrous plague added to the misery of daily life.

Famine   From 1315 to 1322 Europe was hit by famine. One cause was a sudden disparity between an expanding population and its available food supply. No new advances were made in agricultural technology, and after centuries of expansion and clearing of lands there was no new space available for increased agricultural production. To make matters worse, the average annual temperature dropped during this period, with catastrophic consequences for agriculture.

Plague   Near mid-century, Europe's already weakened populations suffered a horrific outbreak of plague. The disease originated in Asia and was transmitted in goods transported by Mongol traders in the 1330s. It spread westward along trade routes to the Black Sea and was introduced to the West when grain-carrying Genoese merchant ships, infested with rats, sailed from the Crimea to ports in Sicily and northern Italy in 1346–1347. Within a year, the plague had spread into northern Europe via trade routes, carried by infected rats and fleas, fanning out across Europe north of the Alps. People with infected lungs inadvertently spread the disease by close contact with others and by frequent coughing.

The disease took its name "Black Death" from the appearance of blackened body sores, called *buboes* (hence the name "bubonic plague"). Once the sores appeared, infected people suffered with high fevers, swollen lymph nodes, and painfully aching joints and usually died within 3 days. The plague ravaged Europe from 1348 to 1352 and returned sporadically in the 1360s, 1370s, and 1390s.

The highly contagious disease was next to impossible to contain. Europe's population was weakened as a consequence of famine, and overcrowded and unsanitary European cities created ideal conditions for the rapid spread of the disease. Moreover, medieval medicine was lacking when it came to the treatment of illnesses and diseases.

It has been estimated that England alone may have lost nearly 1 million from a total population of around 4 million. Urban areas were the hardest hit; Florence suffered losses amounting to around 50,000 out of a total population of 85,000. An estimate of the number of people who died throughout Europe as a result of the first wave of the plague puts the total loss at about one-third of the entire population (see Map 11.4).

There was economic and social fallout from the Black Death across Europe. It was widely believed that the plague was provoked by a wrathful God who punished Christians for their sins. A more sinister response was a wave of anti-Semitism, which targeted Jews as scapegoats and accused them of poisoning wells, perhaps an ominous foreshadowing of the Spanish Inquisition (see Chapter 16). The decline of Europe's population caused a downturn in commerce and trade, and in rural areas a decline in demand for grain products. The reduction in the number of agricultural workers made their labor more sought after than before the plague. The result of these increasing tensions between the well-off and those less well-off was a series of social uprisings throughout Europe. The most serious social revolt occurred in London in 1381. Known as the Peasants' Revolt, the uprising included wealthy country residents as well as participants from the ranks of the urban working classes.

The Hundred Years' War   From the mid-fourteenth to the mid-fifteenth century, Europe was embroiled in a disastrous conflict dubbed the "Hundred Years' War" by nineteenth-century historians. At issue was a dispute over English landholdings in France, the result of the Norman Conquest. When the English king Edward III (r. 1327–1377) laid claim to the vacant French throne in 1328, his claim was rejected in favor of Charles IV (r. 1322–1328), the first of the Valois rulers. These issues came to a head in 1337 when Philip VI (r. 1328–1350) seized control of Gascony, and fighting erupted between the two countries.

The conflict was fought in three phases. Early on, English forces triumphed at the Battle of Crécy in 1346, the Battle of Poitiers in 1356, and the Battle of Agincourt

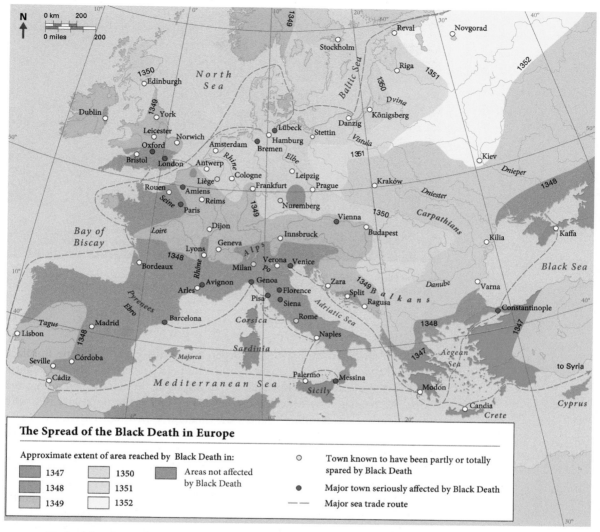

The Spread of the Black Death in Europe

Approximate extent of area reached by Black Death in:

1347	1350	Areas not affected by Black Death
1348	1351	
1349	1352	

○ Town known to have been partly or totally spared by Black Death

● Major town seriously affected by Black Death

‑ ‑ ‑ Major sea trade route

MAP 11.4 **The Spread of the Black Death in Europe**

map analysis

in 1415. Just as it seemed that English forces were on the verge of declaring victory, a 17-year-old peasant girl named Joan of Arc (ca. 1412–1431) encouraged the uncrowned Charles VII (r. 1422–1461) to relieve the siege of Orléans in 1429, where English forces were routed. The victory at Orléans inspired the French to continued victories. The conflict finally came to an end in 1453, when the English conceded a French victory in terms agreed to in the Treaty of Paris, leaving the English in possession of only the port of Calais.

The economic consequences of the war were serious. The war—fought entirely on French soil—destroyed both crops and small farms. In both England and France, financing the war meant new and increased taxes, especially for the peasantry. The war even affected the religious realm. It prevented the resolution of the **Western Schism** as rival popes sought the support of contending French and English kings and their subjects.

Western Schism: The period 1378–1417, marked by divided papal allegiances in Latin Christendom.

Burial of Plague Victims. With up to 50 percent of the people in some places in Europe dying of the plague, burial scenes, such as this one depicted in a Flemish manuscript, were common throughout the middle and late fourteenth century.

image analysis

Crises in the Church Troubles began during the papacy of Pope Boniface VIII (r. 1294–1303), who clashed with Philip IV (r. 1285–1314) of France. Philip levied a tax on the French clergy. In response, Boniface excommunicated Philip; he retaliated by ordering the imprisonment of the pope in 1303, who subsequently died. Boniface's successor, Clement V (r. 1305–1314), left Rome and took up residence in Avignon, on the French border. Clement appointed a number of French clergymen to the College of Cardinals. From 1305 to 1378 successive French popes continued to reside at Avignon, a period known as the *Avignon Papacy*.

In 1378 Pope Gregory XI (r. 1370–1378) returned to Rome, but he died shortly after his arrival there. Perhaps in response to pressure from a Roman mob to elect either a Roman or an Italian as the next pope, the predominantly French College of Cardinals elected an Italian archbishop, Urban VI (r. 1378–1389). The cardinals, regretting their selection of Urban, returned to Avignon and elected a Frenchman as the new pope, Clement VII (r. 1378–1394). The Council of Pisa in 1409 deposed both reigning popes and named a new one, Alexander V (r. 1409–1410). However, the two reigning popes refused to step down, with the result that the church had not one or two but *three* popes.

Adding to the church's problems were outspoken critics, including John Wycliffe (ca. 1330–1384), an Oxford theologian. Wycliffe railed against the wealth and abuses of the clergy, denied the power of priests to act as intermediaries between believers and God, and disputed the validity of many **sacraments**. Wycliffe also oversaw the translation of the Bible into Middle English. Wycliffe's teachings reached Bohemia in central Europe when the English king Richard II (r. 1377–1399) married the princess Anne of Bohemia. John Huss (1370–1415), a radical religious reformer at Prague, enthusiastically supported Wycliffe's ideas (see Map 11.5).

Sacrament: An outward and physical sign of an inward and spiritual grace.

Signs of a New Era in the Fifteenth Century

Dire circumstances of the fourteenth century prompted adaptations and subsequent transformations in the succeeding century that prefigured the transition to the Renaissance. We can observe these adjustments in political, economic, and cultural aspects of fifteenth-century Europe.

Political Reorganization in France and England After the Hundred Years' War, new conceptions of royal authority arose in both England and France. In France, fifteenth-century rulers utilized warfare as an opportunity to centralize their authority. One outcome was to enhance the efficiency and power of the royal bureaucracy. Another was the raising of new taxes without consulting the Estates-General.

The state of politics in England was similarly affected by the course of the Hundred Years' War. Across the course of the war English monarchs were repeatedly forced to convene Parliament in order to gain access to funds to prosecute the war effort. Before granting monies to the crown, however, the House of Commons, consisting of merchants and lesser nobility, insisted on "redress of grievances before consent to taxation." As a result, the House of Commons eventually gained the right to introduce all important tax legislation in Parliament.

European Commerce and Trade When France regained control of Flanders during the course of the Hundred Years' War, England—then at war with the French—was forced to abandon its profitable wool trade with Flemish merchants. As a result, England developed a far more lucrative trade in manufactured cloth products, of which by 1500 it had become a leading exporter.

When the Hundred Years' War disrupted trade in France, new lanes of commerce opened up across Europe. Germanic towns in northern Europe had formed a trading alliance, known as the **Hanseatic League** (from *hansa*, meaning "company"), as early as the thirteenth century. The league reached its peak of influence during the later fourteenth and fifteenth centuries. A new commercial axis extended from the cities of the Hanseatic League in the north southward to the northern Italian cities of Venice and Genoa.

Of crucial importance for the future of European trade was the collapse of the so-called Pax Mongolica in 1368. Following the expansion of the Mongol Empire during the thirteenth and fourteenth centuries, travel and trade networks flourished between China and the West across the Silk Road. Thus, the Mongols facilitated the transfer of technological innovations from China to Europe. When, however, Mongol rule in China dissolved and was replaced by the Ming dynasty, travel on the Silk Road was no longer profitable. European merchants were forced to resort to southern maritime routes, in use from the 750s onward.

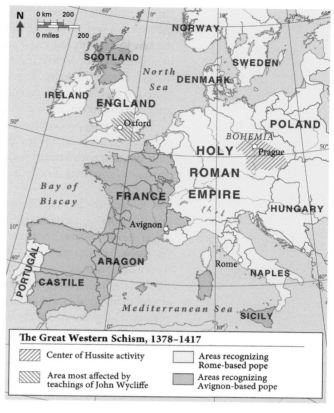

The Great Western Schism, 1378–1417

▨ Center of Hussite activity	▢ Areas recognizing Rome-based pope
▨ Area most affected by teachings of John Wycliffe	▨ Areas recognizing Avignon-based pope

MAP **11.5 The Great Western Schism, 1378–1417.**

Hanseatic League: A trade network of allied ports along the North Sea and Baltic coasts, founded in 1256.

Innovations in Business Techniques   Several innovative economic practices contributed to a revitalization of Europe's economy during the fifteenth century. Smaller markets brought on increased competition among merchants, who sought new business methods in order to remain solvent. New accounting procedures increased the efficiency of record keeping. In addition, the introduction of maritime insurance, which protected investments in seaborne trade, fueled an increase in trans-Mediterranean trade and commerce, while at the same time increasing profits for individual investors.

New banking procedures also facilitated the expansion of Europe's economy by providing loans to merchants and manufacturers. Florence emerged as the center of huge banking partnerships such as the Medici Bank; the Medici family went on to dominate Florentine civic affairs by 1450.

Developments in the Church   As a consequence of the disintegration of papal leadership during the fourteenth century, the church was controlled by councils of bishops in the early fifteenth century. In order to resolve the crises of the fourteenth century, the Council of Constance (1414–1417) was convened by the Holy Roman emperor. Its first order of business was to depose the three reigning popes and to restore papal authority to a single pontiff, who took the name Martin V (r. 1417–1431). Second, to put an end to heretical movements, principally the teachings of John Wycliffe, the council convicted John Huss of heresy and burned him at the stake. The execution of Huss had momentous implications for the future of the church, especially in Germany. Finally, to improve the management of the church, the council declared that councils of bishops would meet frequently in order to keep popes under their strict control.

The popes resisted the increasing power of the bishops, but had to make concessions to secular rulers to gain their support. The result was the further weakening of the Roman Church and the creation of national churches, independent of control from Rome.

Vernacular: The native, common spoken language of a particular region.

Literature   Literary expression flourished, in large part due to the growing popularity of cultural expression in **vernacular** languages instead of Latin. Education in the vernacular was especially popular in the city-states of northern Italy, where the emphasis was on educating students for productive careers in the secular world, rather than training them to become priests.

A number of Italian authors chose to write in the vernacular rather than in Latin. Noteworthy examples include the poet Dante Alighieri (1265–1321), author of *The Divine Comedy*, a long epic poem written in Italian and completed in 1321; Francesco Petrarch (1304–1374), known as the "father of Renaissance humanism," who wrote a series of love sonnets to his beloved Laura; and Giovanni Boccaccio (1313–1375), whose *Decameron* draws its inspiration from the first-century Roman author Petronius.

English and French writers of the fourteenth century also produced works in their native languages. *Piers Plowman*, composed in Middle English by William Langland (ca. 1332–1400), presents a series of complaints and laments about the aristocracy and the clergy in late-fourteenth-century England. Geoffrey Chaucer (ca. 1340–1400), a friend and contemporary of Langland's, also satirized abuses in contemporary society, most famously in his *Canterbury Tales*. Christine de Pizan (ca. 1364–1430) of France composed both poetry and prose; she was primarily concerned with advancing the status of women, and for her criticisms of male behaviors is often considered the first feminist writer.

Canto XIX of Dante's *Inferno*

"The Wife of Bath's Tale," from *The Canterbury Tales*

Philosophy The era's philosophy challenged basic medieval theological beliefs. In place of Aquinas's attempt to reconcile differences between the truths of faith and reason, the intellectuals of the time turned toward the latter, especially toward Aristotle. The earliest philosopher to take this approach was the Oxford Franciscan John Duns Scotus (ca. 1266–1308), who argued for the separation of reason from theology. William of Ockham (ca. 1285–1349), another Oxford Franciscan, carried the assault on the Aquinas synthesis even further. He was an extreme nominalist, arguing that concrete things alone are real and general concepts exist only in the mind.

≫ Putting It All Together

Following the collapse of the Mediterranean Roman Empire, a new Christian religious civilization developed in western Europe during the period ca. 600–1400. The Germanic invasions that brought down Roman rule in the western provinces destroyed imperial unity in the West and created in Europe a series of smaller political entities. After a brief period of centralized imperial rule during the reign of Charlemagne in the later eighth century, medieval Europe fell back in the ninth and tenth centuries into a pattern of decentralized political entities. Feudalism prevented the reassertion of a centralized European empire and prepared Europe for the appearance of several highly centralized, competing kingdoms.

interactive concept map

In terms of cultural developments, the Germanic invasions and subsequent destruction of Roman rule in the West were immensely disruptive, forcing the formation of a new, distinctly European culture based on Roman legacies, Germanic customs, and Christian institutions. Of these, the Christian Church would prove the most important in shaping a new European religious civilization.

During the fourteenth century Europe experienced several transforming events. The horrors of famine and plague, accompanied by over a century of warfare between England and France, led Europeans to question traditional medieval values. In addition, internal problems in the church resulted in a lessening of its authority and prestige. At the same time, however, several developments—particularly in the cultural sphere—prepared Europe for the transition to Renaissance secularism and humanism.

Review and Relate

| Thinking Through Patterns

Examine the ways historians approach the big questions of this chapter.

The Merovingians and Carolingians constructed a new Christian European civilization during the seventh and eighth centuries by utilizing the support of the Christian Church. Through their conversion to Christianity, as well as their support and encouragement of monastic expansion, they earned the support of bishops, priests, and monks. In addition, the creation of the Franco-papal alliance during the eighth century, followed by Charlemagne's personal involvement in church affairs, ensured the emergence of a new Christian foundation for Europe.

≫ **How did the Merovingians and Carolingians construct a new Christian European civilization during the seventh and eighth centuries CE?**

> **What were key factors in the political, economic, and social recovery of Europe during the eleventh and twelfth centuries?**

> **What were some cultural and intellectual developments during the "twelfth-century renaissance," and how did they contribute to medieval civilization?**

> **How did the church influence political developments in Europe during the twelfth and thirteenth centuries?**

> **What events made fourteenth-century Europe so dismal? How did these combine to spell the gradual demise of medieval institutions and perspectives?**

S ome key factors in the political, economic, and social recovery of Europe during the eleventh and twelfth centuries included the emergence of centralized kingdoms in France and England. The expansion of agricultural advances and the development of commerce and trade produced a population surge, which in turn resulted in urbanization and the emergence of a new bourgeois middle class of merchants and traders.

D uring the "twelfth-century renaissance," urban cathedral schools developed into universities in Europe. In order to serve the needs of an expanding urban and commercial economy, more practical disciplines like law and medicine were studied. Aristotelian logic and science, assimilated from contacts in Spain and Sicily, resulted in a debate between the truths of reason and the truths of faith. Although temporarily resolved by Aquinas in the late thirteenth century, Aristotelian nominalism dominated philosophy and theology in the fourteenth century. Another result of the fascination with Aristotle was the development of natural science at Oxford and Paris, which during the later thirteenth and early fourteenth centuries began to uncover flaws in Aristotelian scientific conceptions.

A s a result of a series of ecclesiastical reforms in both the monastic and episcopal arms of the church, a series of increasingly powerful popes began to assert papal primacy over secular rulers, and, indeed, over all European institutions. Pope Gregory VII humbled the German emperor Henry IV in the eleventh century, and Pope Innocent III did the same with King John of England in the beginning of the thirteenth century.

T he fourteenth century witnessed several calamitous setbacks that, taken together, signaled the end of the medieval era and the early stages of the Renaissance era. Among these events were the Black Death, the Hundred Years' War, and the Avignon papacy, followed by the Western Schism, which produced not one, not two, but eventually three popes. At the same time philosophers as well as theologians began to challenge earlier assertions of papal authority, resulting in the Council of Constance (1414–1417), which ultimately replaced papal control of the church with councils of bishops during the fifteenth century.

Against the Grain

Consider this as a counterpoint to the main patterns examined in this chapter.

The Cathar Heresy

- In what ways does Catharism represent a contrast to the patterns of development of medieval Europe?

I n 1144, the dedication of the Gothic abbey church at St. Denis illustrated the power and glory of Roman Christianity in European Christendom. And yet, only one year earlier—in 1143—a heretical cult had posed the most dangerous challenge to Catholic Christianity in its history.

Known as Cathars (from the Greek *katharoi*, "pure ones"), or Albigensians (from Albi, a region in southwestern France), this heretical movement reflected anticlerical sentiments emanating from educated urbanites and rural laity alike, dismayed by the materialism, corruption, and worldliness of the clerical establishment. It was derived from a combination of Persian Zoroastrianism and Manichaeanism, dualistic religions in which forces of good and light (represented by God and the spiritual world) struggle against forces of evil and darkness (represented by Satan) for dominance. Cathars believed that the only way to escape from Satan's grasp was to forego all material things of this world, including marriage, sex, and certain foods. And because Christ was, in part, of the material world, Cathars rejected major elements of Orthodox Christianity.

Alarmed at its growing influence, Pope Innocent III moved to suppress Catharism. He ordered the Albigensian crusade (1209–1229), which resulted in the brutal suppression of the movement. When a force of French knights stormed the center of Cathar resistance at Beziers, they were ordered by the presiding bishop to slaughter all of its inhabitants, both Catholic and Cathar. Further efforts to eliminate Catharism included an Inquisition in 1234, and the movement finally dissolved in 1329, when the last of the Cathars were burned at the stake.

- How does the Cathar heresy compare with other heresies in world religions?

Key Terms

audio flashcards

Baron 250	Estates-General 250	Sacrament 264
Bourgeoisie 254	Feudalism 249	Scholasticism 258
Canon law 259	Guilds 254	Unction 246
Capitalism 253	Hanseatic League 265	Vernacular 266
Coronation 246	Latin Christendom 245	Western Schism 263
Demesne 250	Manorialism 249	Writ 251
Easter 256	Parliament 251	

For additional resources, please go to
www.oup.com/us/vonsivers.
Please see the Further Resources section at the back of the book for additional readings and suggested websites.

» Chapter 12   600–1600 CE

Sultanates, Song, and the Mongol Super Empire

CONTRASTING PATTERNS IN INDIA AND CHINA

In the mid-seventh century CE, Arab armies described northwest India as a desert waste with a hostile populace. Every attempt they made to invade the northwest Indian region of Sind was defeated. Following these failed attempts, a more ambitious invasion was mounted by Muhammad Ibn Qasim, a cousin of the governor of Iraq who was responsible for the conquest of eastern lands.

Ibn Qasim's army brutally pursued the move into India. Wearing coats of chain-mail armor and equipped with siege machinery, they decimated the major cities, executed most of the defenders, and extracted plunder and slaves before completely occupying the area in 711. Though Ibn Qasim's rule in the wake of his violent conquest was considered relatively moderate, he met his death through the duplicity of his new subjects.

When the daughters of Dihar, the ruler of the conquered city of Dehal (Karachi in modern Pakistan), were taken back to the governor of Iraq as tribute, they accused Ibn Qasim of making sexual advances toward them. The governor immediately ordered his cousin Ibn Qasim to be sewn up in a

ABOVE: Completed in 1192, the *Lugouqiao* on the outskirts of modern Beijing acquired its Western association as Marco Polo Bridge because of a mention in Marco Polo's *Travels*. It was also the site of the incident that opened the Japanese invasion of China in 1937.

raw leather sheath and transported home. This was meant to inflict maximal suffering, and, indeed, Ibn Qasim died 2 days into the journey. When his putrefied body was shown to the women who had accused him, they proudly admitted to their deception and revenge on their conqueror.

The clash of cultures and religions has marked the history of the Indian subcontinent. In this contested area, the Hindu vision of Islam has remained one of ruthless conquest. Muslims, on the other hand, have tended to view Hindus as treacherous infidels. Such competing visions have created a pattern of fragile *syncretic* social and political formation (a pattern in which attempts are made to reconcile two different traditions with little or no common ground). In this case, the two cultures actually coexist with considerable hostility toward one another. The dominant pattern has been that each has used the differences of the other to define its own religious civilization more distinctly.

The case of China provides a useful contrast. Here, despite the belief of officials and scholars of the Song dynasty (960–1279) that the fall of the previous dynasty, the Tang, was partly due to the "foreign" Buddhism's influence, there were no persecutions or forced conversions. Song Confucian scholars borrowed from Buddhist cosmological perspectives and Daoist beliefs to create a pattern of *synthetic* social and political formation (a pattern in which the most durable opposing elements merge together into a compatible whole). The result was a coherent Chinese religious civilization for the next 1,000 years.

India: The Clash of Cultures

The early centuries of the Common Era saw the maturing of two divisions among the religious and cultural experiences of India. The first was the spread of Buddhism out of northern India into central Asia, China, and ultimately to Korea, Japan, and Vietnam.

More important for Indian history, however, was the maturation from the fourth to the sixth centuries of the religious practices that we know as "Hinduism." For it was Hinduism, rather than Buddhism, that would dominate Indian life until Islam ultimately established itself in the north. India was transformed from a Hindu religious civilization into a frontier between the competing religious civilizations of Islam and Hinduism.

Following the Gupta era, India experienced nearly 1,000 years of failed attempts to unify the subcontinent. Adding to the confusion were conflicting religious policies on the part of native Hindus and invading Muslims.

Buddhist and Hindu India after the Guptas
By the 500s CE, the last Gupta monarchs were pressured on their borders by central Asian Huns. Moving through the Khyber Pass into northern India, the Huns established themselves in the Punjab and adjacent regions, creating new states as the Gupta lands disappeared.

Harsha Vardhana   One stable regime in the north following the Guptas was that of Harsha Vardhana (r. 606–647). Harsha's life and reign are known to us via the *Life of Harsha*, by the poet Bana, and the account of the famous Chinese Buddhist pilgrim Xuan Zang (see Chapter 9).

Seeing Patterns

≫ How did interactions between Muslims and Hindus in India lead to attempts at religious syncretism?

≫ What steps were taken by Hindus and Muslims to lessen the conflicts between the two rival religious traditions?

≫ How was the Tang dynasty in China different from its predecessors and successors?

≫ How effectively did the religious and philosophical traditions of Buddhism, Confucianism, and Daoism blend together in creating Neo-Confucianism? Where did they clash?

Xuan Zang met Harsha and discovered that the ruler was a devout Buddhist. Xuan Zang notes that Buddhism had once permeated the land, despite the favoritism shown by the Guptas earlier toward Hinduism. However, Buddhism was in decline as the new devotional strains of Hinduism gained adherents.

Still, Xuan Zang found Harsha's kingdom in many ways a model state. The state, however, barely outlived its ruler. The middle years of Harsha's reign saw the Arabs probing the borders of Sind in advance of their full conquest in 711. Meanwhile, following Harsha's reign, northern India was once again divided into regional kingdoms (see Map 12.1).

The Hindu States of the South   The political center of the subcontinent shifted south. By the latter part of the ninth century, a Chola [KO-luh] state based in Tanjore [tan-JO-ray] captured Kanchipuram [kan-chih-POOR-um], advanced south into the Pandya kingdom, and captured their capital at Madurai. In the next century, the Cholas conquered Kerala, invaded Sri Lanka, and expanded their control of the trade with Southeast Asia. The Cholas then advanced northward, allying themselves with the eastern Chalukyas in 1030. In the west, however, the revived western Chalukyas fought the Cholas to a standstill.

The clove trade of the Molucca Islands (in what is now Indonesia) increased the strategic value of that area, which the Indian-influenced Sumatran state of Srivijaya exploited in the tenth and eleventh centuries. In response to the threats Srivijaya posed, the Cholas sent a maritime expedition in 1025 that temporarily reduced its power. In this context, the coming of the Arabs to northern India resulted in a broadening of the subcontinent's position in the world economy. Arab merchants continued their trade in the western ports of India, and despite the religious antagonisms, caravan traffic also continued. India now became part of a triangle of trade that spanned Eurasia (see Map 12.2).

Vijayanagar   A new Hindu state emerged in 1336 with the founding of the city of Vijayanagar ("City of Victory"). Its rulers presided over a political arrangement that, like the Gupta Empire, some scholars have described as feudal, as it absorbed the remnants of the older southern kingdoms. Local leaders collected taxes and provided men and provisions for the army, while retaining considerable autonomy.

For more than 200 years the state of Vijayanagar resisted the Islamic sultanates of the north. In 1564, however, their armies were decimated by a regional coalition of northern Muslim sultanates equipped with the newest technologies—cannon and small arms. The city of Vijayanagar was abandoned.

Islam in India, 711–1398

While conquering Arabs incorporated much of modern Afghanistan, Pakistan, and some parts of northwest India into their empire during

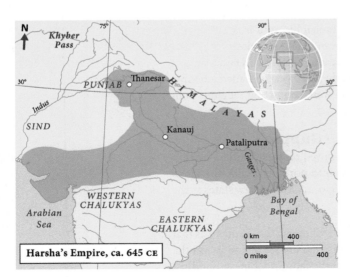

MAP **12.1** **Harsha's Empire, ca. 645 CE.**

the early 700s, the rest of India experienced contact with Islam more peacefully through maritime trade with Muslim merchants. In central Asia, Arab armies moving eastward along the caravan routes advanced through conquest, settling in the cities of Turkestan and raiding into the territories of Turkic nomadic tribes. During 700–1000, first Arab governors and later Persian autonomous rulers supported slave trade.

The Career of Mahmud of Ghazna   The Persian rulers in Iran and central Asia enrolled Turkic slaves in their palace guards and converted them to Islam. The son of one of these slave officers was Sultan Mahmud of Ghazna, who declared himself independent of his Persian overlord. In 997 Mahmud embarked on a career of expansion lasting until his death in 1030. Early in his career, Mahmud conquered territory comprising part of Iran, as well as Afghanistan and Turkestan. Later expeditions moved into the old Ganges River states.

The Northern Sultanates   Mahmud and his successors, the Ghaznavids, ruled for nearly two centuries. But their empire was too large to hold together, and a Persian ruler subject to the Ghaznavids, Muhammad of Ghur, declared his independence and conquered most Ghaznavid lands. In 1192, he defeated the Rajputs, considered Hindu India's most ferocious warriors. Striking deep into northern India, Muhammad set up a Muslim state at Delhi, which endured (1181–1526) under the name of the Sultanate of Delhi. The founders of this state were Turkic generals of slave origin. Their successors were Turkic and Afghan dynasties which ruled until the invasion of Babur, the Mongol-descended founder of the Mughal Empire of India in 1526 (see Map 12.3).

Among the more colorful rulers of the Delhi Sultanate was the female sultan Raziya (r. 1236–1240), who seized the throne from her brother and wore male attire on the battlefield. During her short reign, she pressed south and east to Bengal and settled Muslim refugees from Mongol-controlled lands within her own domains.

The renewed Mongol expansion which led to the destruction of the Abbasid caliphate in 1258 was accompanied by raids along the Delhi Sultanate's borders.

Rajarajeshwara Temple, Tanjore, India. This early-eleventh-century Hindu temple is the largest in all of India and one of the most beautiful. It was richly endowed with spoils taken from Chola conquests.

interactive timeline

India				
ca. 600–711 Reign of Harsha Vardhana, Buddhist king	**ca. 750–1100** Muslim trading at Indian seaports	**1206–1526** Muslim Delhi Sultanate	**1398** Timur sacks Delhi	
ca. 600–1100 Prominence of Cholas and Pallavas in the south	**997–1030** Invasions of Mahmud of Ghazna	**1336–1564** Dominance in the south of Hindu Vijayanagar		

China			
618–907 Tang dynasty, China's most cosmopolitan dynasty	**1127–1279** Southern Song dynasty	**1368–1644** Ming dynasty	
960–1127 Northern Song dynasty	**1280–1368** Yuan dynasty—China briefly part of a vast Mongol Empire	**1405–1433** Zheng He's naval expeditions	

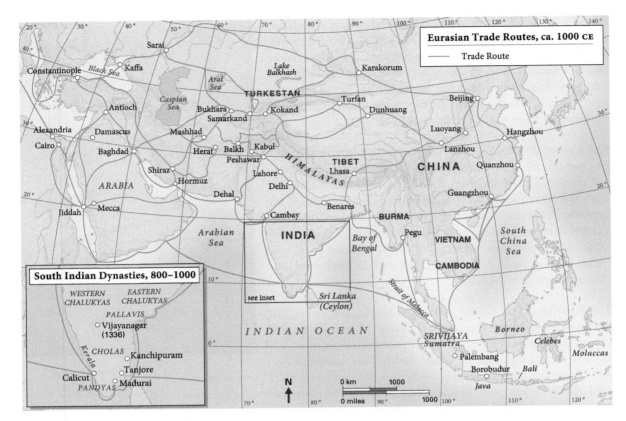

MAP **12.2** **Eurasian Trade Routes, ca. 1000 CE.**

Alberuni's observations of
India, ca. 1030 CE

Out of this period came the reign of Balban from 1266 through 1287. Balban's suppression of rivals resulted in a succession struggle at his death, and a new set of sultans, the Khalijis, came to power in 1290. The Khalijis soon expanded into southern India.

After a period of turmoil the Tughluq rulers rose in 1320 and held power until 1413. Perhaps the most controversial ruler of the line was Muhammad ibn Tughluq (d. 1351), named by his detractors "Muhammad the Bloody." Discontent over high taxes, debased coinage, famine, and ruthless atrocities against his enemies was prevalent during his reign. Within a few decades of his death, powerful forces from the north brought an end to Tughluq rule and altered the region's politics for generations to come.

Toward the Mughal Era, 1398–1450

In 1398, the central Asian nomad Timur (r. 1370–1405) descended on northern India and southwest Asia (see Chapter 20). Though himself a Muslim, Timur did not spare the Muslim capital of Delhi. His invasion broke the power of the Tughluqs. Two smaller sultanates, those of the Sayyids (1414–1451) and the Lodis (1451–1526), held the area around Delhi. The coming of the Mughals in 1526, however, would usher in both stability and imperial aspirations.

The Economy of Islamic India India's wealth continually attracted invasions by outsiders. The turnover of goods acquired by Turkic and Arab incursions financed the emerging northern Muslim sultanates. Even after these states became financially stable, the attraction of the wealth of the southern states resulted in frequent expeditions against them.

The northern sultanates also supported their economies through heavy taxation. Ala-ud-din of the Tughluqs embarked on an ambitious campaign to institute wage and price controls in order to keep food prices low and urban granaries full. In this, Ala-ud-din was surpassed in zeal by Muhammad "the Bloody" Tughluq.

Muhammad also instituted price controls and attempted to stabilize the currency. Despite the sultans' constant need for money, however, Muslim prohibitions against usury kept banking and capital in the hands of Hindus, Buddhists, and *Parsees* (descendants of Zoroastrian emigrants from Persia).

Muslims and Caste Islam appealed to those most discontented with the caste system. Islam's minority status in India, however, meant that it was never possible to carve out an Islamic-majority state within the sultanates.

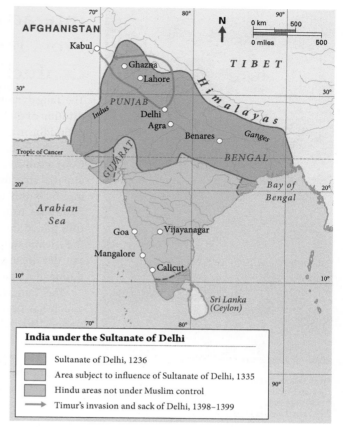

MAP 12.3 **India under the Sultanate of Delhi.**

Over time, cross-cultural compromise was reluctantly granted by both sides. Nearly all Hindu and Muslim sects were eventually allowed to practice to some degree. Muslim repugnance toward some Hindu customs gradually became less overt. At the same time, Hindus in some areas adopted the Muslim practice of veiling women.

The Sikhs By the fifteenth century the unique position of the Muslim sultanates of northern India as havens for refugees from the ravages of the Mongols, as well as for Sufis (practitioners of Islamic mysticism) and Muslim dissidents, provided a rare opportunity for interchange between Muslim and Hindu sects.

The climax of this movement came with the guru ("teacher") Nanak (1469–1539), who founded the faith of **Sikhism**. Combining elements of Hinduism and Islam, the Sikhs, due to religious persecution in the seventeenth century, eventually became more of a fighting faith.

While Sikhism appeared to be a step toward reconciliation between Islam and Hinduism, in fact both Hindus and Muslims opposed the Sikhs, and they were persecuted a number of times under the Mughals. India thus remained a tenuously syncretic religious and cultural society among the world's religious civilizations.

Sikhism: Indian religion founded by Guru Nanak that combines elements of Hindu and Muslim traditions.

Qutb Minar, Delhi. The sense of the northern Indian sultanates being a sanctuary for Muslims from other locales translated into efforts on the part of rulers to outperform their counterparts. The wealth of the area allowed them the resources with which to build a number of spectacular structures. The Qutb Minar, built next to Delhi's first mosque, is said to still be the world's largest minaret, requiring the efforts of two rulers before being finished by the Tughluq sultan Feroz Shah (d. 1388).

image analysis

Tang Taizong, "On Effective Government"

Interactions and Adaptations: From Buddhism to Neo-Confucian Synthesis in China

The Tang dynasty (618–907) marked the completion of the reconstitution of the Chinese empire begun under the Sui. The influence of Buddhism at the imperial court made China a Buddhist empire. Since the Han, China's ideology had been based on the ethics of Confucianism and some elements of Daoism combined with the imperial structure inherited from the Qin (see Chapter 9). By the mid-600s this ideology of statehood had fused with Mahayana Buddhism to give China an overtly religious civilization. China thus joined the ranks of Hindu India (soon to be split by Islam), the Islamic caliphates, the Christian eastern Roman Empire, and the developing states of Western Christian Europe as polities dominated by a universal religion.

The Tang were succeeded by the Song dynasty (960–1279), which has been seen as the beginning of China's early modern period. The political system that marked China from this period until the twentieth century was a departure from Buddhism, which was blamed for the downfall of the Tang. Instead, the new synthesis of official beliefs blended three ethical-religious schools—Confucianism, Daoism, and Buddhism—to create a system called "Neo-Confucianism." Neo-Confucianism in China had no real religious competitors inside or outside the empire

Creating a Religious Civilization under the Tang

For 150 years after its founding, the Tang dynasty expanded into central Asia and made incursions into Korea and Vietnam.

Expansion and Consolidation   Determined to complete the consolidation begun under the Sui, the Tang led military expeditions into central Asia. The Tang reestablished rule in Korea and opened diplomatic relations with Japan, which in 645 adopted Tang imperial institutions, Buddhism, and Confucian bureaucracy. The Tang Empire's position as the eastern terminus of the Silk Road; its maritime trade with India, Japan, Southeast Asia, the Middle East, and Africa; and its integration of Buddhist culture led to China's first extensive encounter with the major agrarian–urban societies to the west. During the seventh century, Muslim conquests in southwest Asia brought China into contact with the Arab Empire. In 674, members of the Sasanid Persian royal house fled the Arabs to the Tang capital at Chang'an, introducing the Tang elites to Arab, Persian, and central Asian goods and cultural forms.

With the Tang Empire expanding, the capital of Chang'an (the present city of Xi'an) grew into perhaps the largest city in the world, with perhaps 2 million people. It became the model for urban planning throughout eastern Asia (see Map 12.4).

The Examination System   The Tang refined Han bureaucracy into a form that survived into the twentieth century. The Tang bureaucratic structure introduced an

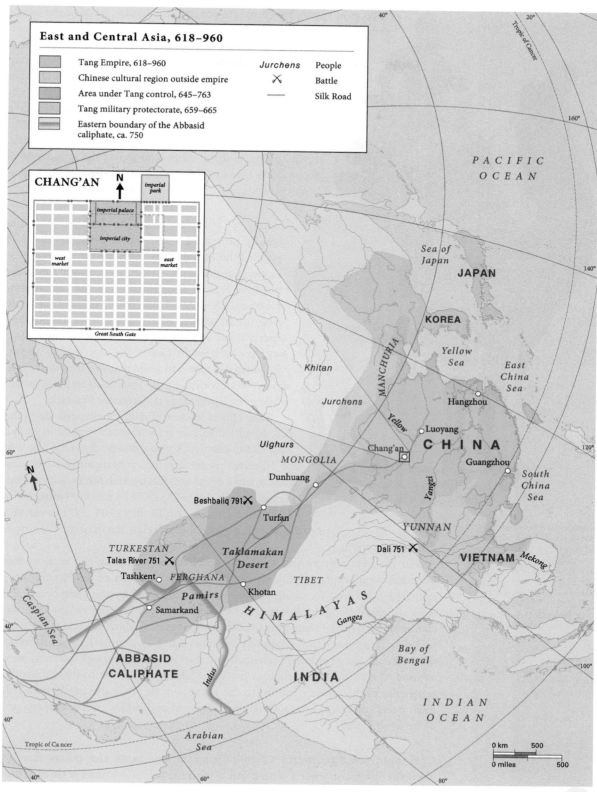

East and Central Asia, 618–960

▨	Tang Empire, 618–960
▨	Chinese cultural region outside empire
▨	Area under Tang control, 645–763
▨	Tang military protectorate, 659–665
▨	Eastern boundary of the Abbasid caliphate, ca. 750

Jurchens   People
✕   Battle
─   Silk Road

CHANG'AN

N

imperial park
imperial palace
imperial city
west market   east market
Great South Gate

PACIFIC OCEAN

Sea of Japan   **JAPAN**

KOREA

Yellow Sea   *East China Sea*

Hangzhou

Khitan

MANCHURIA

Jurchens

Yellow   Luoyang

Uighurs   Chang'an   **C H I N A**

MONGOLIA   Guangzhou

Dunhuang   *South China Sea*

Yangzi

Beshbaliq 791 ✕

Turfan   **YUNNAN**

Dali 751 ✕   **VIETNAM**   *Mekong*

TURKESTAN   *Taklamakan Desert*

Talas River 751 ✕   *TIBET*

Tashkent   *FERGHANA*

Pamirs   Khotan   H I M A L A Y A S

Samarkand   *Ganges*

Caspian Sea

ABBASID CALIPHATE   Indus   **I N D I A**

Bay of Bengal

Arabian Sea   *INDIAN OCEAN*

Tropic of Cancer

0 km   500
0 miles   500

MAP **12.4 East and Central Asia, 618–960.**

map analysis

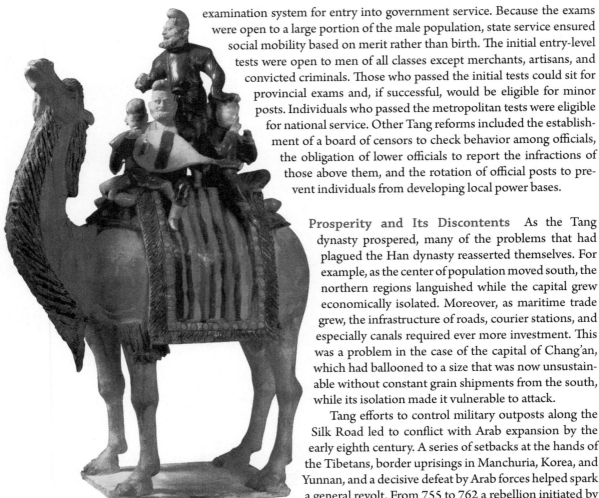

Camel with Musicians.
Music played an important role in Tang China and was enjoyed privately as well as on public occasions. This brightly colored glazed earthenware sculpture, dated to 723 CE, shows three musicians riding a Bactrian (two-humped) camel. Their long coats, facial hair, and hats indicate that they are from central Asia; indeed, the lute held by one of the figures is an instrument that was introduced to China from central Asia in the second century CE.

examination system for entry into government service. Because the exams were open to a large portion of the male population, state service ensured social mobility based on merit rather than birth. The initial entry-level tests were open to men of all classes except merchants, artisans, and convicted criminals. Those who passed the initial tests could sit for provincial exams and, if successful, would be eligible for minor posts. Individuals who passed the metropolitan tests were eligible for national service. Other Tang reforms included the establishment of a board of censors to check behavior among officials, the obligation of lower officials to report the infractions of those above them, and the rotation of official posts to prevent individuals from developing local power bases.

Prosperity and Its Discontents As the Tang dynasty prospered, many of the problems that had plagued the Han dynasty reasserted themselves. For example, as the center of population moved south, the northern regions languished while the capital grew economically isolated. Moreover, as maritime trade grew, the infrastructure of roads, courier stations, and especially canals required ever more investment. This was a problem in the case of the capital of Chang'an, which had ballooned to a size that was now unsustainable without constant grain shipments from the south, while its isolation made it vulnerable to attack.

Tang efforts to control military outposts along the Silk Road led to conflict with Arab expansion by the early eighth century. A series of setbacks at the hands of the Tibetans, border uprisings in Manchuria, Korea, and Yunnan, and a decisive defeat by Arab forces helped spark a general revolt. From 755 to 762 a rebellion initiated by the Tang commander An Lushan (703–757) devastated large sections of the empire. As with the later Han, the dynasty was now in a downward spiral.

For the next century and a half the problems of rebuilding and revenue loss persisted. Confucians questioned a number of the premises of the regime. They criticized Buddhism for being patronized and subsidized by the Tang court, and were critical of Buddhism's "foreign" ideas and practices that contradicted Confucian standards. At the same time, Buddhist monasteries, which paid no taxes, were tempting targets for a cash-strapped government. In 845, despite Tang sponsorship of Buddhism, the government seized all Buddhist holdings, although followers were allowed to continue their religious practices. Sporadic civil war continued for the remainder of the century, leading to the collapse of the Tang dynasty in 906. Following this collapse, China again entered a period of disunity until the emergence of the Song in 960.

Cosmopolitan Commerce From Chang'an, merchants and others traveled along the Silk Road, while Chinese, Indian, and Arab ships ventured as far as Africa.

The compass, a Chinese invention, guided ships throughout the Indian Ocean and Southeast Asia. Drawn by lucrative opportunities, colonies of Chinese merchants could be found throughout the Indian Ocean and Southeast Asia.

Among the export items most coveted by foreign merchants were tea and silk. Tea was the beverage of choice during the Tang and vied with silk for supremacy as a cash crop during the Song. With its medicinal properties tea had a profound effect on the overall health of the population in China, Vietnam, Korea, Japan, and central Asia, and for hundreds of years tea remained China's most lucrative export item.

The influence of foreigners in arts and culture marks a radical departure from the Chinese styles that came before and after. Indeed, the period saw controversial trends regarding the role and deportment of women. As exemplified in the person of the famous Empress Wu (r. 690–705), China's first **empress dowager**, women occasionally exercised considerable authority in political affairs during this time (see below, "Against the Grain").

Tang Poetry   Tang poetry attempts to suggest powerful emotions or themes in minimalist fashion. For example, the Confucian sensibilities of the Tang poet Du Fu (ca. 721–770) are often detectable in his poems such as "Mourning Chen Tao." His friend Li Bai (or Li Bo, 701–762)—carefree, witty, and a lover of wine and women—was in many ways his opposite. Li Bai's poetry evokes happier moments, but frequently conveys them as fleeting and bittersweet.

For all the accomplishments of the Tang, however, the role of Buddhism left the dynasty vulnerable to criticism. With the coming of the Song, China would become a religious civilization that reemphasized the indigenous traditions of Confucianism and Daoism, with elements of Buddhism reduced.

The Song and Yuan Dynasties, 960–1368

During the Song dynasty, China achieved great sophistication in terms of material culture, technology, ideas, economics, and urban living. Its incorporation into the Mongol empire opened the country to influence from neighboring peoples and helped to spread Chinese influence westward. Finally, the new synthesis of Neo-Confucianism would carry China as a religious civilization into the twentieth century.

Reforms of Wang Anshi   The Song instituted a government based on merit rather than heredity. The Song, however, broadened the eligibility of those seeking to take the civil service exams, and an increasingly unwieldy bureaucratic system emerged.

The need for administrative reform spurred the official Wang Anshi ([wahng ahn-SHIR] 1021–1086) to propose initiatives to increase state control over the economy and reduce the power of local interests. He also urged cutting the number of bureaucratic positions in order to lessen the power of local officials and clan heads. Opposition to these proposed reforms, however, forced Wang from office in 1076.

The Song also faced external problems. Because the Tang had lost much of northern China to nomadic groups, Song lands were substantially smaller than those of the Tang. Although the Song maintained a professional army as well as a formidable navy, this massive force was ineffective against the swift militaries of invading

Travel account of an Arab merchant who visited China in the ninth century CE

Empress dowager: In monarchical or imperial systems in which succession is normally through the male line, the widow of the ruler.

Empress Wu. Wife of Emperor Gaozong, Wu Zetian declared herself empress dowager after his death in 684 and founded a new Zhou dynasty in 690. She is the only woman in Chinese history until Empress Dowager Cixi at the turn of the twentieth century to have exercised so much power.

Gunpowder

The most momentous invention to emerge from the Song era was gunpowder. The substance was originally used as a medicine for skin irritations until its propensity to burn rapidly was established. The early Chinese term for gunpowder, *huoyao* (火药) "fire medicine," preserves this sense of its use.

It is unclear when the first weapons employing gunpowder were used. By the Southern Song, however, the Chinese army and navy had weapons that utilized gunpowder either as a propellant or as an explosive. The use of "fire arrows"—rockets mounted to arrow shafts—was recorded during a battle with the Mongols in 1232. The Song navy launched missiles and even employed ships with detachable sections filled with explosives with which to ram other ships. By the end of the century, primitive cannon were also employed as well as gunpowder satchels to blow open city gates and fortifications.

The use of gunpowder weapons by the Song against the Mongols caused the invaders to adopt them for themselves. Indeed, toward the end of the war, the Mongols increasingly employed explosives in their siege operations against Chinese walled cities. They also used them in the 1270s and 1290s during their failed invasions of Japan. The need for these weapons pushed their dispersion throughout the Mongol holdings and beyond.

Korean Rocket Launcher. Adapting Mongol and Chinese military technology, the Koreans repelled a Japanese invasion in 1592 with *hwacha*, mobile rocket launchers that were used with great effect against both enemy land forces and ships.

nomadic groups. The Song also tried diplomacy and bribery to maintain China's dominance. Such efforts, however, were unable to keep the northern part of the empire from falling to the nomadic Jurchens in 1127.

The decreased size of the Song Empire resulted in a more southern-oriented and urbanized economy, with a new capital at Hangzhou [hahng-jo]. Despite the bureaucracy's disdain for the merchant and artisan classes, the state had always recognized the potential of commerce to generate revenue. Thus, while attempting to bring the largest enterprises under state control, the government pursued measures to facilitate trade. These practices, combined with excellent roads and canals, fostered the development of an internal Chinese market. The Song conducted a lively overseas trade, and Chinese merchants established colonies in major ports throughout Southeast Asia and the Indian Ocean.

Genghis Khan

The Mongol Conquest Commercial success, however, could not save the Song from invasion by nomadic peoples. For centuries, disparate groups of nomadic Mongols had lived in tribes and clans in eastern central Asia. There was no real push to unite these groups until the rise to power of the Mongol leader Temujin (ca. 1162–1227), who united the Mongols into one confederation in 1206. Temujin gave himself the title Genghis Khan ("Universal Ruler") of the united Mongol confederation.

Following confederation, the Mongols launched a half-century of steady encroachment on northern China. Genghis Khan's grandson Khubilai Khan [KOO-bleh con] (1215–1294) resumed the Mongol offensive in southern China. In 1267 he moved his capital from Karakorum to Khanbaligh, called by the Chinese "Dadu"—the future city of Beijing. Hangzhou fell to the Mongols in 1276; the death of the Song emperor in 1279, as he attempted to flee, brought the dynasty to an end.

It is difficult to overestimate the importance of gunpowder in human affairs. The Ottomans, Safavids, and Mughals made its use in warfare so central to their efforts that historians often refer to them as "the gunpowder empires." But it was among the states of Europe that these weapons were to achieve their highest levels of development. Incessant warfare among the European states and against the Ottomans fueled the development of bigger and deadlier cannon and lighter and more accurate small arms. The use of these weapons brought on the age of the infantry armed with muskets. By the end of the eighteenth century, even though muskets and artillery were technologically similar the world over, a high degree of drill among bayonet-equipped grenadiers gave European armies an edge against the Ottomans, Mughals, and Africans.

Questions

- How do gunpowder's origins as a medicine complicate the way we typically view technological and cultural adaptations?

- What would have been the consequence for world history if the military uses of gunpowder had never been discovered?

The Yuan Dynasty   In 1280 Khubilai Khan proclaimed the Yuan dynasty, taking the reign name of Shizu. This dynasty pulled China into an empire spanning all of Eurasia from Korea to the interior of Poland and probing as far as Hungary, Java, and Japan. In a way, however, the acquisition of China also signaled a significant change in Mongol fortunes. On the one hand, many of the world's richest, most populous, and commercially vibrant areas were now under the control of what was nominally a unified empire. In terms of all the constituent khans encouraging trade, building infrastructure along land routes, and sponsoring and protecting caravans—including pioneering innovations in insuring them and in limiting liability for investors and traders—it did represent a prototype free trade zone. Politically, however, it became increasingly fragmented. By Khubilai's death in 1294 what had been one empire was now essentially four squabbling khanates: The Ilkhans in Persia and the Middle East, whose advance had been halted by the Mamluks of Egypt; the Golden Horde, occupying a vast stretch of territory in what is now Ukraine and Russia; the khanate of Chagatai, centered at Samarkand and occupying a pivotal position along the Silk Road in central Asia; and the Yuan Dynasty of Khubilai Khan, stretching from Mongolia into Korea, through most of China and down into Tibet and Vietnam.

The necessity of adopting and inhabiting the institutions they now commanded required adaptation on an unprecedented scale in order to make them function in an orderly way. This was especially true for the Mongols, because their tiny population of about a million had to rule as many as one hundred times that number of people. Moreover, the brilliant governmental improvisations of Genghis Khan in conquering his empire now came up against institutions that in some cases had functioned for over a thousand years, and were based on philosophical and ethical systems even older. Thus, the Mongols, like the Manchus who came after them, found themselves reluctantly adapting to Chinese culture to keep the existing systems in operation while struggling to maintain the culture, mores, and belief systems of the steppes.

In some ways this was an easier transition for Shizu than for those of Genghis Khan's generation. The grandson khans had come of age when their families were already fabulously wealthy and powerful, and in this respect it was hardly a leap for Khubilai to take on the trappings and dynastic rituals of a Chinese emperor. Moreover, the rigorous life of the steppe was now a distant memory, replaced with opulent ceremonial commemorations of those days. Even military campaigning was far less rigorous for the khans than in former times, and so the skills so necessary to the Mongols' early successes were already eroding.

Mongol toleration of religious traditions now also left them free to experiment with foreign faiths. To a considerable extent, the fragmentation of the Mongol Empire broke down the idea of Genghis Khan that the leadership should not adopt any particular one of the existing systems of religious, cultural, and political traditions because none of them could be satisfactorily stretched to fit the needs of universal empire. Thus, the Ilkhans in southwest Asia now converted to Islam, married into the local population, and eventually disappeared as a distinct ethnicity. Likewise, the descendants of Chagatay converted to Islam and, though their line did not stay intact, attempted to maintain their genealogy. From this line the fourteenth-century conqueror Timur (Tamerlane) claimed Genghis Khan as his ancestor; Tamerlane's putative descendent, Babur, also claiming the legacy of Genghis Khan, became the progenitor of the Timurids (from Tamerlane), the dynasty in India called the Mughals (see Chapter 20). For their part, some of the Mongols in Yuan territories (as well as Han Chinese and members of other minority groups) also converted to Islam. Others converted to Buddhism, with the Tibetan varieties, such as the Yellow Hat sect later headed by the Dalai Lama, proving especially attractive.

In the Yuan territories, administrative needs ultimately trumped Mongol practices of circulating officials of different nationalities throughout the entire empire. Initially, a number of senior Chinese officials were purged and others resigned in protest to the new order. These changes even spawned a new genre of Chinese landscape painting, which featured a solitary figure in official's robes sitting in exile in his mountain fastness. The practice of bringing in officials and advisors from other regions in the empire had proved only partially successful and caused widespread consternation among the remaining Chinese officials and aspiring scholar-gentry. Ultimately, the examination system was reinstated in 1315, and continued until 1905.

While contemporary source material on the rise of the Mongols under Genghis Khan is scarce—the Persian accounts were written later and even the *Secret History of the Mongols* was composed around 1240, long after Genghis Khan had died—a number of accounts make their appearance from the second half of the thirteenth century on. Though the four large khanates competed for prestige and resisted Kubilai's claim to the title of Great Khan, the relative ease of travel and enhanced commerce continued. China was open on an unprecedented scale to a variety of foreign goods, ideas, and travelers, while Chinese goods like paper money, gunpowder, coal, the compass, and dozens of other innovations circulated in greater variety and profusion than ever before. Emissaries and missionaries from the developing states of Europe for the first time now traveled east to the capital city of Khanbaligh. The two most famous travel accounts of the era, those of the Venetian Marco Polo

selections from the
Travels of Marco Polo

(1254–1324) and Ibn Battuta of Tangier (1304–1369), who lived and traveled throughout the Mongol Empire, are testaments to the powerful impact of Mongol rule in facilitating travel over such a vast area. Indeed, it was during the brief rule of the Mongols that the European image of China as a fairyland of exotica, fabulous wealth, and wondrous inventions was firmly set (see Map 12.5).

The End of the Khans The Yuan period is almost universally regarded by the Chinese as one of imperial China's darkest times. Although the Mongols quickly restored order and allowed a relative tolerance of religious practice and expression, the Yuan period was seen as an oppressive time of large standing armies, withdrawal from service of many Chinese officials, ineffective administration, forced labor, and heavy taxes. Compounding the intensity of the tensions between Mongols and their subjects was perhaps the single worst disaster of the fourteenth century, the bubonic plague—known in Europe as the Black Death. While scholars have only recently begun to examine Chinese mortality rates resulting from the plague, Chinese accounts suggest that they were in all likelihood similar to those of Europe in some areas, with perhaps one third of the population of about 100 million being carried off from the 1340s until the end of the century. One thing that seems clear, however, was that by facilitating travel and commerce, the Mongol regimes unknowingly opened the door for the disease to go from being a regional disaster to a continent-wide pandemic.

Over the following decades, the power of the Mongols continued to decline, both at the center and one by one in the peripheral states as well. Perhaps the first and most dramatic event was the overthrow of the Yuan in China and the restoration of Chinese rule under the Ming Dynasty. This was accompanied by an exodus of refugee officials and Mongol civilians, though many Mongols who had settled in China decided to take their chances and stay. As mentioned above, many had also converted to Islam. By mid-century, all of these factors contributed to outbreaks of rebellion in China. In 1368, a coalition led by a soldier–Buddhist monk named Zhu Yuanzhang [JOO yuwen-JAHNG] (1328–1398) drove the Mongols from the capital at Khanbaligh and proclaimed a new dynastic line, the Ming.

How should we assess the Mongol era as a whole? Although it was once considered a byword for barbarism on a stupendous scale, recent scholars have recalibrated their views considerably. Mongol emphasis on destroying feudal aristocracies, elevating artisans and merchants, facilitating trade, and tolerating multiple religions have all been cited as paving the way for the early modern era. Some have gone so far as to claim that the Mongols in effect brought on the Renaissance in Europe. Most agree that the *Pax Mongolica* in creating a super-regional empire and trading sphere paved the way in some respects for new patterns to come. Yet it is undeniable that the creation of the empire and repeated wars among the later khans were accompanied by unprecedented death and destruction. Though we have no reliable figures for the region as a whole, rough estimates put the population of the areas touched by the Mongols at perhaps 150 million, of which perhaps 18 to 30 million may have died, excluding those killed during the bubonic plague.

Khubilai Khan as the First Yuan Emperor, Shizu (Shih-tzu).

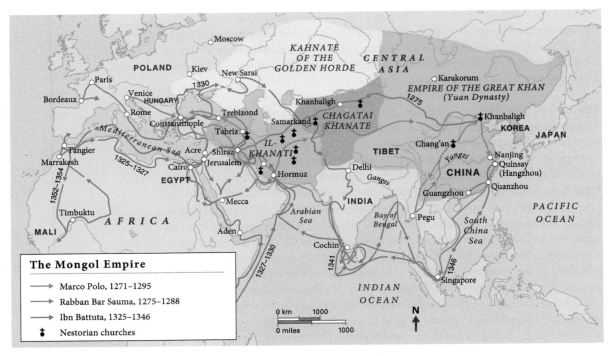

MAP **12.5** **The Mongol Empire.**

Thus, while many modern historians have come to see the Mongol era as a key—perhaps *the* key—to the transition from the medieval to the early modern world, the cost was for many unacceptably high.

The Ming to 1450: The Quest for Stability

Zhu took the reign name of "Hongwu." Under his leadership, Chinese politics and customs were restored and a centralized government was established. This new imperial state would, with minor modifications, see China into the twentieth century.

The Grand Secretariat   Hongwu streamlined this bureaucracy by concentrating power around the emperor. He created the Grand Secretariat, a group of senior officials who served as an advisory board for the emperor; it remained at the apex of imperial Chinese power into the twentieth century. Ming emperors now had a base from which to take measures to protect the empire from incursions by nomadic groups in the north. One step to protect against invasion was taken in 1421, when the capital of the empire was moved from Nanjing to Khanbaligh, now renamed Beijing ("Northern Capital"), so that a strong Chinese presence in the region would discourage invasion. Further safeguards against invasion included fortifications along the Great Wall.

Population Recovery   While the country fortified its borders and reinstated political systems dismantled by the Mongols, it also contended with a drop in population. The population rebound, however, did not assume significant proportions until it was aided by new food crops in the sixteenth and seventeenth centuries.

pictorial map of the
Yellow River, ca. 1370

With the coming of new crops from the Americas by way of Spanish and Portuguese merchants, the country's population grew. The efficiency of Chinese agriculture and the growth of the empire's internal trade contributed to another doubling of the population.

The Interlude of Naval Power Thanks to the foundation laid by Hongwu [hoong-WOO], the dynasty's third emperor, Yongle [young-LUH], inherited a state in 1403 recovering its economic dynamism. He ordered China's first and last great naval expeditions. These voyages, sent out from 1405 to 1433, were perhaps the most remarkable feats of their day.

The first voyages were aimed at overawing any foreign powers harboring pretenders to Yongle's throne. As the realization set in that these foreign threats were nonexistent, the voyages became focused on trade and exploration, covering the Indian Ocean, the Persian Gulf, and the East African coast. Along the way they planted or reestablished contact with Chinese merchants in South and Southeast Asia.

Yongle's successors put an end to the expeditions. The reasons for this abrupt turnabout were both political and strategic. By the 1430s the Mongols were again threatening the northern frontiers. The expense of the voyages and the realization that there were no significant naval rivals were reasons to discontinue them in the face of the Mongol threat. In addition, the Confucian officials argued that maritime trade was not useful to the overall welfare of the empire.

Toward the Ming Decline The activist style of Hongwu and Yongle proved to be the exception rather than the rule during Ming rule. Through most of the sixteenth century, a succession of weak emperors would erode the stability of the reformed Ming imperial system. To compensate for the weakness at the center, power was increasingly diffused throughout the system. Over time, much of it was acquired by the grand secretaries and provincial governors, while at the village level, magistrates and village headmen assumed the bulk of power and responsibility.

Society, Family, and Gender

With the refinement of the examination system and the elaboration of the bureaucracy during the Song, which was renewed during the Ming, the key point of intersection between the people and the government was the district magistrate.

The Magistrate The position of magistrate brought with it enormous responsibility. Assisted by clerks and secretaries, messengers, and constables, he supervised all aspects of local government. He presided over all official ceremonies, conducted the local Confucian examinations, and set a moral example for his constituents.

The Scholar-Gentry and Rural Society While China boasted some of the world's largest cities, more than 85 percent of the country remained rural during the period from the Song to the Ming. At the top of the local structures of power and influence were the *scholar-gentry,* who were the educated and included all ranks of degree holders and their families.

Scholar-gentry membership seldom exceeded 1–2 percent of the population. The chief qualification was attainment of at least the lowest official degree. The demands of memorizing the classical canon, however, were such that the wealthy had a distinct advantage. Still, there were enough poor boys who succeeded to provide a degree of mobility within the system.

Since prestige within the scholar-gentry derived from education, it was not uncommon for individuals to purchase degrees. Thus, there was considerable snobbery among the upper gentry of advanced degree holders and officials toward the lower gentry. This was reinforced by **sumptuary laws** signifying to which of the nine official grades they belonged.

Their position as community leaders and their Confucian ethics placed the scholar-gentry in tension with the official bureaucracy. Along with the district magistrate, they presided over ceremonies at temples and led all clan ceremonies. In addition, the scholar-gentry mingled with the official authorities as social equals; sometimes they outranked the local magistrate.

Local government relied on the cooperation of the gentry and people with the magistrates. The gentry represented a consistent network of people to carry out the day-to-day work of government. They took seriously the Confucian injunction to remonstrate with officials, and could rally the people to subvert the policies of unpopular magistrates. Moreover, as influential men themselves, they could even bring about changes in regional or imperial policy.

Village and Family Life   The tendency toward greater centralization under the Ming also influenced Chinese village life. While life among the peasants still revolved around family, clan, and lineage, institutions perfected under the Ming lasted into the twentieth century.

Originally conceived during the Song dynasty, the *baojia* system of village organization called for families to register all members and be grouped into clusters of 10. One family in each cluster was then assigned responsibility for the others. Each group of responsible families would then be grouped into 10, and a member would be selected from them to be responsible for the group of 100 households, and so on up to the 1,000-household level. The system allowed the authorities to bypass gentry resistance to government directives and guaranteed a rural network of informers.

Peasant Women's Lives   The patterns of work and peasant life changed little from the Song through the Ming. The simple, efficient tools available to farmers had remained fundamentally unchanged from the preceding centuries.

Tensions in village life continued to be magnified in the lives of women and girls. The brief Mongol period of political domination had virtually no impact on Chinese social institutions. Mongol patterns of more egalitarian gender and class relations that had prevailed on the steppe thus remained limited to the Mongols themselves. For the Chinese, on the one hand, the education of upper-class women made them more marriageable. Study of proper Confucian etiquette occupied most of their curriculum. The custom of painful **foot binding** originated during the Song, gained ground during the Ming, and continued until it was banned by the People's Republic of China after 1949. **Female infanticide** also rose in rural areas during times of social stress. As in previous periods, rural girls were frequently sold into servitude by financially pressed families.

Sumptuary laws: Regulations mandating or restricting the wearing of certain clothes or insignia among different classes of people.

Foot binding: The practice of tightly wrapping the feet of young girls in order to break and reset the bones to compress the feet to about one-third of their normal size. Mothers generally did this to their daughters to make them more marriageable, since tiny feet were considered the epitome of female beauty.

Female infanticide: The killing of girl babies.

Perceptions of Perfection: Intellectual, Scientific, and Cultural Life

The period from the Tang to the Ming was marked by technological prowess that subsided after 1500. Indeed, China remained the world's leading producer of new inventions until roughly 1500. One possible answer as to why it suddenly subsided after this time may be that the Chinese felt that they had achieved a degree of perfection in so many areas that there was simply no need to advance them further.

The Neo-Confucian Synthesis The intermingling of Confucianism with Buddhist, Daoist, and other traditions of thought forced its reformulation by the Song period. During the twelfth century, this reformulation matured into Neo-Confucianism, which combined the moral core of Confucian ethics with an emphasis on speculative philosophy borrowed from Buddhism and Daoism. Though the impetus no doubt came in part from these other two systems, Neo-Confucian thinkers were careful to insist that all their key concepts could be found in the ideas of Confucius and Mencius, and in the Classics.

Neo-Confucianism holds that one cannot sit passively and wait for enlightenment, as the Buddhists were alleged to do, but must actively "seek truth through facts" in order to understand the relationships of form and substance (*li*—not to be confused with ritual, which is also pronounced as "*li*") and *qi*, the dynamic force from which things and events are produced as they govern the constitution of the totality of the universe. Indeed, the ethical self and the epistemological self spring from the same source and are different manifestations of the same unity. Exploration of the physical universe undertaken in this spirit is thus the ultimate act of Confucian self-cultivation in that one apprehends the Way (*Dao*) on every level. Indeed, this method came to be called *daoxue*, "the study of the way (dao). This vision of Neo-Confucianism was perfected by Zhu Xi [joo SHEE] (ca. 1129–1200).

Zhu Xi's speculative Neo-Confucianism faded during a Buddhist revival in the Ming era, which favored the more direct ethical action favored by Wang Yangming [wahng yahn-MING] (1472–1529). For Wang, as for Zhu Xi, truth was unitary. He believed that all people carry within them an intuitive sense of the fundamental order of the universe. It is out of this instinct toward the right that one investigates the universe in order to refine one's conclusions.

selections from the writings of Wang Yangming

Wang's other area of emphasis was the unity of knowledge and action. The sage, he argued, must take action in the world, both to be a moral example to others and to complete his own self-cultivation.

Technological Peaks The notion of perfectibility woven through Song and Ming philosophy can also be seen in the scientific and technical realms. While a number of previous innovations were refined, in other cases high points had been achieved early and continued unchanged. For example, Zheng He's innovative ships of the fifteenth century remained unsurpassed triumphs of Chinese naval architecture until the mid-nineteenth century. And while new firearms were introduced in the seventeenth and eighteenth centuries, they remained essentially unchanged until the 1840s.

From the Tang through the Southern Song, China produced technological innovations that would have a profound effect inside and outside the empire, including the horse collar, moldboard plow, wheelbarrow, compass, gunpowder, porcelain,

Song Porcelain. Porcelain reached its full maturity during the Song dynasty, and objects from that period are highly coveted even today. This celadon (sea-green, sometimes with a delicate crackle glaze) ewer with a double phoenix head and peony decorations dates from the Northern Song (960–1127).

early example of a printed map, Song Dynasty

paper, and advanced iron casting. By the height of the Song period, China dominated production and distribution of tea, sugar, silk, porcelain, paper, and cotton cloth. An infrastructure of commercial credit, printed paper money, and insurance supported China's network of industry and trade.

Porcelain and Literature   Many of the advances in technology, such as the production of true porcelain, revolved around luxury items. Following centuries of experimentation, Song craftspeople hit upon the formula for creating the world's most celebrated ceramics. Surviving examples of elegant white and celadon (a shade of green) Song porcelain vessels are among the world's most precious art treasures. Techniques for using blue cobalt oxide pigments were originally introduced from Iraq in the ninth century and were being utilized by Song and Ming potters to brighten their porcelain ware. Government-sponsored and government-run kilns allowed for unprecedented volume and quality control.

The growing wealth, leisure, and literacy of the scholar-gentry and urban classes also created a demand for popular literature. The novel as a literary genre first made its appearance in China during the Yuan period, but emerged as a form of mass entertainment only in the sixteenth century. These novels, written in a combination of classical and colloquial language, captured the imaginations of seventeenth- and eighteenth-century readers.

⟫ Putting It All Together

The experiences of India and China during the period from the seventh through the fifteenth centuries provide us with important areas of comparison. In the realm of political continuity, India was subject to a succession of governments set up by invaders from the north and west, while the kingdoms to the south jockeyed for power among themselves and over the Indian-influenced states of Southeast Asia. While there was cultural and religious continuity in the south, the north was dominated alternately by Hinduism and Buddhism, and ultimately by Islam. In the end, none of these claimed full dominance, though Islam remained the religion of the rulers after the twelfth century.

In the case of China, despite the Mongol invasion during the fourteenth century, the basic political structure reemerged with greater centralization than ever during the Ming dynasty. Culturally, the Mongols' influence on China was negligible; moreover, the Mongols made themselves culturally "Chinese" in order to rule, despite their efforts to maintain their ethnic autonomy. Chinese leadership in technical innovation kept up its former pace, and the brief incorporation into the Mongol Empire facilitated other cultures' interaction with Chinese advances.

The most dramatic difference, however, came in the realm of religion. India, from the time of Mahmud of Ghazna, never completely adapted itself to Islam. Northern India became an uneasily *syncretic* area where Hindus and Muslims attempted to coexist with each other. Even attempts to bridge the gulf between Hindus and Muslims, such as Sikhism, were not successful in attaining widespread acceptance.

In China, however, the dominant political structures of empire and the cultural assumptions of Confucianism not only resisted Mongol attempts to circumvent them but in the end were largely adopted by the conquerors. Unlike the Muslim conquerors in India, the Mongols proved receptive to several of the religious traditions they encountered in their conquests. Tensions between Buddhism and Confucianism in China resulted not in persecution of the Buddhists but in Confucian thinkers borrowing Buddhist approaches to speculative philosophy and creating an expanded synthetic ideology, Neo-Confucianism.

These religious and cultural trends would continue until the nineteenth century. India would struggle to balance the tensions of syncretism; the Chinese continued to pursue their policy that all outsiders could ultimately "become Chinese." Ultimately, both empires would be reduced by the British and European powers, whose centuries-long rise was shortly to begin.

interactive concept map

Review and Relate

| Thinking Through Patterns

Examine the ways historians approach the big questions of this chapter.

⟫ **How did interactions between Muslims and Hindus in India lead to religious syncretism?**

In contemplating this question, we must consider the fundamental beliefs of these two religious traditions and what kinds of changes take place as religions interact with other long-established beliefs. Hinduism encompasses many different religious assumptions and has long tried to fit newly arrived belief systems into its own traditions. This is where the clash with Islam is most evident. Islam teaches that there is no God but God (Allah); Hinduism would place Allah next to its other gods, which Muslims find intolerable. This fundamental clash of views makes any compromise difficult. As Muslim leaders find that they cannot force their Hindu subjects, who vastly outnumber them, to accept the new religion, they must therefore find ways to lessen its impact while holding true to Islam. Thus, some leniency must be given, or rule becomes impossible, but each side keeps its distance from the other in an uneasy coexistence.

>> **What steps were taken by Hindus and Muslims to lessen the conflicts between the two rival religious traditions?**

Some compromises were made to lessen conflict between the major traditions. Muslim rulers routinely suspended their insistence on governing by Islamic law and let the Hindu majority govern itself according to its own traditions. In some cases, Hindu women even adopted the veil, like their Muslim counterparts. The most spectacular steps were the founding of new religious traditions incorporating both Hindu and Muslim elements—Sikhism, for example, as we will see in Chapter 20, the Mughal ruler Akbar's attempt at a synthetic religion.

>> **How was the Tang dynasty in China different from its predecessors and successors?**

The Tang was China's most cosmopolitan dynasty, which made it quite different from its predecessors. This cosmopolitanism largely resulted from the widespread practice of Buddhism. China was now integrated into a Buddhist cultural sphere that allowed circulation of ideas and goods. Thus, China's rulers knew more about their neighbors, and through Buddhism, shared a community of religious interest with them. The reaction to Buddhism as a "foreign" faith in the Song period made China turn more inward; consequently, its larger ties with the Buddhist world deteriorated, never to reach Tang-level connections again.

>> **How effectively did the religious and philosophical traditions of Buddhism, Confucianism, and Daoism blend together in creating Neo-Confucianism? Where did they clash?**

The longevity and diversity of Neo-Confucianism over time suggest that the blending was quite effective. The synthesis of Confucian, humanist-based morality coupled with the speculative ventures of Daoists and Buddhists created a complete, self-sustaining system.

Against the Grain

Consider this as a counterpoint to the main patterns examined in this chapter.

Empress Wu

- In what ways does Empress Wu appear as a classic nonconformist?

The Tang ruler Wu Zetian, or Empress Wu (r. 690–705), exemplified her era's contradictory trends toward both greater restrictiveness and wider latitude in personal behavior, particularly in the case of women. The daughter of a public works official, she spent a brief period at court as a servant to the empress. Disillusioned by life in the capital and drawn to the austerities of Buddhism, she joined a women's monastery, only to return to the palace when her beauty piqued the interest of an imperial prince. She deftly exploited the opportunity.

Hostile chroniclers in subsequent dynasties attributed much of her success, like that of Cleopatra in Egypt, to her sexual exploits, though the records also note that she was well educated, shrewd in her dealings with ministers, and a polished hand at employing imperial spectacle. In 684, after the death of her husband, who had become the emperor, she ruled as empress dowager and as regent for her son. In reality, however, she held all the actual power. A devout Buddhist, she declared Buddhism the state religion. In 690, she inaugurated the new Zhou dynasty, and in 693 took the Buddhist title Divine Empress Who Rules the Universe.

Though she was an able ruler according to the Tang official histories, the act of creating her own dynasty and new titles for herself—including an insistence on the "male" title of "emperor"—was considered usurpation by many of her subjects, and a resistance soon followed. To many Tang leaders, Wu's empowering of Buddhists and Daoists over Confucians was deplorable. As a result, scurrilous accusations were laid against her, including allegations of sexual depravity, the torture and execution of her opponents, and even the murder of her own child in her quest to achieve political power. However, she was able to stifle revolts and to preserve the continuity of the dynasty, only succumbing to natural causes in 705.

Following the Confucian backlash of the Song era, no woman in imperial China would wield this kind of power again until the reign of the empress dowager Cixi in the late nineteenth and early twentieth centuries. Even today, however, Wu remains a controversial figure; while she is celebrated in China as an early feminist role model, she is also seen as an ambitious, cruel, and self-serving schemer.

- In what ways does Empress Wu resemble other ambitious women in history?

Key Terms

Empress dowager 279	Foot binding 286	Sumptuary laws 286
Female infanticide 286	Sikhism 275	

audio flashcards

For additional resources, please go to
www.oup.com/us/vonsivers.
Please see the Further Resources section at the back of the book for additional readings and suggested websites.

Religious Civilizations Interacting

KOREA, JAPAN, AND VIETNAM

Syllabary: A system of written symbols representing the sounds of syllables, rather than individual consonants and vowels.

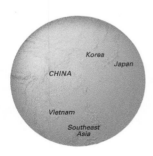

T he brushstrokes flowed across the paper, as they had since she began practicing them as a young girl. For Murasaki Shikibu (ca. 973–1025), the daughter of a minor noble in the court at Heian-Kyo in central Japan, the words had become her refuge from palace life, where a woman's every move was carefully prescribed. The court women of Heian Japan (794–1185 CE), in their thick, stiff winter kimonos, their teeth blackened and faces powdered white to enhance their beauty, were monitored by palace chamberlains and commented on by court gossips. Murasaki's older contemporary Sei Shonagon had responded to this restricted life by skewering its pretentions in her scandalous *Pillow Book*.

Murasaki's literary interests, however, were different. Though trained in *kanji*, the literary Chinese that functioned as Japan's first written language, her private writings were written in the simpler *kana* script based on a **syllabary** of sounds in the Japanese spoken language. Like Sei's, her work also centered on court life. But her subject was the adventures a fictional prince named Genji. Scholars have recognized her *Genji Monogatari*, the *Tale of Genji* (ca. 1000), as the world's first novel. It remains even today Japan's most popular work of fiction and one of the world's great literary masterpieces.

ABOVE: Detail from twelfth-century Japanese scroll depicting The Tale of Genji.

The story of Murasaki, the court women of Heian-Kyo (today's Kyoto), and eleventh-century Japan all help to illustrate the patterns of world history featured in this book.

In the sixth century CE, Chinese writing, culture, thought, and Buddhism were adopted by the ambitious Japanese state of Yamato. Sensing that power and prestige would grow from adapting China's centralized imperial institutions, Yamato leaders remade their state along these lines over the next two centuries. But the suitability of these institutions to Japan's clan-based society was at best uneven.

The tensions in state formation created by this situation were noticeable as well in Korea and Vietnam, which also adapted Chinese institutions. Like the Japanese, the Koreans and Vietnamese would create their own writing systems while retaining Chinese as a literary language. They would also struggle, like the Japanese and Chinese, to balance Buddhism with a Confucian government. The dynamism within these tensions would allow each to make imported Chinese culture their own as they followed distinct courses of state formation—Korea and Vietnam often struggling under China's political shadow, and Japan clinging fiercely to its independence.

» How was the history of Korea affected by its relations with China? With Japan?

» Which important elements of Chinese culture were adapted by the Japanese for their own purposes? What advantages did Japan have over Korea and Vietnam in this regard?

» Which Japanese adaptations of Chinese institutions did not work well in Japan? Why?

» In what ways was the experience of Vietnam similar to that of Japan and Korea? How was it different?

Korea to 1450: Innovation from Above

The influence of imperial China spread throughout east, northeast, and Southeast Asia. Chinese writing, literature, law, government, and thought, as well as imported religions such as Buddhism, shaped local customs and practices. But as these imports were often imposed from the top down, they met frequent resistance at the village and clan levels. Thus, tensions between elites and locals in the assorted Korean kingdoms emerged against a backdrop of invasion and collaboration. From the beginning these societies asserted their political independence from the Chinese. However, their position on or near the Chinese border, their role as havens for refugees, and the pressures of potential invasion provided a conduit for the spread of Chinese innovations—even to the islands of Japan. For the Koreans themselves, shifting relations with China shaped the struggles of different kingdoms for dominance.

People and Place: The Korean Environment

The terrain of the Korean peninsula resembles that of the adjacent region of Manchuria to the north. The Amnokkang (Yalu) River and the Kangnam Mountains form the present dividing line with Manchuria, but Korean kingdoms have at times extended beyond them into modern China's northeast. The areas south of the modern city of Seoul are somewhat flatter. Agriculture has historically been concentrated in the river floodplains and coastal alluvial flats.

Climate and Agriculture   The climate of Korea is continental in the north but influenced by the monsoon system in the south. As in northern China, summer and winter temperatures are extreme, with distinct rainy (summer) and dry (winter) seasons. Annual rainfall amounts differ widely: from average lows of 30 inches in the northeast to 60–70 inches in the southwest. Like the western side of the Japanese islands, however, Korea is largely blocked by Japanese mountain ranges from the moderating effects of the Japan Current.

Altaic: In linguistics, the family of languages descended from that spoken by inhabitants of the region of the Altai Mountains in central Asia. Examples include the Turkic languages, Mongolian, and Manchu.

Striated: Having thin lines or bands.

The difficulties of the terrain and the possibility of drought pose challenges similar to those facing agriculturalists in northern China, with crops such as millet and wheat dominating and rice farming catching on only much later in the south, where rainfall and the terracing of hillsides made it feasible (see Map 13.1).

Ethnic Origins   The ethnic origins of the Koreans are obscure, though some evidence points to a central Asian homeland and links to the **Altaic**-speaking peoples. East and northeast Asia was home to some of the world's first pottery, though the potter's wheel did not arrive in the area for millennia. On the Korean peninsula, pot shards dating from 4000 BCE have been uncovered in **striated** styles not unlike the Jomon wares of Japan, which some scholars have suggested points to early interaction or perhaps a common ancestry.

Conquest and Competition: History and Politics to 1450

The first Korean state predated any Chinese influence. Zhou Chinese annals contain apparent references to the kingdom of Choson—"The Land of the Morning Calm." Choson seems to have extended into southern Manchuria, with its capital located on the site of the modern city of Pyongyang. It is believed to have been founded after 1000 BCE. No indigenous records exist of its early years.

The "Three Kingdoms"   The first attempt by the Chinese at invasion was under the Qin (221–206 BCE). By 108 BCE, their successors, the Han, briefly brought much of the peninsula under their sway. It is from this period that the first written records of the Koreans, Japanese, and Vietnamese appear in Han histories. As related in Sima Qian's *Records of the Grand Historian*, the Han conquest of "Chaoxian" (Choson) was rife with chaos.

Long before this, however, Chinese agricultural techniques, methods of bronze and iron smelting, and other technologies found their way to Choson and beyond. Early contacts between Choson and the Zhou Chinese states from the ninth century BCE on saw the arrival of bronze tools, coins, and weapons. By the fifth century BCE, the technology of iron smelting was also established on the Korean peninsula.

Following the Han conquests, a more systematic Chinese transformation was attempted. The Han incorporated most of the peninsula into their empire, with Pyongyang as their regional capital. They encouraged Chinese settlement in the newly acquired territories. An indirect effect of the conquest was a stream of refugees into the unoccupied regions of the south and to Japan. This traffic across the narrow strait separating the Japanese islands from the mainland facilitated cultural exchanges. Koreans were important actors in early Japanese history, and with the founding of the small Japanese holding of *Kaya* (Gaya) in 42 CE, Japanese territorial claims were established on the peninsula.

At the same time, the foundations had been laid for the so-called Three Kingdoms of Korea: *Koguryo* [go-GUR-yo] (37 BCE–668 CE), *Paekche* [BAAK-chih] (18 BCE–660 CE), and *Silla* [Si-lah] (57 BCE–935 CE). By the fourth century CE, the dissolution of the Han Empire encouraged the Koreans to push the Chinese out of the peninsula. In the wake of their retreat, the three rival kingdoms began a struggle for dominance. Koguryo, in the extreme north, formed the largest state as the Chinese evacuated, moving into southern Manchuria. In the south, the areas that had never been under Chinese control had a history of ties to Japan and, consequently, tended to be more outward-looking.

In 372 the Chinese state of Jin sent Buddhist missionaries to Koguryo. With them came Chinese writing and Confucian thought. In 427, Koguryo remade itself along Chinese lines with a central Confucian bureaucracy, examinations, a reconstituted land tax, and a conscription system.

Meanwhile, the two southern kingdoms continually fought off domination by their northern rival. Paekche's maritime contacts with south China and its wars with Koguryo aided the spread of Buddhism there from 364 to 371. While Buddhism had also come to Silla, its clan-based, autocratic monarchy adopted a Chinese-style bureaucracy that left power largely in the hands of warrior aristocrats.

The struggle among the peninsular states from time to time involved China. In 550, Silla allied with Paekche Koguryo, in the course of which Kaya was eliminated in 562. The reunification of China under the Sui dynasty in 589 soon resulted in another invasion of the north. After several Tang campaigns were repulsed, the Chinese concluded an alliance with Silla in 660, spelling the immediate end of Paekche. Threatened along two fronts, Koguryo itself finally submitted in 668. Silla was ultimately recognized by the Chinese as a client state controlling all of Korea south of Pyongyang in 735.

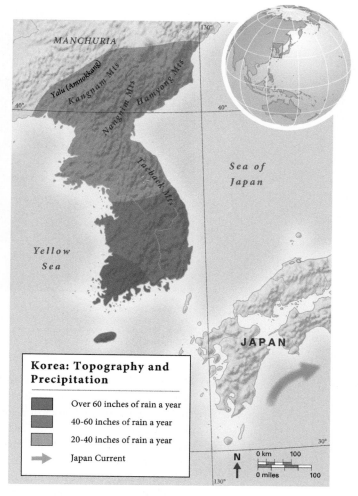

Korea: Topography and Precipitation

- Over 60 inches of rain a year
- 40–60 inches of rain a year
- 20–40 inches of rain a year
- → Japan Current

0 km   100
0 miles   100

MAP 13.1 **Korea: Topography and Precipitation.**

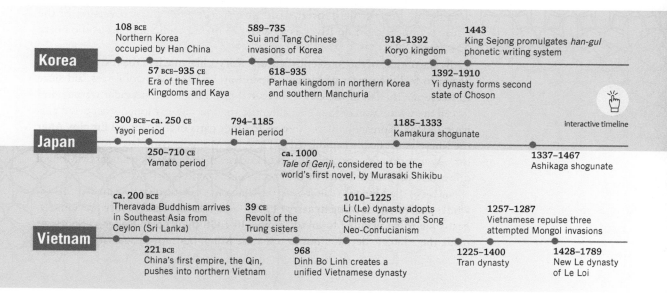

Korea

108 BCE
Northern Korea occupied by Han China

57 BCE–935 CE
Era of the Three Kingdoms and Kaya

589–735
Sui and Tang Chinese invasions of Korea

618–935
Parhae kingdom in northern Korea and southern Manchuria

918–1392
Koryo kingdom

1392–1910
Yi dynasty forms second state of Choson

1443
King Sejong promulgates *han-gul* phonetic writing system

Japan

300 BCE–ca. 250 CE
Yayoi period

250–710 CE
Yamato period

794–1185
Heian period

ca. 1000
Tale of Genji, considered to be the world's first novel, by Murasaki Shikibu

1185–1333
Kamakura shogunate

1337–1467
Ashikaga shogunate

interactive timeline

Vietnam

ca. 200 BCE
Theravada Buddhism arrives in Southeast Asia from Ceylon (Sri Lanka)

221 BCE
China's first empire, the Qin, pushes into northern Vietnam

39 CE
Revolt of the Trung sisters

968
Dinh Bo Linh creates a unified Vietnamese dynasty

1010–1225
Li (Le) dynasty adopts Chinese forms and Song Neo-Confucianism

1225–1400
Tran dynasty

1257–1287
Vietnamese repulse three attempted Mongol invasions

1428–1789
New Le dynasty of Le Loi

Pulguksa Temple. Buddhism put down strong roots in Silla after its introduction in the fourth century. The Pulguksa temple was first built in Kyongjiu, the Silla capital, in 535 as part of the state Buddhist school. The stone pagodas were built in the ninth century under the auspices of the new Son school, better known by its Japanese name, Zen.

Korea to the Mid-Fifteenth Century   By the middle of the eighth century, Silla was in decline. In 780 the king was assassinated, and revolts threatened stability for some time to come. Among the most restive members of Silla society were the merchants, who, like their counterparts in China, were both aware of their economic power and sensitive to the contempt of the Confucian-influenced aristocracy and bureaucrats.

One such merchant, Wong Kon (d. 943), subdued the kingdom and reconstituted it as Koryo—from which comes the name "Korea." The Chinese imperial model of state formation proved attractive to Wong, who, after the practice of Chinese emperors, was accorded a posthumous reign name, Taejo. He moved the capital to Kaesong and adopted Chinese-style bureaucratic and tax systems, with military and labor conscription. Koryo even built its own version of the Great Wall near the Yalu River as a barrier to the nomadic peoples to the north (see Map 13.2).

By the middle of the thirteenth century, Koryo, like much of the rest of Asia, had begun to feel the power of Mongol expansion. In 1231, Mongol forces laid siege to Kaesong. The fall of the city inaugurated four decades of irregular warfare and forced the withdrawal of the government to the south. The Mongols deported perhaps 250,000 Koreans as slave laborers to other parts of the Mongol Empire. After the Koryo court finally capitulated in 1259, the Mongols assimilated to Korean culture. As in most of the occupied areas of Eurasia, the advantages brought by Mongol unity were eclipsed in Korea by the cruelty of the conquest itself.

In 1368, the Mongol Yuan dynasty in China was overthrown by Zhu Yuanzhang, who inaugurated the Ming dynasty (1368–1644). As had nearly every previous dynasty, the Ming planned to invade Korea. In 1388 the Korean leader Yi Song-gye made the strategic decision not to resist the Ming, but moved against the Korean court instead, founding the Yi dynasty in 1392 and resurrecting the name of Choson for the new state. The Yi concluded a diplomatic/commercial agreement with China that formed what is often referred to as the Ming "tribute system" (see Chapter 21).

Meanwhile, the Yi polity adapted to Chinese-style institutions. The centralized government of the Ming was echoed in Choson, and the adoption of Neo-Confucianism drove out older local customs. A new capital was established, and the state was divided into eight provinces following the Chinese model of prefectures and districts. A uniform law code was promulgated in 1485, and the Confucian exam structure was broadened to include a two-tiered official class, the *yongban* and *chungin*.

The new class structure was not without problems. To stabilize the *yongban* class, Yi rulers made large land grants to the great officials of the kingdom. These landholders, however, used their grants to amass local power. Unlike Chinese officials, who were moved from place to place to avoid just this, they tended to remain in their own territories and resisted attempts from the throne to rein in their excesses. Over time, many became like regional rulers.

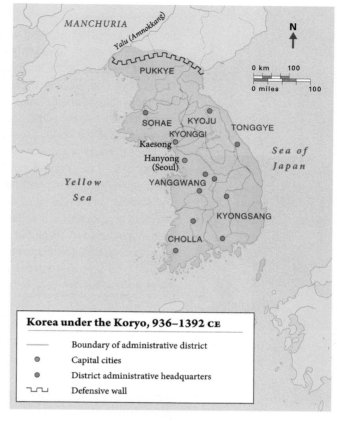

MAP 13.2 **Korea under the Koryo, 936–1392.**

Economy, Society, and Family

Like their counterparts in China, rulers in the Korean kingdoms were preoccupied with problems of landlordism and tenancy, land reform, maintenance of local infrastructures, and alleviating want during times of shortage.

Land Reform   Rulers under Chinese influence proposed schemes of land redistribution based on the Chinese "well-field" model (see Chapter 4). More ambitious was the *chongjon* system of Silla, begun in 722. This system mandated a government-sponsored distribution of land, with taxes paid in kind. Additionally, peasants were instructed to develop specialized cash crops or engage in small-craft manufacture. A prime example was sericulture—the planting of mulberry trees as food for silkworms, the raising of silkworms, and the production of silk.

The Yi dynasty of Choson prioritized the implanting of Neo-Confucian values in the countryside as well as among elites. A new system of land tenure was made part of a more general stabilizing of all classes. Peasant rents were fixed at half the crop, and, as in the Chinese system, a hierarchy of village headmen, bureaucrats, and magistrates was set up to collect taxes, settle disputes, and dispense justice.

The institution of Chinese systems in Korea attracted the elites more than the peasant and artisan classes. This aggravated societal tensions, despite the governmental efficiencies they created. One factor was the bureaucracy's attempt to enhance its power at the expense of the merchant and artisan classes. In the countryside, power

Printing

Seven centuries before the invention of the printing press and movable type revolutionized the intellectual life of early modern Europe, these developments in East Asia had a similar effect. In many respects, the consequences of these innovations were different, because of the languages and the technical media with which printers in China, Korea, Japan, and Vietnam worked, and the cultural patterns of handwriting and calligraphy as artistic skills cultivated by elites slowed the spread of printing. Yet by the fourteenth century, the societies of East Asia achieved the highest preindustrial literacy rates in the world. These would be unmatched in Europe for centuries.

The earliest remnant examples of woodblock printing date to the fall of the Han dynasty in 220 CE. Printers carved blocks of text on book-sized boards, inked them, and pressed the cloth or paper pages on them to get copies. The boards could then be shaved down and carved again as needed. By the eighth century the Chinese had also begun to experiment with copper movable type inserted vertically into standardized rows in a system very much like the one Gutenberg devised centuries later. But, ironically, these presses remained more curiosities than practical devices. The obstacle was

The Korean Printing Industry. Because of its position as the northern crossroads of the Buddhist and Chinese literary world, Korea was a major center of printing. Printing with carved wooden blocks had been developed during the eighth century, and large publishers and academies kept great numbers of them on hand. The most famous collection is in this storehouse, which still preserves the 80,000 blocks of the *Tripitaka*, carved between 1237 and 1257.

remained in the hands of the landholder aristocracy, which meant conditions for peasants resembled the serfdom of their European contemporaries.

Neo-Confucian Influence   Particularly in the cities, Song Chinese–influenced material culture was evident by the eleventh and twelfth centuries. Interregional trade was brisk, and Korea's position at the center of the east Asian Buddhist world made it a trade and pilgrimage crossroads. Korean artisans became proficient in porcelain making and book printing; many of the oldest Chinese, Korean, and Japanese works extant were printed by Korean publishers.

Under the Yi, the Confucian exams became more open, though the new social arrangements called for two official classes, the *yongban*, or scholar-gentry, and the *chungin*, or minor officials. Below these were the *yangmin*, commoners of different professions as well as peasants and serfs, while the lowest group, the *chonmin*, consisted of bond slaves, laborers, and prostitutes.

Though the Confucian exams theoretically allowed for some degree of social mobility, they were monopolized by the *yongban*. The institution of hereditary classes, intended to create a stable and harmonious social structure, instead concentrated wealth in the hands of the rural gentry. In many places, the older patterns of aristocratic local power continued. Thus, by the end of the fifteenth century, the divide between the wealthy, educated, sophisticated capital and large provincial cities and the tradition-bound countryside was increasing.

Women and Society   Until the arrival of Confucian institutions in the Korean countryside, local village life, as in Vietnam and Japan, tended toward more equality between men and women than would later be the case. In Korea, this egalitarianism

the Chinese written language—and, at this time, the written languages of Korea, Japan, and Vietnam as well. Unlike the English alphabet with its 26 letters, literary Chinese has thousands of different characters. It was simply impractical for typesetters to cast adequate supplies of characters, organize them, and sort through them to compose the text to be copied. It was far less work to just carve the text blocks from scratch.

One catalyst for printing was the growing popularity of Buddhism throughout East Asia. As would be the case centuries later with the spread of religious tracts during the Protestant Reformation, the desire of Buddhists to read scriptures proved a stimulus to literacy, though in practical terms only those with considerable leisure could master the literary Chinese of the scriptures. Still, the establishment of woodblock printing as a major industry in East Asia by the fourteenth century has been seen by a variety of scholars as one of the hallmarks of early modernity centuries before that term is applied to Europe.

Questions

- How did the innovation of woodblock printing facilitate the spread of Buddhism throughout East Asia?

- What does the use of *han-gul* script in Korea say about the relationship between literacy and state formation?

persisted despite Neo-Confucian precepts. Until the sixteenth and seventeenth centuries, for example, bilateral and **matrilocal** marriage patterns tended to be the norm. As in Japan and Vietnam, the communal nature of rice agriculture made women and girls more equal partners in local rural society. Women's property and inheritance rights, far more expansive than in Confucian China, also reflected this.

Matrilocal: Living with the family of the bride.

Under the Neo-Confucian reforms of the Yi, these practices changed. Strictly delineated gender roles, long a staple among the urban elites and official classes, became a cornerstone of moral training in rural academies and in the home.

Religion, Culture, and Intellectual Life

Early Korean religion appears to have been nature-spiritual. One could appeal to the spirits through shamans or animals believed to have certain powers. Like Shinto in Japan, these beliefs continued at the local level long after the introduction of more formalized systems. The invasion of the Han brought the Chinese concepts of heaven, earth, and humankind along with imperial rituals. Most importantly, Buddhism was introduced to the Three Kingdoms during the fourth century CE.

A Korean Foundation Myth

Buddhism, Printing, and Literacy All the Korean kings seized the combination of Buddhism, Han Confucianism, and their institutions as a way to enhance their states. In Silla, the court pursued a course of striving for Buddhist "perfection." It built the 210-foot Hwang Nyonsu temple in 645. Others sponsored the publication of Buddhist works: Koryo produced a version of the *Tripitaka* printed on 80,000 hand-carved wood blocks. This contributed to the high level of functional literacy in written Chinese among Korean elites. Due to the demand for Buddhist works, twelfth-century Korea developed into one of the world's early centers of publishing (see "Patterns Up Close").

Korean woodblock printing of the *Tripitaka*, 1251 CE

Han-gul: Korean
phonetic script,
introduced in the middle
of the fifteenth century.

Korea's literacy received a further boost during the reign of King Sejong (r. 1418–1450). Here, the development of the Korean phonetic script **han-gul**, like the use of *kana* in Japan, made the introduction of writing much simpler than literary Chinese. Yet, like *kana* in Japan, it also created a two-tiered system of literacy: Chinese remained the written medium of choice among the elites, while *han-gul* became the written language of the commoners and, increasingly, women. Such divisions notwithstanding, the explosion of vernacular literature contributed to Korea attaining, with Japan, some of the highest levels of functional literacy in the preindustrial world.

Japan to 1450: Selective Interaction and Adaptation

The case of Japan raises exciting questions about the effects of isolation. Like Britain, Japan's geographical position allowed it to selectively interact with and adapt to continental innovations. Acculturation in Japan—which had never experienced a successful invasion—was almost completely voluntary, a characteristic unique among the societies of Eurasia.

The Island Refuge

Japan's four main islands, Honshu, Hokkaido, Kyushu, and Shikoku, are varied in climate. The northernmost island of Hokkaido has cold winters and cool summers; the central island of Honshu, bisected north to south by mountain ranges, has a temperate to subtropical climate on the eastern side, where it is moderated by the Japan Current, and a colder, more continental climate on the western side that faces Korea and northeastern China. The small southern island of Shikoku and the southernmost island of Kyushu have warm, moist weather governed by the Pacific monsoon system (see Map 13.3).

The Limitations of the Land   Only about one-fifth of the territory of Japan's islands is arable. In the narrow plains and valleys, the majority of which are on the temperate Pacific side of the mountains, the soil is mineral-rich and the rainfall abundant. But islanders face the limitations of the land in supporting a growing population. Like the Korean peninsula, the ruggedness of the land forced its people to live in politically isolated, culturally united communities. Communication by water was often most convenient, both among the Japanese home islands and across the strait to Korea.

Adaptation at Arm's Length: History and Politics

The origins of the Japanese are obscure. Two groups appear to have migrated to the islands from the Asian mainland via Ice Age land bridges, perhaps 10,000–20,000 years ago. Their descendants, the Utari or Ainu, are today regarded as Japan's aboriginal peoples. Details of their religious practices and recent DNA typing have led some anthropologists to link them to the peoples of central Asia, Siberia, and the Americas.

The later inhabitants may have originally come from the peoples who migrated into Southeast Asia, Indonesia, and eventually the central Pacific. They may also have been descended from Polynesian travelers and migrants from the Asian mainland.

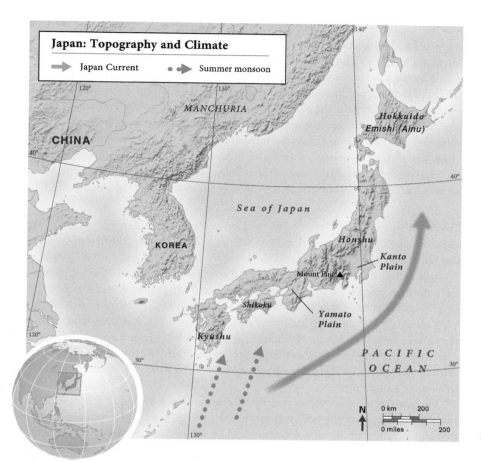

Japan: Topography and Climate

→ Japan Current   •→ Summer monsoon

MANCHURIA

CHINA

Sea of Japan

KOREA

Hokkaido
Emishi (Ainu)

Honshu

Kanto
Plain

Mount Fuji ▲

Shikoku

Yamato
Plain

Kyushu

PACIFIC
OCEAN

N
0 km   200
0 miles   200

map analysis

Microlith: A very small blade made of flaked stone and used as a tool, especially in the Mesolithic era.

Matriarchal: A social system in which the mother is head of the family.

Matrilineal: Relating to, based on, or tracing ancestral descent through the maternal line.

MAP **13.3** **Japan: Topography and Climate.**

Linguistic evidence suggests a very tenuous connection to Korean and even to the Altaic language family.

Jomon and Yayoi   Japan's prehistory (ca. 10,000–300 BCE) has been designated by archaeologists as the Jomon period. Artifacts of this period include lightly fired clay vessels and **microlith** items: arrowheads, spear points, tools made of bone and antler, and nets and fishhooks. **Matriarchal** and **matrilineal** clans appear to have dominated society, clustered mostly near the sea or slightly inland. Fishing and harvesting seaweed were the major forms of subsistence. As among the American peoples of the Pacific Northwest, the bounty of the sea and forests enabled village life to develop in the absence of an early agricultural revolution.

During the final half-millennium before the Common Era, increased intercommunication among Japanese, Koreans, and the Late Zhou Chinese coastal states laid the groundwork not only for the introduction of agriculture to the Japanese islands but for an almost simultaneous Bronze Age, as well. During the last centuries of the Jomon period, it appears that some of the grain crops of northern Asia found their

Jomon Jar and Yamato Sharinseki Disk. The distinctive herringbone pattern and flared top mark this pottery as Middle Jomon, perhaps 5,000–6,000 years old. The disk made of finely worked steatite was taken from a third-century CE *kofun* burial mound in central Japan. It may be related as a religious object to similar kinds of ornaments found in China.

way to the islands. During a 600-year period designated Yayoi (300 BCE–300 CE), imported and domestically manufactured bronze and iron articles appeared. Southern Honshu and Kyushu also saw the cultivation of rice. These changes were introduced by the dislocations resulting from the creation of China's first empire in 221 BCE and the influx of Korean refugees after the initial Chinese invasion of Korea.

As elsewhere in Asia, the rice revolution allowed for population growth in Japan. The movement away from fishing and gathering combined with the efficiency of metal tools and weapons also fostered state formation among the larger and more powerful clans, or *uji*. Thus, sometime after 250 CE, Japan's first fully evolved state, Yamato, centered on the Kanto Plain near modern Tokyo, emerged. Japan's first monumental architecture, enormous burial mounds called *kofun*, date from this period.

Toward the Imperial Order The earliest written records describing Japan were composed by Chinese chroniclers in 57 CE. In 297 CE, we have the first mention of the Yamato state.

Although there had been diplomatic and cultural contact across the Sea of Japan from the first century CE, a high level was reached during the later sixth century CE. In 552, tradition has it that Buddhism was introduced to the islands from Paekche. With it came the Chinese writing system and written works. A decade later, in 562, the Korean kingdom of Silla eliminated the Japanese colony of Kaya on the peninsula, precipitating a new flow of refugees to Japan. From 589 into the early seventh century, continued Chinese attempts to dominate the Korean kingdoms increased the level of emigration.

The growing power of China and Silla prompted the Soga *uji*'s Empress Suiko (r. 592–628) and her nephew, Prince Shotoku (ca. 573–621), to connect Yamato to mainland conceptions of politics, culture, literature, and, ultimately, the imperial system itself. Yamato adoptions included Buddhism as a state religion (594), the Chinese lunar calendar for state record keeping (604), and the prince's constitution modeled on Confucian and Buddhist precepts (604).

selections from the *Taika*

The most far-reaching changes came later in the century, with the *Taika*, or Great Reform, of 645. The remaking of the Yamato regime along Chinese lines in the wake of the *Taika* marks the beginning of the imperial Japanese state. Soga clan control of the court was overturned, and Fujiwara No-Kamatari, an adviser to the new emperor, Tenchi, ushered in a connection between his family and the imperial court that continued into the twentieth century. In less than a century the first Chinese-style imperial histories were composed; the concept of the Mandate of Heaven was adopted to justify the overthrow of the Sogas; the emperor as the center of a hierarchical system of government was institutionalized; and a census, uniform taxation, and conscription and labor service were enacted. The edicts mandating these changes were promulgated as the Taiho Code of 702, which remained the basis of Japanese law until the late nineteenth century.

Yamato's spiritual roots in Shinto, with its connection to nature, had dictated that the seat of the state be frequently moved. Because of the requirements of a far larger system of government, however, it was decided that a permanent capital be built. The first site selected, at Nara, saw the creation in 710 of a close replica of the Tang capital at Chang'an. In 794, a larger capital was completed nearby along the same lines called Heian-kyo, the future city of Kyoto. The era of imperial rule from this capital, which lasted until 1185, is referred to as the "Heian" period (see Map 13.4).

Heian Japan As the imperial order penetrated all the Japanese home islands except Hokkaido and the adoption of Buddhist culture connected Japan to an interconnected Asian sphere, Heian Japan became a land of contrasts, with local rumblings of discontent. The elites of the capital and provincial administrative centers saw themselves as part of a cosmopolitan world, as fashions in poetry, literature, fine arts, calligraphy, music, and clothing all found their way to court and beyond.

For the members of the new classes into which the majority of Japan's people had been placed (peasants, artisans, merchants, and Buddhist monks) many of the changes had been disruptive. Power and military strength was diffusing from the court and capital out into the countryside. This was particularly true in more remote regions where the most aggressive *uji* had assembled forces. The bureaucracy became weaker as the local *uji* began to reassert power and especially in the wake of a smallpox epidemic (735–737) that reduced the population by as much as one-third.

MAP **13.4 Heian Japan.**

Despite court attempts to create a Chinese-style "well-field" system, tenancy became a chronic problem. Clan estates were given tax-exempt status because of their military contributions, and the estates of Buddhist monasteries were similarly exempt. By the late eleventh century, perhaps half of the land in the empire had become exempt from taxes. As the countryside became more self-sufficient, the capital became more isolated—and more reliant on local military cooperation.

The court was often divided by factional disputes. Three decades of civil war between factions supporting the claims of the Taira clan and those pledged to the Minamoto, or Genji, finally ended in 1185 with the defeat of the Taira. Shortly thereafter, Minamoto Yoritomo was given the title Sei-i-tai **Shogun**, and the period of the **Shogunates** was inaugurated, lasting until 1867.

Japan under the Shoguns Though the emperor at Kyoto theoretically remained in charge with the shogun as his deputy, the arrangement in fact hastened the drain of power from the capital. In order to restore order, Yoritomo set up his headquarters at Kamakura in 1192, several hundred miles from Kyoto near present-day Tokyo. Thus began an interval known as the Kamakura shogunate, which officially lasted till 1333. The court itself remained the center of religious and ceremonial life, but the real center of power was the shogun's headquarters. Meanwhile, in 1274, the Mongols launched the first of two major attempts to invade Japan. Their first armada was defeated, while in 1281 their fleet was smashed by a typhoon, known ever after by the Japanese as *kamikaze,* the "divine wind."

Emperors occasionally led unsuccessful attempts to reassert their own power. The most ambitious of these was the revolt by Emperor Go-Daigo in 1333. Securing the support of the powerful leader Ashikaga Takauji [ah-shee-KAH-gah tah-kah-OO-jee],

Heian Japan

○   Capital

■   Buddhist temple

●   Shinto shrine

——   Provincial border, ca. 800

Japanese rice field survey, eighth century CE

Shogun: The chief military official of Japan. The office was hereditary under the Tokugawa family from 1603 until 1867.

Shogunate: The government, rule, or office of a shogun.

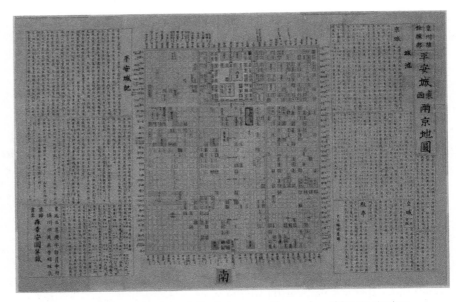

Plan of the Capital at Heian-kyo (Kyoto). The desire to copy the grandeur of Tang institutions extended even to city planning for the eighth-century Japanese court. The capital city at Heian was a faithful copy of the plan of the Tang capital of Chang'an, at the time one of the world's largest cities. The city grid was strictly laid out on a north–south axis, with the most important structures, like the imperial palace, placed in the northern section and their courtyards and main gates all facing south, the most propitious direction, indicated by the Chinese character highlighted in red at the bottom of the page, meaning "south." The placement of gardens and outlying structures was also carefully calculated according to Chinese notions of *feng shui* geomancy regarding trees, hills, and water.

Go-Daigo's faction was crippled when the opportunistic Ashikaga switched sides twice during the conflict. Ashikaga finally placed his own candidate on the throne, drove Go-Daigo into exile, and moved his headquarters to Kyoto. For the first time in nearly 200 years, the seats of political and cultural influence were reunited in the same city, and the refinements of court life were now available to the warrior classes. There thus was born the "dual way" of the sword and writing brush. The patronage of the *daimyo*, or regional lords, and their retainers, the **samurai**, ensured development of the Chinese-inspired arts of painting, poetry, and calligraphy. Zen and tea, introduced in the twelfth century, forged an armature of discipline in both the martial and courtly arts.

> **Samurai:** A Japanese warrior who was a member of the feudal military aristocracy.

Daimyo and samurai prided themselves on a strict system of loyalty and honor—*bushido*, the "Way of the Warrior." Indeed, the tradition of *seppuku* or *hara-kiri*—ritual suicide—developed originally as a way to show one's "sincerity" and disdain for death and capture on the battlefield. One was also expected to show honor and respect to one's opponents.

By the fifteenth century, however, armies increasingly dominated by massed ranks of infantry. By the middle of the following century, the adoption of firearms and advances in fortification made Japan perhaps the most heavily armed country on earth. The fluidity of the military situation had social consequences, and by the middle of the sixteenth century it was increasingly possible for commoners to rise through the ranks and become commanders and even *daimyo*.

One important reason for these conditions was the instability of the Ashikaga Shogunate. In 1467, factional struggles would finally erupt into all-out war for 10 years, the effects of which would last more than a century.

Economy, Society, and Family

The diversification of Japan's economy began with the Yayoi period, around 300 BCE. Wet rice and vegetable agriculture allowed early Japanese communities to sustain the sedentary population necessary for assimilating new technologies and concentrating power for state formation. The limited amount of arable land also meant that the populations of large open areas (like the Kanto Plain) were in an advantageous position to subdue their neighbors. By the high point of the Yamato period, Chinese accounts describe an economy with the majority of inhabitants engaged in agriculture and emerging merchant and artisan classes.

The New Economy By the sixth century, nearly every domesticated plant and animal from the mainland suitable to the environment had been introduced to Japan. Like their counterparts on the mainland, the Yamato court and its successors regulated economic activity in the form of land and produce taxes, taxes on trade, monopolies on strategic commodities, and requisitions of labor for infrastructural projects.

Yet these efforts at centralization were only partially effective. The larger *uji*, whose power had theoretically been reduced by the creation of a state bureaucracy, got around the problem by supplying many of the officials for the new body. They took advantage of government incentives to reclaim land. By such means the large *shoen* holdings and monastery estates with their tax exemptions acquired regional political and military power.

The period from 1250 to 1450 saw cycles of expansion in overseas commerce, with colonies of Japanese merchants operating in the Philippines, Java, and Malacca, as well as in Korea and China. Through their wares, the *daimyo* and samurai became sophisticated connoisseurs of luxury goods. As the early ports and towns grew, Japanese craftspeople imitated and refined Chinese crafts. Moreover, a diverse middle class organized into trade guilds were also consumers of luxury items. Their increased demand for capital spurred a monetization of the economy and the beginnings of banking and credit systems.

Advances in Agriculture The period from 1250 to 1600 saw an increase in both cultivation of Japan's arable land and the introduction of new crops. As it had throughout East Asia, the use of fast-ripening rice strains from Southeast Asia vastly enhanced stocks of this staple. In some areas, the wet paddy fields it required allowed dry raised beds for vegetables to be made from the soil taken out of the paddies. The introduction of the Chinese "dragon pump" (see Chapter 9) facilitated irrigation. Finally, a triple-cropping system with vegetables grown on the raised beds in between fields allowed families to subsist on only a few acres of land.

With this enhanced productivity, the population of about 5 million in 1100 doubled, perhaps as early as 1300; by 1450 it was on its way to doubling again.

Family Structure As in Korea, the earliest social structures of Japan appear to have been matrilocal and, most likely, matriarchal. *Uji* before the sixth century were organized around female lineages. This was to change with the coming of Chinese institutions. During the sixth and seventh centuries, women at the top, like Empress Suiko of the Soga clan, could still wield considerable political power. By the height of the power of the Heian court, Confucian patriarchal institutions had greater

Japanese *Daimyo* Armor. This extraordinarily well-preserved torso armor and helmet is believed to date from the fourteenth century and may have belonged to the shogun Ashikaga Takauji (r. 1338–1358). The helmet is bronzed iron, while the cuirass is made of thousands of overlapping iron and lacquered leather scales held together in horizontal rows by means of rivets. The combination made for effective protection against swords and arrows while allowing considerable freedom of movement.

influence but were moderated by Buddhism and Shinto. Aristocratic women controlled property, though they increasingly tended to wield political power through men. They were sequestered at court and forced into a highly refined ritual life, yet they created their own influential cultural world.

Outside the court, the moderating institution for commoners, and particularly women, was the Buddhist monastery. As in China and Korea, the monasteries provided havens for women and men who did not marry or had fled bad marriages. They provided education, thus helping to increase literacy. They also provided avenues of political power.

The family life of commoners was governed by a mix of Confucian filial piety, local clan relations, and the desire to improve the family's position through marriage. As in China, girls came to be considered expendable because they would move in with their husband's family. Arranged marriages were the norm, and by way of forcing such issues, rape, kidnapping, and family vendettas were all too common. Under the Tokugawa shogunate, strictly regulated Neo-Confucian family codes were enforced by the shogun's local officials.

Religion, Culture, and Intellectual Life

The foundations of Japan's original religion, Shinto, go far back into remote antiquity. Scholars have used the word "vitalism" to describe Shinto belief in the power of *kami*—spirits of divinities, beings living and departed, nature as a whole, and even inanimate objects like mountains and streams. Reverence for these forces extended to fertility and earthly vitality.

The importance of vitality was reinforced by an emphasis on ritual purity. On the other hand, death and corruption were things to be separated from as much as possible.

The Way of the Gods   Shinto means "the way of the gods," and Japanese mythology recognized an array of deities. Chief among these were Izanagi and Izanami, whose initial sexual act created the Japanese home islands, as well as Amaterasu, the sun goddess, considered the ancestor of Japan's emperors, purportedly starting with Jimmu in 660 BCE. Until the emperor Hirohito renounced his divinity at the end of World War II, every Japanese emperor was considered a god in the Shinto pantheon by believers.

Although it had undoubtedly arrived some time before, the customary dating of the introduction of Buddhism to Japan is 552 CE, when the king of Paekche sent a collection of Buddhist scriptures as a present to Yamato. The new religion soon became well established among Japanese elites, and Buddhism became the state religion of Yamato in 594. Buddhism and Shinto were ultimately able to coexist. The ability of Buddhism to adapt the cosmologies of other traditions to its core beliefs made it an easy fit for Shinto. For their part, Shinto believers could add Buddhist entities to the list of *kami*. Such accommodations facilitated the spread of the religion.

Most of the schools of Buddhism established in Japan had first become popular in China. The first to establish itself at Nara was the Hosso school, based on texts brought back from India. This was shortly displaced by the Tendai school and the Shingon sect, which dominated the imperial court for most of the Heian period.

As noted in Chapter 9, for Tendai followers, the most important scripture was the Lotus Sutra, which includes the key revelation that all beings possess the potential

The Miracles of Kannon. Amida Buddhism was the most popular school throughout East Asia, and the most popular figure of the many bodhisattvas was Kannon (Guanyin in China). On this long-hand scroll dated to 1257, Kannon saves her followers from assorted tribulations: Here, she appears to two men set upon by soldiers or brigands.

for salvation. Esoteric Buddhism, on the other hand, placed more emphasis on scriptural study and aesthetics. The popular devotional schools of Buddhism also came to Japan during the eighth and ninth centuries. Their simplicity and optimism ensured widespread adherence.

Though neither achieved widespread popularity, two other Buddhist schools deserve mention because of their influence. The first is a wholly Japanese development. Nichiren (1222–1282) advocated a Japan-centered, patriotic form of Buddhism. Perhaps more influential was the practice of Zen. Arriving in Japan from China in the twelfth century, it spread among the *daimyo* and samurai, who had the discipline to pursue its rigors. Zen seeks to achieve *satori*, a flash of enlightenment signaling the recovery of one's Buddha nature. Zen adherents follow the instructions of an experienced master rather than engage in prolonged scriptural study. Practitioners seek to open themselves to enlightenment by lowly, repetitive tasks, contemplating paradoxes and sitting in meditation. All of these practices can be useful to a warrior.

One final area in which Zen permeated the life of the warrior classes was in the use of tea. Introduced from China by the Zen monk Eisai (1141–1215), tea drinking in Japan spread as an aid to discipline and meditation among monks in the twelfth

excerpt from *The Tale of the Heike*

century. Soon, it became popular among the upper classes. Its presentation was refined by the sixteenth-century tea master Sen-no Rikyu (1522–1591), whose ritual of the tea ceremony became a popular preparation for battle among *daimyo* and samurai.

Forging a Japanese Culture The Chinese influence on Japan included an understanding of the importance of histories and record keeping. The first Chinese-influenced Japanese histories, the *Nihongi* (*Chronicles of Japan*) and *Kojiki* (*Records of Ancient Matters*), made their appearance during the early eighth century. At about the same time, the first collection of Japanese poetry published in Chinese, the *Man'yoshu* (*The Ten Thousand Leaves*) appeared. It illustrated the problems inherent in using Chinese characters as a method of rendering Japanese sounds.

The *Man'yoshu* uses one-syllable Chinese characters picked for their similarity to Japanese sounds and strings them together into Japanese words. If one can follow the *sounds* of the words, one can grasp the meaning of the poems; if, however, one attempts to read them based on the *meaning* of the characters, they become gibberish. This problem was solved by devising the *kana* syllabary, a system of 50 symbols that form the building blocks of Japanese words. By the late ninth century, a social divide had arisen between predominantly male, Buddhist, elite users of literary Chinese and literate women and members of the lower elites who favored the *kana* system. As in China and Korea, the technology of printing spurred the circulation of these works and pushed functional literacy to some of the highest premodern levels in the world.

The most important literary developments to come from the use of *kana* were the novel and the prose diary. The former is credited to Murasaki Shikibu, whose *Tale of Genji* is often considered the world's first novel. Seclusion for court women fostered self-analysis, and Murasaki's writing illuminates the tension between Buddhist ideas and the requirements of the court.

Vietnam: Human Agency and State Building

Modern scholars of Southeast Asia emphasize the similarities of the lived experience of the common people on both sides of the cultural divide between areas influenced by India and those influenced by China. This approach considers the *agency* of people: their taking of the initiative in deciding matters of acculturation, political systems, and so forth. Here, we explore the agency of people in their acceptance and rejection of certain influences and innovations.

The Setting and Neolithic Cultures

Southeast Asia stretches from the borders of Assam in India to the Mekong delta in the south of what is now Vietnam. The region is divided into watersheds separated by mountain ranges running generally parallel to them. Even today much of the region is heavily forested, with abundant rainfall supplied by the summer monsoon, which acts as the region's principal climatic regulator. The river valleys and coastal plains are believed to have supplied the wild ancestors of the first rice plants (see Map 13.5).

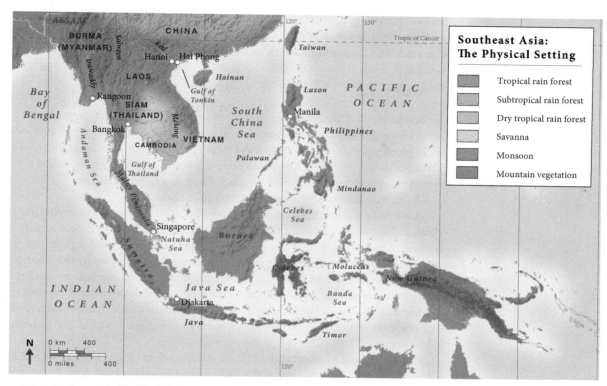

MAP 13.5 **Southeast Asia: The Physical Setting.**

The Neolithic revolution appears to have taken place in Southeast Asia at about the same time as it did in southwest Asia. The origins of these peoples are obscure, with speculation centering on a homeland perhaps in southern China. Out of the fertile subtropical and tropical regions in which they settled, it is believed that the basics of wet rice agriculture and the domestication of chickens and pigs may well have diffused north into China and perhaps west to northern India.

Village Society and Buddhism The earliest records of the peoples and states in the region are likewise fragmentary. Late Zhou Chinese references frequently mention the state of Yue, but its southern borders appear to have been fluid. The social structure suggests a village-based agricultural system in which women enjoyed far more equality than would later be the case. Villages and clans were often bilateral or matrilineal and matrilocal. Men paid a **bride-price** to the families of their wives, and divorce for either spouse appears to have been relatively easy. As in other places in East Asia during the first millennium BCE, women occupied roles as officials, diplomats, merchants, and small-business operators. The area also became one of the first outposts of Theravada Buddhism, which would come to be the majority religion in the region for the next 2,000 years.

Bride-price: Amount negotiated between the family of the groom and the family of the bride to be paid by the former to the latter in some marriage traditions, as compensation for the loss of her labor.

The "Far South": History and Politics to 1450 With the unification of China under the Qin in 221 BCE, Yue was incorporated into the First Emperor's new state. Thus began a period of Chinese occupation and local resistance in the area lasting over 1,000 years. As in Korea, the occupation brought with it Chinese culture, including writing, political ideas, and cultural preferences. Like their counterparts in Korea and Japan, the new Vietnamese literate elites were incorporated into the world of Chinese civilization and the Buddhist cultural and religious sphere. Southeast Asia's geographical position in the center of the maritime portion of this sphere encouraged openness to outside influences.

Sinicization and Resistance   Repeated invasions from the north also encouraged a Vietnamese ethnic identity. The collapse of the Qin in the period 206–202 BCE encouraged a rebellion against the local Chinese officials of "Nam Viet"—the Vietnamese name for the Chinese *Nanyue* ("Far South"), as the Qin had called their new southern province. The Han emperor Wudi reoccupied northern Vietnam in 111 BCE, and reimposed Chinese institutions on the region.

Han attempts at sinicization raised tensions between the new Chinese-influenced elites and those who retained their cultural independence. In 39 BCE a rebellion began that to this day is commemorated as helping to form the modern Vietnamese national identity. Trung Trac, the widow of a local leader executed by the Chinese, and her sister Trung Nhi (both ca. 12–43) led their local militia and defeated the Han garrison, sparking a general revolt. The Chinese, however, soon overpowered the forces of the Trung sisters, who drowned themselves rather than be taken alive. For the next millennium, northern Vietnam would remain within the imperial Chinese orbit.

In the three and a half centuries following the breakup of the Han Empire in 220 CE, the region gained some political autonomy, but the power of Vietnam's sinicized elites continued to ensure their loyalty to China. With the reunification of China under the Sui and Tang, the drive for Chinese political control of the Vietnam region as well as Korea was taken up again, and the north was soon fully reincorporated into imperial China. During the political chaos following the fall of the Tang, however, the long-awaited opportunity for independence arrived again.

Independence   Dinh Bo Linh, the first emperor of Vietnam, solidified his control of the region in 968. Though politically independent of China, Vietnam's new Li dynasty (1010–1225), long immersed in Chinese notions of Confucianism and statecraft, instituted Song-style institutions and created its own bureaucracy. Continuing a pattern of expansion, the Li pushed south during their two centuries of control.

With the fall of the Li dynasty, the Tran dynasty (1225–1400) soon faced the threat of the Mongols, who in 1280 would subdue the southern Song in China and form the Yuan dynasty. The Mongols made three attempts at invasion, but the unsuitability of Mongol strategy and tactics and the resistance of the Vietnamese ultimately prevented further Mongol expansion and allowed the Tran to keep the dynasty intact.

Cultural and Political Conflict   Even during the height of the Mongol threat, the Tran continued to push southward. Much of this drive was aimed at the state of Champa, which itself had ambitions to achieve regional dominance. Centuries before, the Vietnamese had expanded at the expense of Champa. Champa and the Khmers, influenced by India, had briefly united to subdue another Indian-influenced state, the trading kingdom of Funan, in the 600s. A reconstituted Champa now represented not just a strong political threat but—as a Sanskrit, Hindu, and Theravada Buddhist state—a cultural rival, as well. In the resulting war, the new Le dynasty of Dai Viet

("Great Viet"), founded in 1428 by Le Loi, decisively broke the power of the Champa in 1471. The remnants of their state were incorporated into Vietnam in 1720.

Economy, Society, and Family

Since the Neolithic domestication of rice, Vietnam has been one of the world centers of wet rice cultivation. In the eighteenth century, roughly 90 percent of the people were engaged in agriculture, a figure consistent with other east Asian agrarian-based societies. As in those societies, the rhythms of the agricultural year were governed by the monsoon cycle. During the long rainy season of the summer, rice, vegetables, and commercial crops would be cultivated.

As in southern China and Japan, families could be sustained on relatively small amounts of land and required few complex tools. Along with draft animals like water buffalo, these would often be held communally by clans within the village. Villages consisted of raised, thatch-roofed dwellings, surrounded by a bamboo fence and centered on a shrine to the ancestral spirits.

Politics, Labor, and Trade   Two key political institutions kept order. The village headman was elected, but had to be approved by the imperial court, which, like its Chinese counterpart, ruled through a Confucian bureaucracy of provincial governors, prefects, and magistrates. The headman collected the taxes and dues and sat with a council of notables. His powers, however, were checked by the council itself, which consisted of members of a scholar-gentry class. Thus, there was a balanced tension between the power of the central government and local interests.

One legacy of the Chinese occupation was the use of conscription and corvée (unpaid, forced) labor by Vietnamese dynasties. Peasants were required to serve in the army 4 months per year—indefinitely during national emergencies. They could also be sentenced to slave labor for various offenses. In many cases, they would be sent to open up virgin land for agriculture, which would be theirs to keep upon the expiration of their sentences.

Changing Position of Women   One pattern of history the Vietnamese shared with the other societies we have examined in this chapter is that of changes in the status of women over time. The nature of the agricultural work undertaken was communal, and men and women worked in the fields together. As in Korea and Japan, kinship lines were bilateral—traced through either spouse—or matrilineal. Chinese influence and Neo-Confucian emphasis on filial piety, hierarchy, and separate roles for men and women eroded this equality, though less markedly in Vietnam than in Korea or Japan. In villages, ports, and market cities, women were merchants, entrepreneurs, and craftspeople. This was reinforced by the prominence of the different Mahayana schools of Buddhism. Buddhist nuns and abbesses wielded considerable power, though their positions were often at odds with the Confucian precepts of the elites. Still, women's rights to divorce and property ownership were upheld in the Neo-Confucian law code of 1460.

Religion, Culture, and Intellectual Life

As they struggled to maintain their political independence, the Vietnamese developed their own cultural distinctiveness. While the porous border region with southern China and geographical and ethnic ties to other Southeast Asian peoples ensured a flow of influences, not all were readily absorbed.

Mahayana Buddhism   Whether the practice of ancestor veneration arrived with the Chinese or whether it was present before is as yet unsettled. Nearly all villages had a shrine for a founding ancestor where periodic ceremonies honoring him would take place. As in Korea, the coming of the Han emperor Wudi's armies in the second century BCE brought the imperial system of the Son of Heaven as intermediary between heaven and earth. At about the same time, however, Theravada Buddhism was being established in the Indianized ports of Southeast Asia. Although the Han retreat from the north allowed for the emergence of Mahayana Buddhism in the area, it was Indian-influenced Theravada that would dominate the religious and cultural life of Vietnam for centuries to come.

Later, the Tang occupation brought an infusion of Mahayana influence as well as the entire spectrum of Confucian and Daoist ideas. While Mahayana became the dominant division from this time on, the Vietnamese at the local level tended to pursue a synthesis of all of these systems in their beliefs. Similarly, the Vietnamese court sought to reconcile the differences among the systems by promulgating edicts on their compatibility. Indeed, some emperors sought to take a leading role in developing a unique strain of Vietnamese Buddhism.

Chu Nom   During the fifteenth-century consolidation of Dai Viet, the Le dynasty undertook a sinicization of the country, adopting Chinese law codes and dress. As in Korea and Japan, Chinese-style histories were compiled and court-sponsored literary projects commissioned. Yet here again, the literary language favored by the court for such projects continued to be the Chinese of the elites. As in Korea and Japan, an attempt was made during the tenth century to develop a vernacular writing system. Called *chu nom* ("southern characters"), the new script combined existing Chinese characters picked for the similarity of their sounds to Vietnamese words with newly invented Chinese-style characters for meaning. In theory, it would be easier to use as a tool for literacy. However, it never had the widespread circulation of *han-gul* or *kana* in Korea or Japan.

❯ Putting It All Together

interactive concept map

While there are commonalities among the patterns of state formation and religious interaction along the outer ring of Chinese influence, each state responded to that influence in its own way. From the beginning, each state sought to maintain its political independence, though all acculturated to some degree to Chinese models. The attractiveness of those models was related to their usefulness in state building. That is, while the Koreans and Vietnamese struggled to throw off the Chinese political yoke, the systems and values of the invaders also gave tools to the invaded, allowing them to organize their new regimes after they had won independence. The invaders also came with moderating institutions like Mahayana Buddhism. They were therefore equipped with a wide range of options to adopt or discard, as the situation demanded. In that sense, the cultural intrusion was far more successful than the political one.

In the case of Japan, since the early Yamato state did not have Chinese traditions imposed on it from the outside, its leaders could afford to be more selective in what to adopt. However, the wholesale adoption of Chinese institutions proceeded even more quickly in Japan than on the mainland. Part of this may be attributed to the power that such institutions could provide to a government; part of it may also have been a sense on the part of the Japanese that states on the mainland based on these institutions were a potential threat.

By the end of the fifteenth century, all three of these states were in the process of consolidating civilizations based on Chinese models and prominently including Neo-Confucianism and Buddhism among their governing traditions. They may therefore be considered part of the dominant trend toward the formation of religious civilizations, a pattern we have emphasized in Part 3 of this volume. However, given the specific adaptations to local conditions, the three states were quite different from each other and from China. Yet faced with varying degrees of dislocation, foreign intrusion, or rebellion, all would seek similar solutions to solve these problems.

Review and Relate

| Thinking Through Patterns

Examine the ways historians approach the big questions of this chapter.

The various Korean kingdoms were affected by China through conquest. Chinese culture and institutions were planted in Korea during the Qin, Han, Sui, and Tang eras. This also prompted the Korean kingdoms to assert their political independence and to be discriminating about which Chinese institutions to adopt. Thus, Neo-Confucianism was adopted because of its use as a state-supporting ideology. Chinese writing, though useful as the means of acquiring the literature of China, ultimately yielded to the *han-gul* system as more convenient.

Korea served as both a cultural intermediary between Japan and China and as a mainland target for conquest. Thus, Korea's status as a buffer between the two regional powers made its position precarious.

In addition to the Bronze Age elements of wet rice cultivation and bronze implements, cultural elements, beginning with the Chinese writing system, were the most influential. With the writing system came ideas of government, ethics, philosophy, literature, and Buddhism. Unlike Korea and Vietnam, Japan acquired all of these more or less voluntarily and had the leisure to adopt them according to its own needs, rather than have them imposed by conquest.

While the Chinese writing system gave Japan a ready-made literature, the language itself was not well suited to the Japanese vernacular. Thus, by the 800–900s it had to be supplemented with the *kana* system. More serious was the less-than-perfect fit of the Chinese governmental structures with Japan's clan-based society. Cleavages developing during the Heian period would cause the social breakdown that resulted in the era of the shoguns, which lasted until 1867.

> » How was the history of Korea affected by its relations with China? With Japan?

> » Which important elements of Chinese culture were adapted by the Japanese for their own purposes? What advantages did Vietnam have over Korea and Japan in this regard?

> » Which Japanese adaptations of Chinese institutions did not work well in Japan? Why?

≫ **In what ways was the experience of Vietnam similar to that of Japan and Korea? How was it different?**

Like Japan and Korea, much of Vietnam was influenced by the importation of Chinese culture, including Buddhism, the imperial system, and Confucianism. Like Korea, and unlike Japan, Vietnam suffered centuries of Chinese invasion and occupation. But Vietnam, positioned on the border with the Indianized states of Southeast Asia, also was influenced by Indian culture in its southern and western areas, causing interactions and adaptations that did not take place in the other states inside the Chinese sphere of cultural and political influence.

| Against the Grain

Consider this as a counterpoint to the main patterns examined in this chapter.

Zen and Bushido

- Are there other religions in Japan (such as Shinto) that might work equally well for warriors? Why?

- Is Japan unique in adapting a pacifistic religion for use by warrior classes? Can you think of ways that, for example, Christian warriors adapted their beliefs to support their profession?

One seemingly counterintuitive development in the political and religious history of Japan is the marriage of a sect of Buddhism—a pacifistic belief system—to the warrior nobility of Japan, the *daimyo*, and their retainers, the samurai. Zen Buddhism became the central religious practice of the warrior classes. The adoption by warriors of a pacifistic creed is not unique to Japan—one need only consider the history of Christianity to see some broad parallels. But Christianity, as the state religion of Rome and its successor empires and kingdoms, was the only approved religion for all classes. Zen was one of many competing variants of Buddhism available to Japanese warriors. So how does one account for its appeal?

Perhaps we may view it this way: While Buddhism teaches respect for all sentient beings, the duties of a warrior might induce one to extend the ideal of "nonattachment" to a state of indifference toward one's own life or death—and by extension to that of others. Moreover, the rigors of Zen training and practice are not unlike those of military training: breaking down the ego by performing humbling tasks, being remade by strict discipline and constant repetition, and finally achieving a new "self" as a result of a rigorous training process. There is also an element of elitism in becoming one of the few who achieve the highest levels, though those who do reach them are expected to be humble in their bearing. Zen thus provides a balance of opposites—the strict discipline to fight without regard for one's own safety on the battlefield, and in the process to transcend the self, reaching a state that brings the flash of enlightenment—*satori*. This condition of disciplined mindfulness extended to poetry, painting, and calligraphy, providing the basis for yet another unity of opposites: the dual way of the sword and the writing brush unique to Japan.

Key Terms

Altaic   294
Bride-price   309
Han-gul   300
Matriarchal   301

Matrilineal   301
Matrilocal   299
Microlith   301
Samurai   304

Shogun   303
Shogunate   303
Striated   294
Syllabary   292

audio flashcards

For additional resources, please go to
www.oup.com/us/vonsivers.
Please see the Further Resources section at the back of the book
for additional readings and suggested websites.

Patterns of State Formation in Africa

According to local tradition, the founder of the gold-trading kingdom of ancient Ghana (ca. 400–1200) in West Africa was Dinga. He was a descendant of Bilal, the Ethiopian whom, according to tradition, the Prophet Muhammad chose as the first *muezzin*, the person who calls the Muslim faithful to prayer. When Dinga arrived from Arabia to the Sahel, south of the Sahara Desert in West Africa, he asked a many-headed snake at a well for water. The snake refused, and Dinga subdued her through magic to receive his drink. After marrying the snake's three daughters, he fathered three sons, the eldest of whom was a half-human, half-serpent being who went to live underground. The two younger sons were still growing when their father returned to Arabia.

The second son grew into an inconsiderate man who mistreated his father's old servant. The third son turned into a much kinder person, giving the same servant his leftover meals. Years later, Dinga felt his end coming and summoned his two sons to give them their respective inheritances. The elderly servant, who had never forgotten the kindness of the younger son, persuaded the youngest son to go first, disguised as his older brother, to receive the lion's share of Dinga's estate. The father bestowed his power of magic as well as the kingdom on the youngest son, while the older son received the more modest power of rain making.

ABOVE: **Detail from the** *Catalan Atlas* **(1375), showing Mansa Musa, the king of Mali, on his throne.**

The two sons struck a deal whereby Ghana would receive enough rain and gold as long as its people would sacrifice a virgin and a colt every year. After many years of sacrifices, a Wagadu man and admirer of a virgin about to be sacrificed slew the snake brother. As he was dying, the snake brother cursed the people of Wagadu, which lost its abundance of rain and gold. A parched and impoverished Ghana fell to its enemies.

This story gives us a glimpse of a main pattern underlying the history of sub-Saharan Africa between 600 and 1450: adaptation of African spirituality to Islam. The pattern played itself out particularly in West and East Africa, whose rulers converted to Islam and incorporated Islamic beliefs and practices into their traditional **African spirituality**.

While the Eurasian and North African pattern during 600–1450 was that of the formation of religious civilizations that contained commonwealths of states, the pattern of sub-Saharan Africa in the same period was that of religious kingdom and empire formation. In the northeast of sub-Saharan Africa, kingdoms had already adapted to Christianity prior to 600. In West Africa, Mali, the successor of ancient Ghana, adapted to Islamic imperial traditions and became an empire. On Africa's east coast, Islamic merchant states emerged, under either kings or councils of notables. Finally, in the interior of central and southern Africa, indigenous kingdoms arose on the basis of the African tradition of magic-empowered authority.

Christians and Muslims in the Northeast

Between 600 and 1250, Nubia was a Christian kingdom along the middle Nile in the Sahara and sub-Saharan steppe built on agriculture and trade. Ethiopia, Nubia's neighbor in the highlands to the southeast, was similarly Christian but, unlike Nubia, was a collection of decentralized chiefdoms until one of the chiefs centralized rule in 1137. Both Nubia and Ethiopia were cases of sub-Saharan polities adopting patterns of state formation from the Middle East into their African heritage.

Nubia in the Middle Nile Valley
About a century after the end of the kingdom of Meroë (see Chapter 6), small Nubian successor states dominated the middle Nile valley. In the course of the mid-500s, these states converted to Coptic Christianity and united into a single kingdom. Open to trade with the empire of the Arab Umayyads, Arab merchants came to dominate Nubian commerce. The position of these merchants led to Muslim political control: In 1276, the Egyptian Mamluks defeated the Christian king of Nubia and installed a puppet regime. By around 1450 Christianity in Nubia had largely given way to Islam.

The Rise of Christian Kingdoms in Nubia In the early centuries of the Common Era, the use of the camel created a transportation revolution in the Sahara and opened up new routes for commerce and invasion. As a result, a new ruling class

Seeing Patterns

≫ What patterns of adaptation did the Christian kingdoms of northeast Africa demonstrate in their interactions with the civilizations of the Middle East and eastern Mediterranean?

≫ What were the responses of Africans to Muslim merchants who connected them with the trading zone of the Indian Ocean and Mediterranean? As these Africans adapted to Islam, which forms of political organization did they adopt?

≫ In what ways did the economic and political transformations on the East African coast and West Africa affect developments in the interior?

African spirituality: The experience of and/or belief in the presence of a life substance or spirit shared by all living beings and things in nature. People or ancestors, therefore, could influence each other, positively or negatively. A human or animal mask allowed a person to assume a different identity.

of Nubians arose in the middle Nile valley during the 400s. Nubian chiefs and their followers established three small kingdoms along the middle Nile that prospered in large part as the result of the rapid spread of the animal-driven waterwheel invented in Egypt in the first century CE.

In the 500s, Egyptian missionaries converted the Nubians to Christianity. New churches and monasteries were built, and kings and members of the ruling class sponsored these Christian institutions. As did their contemporaries in the Mediterranean and Middle East, the Nubian rulers appreciated the unifying effect of a single state religion over the multiplicity of local cults.

Barely Christianized, Nubia now had to withstand an invasion of Arabs from Egypt. After the establishment of the Arab emirate of Syria, Iraq, and Egypt (see Chapter 10), the new governors in Egypt organized military campaigns into neighboring countries. In 652, one of these campaigns penetrated deep into Nubia. But an army of Nubian archers defeated the Arabs, forcing them to retreat. In a subsequent agreement, the two sides formally recognized each other. Later Muslim historians reinterpreted this pact, ignoring the defeat and presenting it as a treaty of submission to Islamic hegemony. Nevertheless, the pact endured and blocked the advance of Islam into East Africa for 600 years.

Royal Power and Governance   In the 700s, the three Nubian kingdoms were unified by a "great king." Power remained largely decentralized, however, with an official called an "eparch" who governed the northern subkingdom. The Coptic patriarch of Alexandria appointed the bishops, who were independent from the kings, in contrast to bishops in Catholic Europe at the same time (see Chapter 11).

In terms of financial administration, vassal rulers were probably powerful landlords who sent presents to the great king. As in Europe, abbots of monasteries were also landlords to whom peasant farmers paid rent. Most likely, in the vicinity of the great king's residence some basic fiscal mechanisms existed whereby village headmen delivered taxes in kind. Another source of income for the kings and eparchs was long-distance trade. In this respect, the Christian great kings of Nubia were similar to their Islamic counterparts in eastern and western Africa.

Agriculture   The farmland of the Nubian villages consisted of arable land on the fertile banks of the Nile. The annual summer floods between June and September left this land covered with rich sediment. Palm orchards helped to anchor the silt, and stone walls and jetties built into the Nile captured additional amounts of alluvial soil. As the floods receded in fall, villagers grew sorghum, millet, barley, wheat, and cotton.

Higher fields away from the banks required waterwheels for irrigation, and were planted during the winter. In the spring, farmers planted second crops on the banks and at higher elevations. Vineyards and wine-making became more important as the kingdoms evolved. Farmers also kept cattle, donkeys, sheep, goats, and pigs.

Long-Distance Trade   The pact of 652 between the Arabs and Nubia included clauses concerning the trade of Egyptian goods for ivory and slaves. The latter two items came from the tropical territories on the White Nile, and the kings taxed the merchant caravans at various resting places along the way.

In the period between 800 and 1200, long-distance trade attracted Muslim merchants and craftspeople to the northern province of the Nubian kingdom.

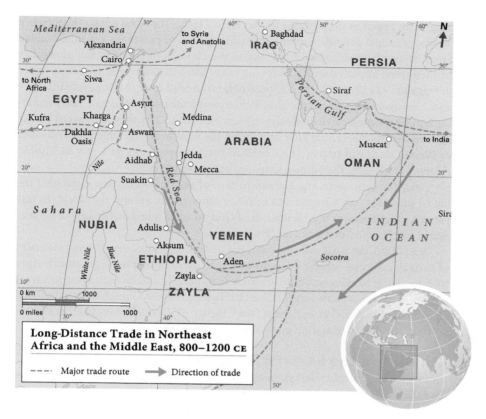

MAP 14.1 **Long-Distance Trade in Northeast Africa and the Middle East, 800–1200.**

A money economy emerged, based on Islamic gold dinars. Muslim merchants also settled along the Red Sea coast, especially once the North African Fatimid caliphs had conquered Egypt in 969. To compete with the Iraqi Abbasid caliphs on the Persian Gulf, the Fatimids developed maritime trade with India through the Red Sea (see Map 14.1).

From Christian to Islamic Nubia   In the mid-1000s, Egyptian rulers resettled unruly nomadic migrants from Arabia to Upper Egypt. These migrants and their

interactive timeline

ca. 450–1450 Kingdom(s) of Nubia on Middle Nile	**ca. 750–nineteenth century** Swahili city-states in coastal East Africa	**ca. 1000–1400** Kingdom of Ife in West African rain forest	**1137–1270** Kingdom of Ethiopia under the Zagwe
	ca. 650–1137 Kingdom of Aksum in northeast Africa	**ca. 750–1240** Kingdom of ancient Ghana in West Africa	**1070–1300** Kingdom of Mapungubwe in southern Africa

		ca. 1300–1885 Kingdom of Luba in central Africa
ca. 1217–1255 Mansa Sundiata of Mali	**1235–1645** Empire of Mali in West Africa	
1250–1505 Kingdom of Great Zimbabwe in southern Africa	**1270–1974** Kingdom of Ethiopia, Solomonid dynasty	

neighbors began raiding Nubia in the early 1100s. The local rulers in northern Nubia, principal defenders against the raids, gained in power vis-à-vis the Nubian kings. Dynastic rivalries broke out, and in the 1200s both usurpers and pretenders to the throne appealed to Egypt for support. The Mamluks, who governed Egypt at this time (1250–1517, see Chapter 17), responded by including Nubia in their anti-Christian holy war efforts. They reinterpreted the pact of 652 as a treaty requiring regular tributes, particularly slaves, from Nubia. In 1276, they conquered Nubia, installed a Christian vassal king, and levied the *jizya* head tax, which non-Muslims in Islamic lands had to pay. The Christian dynasty eventually gave way to Muslim rulers; and by 1365, the Nubian kingdom had ceased to exist.

Viewed in retrospect, the Nubian pattern of political formation resembled the feudal practices (see Chapter 11) of many other places around the world. In this pattern, kings acting as representatives of God on earth relied on the support of federated chiefs, who functioned much like vassals.

Coptic Christianity: A branch of Christianity centered in Egypt that stresses the divine nature of Jesus, in contrast to Catholic Western and Orthodox Eastern Christianities, in which his human as well as divine nature are emphasized.

In addition, the patriarch of Alexandria never lost control over the appointment of Nubian bishops—unlike the pope in his struggles during the high Middle Ages with the Holy Roman emperors over lay investiture—and Nubian churches were outposts of the Egyptian **Coptic** Church. Had the Nubian Church been a "national church" like the churches in Europe (see Chapter 17), it might have been in a better position to resist Islamization once Muslim rulers took over.

Ethiopia in the Eastern Highlands

Although the Christian kingdom of Aksum had diminished to a chiefdom by the 600s, it continued (in cooperation with the Coptic Church) to represent the church's mission to convert the southern highland Africans. Eventually, new dynasties revived the mission, among which the Solomonids and their Christian Crusades were the most successful. In Ethiopia, the adaptation to Christianity was more thorough than in Nubia. The Ethiopians embarked on a pattern of forming an African Christian civilization.

Christianity in the Highlands   The kings of Aksum and the patriarch of the Coptic Church abandoned their capital by the mid-600s. They continued to trade ivory, ostrich feathers, musk, and myrrh for linen and cotton textiles and spices on the Red Sea, but no longer issued coins. When Muslim rulers in Egypt in the late 800s occupied ports on the west coast of the Red Sea and expanded trade with India and East Africa, Aksum became a partner in this trade and sold slaves captured in raids to the south. The Aksum kings campaigned southward, taking priests and settlers with them to convert the highland Africans. Reduced as it was, Aksum continued to be a factor in highland politics.

However, in the 970s the Africans subjected to conversion struck back. A queen, Gudit (Judith), led destructive campaigns in which churches and monasteries were burned, towns destroyed, and thousands of people killed or enslaved. After her reign of terror of a purported 40 years, a remnant of the Aksumite kingdom recovered and survived modestly for another century, but little is known about it.

State and Church under the Zagwe Kings   Political stability returned to the highlands with the Zagwe dynasty (1137–1270), some 300 miles south of Aksum. To its neighbors, the Zagwe kingdom was known as Ethiopia or Abyssinia, names rooted in the Hebrew and Christian Bibles. The Zagwe continued the Aksumite tradition of church sponsorship and missionary work in the south.

One king in the mid-twelfth century attempted to create an Ethiopian Church independent of the patriarch of Alexandria, but the Egyptian sultan refused the split. The Muslims were not about to relinquish the indirect leverage they possessed in Ethiopia through their political control over the patriarchs in Egypt. Had Ethiopia succeeded, the development of a "national church" would have occurred—the opposite of the situation in Europe at that time (see Chapter 11).

Church sponsorship expressed itself in the construction of 11 churches carved from subterranean rock during the early 1200s, called the Lalibela churches. The churches were arranged in two groups, separated by a stream named the Yordanos, after the biblical Jordan River. The policy of the Zagwe dynasty was the recreation of Zion, perhaps in succession to Jerusalem, which the Muslims reconquered in 1187 from the western European crusaders. Accordingly, the dynasty used these churches during Holy Week for elaborate masses and processions.

Under the Zagwe kings, the conversion of the peoples in the central and southern highlands to Christianity resumed, and Christian settlers from the north were encourage to colonize those lands. The central and southern highlands offered opportunities for the establishment of new villages, fields, and pastures. With its fertile volcanic soil, southern Ethiopia became one of the most productive agricultural regions of sub-Saharan Africa.

The political system that emerged in the center and south was an extension of what Aksum had pioneered in the north. Under a king ruling by divine right, Ethiopia was a confederation of provincial lords who lived in villages among their farmers and collected rents. Legally, ownership of the land was vested in families and had the status of inalienable property, with the family lords holding the right to collect rents.

Church of St. George, Lalibela, Ethiopia. Stonemasons cut this church and its interior from the surrounding rock formation. This and 10 other churches, built in the early 1200s, are part of a pilgrimage center created in the image of the Holy Land in Palestine.

image analysis

MAP 14.2 **The Ethiopian Highlands, ca. 1450.**

selection from *The Glorious Victories of Amda Seyon*

The Solomonid Dynasty Christians from the north now shifted their missionary efforts southward. In 1270, a new dynasty of kings, the Solomonids, emerged some 300 miles south of Aksum, in the region of today's capital of Ethiopia, Addis Ababa. These new kings claimed descent from a union between the queen of Sheba and the Israelite king Solomon. They also claimed to have inherited the Israelite Ark of the Covenant after the destruction of the First Temple by the Neo-Babylonians. The religious heritage of the Solomonids still lives on in Ethiopia. Outside Africa, this heritage has been embraced by the *Rastafarians*—Afrocentric Christians who form a small minority in Jamaica.

Ethiopian Christians and Coastal Muslims During the 1300s and most of the 1400s, Ethiopia was a powerful kingdom. The kings commanded a sizable mercenary army, with which they extended their authority over small principalities of Christians, traditional Africans, and Muslims in the southern highlands and Rift Valley, as well as Muslim sultanates along the Red Sea coast.

This extension began with the conquests of King Amda Seyon (r. 1314–1344). A century after the Mamluks had eradicated the crusader kingdom of Jerusalem in the Middle East (1291), Solomonid Ethiopia was carrying on the Christian holy war in sub-Saharan Africa (see Map 14.2).

The Muslim sultanates along the Red Sea coast relied principally on trade, linking East Africa via the Rift Valley with the India–Mediterranean sea lane. Farther away from the coast, the lands were too dry to support more than populations of camel nomads. Urban dwellers, nomads, and pastoralists had converted to Islam in the centuries after 800 when autonomous Muslim rulers in Egypt began the expansion of trade via the Red Sea with India and East Africa.

Initially, the Ethiopian kings were ruthless in their efforts to subdue the sultans. But the kings were also pragmatic enough to exempt Muslim merchants and pastoralists from the church's missionary efforts in the south of the kingdoms. Similarly, in the end, the kings had little choice but to tolerate the sultans as Muslim vassals. Ethiopia became a multiethnic, multilinguistic, and multireligious empire in which the kings limited the church's conversion efforts.

Adaptation to Islam: City-States and Kingdoms in East and Southern Africa

During the period 600–1450, the Swahili people emerged as an indigenous African population of Muslims. They were divided into dozens of city-states along a 2,000-mile stretch of the African east coast, from today's Somalia in the north to Mozambique in the south. Swahili merchants were middlemen between the interior of East Africa and the Middle East as well as India. In the interior, increasing agricultural resources and trade with the Swahilis encouraged the expansion of chiefdoms but not yet the rise of kingdoms, except in the far south, in the middle Limpopo valley, and on the Zimbabwean plateau, where local people mined gold. Here, beginning around 1075, towns, cities, and kingdoms arose, the best known of which was Great Zimbabwe (ca. 1250–1505).

The Swahili City-States on the East African Coast

Arabs first established trade contacts in the 700s with Bantu-speaking villagers in coastal East Africa. In the following centuries, these villagers adapted themselves to long-distance trade and Islamic civilization. They evolved into an urban society of kings, **patricians**, religious scholars, sailors, fishermen, and farmers based in small port cities. The kings and patricians were consumers of luxury goods brought to them by Middle Eastern and Indian merchants. The patricians acquired goods from the interior, which the Muslim merchants from overseas took back home.

Swahili Beginnings The East African coast has few bays and natural harbors. Many small rivers open into the Indian Ocean, and their estuaries provide some room for anchorage. Only the Zambezi River in the south was large enough to allow longer-range water traffic and the building of inland towns. Islands, reefs, and mangrove swamps were numerous and favored the use of small vessels among the Swahilis for communication along the coast. Monsoons blowing from the southwest from April to September bring the northern half of the East African coast most of its annual rain. These monsoon winds facilitated sea voyages between Africa, the Middle East and India. The southern half of the coast has no reliable seasonal winds, making sailing conditions less predictable.

The main ethnic group in the interior of sub-Saharan Africa was that of the Bantus, who possessed a diversified agriculture and iron implements. In the mid-700s CE, a cultural differentiation between the Bantus of the interior and the east coast began to emerge, as the coastal population adapted to Islam, while traditional African spirituality persisted in the hinterland. The earliest Muslim merchants in East Africa were Khariji dissidents from the Middle East. They had opposed the caliphs shaping the emergent Islamic state religion. The caliphs pushed the dissidents into political insignificance in distant provinces with limited agriculture. Given the challenges of these regions, the Kharijis took to trade.

Early on, the Kharijis were mostly interested in slaves, who were in great demand for agricultural labor in the Islamic empire. After a slave revolt from 868 to 883 disrupted the Abbasid Empire's entire trade through the Persian Gulf, large-scale agricultural slavery in the region ended. Black slave imports from East as well as West Africa continued on a smaller scale, however.

Adapting to Islam After the Kharijis lost their trade advantage, Muslim merchants from the heartland of the Islamic empire traveled to East Africa to purchase luxury goods such as ivory, hardwoods, and skins. One of the heartland cities was Shiraz, the capital of the Shiite dynasty of the Buyids (945–1055) in Iran. Wealthy Swahili merchant families associated themselves with them, claiming Shirazi

Patrician: Term used in this chapter to denote Muslims in Swahili society claiming Middle Eastern descent and, by virtue of profiting from long-distance trade with the countries around the Indian Ocean, either ascending to the throne of their cities as kings or governing their cities in councils, together with other patricians.

descent. Members of these families migrated southward and founded new trading centers as far away as the Comoros Islands.

After 1050, mainstream Islam rose in prestige. *Sharifian* descent—that is, the possession of a genealogy going back to the Prophet Muhammad—began to rival Shirazi descent. Islamic families claiming Shirazi or Sharifian descent thus assumed dominant positions in the Swahili cities.

selection from The Swahili saga of Liyongo Fumo

Urbanism   Swahili urbanism along the East African coast encompassed several hundred towns and about two dozen city-states of up to 10,000 inhabitants, either on the mainland or on islands off the coast (see Map 14.3). Many cities featured a central open space containing the Friday mosque for the congregational noon prayer, the main city well, and tombs of Islamic saints. Around the mosque were the inner cities of the patricians. Craftspeople lived in the less densely settled outskirts.

Separate commoner towns housed fishermen, boat builders, and sailors. Further inland lived non-Muslim client populations who traded meat and food staples to the cities. Cities, towns, and inland people thus formed loosely organized city-states under the leadership of the patricians.

Governance   In the period 600–1450, the Swahili city-states were governed by kings and/or councils of patrician elders. Mainland cities were more vulnerable and, therefore, more dependent on inland alliances than cities located on islands. Both hinterland and inland populations were trade partners whom the Swahili patrician merchants visited but among whom they did not settle. The merchants did not establish mosques in the interior, and the interior population did not convert to Islam.

The office of chieftainship as the traditional African institution binding lineage federations together served to express the communality of the cities and surrounding rural peoples. The mainland kings were Muslims, but in the dealings with their non-Muslim allies they acted more like traditional chiefs. By contrast, the patrician councils in the island cities had no inland allies and at times even dispensed with kings.

The Swahili city-states and port states were considerably smaller than the Christian or Islamic kingdoms of Nubia, Ethiopia, and southern, central, and western Africa. Nevertheless, the patricians' regalia clearly expressed royal aspirations. The most important royal prerogative was the minting of coins. Given, however, that power on the Swahili coast was based on commercial, and not landed, wealth from which to collect taxes, in administrative practice the kings were never more than firsts among equals in the patriciate.

One prominent visitor was Zheng He, the admiral whom the Ming emperors entrusted with an Indian Ocean expedition and who in 1405 explored among other areas the Swahili coast (see Chapter 12). Even though his journey was principally for the purpose of displaying Ming power after the Mongol interlude, it can be seen as falling within the pattern of routine merchant journeys across the Indian Ocean and the South China Sea.

Traditional Kingdoms in Southern and Central Africa

The first region in the interior with a pattern of increasing wealth and population density during the period 600–1505 was southern Africa, on and around the Zimbabwean plateau. Here, the original foragers of the grasslands were adapting to the Bantu culture arriving from the north (see Chapter 6). Chiefs became powerful on

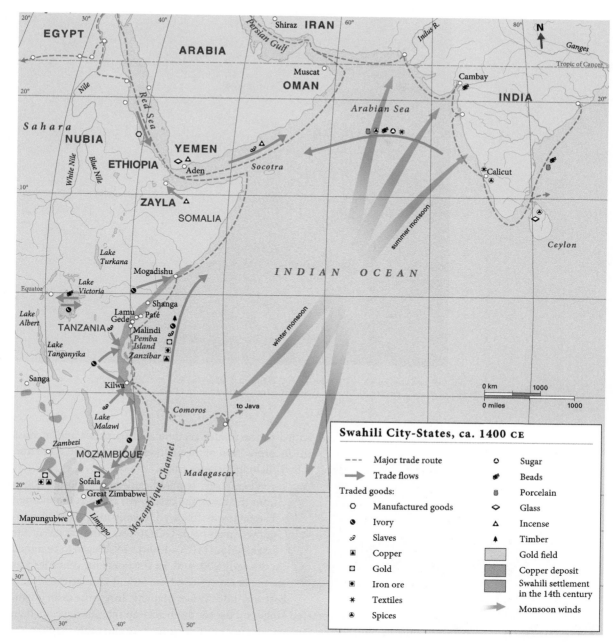

MAP **14.3 Swahili City-States, ca. 1400.**

the basis of large herds of cattle. Later, by trading with coastal Swahili merchants, the chiefs initiated a pattern of political formation, building cities and kingdoms, such as Mapungubwe and Great Zimbabwe.

The Kingdom of Mapungubwe   Khariji Swahili merchants from the north had founded the coastal town of Chibuene for the purpose of buying ivory. This trade

Gift of a Lion by a Swahili Merchant. This painting, which dates from the Ming Dynasty (1368–1648), depicts the exchanges between East Africa and the Ming court in China.

Golden Rhinoceros. This golden rhinoceros was found among the items of the royal dynasty of Mapungubwe, signifying the power and magic of the kings. The kingdom was organized around the mining and trading of gold with the Swahili cities and, from there, with the Islamic Middle East.

added to the wealth accumulated by chiefs and marked the incorporation of the southern African hinterland into Swahili long-distance trade.

When chiefs acquired cattle and imported goods from the coast, the first towns arose in the interior. Larger towns followed, culminating with Mapungubwe [mah-poon-GOOB-way], the capital of the first kingdom (1070–1300). Gold began to be mined in the early 900s and for the next four centuries was the major export item from Swahili cities to the Middle East and India. When Mapungubwe arose as an urban-centered kingdom, the southern African interior developed an urban craftspeople class who did not practice agriculture and cattle herding.

Excavations in Mapungubwe and ethnographic studies have yielded important insights into the institution of southern African kingship. The king resided on a hill that had previously been used for rainmaking ceremonies. He and his family were in ritual seclusion from the commoners, who lived in the town at the foot of the hill. The hill also contained residences for a few senior wives. Many female members of the royal family resided in villages outside Mapungubwe, where they were married to allies and clients of the kings.

The king was in charge of rainmaking ceremonies and harvest feasts, but the actual rituals were conducted by the diviner, an expert in spirituality. Although royal power was associated with spiritual authority, there was an institutional division between the king's power over life and death and the diviner's authority to summon the spirits. Thus, African kingship shared the pattern of rulership development encountered also in Eurasia and the Americas: Royal power was legitimate only if combined with spiritual or divine authority.

The Kingdom of Great Zimbabwe The kingdom of Great Zimbabwe (1250–1505) represents the culmination of the southern African kingdoms. Initially a tributary state of Mapungubwe, Great Zimbabwe emerged as a kingdom in its own right when the cooling and drying trend in the climate made agriculture in the Limpopo valley more difficult. Inhabitants abandoned Mapungubwe in the second half of the 1200s, with evidence of some royalty migrating north to Great Zimbabwe.

Great Zimbabwe was located at the southern end of the Zimbabwean plateau where gold was found. Granite for the construction of stone walls could be quarried easily, using heat from fires to split off layers of rock. At its height, the capital was the seat of a kingdom extending northward across the Zimbabwean plateau. Most settlements in the kingdom were dedicated to gold mining and trading, but the primary sources of income were cattle and grain.

Today, the best-known structure remaining of the capital is the so-called Great Enclosure within the Western Enclosure complex, an imposing 36-foot-high circular wall built of granite. The royal palace precinct contained buildings similar to those in Mapungubwe. All enclosures were once densely packed with houses, presumably occupied by the kings and/or the ruling classes. Commoners lived in simple thatched huts built with timber and plastered with clay.

The kingdom of Great Zimbabwe ended around 1505 when Swahili merchants replaced the initial southern Limpopo trade route with the shorter northern Zambezi route.

Great Zimbabwe, Passageway. The person in the center, visible at the end of the curve, provides an idea of the scale of the massive urban structures erected under the kings. The stonemasons were highly specialized craftspeople, who constructed walls that outlasted the demise of the Zimbabwe kingdom in the middle of the fifteenth century.

Central African Chiefdoms and Kingdoms

The central African rain forest and savanna participated in the general pattern of increased agricultural production and population expansion between 600 and 1450. In the Congo Basin, relatively favorable agricultural conditions supported the formation of kingdoms. One savanna site, the Lake Upemba depression in the south of today's Democratic Republic of the Congo, was the home of the Luba people, who founded a kingdom sometime in the period between 1000 and 1300 (see Map 14.4).

Luba Origins Archaeologists date the earliest evidence for the existence of permanent agricultural and fishing settlements around Lake Upemba to the period around 800. Villagers relied on fish, sorghum, millet, chickens, goats, and sheep. Locally produced iron and salt added to the resources. Hunting groups formed the nucleus, around 1000, for the emergence of chiefs.

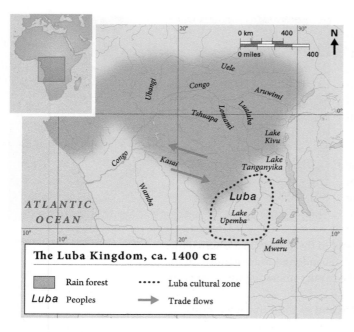

The Luba Kingdom, ca. 1400 CE

	Rain forest	⋯⋯	Luba cultural zone
Luba	Peoples	→	Trade flows

MAP **14.4** **The Luba Kingdom, ca. 1400.**

Similar to the kings of Mapungubwe and Zimbabwe, Luba kings possessed magic powers, which entitled only the descendants from their bloodline to succeed to the throne. The chieftains of other clans were excluded from the succession. A stable balance was established between the king and the chieftains, making Luba the model for subsequent kingdoms in the savanna of central Africa. The Luba kingdom itself survived until the beginning of Belgian colonialism at the end of the nineteenth century.

Cultural Encounters: West African Traditions and Islam

A pattern of regional trade, urbanization, and chiefdom formation was also characteristic for West Africa from the middle of the first millennium CE onward. Around 600, chiefs became kings when they unified their clans, conquered some neighbors from whom they collected tributes, and arranged alliances with others. Like their later African colleagues in the eastern half of Africa, they claimed to possess magic powers and adopted royal customs of seclusion. Two kingdoms, ancient Ghana and Mali, followed each other in the period 600–1450. Their royal–military ruling clans gradually converted to Islam, while the general population remained faithful to their African religious traditions.

The Kingdom of Ancient Ghana

Ancient Ghana emerged in the 600s and advanced to the status of a kingdom after 750, when it became the center for trade across the Sahara with the North African Islamic states. In the 1100s, however, drought and provincial unrest weakened Ghana. The kingdom gave way in 1240 to Mali, an empire which began its rise in the upper Niger rain forest and savanna.

Formation of Ancient Ghana   A period of progressive desertification (3000–300 BCE) had driven the inhabitants of the southern Sahara southward into what became the Sahel, a belt of steppe, grassland, and marginal agriculture. During the period 600 BCE–600 CE, the climate stabilized, and village formation expanded across the Sahel and northern savanna from Lake Chad in the east to the Senegal valley in the west. The city of Jenné-jeno emerged around 300 and was a center of regional trade of urban manufactures in exchange for iron and gold from the upper Niger and Senegal valleys and copper from the Sahara.

After 300, the regional trade became a long-distance trade. With the arrival of the Arabian camel, it became possible to travel through the desert. Long-distance merchants from the cities of Roman North Africa made contact with Soninke merchants in the Sahel and exchanged Roman manufactures as well as Saharan copper and salt for gold. Cowrie shells, imported by Rome from the Indian Ocean and exported to West Africa, attest to trade connections even farther than the Mediterranean.

It took some time for the trans-Saharan exchanges to become regular. Only after the loss of their gold mines in northwestern Iberia to Germanic migrants did the Romans regularize the trans-Saharan trade, beginning in the mid-500s. The regularization had a profound effect in the Sahel. In the 600s, Soninke chiefs, enriched by the Saharan trade, equipped their followers with swords and lances and subjugated more distantly related Soninke groups in the Sahel between the Niger and Senegal valleys. In the mid-700s, one of the chiefs proclaimed himself king in Wagadu, a city in the Sahel northwest of the inland delta, and founded the kingdom of ancient Ghana (as distinguished from the modern state of Ghana).

Ancient Ghana lasted through the wet period of the first millennium (300–1100) and eventually succumbed to the successor state of Mali, when it could not adapt in the Sahel to the emerging dry period (1100–1500).

From Roman to Islamic Trade   Ancient Ghana received its gold from Bambuk, a region in the rain forest at the western edge of the kingdom. The Bambuk gold fields occupied a no-man's-land between the kingdom of ancient Ghana and the chiefdom of Takrur on the lower Senegal. Soninke merchants went no farther than nearby towns, from which they conducted their trading activities with the villagers.

Romanized Berbers gave way to Islamized Berbers in the trans-Saharan trade after about 750. As was the case in Swahili East Africa, Khariji merchants pushed by the emerging Islamic empire into the outer provinces were the first Muslims to travel to the African interior. According to an eleventh-century Arabic source, Wagadu was a twin city, with its merchant and royal halves several miles apart. In contrast to their Swahili colleagues, the kings of Ghana avoided a combination of traditional kingship with Islam. Even though they benefited from including Muslims in their administration, they were not about to surrender their exalted, magical royal authority over life and death to the supremacy of Islamic law.

From African Spirituality to Islam in the Ruling Class   While the kings of Ghana retained traditional African spirituality, the Soninke merchants converted to Islam, which made business with the North African and Middle Eastern merchants easier to transact. By the early 1000s, the merchants in the trading towns near the Bambuk villages were Muslims, and the adjacent state of Takrur had also become Islamic. The sectarian Khariji Islam gave way to mainstream Sunnism.

In the early 1100s the kings of Ghana followed their merchants by also converting to Islam. The Sahel and savanna villagers, however, retained their African spirituality. As a result, Ghana now resembled the states on the Swahili coast and their hinterlands, where only the rulers and merchants were Muslim. In addition to the villagers, a number of allied Soninke chiefs remained faithful to traditional spirituality; and during the second half of the 1100s the cohesion of the kingdom began to weaken. In 1180, the founding clan of ancient Ghana ceded power to another clan, which established a new dynasty in Wagadu and adopted a policy of conquest of the southern savanna. For the next half century Ghana was an imperial power, trading gold not only from the Senegal River in the west but also from the upper Niger and Black Volta Rivers (see Map 14.5).

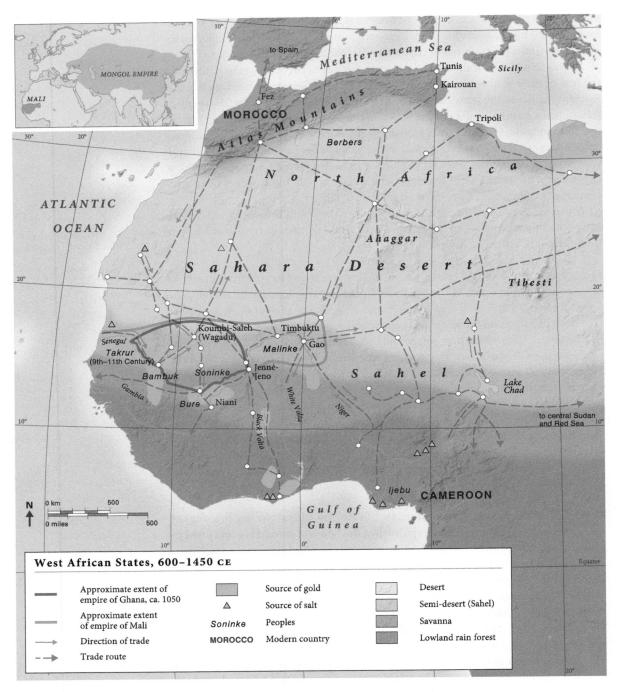

MAP **14.5** **West African States, 600–1450.**

map analysis

The Empire of Mali

The opening of new gold exposed hitherto marginal peoples to the influence of long-distance trade, royal rule, and Islam. One of these peoples, the Malinke, built the empire of Mali, a polity of many ethnic, linguistic, and religious groups. At its height, Mali stretched from the Atlantic to the Niger bend and from the Sahara to the rain forest.

Increased Trade   Mali was the beneficiary of the demand for gold in the Islamic realm on the other side of the Sahara. In addition to the existing Islamic mints, Christian mints began to stamp gold coins. In response to the increased demand for gold, merchants encouraged the opening of new gold fields in the upper Niger and its tributaries.

The people in this region were Malinke villagers who spoke a language related to that of the Soninke in the north, but who were ethnically distinct. In the course of the 1000s, these villagers had acculturated to ancient Ghana, which they recognized as overlord. When the new dynasty of Ghana conquered much of the Malinke lands at the end of the 1100s, resistance against the new rulers rose quickly. In a rebellion in 1230–1235, the Malinke not only liberated themselves but went on to conquer ancient Ghana.

The leader of the conquest was the inspiring hero Sundiata (ca. 1217–1255). He and his adventures were at the center of an **oral tradition**, with stories handed down from generation to generation. In the nineteenth and twentieth centuries, anthropologists recorded and translated these traditions. According to this tradition, Sundiata defeated ancient Ghana in 1235 and founded the empire of Mali, with its capital, Niani, on an upper Niger tributary in modern Guinea.

The Epic of Sundiata

Oral traditions: Myths, tales, and stories (e.g., the foundation myth of Wagadu) handed down from generation to generation. In the absence of other sources, oral traditions should not be equated with history.

The Malian Empire   Mali was the first enduring empire in sub-Saharan Africa (1235–1645). At its height in the early 1300s, the territory of Mali was surpassed only by that of the contemporary Mongol Empire. At the core of the empire were Malinke clans whose kings and chiefs met in an assembly under the emperors who assumed the title of *mansa*. Oral tradition records the laws, customs, and traditions of which the assembly was the guardian and according to which the empire was governed.

As in ancient Ghana, Mali's power rested on a large, horseborne army recruited from the Soninke clans. And like their royal predecessors in ancient Ghana, the Malian emperors relied on a small central administration run by Muslims as well as by slaves. The empire financed itself with tributes from vassal kingdoms in the Sahel and river chiefdoms with villagers and fishermen, as well as taxes on commerce of goods and manufactures. Since the new gold fields and the capital of Niani were located on a tributary of the Niger, the rulers relied on water transport downriver to the cities of Jenné-jeno, Timbuktu (founded in 1100), and Gao. In the mid-1300s, these three cities replaced Wagadu as the main transshipment centers of goods for the Saharan caravans.

In 1324, the Malian ruler Mansa Musa (r. ca. 1312–1337) annexed the city of Timbuktu from its Touareg Berber founders. There he founded a college and a library, part of the Sankoré Mosque. Timbuktu became a center of learning, focused on Islamic law but also offering ancillary fields of study which judges and independent scholars were required to know. The independent scholars were often members of merchant families who kept private libraries in their residences. In the mid-1400s, with some 100,000 inhabitants, the commercial and scholarly hub of Timbuktu was one of the larger cities in the world.

Mansa Musa, from the Catalan Atlas

The Decentralization of Mali   Timbuktu flourished even while its imperial overlord, Mali, unraveled in the later 1300s. Dynastic disputes broke out, and outsiders, including rain-forest groups and Touareg nomads, attacked from the south and north. As a result, some of the Sahel provinces broke away and established

The Sculptures of Ife

Forager, villager, and pastoral societies developing in the direction of chiefdoms, but not yet kingdoms, preserved traditional ancestor cults within their African spirituality. The sculptures, figures, and figurines of Africa played a role in that preservation.

As lineages evolved, generations of ancestors became an anonymous collective. The spirits of the ancestors in the invisible world, therefore, were conceived as being collectively present, to be consulted and nourished through sacrifices. One could "trap" them in sculptures, figures, and figurines, which emphasized the head, believed to be the seat of the spirit, at the expense of the torso and limbs, which were indicated in rudimentary fashion. The heads were generally fashioned in abstract ways, corresponding to the collective nature of the ancestors. These artifacts, therefore, were not "primitive;" their style was generic because the collective of the ancestors was generic.

When societies reached the level of kingdoms, kings became exceptional persons, endowed with ancestral magic (in Africa) or a transcendent divine mandate (in Eurasia) to exercise power, not merely chiefly authority. Generic ancestor "traps" would not do: Artists had to apply the techniques of naturalistic representation so that the kings would recognize themselves in them. Of course, after a while sculptures turned into generic likenesses again (image *a*), as they did in Mesopotamia and Egypt, since kingship became an ordinary institution with undistinguished kings not worth remembering.

(a) Guardian Figure, Bakota Area, Gabon, Nineteenth–Twentieth Century. The abstract Bakota figure, above, with its generic geometric elements, represents the collective lineage spirit; the much more realistic Nigerian figure on the next page represents royalty who wished to be remembered individually.

The Sankoré Mosque of Timbuktu, Mali. The mosque evolved in the fourteenth century into a large university with a library housing hundreds of thousands of manuscripts. A preservation program under UN auspices seeks to restore and preserve these manuscripts today.

independent kingdoms. Deepening drought conditions eventually caught up with Mali, and by 1450, Mali had shrunk to a kingdom in the savanna.

Rain-Forest Kingdoms

The West African rain forest stretches from modern Guinea above the southwestern corner of West Africa to Cameroon on the bend to central Africa, where it transitions to the Congo rain forest. In the earlier period of 600 BCE to 600 CE, savanna peoples with iron implements had entered the rain forest and founded villages in clearings. As elsewhere in Africa, the region saw a pattern of political formation that included village clusters, chiefdoms, and kingdoms with urban centers and sophisticated crafts, such as bronze casting in Nigeria.

The Kingdom of Ife   The earliest village cluster to urbanize was that of Ife [EE-fay] the spiritual center of the Yoruba ethnic group and its oral traditions. By 1000 it was a kingdom with a walled capital with a palace, shrines, houses, and craft workshops. One highly developed art was sculpting, in terra-cotta, copper, or bronze.

Sungbo's Eredo   Ife set the example for other chiefdoms to develop as kingdoms between 1000 and 1450. Oyo, which expanded from the rain forest northward,

The Ife terra-cotta, copper, and bronze royal heads stem from that innovative time period of about 200 years (1100–1300) when kingship was new in Ife. The naturalism of these figures is striking, especially when one takes into consideration that Christian and Muslim figurative art during the same period was still nonrepresentative, in the sense of being hieratic—that is, it typically represented standardized ideas about how biblical and prophetic figures should look, so that their God-pleasing nature was immediately recognizable. The stripes on the faces of some Ife figures (image *b*) are believed to represent scarifications, or scars marking the passage from youth to adulthood or distinguishing one lineage from another, as practiced in parts of Africa.

(*b*) Ife Shrine Head, Terra-Cotta, Nigeria, ca. 1200.

Questions

- How does the history of African sculptures, such as those from Ife, provide evidence for studying the patterns of state building in this period?

- Why does material culture represent such an important dimension in understanding the African past?

arose as a trade center, trading with first Ghanaian and then Malian merchants. In the other chiefdoms, leaders mobilized villagers for the construction of earthworks, including Sungbo's Eredo. One of these chiefdoms, Ijebu, encompassed a capital and villages on a territory of 22 square miles, surrounded by a combined moat and rampart up to 70 feet deep/high and 100 miles long. In nearby Benin, smaller earthworks around villages became the nucleus for an important kingdom in 1440. In both Ijebu and Benin, the moats and ramparts required centuries of hard labor with nothing more than iron shovels.

Scholars are still undecided over the purpose of these constructions: protection, boundary markers, toll collection, or perhaps all three? Equally difficult is an explanation for the collective labor: How were chiefs able to motivate workers? As in the Americas and Pacific, where followers built huge temples or transported heavy stone sculptures across distances, authority buttressed by ancestral pedigree and spirituality can be seen as a powerful motivator.

❯ Putting It All Together

Africa in the period 600–1450 displayed patterns of political and cultural development that included the creative adaptation of African spirituality to Christianity and Islam and indigenous kingdom formation. Adaptation depended on regional

interactive concept map

conditions and the degree of integration into Eurasian long-distance trade. The Nile valley and northeastern highlands incorporated Christianity into their local traditions. They adopted the Christian institutional division between kingship and church, in which kingship was a sacred office but subject to Christian law and ethics. The church, for its part, was an autonomous, hierarchical body. As in post-1000 Christian western Europe, the Nubian and Ethiopian churches were subject to a distant religious authority.

Coastal East and West Africa adopted Islam, which arrived through merchants. In eastern Africa, Islam took root among the coastal people and did not penetrate inland. In western Africa, only merchants and kings converted but did so across the interior.

In the same period, African kingship was a new institution with roots in the traditions of chieftainship in villages and village clusters. The kings emphasized their royal powers over life and death but also continued to claim the traditional chiefly powers of spirituality and magic. It is important to emphasize that Africa needed neither Christianity nor Islam to embark on its own distinctive pattern of kingdom formation.

Between 600 and 1450, however, this pattern clearly remained an exception amid the sub-Saharan population, the majority of whom remained stateless. They possessed chiefs but did not unite into larger polities or trade farther away than regionally. The silent presence of this unrecorded majority of stateless Africans should be kept in mind, alongside the kingdoms and empires, in seeking to understand Africa's significance in world history during this period.

Review and Relate

| Thinking Through Patterns

Examine the ways historians approach the big questions of this chapter.

» **What patterns of adaptation did the Christian kingdoms of northeast Africa demonstrate in their interactions with the civilizations of the Middle East and eastern Mediterranean?**

In the period 600–1450, the northeast of sub-Saharan Africa was drawn into the orbit of Eastern Christian and Islamic civilizations without fully adopting their formative patterns. Perhaps the most extensive adaptation occurred in the sphere of trade. Beginning in 1250 in Nubia, the expansionist regime of the Muslim Mamluks in Egypt put the African Christians on the defensive. By 1450 the middle Nile region was Islamized. In contrast, an expansionist Christian Ethiopia put Muslims on the coast of the Red Sea on the defensive and Christianized the pagan southern highlands.

» **What were the responses of Africans to Muslim merchants who connected them with the trading zone**

The inclusion of the East African coast and sub-Saharan West Africa into the Muslim Indian Ocean and Mediterranean trading zone resulted in the rise of small coastal Swahili states and two large West African polities: the kingdom of ancient Ghana and the empire of Mali. Muslim mariners and merchants interacted with Islamized local African rulers and merchants to exchange Middle Eastern manufactures for African luxury commodities as well as slaves. Adaptation to Islamic religious civilization was a phenomenon limited to the ruling classes and associated merchant circles.

The adaptation of coastal East Africa to Islamic religious civilization had an indirect effect on the interior of southern Africa. Here, chiefs in Zimbabwe used the wealth from the Swahili trade network for the transformation of their chiefdoms into kingdoms. The East and West African expansion of trade under the impact of Islam may have also indirectly led to a population increase in the interior of Africa. Such an increase became noticeable toward the 1300s, especially in the Congo basin, where the Luba kingdom was the first to emerge.

of the Indian Ocean and Mediterranean? As these Africans adapted to Islam, which forms of political organization did they adopt?

≫ In what ways did the economic and political transformations on the east African coast and West Africa affect developments in the interior?

| **Against the Grain**

Consider this as a counterpoint to the main patterns examined in this chapter.

Sundiata's Rise to Power

The Sundiata epic is the story of a disadvantaged hero who emerges triumphant. It begins with a king's sister: Insulted by not receiving her fair share of a meal during a royal feast, she turns herself into a forest buffalo and devastates the fields of the kingdom's villages. Hunters from the neighboring kingdom of the Malinke slay her. The king rewards them with an ugly hunchback woman, heir of the buffalo spirit's forest powers. The reward is in fulfillment of a prophecy according to which the Malinke king has to find an ugly hunchback to give him a successor. But a jealous co-wife casts a spell, and Sundiata, the successor, is born a cripple. During puberty, thanks to the inheritance of his mother's forest powers, Sundiata stands, uproots a tree, and becomes a physically superior hunter.

But the king's co-wife forces Sundiata into exile. Her own son, succeeding to the throne, is unable to withstand conquest by a neighboring king. A former blacksmith, this king is endowed with forest powers and tyrannizes the Malinke. In despair, the Malinke recall Sundiata from exile. Sundiata prevails in the end because his beautiful sister sacrifices her honor. During a one-night stand in the tyrant's chamber she discovers his dark secret: A cock's spur attached to an arrow can break his invulnerability. Shooting one such arrow, Sundiata achieves his final victory and creates the empire of Mali.

Traditional West African spirituality is built on the conceptualization of a world created by a remote god, in which civilization and nature mingle. Accordingly,

- What are the similarities and differences between the epics of Sundiata and Homer (Chapter 7)?

- Compare the messages of the Epic of Sundiata and Machiavelli's *The Prince* (Chapter 17). In what ways are they comparable, even if separated by time and region?

existence is embedded in pairs of opposing but complementary elements. These opposing pairs are skillfully woven into the epic, suggesting that figures marginal to village life, such as hunters or blacksmiths, can cut across the established social order with its jealousies and intrigues and tap into the forces of nature, and found new kingdoms and empires.

Key Terms

audio flashcards

African spirituality   317

Coptic Christianity   320

Oral traditions   331

Patrician   323

For additional resources, please go to
www.oup.com/us/vonsivers.
Please see the Further Resources section at the back of the book
for additional readings and suggested websites.

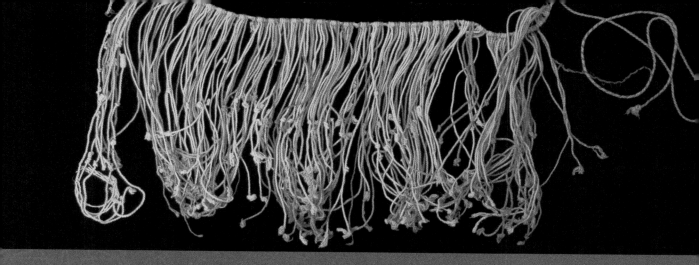

The Rise of Empires in the Americas

Just outside Lima lies the shantytown of Túpac Amaru, named after the last Inca ruler, who died in 1572. People fleeing the Maoist Shining Path guerillas southeast of Lima settled here during the 1980s. Archaeologists knew that the site was an ancient burial place called Puruchuco (Quechua "Feathered Helmet") but could not prevent the influx of settlers. By the late 1990s, the temporary shantytown had become an established settlement. However, residents realized that archaeologists had to be consulted before the shantytown could be officially recognized.

During excavations from 1999 to 2001, archaeologists unearthed one of the most astounding treasures in the history of American archaeology. The team discovered some 2,200 mummies, most of them bundled up in blankets and perfectly preserved. Many bundles also contained burial gifts of food and jewelry.

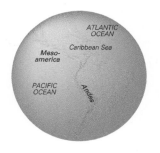

Scholars hope that when all of the mummies have been unwrapped, more will be learned about the social characteristics of the buried people, as so much about the Inca Empire that ruled the Andes from 1438 to 1533 remains unknown.

The Inca Empire and the Aztec Empire (1427–1521) grew from patterns that began to form around 600 CE in Mesoamerica and the Andes (see Chapter 5). After 600, kingdom formation spread across Mesoamerica

ABOVE: This kind of knotted string assembly (a quipu) was used in the Andes from ca. 2500 BCE onward for the recording of taxes, population figures, calendar dates, troop numbers, and other data.

Seeing Patterns

≫ **Within the patterns of state formation basic to the Americas, which types of states emerged in Mesoamerica and the Andes during the period 600–1550? What characterized these states?**

≫ **Why did the Tiwanaku and Wari states have ruling classes but no dynasties and central bureaucracies? How were these patterns expressed in the territorial organization of these states?**

≫ **What patterns of urban life characterized the cities of Tenochtitlán and Cuzco, the capitals of the Aztec and Inca Empires? In which ways were these cities similar to those of Eurasia and Africa?**

and arose for the first time in the Andes. These kingdoms were states with military ruling classes that could conquer larger territories than was possible prior to the 600s. Military competition prepared the way for the origin of empires. Even though empires arrived later in the Americas than in Eurasia, they demonstrate that humans, once they had adopted agriculture, followed similar patterns of social and political formation across the world.

The Legacy of Teotihuacán and the Toltecs in Mesoamerica

The city-state of Teotihuacán had dominated northern Mesoamerica from 200 BCE to the late 500s CE. After its collapse, the surrounding towns and villages perpetuated the cultural legacy of Teotihuacán. Employing this legacy, the conquering state of the Toltecs unified part of the region from 900 to 1180. At the same time, after an internal crisis, the southern Maya kingdoms on the Yucatán Peninsula reached their late flowering, together with the northern state of Chichén Itzá.

Militarism in the Mexican Basin

After the ruling class of Teotihuacán disintegrated at the end of the sixth century, the newly independent small successor states of Mesoamerica continued Teotihuacán's cultural heritage. The Toltecs, migrants from the north, militarized the Teotihuacán legacy and transformed it into a program of conquest.

Ceremonial Centers and Chiefdoms   In the three centuries after the end of Teotihuacán, the local population declined from some 200,000 to about 30,000. However, other places around the Mexican Basin and beyond rose in importance. The region to the northwest of the valley had an extensive mining industry that produced a variety of gemstones. Independent after 600, inhabitants built small states and traded their gemstones to their neighbors.

To the north were the Pueblo cultures in today's southwestern United States. These cultures, which flourished between 700 and 1500, were based on irrigated farming systems and are known for their painted pottery styles. These cultures might have been in contact with the Mississippi cultures, of which the city of Cahokia (650–1400) near modern St. Louis is the best-known site (see Map 15.1).

To the south, in western Mesoamerica, chiefdoms flourished on the basis of metallurgy (especially copper), which arrived with Ecuadoran seaborne merchants ca. 600–800. Copper, too soft for agricultural implements or military weapons, was used mostly in household objects and as jewelry. A number of small, fortified hilltop states also flourished in the south. More than in other Mesoamerican states, the ruling classes in the west were embroiled in fierce wars during 600–900.

The Toltec Conquering State   Soon after the collapse of Teotihuacán, craftspeople and farmers migrated north to Tula. They founded a ceremonial center and town with workshops known for tools fabricated from the local Pachuca obsidian. Around 900, new migrants arrived from northwest Mexico as well as the Gulf Coast. The northerners spoke Nahuatl [NAH-huaw], the language of the later Aztecs, and after taking possession of Tula, they made it their ancestral city.

The integration of the new arrivals resulted in the abandonment of the temple and the departure of a defeated party of Tulans.

The new Tula of 900 developed quickly into a large city with a new temple. It later became the capital of the conquering state of the Toltecs, whose warrior culture influenced Mesoamerica from around 900 to 1180 (see Map 15.1).

The Toltecs introduced two innovations in weaponry that improved the effectiveness of hand-to-hand combat: a short sword made of hardwood with inlaid obsidian edges could slash as well as crush; and obsidian daggers with wooden handles worn inside a band on the left arm. Traditional dart throwers and slings for stone projectiles completed the offensive armament of the warriors.

The Toltec army was sufficiently large to engage in battles of conquest within 4 days' march from Tula. Any target beyond this range was beyond their capabilities, given the logistics—and, of course, Toltecs did not have the benefit of wheeled vehicles. Thus, the only way of projecting power beyond the 4-day range was to establish colonies and to have troops accompany traders. As a result, the Toltec state projected its power through the prestige of its large military, rather than through an administrative imposition of governors, tributes, and taxes.

Trade The Toltecs established a large trade network based on Tula's obsidian. Merchants moved southward into the cacao, vanilla, and bird-feather production centers of Chiapas and Guatemala; to the north into gemstone mining regions; and westward into centers of metal mining. Metallurgy advanced around 1200 with the development of the technology of bronze casting. Bronze was preferable to copper for axes and bells; both were prized by the elites in Tula.

The Late Toltec Era Toltec military power declined in the twelfth century when the taxable grain yield around the city diminished. Sometime around 1180, foraging peoples from the northwest invaded, attacking Toltec communication lines. The disruptions caused an internal revolt, which brought down the ceremonial center and its palaces. By 1200, Mesoamerica relapsed into a period of small-state coexistence.

Late Maya States in Yucatán

Teotihuacán's demise at the end of the sixth century was paralleled by a realignment of the balance of power among the Maya kingdoms in the southern Yucatán lowlands of Mesoamerica. This realignment was resolved by around 650. A period of late flowering spanned the next two centuries, followed by a shift of power from the southern to the northern part of the peninsula.

The Southern Kingdoms At its height during the fourth and fifth centuries, Teotihuacán had interjected itself into the balance of power among the Maya kingdoms of southern Yucatán. Alliances shifted, and wars racked the lowlands, destroying

Chapter Outline

- The Legacy of Teotihuacán and the Toltecs in Mesoamerica

- The Legacy of Tiwanaku and Wari in the Andes

- American Empires: Aztec and Inca Origins and Dominance

- Imperial Society and Culture

- Putting It All Together

Mayan ceremonial ball game scene, Late Classic Period

interactive timeline

600	600–900		850–1000	1427–1521
End of city-state of Teotihuacán in Mexican Basin	Late Maya kingdoms in Yucatán Peninsula		City-state of Chichén Itzá in northern Yucatán Peninsula	Aztec Empire in Mesoamerica
	600–1100	700–1000	900–1170	1438–1533
	Conquering state of Tiwanaku in Andes (southern Peru/Bolivia)	Conquering state of Wari in Andes (central Bolivia)	Toltec conquering state, north of Mexican Basin	Inca Empire in Andes

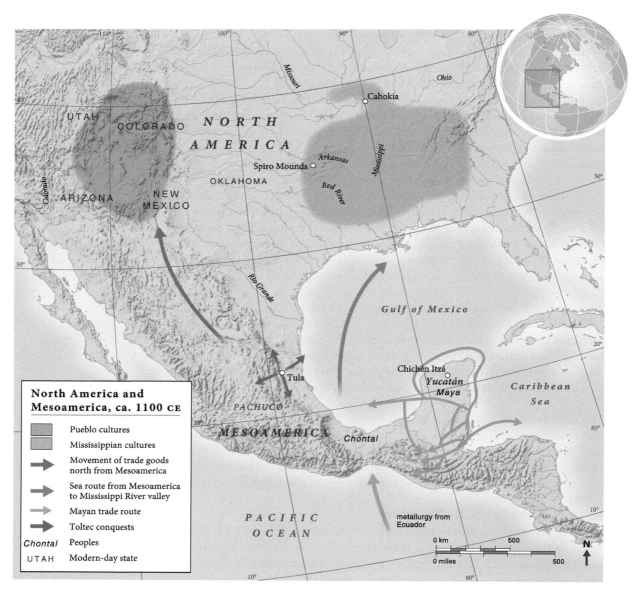

MAP 15.1 **North America and Mesoamerica, ca. 1100.**

Mayan city-state
of Palenque

several older states. A dozen new kingdoms emerged and established a new balance of power among themselves. After a lengthy hiatus, Maya culture entered its final period (650–900).

The final period in the southern, rain forest–covered lowlands and adjacent highlands was marked by agricultural expansion and ceremonial monument construction. The rain forest on hillsides was cut down and terraces were built for soil retention. The largest kingdoms grew to 50,000–60,000 inhabitants and reached astounding rural population densities of about 1,000 persons per square mile. Although the late Maya states were geographically small, they were administratively the most centralized polities ever created in indigenous American history.

The late Maya states did not last long. Torrential downpours washed the topsoil from the newly built hillside terraces. Malnutrition resulting from the shrinking agricultural surface began to reduce the labor force. In the end, even the ruling classes suffered, with members killing each other for what remained of agricultural surpluses. By about 900, the Maya kingdoms in southern Yucatán had shriveled.

Chichén Itzá in the North   A few small Maya states on the periphery survived. The most prominent among them was Chichén Itzá [chee-CHEN eet-SAH], which flourished from about 850 to 1000. The region would appear to be inhospitable, as the climate was very dry and the surface was rocky or covered with thin topsoil. There were no rivers, but many sinkholes in the porous limestone underneath the soil held water. Cisterns to hold additional amounts of water for year-round use were cut into the limestone; this water, carried in jars to the surface, supported a productive garden agriculture.

Chichén Itzá was founded during the phase of renewed urbanization in 650. The population was composed of local Maya as well as the Maya-speaking Chontal from the Gulf Coast farther west. Groups among these people engaged in long-distance trade, both overland and in boats along the coast. Since trade in the most lucrative goods required contact with people outside even the farthest political reach of either Teotihuacán or Tula, merchants traveled in armed caravans.

Chontal traders adopted Toltec culture, and in Chichén Itzá around 850 they superimposed their adopted culture over that of the original Maya. At the very end of the period of Teotihuacán, Maya, and Toltec cultural expansion, the three cultures finally merged on the Yucatán Peninsula. This merger did not last long: Already around 1000 the ruling-class factions left the city-state for unknown reasons, and the city-state diminished in size and power.

Chacmool (Offering Table) at the Entrance to the Temple of Warriors, Chichén Itzá. Chacmools originated here and spread to numerous places in Mesoamerica, as far north as Tenochtitlán and Tula. Offerings to the gods included food, tobacco, feathers, and incense. Offerings might have included also human sacrifices. The table in the form of a prostrate human figure is in itself symbolic of sacrifice.

The Legacy of Tiwanaku and Wari in the Andes

Mesoamerica and the Andes shared the tradition of regional temple pilgrimages. In the Andes, the chiefdoms remained mostly coastal. Around 600 CE, the two conquering states of Tiwanaku in the highlands of what are today southern Peru and Bolivia and Wari in central Peru emerged. Both states represented a major step in the formation of larger, militarily organized polities.

The Expanding State of Tiwanaku

Tiwanaku was a political and cultural power in the south-central Andes during the period 600–1100. It began as a ceremonial center and developed into a state

Tiwanaku, Kalassaya Gate.
Within the Temple of the Sun, this gate is aligned with the sun's equinoxes and was used for festive rituals. Note the precise stone work, which the Incas later developed further.

dominating the region around Lake Titicaca. At its apogee it planted colonies in regions far from the lake and conveyed its culture through trade to peoples even farther away.

Agriculture on the High Plain   The Andes consist of two parallel mountain chains along the west coast of South America. In southeastern Peru and western Bolivia an intermountain plain, 12,500 feet above sea level, extends as wide as 125 miles. At its northern end lies Lake Titicaca, which has one outlet at its southern end, a river flowing into Lake Poopó [po-PO], a salt lake 150 miles south. The Lake Titicaca region receives winter rains sufficient for agriculture and grazing.

The region around Lake Titicaca offered nearly everything necessary for an advanced urbanization process. The lake's freshwater supported fish and resources such as reeds from the swamps, which served for the construction of boats and roofs. The food staples were potatoes and quinoa. The grasslands of the upper hills served as pastures for llama and alpaca herds. Llamas were used as transportation animals, and alpacas provided wool; the meat of both animals was a major protein source.

Farmers grew their crops on hillside terraces or on raised fields close to the lake. The raised-field system, which farmers adopted from peoples of the Maya lowlands, consisted of a grid of narrow strips of earth, separated from each other by channels. Mud from the channels, heaped onto the strips, replenished their fertility. By 700, the city of Tiwanaku had 20,000 inhabitants.

Ceremonial feasts brought together elite lineages and clients, or ordinary craftspeople and villagers. Elites and clients cohered through **reciprocity**—that is, communal labor by clients rewarded by the elites with feasting. Forced labor through conscription or taxation did not appear until shortly before the collapse of the state.

Reciprocity: In its basic form, an informal agreement among people according to which a gift or an invitation has to be returned after a reasonable amount of time; in the pre-Columbian Americas, an arrangement of feasts instead of taxes shared by ruling classes and subjects in a state.

Expansion and Colonization   The region around southern Lake Titicaca housed related but competing elite–client hierarchies. Ruling clans and ordinary farmers comprised a state capable of imposing military power beyond the center. Counterbalancing clans at the head of similar hierarchies prevented the rise of permanent, unified central administrations and military forces.

The hallmark of Tiwanaku authority was the prestige of its ceremonial center, rather than military might. Tiwanaku feasting ceremonies could be considered expressions of Tiwanaku authority—and pilgrims who partook in the feasts came into its orbit.

Yet military force did play a role in the western valleys of the Andes. Merchants accompanied by warriors traveled hundreds of miles. Settler colonies were additional forms of power projection, especially those established in the Moquegua [mow-KAY-gah] valley to the west. Here, Tiwanaku emigrants established villages, which

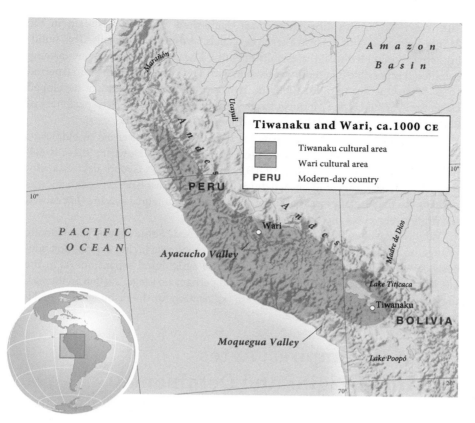

MAP 15.2 **Tiwanaku and Wari, ca. 1000.**

sent some of their corn or beer to the capital in return for salt and obsidian tools. Although overall less militarily inclined than the Mesoamerican states of the same time period, Tiwanaku wielded a visible influence over southern Peru (see Map 15.2).

The Expanding City-State of Wari

Little is known about early settlements in central Peru. The state of Wari emerged around 600, and expansion to the south put Wari into direct contact with Tiwanaku. The two states came to some form of mutual accommodation, and it appears that neither embarked on an outright conquest of the other. Their military postures remained limited to their regional spheres of influence.

Origins and Expansion   Wari was centered on the Ayacucho valley, a narrow plain in the highlands of northern Peru. The land is mountainous, interspersed with valleys and rivers. Farmers grew potatoes, corn and cotton. In the seventh century, Wari grew to 30,000 inhabitants and brought neighboring cities under its control. It also expanded terrace farming. Like Tiwanaku, Wari became the center of a developed urbanism and a diversified agriculture.

In addition to maintaining control over the cities in its vicinity, Wari constructed new towns with plazas, housing for laborers, and halls for feasting. Outside the core area, Wari elites established colonies. It appears that Wari exercised much stronger political control over the chiefs of its core region than Tiwanaku and was more active in founding colonies.

The Wari–Tiwanaku Frontier   Wari established a colony upstream in the Moquegua valley with extensive terraces, canals, and protective walls. This building activity coincided with the establishment by Tiwanaku of downstream farming colonies. It is possible that there was tension with Tiwanaku during the initial period (650–800), but during 800–1000 the two agricultural communities developed closer ties. Very likely, the Moquegua valley was politically so far on the periphery of both states that neither had the means to impose itself on the other.

Wari, like Tiwanaku, was an expanding state. Both were governed by elite clans who benefited from reciprocal patron–client organizations.However, there is evidence of increased internal tension after 950 in the two states. Groups defaced sculptures, destroyed portals, and burned down edifices. Scholars have argued that it was perhaps the fragility of power based on an increasingly unequal sharing that caused the rift between elites and subjects.

Why would elites allow reciprocity to be weakened? Some suggest that climatic change made large feasts no longer possible. A more convincing explanation suggests environmental degradation as the result of agricultural expansion. As in the late Maya kingdoms, the exhausted land could perhaps no longer sustain an increasing population. Unfortunately, an ultimate explanation for the disintegration of Tiwanaku and Wari remains elusive.

American Empires: Aztec and Inca Origins and Dominance

States in the Andes and Mesoamerica gave way in the early fifteenth century to empires. As in Eurasia, they were centralized multireligious, multiethnic, and multilinguistic polities: empires in every sense of the word.

The Aztec Empire of Mesoamerica

The ancestors of the Aztecs left Tula and arrived at the Mexican Basin at an unknown time. They eventually conquered the Mexican Basin, the site of today's Mexico City. In the fifteenth century they conquered an empire that encompassed Mesoamerica from the Pacific to the Gulf of Mexico and from the middle of modern northern Mexico to the Isthmus of Panama.

The Founding of Tenochtitlán

Settlement in the Mexican Valley   According to the Aztecs' founding myth, the first Aztec was born on an island in a lake or in a mountain cave northwest of the Mexican Basin. This Aztec ancestor and his descendants migrated south, guided by their hunter–warrior patron god Huitzilpochtli [hoo-it-zil-POSHT-lee] to a land of plenty.

When the ancestors arrived at the Mexican Basin, an eagle perched on a cactus commanded the Aztecs to settle and build a temple to their god. In this temple, they were to sacrifice to the god the blood of humans captured in war.

The historical record in the Mexican Basin becomes clearer in the fourteenth century, during which the Aztecs appeared as clients of two Toltec-descended overlords in city-states on the southwestern shore. Here, they created two islands, founded a city with a ceremonial center and rendered military service to their overlords. Aztec leaders married into the elites of the neighboring city-states and gained the right to have their own ruler presiding over a council of the elite and priests.

The Rise of the Empire After the successful rebellion in 1428 of a triple alliance among the Aztec city-state and two other vassal states against the reigning city-state in the Mexican Basin, the Aztec leader Itzcóatl [its-CO-aw] (r. 1428–1440) emerged as the dominant figure. Tenochtitlán, the Aztec city on one of the islands, became the capital of an empire that consisted of a set of six "inner provinces" in the Mexican Basin. Local elites were required to attend ceremonies in Tenochtitlán, bring and receive gifts, leave their sons as hostages, and intermarry with the elites of the triple alliance. Farmers had to provide tribute, making the imperial core self-sufficient.

After further conquests by the middle of the fifteenth century, the triple alliance created an imperial polity from the Pacific to the Gulf (see Map 15.3). This state was more centralized than the Teotihuacán and Toltec city-states. In this empire, local ruling families were generally left in place, but commoners had to produce tributes of goods and materials.

In some provinces, Aztec governors replaced the rulers; in others, Aztec tribute collectors (supported by troops) held local rulers in check and supervised the transportation of the tributes. Although reciprocity continued, it was now clearly subordinate to military considerations.

The resulting multiethnic, multireligious, and multilinguistic empire was still developing in the early sixteenth century when the Spanish arrived. The state of Tlaxcala [tlash-KAH-lah], held out in opposition, together with enemy states on the periphery. Although the triple alliance did everything to expand, pockets of anti-Aztec states survived and eventually became allies of the Spanish.

The key policy of continued expansion of Aztec central control was the threat of warfare. This fear-inducing tactic was an integral innovation in the imperialism of the Aztecs.

The Military Forces The triple alliance ruled 1.5 million inhabitants in the Mexican Basin. This number yielded up to a quarter of a million potential soldiers. Initially, the army was recruited from among the elite of the Aztecs and their allies. But toward the middle of the fifteenth century, Aztec rulers set up separate military school systems for the sons of the elite and the commoners. After graduation, soldiers rose in the army hierarchy on the basis of merit, particularly their success in the capture of enemies for future sacrifice.

The Aztecs inherited the weaponry and armor of the Toltecs, and they also made innovations, including the bow and arrow, which arrived from northwest Mexico at the end of Toltec rule, and the obsidian-spiked broadsword, derived from the Toltec short sword. Clubs, maces, and axes declined in importance in the Aztec arsenal. Body armor, consisting of quilted, sleeveless cotton shirts, thick

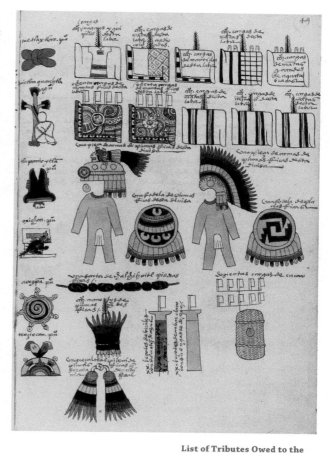

List of Tributes Owed to the Aztecs. The list includes quantities of cotton and wool textiles, clothes, headgear with feathers, and basketry. The Aztecs did not continue the complex syllabic script of the Maya, but used instead images, including persons with speech bubbles, for communication. Spanish administrators and monks who copied the Aztec manuscripts added their own explanations to keep track of Native American tributes.

image analysis

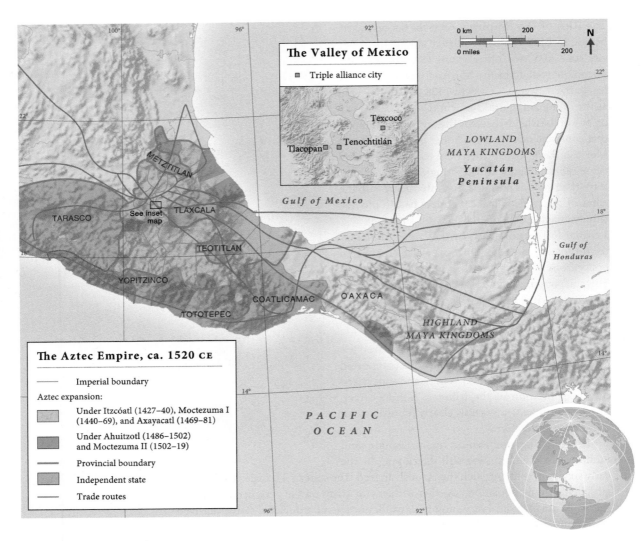

MAP 15.3 **The Aztec Empire, ca. 1520.**

cotton helmets, and round wooden or cane shields, was adopted from the Toltecs. With the arrival of the Aztecs, the Americas had acquired the heaviest infantry weaponry in their history.

The Inca Empire of the Andes

After the disintegration of Tiwanaku and Wari around 1100, the central Andes returned to local chiefdoms in small city-states with ceremonial centers and agricultural hinterlands. Tiwanaku cultural traditions, however, remained dominant.

The southern Peruvian city-state of Cuzco, with its Inca elite, emerged in the early fifteenth century at the head of a militaristic conquering polity. Within another century, the Incas had established an empire, called Tawantinsuyu [ta-wan-tin-SOO-yuh] (Quechua "Four Regions"), symbolizing its geographical expanse. It stretched from Ecuador in the north to central Chile in the south, with extensions into the upper Amazon and western Argentina (see Map 15.4).

The Incas, like the Aztecs, have a founding myth. In one version, the creator god Viracocha [vee-rah-KO-chah] summoned four brothers and four sisters, pairing them as couples and promising them a land of plenty. They would find this land when a golden rod would get stuck in the soil. Alternatively, the sun god Inti [IN-tee] did the pairing of the couples before sending them with the golden rod to their promised land. In Cuzco, where the rod plunged into fertile soil, the Incas drove out the existing farmers.

In the fourteenth century, Cuzco became a serious contender in the city-state competition. Eight rulers are said to have succeeded each other in the consolidation of Cuzco as a regional power, although little is known about them. Firm historical terrain is reached with the ninth ruler, Pachacuti (r. 1438–1471). The history of the Incas from 1438 onward is known much better, primarily because of the records of the Spanish conquerors.

Aztec Weapons. Aztec weapons were well-crafted hardwood implements with serrated obsidian edges, capable of cutting through metal, including iron. As slashing weapons they were highly effective in close combat.

Imperial Expansion   The system of reciprocity that characterized earlier Mesoamerican and Andean history continued under the Incas. *Ayllu* [AY-yoo], the Quechua term for a household with an ancestral lineage, implied mutual obligations among groups of households, neighborhoods, villages, and city-states. The most important social expression of reciprocity remained the feast. In the Incan Empire, the state collected more from the *ayllus* than Tiwanaku and Wari had done, but whether it returned comparable amounts through feasts and celebrations was a matter of contention, often leading to armed rebellion.

The earliest conquests under Pachacuti were around Lake Titicaca, as well as the north of the former Wari state. The Incas then expanded 1,300 miles northward to southern Ecuador and 1,500 miles southward to Chile. The final provinces, added in the early sixteenth century, were in northern Ecuador as well as on the eastern slopes of the Andes. The capital, Cuzco, with some 100,000 inhabitants in the early sixteenth century, was laid out in a grid of four streets. Symbolically, the capital reached out to the four regions of the empire—coast, north, south, and Amazon rain forest.

Administration   Ethnic Inca governors administered the four regions, which were subdivided into provinces, each with an Inca subgovernor. Most provinces were composites of former city-states, which remained under their local elites. A system of population organization was imposed by the Inca rulers. According to this system, members of the local elites commanded 10,000, 1,000, 100, and 10 household heads for the *mit'a* [MIT-ah] ("to take a turn," in reference to service obligations rotating among the subjects). The services were owed by subjects to the empire as a form of taxes.

The **mit'a** was an important innovation the Incas contributed to the history of the Americas. In contrast to the Aztecs, who shipped taxes in kind to their capital by boat, the Incas had no efficient means of transportation for long distances. The only way to make use of the taxes in kind was to store them locally. The Incas built storehouses and required subjects to deliver a portion of their goods and harvests under *mit'a* obligations to the nearest storehouse. These supplies enabled the Incas to conduct military campaigns far from Cuzco. In addition, it was through the *mit'a* that

Mit'a: Innovation of the Incas in which subjects were obligated to deliver a portion of their harvests, animal products, and domestically produced goods to nearby storehouses for use by Inca officials and troops. The *mit'a* also provided laborers for construction projects as well workers on state farms or mines.

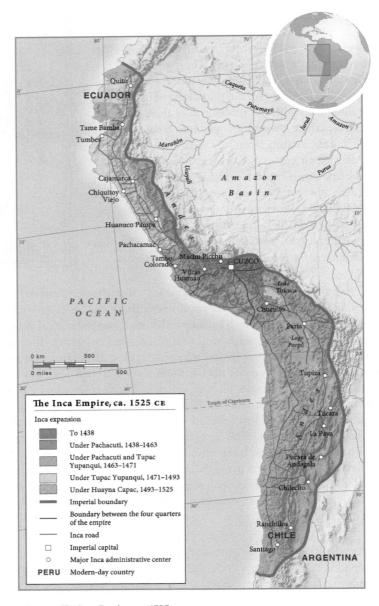

MAP 15.4 **The Inca Empire, ca. 1525.**

map analysis

Quipu: Knotted string assembly, used in the Andes from ca. 2500 BCE onward for the recording of taxes, population figures, calendar dates, troop numbers, and other data.

laborers were assembled for construction projects, often far from the urban center. Finally, *mit'a* provided laborers for mines, quarries, farms, and colonies.

To keep track of *mit'a* obligations, officials used bundles of knotted cord (**quipu**, or *khipu* [KEE-poo], "knot"). The numbers of knots on each cord in the bundles contained information on population figures and service obligations. The use of *quipus* was widespread in the Andes long before the Inca. Although some 700 have been preserved, attempts to decipher them have so far failed.

Military Organization   Under the *mit'a* system of the Inca empire, men were required to serve in the military. As in the Aztec Empire, administrators made sure that

Inca Roads. Inca roads were paths reserved for runners and the military. They were built on beds of rocks and rubble and connected strategic points in the most direct line possible.

enough laborers remained in the villages to take care of their other obligations of farming, herding, transporting, and manufacturing. Intermediate commanders came from the local and regional elites, and the top commanders were members of the two upper and lower Inca ruling elites.

Inca weaponry was comparable to that of the Aztecs, consisting of bows and arrows, dart throwers, slings, clubs with spiked bronze heads, wooden broadswords, bronze axes, and bronze-tipped javelins. The Incas also used a snare to entangle the enemy's legs. Protective armor consisted of quilted cotton shirts, copper breastplates, cane helmets, and shields.

During the second half of the fifteenth century, the Incas turned from conquest to consolidation. Faced with rebellions, they deemphasized the draft and recruited longer-serving troops from a smaller number of trusted peoples. These troops garrisoned forts throughout the empire and were part of the settler colonies in rebellious provinces and border regions. Personal guards recruited from non-Inca populations accompanied leading ruling-class members. The professionalization of the Inca army, however, lagged behind that of the Aztecs, since the Incas did not have military academies open to their subjects.

Communications   The Incas created an excellent imperial communication and logistics structure. They improved on the road network that they inherited from Tiwanaku, Wari, and other states. Roads extended from Cuzco nearly the entire length of the empire. The roads often required extensive grounding, paving, staircasing, and tunneling. In many places, the 25,000-mile road network still exists today.

The roads were reserved for troops, officials, and runners carrying messages. For their convenience, every 15 miles, or at the end of a slow 1-day journey, an inn provided accommodation. Larger armies stopped at barracks or pitched tents. Despite the fact that they did not have wheeled transport, the Incas were aware of how crucial paved and well-supplied roads were for infantry soldiers.

Imperial Society and Culture

As Mesoamerica and the Andes entered their imperial age, cosmopolitan capitals with monumental ceremonial centers and palaces emerged. Ceremonies and rituals impressed on enemies and subjects alike the irresistible might of the empires.

Imperial Capitals: Tenochtitlán and Cuzco

In the fifteenth century, the Aztec and Inca capitals were among the largest cities of the world, encompassing between 100,000 and 200,000 inhabitants. Although their monumental architecture followed different artistic traditions, both emphasized platforms and sanctuaries atop large pyramid-like structures as symbols of elevated power as well as closeness to the gods.

Tenochtitlán as an Urban Metropolis More than half of the approximately 1.5 million people living during the fifteenth century in the Mexican Basin were urban dwellers. Such an extraordinary concentration of urban citizens was unique in the agrarian world prior to the industrialization of Europe, when cities usually held no more than 10 percent of the total population (see Map 15.5).

The center of Tenochtitlán, on the southern island, was a large platform. In an enclosure on this platform were the main pyramid, with temples to the Aztec gods on top, and smaller ceremonial centers. Also on the platform were a food market, palaces of the ruling elite, courts of law, workshops, a prison, and councils for teachers and the military. Aztecs and visitors assembled each day to pay respect to the ruler and to trade in the market.

In 1473, the southern island was merged with the northern island. At the center of the northern island was the principal market of the combined islands, which attracted as many as 40,000 people each day. The sophistication of the market was comparable to that of any market in Eurasia during the fifteenth century.

Causeways linked the capital with the lakeshore, and people traveled inside the city on a system of canals. Dikes with sluices regulated both the water level and the salinity of the lake. Potable water arrived from the shore via an aqueduct on one of the western causeways. Professional water carriers took fresh water from the aqueduct to commoners in the city; professional waste removers collected human waste from urban residences and took it to farmers for fertilizer.

The two city centers—the pyramid and palaces in the south and the market in the north—were surrounded by residential

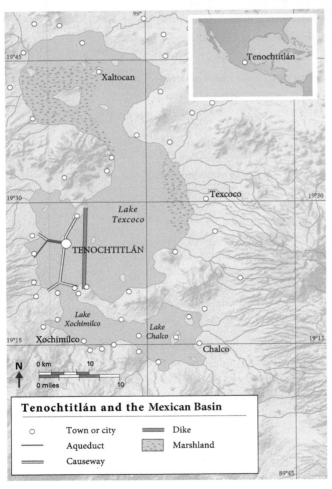

MAP **15.5 Tenochtitlán and the Mexican Basin.**

Tenochtitlán and the Mexican Basin

○ Town or city ▬ Dike
─ Aqueduct ▨ Marshland
═ Causeway

quarters, many of which were inhabited by craftspeople of a shared profession. The rooms of the houses surrounded a central patio—an architectural preference common to Meso-america and the Andes, as well as the Middle East and Mediterranean.

Residents of quarters farther away from the center were farmers. Here, a grid of canals encased small, rectangular islands devoted to housing compounds and/or farming. A raised-field system prevailed, whereby farmers dredged the canals and heaped the fertile mud on top of the rectangular islands, called **chinampas**.

Aqueduct from the Western Hills to Tenochtitlán. This aqueduct, still standing today, provided fresh water to the palace and mansions of the center of the island, to be used as drinking water and for washing.

In contrast to the luxurious palaces of the elite, housing for farmers consisted of humble plastered huts. As in all agrarian societies, farmers—subject to high taxes or rents—were among the poorest folk.

On the surface of the *chinampas*, farmers grew seed plants as well as *maguey* [mag-AY], a large succulent agave. This evergreen plant has a large root system, which stabilizes the ground, and produces fiber for weaving and pulp for making *pulque* [POOL-kay], a fermented drink.

Ownership of the *chinampas* was vested in clans, which, under neighborhood leaders, were responsible for the allocation of land and adjudication of disputes as well as the payment of taxes in kind to the elite. There were also members of the elite who possessed estates and employed managers to collect rents from the farmers. Whether there was a trend from taxes to rents is unknown.

Chinampas: Small, artificial islands in Lake Texcoco created by farmers for raising agricultural crops.

Cuzco as a Ceremonial-Administrative City   The site of the Inca city of Cuzco was a triangle formed by the confluence of two rivers. At one end was a hill on which were built the imperial armory and a temple dedicated to the sun god. Enormous stone walls followed the contours of the hill.

Below, the city was laid out in a grid pattern. The residents of the city, all belong-ing to the Inca ruling class, lived in adobe houses arranged in a block-and-courtyard pattern similar to that of Wari. Squares and temples served as ceremonial centers. The Coricancha [co-ri-CAN-tsha], the city's main temple, stood near the conflu-ence of the rivers. This temple was a walled compound set around a courtyard. Each year priests of the empire's ceremonial centers sent a sacred object to the Corican-cha, to demonstrate their obedience to the central Inca temple.

Across the rivers were settlements for commoners with markets and store-houses. In the fields, interspersed stone pillars and shrines were aligned on sight lines radiating from the Coricancha, tying the countryside closely to the urban center. Farther away were imperial estates with unfree laborers from outside the *mit'a* system. In contrast to the Aztec elite, which allowed meritorious generals to rise in the hierarchy, the Inca elite remained exclusionary, allowing no commoners to reside in Cuzco.

Power and Its Cultural Expressions

Ruling elites emphasized the display of power during the period 600–1500. This was particularly true with the Aztecs and Incas during the fifteenth century.

Patterns Up Close | Human Sacrifice and Propaganda

In the first millennium CE, Mesoamerica and the Andes evolved from their early religious spirituality to polytheism. The spiritual heritage, however, remained a strong undercurrent, as seen in human as well as animal and agricultural sacrifices. Rulers appeased the gods also through self-sacrifice—that is, the piercing of tongue and penis. The feathered serpent god Quetzalcóatl was the Mesoamerican deity of self-sacrifice, revered in the city-states of Teotihuacán (200 BCE–570 CE) and Tula (ca. 900 CE). Under the Toltecs and the Aztecs, this god receded, in favor of warrior gods such as Tezcatlipoca and Huitzilpochtli. The survival of traditional blood rituals within polytheism was a pattern that distinguished the early American empires from their Eurasian counterparts.

Whether human sacrifices were prolific under Aztec and Inca imperialism is questionable. Archaeological evidence does not support the impression created by

52.

Human Sacrifice. Human sacrifice among the pre-Columbian Mesoamericans and Andeans was based on the concept of a shared life spirit or mind, symbolized by the life substance of blood. In the American spiritual-polytheistic conceptualization, the gods sacrificed their blood, or themselves altogether, during creation; rulers pierced their earlobes, tongues, or penises for blood sacrifices; and war captives lost their lives when their hearts were sacrificed.

Inca Ruling-Class Gender Relations   The greatest honor for Inca girls in Cuzco and provincial colonies was to enter at age 10–12 into the service of a "House of Chosen Women." An inspector from Cuzco visited villages to select attractive young girls for the service. These houses had female instructors who provided the girls with an education in cooking, beer making, weaving, and officiating in the ceremonies of the Inca religion. After their graduation, the young women became virgin temple priestesses, were given in marriage to non-Incas honored for service to the rule, or became servants or concubines of the Inca elite. The collection of this girl tribute was separate from the reciprocity system.

The form of agriculture in Mesoamerica and the Andes gave males fewer opportunities to accumulate wealth and power than plow agriculture did in Eurasia. Nevertheless, the gradual agrarian–urban diversification of society, even if it was slower in the Americas than in Eurasia, proceeded along similar paths of increasing male power concentration. An emphasis on gender differences, therefore, should be viewed as a characteristic phenomenon arising in imperial contexts.

Inca Mummy Veneration   Other houses in Cuzco were ghostly residences in which servants catered to the needs of deceased, mummified Inca emperors and their principal wives. During the mummification process, attendants removed the cadaver's internal organs, placed them in special containers, and desiccated the bodies until they were completely mummified. Servants dressed the mummies in their finest clothing and placed them back into their residences amid their possessions, as if they had never died. The mummies received daily meals and were carried around by their retinues for visits to their mummified relatives. On special occasions, mummies were lined up according to rank on Cuzco's main plaza to participate in ceremonies and processions. In this way, they remained fully integrated in the daily life of the elite.

the Spanish conquerors and encourages doubts about the magnitude of human sacrifices in temple ceremonies.

Could it be that there was no significant increase in human sacrifice under the Aztecs and Incas, as the self-serving Spanish conquerors alleged? Were there perhaps, instead, imperial propaganda machines in the Aztec and Inca Empires, employed in the service of conquest and consolidation who sought to intimidate their enemies? If the answer to these questions is yes, the Aztec and Inca Empires would be but two typical examples of the general world-historical pattern of competitive militaristic states during the early agrarian era using propaganda to further their imperial power.

Questions

- In examining the question of whether empires such as the Inca and the Aztec employed human sacrifice for propaganda purposes, can this practice be considered an adaptation that evolved out of earlier rituals, such as royal bloodletting?

- If the Aztec and the Inca did indeed employ human sacrifice for propaganda purposes, what does this say about the ability of these two empires to use cultural and religious practices to consolidate their power?

In Andean society, mummies were a crucial ingredient in the religious heritage, in which strong spiritual elements survived underneath the polytheistic overlay of astral gods. In the spiritual tradition, a dead person's spirit, while no longer in the body, remains nearby and needs daily nourishment in order not to be driven away. Hence, even though non-Incan Andean societies removed the dead from their daily living spaces, descendants had to visit tombs regularly with food and beer.

The expenses for the upkeep of the mummy households were the responsibility of the deceased emperor's bloodline, headed by a surviving brother. As heirs of the emperor's estate, the members of the bloodline formed a powerful clan within the ruling class. The new emperor was excluded from this estate and had to acquire his own new one in the course of his rule. In the early sixteenth century, however, this mechanism of keeping the upper and lower rungs of the ruling class united became counterproductive. Emperors lacking resources had to contend with brothers richly endowed with inherited wealth and ready to engage in dynastic warfare—as actually occurred shortly before the arrival of the Spanish (1529–1532).

≫ Putting It All Together

The Aztec and Inca Empires unleashed extraordinary creative energies. Sculptors, painters, and (after the arrival of the Spanish) writers recorded the traditions as well as the innovations of the fifteenth century. Aztec painters produced codices, or illustrated manuscripts, that present the cultural and administrative activities of their societies in exquisite detail. Today, a handful of these codices survive, preserved in Mexican and European libraries.

interactive concept map

The Aztec and Inca Empires were polities that illustrate how humans not in contact with the rest of the world developed patterns of innovation that were remarkably similar. On the basis of an agriculture that produced ample surpluses, humans made the same choices as their cousins in Eurasia and Africa. Specifically, in the period 600–1500, they created temple-centered city-states, just like their Sumerian and Hindu counterparts. Their military states were not unlike the Chinese warring states. And, finally, their empires were comparable to those of the New Kingdom Egyptians or the Assyrians. The Americas had their own unique variations of these larger historical patterns, but they nevertheless displayed the same humanity as found elsewhere.

Review and Relate

>> Within the patterns of state formation basic to the Americas, which types of states emerged in Meso-america and the Andes during the period 600–1550? What characterized these states?

>> Why did the Tiwa-naku and Wari states have ruling classes but no dynasties and central bureaucracies? How were these patterns expressed in the territorial organization of these states?

>> What patterns of urban life characterized the cities of Tenochtitlán and Cuzco, the capitals of the Aztec and Inca Empires? In which ways were these cities similar to those of Eurasia and Africa?

Thinking Through Patterns

Examine the ways historians approach the big questions of this chapter.

The basic pattern of state formation in the Americas was similar to that of Eurasia and Africa. Historically, it began with the transition from foraging to agriculture and settled village life. As the population increased, villages became chiefdoms, which in turn became city-states. American city-states often became conquering states, beginning with the Maya kingdoms and Teotihuacán. Military states in which ruling classes sought to expand territories, such as Tula and Tiwanaku and Wari, were characteristic of the early part of the period 600–1550. Their successors—the Aztec and Inca Empires—were multiethnic, multilinguistic, and multireligious polities that dominated Meso-america and the Andes before the Spanish conquest brought them to a premature end.

The states of Tiwanaku and Wari had cohesive ruling classes but no dynasties or centralized bureaucracies. These ruling classes and their subjects were integrated through systems of reciprocity. Over time, tensions arose, either between stronger and weaker branches of the ruling classes or between rulers and subjects over questions of obligations and justice. When these tensions erupted into internal warfare, the states disintegrated, often in conjunction with environmental degradation and climate change.

Tenochtitlán and Cuzco, the capitals of the Aztec and Inca Empires, were urban centers organized around temples and associated residences of the ruling dynasties and their priestly classes. They also contained quarters inhabited by craftspeople, and large central markets. Armed caravans of merchants and porters transported luxury goods across hundreds of miles. Tenochtitlán had an aqueduct for the supply of drinking water, and Cuzco was traversed by a river. Both capitals had agricultural suburbs in which farmers used irrigation for their crops.

Against the Grain

Consider this as a counterpoint to the main patterns examined in this chapter.

Amazon Rain Forest Civilizations

For years, scholarly opinion held that the Amazonian river basin, covered by rain forest, was too inhospitable to allow for more than small numbers of widely dispersed foragers. Even farmers, living in populated villages, could not possibly have founded complex societies. Slash-and-burn agriculture prevented the advance of urban life: After exhausting the soil, whole villages had to pack up and move.

However, scholars now realize that this belief was erroneous. Modern farmers, encroaching on the rain forest, noticed two hitherto neglected features. First, these farmers found in stretches of forest and savanna a black soil so fertile that it did not require fertilizers. Second, as they slashed and burned the rain forest and savanna with their modern tools, the farmers exposed monumental earthworks that had previously escaped attention. The two features were connected. *The black soil* was the result of centuries of soil enrichment by indigenous people who also built the earthworks. Instead of slashing and burning, these people had engaged in "slashing and charring"—that is, turning the trees into nutrient-rich charcoal rather than quickly depleted ash.

Scholars have now documented large-scale settlements in areas along the southern tributaries to the Amazon. In the Purus region, for example, researchers employing aerial photography revealed a huge area home to perhaps 60,000 inhabitants during a period around the late thirteenth century. This area is adjacent to the farthest northeastern extension of the Inca Empire into the Amazon. Thus, when the Incas expanded into the rain forest, they clearly did so to incorporate advanced societies into their empire. Thanks to scholars who challenged the orthodoxy of the "empty rain forest," we are rediscovering the Amazonian past.

- Which is more important: to save the rain forest or uncover its archaeological past? Can the two objectives be combined?

- Compare the Amazonian earthworks to those of Benin in Africa during the same period (Chapter 14). Which similarities and differences can you discover?

Key Terms

Chinampas 351
Mit'a 347

Quipu 348
Reciprocity 342

audio flashcards

For additional resources, please go to
www.oup.com/us/vonsivers.
Please see the Further Resources section at the back of the book for additional readings and suggested websites.

PART FOUR

Interactions across the Globe

1450–1750

Around 1450, important changes occured in the patterns of world history. While religious civilizations continued to evolve, the competing states that constituted these civilizations began to give way to new empires. Smaller European countries were creating the first global seaborne empires. The new empires reorganized themselves as centralized polities based on money economies, large bureaucracies, and professional armies possessed of firearms. Competing for resources, markets, and ideological influence, they interacted with each other with increasing intensity.

Two new phenomena appeared between 1450 and 1750 that would have far-reaching implications: the New Sciences (or Scientific Revolution) and the Enlightenment. Attempts to found an understanding of the universe on mathematics and experimentation would lead to science as the chief mode of interpreting the physical realm. Attempts to apply principles of science to understanding human societies would lead to the concepts of individual rights, natural law, and popular sovereignty. The combination of these two trends created the foundations of the *scientific–industrial society* that dominates contemporary global culture.

The process by which this formation of *scientific–industrial society* took place was extremely complex, and it is impossible for us to do more than suggest some of the larger patterns of it here. Moreover, because of the long-standing argument

1440–1897
Benin kingdom, West Africa

1492
Spanish conquest of Granada, expulsion of Jews, and discovery of the Americas

ca. 1500
Beginning of Columbian Exchange

1514
Nicolaus Copernicus formulates the heliocentric model

1453
Ottoman capture of Constantinople

1498
Vasco da Gama's circumnavigation of Africa and journey to India

1511
First African slaves taken to Caribbean

1517
Martin Luther publishes his 95 theses; beginning of Protestant Reformation

in Western historiography for European exceptionalism, we must be careful to explore this process without easy assumptions about their inevitability. For example, one question is "To what extent did the societies of western Europe (what we have termed the 'religious civilization' of Western Christianity) part ways with the other religious civilizations of the world?" Aspects of the question have recently been the subject of debate:

- On one hand, there appears to have been no movement comparable to that of the European Renaissance or Reformation arising during this time in the other parts of the world to create a new culture similar to that of Europe. The Middle East, India, and China for the most part continued ongoing cultural patterns, although often on considerably higher levels of refinement and sophistication.

- On the other hand, Europe, like much of the rest of the world, remained rooted in agrarian–urban patterns until the effects of the Industrial Revolution began to be felt sometime after 1800. Furthermore, through nearly this entire period, China and India were more populous and at least as wealthy and diversified in their economies and social structures as their European counterparts. Nonetheless, the overall wealth of European countries involved in the conquest and exploitation of the resources of the Americas and the development of global trading systems advanced immensely. Thus, while India and China had possessed these resources for a long time, European countries were now utilizing them at an accelerating rate. This wealth and the patterns of its acquisition and distribution would eventually have far-reaching consequences.

For the great majority of people, even in 1750, much seemed to go on as before. Everywhere in the world empires continued to grow and decline, religious tensions continued to erupt into warfare, and rulers continued to ground their authority not in their peoples but in the divine. Thus, for a full understanding of world history during 1450–1750, one has to keep in mind that although change was certainly occurring, it was often too imperceptible for contemporaries to detect.

Thinking Like a World Historian

≫ What new and different patterns characterized the development of states and empires in the period 1450–1750?

≫ How did the emergence of centralizing states lead to more intensive and frequent interactions among empires in the period 1450–1750?

≫ How did the New Sciences and the Enlightenment lay the foundation for the scientific–industrial society that dominates our global culture today?

≫ To what extent did the societies of western Europe diverge from other civilizations in the period 1450–1750? Why is the notion of "exceptionalism" problematic in examining this question?

interactive timeline

1521, 1533
Spanish conquest of the Aztec and Inca Empires

1577
Matteo Ricci, first Jesuit missionary to arrive in China

1607
Founding of Jamestown, Virginia

1720
Edo, capital of Japan, world's largest city

1542–1605
Akbar, the most innovative of the Mughal rulers (India)

1604
Galileo Galilei formulates the mathematical law of falling bodies

1687
Isaac Newton unifies physics and astronomy

1736–1795
Reign of Qianlong emperor, China

Western European Overseas Expansion and the Ottoman–Habsburg Struggle

A l-Hasan Ibn Muhammad al-Wazzan (ca. 1494–1550) was born in Muslim Granada soon after the Christian conquest of this kingdom in southern Iberia in 1492. Unwilling to convert to Christianity, Hasan's family emigrated to Muslim Morocco around 1499–1500. Here, Hasan received a good education and entered the administration of the Moroccan sultan, traveling to sub-Saharan Africa and the Middle East on diplomatic missions.

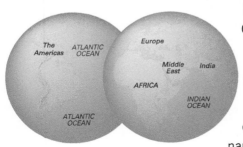

In 1517, as he was returning home from a mission to Istanbul, Christian **corsairs** kidnapped him. Like their Muslim counterparts, these corsairs roamed the Mediterranean to capture travelers, whom they then held for ransom or sold into slavery. For a handsome sum of money, they turned Hasan over to Pope Leo X (1513–1521), who ordered Hasan to convert to Christianity and baptized him with his own family name, Giovanni Leone di Medici. Hasan became known in Rome as Leo Africanus ("Leo the African"). He stayed for 10 years

ABOVE: This 1630 map by João Teixeira Albernaz the Elder (late 1500s–ca. 1662), member of a prominent family of Portuguese map makers, shows Arabia, India, and China.

in Italy, initially at the papal court and later as a scholar in Rome. During this time, he taught Arabic to Roman clergymen and compiled an Arabic–Hebrew–Latin dictionary. His most enduring work was a travelogue, *Description of Africa*, which was for years the sole source of information about sub-Saharan Africa in the Western Christian world.

In 1527 Charles V (r. 1516–1558), king of Spain and emperor of the Holy Roman Empire of Germany, invaded Italy and sacked Rome. Hasan survived but departed for Tunis sometime after 1531, seeking a better life in Muslim North Africa. Unfortunately, all traces of Hasan after his departure from Rome are lost. It is possible that he perished in 1535 when Charles V attacked and occupied Tunis (1535–1574), although it is generally assumed that he lived there until around 1550.

The world in which Hasan lived was a Muslim–Christian world composed of the Middle East, North Africa, and Europe. Although Muslims and Christians traveled with relative freedom in much of this world, the two religious civilizations were locked in a pattern of fierce competition. During 800–1050, the Muslims justified their conquests as holy wars (*jihads*), and during 1050–1300 the Christians retaliated with their Crusades and the reconquest (*Reconquista*) of Iberia.

By the fifteenth century, the Christians sought to rebuild the crusader kingdom of Jerusalem, which had been lost to the Muslims in 1291. Searching for a route that would take them around Africa, they hoped to defeat the Muslims in Jerusalem with an attack from the east. In the process, the Christians discovered the Americas. For their part, the Muslims sought to conquer eastern and central Europe while defending North Africa and driving the Portuguese out of the Indian Ocean. After a hiatus of several centuries, imperial polities reemerged in the form of the Ottoman and Habsburg Empires.

The Muslim–Christian Competition in the East and West, 1450–1600

In the second half of the fifteenth century the Christian kings resumed the *Reconquista* of Iberia. During the same period, the small principality of the Ottomans took advantage of Mongol and Byzantine weakness to conquer lands in both Anatolia and the Balkans. After the Muslim conquest of Constantinople in 1453 and the Western Christian conquest of Granada in 1492, the Ottoman and Habsburg Empires emerged.

Iberian Christian Expansion, 1415–1498

Portugal resumed its *Reconquista* policies by expanding to North Africa in 1415. Looking to circumvent the Muslims, collect West African gold, and reach the Indian spice coast, the Portuguese established fortified harbors along the African

≫ **What patterns characterized Christian and Muslim competition in the period 1300–1600? Which elements distinguished them from each other, and which elements were similar? How did the pattern change over time?**

≫ **How did centralizing states in the Middle East and Europe function in the period 1450–1600? How did economics, military power, and imperial objectives interact to create the centralizing state?**

≫ **Which patterns did cultural expressions follow in the Habsburg and Ottoman Empires? Why did the ruling classes of these empires sponsor these expressions?**

Corsairs: In the context of this chapter, Muslim or Christian pirates who boarded ships, confiscated the cargoes, and held the crews and travelers for ransom; they were nominally under the authority of the Ottoman sultan or the pope in Rome, but operated independently.

map of the known world by Martellus, ca. 1489

Military orders: Ever since the early 1100s, the papacy encouraged the formation of monastic fighting orders, such as the Hospitalers and Templars, to combat the Muslims in the crusader kingdom of Jerusalem; similar *Reconquista* orders, such as the Order of Santiago and the Order of Christ, emerged in Iberia to eliminate Muslim rule.

Apocalypse: In Greek, "revelation"—that is, the unveiling of events at the end of history, before God's judgment; during the 1400s, expectation of the imminence of Christ's Second Coming, with precursors paving the way.

coastline. Castile and Aragon conquered Granada in 1492, occupied ports in North Africa, and sent Columbus to discover an alternate route to India. Columbus's discovery of America, instead, delivered the prospect of a new continent to the rulers of Castile and Aragon (see Map 16.1).

Maritime Explorations   In 1277–1281, mariners of the Italian city-state of Genoa pioneered commerce by sea between the Mediterranean and northwestern Europe. In Lisbon, Portuguese shipwrights and their Genoese teachers developed ships suited for Atlantic seas. In the early fifteenth century they developed the *caravel*, a ship with upward-extending fore and aft sides, a stern rudder, and square as well as triangular lateen sails. The Portuguese became important traders between England and the Mediterranean countries.

The sea trade stimulated an exploration of the eastern Atlantic. By the early fifteenth century, the Portuguese had discovered the Azores and Madeira, while the Castilians began a conquest of the Canary Islands. Here, the indigenous inhabitants, the Guanches, put up a fierce resistance. But settlers carved out colonies on conquered parcels of land, enslaving the Guanches to work in sugarcane plantations. They thus introduced the sugarcane plantation system from the eastern Mediterranean, where it had Byzantine and Crusader roots on the island of Cyprus, to the Atlantic.

Apocalyptic Expectations   The loss of the crusader kingdom in Palestine to the Muslim Mamluks in 1291 stirred deep feelings of guilt among Western Christians. Efforts to reconquer Jerusalem failed, however, because rulers in Europe were warring against each other for territorial gain. The failure did not dampen spiritual revivals, however, especially in the Franciscan and **military orders** of Iberia. These monks, often well connected with the Iberian royal courts, were believers in apocalypse—that is, the imminent end of the world and the Second Coming of Christ.

According to the **Apocalypse**, Christ's return could happen only in Jerusalem. This made it urgent for the Christians to reconquer the city. Christians as well as Muslims saw no contradiction between religion and military conquest. A providential God, so they believed, justified the conquest of lands and the enslavement of the conquered. The religious justification of military action, therefore, was a declaration by believers that God was on their side to help them convert and conquer.

In Portugal, political claims in the guise of apocalyptic expectations guided the military orders in "reconquering" Ceuta, a northern port city of the Moroccan sultans. Accordingly, a fleet under Henry the Navigator (1394–1460) took Ceuta in 1415, capturing a stock of West African gold. Henry, a brother of the ruling Portuguese king, was searching for the West African source of Muslim gold. By the middle of the fifteenth century, Portuguese mariners had reached the "gold coast" of West Africa, where local rulers imported gold from the interior Akan fields.

Reforms in Castile   The Portuguese renewal of the *Reconquista* stimulated a similar revival in Castile, which occurred after the dynastic union of Castile and Aragon–Catalonia under their respective monarchs, Queen Isabella (r. 1474–1504) and King Ferdinand II (r. 1479–1516). The two monarchs used the reconquest ideology to speed up political and religious reforms.

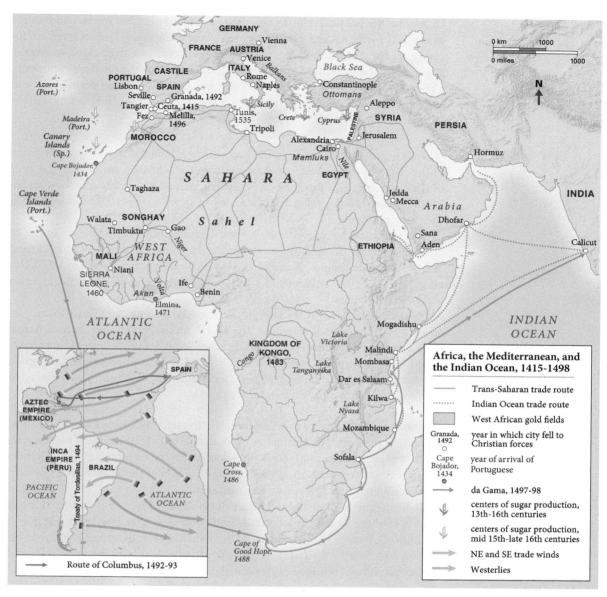

MAP **16.1 Africa, the Mediterranean, and the Indian Ocean, 1415–1498.**

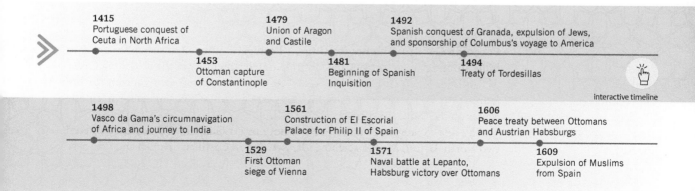

1415
Portuguese conquest of
Ceuta in North Africa

1453
Ottoman capture
of Constantinople

1479
Union of Aragon
and Castile

1481
Beginning of Spanish
Inquisition

1492
Spanish conquest of Granada, expulsion of Jews,
and sponsorship of Columbus's voyage to America

1494
Treaty of Tordesillas

interactive timeline

1498
Vasco da Gama's circumnavigation
of Africa and journey to India

1529
First Ottoman
siege of Vienna

1561
Construction of El Escorial
Palace for Philip II of Spain

1571
Naval battle at Lepanto,
Habsburg victory over Ottomans

1606
Peace treaty between Ottomans
and Austrian Habsburgs

1609
Expulsion of Muslims
from Spain

Among the political reforms was the recruitment of urban militias and judges to check the military and judicial powers of the aristocracy. Religious reform focused on education for the clergy and enforcement of Christian doctrine among the population. The institution entrusted with the latter was the Spanish Inquisition, a body of clergy appointed in 1481 to discover and punish those deemed to be in violation of Christian theology and church law. These reforms laid the foundations for increased state power.

The Conquest of Granada

The *Reconquista* culminated in a 10-year campaign (1482–1492) that resulted in Granada falling into Christian hands. The last emir of Granada negotiated terms for an honorable surrender. According to these terms, Muslims who stayed as subjects of the Castilian crown were permitted to worship in their own mosques.

The treaty did not apply to the Jews of Granada, however, who were forced to either convert to Christianity or emigrate. Many emigrated in 1492 to Portugal and the Ottoman Empire. Portugal adopted its own expulsion decree in 1497. This ended the nearly millennium-and-a-half-long Jewish presence in Sefarad, as Spain was called in Hebrew.

After the expulsion of the Jews, it did not take long for the Christians to violate the Muslim treaty of surrender. The church forced conversions, burned Arabic books, and transformed mosques into churches. In 1499 the Muslims of Granada rebelled. Christian troops crushed the uprising, and Isabella and Ferdinand abrogated the treaty of surrender. During the early sixteenth century, Muslims were forced to convert, disperse to other provinces, or emigrate.

Columbus's Journey to the Caribbean

In early 1492, Isabella and Ferdinand authorized the mariner Christopher Columbus (1451–1506) to build two caravels and a larger carrack and sail across the Atlantic. Columbus promised to reach India ahead of the Portuguese. Money for the construction of ships came from Castilian and Aragonese Crusade levies on the Muslims.

In September, Columbus and his mariners departed from the Castilian Canary Islands, catching the favorable South Atlantic easterlies. After a voyage of a little over a month, Columbus landed on one of the Bahaman islands, mistakenly assuming that he was close to the Indian subcontinent. After 3 months, he left a colony of settlers behind and returned to Iberia with seven captured Caribbean islanders and some gold.

Although disappointed by the meager returns of Columbus's first and subsequent voyages, Isabella and Ferdinand were delighted to have acquired new islands in the Caribbean, in addition to the Canaries. In one blow they had drawn even with Portugal.

Vasco da Gama's Journey to India

Portugal continued to search for a way to India around Africa. In 1498, the king appointed a member of the crusading Order of Santiago, Vasco da Gama (ca. 1469–1524), to command four caravels for the journey to India. After 6 months, the ships arrived in Calicut, the main spice trade center on the Indian west coast.

The first Portuguese mariner sent ashore by da Gama in Calicut encountered two North African Muslims, who addressed him in Castilian Spanish and Genoese

Italian: "The Devil take you! What brought you here?" The mariner replied: "We came to seek Christians and spices." The Muslim and Hindu merchants were un-interested in the goods designed for the African market offered by da Gama and demanded gold or silver, which the Portuguese had only in small amounts. As rumors spread about a Muslim and Hindu plot against him, da Gama prudently sailed home.

However, Portugal soon mastered the India trade. The Portuguese crown or-ganized regular journeys around Africa, and when Portuguese mariners ventured in the other direction to northeast Brazil, they claimed it for their expanding com-mercial network. During the early sixteenth century, as the Portuguese India fleets brought considerable amounts of spices from India back to Portugal, the project of retaking Jerusalem receded into the background.

Pedro Reinel's map of East Africa and the Indian Ocean, ca. 1507

Rise of the Ottomans and Struggle with the Habsburgs for Dominance, 1300–1609

While Muslim rule was disappearing from the Iberian Peninsula in the late fifteenth century, the opposite was happening in the Balkans. Here, the Ottoman Turks ex-panded Islamic rule over Christians. By the late sixteenth century, when conflict be-tween the Habsburgs and Ottomans reached its peak, entire generations of Croats, Germans, and Italians feared a Muslim conquest of all of Christian Europe.

Late Byzantium and Ottoman Origins   The rise of the Ottomans was re-lated to the decline of Byzantium. The emperors of Byzantium had reclaimed their "empire" in 1261 from its Latin rulers and Venetian troops. This empire was a mid-size kingdom with modest agricultural resources. But it was still a valuable trading hub, given Constantinople's strategic position. Thanks to its commercial wealth, Byzantium experienced a cultural revival that influenced the Western Renaissance in Italy (see Chapter 10).

Both Balkan Slavs and Anatolian Turks appropriated Byzantine provinces in the late thirteenth century, further reducing the empire. One of the lost provinces was Bithynia, where, in 1299, the Turkish warlord Osman (1299–1326) declared him-self an independent ruler. Osman and other Turkish lords in the region were nomi-nally subject to the Seljuks, the Turkish dynasty that had conquered Anatolia from the Byzantines two centuries earlier but by the early 1300s was disintegrating.

During the first half of the fourteenth century, Osman and his successors con-quered further Anatolian provinces from Byzantium. In 1354, the Ottomans gained their first European foothold on a peninsula about 100 miles southwest of Constan-tinople. Thereafter, it seemed only a matter of time before the Ottomans would con-quer Constantinople.

Through skillful mixture of defense and diplomacy, however, the Byzantine em-perors salvaged their rule for another century. They were also helped by Timur the Great (r. 1370–1405), a Turkish-descended ruler from central Asia who sought to rebuild the Mongol Empire. He defeated the Ottomans in 1402. Timur and his suc-cessors were unsuccessful with their dream of Mongol world rule; the Ottomans needed nearly two decades (1402–1421) to reconstitute their empire in the Balkans and Anatolia. Under Mehmet II, "the Conqueror" (r. 1451–1481), they finally laid siege to the Byzantine capital.

Patterns Up Close | Shipbuilding

With the appearance of empires during the Iron Age, four regional but interconnected shipbuilding traditions—Mediterranean, North Sea, Indian Ocean, and China Sea—emerged.

In the Mediterranean, around 500 BCE, shipwrights began to use nailed planks for their war galleys as well as for cargo transports. In the Roman Empire (ca. 200 BCE–500 CE), nailed planking allowed the development of the roundship (image *a*), a large vessel 120 feet in length with a capacity of 400 tons of cargo for the transport of grain from Egypt to Italy. The roundship and its variations had double planking, multiple masts, and multiple square sails. After 100 BCE, the triangular (lateen) sail allowed for tacking (zigzagging) against the wind, greatly expanding shipping during the summer sailing season.

The Celtic North Sea tradition adapted to the Mediterranean patterns of the Romans. Shipwrights in Celtic regions shifted to frame-first construction for small boats in the 300s. At the same time, Norsemen, or Vikings, innovated by introducing overlapping (clinkered) plank joining for their seagoing boats. The North Sea innovations, arriving as they did at the end of the western Roman Empire, remained local for nearly half a millennium.

China made major contributions to ship construction. In the Han period (206 BCE–220 CE) there is evidence from clay models for the use of nailed planks in riverboats. One model, dating to the first century CE, shows a central steering rudder at the end of the boat. At the same time, similar stern rudders appeared in the Roman Empire. Who adopted what from whom, if there was any borrowing at all, is still an unanswered question.

Patterns of Shipbuilding. Left to right: (*a*) Hellenistic-Roman roundship, (*b*) Chinese junk, (*c*) Indian Ocean dhow.

From Istanbul to the Adriatic Sea   Mehmet's siege and conquest of Constantinople (April 5–May 29, 1453) is one of the stirring events of world history. The Byzantines were unable to defend the land walls that protected the city. Using their superiority in troop strength, the Ottomans bombarded Constantinople's walls with heavy cannons. A weak section was on the northeastern side, along the harbor in the Golden Horn, where the walls were low. Here, the Byzantines had blocked off the entrance to the Golden Horn with a huge chain. Mehmet circumvented the chain by having troops drag ships on rollers over a hillside into the harbor. The soldiers

Shipbuilding innovations continued after 600 CE. In Tang China, junks with multiple bulkheads (watertight compartments) and layers of planks appeared. The average junk was 140 feet long, had a cargo capacity of 600 tons, and could carry on its three or four decks several hundred mariners and passengers (see image *b*). Junks had multiple masts, and their trapezoidal (lug) and square sails made of matted fibers were strengthened (battened) with poles sewed to the surface. The Middle Eastern, eastern African, and Indian dhow was built with sewed or nailed planks and rigged with lateen and square sails, traveling as far as southern China (see image *c*).

In western Europe, the patterns of Mediterranean and North Sea shipbuilding merged during the thirteenth century. At that time, northern shipwrights developed the cog, a ship of some 60 feet in length and 30 tons in cargo capacity, with square sails and flush planking below and clinkered planking above the waterline. Northern European crusaders traveled during 1150–1300 on cogs via the Atlantic to the Mediterranean. Builders adapted the cog's clinker technique to the roundship tradition that Muslims as well as Eastern and Western Christians had modified in the previous centuries. Genoese clinkered roundships pioneered the Mediterranean–North Sea trade in the early fourteenth century (see image *d*).

Lisbon shipwrights in Portugal developed the caravel around 1430. The caravel was a 60-foot-long ship with a 50-ton freight capacity, a stern rudder, square and lateen sails, and a magnetic compass (of Chinese origin). The caravel and, after 1500, the similarly built but much larger galleon were the main vessels the Portuguese, Spanish, Dutch, and English used during their oceanic voyages from the mid-fifteenth to mid-eighteenth centuries (see image *e*).

Patterns of Shipbuilding (*Continued*). From top: (*d*) Baltic cog, (*e*) Iberian caravel. These ships illustrate the varieties of shipbuilding traditions that developed over thousands of years.

Questions

- How does the history of shipbuilding demonstrate the ways in which innovations spread from one place to another?

- Do the adaptations in shipbuilding that flowed between cultures that were nominally in conflict with each other provide a different perspective on the way these cultures interacted?

massed on these ships were ready to assault the walls with the help of ladders. On the first sign of cracks in the northeastern walls, the Ottoman besiegers stormed the city. The last Byzantine emperor, Constantine XI, perished in the massacre that followed the Ottoman occupation of the city.

Mehmet repopulated Constantinople ("Istanbul" in Turkish) and appointed a new patriarch at the head of the Eastern Christians, to whom he promised full protection as his subjects. He ordered the construction of the Topkapı Palace (1459), the transfer of the administration to Istanbul, and the resumption of expansion in

Siege of Constantinople, 1453.
Note the soldiers on the left pulling boats on rollers and wheels over the Galata hillside. With this maneuver, Sultan Mehmet II was able to circumvent the chain stretched across the entrance to the Golden Horn (in place of the anachronistic bridge in the image). This allowed him to speed up his conquest of Constantinople by forcing the defenders to spread their forces thinly over the entire length of the walls.

a Safavid battle tunic

the Balkans, where he forced the majority of rulers into submitting to vassal status.

Mehmet's conquests brought him to the Adriatic Sea, from where the Ottomans were poised to launch a full-scale invasion of Italy. When the sultan died unexpectedly, his successor turned back, preferring instead to consolidate the Ottoman Empire in the Middle East, North Africa, and the Balkans.

Imperial Apogee   Between 1500 and 1600 the Ottomans consolidated their empire. In 1514, they defeated the Persian Safavids in Iran, who had risen in 1501 to form a rival Shiite empire in opposition to the Sunni Ottomans. In the southern Middle East, tensions between the Ottomans and the Mamluk Turks erupted in war in 1517. The Ottomans defeated the Mamluks and took control of western Arabia, including the holy pilgrimage city of Mecca. A year later, in 1518, Sultan Süleyman I, "the Magnificent" (r. 1520–1566), drove the Spanish from much of North Africa, which the latter had conquered in the name of the *Reconquista* in the 1490s and early 1500s.

In the Balkans, the Ottomans completed their conquests of Serbia and Hungary with the annexation of Belgrade and Buda (now part of Budapest) as well as a brief siege of Vienna in 1529. By the second half of the sixteenth century, the Ottoman Empire was a vast multiethnic and multireligious state of some 15 million inhabitants extending from Algeria in the Maghreb to Yemen in Arabia and from Upper Egypt to the Balkans and the northern shores of the Black Sea (see Map 16.2).

Morocco and Persia   In the period 1450–1600, the Ottomans and Indian Mughals dominated Islamic civilization. Two smaller realms existed in Morocco and Persia, ruled by the Saadid (1509–1659) and Safavid (1501–1722) dynasties, respectively. The Saadid sultans defended themselves successfully against the Ottoman expansion and liberated themselves from the Portuguese occupation of Morocco's Atlantic ports. In 1591, the Saadids sent an army to West Africa in an unsuccessful attempt to revive the gold trade. Moroccan army officers assumed power in Timbuktu, and their descendants, the Ruma, became provincial lords independent of Morocco. The Saadids split into provincial realms. The still-reigning Alaouite dynasty of Moroccan kings replaced them in 1659.

The Safavids grew in the mid-1400s from a mixed Kurdish-Turkish mystical brotherhood in northwestern Iran into a Shiite warrior organization that carried out raids against Christians in the Caucasus. In 1501, the leadership of the brotherhood put forward a 14-year-old boy named Ismail as the Hidden Twelfth Imam. According to Shiite doctrine, the Hidden Imam, or Messiah, was expected to arrive and establish a Muslim apocalyptic realm of justice at the end of time, before God's Last Judgment. This realm would replace the "unjust" Sunni Ottoman Empire. The Ottomans, however, crushed the Safavid challenge in 1514 at the Battle of Chaldiran. Ismail dropped his claim to messianic status, and his successors assumed the more modest title of king (Persian *shah*) as the head of state.

The Safavids recruited a standing infantry from among young Christians on lands conquered in the Caucasus. They held fast to Shiism, thereby continuing their

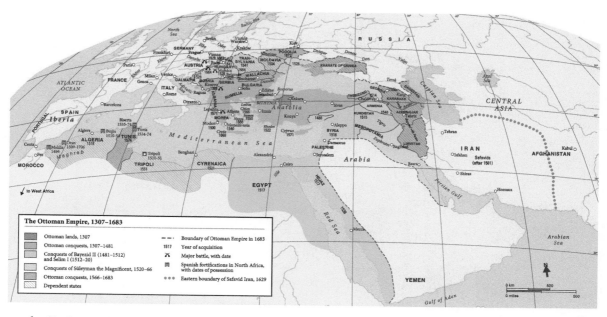

MAP 16.2 **The Ottoman Empire, 1307–1683.**

map analysis

opposition to the Sunni Ottomans, and made this form of Islam dominant in Iran. They moved the capital from Tabriz to the centrally located Isfahan in 1590, and built a palace, administration, and mosque complex in the city. They also held the monopoly in the production of Caspian Sea silk, a high-quality export product.

Not everyone accepted Shiism, however. An attempt to force the Shiite doctrines on the Afghanis backfired badly when enraged Sunni tribes formed a coalition, defeated the Safavids, and ended their regime in 1722.

Rise of the Habsburgs   On the Iberian Peninsula, Castile-Aragon evolved into the center of a vast empire. A daughter of Isabella and Ferdinand married a member of the Habsburg dynastic family, which ruled Flanders, Burgundy, Naples, Sicily, and Austria, as well as Germany (the "Holy Roman Empire of the German Nation," as this collection of principalities was called). Their son, Charles V (r. 1516–1558), not only inherited Castile–Aragon, now merged and called "Spain," and the Habsburg territories but also became the ruler of the Aztec and Inca Empires in the Americas. In both Austria and the western Mediterranean the Habsburgs were direct neighbors of the Ottomans (see Map 16.3).

After a victorious battle against France in 1519, Charles V also won the title of emperor from the pope, which made him the overlord of all German principalities and supreme among the monarchs of Western Christianity. He was now the titular political head of Western Christianity and thereby the direct counterpart of Sultan Süleyman in the struggle for dominance in the Christian–Muslim world of Europe, the Middle East, and northern Africa. Both the Habsburgs and the Ottomans renewed the traditional Islamic–Christian imperialism which had characterized the period 628–950 and which had been replaced by the Muslim and Christian commonwealths of 950–1450.

MAP 16.3 **Europe and the Mediterranean, ca. 1560.**

Habsburg Distractions   Charles V faced a daunting task in his effort to prevent the Ottomans from advancing against the Christians in the Balkans and the Mediterranean. Problems in his European territories diverted his attention from what Christians in most parts of Europe perceived as a pervasive Ottoman–Muslim threat. During the first three decades of the sixteenth century, revolts in Iberia, the Protestant Reformation in the German states, and renewed war with France commanded Charles's attention.

The emperor's distractions increased further in 1534 when, in an attempt to drive the Habsburgs out of Italy, France forged an alliance with the Ottomans. While this alliance horrified western Europe, it demonstrated that the Ottomans had become crucial players in European politics.

Habsburg and Ottoman Losses   These diversions strained Habsburg resources against the Ottomans, who pressed ahead on the two fronts of the Balkans and North Africa. Although Charles V deputized his younger brother Ferdinand I to shore up the Balkan defenses, he was unable to send him enough troops. After a series of defeats, Austria had to pay the Ottomans tribute and, eventually, sign a humiliating truce (1562). On the western Mediterranean front, by 1556, at the end of Charles V's reign, only two of eight Habsburg garrisons had survived Ottoman onslaught.

A third frontier of the Muslim–Christian struggle for dominance was the Indian Ocean. After Vasco da Gama had returned from India in 1498, the Portuguese kings sought to break into the Muslim-dominated Indian Ocean trade. In response, the Ottomans protected existing Muslim commercial interests in the Indian Ocean. They blocked Portuguese military support for Ethiopia and strengthened their ally, the sultan of Aceh on the Indonesian island of Sumatra, by providing him with troops and weapons. War on land and on sea raged in the Indian Ocean through most of the sixteenth century.

In the long run, the Portuguese were successful in destroying the Ottoman fleets sent against them, but smaller convoys of Ottoman galleys continued to harass Portuguese shipping interests. By 1570 the Muslims traded as much via the Red Sea route to the Mediterranean as the Portuguese did by circumnavigating Africa. In addition, the Ottomans now benefited from the trade of coffee, produced in Ethiopia and Yemen. Both Portugal and the Ottomans reduced their by now unsustainable military presence in the Indian Ocean, which allowed the Netherlands in the early seventeenth century to overtake both Portugal and the Ottoman Empire in the Indian Ocean spice trade (see Map 16.4).

Portuguese trading posts in the Indian Ocean, 1630

Habsburg–Ottoman Balance   In the 1550s, Charles V decided to ensure the continuation of Habsburg power through a division of his western and eastern territories. Accordingly, he bestowed Spain, Naples, the Netherlands, and the Americas on his son Philip II (r. 1556–1598). The Habsburg possessions of Austria, Bohemia, and the remnant of Hungary not lost to the Ottomans, as well as the Holy Roman Empire (Germany), went to his brother Ferdinand I (r. 1558–1564). Charles hoped that his son and brother would cooperate and help each other militarily against the Ottomans.

When Philip took over the Spanish throne, he realized that most of the Habsburg military was stationed outside Spain, leaving that country vulnerable to attack—especially as the Ottomans had recently conquered Spanish strongholds in North Africa. Fearful of **morisco** support for an Ottoman invasion of Spain, Philip's administration and the Inquisition renewed their decrees of conversion.

This sparked a revolt among the moriscos of Granada in 1568–1570, which Philip was able to suppress only after recourse to troops and firearms from Italy. To break up the large concentrations of Granadan moriscos in the south of Spain, Philip ordered them to be dispersed throughout the peninsula. At the same time, to alleviate the Ottoman naval threat, Philip, the pope, Venice, and Genoa formed a Holy Christian League. The fleet succeeded in 1571 in destroying the entire Ottoman navy at Lepanto, in Ottoman Greece.

The Ottomans, however, rebuilt their navy and captured the strategic port city of Tunis in 1574 from the Spaniards. After this date, Venice was the only naval enemy of the Ottomans. The Ottomans turned their attention to the rival Safavid Empire,

Moriscos: From Greek *maurus* ("dark"); Castilian term referring to North Africans and to Muslims under Spanish rule.

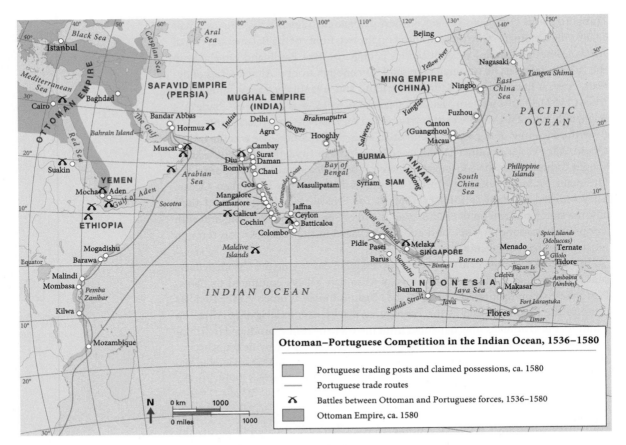

MAP 16.4 **Ottoman–Portuguese Competition in the Indian Ocean, 1536–1580.**

where they exploited a period of dynastic instability for the conquest of territories in the Caucasus (1578–1590). The Catholic Philip II, for his part, was faced with the Protestant war of independence in the Netherlands. This war was so expensive that Philip II had to declare bankruptcy and sue for peace with the Ottomans (1580).

The Limits of Ottoman Power   After their victory over the Safavids, the Ottomans looked again to the west, where a long peace with Ferdinand I in Austria (since 1562) was ready to collapse. A series of raids and counter-raids at the Austrian and Transylvanian borders had inflamed tempers, and in 1593 the Ottomans went on the attack.

Eventually, the Ottomans were only able to draw on the battlefield with the Austrians. In 1606, the Ottomans and Austrian Habsburgs made peace again. With minor modifications in favor of the Austrians, the two sides returned to their earlier borders. The Austrians made one more tribute payment and then let their obligation lapse. Officially, the Ottomans conceded nothing, but in practical terms Austria was no longer a vassal state.

Expulsion of the Moriscos   Although the peace between the Ottomans and Spanish Habsburgs held, Philip and his successors were aware of the possibility of renewed Ottoman aid to the Iberian Muslims, or moriscos, who continued to resist conversion. The church advocated the expulsion of the moriscos, arguing that the allegedly high Muslim birthrate was a serious threat.

Fierce resistance against the proposed expulsion, however, rose among the Christian landowners in the southeastern province of Valencia. These landowners benefited from the skills of morisco tenant farmers. Weighing the potential Ottoman threat against the possibility of economic damage, the government decided in 1580 in favor of expulsion.

It took until 1609, however, before a compensation deal with the landowners in Valencia was worked out. In the following 5 years, some 300,000 moriscos were forcibly expelled from Spain, under often appalling circumstances: As in the case of the Jews a century earlier, Spain's loss was the Ottoman Empire's gain, this time mostly in the form of skilled irrigation farmers.

Paolo Veronese, *Battle of Lepanto,* **altar painting with four saints beseeching the Virgin Mary to grant victory to the Christians (ca. 1572).** In the sixteenth century, the entire Mediterranean, from Gibraltar to Cyprus, was a naval battleground between Christians and Muslims. The Christians won the Battle of Lepanto thanks to superior naval tactics. At the end of the battle "the sea was entirely covered, not just with masts, spars, oars, and broken wood, but with an innumerable quantity of blood that turned the water as red as blood."

The Centralizing State: Origins and Interactions

The major technological change in the Middle East and Europe during 1250–1350 was the use of firearms. It took until the mid-1400s, however, before cannons and muskets were effective enough to make a difference in warfare. At this time, a pattern emerged whereby rulers created centralized states to finance their shift to firearm-bearing infantries. They resumed the policy of conquest and imperialism. Both the Ottomans and the Habsburgs raised immense amounts of silver and gold to spend on cannons, muskets, and ships for achieving world rule.

State Transformation, Money, and Firearms

In the early stages of their realms, the kings of Iberia (1150–1400) and the Ottoman sultans (1300–1400) compensated military commanders for their service with land grants. Once the Iberian and Ottoman rulers had conquered cities and gained control over long-distance trade, however, patterns changed. Rulers began collecting taxes in cash, with which they paid regiments of personal guards to supplement the army of land-grant officers. This centralizing state was the forerunner of the absolutist state of the early seventeenth century.

The Land-Grant System In the 1300s, Ottoman military lords created personal domains on lands they had conquered and took rents in kind from villagers to finance their dynastic households. Members of their clan or adherents (many of whom were holy warriors and/or adventurers), received other conquered lands, from which they collected rents. As the Ottomans conquered Byzantine cities, they gained access to the **money economy**. They collected taxes in coins from the markets and tollbooths at city gates, as well as from the Christians and Jews subject to the head tax.

After the conquest of the southern Balkans by the Ottoman Empire in the fifteenth and sixteenth centuries, both the land-grant system and the money economy expanded. A military ruling class of grant holders emerged, cavalrymen who

Money economy: Form of economic organization in which mutual obligations are settled through monetary exchanges; in contrast, a system of land grants obliges the landholders to provide military service, without payment, to the grantee (sultan or king).

Janissaries: Infantry soldiers recruited among the Christian population of the Ottoman Empire and paid from the central treasury.

Devşirme: The levy on boys in the Ottoman Empire; that is, the obligation of the Christian population to contribute adolescent males to the military and administrative classes.

lived with their households of retainers in the interior of Anatolia and the Balkans. Most of the time, they were away on campaign with the sultans, leaving managers in charge of the collection of rents. By the early years of the sixteenth century, the landed ruling class of cavalrymen constituted a reserve of warriors for the mobilization of troops each summer.

The Janissaries   The military institution of the **Janissaries**—troops who received salaries from the central treasury—is first documented in 1395. It was based on a practice (called ***devşirme*** [dev-SHIR-meh]) of conscripting young boys from the empire's Christian population. Boys between the ages of 6 and 16 were sent to Istanbul, where they were converted to Islam and trained as future soldiers and administrators. The youth then entered the system of manumitted palace slaves under the orders of the sultan and his ministers.

The practice of *devşirme* contradicted Islamic law, which forbade the enslavement of "peoples of the Book" (Jews, Christians, and Zoroastrians). Its existence, therefore, documents the extent to which the sultans reasserted the Roman–Sasanid–Arab imperial traditions of the ruler making doctrine and law.

Toward the first half of the fifteenth century, the sultans equipped their Janissaries with cannons and matchlock muskets. By this point, firearms had undergone some 150 years of development in the Middle East and North Africa. By the mid-1400s, gigantic siege cannons and slow but reliable matchlock muskets were the standard equipment of Ottoman and other armies, and the sultans relied on indigenous, rather than European, gunsmiths.

Boy Levy (*devşirme*) in a Christian Village. This miniature graphically depicts the trauma of conscription, including the wailing of the village women and the assembly of boys waiting to be taken away by implacable representatives of the sultan.

Revenues and Money   The maintenance of a salaried standing army and a central administration would have been impossible without precious metals. Therefore, the Ottoman imperial expansion was driven by the need to acquire mineral deposits. During the fifteenth century the Ottomans captured the silver, lead, and iron mines of Serbia and Bosnia. Together with Anatolian copper, iron, and silver mines, the Balkan mines made the Ottomans the owners of the largest precious metal production centers prior to the Habsburg acquisition of the Mexican and Andean mines in the mid-1500s.

The sultans left the Balkan mining and smelting operations in the hands of preconquest Christian entrepreneurs who were integrated into the Ottoman imperial money economy as tax farmers. **Tax farming** was the preferred method of producing cash revenues for the central administration. The holders of tax farms delivered the profits from the production of minerals to the state, minus the commission they were entitled to subtract for themselves. Thus, tax farmers were crucial members of the ruling class.

The right to mint silver was part of the tax-farm regime, as were the market, city gate, and port duties. The tax-farm regime was dependent on a strong sultan or chief minister, the grand vizier. Without close supervision, this regime could easily become decentralized, which indeed eventually happened in the Ottoman Empire.

Süleyman's Central State   The Ottoman state reached its apogee under Sultan Süleyman I, "the Magnificent." The sultan financed a massive expansion of the military and bureaucracy and formed a centralized state, the purpose of which was to project power and cultural splendor toward its subjects as well as Christian enemies outside the empire.

The bureaucrats were recruited from two population groups. Most top ministers and officers in the fifteenth and sixteenth centuries came from the *devşirme* among the Christians. The empire's other recruits came from colleges to which the Muslim population of the empire had access. Ambitious villagers far from urban centers could gain upward mobility through the colleges. Muslims of Christian parentage made up the top layer of the elite, while Muslims of Islamic descent occupied the middle ranks.

Under Süleyman, the Janissaries comprised musket-equipped troopers, a cavalry, and artillery regiments. Most were stationed in Istanbul, while others served in provincial cities and border fortresses.

Typical military campaigns required sophisticated logistics. Wages, gunpowder, weapons, and foodstuffs were carried on wagons and barges, since soldiers were not permitted to provision themselves from villagers, whether friend or foe. Although the state collected heavy taxes, it had a strong interest in not destroying village productivity.

Charles V's Centralizing State   The centralizing state began in Iberia with the reforms of Isabella and Ferdinand and reached its mature phase under Charles V. From the late fifteenth century onward, Castile and Aragon shared fiscal characteristics with the Ottomans, such as tax farming. In addition, Muslims paid head taxes in cash. Most of the money taxes were also enforced in Flanders, Burgundy, Naples, Sicily, and Austria, after Iberia's incorporation into the Habsburg domain in 1516. Together, these taxes were more substantial than those of Spain.

From 1521 to 1536, the Spanish crown enlarged its money income from looted Aztec and Inca gold and silver. Under Charles V, Habsburg imperial revenues doubled, reaching about the same level as those of the Ottomans. At the height of their struggle for dominance in the Muslim–Christian world, the Habsburgs and the Ottomans expended similar resources in wars with each other.

In one significant respect, however, the two empires differed. The cavalry ruling class of the Ottoman Empire was nonhereditary. By contrast, Iberian landholders possessed a legal right to inheritance. When Isabella and Ferdinand embarked on state centralization, they had to wrestle with a powerful, landed aristocracy that had taken over royal jurisdiction and tax prerogatives on their vast lands. The two monarchs took back much of the jurisdiction but were unable to do much about the taxes.

Ottoman Siege of a Christian Fortress. By the middle of the fifteenth century, cannons had revolutionized warfare. Niccolò Machiavelli, ever attuned to new developments, noted in 1519 that "no wall exists, however thick, that artillery cannot destroy in a few days." Machiavelli could have been commenting on the Ottomans, who were masters of siege warfare. Sultan Mehmet II, the conqueror of Constantinople in 1453, founded the Imperial Cannon Foundry shortly thereafter; it would go on to make some of the biggest cannons of the period.

Tax farming: Governmental auction of the right to collect taxes in a district. The tax farmer advanced these taxes to the treasury and retained a commission.

The Habsburgs sought to overcome their lack of power over the aristocracy and the weakness of their Spanish tax base by exploiting the Italian and Flemish cities and the American colonies. But in the long run their finances remained precarious. Spanish aristocrats seldom fulfilled their obligation to unpaid military service. As a result, the kings hired as many Italians, Flemings, and Germans as possible, and at times, they deployed these mercenaries to Spain in order to maintain peace there.

Although the Ottoman and Habsburg patterns of centralized state formation bore similarities to patterns in the earlier Roman and Arab Empires, the centralizing states of the period after 1450 were much more potent enterprises because of firearms. They were established polities, evolving into absolutist and eventually national states.

Imperial Courts, Urban Festivities, and the Arts

Ottoman and Habsburg rulers projected the splendor of their states to subjects at home as well as enemies abroad. Although Christian and Muslim artists and artisans belonged to different religious and cultural traditions, their artistic achievements were inspired by the same impulse: to glorify their states through religious expression.

The Ottoman Empire: Palaces, Festivities, and the Arts

The Ottomans built palaces and celebrated public feasts to demonstrate their imperial power and wealth. Many mosques were built during the sixteenth century. Painting and illustration was found only inside the privacy of the Ottoman palace and wealthy households. Theater and music were enjoyed on the popular level, in defiance of religious restrictions.

The Topkapı Palace   When the Ottoman sultans conquered the Byzantine capital Constantinople in 1453, it was dilapidated and depopulated. The sultans initiated large construction projects and populated the city with craftspeople and traders from across their empire. By 1600 Istanbul was again an imposing metropolis, easily the largest city in Europe at that time.

One of the construction projects was a new palace for the sultans, the Topkapı Sarayı, or "Palace of the Gun Gate," begun in 1459. The Topkapı complex included the main administrative school, military barracks, an armory, a hospital, and living quarters, or harem, for the ruling family.

The institution of the harem arose during the reign of Süleyman. At that time, sultans no longer pursued marriage alliances with neighboring Islamic rulers. Instead, they chose slave concubines (often Christian) for the procreation of children. A concubine who bore a son to the reigning sultan acquired privileges.

The head eunuch of the harem guard evolved into a powerful intermediary for diplomatic and military decisions between the sultan's mother, who was confined to the harem, and those she sought to influence. In addition, the sultan's mother arranged marriages of her daughters to high-ranking officials. In the strong patriarchal order of the Ottoman Empire, such women exercised considerable power.

Public Festivities   As in Habsburg Spain, feasts and celebrations were events that displayed the state's largesse. Typical festivities commemorated Muslim holidays. Other feasts were connected with the birthday of the Prophet Muhammad and his journey to heaven and hell. Processions and communal meals commemorated the birthdays of local Muslim saints in many cities. As in Christian Spain, these feasts attracted large crowds.

Wrestlers, ram handlers, and horsemen performed in the Hippodrome, the stadium for public festivities. At the harbor of the Golden Horn, tightrope artists performed high above the water. Court painters recorded the procession and performance scenes in picture albums. The sultans incorporated these albums into their libraries, together with history books recording their military victories against the Habsburgs.

Imperial Hall, Topkapı Palace. The Ottomans never forgot their nomadic roots. Topkapı Palace, completed in 1479 and expanded and redecorated several times, resembles in many ways a vast encampment, with a series of enclosed courtyards. At the center of the palace complex were the harem and the private apartments of the sultan, which included the Imperial Hall, where the sultan would receive members of his family and closest advisors.

image analysis

Popular Theater   The evenings of the fasting month of Ramadan were filled with festive meals and a special form of entertainment, the Karagöz ("Black Eye") shadow theater. This form of theater came from Egypt, although it probably had Javanese–Chinese roots. For boys, a performance of the Karagöz theater accompanied the ritual of circumcision, a rite of passage from the ancient Near East adopted by Islamic civilization. Circumcision signified the passage from the nurturing care of the mother to the educational discipline of the father.

Mosque Architecture   During the sixteenth century, the architect Sinan (ca. 1492–1588) filled Istanbul and the earlier Ottoman capital Edirne with imperial mosques, defined by their slender minarets. Sultan Süleyman, wealthy officials, and private donors provided the funds. Sinan was able to hire as many as 25,000 laborers, enabling him to build each of his mosques in six years or less.

Sinan's most original contribution to architecture was the replacement of the highly visible and massive four exterior buttresses, which marked the square ground plan of the Hagia Sophia, with up to eight slender pillars as hidden internal supports of the dome. His intention was not massive monumentality but elegant spaciousness.

The Spanish Habsburg Empire: Popular Festivities and the Arts

The culture of the Habsburg Empire was strongly religious, and both state-sponsored spectacles and popular festivities displayed devotion to the Catholic faith. More secular tendencies, however, emerged as a result of the Renaissance. Originating in Italy and the Netherlands, Renaissance aesthetics emphasized pre-Christian Greek and Roman heritages.

Capital and Palace   The Habsburgs were relatively late in establishing a capital city and a palace. Catholicism was the majority religion by the sixteenth century and a powerful unifying force, but there were strong linguistic differences among the provinces of the Iberian Peninsula. Charles V resided for a while in a palace in

Granada next door to the formerly Muslim Alhambra palace—but Granada was too Moorish and, geographically too far away from the north for many Spanish subjects to be properly awed.

Only a few places in Spain were suited for the location of a central palace and administration. Philip II eventually found such a place near the city of Madrid, which had once been a Muslim provincial capital. There, royal architect Juan Bautista de Toledo (ca. 1515–1567) built the Renaissance-style palace and monastery complex of El Escorial (1563–1584). As a result, Madrid became the seat of the administration and later of the court.

Christian State Festivities   Given the close association between the state and the church, the Spanish crown expressed its glory through the observance of feast days of the Christian calendar. These feasts were the occasion for processions and/or **passion plays**, during which urban residents affirmed their Catholic faith. During Holy Week, the week preceding Easter, Catholics marched through the streets, carrying heavy crosses or shouldering wooden platforms with statues of Jesus and Mary. The physical rigors of the Holy Week processions were collective reenactments of Jesus's suffering on the Cross.

Passion play: Dramatic representation of the trial, suffering, and death of Jesus Christ; passion plays are still an integral part of Holy Week in many Catholic countries today.

By contrast, the processions that took place several weeks after Easter were joyous celebrations. Costumed marchers participated in jostling and pushing contests, played music, performed dances, and enacted scenes from the Bible.

The Auto-da-Fé   The investigation or proceeding of faith (Portuguese *auto-da-fé*, "act of faith") was a show trial in which the state, through the Spanish Inquisition, judged a person's commitment to Catholicism. The Inquisition employed thousands of state-appointed church officials to investigate anonymous denunciations of individuals failing to conform to the Catholic faith.

Suspected offenders, such as Jewish or Muslim converts to Catholicism or perceived deviants from Catholicism, had to appear before a tribunal. In secret trials, officials determined the offense and the appropriate punishment. These trials often employed torture. However, scholarship has emphasized that in the great majority of cases the punishments were minor, or the investigations did not lead to convictions.

Popular Festivities   *Jousts* (mock combats between contestants mounted on horseback) were secular, primarily aristocratic events. Contestants rode their horses into the city square and led their horses through a complex series of movements. At the height of the spectacle, contestants galloped past each other, hurling their javelins at one another while protecting themselves with their shields. The joust evolved eventually into exhibitions of dressage ("training"), cultivated by the Austrian Habsburgs, who in 1572 founded the Spanish Court Riding School in Vienna.

Bullfights often followed the jousts. During the Middle Ages, bullfights were aristocratic pastimes that drew spectators from local estates. Bullfighters, armed with detachable metal points on 3-foot-long spears, tackled several bulls in a town square. The bullfighter who stuck the largest number of points into the shoulders of the bull was the winner.

Theater, Literature, and Painting   The dramatic enactments of biblical scenes in the passion plays and religious processions were the origin of secular theater in Italy and Spain. Stationary theaters appeared in the main cities of Spain during the

Auto-da-Fé, Madrid. This detail from an 1683 painting by the Italian-born painter Francisco Rizi shows a huge assembly in the Plaza Mayor of Madrid. It captures the solemn spectacle of the trial: In the center, below a raised platform, the accused stand in the docket waiting for their convictions to be pronounced; ecclesiastical and civil authorities follow the proceedings from grandstands. On the left, an altar is visible: The celebration of mass, often lasting for hours, was a common feature of the auto-da-fé.

sixteenth century. A performance typically began with a musical prelude and a prologue describing the piece, followed by the three acts of a drama or comedy. Many were hugely successful, enjoying the attendance or even sponsorship of courtiers, magistrates, and merchants.

An important writer of the period was Miguel de Cervantes (1547–1616). His masterpiece, *Don Quixote*, describes the adventures of a poverty-stricken knight and his attendant, the peasant Sancho Panza, as they wander around Spain searching for the life of bygone *Reconquista* chivalry. *Don Quixote* is an example of a new literary form: the novel.

The outstanding painter of Spain during Philip II's reign was El Greco (Domenikos Theotokopoulos, ca. 1546–1614), a native of the island of Crete. El Greco's works reflect the spirit of Spanish Catholicism, with its emphasis on strict obedience to traditional faith and fervent personal piety. His characteristic style represents a variation of Mannerism (with its perspective exaggerations), which succeeded the Renaissance style in Venice during the later sixteenth century.

❯❯ Putting It All Together

The Ottoman–Habsburg struggle can be seen as another chapter in the long history of competition that began when the Achaemenid Persian Empire expanded into the Mediterranean and was resisted by the Greeks in the middle of the first millennium BCE. There were obvious religious and cultural differences between the Islamic and Western Christian civilizations as they encountered each other during this period. But their commonalities are equally interesting. Both Ottomans and Habsburgs were representatives of the return to imperialism, and in the pursuit of their imperial goals, both adopted the policy of the centralizing state with its firearm infantries and

interactive concept map

urban money economy. Both found it crucial to project their glory to the population and to sponsor artistic expression. In the long run, however, the imperial ambitions of the Ottomans and Habsburgs exceeded their ability to raise cash. Although firearms and a monetized urban economy made them different from previous empires, they were as unstable as all their imperial predecessors. Eventually, around 1600, they reached the limits of their conquests.

Review and Relate

Thinking Through Patterns

> **What patterns characterized the Christian and Muslim imperial competition in the period 1300–1600? Which elements distinguished them from each other, and which elements were similar? How did the pattern change over time?**

> **How did the centralizing state in the Middle East and Europe function in the period 1450–1600? How did economics, military power, and imperial objectives interact to create the centralizing state?**

> **Which patterns did cultural expressions follow in the Habsburg and Ottoman Empires? Why did the ruling classes of these empires sponsor these expressions?**

Examine the ways historians approach the big questions of this chapter.

In 1300, the Ottomans renewed the Arab-Islamic tradition of jihad against the Eastern Christian empire of Byzantium, defeating the empire with the conquest of Constantinople in 1453. They also carried the war into the western Mediterranean and Indian Ocean. In Western Christian Iberia, the rekindling of the reconquest was more successful. Invigorated by a merging of the concepts of the Crusade and the *Reconquista*, the Iberians expanded overseas to circumvent the Muslims and trade for Indian spices directly. The so-called Age of Exploration is rooted in the Western traditions of war against Islamic civilization.

In the mid-1400s, the Middle East and Europe returned to the pattern of imperial state formation after a lull during which states had competed against each other within their respective commonwealths. The element which fueled this return was gunpowder weaponry. The use of cannons and handheld firearms became widespread during this time but required major financial outlays on the part of the states. The two empires became states based on a money economy: Bureaucracies maintained centralized departments that regulated the collection of taxes and the payroll of soldiers.

The rulers of these empires were concerned to portray themselves, their military, and their bureaucracies as highly successful and just. The state had to be as visible and benevolent as possible. Rulers, therefore, were builders of palaces, churches, or mosques. They celebrated religious and secular festivities with great pomp and encouraged ministers and the nobility to do likewise. In the imperial capitals, they patronized architects, artists, and writers, resulting in a veritable explosion of intellectual and artistic creativity. In this regard, the Ottomans and the Habsburgs followed similar patterns of cultural expression.

| Against the Grain

Consider this as a counterpoint to the main patterns examined in this chapter.

Tilting at Windmills

Cervantes's *The Ingenious Gentleman Don Quixote of La Mancha* contributed to the rise of the novel as a characteristic European form of literary expression. Cervantes composed his novel in opposition to the dominant literary conventions of his time—as he wrote, to "ridicule the absurdity of those books of chivalry, which have, as it were, fascinated the eyes and judgement of the world, and in particular of the vulgar."

Every episode in this novel parodies one or another absurdity in society. The frame is provided by the fictional figure of Cide Hamete Benengeli, a purportedly perfidious Muslim and historian who might have been lying when he chronicled the lives of the knight Don Quixote and his squire Sancho Panza. Don Quixote's joust, or "tilting," against windmills has become a powerful metaphor for rebelling against the overpowering conventions of society.

Don Quixote is today acclaimed as the second-most-printed text after the Bible. Over the past four centuries, each generation has interpreted the text anew. Revolutionary France saw Don Quixote as a doomed visionary; German Romantics, as a hero destined to fail; Communists, as an anti-capitalist rebel before his time; and secular progressives, as an unconventional hero at the dawn of modern free society. For Karl Marx, Don Quixote was the hidalgo who yearned for a return to the feudal aristocracy of the past. Sigmund Freud saw the knight-errant as "tragic in his helplessness while the plot is unraveled." In our own time, Don Quixote has become the quintessential postmodern figure; in the words of Michel Foucault, his "truth is not in the relation of the words to the world but in that slender and constant relation woven between themselves as verbal signs." As a tragic or comic figure, Don Quixote continues to be the irresistible symbol of opposition.

- What explains the lasting literary success of Don Quixote?

- Why has the phrase "tilting at windmills" undergone a change of meaning from the original "fighting imaginary foes" to "taking on a situation against all seeming evidence" in our own time?

Key Terms

audio flashcards

Apocalypse 360	Janissaries 372	Moriscos 369
Corsairs 358	Military orders 360	Passion play 376
Devşirme 372	Money economy 371	Tax farming 372

For additional resources, please go to
www.oup.com/us/vonsivers.
Please see the Further Resources section at the back of the book for additional readings and suggested websites.

AXIOMATA
SIVE
LEGES MOTUS

Lex. I.

Corpus omne perseverare in statu suo quiescendi vel movendi uniformiter in directum, nisi quatenus a viribus impressis cogitur statum illum mutare.

Projectilia perseverant in motibus suis nisi quatenus a resisten-

Actioni contrariam semper & æqualem esse reactionem : sive corporum duorum actiones in se mutuo semper esse æquales & in partes contrarias dirigi.

Quicquid premit vel trahit alterum, tantundem ab eo premitur vel trahitur. Siquis lapidem digito premit, premitur & hujus digitus a lapide. Si equus lapidem funi alligatum trahit, retrahetur etiam & equus æqualiter in lapidem: nam funis utrinque distentus eodem relaxandi se conatu urgebit Equum versus lapidem, ac lapidem versus equum, tantumque impediet progressum unius quantum promovet progressum alterius. Si corpus aliquod in corpus aliud impingens, motum ejus vi sua quomodocunque mutaverit, idem quoque vicissim in motu proprio eandem mutationem in partem contrariam vi alterius (ob æqualitatem pressionis mutuæ) subibit. His actionibus æquales fiunt mutationes non velocitatum sed motuum, (scilicet in corporibus non aliunde impeditis:) Mu-

» Chapter 17   1450–1750

The Renaissance, New Sciences, and Religious Wars in Europe

One of the most remarkable scientific minds of the seventeenth century was Maria Cunitz (ca. 1607–1664). Under the tutorship of her father, a physician, she became accomplished in six languages, the humanities, and the sciences. During the Thirty Years' War (1618–1648), as Cunitz and her Protestant family sought refuge in a Cistercian monastery, she wrote *Urania propitia* (*Companion to Urania*), in praise of the Greek muse and patron of astronomy. When the family returned home, Cunitz continued to devote her life to science through her careful astronomical observations.

Cunitz's book is a popularization of the astronomical tables of Johannes Kepler (1571–1630), who discovered the elliptical trajectories of the planets. Cunitz's book, published privately in 1650, makes corrections in Kepler's tables and offers simplified calculations of star positions. It was generally well received, although there were a few detractors who found it hard to believe that a woman could succeed in the sciences.

Cunitz lived in a time when Western Christianity had entered the age of early global interaction, from 1450 until 1750. Europe remained

URBAN POPULATION OF EUROPE IN 1700

London   Amsterdam
Paris

Naples

- Over 30%
- 25–30%
- 10–15%
- 5–10%
- 1–5%
- 0–1%
- city with population over 200,000

ABOVE: In his *Principia Mathematica*, first published in 1687, Isaac Newton (1643–1727) unified physics and astronomy into a single mathematic system.

institutionally similar to the other parts of the world, especially the Middle East, India, China, and Japan. Rulers throughout Eurasia governed by divine grace. All large states followed patterns of political centralization, and their economies depended on the productivity of agriculture.

Culturally, however, northwestern Europe began to move in a different direction from Islamic, Hindu, Neo-Confucian, and Buddhist civilizations after 1500. New developments in the sciences and philosophy in Europe initiated new cultural patterns. As significant as these patterns were, these new mathematized sciences remained limited to a relatively few educated persons, largely outside the ruling classes. Their ideas diverged substantially from those represented by the Catholic and Protestant ruling classes and resulted in tensions or even repression of scientists by the authorities. The new scientific and intellectual culture broadened after 1750 and eventually led to the Industrial Revolution.

The European Renaissance, Baroque, and New Sciences began with the appropriation of the Greek and Roman cultural heritage, allegedly absent from the Middle Ages, by an educated elite. However, this elite overestimated the extent of their break from the Middle Ages. Scholars today understand this break as far less radical, with much in culture remaining unchanged. Similarly, the political and social changes of the period 1400–1750 have to be balanced against inherited continuities. While the seeds of a departure of Western Christianity from the general patterns of agrarian–urban society were planted around 1500, the "great divergence" from the agrarian–urban patterns of Islamic, Hindu, and Chinese civilizations began only after 1750.

Cultural Transformations: Renaissance, Baroque, and New Sciences

The **Renaissance** was a period of cultural transformation in the fifteenth century that followed the scholastic Middle Ages in Western Christianity. Its thinkers and artists considered their period a time of "rebirth" (which is the literal meaning of "renaissance" in French). They were powerfully influenced by the writings of Greek and Hellenistic-Roman authors who had been unknown during the scholastic age. In the sixteenth century, the Renaissance gave way to the Baroque in the arts and the **New Sciences**.

The Renaissance and Baroque Arts
An outpouring of learning, scholarship, and art began around 1400 in Italy and spread through northwestern Europe. Thinkers and artists benefited from Greek and Hellenistic-Roman texts that scholars had discovered in Byzantium. The emerging cultures of the Renaissance and Baroque were creative adaptations of those Greek

Seeing Patterns

≫ What were the reasons for the cultural change that began in Europe with the Renaissance around 1400? In which ways were the subsequent patterns of cultural change different from those in the other religious civilizations of Eurasia?

≫ When and how did the mathematization of the sciences begin, and how did it gain popularity in northwestern Europe? Why is the popularization of the sciences important for understanding the period 1500–1750?

≫ What were the patterns of centralized state formation and transformation in the period 1400–1750? How did the Protestant Reformation and religious wars modify these patterns?

Renaissance: "Rebirth" of culture based on new publications and translations of Greek, Hellenistic, and Roman authors whose writings were previously unknown in Western Christianity.

New Sciences: Mathematized sciences, such as physics, introduced in the 1500s.

and Hellenistic-Roman writings to the cultural heritage of Western Christianity. This vibrant mixture led to the movement of **humanism**.

New Manuscripts and Printing   Eastern Christian Byzantium experienced a cultural revival between 1261 and the 1453 Muslim Ottoman conquest of Constantinople. Italian scholars, aware of how much of Greek literature was still absent from Western Christianity, invited Eastern Christian scholars to bring manuscripts to Italy for teaching and translation. Their students became fluent in Greek and translated Hesiod and Homer, Greek plays, Plato and the Neo-Platonists, the works of Aristotle, Hellenistic scientific texts, and the Greek church fathers.

The dissemination of these works was helped by the development of paper. Experimentation in the 1430s with movable metal typeface led to the printing press. A half century later, a printing revolution had taken place in Europe.

Philology and Political Theory   This examination of manuscripts encouraged the study of Greek, Latin, and Hebrew philology. The best-known philologist was the Dutchman Desiderius Erasmus (1466–1536), who published an edition of the Greek and Latin New Testaments in 1516.

Another approach emerged as a central element in political thought. In *The Prince*, Niccolò Machiavelli (1469–1527) argued that what Italy needed was a unifier who possessed what Aristotle discussed in Book 5 of his *Politics*: a person of indomitable spirit (Italian, *virtù*) to take the proper steps when political success was to be achieved. Many Renaissance scholars preferred Plato, but Machiavelli remained faithful to Aristotle—an Aristotle later esteemed by the American founding fathers.

The Renaissance Arts   In Italy, a new artistic way of looking at the Roman past and the natural world emerged. The first artists to adopt this perspective were the sculptor Donatello (ca. 1386–1466) and the architect Filippo Brunelleschi (1377–1446), who received their inspiration from Roman imperial statues and ruins. The artistic triumvirate of the high Italian Renaissance was composed of Leonardo da Vinci (1452–1519), Michelangelo (1475–1564), and Raphael (1483–1520). Inspired by the Italian creative outburst, the Renaissance flourished also in Germany, the Netherlands, and France.

For musical composers of the Renaissance, the difficulty was that the music of the Greeks or Romans was completely unknown. A partial solution for this difficulty

---

Chapter Outline

- Cultural Transformations: Renaissance, Baroque, and New Sciences

- Centralizing States and Religious Upheavals

- Putting It All Together

Humanism: Intellectual movement focusing on human culture, in such fields as philosophy, philology, and literature, and based on the corpus of Greek and Roman texts.

---

interactive timeline

| 1506–1558 Reign of King Charles V of Spain | 1517 Martin Luther posts his 95 theses; beginning of Protestant Reformation | 1545 Beginning of Catholic Reformation | 1565–1620 Dutch Protestant war of liberation from Spain | 1589–1610 Reign of King Henry IV of France |

| 1514 First formulation of the heliocentric solar system by Nicolaus Copernicus | 1524–1525 German Peasants' War | 1562–1598 French war of religion | 1571–1630 Johannes Kepler, discoverer of the elliptical paths of the planets |

| 1556–1598 Reign of King Philip II of Spain, the Netherlands, and the Americas | 1618–1648 Thirty Years' War in Germany | 1643–1715 King Louis XIV of France | 1688 "Glorious Revolution" in England | 1740–1786 Frederick II, builder of the centralizing state of Prussia |

| 1604 Galileo Galilei's first formulation of the mathematical law of falling bodies | 1639–1660 Religious wars and aftermath in England, Scotland, and Ireland | 1687 Isaac Newton unifies physics and astronomy | 1690 Denis Papin's first steam engine |

was found through emphasizing the relationship between the word—that is, rhetoric—and music. In the sixteenth century this emphasis coincided with the Protestant and Catholic demand for liturgical music, such as hymns and masses.

The theater was a relatively late expression of the Renaissance. The popular mystery, passion, and morality plays from the centuries prior to 1400 continued in Catholic countries. In Italy, in the course of the fifteenth century, the *commedia dell'arte* (a secular popular theater) emerged. In England during the sixteenth century, theater troupes became stationary and professional. Sponsored by the aristocracy and the Elizabethan court, the best-known playwright was William Shakespeare (1564–1616).

Albrecht Dürer, *The Fall of Man (Adam and Eve)*, 1504

The Baroque Arts The Renaissance gave way around 1600 to the Baroque, which dominated the arts until about 1750. Two factors influenced its emergence. First, the Protestant Reformation, Catholic Reformation, and religious wars changed the nature of patronage, on which artists depended. Many Protestant churches, opposed to imagery as incompatible with their view of early Christianity, did not sponsor artists for the adornment of their buildings with religious art.

Second, the predilection for Renaissance balance and restraint gave way to greater spontaneity and dramatic effect. Church and palace architecture shifted to the "baroque" voluptuousness of forms and decorations seen in Bavarian and Austrian Catholic churches, the Versailles Palace, and St. Paul's Cathedral in London, all completed between 1670 and 1750. Baroque composers, as exemplified by the Italian Antonio Vivaldi (1678–1741) and the German Johann Sebastian Bach (1685–1750), benefited from ample church and palace patronage.

The New Sciences

Italian Renaissance scholars were divided between those who continued to adhere to the scholastic Aristotelian scientific method and those (such as Copernicus) who were more interested in newly translated Hellenistic mathematical, astronomical, and geographical texts. In the 1600s, two scientists—Galileo and Newton—abandoned much of the *qualitative* scientific method of Aristotelian scholasticism in favor of the *mathematized* science of physics. In the eighteenth century, Newton's science of a mechanical, deterministic universe became the foundation of modern scientific–industrial society.

Copernicus's Incipient New Science Nicolaus Copernicus (1473–1543) was born in Torún, a German-founded city under Polish rule. He studied at the University of Kraków, the only eastern European school to offer courses in astronomy. During the years 1495–1504, he continued his studies at Italian universities. In 1500 he taught mathematics in Rome and perhaps read Greek astronomical texts translated from Arabic. After he graduated with a degree in canon law, Copernicus took an administrative position at the cathedral of Torún, which allowed him time to pursue astronomical research. One text Copernicus did read, the *Geography* written by the Hellenistic cosmographer Ptolemy, proposed the geographical concept of Earth as a globe composed of a single sphere of intermingled earth and water.

Between 1507 and 1514 Copernicus realized that the discovery of the Americas in 1492 provided empirical proof for the theory of the world as a single earth-water sphere. It is likely that he saw the new world map by the German cartographer

Renaissance Art. Brunelleschi's cupola for the cathedral of Florence, completed in 1436, was one of the greatest achievements of the early Renaissance (a). Raphael's School of Athens (1509–1510) depicts some 50 philosophers and scientists, with Plato (in red tunic) and Aristotle (blue) in the center of the painting (b).

Copernicus's heliocentric universe

Martin Waldseemüller (ca. 1470–1520), which made him aware of the Americas as hitherto unknown inhabited lands on the other side of the world.

As a result, Copernicus firmly espoused the Ptolemaic theory of the single intermingled water-earth sphere. A globe with well-distributed water and landmasses is a perfect body that moves in perfect circular paths, he argued further. He formulated a hypothesis, according to which the earth is a body that has the same appearance and performs the same motions as the other bodies in the planetary system, especially the sun with its similar path. This revolutionary idea removed the earth from the center of the planetary system and made it revolve around the sun.

Galileo's Mathematical Physics   In the decades between the births of Copernicus and Galileo Galilei (1564–1642), mathematics improved considerably. Euclid's *Elements* was retranslated correctly from the original Greek in 1543. A translation in 1544 of a text on floating and descending bodies by the Hellenistic scholar Archimedes (287–212 BCE) also attracted intense scholarly attention.

In 1604, Galileo combined geometry, algebra, and Archimedean physics to formulate his mathematical "law of falling bodies." While earlier scholars reflected on the logical and/or geometric properties of motion only "according to imagination," Galileo systematically combined imagination with empirical research and experimentation. He thereby established what we now call the (mathematized) New Sciences.

Running Afoul of the Church   Galileo was one of the first astronomers to use a telescope, which had been recently invented in Flanders. On the basis of his astronomical work, in 1610 he became chief mathematician and philosopher at the court of the Medici, the ruling family of Florence. But his increasing fame also attracted the enmity of the Catholic Church.

As a proponent of Copernican heliocentrism, Galileo seemed to contradict the passage in the Hebrew Bible where God recognized the motion of the sun around

Waldseemüller's 1507 World Map. The German mapmaker Martin Waldseemüller was the first western Christian to draw a world map which included the newly discovered Americas. He gave them the name "America" after the Italian explorer Amerigo Vespucci (1454–1512), who was the first to state that the Americas were a separate landmass, unconnected to Asia. The single copy of Waldseemüller's map still extant is among the holdings of the US Library of Congress.

image analysis

the earth. (In Joshua 10:12–13, God stopped the sun's revolution for a day.) In contrast to the more tolerant pope at the time of Copernicus, the Roman Inquisition favored a strictly literal interpretation of this passage. In 1632 Galileo was condemned to house arrest and forced to make a public repudiation of heliocentrism.

The condemnation of Galileo had a chilling effect on scientists in countries where the Catholic Reformation was dominant. During the seventeenth century, interest in the New Sciences shifted to France, Germany, the Netherlands, and England. In these countries, no single church authority was sufficiently dominant to enforce the literal understanding of scripture. As a result, these countries produced mathematicians, astronomers, physicists, and inventors, Catholic as well as Protestant. It was this relative intellectual freedom, not sympathy on the part of religious authorities for the New Sciences, which allowed the latter to flourish, especially in the Netherlands and England.

Galileo's views of the moon

Iberian Natural Sciences   Southern European countries were still well situated to make substantial scientific contributions, even if not in the New Sciences. Botanists, geographers, ethnographers, physicians, and metallurgists fanned out across the new colonies to research the new plants, diseases, peoples, and mineral resources of the New World, Africa, and Asia. They used the traditional methods of the natural sciences and accumulated a voluminous amount of knowledge. For long periods, the Habsburg monarch kept these discoveries hidden, fearful that colonial competitors would benefit from them. It is only recently that the Iberian contributions to the sciences in the 1500s and 1600s have become more widely known.

Isaac Newton's Mechanics   In the middle of the English struggles between the Protestants and the Catholic/Catholicizing Stuart monarchs, Isaac Newton (1643–1727) brought the New Sciences of Copernicus and Galileo to their culmination. As a professor at the University of Cambridge, his primary early contribution was calculus, which he developed at the same time as the German philosopher Gottfried Wilhelm Leibniz (1646–1716). Later in his career, Newton unified the fields of physics and astronomy, establishing the so-called Newtonian synthesis. His *Mathematical Principles of Natural Philosophy*, published in 1687, established a deterministic universe following mathematical rules and formed the basis of science until the early twentieth century, when Albert Einstein's theory of relativity superseded Newtonianism.

The New Sciences and Their Social Impact

Scientists in the seventeenth century met each other in scientific societies or residential salons. Popularizers introduced the public to the New Sciences. Scientific instruments such as telescopes, microscopes, thermometers, and barometers were constantly improving. Experimentation with barometers, vacuum chambers, and cylinders operating with condensing steam culminated with the invention of the steam engine in England in 1712.

New Science Societies   When the Catholic Reformation drove the New Sciences to northwestern Europe, chartered scientific societies, such as the Royal Society of London (1660) and the Paris Academy of Sciences (1666), were established. These societies co-opted scientists as fellows, held regular meetings, challenged their fellows to answer scientific questions, awarded prizes, and organized expeditions. They also published their findings. Many societies attracted thousands of members representing an important cross section of seventeenth-century urban society in northwest Europe (see Map 17.1).

The New Science triumphed in northwestern Europe in a large, scientifically and technically interested public of experimenters, engineers, instrument makers, artisans, business people, and lay folk. Popularizers lectured to audiences of middle-class amateurs, instrument makers, and craftspeople, especially in England and the Netherlands. Coffeehouses allowed the literate urban public to meet, hear lectures, read the daily newspapers (first appearing in the early seventeenth century), and exchange ideas. Wealthy businessmen endowed public lectures and supported elaborate experiments and expensive laboratory equipment. Male urban literacy is estimated to have exceeded 50 percent in England and the Netherlands during this period, although it remained considerably lower in France, Germany, and Italy.

Women, Social Salons, and the New Science   Women were part of this scientifically inclined public. In the fields of mathematics and astronomy, Sophie Brahe (1556–1643), sister of the Danish astronomer Tycho Brahe (1546–1601), and Maria Cunitz (p. 380) made contributions to the new astronomy of Copernicus and Kepler. According to estimates, in the second half of the seventeenth century some 14 percent of German astronomers were women. A dozen prominent female astronomers practiced their science privately in Germany, Poland, the Netherlands, France, and England.

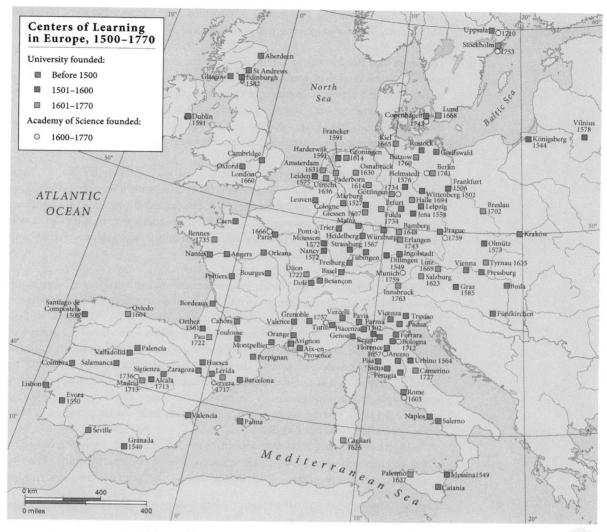

Centers of Learning in Europe, 1500–1770

University founded:
- ■ Before 1500
- ■ 1501–1600
- ■ 1601–1770

Academy of Science founded:
- ○ 1600–1770

MAP **17.1 Centers of Learning in Europe, 1500–1770.**

map analysis

Another institution that helped in the popularization of the New Sciences was the salon. As the elegant living room of an urban residence, the salon was a meeting place for the urban social elite to engage in conversations, presentations, and experiments. The culture of the salon emerged first in Paris. Since the Catholic French universities were hostile to many new ideas, educated urban aristocrats and middle-class professionals turned to the salons as places to learn about new scientific developments. Furthermore, French universities and scientific academies refused to admit women, in contrast to Italian and German institutions. The French salon, therefore, became a bastion of female scholars.

One example of a French woman scientist was Gabrielle-Émilie du Châtelet (1706–1749). In a Paris salon she met François-Marie Arouet, known as Voltaire (1694–1778), a writer, skeptic, satirist, and amateur Newtonian. Although Voltaire published prolifically, Châtelet eventually outstripped him in both research and scientific understanding. Her lasting achievement was the translation of Newton's *Mathematical Principles* into French, published in 1759.

Discovery of the Vacuum   Of all the scientific instruments available at the time, it was the barometer that would prove crucial for the exploration of the properties of the vacuum and condensing steam, eventually leading to the invention of the steam engine. The scientist who laid the groundwork for the barometer was Evangelista Torricelli (1608–1647), an assistant of Galileo. He experimented with mercury-filled glass tubes, demonstrating that atmospheric pressure produced a vacuum inside these tubes.

A few years later, the French mathematician and philosopher Blaise Pascal (1623–1662) used a mercury barometer to demonstrate lower air pressures at higher altitudes. Soon thereafter, scientists discovered the connection between changing atmospheric pressures and the weather. The discovery of the vacuum was an important step toward the practical application of the New Sciences to mechanical engineering in the eighteenth century.

The Steam Engine   The French Huguenot scientist and engineer Denis Papin (ca. 1647–1712) made the first step from the vacuum chamber to the steam engine. In 1690, Papin constructed a cylinder with a piston. Weights, via a cord and two pulleys, held the piston at the top of the cylinder. When heated, water in the bottom of the cylinder turned into steam. When subsequently cooled through the injection of water, the steam condensed, forcing the piston down and lifting the weights up. The Royal Society of London held discussions of his papers, thereby alerting engineers, craftspeople, and entrepreneurs in England to the steam engine as a labor-saving machine. In 1712, the mechanic Thomas Newcomen built the first steam engine to pump water from coal mine shafts.

Altogether, it took a little over a century for Europeans to apply the New Sciences to engineering—that is, to the construction of the steam engine. Prior to 1600, mechanical inventions—such as the wheel, the compass, the stern rudder,

Vacuum Power. In 1672, the mayor of Magdeburg, the New Scientist Otto von Guericke, demonstrated the experiment that made him a pioneer in the understanding of the physical properties of the vacuum. In the presence of German emperor Ferdinand III, two teams of horses were unable to pull the two sealed hemispheres apart. Guericke had created a vacuum by pumping out the air from the two sealed copper spheres.

and the firearm—had been constructed by anonymous tinkerers. By 1700, engineers needed at least a basic understanding of mathematics and such abstract physical phenomena as inertia, gravity, vacuums, and condensing steam in order to build a steam engine or other complex machinery.

The New Sciences: Philosophical Interpretations

The New Sciences engendered a pattern of radically new intellectual, religious, and political thinking. This thought evolved into a powerful instrument of critique of Christian doctrine and the constitutional order of the absolutist states. Through the new concept of the social contract, these ideas became a potent political force in the course of the 1700s.

Descartes's New Philosophy The first major New Scientist who started a radical reconsideration of philosophy was the Frenchman René Descartes (1596–1650). In the service of the Dutch and Bavarian courts, he bore witness to the atrocities committed in the name of religious doctrines during the Thirty Years' War. He spent two decades in the Netherlands, studying and teaching the New Sciences. His principal innovation in mathematics was the discovery that geometry could be converted, through algebra, into analytic geometry.

Descartes, selections from *A Discourse on Method* (1637)

Descartes was shocked by the condemnation of Galileo and decided to abandon all traditional propositions and doctrines of the church. Realizing that the five senses of seeing, hearing, touching, smelling, and tasting were unreliable, he determined that the only reliable body of knowledge was thought, especially mathematical thought. As a person capable of thought, he concluded—bypassing his unreliable senses—that he existed: "I think, therefore I am" (*cogito ergo sum*). A further conclusion from this argument was that he was composed of two radically different substances, a material substance consisting of his body (that is, his senses) and another, immaterial substance consisting of his thinking mind.

Variations on Descartes's New Philosophy Descartes's radical distinction between body and mind stimulated a lively debate. Was this distinction only conceptual, while reality was experienced as a unified whole? If the dualism was real as well as conceptual, which substance was more fundamental, sensual bodily experience or mental activity, as the creator of the concepts of experience? The answers of three philosophers—Baruch Spinoza, Thomas Hobbes, and John Locke—set the course for two major directions of philosophy during the so-called Enlightenment of the 1700s (see Chapter 23), one Continental European and the other Anglo-American.

For Baruch Spinoza (1632–1677), Descartes's distinction between body and mind was to be understood only in a conceptual sense. He therefore abandoned Descartes's distinction and developed a philosophical system that sought to integrate Galilean nature, the ideas of God, the Good in ethics, and the Just in politics into a unified whole. The Jewish community of Amsterdam, into which he had been born, excommunicated him for heresy, since he seemed to make God immanent in the world.

Both Thomas Hobbes (1588–1679) and John Locke (1632–1704) not only accepted Descartes's radical distinction; they furthermore made the body the fundamental reality and the mind a dependent function. Consequently, they focused on the bodily passions, not reason, as the principal human character trait. Hobbes

Mapping the World

In 1400, no accurate map of the world existed anywhere. Prior to the first Portuguese sailing expeditions down the west coast of Africa in the 1420s and 1430s, mariners relied upon local knowledge of winds, waves, and stars to navigate. The Portuguese were the first to use science to sail, adapting scholarship in trigonometry, astronomy, and solar timekeeping developed by Jewish and Muslim scientists in Iberia.

Crucial to this approach was latitude, which required precise calculations of the daily changes in the path of the sun relative to the earth and determination of the exact height of the sun. The invention of the nautical astrolabe in 1497 by the Jewish scientist Abraham Zacuto aided this process. To determine longitude, Jewish scientists in Portugal adapted a method based on the work of the Islamic astronomer al-Biruni (973–1048).

The new maps of the fifteenth century also drew upon an innovation from another part of the world: the compass. Originating in China, the compass was used as a navigational instrument by Muslim sailors during the twelfth century. In the thirteenth century, mapmakers in the Mediterranean began to include compasses

frontispiece to *Leviathan*

Locke, *An Essay Concerning Human Understanding* (1690)

speculated that individuals in the primordial state of nature were engaged in a "war of all against all." To survive, they forged a social contract in which they transferred all power to a sovereign. Hobbes's book *Leviathan* (1651) can be read as a political theory of absolute rule, but his ideas of a social contract and transfer of power nevertheless move toward constitutionalism.

Locke focused on the more benign bodily passion of acquisitiveness. Primordial individuals, so he argued, engaged as equals in a social contract for the purpose of erecting a government that protected their properties and established a civil society governed by law. With Hobbes and Locke a line of new thought came to its conclusion, leading from Descartes's two substances to the ideas of absolutism as well as democratic constitutionalism.

Centralizing States and Religious Upheavals

The pattern of the centralizing state transforming the institutional structures of society was characteristic not only of the Ottoman and Habsburg Empires during 1450–1750, but also of other countries of Europe, the Middle East, and India. The financial requirements for such a state required a reorganization of the relationship between rulers, ruling classes, and regional forces. Although the Protestant Reformation and religious wars slowed the pattern of central state formation, two types of states eventually emerged: the French, Russian, and Prussian landed centralizing state and the Dutch and English naval centralizing state.

The Rise of Centralized Kingdoms

The shift from feudal knights to firearm-equipped professional infantries led to states whose rulers sought to strengthen their administrations. Rulers centralized state

on portolans, or nautical charts, enabling sailors to follow their direction on a map.

With an accurate science for fixing latitude and improved knowledge for longitude, the science of cartography was transformed in the fifteenth and sixteenth centuries. Any place on earth could be mapped mathematically in relation to any other place, and the direction in which one place lay in relation to another could be plotted using compass lines. By 1500 mapmakers could locate any newly discovered place in the world on a map.

Portolan by Pedro Reinel.
Drawn in 1504 by the great Portuguese cartographer Pedro Reinel (ca. 1462–ca. 1542), this nautical chart (portolan) shows compass lines and is the earliest known map to include lines of latitude.

Questions

- How were adaptations from various cultural traditions essential to the transformation of cartography in the fifteenth and sixteenth centuries?

- How are developments in cartography in this time period an example of the shift from descriptive science to mathematical science?

power, collected taxes, and curbed the decentralizing forces of the nobility, cities, and local institutions. Not all city-states, city-leagues, and religious orders dating to the previous period (600–1450) survived the race to centralization. A winnowing process during 1450–1550 left only a few kingdoms in control of European politics.

The Demographic Curve Following the demographic disaster of the Black Death, the population of the European states expanded again after 1470 and continued to grow until about 1600, when it entered a half century of stagnation during the coldest and wettest period in recorded history, the Little Ice Age (1550–1750).

During 1650–1750, the population rose slowly at a moderate rate from 105 to 140 million. The overall population figures for Europe demonstrate that Western Christianity had risen by 1750 to demographic equivalence to the two leading religious civilizations of India (155 million) and China (225 million).

A Heritage of Decentralization Bracketed between the two empires of the Ottomans and Habsburgs, Western Christian Europe during the second half of the fifteenth century was comprised of independent or autonomous units, including the centralizing kingdoms of France and England; the Hanseatic League of trading cities; the territory ruled by the Catholic crusading order of Teutonic Knights; and the small kingdoms of Denmark, Sweden, Norway, Poland–Lithuania, Bohemia, and Hungary. It furthermore comprised the principalities and cities of Germany, the duchy of Burgundy, the republic of Switzerland, and the city-states of Italy. At the northeastern periphery was the Grand Duchy of Moscow, representing Eastern Christianity after the fall of Byzantium to the Ottomans in 1453. These units competed with each other.

Military and Administrative Capacities In the course of the sixteenth century, some kingdoms turned their mercenary troops into standing armies and stationed them in star-shaped forts. Habsburg imperial as well as Dutch troops introduced the line infantry in the course of the sixteenth century. Since the line formation required peacetime drills and maneuvers, the regimental system came into use. Soldiers formed permanent regiments and wore standardized uniforms.

The French-invented flintlock gradually replaced the matchlock musket during 1620–1630. Similarly, during 1660–1700 the French introduced and improved the bayonet. By 1750, armies in the larger European countries were more uniform in their armaments and increased to tens of thousands of soldiers (see Map 17.2).

The military forces were expensive, and taxes expanded during the period 1450–1550. But rulers could not raise taxes without the assent of the ruling classes and cities. Villagers simply moved when taxes became too oppressive. The taxation limits were reached in most European countries in the mid-sixteenth century, and for the next two centuries rulers could raise finances only to the detriment of their central powers, such as by borrowing from merchants and selling offices.

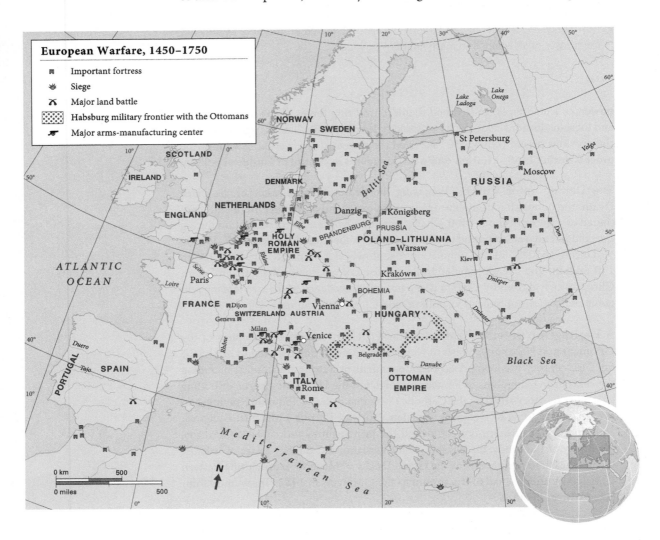

MAP **17.2** **European Warfare, 1450–1750.**

The Netherlands was an exception. Only there did the urban population rise from 10 to 40 percent, willing to pay higher taxes on expanded urban manufactures and commercial suburban farming. The Dutch government also derived revenues from charters granted to overseas trading companies. Given the severe limits on revenue-raising measures in most of Europe, the eighteenth century saw a general deterioration of state finances, which eventually contributed to the American and French Revolutions.

The Protestant Reformation, State Churches, and Independent Congregations

Parallel to the centralism of the kings, the popes restored the central role of the Vatican in the church hierarchy. The popes undertook expensive Vatican construction projects that aroused criticism, especially in Germany, where the leading clergy was strongly identified with Rome. Growing literacy and lay religiosity nurtured a profound theological dissatisfaction, leading to the **Protestant Reformation**. The Reformation began as a movement in the early sixteenth century that demanded a return to the simplicity of early Christianity. The movement quickly engulfed the kingdoms and resulted in religious wars. The divisions mark the culture of Europe even today.

Background to the Reformation   Religious and political changes in the fifteenth century led to the Protestant Reformation. One religious shift was the growth of popular theology, a consequence of the introduction of the printing press (1454/1455). Devotional tracts catered to the spiritual interests of ordinary people. Many Christians attended Mass daily. Wealthy Christians endowed saint cults and charitable institutions; poor people studied scripture on their own.

A key political change was an increasing inability of the popes to appoint archbishops and bishops outside Italy. The kings of France, Spain, England, and Sweden were transforming their kingdoms into centralized states, reducing the influence of the popes. (The popes' influence remained strong in a politically splintered Germany.) What remained to the popes was the right to collect dues, which they used to finance their expensive administration in Rome. One of the dues was the sale of **indulgences**, which, in popular understanding, were tickets to heaven. Those disturbed by the discrepancy between declining papal power and the remaining financial privileges demanded reforms.

Luther's Reformation   One such observer was the German monk, priest, and professor Martin Luther (1483–1546). In 1517 he wrote his archbishop a letter with 95 theses in which he condemned the indulgences and other matters as contrary to scripture. What was to become the Protestant Reformation had begun.

News of Luther's protest traveled across Europe. Sales of indulgences fell off sharply. In a series of writings, Luther spelled out further reforms. One reform was the elevation of original New Testament scripture over canon law and papal decisions. Another reform was the declaration of the priesthood of all Christians, doing away with the privileged position of the clergy. A third reform was a call to German princes to begin church reform through their power over clerical appointments, even if the Habsburg emperor was opposed. Finally, by translating the Bible into German, Luther made the text available to all.

Protestant Reformation: Broad movement to reform the Roman Catholic Church, the beginnings of which are usually associated with Martin Luther.

Erasmus, *Julius Excluded from Heaven* (1514)

Indulgence: Partial remission of sins after payment of a fine or presentation of a donation. Remission would mean the forgiveness of sins by the Church, but the sinner still remained responsible for his or her sins before God.

Reaction to Luther's Demands   Both the emperor and the pope failed to arrest Luther and suppress his call for church reform. Emperor Charles V, a devout Catholic, was distracted by the Ottoman-led Islamic threat in eastern Europe and the western Mediterranean. In addition, his rivalry with the French king precluded the formation of a common Catholic front against Luther. People in Germany exploited Charles's divided attention and abandoned both Catholicism and secular obedience. A savage civil war, called the Peasants' War, engulfed Germany from 1524 to 1525.

Luther and other reformers were horrified by the war. They drew up church ordinances that regulated preaching and other church matters. In Saxony, the duke endorsed this order in 1528, creating the model of Lutheran Protestantism as a state religion with the rulers as protectors and supervisors of the churches in their territories.

Other German princes and the kings of Denmark and Sweden followed suit. In England, Protestants gained strength when Henry VIII (r. 1509–1547) broke with Rome and took over church leadership in his kingdom. Although remaining Catholic, he proclaimed an Anglican state church that combined elements of Catholicism and Protestantism. Switzerland and Scotland also adopted reforms. Thus, most of northern Europe followed a pattern of alliances between Protestant reformers and the state (see Map 17.3).

Calvinism in Geneva and France   In France, King Francis I controlled all church appointments but did not create an independent state church. Since he competed with Charles V of the Habsburg Empire for dominance over the papacy in Italy, he had to appear especially loyal and devout. When Protestants in France demanded church reform, Francis I gave them the choice of exile or burning at the stake.

One reformer who chose exile was John Calvin (Jean Cauvin, 1509–1564). During his exile in Geneva, he began a stormy career as the city's religious reformer. Geneva was unsure about which path of reform to embrace. It was not until the 1550s that Calvin's form of Protestantism prevailed in the city.

A crucial doctrine of Calvin's was *predestination*. According to this doctrine, God has "predestined" each human prior to birth for heaven or hell. Believers could only hope, through faith alone, that they would receive a glimpse of their fate. In contrast to Luther, however, Calvin made the enforcement of a moral code by local authorities, part of his version of Protestantism.

Interestingly, this code did not prohibit the taking of interest on loans. While Luther as well as the Catholic Church, in accordance with scripture, condemned all interest as usury, Calvin placed moneylending into the increasingly urban context of the 1500s. Acquiring wealth with the help of money and thereby perhaps gaining a glimpse of one's fate became a hallmark of Calvinism. Wealth began to become respectable in Christian society.

Calvinist preachers went to France and the Netherlands in the mid-1500s. Under the protection of local magistrates, they organized the first independent Calvinist congregations. Calvinist religious self-organization by independent congregations became an alternative to Lutheran state religion.

The Catholic Reformation   The rivalry between Spain and France made it difficult for the popes to address Catholic reforms in order to meet the Protestant challenge. Finally, at the Council of Trent (1545–1563), they abolished payment for indulgences and phased out other church practices considered to be corrupt.

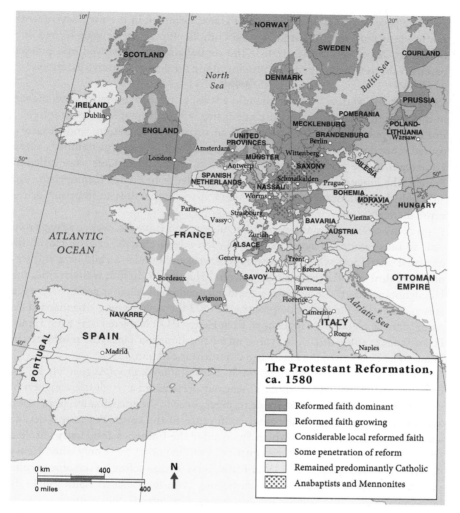

MAP 17.3 **The Protestant Reformation, ca. 1580.**

These actions launched the **Catholic Reformation**, an effort to gain back dissenting Catholics. Supported by the kings of Spain and France, however, the popes made no changes to the traditional doctrines of faith together with good works, priestly mediation between believer and God, and monasticism. They even revived the papal Inquisition and promulgated a new Index of Prohibited Books.

The popes also furthered the work of the priest Ignatius Loyola (1491–1556). At the head of the Jesuits, Loyola devoted himself to the education of the clergy, the establishment of a network of Catholic schools and colleges, and the conversion of Protestants as well as non-Christians by missionaries to the Americas and eastern Asia. Thanks to Jesuit discipline, Catholics regained self-assurance against the Protestants.

Religious Wars and Political Restoration

The growth of Calvinism led to a civil war in France and a war of liberation from Spanish Catholic rule in the Netherlands in the later sixteenth century. In England,

Catholic Reformation: Also known as Counter-Reformation. Reaffirmation of Catholic papal supremacy and the doctrine of faith together with works as preparatory to salvation. Such practices as absenteeism (bishops in Rome instead of their bishoprics) and pluralism (bishops and abbots holding multiple appointments) were abolished.

the slow pace of reform in the Anglican Church erupted in the early seventeenth century into a civil war. In Germany, the Catholic–Protestant struggle turned into the Thirty Years' War (1618–1648). The centralizing states evolved into polities based on absolutism, tempered by provincial and local administrative practices.

Civil War in France   During the mid-1500s, Calvinism in France grew mostly in the western cities, where literate merchants and craftspeople were receptive to Protestant publications. Calvinism was an urban denomination; and peasants, rooted more deeply in traditional ways of life, did not join in large numbers. Some 10 percent of the population were Huguenots, as the Protestants were called in France. The Huguenots posed a formidable challenge to French Catholicism; and although the government persecuted them, it was impossible to imprison or execute them all.

In many cities, relations between Huguenots and Catholics were uneasy. From time to time, groups of agitators crashed each other's church services. Hostilities escalated after 1560, when the government weakened under a child king and was unable to deal with the increasingly powerful Huguenots. In four western cities the Huguenots achieved self-government and full freedom of religious practice from the crown. Concerned to find a compromise, in 1572 the now reigning king married his sister to the leader of the Huguenots, King Henry III of Navarre (later King Henry IV of France, 1589–1610), a Protestant of the Bourbon family in southwestern France. Henry detested the fanaticism that surrounded him.

Only 6 days after the wedding, on St. Bartholomew's Day (August 24, 1572), outraged members of the Catholic aristocracy perpetrated a wholesale slaughter of thousands of Huguenots. This massacre, in response to the assassination of a French admiral, occurred with the apparent connivance of the court. For over a decade and a half, civil war raged, in which Spain aided the Catholics and Henry enrolled German and Swiss Protestant mercenaries. A turning point came only when Henry of Navarre became King Henry IV in 1589. It was 9 years before he was able to calm the religious fanaticism of the French people. With the Edict of Nantes in 1598, he decreed freedom of religion for Protestants. However, Catholic adherents were deeply offended by the edict as well as by the alleged antipapal policies of Henry IV, and the king was assassinated in 1610. In 1685, King Louis XIV revoked the edict and triggered the emigration of Huguenots to the Netherlands, Germany, England, and North America. At last, France was Catholic again.

The Dutch War of Independence   In the Netherlands, the Spanish overlords were determined to keep the country Catholic. When Charles V resigned in 1556 (effective 1558), his son Philip II (r. 1556–1598) became king of Spain and the Netherlands. Like his father, Philip supported the Catholic Reformation. He asked the Jesuits and the Inquisition to aggressively persecute the Calvinists. Philip also subdivided the bishoprics into smaller units and recruited clergymen in place of members of the nobility.

In response, in 1565 the nobility and Calvinist congregations rose in revolt, triggering what was to become a Protestant war of Dutch liberation from Catholic Spanish overlordship (1565–1620). Philip suppressed the liberation movement, reimposed Catholicism, and executed thousands of rebels, many of them members of the Dutch aristocracy.

first Dutch national atlas, 1622

In 1579, rebels renewed the war of liberation. Spain kept fighting the rebellion until acute Spanish financial difficulties prompted the truce of 1609–1621. Although drawn into fighting again during the Thirty Years' War, the Netherlands gained its full independence eventually in 1648.

Civil War in England   The prevalent form of Protestantism in England was Calvinism. During the sixteenth century, the majority of people in England, including Calvinists, belonged to the Anglican Church. English Catholics were a small minority. The percentage of Calvinists was the same as in France before 1685, but the partially reformed Anglican Church under the tolerant queen Elizabeth I (1533–1603) was able to hold them in check.

The Calvinists encompassed moderate and radical tendencies that neutralized each other. Among the radicals were the Puritans, who demanded the abolition of the Anglican clerical hierarchy and a new church order of independent congregations. When Anglican Church reform slowed with the arrival of the Stuart monarchs on the throne of England (1603–1685), unfortunately the balance among the religious tendencies unraveled. As rulers of England, the Stuarts were officially heads of the Anglican state church, but except for the first king, the 3 successors were either Catholics or Catholic sympathizers. Since they were furthermore rulers of what was called the England of the Three Kingdoms they found it impossible to maneuver among the demands of the English Puritans, Scottish Presbyterians (self-governing regional Calvinists), and Catholic Irish. The issue of how little or how far the Anglican Church had been reformed away from Catholicism and how dominant it should be in the three realms became more and more divisive (see Source 17.1).

In addition, the Stuarts were intent on building a centralized state. They collected taxes without the approval of Parliament. Many members of Parliament resented being bypassed. A slight majority in the House of Commons was Puritan, and what they considered the stalled church reform added to their resentment. Eventually, when all tax resources were exhausted, the king had to call Parliament back together. The two sides were unable to come to an agreement, however, and civil war broke out. Since this war was also a conflict among the Three Kingdoms, it had both religious and regional aspects (1639–1651).

Because of widespread pillage and destruction, the indirect effects of the war for the rural population were severe. The New Model Army, a professional body of 22,000 troops raised by the Puritan-dominated English Parliament against the royal forces, caused further upheavals by cleansing villages of their "frivolous" local traditions. In the end, the monarchy was replaced with a republican theocracy, the "Commonwealth of England."

Republic, Restoration, and Revolution   The ruler of this theocracy, Oliver Cromwell (r. 1649–1658), was a Puritan member of the lower nobility and a commander in the New Model Army. After dissolving Parliament, Cromwell handpicked a new parliament but ruled mostly without its consent. Since both Scotland and Ireland were opposed to the English Puritans, Cromwell waged a savage war of submission against the two. The Dutch and Spanish, also opponents of the Puritans, were defeated in naval wars that increased English power in the Atlantic. But fear in Parliament of a permanent centralized state led to a refusal of financial subsidies for the military. After Cromwell's death in 1658, it took just 3 years to restore the Stuart monarchy and the Anglican state church.

The recalled Stuart kings, however, resumed the policies of centralization. As before, the kings rarely called Parliament together and raised funds without its authorization. But their standing army was intended more to intimidate the parliamentarians than to subjugate them. In the "Glorious Revolution" of 1688, a defiant Parliament deposed the king and made his daughter and her Dutch husband the new co-regents.

The Thirty Years' War in Germany Continuing religious tensions in Germany erupted into the Thirty Years' War. Rulers of the German principalities had made either Catholicism or Protestantism their state religion, though most tolerated minorities or even admitted them to offices. The Jesuit-educated Ferdinand II (r. 1619–1637), ruler of the Holy Roman Empire, however, refused to appoint Protestants in majority-Protestant Bohemia. In response, Protestant leaders in 1618 renounced Ferdinand's authority and made the Calvinist prince of the Palatinate in the Rhineland their new king.

In a first round of war (1619–1630), Ferdinand and the Catholic princes suppressed the rebellion and advanced toward northern Germany, capturing Lutheran territories for reconversion to Catholicism and defeating Denmark. In 1630, however, the Lutheran king Gustavus II Adolphus (r. 1611–1632) of Sweden intervened. By aiding the German Lutherans, he hoped to consolidate his predominance in the region. Louis XIII (r. 1610–1643) of France granted Sweden financial subsidies, since he was concerned that Ferdinand's victories would further strengthen the Habsburg grip around France. With the politically motivated alliance between Sweden and France, the German Catholic–Protestant war turned into a war for state dominance in Europe.

The Swedes were initially successful, but withdrew when Gustavus II Adolphus fell. Ferdinand compromised with the Protestant princes of Germany, by reestablishing the prewar divisions, in order to keep the French out of the war. But Louis XIII entered anyway and occupied Habsburg Alsace. Swedish armies, exploiting the French successes against the Habsburgs, fought their way back into Germany. In 1684, the Austrian–German Habsburgs agreed to the Peace of Westphalia.

The agreement provided for religious freedom in Germany and ceded Habsburg territories in Alsace to France and the southern side of the Baltic Sea to Sweden. It granted territorial integrity to all European powers. The Spanish Habsburgs continued their war against France until their defeat in 1659, which accelerated the decline of Spain's overseas power. France emerged as the strongest country in Europe, and the Spanish-dominated Caribbean became an area of open rivalry (see Map 17.4).

Absolutism: Theory of the state in which the unlimited power of the king, ruling under God's divine mandate, was emphasized. In practice, it was neutralized by the nobility and provincial and local communities.

Absolutism in France? During its period of greatest political dominance, France came under the rule of its longest-reigning monarch, King Louis XIV (1643–1715). He made Versailles—a gigantic palace and gardens near Paris, populated with 10,000 courtiers, attendants, and servants—into a site of almost continuous feasting, entertainment, and intrigue. It was here that Louis, the "Sun King," exercised his "absolute" divine mandate upon his aristocracy and commoners alike.

In practice, the **absolutism** of Louis XIV, as well as absolutism in other European countries, was a mixture of centralized and decentralized forces. On one

Centralizing States at War. German imperial troops besiege Swedish troops in the northern German city of Stralsund in 1628. The etching shows typical features of the centralizing state, from top to bottom: galleon-style warships (successors of the caravel); a star-shaped fort (an Italian innovation) designed to withstand artillery barrages; the medieval walls of the city; musket-equipped infantry troops; field cannons; and the colorful Baroque uniforms worn by the musketeers of the period.

hand, after the end of the religious wars in 1648, mercenary armies under autonomous dukes and counts were replaced by permanent armies or navies under the central command of royal relatives or favorites. The kings no longer called assemblies together to have new taxes approved (in France from 1614 to 1789), and thus, many of the nobility's tax privileges disappeared.

On the other hand, kings were aware that true absolutism was possible only if the taxes were collected by centrally salaried employees. However, a centrally paid bureaucracy would have required a central bank with provincial branches, using

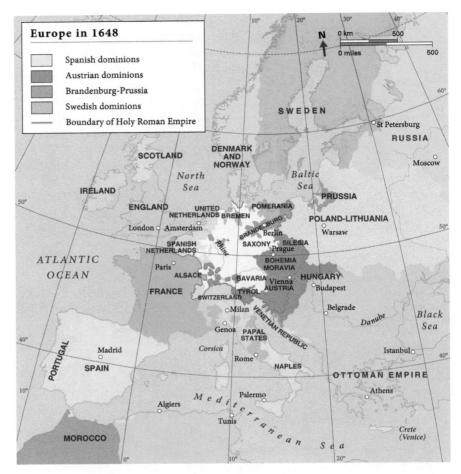

MAP **17.4** **Europe in 1648.**

a credit and debit system. The failed experiment with such a bank in Paris from 1714 to 1720 demonstrates that absolute central control was beyond the powers of the kings.

Instead, the kings had to rely on subcontracting out the collection of taxes to the highest bidders, who then helped themselves to the collection of their incomes. Under Louis XIV anyone who had money or borrowed it from financiers was encouraged to buy an office. The government often forced these officers to grant additional loans to the crown. To retain their loyalty, the government rewarded them with first picks for retaining their offices within the family. They were also privileged to buy landed estates or acquire titles of nobility. By selling offices and titles, the king sought to bind the financial interests of the two nobilities to those of his own.

Louis XIV sent salaried *intendants* to the provinces to ensure that collecting taxes, rendering justice, and policing functioned properly. About half of the provinces had *parlements*—appointed assemblies for the ratification of decrees from Paris—whose officeholders, drawn from the local noble, clerical, and commoner classes, frequently resisted the intendants.

In later years, when Louis XIV was less successful in his wars against the rival Habsburgs and Protestant Dutch, the crown overspent and had to borrow heavily. Louis's successors in the second half of the eighteenth century were saddled with crippling debts.

The Rise of Russia   The ideological embodiment of absolutism in the Versailles of Louis XIV spawned adaptations across Europe. These adaptations were most visible in eastern Europe, which had far fewer towns and cities. Without a large population of urban commoners to aid them in building the centralized state, rulers there had to make do with the landowning aristocracy. As a result, rulers and aristocracy connived to finance state centralization through an increased exploitation of farmers. In the 1600s, the legal status of farmers deteriorated, their tax liabilities increased, and they became serfs.

Peter the Great, "Decree on the Invitation to Foreigners" (1702)

In Russia, **Tsar** Peter I, "the Great" (r. 1682–1725), of the Eastern Christian Romanov dynasty, sought to establish the French-type centralized state. Peter invited western European soldiers, mariners, administrators, craftspeople, scholars, and artists into his service. He built ports on the Baltic Sea and established the new capital of St. Petersburg, with beautiful palaces and official buildings.

Tsar (or Czar): Derived from "Caesar," title used by the Russian rulers to emphasize their imperial ambitions.

The Russian military was completely reorganized by the tsar. Peter made the inherited firearm regiments part of a new army recruited from the traditional Russian landed nobility. Soldiers received education at military schools and academies and were required to provide lifelong service. A census was taken to facilitate the shift from the inherited household tax on the villagers to a new capitation tax collected by military officers. In the process, many farmers now found themselves classified and taxed as serfs, unfree to leave their villages. The result of Peter's reforms was a powerful, expansionary centralizing state (see Map 17.5).

The Rise of Prussia   Similar to Russia, the principality of Prussia-Brandenburg was underurbanized. When the Lutheran Hohenzollern rulers embarked on the construction of a centralized state in the later seventeenth century, they first broke the tax privileges of the landowning aristocracy and raised taxes themselves through agents. As in Russia, farmers who worked on estates held by landlords were serfs. Since there were few urban middle-class merchants and professionals, the kings enrolled members of the landlord aristocracy in the army and civilian administration.

The Hohenzollern monarchs enlarged the army, employing it during peacetime for drainage and canal projects as well as palace construction in Berlin, the capital. Under Frederick II, "the Great" (1740–1786), Prussia pursued an aggressive foreign policy. Frederick also sought to attract immigrants, intensify agriculture, and establish manufacturing. Prussia emerged as a serious competitor of the Habsburgs in the Holy Roman Empire of Germany.

English Constitutionalism   In contrast to Prussia, France, Spain, Austria, and other European states, England had since 1450 a political system ruled by a king or a queen, with a parliament composed of the aristocracy as well as representatives of towns and cities. Only in England did the interests of the nobility and the urban merchants gradually converge: Younger sons, unable to inherit the family estate, sought their fortunes in London. English cities allied with the aristocracy in resisting indirect tax increases and forcing the throne to use the revenues of its royal estates to pay

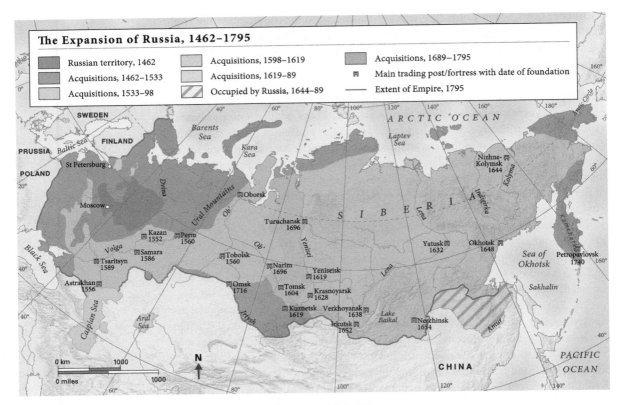

MAP **17.5** **The Expansion of Russia, 1462–1795.**

Prussian Military Discipline. The Prussian line infantry made full use in the mid-1700s of flintlock muskets, bayonets, and drilling.

soldiers. Efforts of the Stuart kings to create a centralized state based on firearm infantries failed. Instead, the ruling class preferred to build a centralized naval state. After the Glorious Revolution of 1688, England became the world's dominant naval power.

After its victory over the Stuart kings, Parliament consolidated its financial powers through the creation of the Bank of England in 1694. When Mary and William died without children, England continued in 1714 with a king from the principality of Hannover in Germany distantly related to the previous royals. Around the same time, England and Scotland united, creating the United Kingdom. Parliament collected taxes and, through its bank, was able to keep its debt service low during the early 1700s. The navy grew twice as large as that of France and was staffed by a well-salaried, disciplined military, while the few land troops were mostly low-paid Hessian-German mercenaries. A two-party system of two aristocracy–merchant alliances emerged. The two parties were known as the Tories and the Whigs, with the Whigs in power for most of the first half of the eighteenth century.

❯ Putting It All Together

Prior to 1500, all religious civilizations possessed mathematics and qualitative sciences. Trigonometry-based astronomy existed in the Islamic, Hindu, and Christian religious civilizations and was practiced also in China. Physics became the second mathematical science in the early 1500s, but only in Western Christianity. This transformation of the sciences had no practical consequences prior to the invention of the steam engine in the 1700s. Furthermore, the mathematization of physics did little to influence the continued prevalence of qualitative description as the methodology of the other sciences.

interactive concept map

Most importantly, the rise of the New Sciences should not be confused with the vast changes, called "modernity" after 1800, which propelled the West to world dominance. Although the West began to acquire its scientific and philosophical identity with the introduction of the mathematical sciences in the century between Copernicus and Galileo (1514–1604), the impact of these sciences on the world was felt only after 1800 when they were applied to industry. Once this application gathered momentum in the nineteenth century, Asia and Africa had no choice but to adapt to modern science and industrialization.

Review and Relate

| Thinking Through Patterns

Examine the ways historians approach the big questions of this chapter.

L ocated far from the traditional agrarian–urban centers of Eurasia, Western Christianity adapted its culture in response to outside stimuli coming from Islamic and Eastern Christian civilizations. Without these stimuli, the Renaissance, Baroque, New Science, and Enlightenment would not have developed. In contrast,

❯ What were the reasons for the cultural changes that began in Europe around 1450? In which ways were the patterns of cultural changes during

1450–1750 different from those in the other religious civilizations of Eurasia?

≫ When and how did the New Sciences begin, and how did they gain popularity in northwestern European society? Why is the popularization of the New Sciences important for understanding the period 1450–1750?

≫ What were the patterns of centralized state formation and transformation in the period 1450–1750? How did the Protestant Reformation and religious wars modify these patterns?

the Middle East, Byzantium, India, and China, originating within the traditional agrarian–urban centers, received far fewer outside stimuli prior to the scientific–industrial age. Scholars and thinkers in these religious civilizations did not feel the same pressure to change their cultural heritage and adapt as their colleagues in Western Christianity did.

The discovery of the two new continents of the Americas prompted Nicolaus Copernicus to posit a sun-centered planetary system. Copernicus's new approach to science continued with Galileo Galilei's discovery of the mathematical law of falling bodies in physics and was completed when Isaac Newton unified physics and astronomy. The New Sciences became popular in educated urban circles in northwestern Europe, where Catholic and Protestant church authorities were largely divided. In southern Europe, where the Catholic Reformation was powerful and rejected Galileo, the adoption of the New Sciences occurred more slowly. Scientists in northwestern Europe discovered the practical applicability of the New Sciences as they experimented with steam engines, a catalyst for the launching of the scientific–industrial age.

European kingdoms expanded their powers of taxation to the detriment of the nobility. With these funds, they hired and salaried mercenary infantries equipped with firearms, using them to conquer land from their neighbors. The religious wars of the 1500s and 1600s strengthened centralization efforts and hastened the demise of the nobility as an obstacle to the centralized state. In England, Parliament blocked the Stuart kings from building a landed central state and instead pursued the construction of a naval state.

| **Against the Grain**

Consider this as a counterpoint to the main patterns examined in this chapter.

The Digger Movement

- Was Winstanley hopelessly utopian in his efforts to establish farmer communities on common land in England?

- How have other figures in world history sympathized with the lot of poor and landless farmers and attempted reform (or revolution) on their behalf?

In April 1649, toward the end of the English Civil War and just 3 months after the execution of King Charles I, a group of farmers and day laborers occupied "common" (public) land south of London to establish a colony. As the farmers and laborers dug up the soil, they came to be called the "Diggers."

Driven off by small landowners who benefited from the use of common land for grazing sheep and cutting timber, a smaller group of Diggers moved on to common land in nearby Cobham in August 1649. This time it was the gentry with their manor rights to the common land who destroyed the Diggers' cottages and fields in the winter of 1650. The Diggers made a much-publicized statement that public land was "the treasure of all people" and should not be reserved for the benefit of anyone—a bold demand that ran counter to the rapidly increasing privatization of land and commercialization of agriculture.

The leader of the group was Gerrard Winstanley (1609–1670), a former cloth merchant in London who had had to abandon his trade in 1643 after he became insolvent. He struggled to regain his solvency in the countryside of Surrey, at one point working as a grazier of cattle. Parts of Surrey had suffered substantial hardship during the Civil War, having been forced to provision and quarter troops. In pamphlets between 1648 and 1650, Winstanley explained the motives and goals of the Diggers, making these affairs relevant, in the religious idiom of Protestantism, for England as a whole. He was the first to identify the problem of the rising numbers of rural landless laborers victimized by the increasing commercialization of agriculture in England—a labor force that continued to increase until the industrializing cities of the later 1700s eventually absorbed them.

Key Terms

audio flashcards

Absolutism   398

Catholic Reformation   395

Humanism   382

Indulgence   393

New Sciences   381

Protestant Reformation   393

Renaissance   381

Tsar (or Czar)   401

For additional resources, please go to
www.oup.com/us/vonsivers.
Please see the Further Resources section at the back of the book for additional readings and suggested websites.

New Patterns in New Worlds

COLONIALISM AND INDIGENOUS RESPONSES IN THE AMERICAS

THE AMERICAS IN 1750

ATLANTIC OCEAN

PACIFIC OCEAN

- Spanish
- Portuguese
- British
- French
- Dutch

Alonso Ortíz fled from his creditors in Spain in the early 1770s to find a new life in the Americas. In Mexico City, he set up shop as a tanner. Eight Native American employees did the actual labor of stomping the hides in the vats filled with tanning acids. A black slave was the supervisor. Ortíz concentrated on giving instructions and hustling his flourishing business.

Ortíz's situation in Mexico City was not entirely legal, however. He had left his wife and children alone in Spain, though the law required that families should be united. The authorities rarely enforced this law, but that was no guarantee for Ortíz. Furthermore, he had not yet sent his family any remittances. And then there was still the debt. Ortíz had reasons to be afraid of the law.

To avoid prosecution, Ortíz wrote a letter to his wife. In this letter, he described the comfortable position he had achieved. He announced that his business partner was sending her a sum of money sufficient to begin preparations for her departure from Spain. To his creditors, Ortíz promised to send 100 tanned hides within a year. Evidently aware of her reluctance

ABOVE: In his monumental *Historia de la conquista de México*, written more than 150 years after the events described, Antonio de Solís (1610–1686) depicted the meeting of Moctezuma and Cortés.

to join him in Mexico, Ortíz closed his letter with a request to grant him 4 more years abroad and to do so with a notarized document from her hand. Unfortunately, we do not know her answer.

The Ortíz family drama gives a human face to European colonialism and emigration to the "New World" of the Americas. Like Alonso Ortíz, some 300,000 other Spaniards left the "Old World" (Europe, contiguous with Asia and Africa) between 1500 and 1800. A few hundred letters by emigrants exist, giving us glimpses of their lives in the parts of the Americas conquered by the Spanish and Portuguese in the sixteenth century. These relatively privileged immigrants hoped to build successful enterprises using the labor of Native Americans as well as black slaves imported from Africa. The example of Ortíz shows that even in the socially not very prestigious craft of tanning, a man could achieve a measure of comfort by having people of even lower status working for him.

Seeing Patterns

≫ What is the significance of western Europeans acquiring the Americas as a warm-weather extension of their northern continent?

≫ What was the main pattern of social development in colonial America during the period 1500–1800?

≫ Why and how did European settlers in South and North America strive for self-government, and how successful were they in achieving their goals?

Beginning in the sixteenth century, the Americas became an extension of Europe. European settlers extracted mineral and agricultural resources from these new lands. A pattern emerged in which gold and silver, as well as agricultural products, were intensively exploited. In this role, the Americas became a crucial factor in Europe's changing position in the world. First, Europe acquired precious metals, which its two largest competitors, India and China, lacked. Second, with agricultural commodities pouring in from the Americas, Europe rose to a position of agrarian autonomy similar to that of India and China.

The Colonial Americas: Europe's Warm-Weather Extension

The European extension into the Americas followed Columbus's pursuit of a sea route to India that would circumvent the Mediterranean and its dominance by Muslim traders. The Spaniards financed their imperial expansion as well as their wars against Ottoman and European rivals with American gold and silver, leaving little for domestic investment. A pattern evolved in which Iberian settlers transformed the Americas into mineral-extracting and agrarian colonies based on either cheap or forced labor.

The Conquest of Mexico and Peru

The Spanish conquerors of the Aztec and Inca Empires exploited internal weaknesses in the empires. They eliminated the top of the power structures, paralyzing the decision-making apparatuses long enough for their conquests to succeed. Soon after the conquests, the Old World disease of smallpox ravaged the Native American population and dramatically reduced the indigenous labor force. To make up for this reduction, colonial authorities imported black slaves from Africa. A three-tiered society of European immigrants, Native Americans, and black slaves emerged in the Spanish and Portuguese Americas.

Bartolomé de las Casas, from *A Short Account of the Destruction of the Indies* (1542)

Land-labor grant
(*encomienda*): Land
grant by the government
to an entrepreneur,
entitling him to use
forced indigenous
or imported slave
labor on that land for
the exploitation of
agricultural and mineral
resources.

From Trading Posts to Conquest   Columbus had discovered the Caribbean
islands under a royal commission, which entitled him to build fortified posts and
to trade with the indigenous Taínos. Trade relations with the Taínos, however, deteriorated into exploitation, with the Spaniards usurping the traditional entitlements of
the Taíno chiefs to the labor of their fellow men. With the help of **land-labor grants**
(Spanish *encomiendas*), the Spanish took over from the Taíno chiefs and, through
forced labor, amassed quantities of gold. What had begun as trade-post settlement
turned into full-blown conquest of land.

The Spaniards conquered the Caribbean islands not only through force. Much
more severe in its consequences was the indirect conquest through disease. Smallpox wiped out an estimated 250,000 to 1 million Taínos as well as the Caribs. Isolated from the rest of humankind, Native Americans possessed no immunity against
smallpox and other introduced diseases.

Protests, mostly among some members of the clergy, arose against both the labor
exploitation and the helplessness of the Taínos against disease. The land-labor grant
system finally came to an end after 1542 with the introduction of the *repartimiento*
system (see p. 414 below).

First Mainland Conquests   Hernán Cortés (1485–1547), upon arriving on
Hispaniola in 1504, advanced from governmental scribe in Hispaniola to mayor of
Santiago in Cuba. Thanks to labor grants, he became rich. When the Cuban governor asked him in 1518 to lead an expedition for trade and exploration to the
Yucatán Peninsula in Mexico, Cortés enthusiastically agreed. He assembled 300
men, considerably exceeding his contract. The gov-
ernor tried to stop him, but Cortés departed quickly
for the American mainland.

As the Cuban governor had feared, Cortés did not
bother with trading posts in Yucatán. The Spanish
had learned of the existence of the Aztec Empire, with
its immense silver and gold treasures. In a first encounter, Cortés's small Spanish force defeated a much
larger indigenous force at Tabasco. The Spaniards'
steel weapons and armor proved superior in hand-to-
hand combat against the defenders.

Among the gifts presented by the defeated
Native Americans in Tabasco was Malinche, a
Nahuatl [NAH-huaw]-speaking woman. Malinche
quickly learned Spanish and became the consort
of Cortés. As a translator, Malinche was nearly as
decisive as Cortés in shaping events. With Tabasco conquered, Cortés quickly
moved on; he was afraid that the Cuban governor would otherwise force him to
return to Cuba.

Cultural Intermediary. The
Tabascans gave Malinche, or
Doña Marina, to Hernán Cortés
as a form of tribute after they
were defeated by the Spanish.
Malinche served Cortés as a
translator and mistress, playing a central role in Cortés's
eventual victory over the Aztecs.
She was in many respects the
principal face of the Spanish and
is always depicted center stage in
Native American visual accounts
of the conquest.

Conquest of the Aztec Empire   On the southeast coast of Mexico, Cortés
founded the city of Veracruz. He had his followers elect a town council, which made
Cortés their head and chief justice, allowing Cortés to claim legitimacy for his march
inland. Marching inland, the Spaniards ran into resistance from indigenous people,
suffering their first losses of horses and men. They pressed onward with thousands

of Native American allies, most notably the Tlaxcalans, traditional enemies of the Aztecs. The support from these indigenous peoples proved essential when Cortés and his army reached the court of the Aztecs.

When Cortés arrived at the city of Tenochtitlán on November 2, 1519, the emperor Moctezuma II (r. 1502–1519) was unsure of how to react to the invaders. To gain time, Moctezuma greeted the Spaniard in person and invited him to his palace. Cortés and his company, now numbering some 600 Spaniards, took up quarters in the palace precincts. After a week of deteriorating discussions, Cortés suddenly put the incredulous emperor under house arrest and made him swear allegiance to Charles V.

However, Cortés was diverted by the need to march back east, where troops from Cuba had arrived to arrest him. After defeating those troops, he pressed the remnants into his own service and returned to Tenochtitlán. During his absence, the Spaniards who had remained in Moctezuma's palace had massacred Aztec nobles. As an infuriated crowd of Tenochtitlán's inhabitants invaded the palace, Moctezuma and some 200 Spaniards died. The rest of the Spanish retreated east to their Tlaxcalan allies. There, after his return, Cortés devised a new plan for capturing Tenochtitlán.

After 10 months of preparations, the Spaniards returned to the Aztec capital. In command now of about 2,000 Spanish soldiers and assisted by some 50,000 Native American troops, Cortés laid siege to the city. After nearly 3 months, much of the city was in ruins, water and food became scarce, and smallpox began to decimate the population. On August 21, 1521, the Spaniards and their allies stormed the city and looted its gold treasury. They captured the last emperor, Cuauhtémoc [coo-aw-TAY-moc] and executed him in 1525, thus ending the Aztec Empire (see Map 18.1).

Conquest of the Inca Empire   A relative of Cortés, Francisco Pizarro (ca. 1475–1541), planned to conquer the Andean empire of the Incas. Pizarro, like Cortés born in Spain, but uneducated, arrived in Hispaniola as part of an expedition in 1513 that went on to discover Panama and the Pacific. He became mayor of Panama City, acquired some wealth, and heard rumors about an empire of gold and silver to the south. After a failed initial expedition, he captured some precious metal from an oceangoing Inca sailing raft. Upon receiving a permit from Charles V to establish a trading post, Pizarro and a team departed in late December 1530.

Cortés and the conquest of the Aztec Empire

"The Capture of Tenochtitlán"

interactive timeline

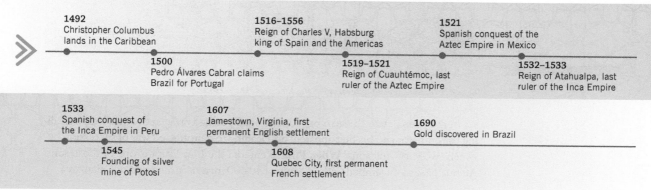

1492	Christopher Columbus lands in the Caribbean
1500	Pedro Álvares Cabral claims Brazil for Portugal
1516–1556	Reign of Charles V, Habsburg king of Spain and the Americas
1519–1521	Reign of Cuauhtémoc, last ruler of the Aztec Empire
1521	Spanish conquest of the Aztec Empire in Mexico
1532–1533	Reign of Atahualpa, last ruler of the Inca Empire
1533	Spanish conquest of the Inca Empire in Peru
1545	Founding of silver mine of Potosí
1607	Jamestown, Virginia, first permanent English settlement
1608	Quebec City, first permanent French settlement
1690	Gold discovered in Brazil

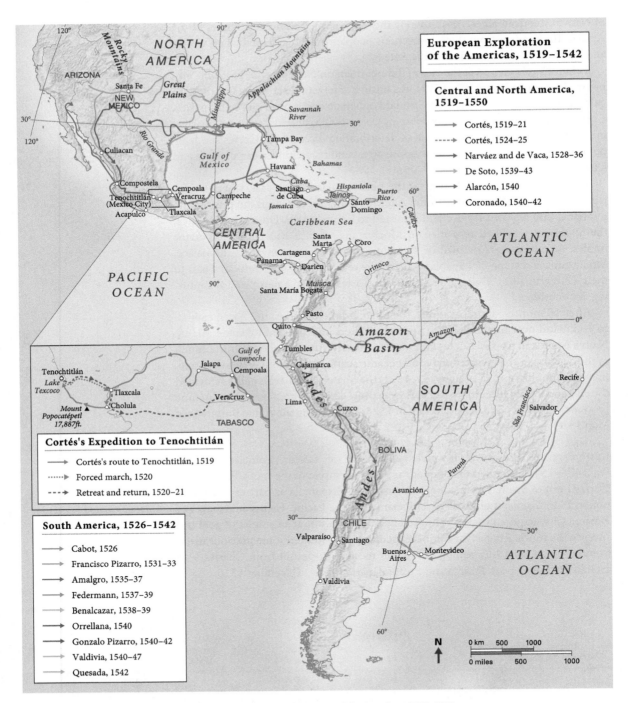

In the years before Pizzaro's expedition, smallpox had ravaged the Inca Empire, killing the emperor and his heir apparent and leading to a protracted war of succession between two surviving sons. When Pizarro entered the Inca Empire, one of those sons, Atahualpa, was encamped with an army of 40,000 men near the town of Cajamarca.

Arriving at Cajamarca, Pizarro arranged an unarmed audience with Atahualpa. On November 16, 1532, Atahualpa came to this audience, surrounded by several thousand unarmed retainers, while Pizarro's soldiers hid nearby. At a signal, these soldiers rushed forward, capturing Atahualpa and massacring his retainers. Not one Spanish soldier was killed.

The ambush paralyzed the Inca Empire at the very top. Atahualpa offered his captors a room full of gold and silver as ransom. In the following 2 months, Inca administrators delivered immense quantities of precious metals to Pizarro. But Spanish officers executed Atahualpa anyway on July 26, 1533, hoping to keep the Incas disorganized.

The Spaniards then captured the Incan capital, Cuzco, massacring the inhabitants and stripping the city of its immense gold and silver treasures. In 1535 Pizarro founded a new capital, Lima, which was more conveniently located on the coast. Although Incas in the south rebuilt a kingdom that held out until 1572, the Spanish eventually gained full control of the Inca Empire.

ATAHUALLPA. INCA XIIII.

Conquest by Surprise. The Spanish conqueror Francisco Pizarro captured Emperor Atahualpa in an ambush. Atahualpa promised a roomful of gold in return for his release, but the Spaniards collected the gold and murdered Atahualpa before generals of the Inca army could organize an armed resistance.

The Portuguese Conquest of Brazil   Navigators from both Spain and Portugal had first sighted the Brazilian coast in 1499–1500, and the Portuguese quickly claimed it for themselves. The majority of Brazil's indigenous population at that time lived in villages based on agriculture, fishing, and hunting.

The Portuguese were interested initially in trade with villagers, mostly for brazilwood, which was used to make a red dye. When French traders appeared, ignoring the Portuguese commercial treaties with the tribes, the Portuguese crown shifted to trading-post settlements. Land grants were made with the obligation to build fortified coastal villages for settlers and to engage in agriculture and friendly trade. By the mid-sixteenth century, inhabitants of some of these villages intermarried with local indigenous chieftain families and established sugarcane plantations.

Explanations for the Spanish Success   The stupendous victories of handfuls of Spaniards over huge empires defies easy explanation. Four factors invite consideration. First, the conquistadors went straight to the top of the imperial pyramid. The emperors expected diplomatic deference, but confronted instead with arrogance and brutality, they were thrown off balance by the Spaniards. Second, in both the Aztec and Inca Empires, individuals and groups contested the hierarchical power structure. The conquistadors either found allies among the subject populations or encountered a divided leadership. Third, European-introduced diseases took a devastating toll. In both empires, smallpox hit at critical moments during or right before the Spanish invasions. Finally, thanks to horses and European steel weapons and armor, small numbers of Spaniards were able to hold large numbers of attacking Aztecs and Incas at bay in hand-to-hand combat. Cannons and matchlock muskets were less important, since they were useless in close encounters.

Malinche directing Spanish forces, from the *Lienzo de Tlaxcala* (1552)

The Establishment of Colonial Institutions

The Spanish crown established administrative hierarchies in the Americas, with governors at the top and lower ranks of functionaries. Some settler autonomy was permitted through town and city councils, but the crown was determined to make the Americas a territorial extension of the European pattern of centralized state formation.

Brazil in 1519. This early map is fairly accurate for the northern coast, but increasingly less accurate as one moves south. First explorations of the south by both Portuguese and Spanish mariners date to 1513–1516. Ferdinand Magellan passed through several places along the southern coast on his journey around the world in 1520–1521. The scenes on the map depict Native Americans cutting and collecting brazilwood, the source of a red dye much in demand by the Portuguese during the early period of colonization.

Creoles: American-born descendants of European, primarily Spanish, immigrants.

Several hundred thousand settlers found a new life in the Americas. By the early seventeenth century, an elite of Spaniards who had been born in America, called **Creoles** (Spanish *criollos*), first assisted and later replaced most of the administrators sent from Spain (see Map 18.2).

From Conquest to Colonialism   The riches of Cortés and Pizarro inspired further expeditions into Central and North America, Chile, and the Amazon. These expeditions, however, yielded only modest amounts of gold and earned more from selling captured Native Americans into slavery. In the north, expeditions penetrated as far as Arizona, New Mexico, Texas, Oklahoma, Kansas, and Florida, but encountered only relatively poor villagers and Pueblo towns. No new golden kingdoms beyond the Aztec and Inca Empires were discovered in the Americas.

In the mid-sixteenth century, the conquistadors shifted from looting to the exploitation of Native American labor in mines and in agriculture. Explorers discovered silver in Bolivia (1545) and northern Mexico (1556), gold in Chile (1552), and mercury in Peru (1563).

Indigenous peoples occasionally resisted incorporation into the Spanish colonies. Notably, the Mapuche in southern Chile repulsed all attempts by the Spanish to subdue them. Initially, in 1550–1553 the Spanish succeeded in establishing forts and opening a gold mine, but they failed to gain more than a border strip with an adjacent no-man's-land. In 1612 they agreed to a temporary peace that left the majority of the Mapuche independent.

Another Native American people who successfully resisted the Spanish conquest were the Asháninka in the Peruvian rain forest. The Asháninka exploited hillside salt veins in their region and were traders of goods between the Andes and the rain forest. It was only in 1737 that the Spanish finally built a fort in the region—a first step toward projecting colonial power into the rain forest.

Bureaucratic Efficiency   During the first two generations after the conquest, Spain maintained an efficient colonial administration to deliver revenues to Spain. In addition, the viceroyalty of New Spain in Mexico remitted another 25 percent of its revenues to the Philippines, the Pacific province for which it was administratively responsible from 1571 onward. Settlers in New Spain had to pay up to 40 different taxes and dues. The only income tax was the tithe to the church, which the administration collected and, at times, used for its own budgetary purposes. Altogether, however, for the settlers the tax level was lower in the New World than in Spain, and the same was true for the English and French colonists in North America.

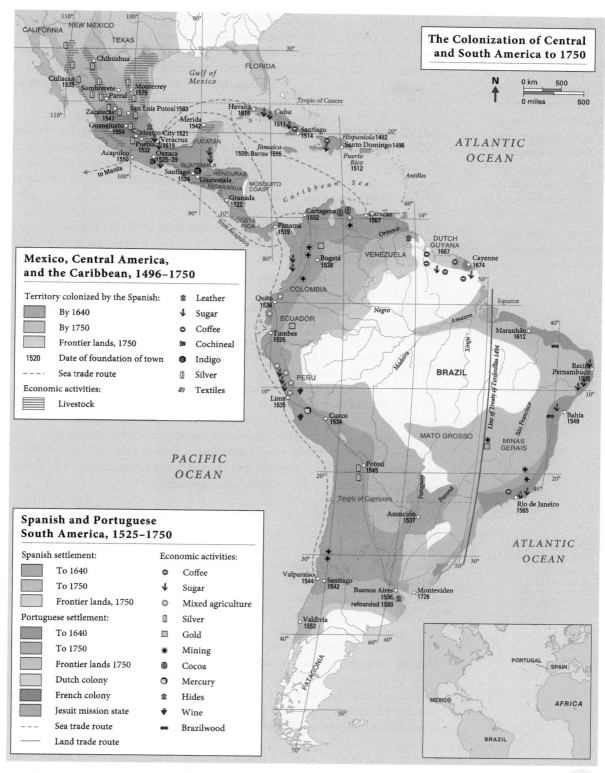

The Colonization of Central and South America to 1750

N   0 km   500
     0 miles   500

Mexico, Central America, and the Caribbean, 1496–1750

Territory colonized by the Spanish:

	By 1640
	By 1750
	Frontier lands, 1750
1520	Date of foundation of town
- - -	Sea trade route

Economic activities:

| | Livestock |

🦌 Leather
⬇ Sugar
⊖ Coffee
🐚 Cochineal
⬤ Indigo
▯ Silver
▨ Textiles

Spanish and Portuguese South America, 1525–1750

Spanish settlement:

	To 1640
	To 1750
	Frontier lands, 1750

Portuguese settlement:

	To 1640
	To 1750
	Frontier lands 1750
	Dutch colony
	French colony
	Jesuit mission state
- - -	Sea trade route
——	Land trade route

Economic activities:

⊖ Coffee
⬇ Sugar
◉ Mixed agriculture
▯ Silver
▢ Gold
✦ Mining
◉ Cocoa
○ Mercury
🦌 Hides
⬇ Wine
— Brazilwood

MAP 18.2 **The Colonization of Central and South America to 1750.**

map analysis

Labor assignment (*repartimiento*): Obligation by villagers to send stipulated numbers of people as laborers to a contractor, who had the right to exploit a mine or other labor-intensive enterprise; the contractors paid the laborers minimal wages and bound them through debt peonage (repayment of money advances) to their businesses.

In the 1540s the government introduced rotating **labor assignments** (*repartimientos*) to phase out the *encomiendas*. This institution of rotating labor assignments was a continuation of the *mit'a* system, which the Incas had devised as a form of taxation (see Chapter 15). Rotating labor assignments meant that a percentage of villagers had to provide labor to the state. Private entrepreneurs could also contract for indigenous labor assignments, especially in mining regions.

In Mexico the *repartimiento* fell out of use in the first half of the seventeenth century due to the toll of smallpox on the Native American population. The replacement for the lost workers was wage labor. In highland Peru, where the effects of smallpox were less severe, the assignment system lasted to the end of the colonial period. Wage labor expanded there as well. Wages for Native Americans and blacks remained everywhere lower than for those for Creoles.

The Rise of the Creoles   Administrative and fiscal efficiency did not last very long. The wars of the Spanish Habsburg Empire cost more than the crown was able to collect in revenues. In order to make up the financial deficit, the crown began to sell offices in the Americas to the highest bidders. By the end of the century, Creoles had purchased life appointments in city councils as well as other important sinecures that allowed them to collect fees and rents. Local oligarchies emerged, effectively ending participatory politics in Spanish colonial America.

The effects of the change from recruitment by merit to recruitment by wealth on the functioning of the bureaucracy were far-reaching. Creoles advanced on a broad front in the administrative positions, while fewer Spaniards found it attractive to buy their American positions from overseas. The only opportunities which European Spaniards still found enticing were positions that gave their owners the right to subject the Native Americans to forced purchases of goods, yielding huge profits. By 1700, the consequences of the Spanish crown selling most of its American administrative offices were a decline in the competence of officeholders, the emergence of a Creole elite able to bend the Spanish administration to its will, and a decentralization of the decision-making processes.

engraving showing English attack on the Spanish settlement of St. Augustine, Florida, 1589

Northwest European Interference   As Spain's administrative grip on the Americas weakened during the seventeenth century, the need to defend the continents militarily against European interlopers arose. European privateers, holding royal charters, harassed Spanish silver shipments and ports in the Caribbean. In the early seventeenth century, the French, English, and Dutch governments occupied the smaller Caribbean islands not claimed by Spain. Privateer and contraband traders stationed on these islands further damaged Spain's monopoly of shipping between Europe and the Caribbean.

Conquests of Spanish islands followed in the second half of the century. England captured Jamaica in 1655, and France colonized western Hispaniola (Saint-Domingue) in 1665. Along the Pacific coast, the galleons of the annual Acapulco–Manila fleet were the targets of English privateers. Over the course of the seventeenth century, Spain allocated one-half to two-thirds of its American revenues to the defense of its annual treasure fleets and Caribbean possessions.

Bourbon Reforms   After the death of the last, childless Habsburg king of Spain in 1700, the new French-descended dynasty of the Bourbons made major efforts to regain control over their American possessions. Fortunately, population increases among the settlers as well as the Native Americans offered opportunities to Spanish manufacturers and merchants. By the middle of the eighteenth century, the Bourbon reform program began to show results.

The reforms aimed to improve naval connections and administrative control between the mother country and the colonies. The monopolistic annual armed silver fleet was reduced. Instead, the government authorized more frequent single sailings. Newly formed Spanish companies, receiving exclusive rights at specific ports, reduced contraband trade. Elections took place again for municipal councils. Spanish-born salaried officials replaced many Creole tax and office farmers. The original two viceroyalties were subdivided into four, to improve administrative control. The sale of tobacco and brandy became state monopolies. Silver mining and cotton textile manufacturing were expanded. By the second half of the eighteenth century, Spain had regained a measure of control over its colonies.

As a result, government revenues rose substantially. In the end, however, the reforms remained incomplete. Since the Spanish economy was not also reformed, the changes did not much diminish the English and French dominance of the import market. Spain failed to produce goods at competitive prices for the colonies; thus the level of English and French exports to the Americas remained high.

Early Portuguese Colonialism   In contrast to the Spanish Americas, the Portuguese overseas province of Brazil developed only slowly during the sixteenth century. The first governor-general arrived in 1549. He and his successors (after 1640 called "viceroys," as in the Spanish colonies) were members of the high aristocracy, but their positions were salaried and subject to term limits. As the colony grew, the crown created a council in the capital of Lisbon for all Brazilian appointments and established a high court for all judicial affairs in Bahia in northern Brazil. In the early seventeenth century, offices became as open to purchase as in the Spanish colonies, although not on the city council level, where an electoral process survived.

Jesuits converted the Native Americans, whom they transported to Jesuit-administered villages. Colonial cities and Jesuits repeatedly clashed over the slave raids of the "pioneers" (*bandeirantes*) in village territories. Although the Portuguese crown and church had, like the Spanish, forbidden the enslavement of Native Americans, the bandeirantes exploited a loophole. The law was interpreted as allowing the enslavement of Native Americans who resisted conversion to Christianity. For a long time, Lisbon and the Jesuits were powerless against this interpretation.

Expansion into the Interior   In the middle of the seventeenth century, the Jesuits and Native Americans pushed many bandeirantes west and north, where they switched from slave raiding to prospecting for gold. In the far north, however, the raids continued until 1680, when the Portuguese administration finally ended Native American slavery, almost a century and a half after Spain.

As a result of gold discoveries in Minas Gerais in 1690 by bandeirantes, the European immigrant population increased rapidly. Brazilians imported slaves from Africa, to work at first in the sugar plantations and, after 1690, in the mines, where their numbers increased to two-thirds of the labor force. The peak of the gold boom came in the 1750s, when the importance of gold was second only to that of sugar among Brazilian exports to Europe.

Early in the gold boom, the crown created the new Ministry of the Navy and Overseas Territories, which greatly expanded the administrative structure in Brazil, and moved the capital from Bahia to Rio de Janeiro in 1736. The ministry in Lisbon ended the sale of offices, increased the efficiency of tax collection, and encouraged Brazilian textile manufacturing to render the province more independent from English imports. By the mid-1700s, Brazil was a flourishing overseas colony of Portugal.

North American Settlements   Efforts at settlement in North America in the sixteenth century were unsuccessful. Only in the early part of the seventeenth century did French, English, and Dutch merchant investors succeed in establishing small communities of settlers on the coast: Jamestown (founded in 1607 in today's Virginia), Quebec (1608, Canada), Plymouth and Boston (1620 and 1630, respectively, in today's Massachusetts), and New Amsterdam (1625, today's New York). Subsistence agriculture and fur, however, were not enough for growth. The settlements struggled through the seventeenth century, sustained either by Catholic missionary efforts or by the Puritans who had escaped persecution in England. Southern places like Jamestown survived because they adopted tobacco as a cash crop for export to Europe. In contrast to Mexico and Peru, the North American settlements were not followed—at least, not at first—by territorial conquests (see Map 18.3).

Native Americans   European arrivals in North America soon began supplementing agriculture with trade, exchanging metal and glass wares, beads, and seashells for furs with the Native American groups of the interior. As a result, smallpox, already a menace during the 1500s in North America, became devastating as contacts intensified.

The introduction of guns contributed an additional lethal factor to trading arrangements, as traders provided Native American trading partners with flintlocks in order to increase the yield of furs. As a result, during the 1600s the Iroquois in the northeast were able to organize themselves into an armed federation, capable of inflicting heavy losses on rival groups as well as on European traders and settlers.

Farther south, in Virginia, the Jamestown settlers encountered the Powhatan confederacy. These Native Americans dominated the region between the Chesapeake Bay and the Appalachian Mountains. Initially, the Powhatan supplied Jamestown with foodstuffs and sought to integrate the settlement into their confederation.

Samuel de Champlain's map of the northeast coast of North America, ca. 1607

Mine Workers. The discovery of gold and diamonds in Minas Gerais led to a boom, but did little to contribute to the long-term health of the Brazilian economy. With the Native American population decimated by disease, African slaves performed the backbreaking work.

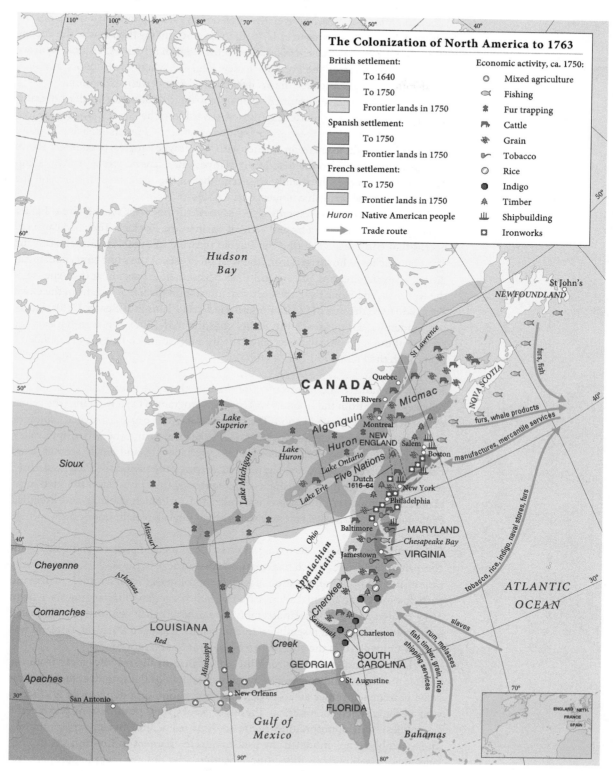

The Colonization of North America to 1763

British settlement:
- To 1640
- To 1750
- Frontier lands in 1750

Spanish settlement:
- To 1750
- Frontier lands in 1750

French settlement:
- To 1750
- Frontier lands in 1750

Huron   Native American people

→   Trade route

Economic activity, ca. 1750:
- Mixed agriculture
- Fishing
- Fur trapping
- Cattle
- Grain
- Tobacco
- Rice
- Indigo
- Timber
- Shipbuilding
- Ironworks

MAP 18.3 **The Colonization of North America to 1763.**

When this attempt failed, however, the confederacy raided Jamestown twice. But the settlers defeated the Powhatan in 1646, thereafter occupying their lands. The decline of the Powhatan in the later 1600s allowed the English settlers of Virginia to move westward, in contrast to the Puritans in New England, where the Iroquois, although allied with the English against the French, blocked any western expansion.

The Iroquois were determined to maintain their dominance of the fur trade, driving smaller Native American groups westward into the Great Lakes region and Mississippi plains, where these groups settled as refugees. French officials and Jesuit missionaries sought to create an alliance with the refugee peoples, to counterbalance the powerful Iroquois to the east. Many Native Americans converted to Christianity, creating a Creole Christianity similar to that of the Africans of Kongo and the Mexicans after the Spanish conquest of the Aztecs.

Major population movements also occurred further west on the Great Plains, where the Apaches arrived from the Great Basin in the Rockies. They had captured horses that had escaped during the Pueblo uprising of 1680–1695 against Spain. The Comanches, who arrived from the west on horses at the same time, had, in addition, acquired firearms and around 1725 began their expansion at the expense of the Apaches. The Sioux from the northern forests and the Cheyenne from the Great Basin added to the mix of federations on the Great Plains in the early 1700s. Smallpox epidemics did not reach the Plains until the mid-1700s, while in the east the ravages of this epidemic had weakened the Iroquois so much that they concluded a peace with the French in 1701.

French Canada   The involvement of the French in the Great Lakes region with refugees fleeing from the Iroquois was part of a program of expansion into the center of North America, begun in 1663. The governor of Quebec had dispatched explorers, fur traders, and missionaries into the Great Lakes region and the Mississippi valley. The French government then sent farmers, craftspeople, and single women from France to establish settlements. The most successful settlement, called "La Louisiane," was at the mouth of the Mississippi, where settlers with African slaves founded sugar plantations. Because immigration was restricted to French subjects and excluded Protestants, Louisiana had far fewer settlers than English North America.

Colonial Assemblies   As immigration to New England picked up, the merchant companies in Europe, which had financed the journeys of the settlers, were initially responsible for the administration of settlement colonies. The first settlers to demand participation in the colonial administration were Virginian tobacco growers, who in 1619 created an early popular assembly. The other English colonies soon followed suit, creating their own assemblies. In contrast to Spain and Portugal, England was initially uninvolved in the governance of the overseas territories.

When England eventually took the governance of the colonies away from the charter merchants and companies in the second half of the seventeenth century, it faced entrenched settler assemblies. Many governors were deputies of aristocrats who never traveled to America. These governors were powerless to prevent the assemblies from appropriating rights to levy taxes and making appointments. The assemblies thus modeled themselves after Parliament in London. As in England, these assemblies excluded poorer settlers who did not meet the property requirements to vote or stand for elections.

Territorial Expansion Steady immigration encouraged land speculators in the British colonies to cast their sights beyond the Appalachian Mountains. In 1749, the Ohio Company of Virginia received a royal permit to develop land, together with a protective fort, south of the Ohio River. The French, however, also claimed the Ohio valley. Tensions over the valley soon erupted into open hostility. Initially, the local encounters went badly for the Virginian militia and British army. In 1755, however, the British and French broadened their clash into a worldwide war for dominance in the colonies and Europe, the Seven Years' War of 1756–1763.

powder horn, ca. 1757

The Seven Years' War Both France and Great Britain borrowed heavily to finance the war. England had the superior navy and France the superior army. Since the British navy succeeded in choking off French supplies to its increasingly isolated land troops, Britain won the war overseas. In Europe, Britain's failure to supply the troops of its ally Prussia against the Austrian–French alliance caused the war on that front to end in a draw. Overseas, the British gained most of the French holdings in India, several islands in the Caribbean, all of Canada, and all the land east of the Mississippi. The costs, however, proved to be unmanageable for all concerned. The unpaid debts became the root cause of the American, French, and Haitian constitutional revolutions that began 13 years later.

The Making of American Societies: Origins and Transformations

The patterns which made the Americas an extension of Europe emerged gradually and displayed characteristics specific to each region. On one hand, there was the slow transfer of the plants and animals native to each continent, called the **Columbian Exchange** (see "Patterns Up Close"). On the other hand, Spain and Portugal adopted different strategies of mineral and agricultural exploitation. In spite of these different strategies, however, the settler societies of the two countries in the end displayed similar characteristics.

Columbian Exchange: Exchange of plants, animals, and diseases between the Americas and the rest of the world.

Exploitation of Mineral and Tropical Resources

The pattern of European expansion into subtropical and tropical lands began with the Spanish colonization of the Caribbean islands. When the Spanish crown ran out of gold in the Caribbean, it exported silver from Mexico and Peru to finance a centralizing state. By contrast, Portugal's colony of Brazil did not at first mine for precious metals, and consequently the Portuguese crown pioneered the growing of sugar on plantations. The North American colonies of England and France had, in comparison, little native industry at first. By moving farther south, however, they adopted the plantation system for indigo and rice.

Silver Mines Two main mining centers emerged in the Spanish colonies: Potosí in southeastern Peru (today Bolivia) and Zacatecas and Guanajuato in northern Mexico. During the eighteenth century, gold mining in Colombia and Chile rose to importance as well.

Innovations such as the "patio" method, which facilitated the extraction of silver through the use of mercury, and the unrestrained exploitation of indigenous labor

The Columbian Exchange

Few of us can imagine an Italian kitchen without tomatoes or an Irish meal without potatoes or Chinese or Indian cuisine without chilies, but until fairly recently each of these foods was unknown to the Old World. Likewise, for millennia apples, as well as many other common fruits, were absent from the New World. It was not until the sixteenth century that new patterns of ecology and biology changed the course of millions of years of divergent evolution.

When considering the long list of life forms that moved across the oceans in the Columbian Exchange, the impact of European weeds and grasses on American grasslands, which made it possible for the North American prairie and the South American pampas to support livestock, should not be overlooked. By binding the soil together with their long, tough roots, the "empire of the dandelion" provided the conditions for the grazing of sheep, cattle, and horses, as well as the planting of crops like wheat.

The other silent invader that accompanied the conquistadors was disease. Thousands of years of mutual isolation between the Americas and Afro-Eurasia rendered the immune systems of Native Americans vulnerable to the scourges that European colonists unwittingly brought with them. By some estimates, the native populations of Mesoamerica and the Andes plummeted by 90 percent in the period 1500–1700. In comparison, the contagions the New World was able to reciprocate upon the Old World—syphilis and tuberculosis—did not unleash nearly the same devastation, and the New World origin of these diseases is still debated.

Therefore, the big winner in the Columbian Exchange was western Europe, though the effects of the New World bounty took centuries to be fully discerned. While Asia and Africa also benefited from the Columbian Exchange, the Europeans got a continent endowed with a warm climate in which they could create new and improved versions of their homelands. The Native Americans were nearly wiped out by disease, their lands appropriated, and the survivors either enslaved or marginalized. The precipitous drop in the population of Native Americans, combined with the tropical and semitropical climate of much of the Americas, created the

made American silver highly competitive in the world market. Conditions among the Native Americans and blacks employed as labor were abominable. Few laborers lasted through more than two forced recruitment (*repartimiento*) cycles before they were incapacitated or dead.

Since the exploitation of the mines was of central importance, for the first century and a half of New World colonization, the Spanish crown organized its other provinces around the needs of the mining centers. The main function of Hispaniola and Cuba in the Caribbean was to feed and protect Havana, the collection point for Mexican and Peruvian silver and the port from where the annual Spanish fleet shipped the American silver across the Atlantic.

A second region, Argentina and Paraguay, was colonized as a bulwark to prevent the Portuguese and Dutch from accessing Peruvian silver. Once established, the two colonies produced goods and foodstuffs to supply the miners in Potosí.

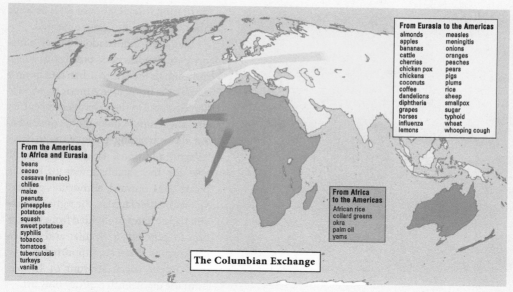

From Eurasia to the Americas

almonds	measles
apples	meningitis
bananas	onions
cattle	oranges
cherries	peaches
chicken pox	pears
chickens	pigs
coconuts	plums
coffee	rice
dandelions	sheep
diphtheria	smallpox
grapes	sugar
horses	typhoid
influenza	wheat
lemons	whooping cough

From the Americas to Africa and Eurasia

beans
cacao
cassava (manioc)
chilies
maize
peanuts
pineapples
potatoes
squash
sweet potatoes
syphilis
tobacco
tomatoes
tuberculosis
turkeys
vanilla

From Africa to the Americas

African rice
collard greens
okra
palm oil
yams

The Columbian Exchange

MAP 18.4 **The Columbian Exchange.**

necessary conditions for the Atlantic slave trade. The population losses from this trade were monumental.

Questions

- Can the Columbian Exchange be considered one of the origins of the modern world? How? Why? How does the Columbian Exchange demonstrate the origins, interactions, and adaptations model that is used throughout this book?

- Weigh the positive and negative outcomes of the Columbian Exchange. Is it possible to determine whether the overall effects of the Columbian Exchange on human society and the natural environment were for the better or for the worse?

A third colonial region, Venezuela, began as a grain and cattle supply base for Cartagena, the port for the shipment of Colombian gold, and Panama and Portobelo, ports for the transshipment of Peruvian silver from the Pacific to Havana. Thus, three major regions of the Spanish overseas empire in the Americas were mostly peripheral as agricultural producers during the sixteenth century. Only after the middle of the century did they begin to specialize in tropical agricultural goods, and they were exporters only in the eighteenth century.

Wheat Farming and Cattle Ranching   To support the mining centers and administrative cities, the Spanish colonial government encouraged the development of agricultural estates (*haciendas*). Native American tenant farmers were forced to grow wheat and raise livestock for the conquerors, who were now agricultural entrepreneurs. In the latter part of the sixteenth century, the land grants gave way

map of Mexican town drawn by indigenous artists, 1579

The Silver Mountain of Potosí.
Note the patios in the left foreground and the water-driven crushing mill in the center, which ground the silver-bearing ore into a fine sand that then was moistened, caked, amalgamated with mercury, and dried on the patio. The mine workers' insect-like shapes reinforce the dehumanizing effects of their labor.

to rotating forced labor as well as wage labor. A landowner class emerged.

Like the conquistadors before, a majority of landowners produced wheat and animals for sale to urban and mining centers. As the Native American population declined in the seventeenth century and the church helped in consolidating the remaining population in large villages, additional land became available for the establishment of estates. From 1631 onward, authorities granted Spanish settler families the right to maintain their estates undivided from generation to generation. Secular and clerical landowning interests supported a powerful upper social stratum of Creoles from the eighteenth century onward.

Plantations and Gold Mining in Brazil   Brazil's economic activities began with brazilwood, followed by sugar plantations, before gold mining rose to prominence in the eighteenth century.

These gold-mining operations were less capital-intensive than the silver mines in Spanish America. Most miners were relatively small operators with a few black slaves as unskilled laborers. Many entrepreneurs were indebted for their slaves to absentee capitalists, with whom they shared the profits. Since prospecting took place on the land of Native Americans, bloody encounters were frequent. Brazil's gold production was a welcome bonanza for Portugal at a time of low agricultural prices.

Plantations in Spanish and English America   The expansion of plantation farming in the Spanish colonies was a result of the Bourbon reforms. Although sugar, tobacco, and rice had been introduced early into the Caribbean and southern Mexico, it was only in the plantation system of the eighteenth century that these and other crops were produced for export to Europe. The owners of plantations invested in African slave labor, with the result that the slave trade hit full stride beginning around 1750.

English Northeast American settlements in Virginia and Carolina exported tobacco and rice beginning in the 1660s. Georgia joined southern Carolina as a major plantation colony in 1750. In the eighteenth century, New England exported timber for shipbuilding and charcoal production in Great Britain. These timber exports illustrate the importance of the Americas as a replacement for dwindling fuel resources across much of northern Europe. Altogether, it was thanks to the Americas that mostly cold and rainy Europe rose into the ranks of the wealthy Indian and Chinese empires.

Social Strata, Castes, and Ethnic Groups

Given the small settler population of the Americas, the temptation to develop a system of forced labor in agriculture and mining was irresistible. Since the Native Americans and African slaves pressed into labor were ethnically so different from the Europeans, however, a social system evolved in which the latter two not only were economically underprivileged but also made up the ethnically nonintegrated lowest rungs of the social ladder. A pattern of legal and customary discrimination evolved which prevented the integration of American ethnicities into settler society.

The Social Elite   The heirs of the Spanish conquistadors and estate owners maintained city residences and employed managers on their agricultural properties. In Brazil, cities emerged more slowly. During the seventeenth century, estate owners intermarried with the Madrid- and Lisbon-appointed administrators, creating the top tier of settler society known as Creoles. They formed a relatively closed society in which descent, intermarriage, landed property, and a government position counted more than money and education.

In the seventeenth and eighteenth centuries, the estate owners farmed predominantly with Native American forced labor. In contrast to the black slave plantation estates of the Caribbean and coastal regions of Spanish and Portuguese America, these farming estates did not export their goods to Europe.

As local producers with little competition, farming and ranching estate owners did not feel market pressures. They exploited their estates with minimal investments and usually drew profits of less than 5 percent of annual revenues. As a result, they were often heavily indebted.

Lower Creoles   The second tier of Creole society consisted of privileged European settlers who, as craftspeople and traders, theoretically worked with their hands. In practice, many of them were owner-operators who employed Native Americans and/or black slaves. Many strove to rise into the ranks of the landowning Creoles.

Wealthy weavers ran textile manufactures mostly concentrated in the cities of Mexico, Peru, Paraguay, and Argentina. On a smaller scale, manufactures also existed for pottery and leather goods. On the whole, the urban manufacturing activities of the popular people, serving the poor in local markets, remained vibrant until well into the nineteenth century, in spite of massive European imports. Prior to the arrival of railroads, the transportation of imports into the interior of the Americas was prohibitively expensive.

Mestizos and Mulattoes   The mixed European–Native American and European–African population had the collective name of "caste" (*casta*), or ethnic group. The two most important castes were the *mestizos* (Spanish), or *mestiços* (Portuguese), who had Iberian fathers and Native American mothers, and *mulatos*, who had Iberian fathers and black mothers. By 1800 the castas as a whole formed the third largest population category in Latin America. In both Spanish and Portuguese America, there were also a small percentage of people descended from Native American and black unions. These intermediate population groups played important neutralizing roles in colonial society, as they had one foot in both the Creole and subordinate social strata (see Figure 18.1).

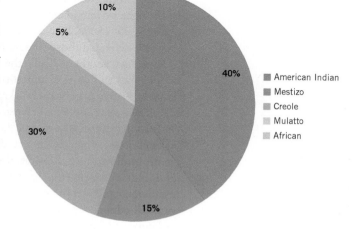

Figure 18.1 Ethnic Composition of Latin America, ca. 1800.

Mestizos and mulattoes filled lower levels of the bureaucracy and the lay hierarchy in the church. They held skilled and supervisory positions in mines and on estates. In addition, in the armed forces mulattoes dominated the ranks of enlisted men; in the defense militias, they even held officer ranks. In Brazil, many mulattoes and black freedmen were farmers. Much of the craft production was in their hands. Many laws kept mestizos and mulattoes in their intermediate social and political positions.

Women The roles played by women depended on their social position. Elite Creole households followed the Mediterranean tradition of secluding women from men. Within the household, Creole women were the owners of substantial dowries and legally stipulated grooms' gifts. Often, they actively managed the investment of their assets. Outside the household, however, even elite women lost all protection. Husbands and fathers could banish daughters or wives to convents for alleged lapses in chastity, or even kill them without punishment. Thus, even elite women were bound by limits set by a patriarchal society.

On the lower rungs of society, gender separation was much less prevalent. Men, women, and children shared labor in the fields and workshops. Girls or wives took in clothes to wash or went out to work as domestics in wealthy households. Older women dominated retail in market stalls. Working families with few assets suffered abandonment by males. Women headed one-third of all households in Mexico City, according to an 1811 census. Among black slaves in the region of São Paulo, 70 percent of women were without formal ties to the men who fathered their children. The most pronounced division in colonial society was that of a patriarchy among the Creoles and a slave society dominated by women, with frequently absent men.

Native Americans In the immediate aftermath of the conquest, Native Americans could be found at all social levels. Social distinctions, however, disappeared during the first 150 years of Spanish colonialism as disease reduced the Native American population by nearly 80 percent. It was only in the twentieth century that population figures reached the preconquest level again in most parts of Latin America.

Apart from European diseases, the Native Americans in the Amazon, Orinoco, and Maracaibo rain forests were the least affected by European colonials during the period 1500–1800. Not only were their lands economically the least promising, but they also defended those lands successfully. In many arid or semiarid regions, such as Patagonia, southern Chile, the Argentine grasslands (*pampas*), the Paraguayan salt marshes and deserts, and northern Mexican mountains and steppes, the semi-nomadic Native Americans quickly adopted the European horse and became highly mobile warrior peoples in defense of their mostly independent territories.

The villagers of Mexico, Yucatán, Guatemala, Colombia, Ecuador, and Peru had fewer choices. When smallpox reduced their numbers in the second half of the sixteenth century, authorities razed villages and concentrated the survivors in *pueblos de indios*. Initially, the Native Americans put up strong resistance against these resettlements. From the middle of the seventeenth century, however, the pueblos were self-administering units, with councils (*cabildos*), churches, schools, communal lands, and family parcels.

The councils were important institutions of legal training and social mobility for Native Americans. Initially, the traditional "noble" chiefly families descending from

Illustration from an Indian Land Record. The Spaniards almost completely wiped out the Aztec archives after the conquest of Mexico; surviving examples of Indian manuscripts are thus extremely rare. Although the example shown here, made from the bark of a fig tree, claims to date from the early 1500s, it is part of the so-called Techialoyan land records created in the seventeenth century to substantiate native land claims. These "títulos primordiales," as they were called, were essentially municipal histories that documented in text and pictures local accounts of important events and territorial boundaries.

the preconquest Aztec and Inca ruling classes were in control as administrators. The many village functions, however, for which the *cabildos* were responsible allowed commoners to move up into auxiliary roles. Native American villages were closed to settlers, and the only outsiders admitted were Catholic priests. Contact with the Spanish world remained minimal, and acculturation went little beyond official conversion to Catholicism. Thus, even in the heartlands of Spanish America, Native American adaptation to the rulers remained limited.

Unfortunately, however, tremendous demographic losses made the Native Americans in the pueblos vulnerable to the loss of their land. Estate owners expanded their holdings, and when the population rebounded, many estates had grown to immense sizes. Villages began to run out of land for their inhabitants. Increasing numbers of Native Americans had to rent land from estate owners or find work on estates as farmhands. They became estranged from their villages, fell into debt peonage, and entered the ranks of the working poor.

New England Society   In the early modern period, the small family farm remained the norm for the majority of New England's population. An acute lack of money and cheap means of transportation hampered the development of market networks in the interior well into the 1770s. The situation was better in the agriculturally more favored colonies in the Mid-Atlantic, especially in Pennsylvania. The number of plantations in the south rose steadily, demanding a substantial increase in numbers of slaves, although world market fluctuations left planters vulnerable. Except for boom periods in the plantation sector, the rural areas remained largely poor.

Real changes occurred during the early eighteenth century in the urban regions of New England. Large port cities emerged which shipped in goods from Europe in return for timber. A wealthy merchant class formed, spawning urban strata of professionals. Primary school education was provided by municipal public schools as well as by some churches, and evening schools for craftspeople also existed. By the middle of the eighteenth century, a majority of men could read and write. Finally, in contrast to Latin America, social ranks in New England were less elaborate.

The Adaptation of the Americas to European Culture

European settlers brought two distinct cultures to the Americas. In the Mid-Atlantic, Caribbean, and Central and South America, they brought with them the Catholic Reformation, a culture that resisted the New Science and the Enlightenment until the late eighteenth century. In the northeast, colonists implanted dissident Protestantism as well as the Anglicanism of Great Britain and the Presbyterianism of Scotland.

earliest representation of the Madonna and Child created by Indians in the New World (1531)

Catholic Missionary Work   Spanish and Portuguese monarchs relied on the Catholic Church for their rule in the new American provinces. A strong motive driving many in the church and society was the belief in the imminent Second Coming of Jesus. This belief was one inspiration for the original Atlantic expansion (see Chapter 16). When the Aztec and Inca Empires fell, members of the Franciscan order, the main proponents of the belief in the imminence of the Second Coming, interpreted it as a sign of the urgent duty to convert the Native Americans to Christianity.

Thousands of preaching monks, later followed by the Jesuits, fanned out among the Native Americans. They baptized them, introduced the sacraments, and taught them basic theological concepts. The missionaries learned native languages, translated the catechism and New Testament into those languages, and taught the children of the ruling native families how to read and write.

The role and function of saints formed one element of Catholic Christianity to which Native Americans acculturated early. Good works as God-pleasing human efforts to gain salvation in the afterlife formed another. The veneration of images of the Virgin Mary and pilgrimages to the chapels and churches where they were kept constituted a third element. On the other hand, the Spanish Inquisition also operated in the Spanish and Portuguese colonies, seeking to limit the degree to which Catholicism and traditional religion mingled.

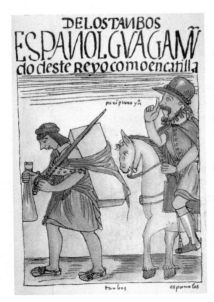

Spanish Cruelty to Incas. Felipe Guamán Poma de Ayala, a Peruvian claiming noble Inca descent, was a colonial administrator, well educated and an ardent Christian. He is remembered today as a biting critic of the colonial administration and the clergy, whom he accused of mistreating and exploiting the Andean population, as in this colored woodcut print.

Education and the Arts   The Catholic Reformation also influenced the organization of education. The Franciscans and Dominicans had offered education to the children of settlers early on and, in colleges, trained graduates for missionary work. New World universities taught theology, church law, and Native American languages. Under the impact of the Jesuits, universities broadened the curriculum. Although the universities did not teach the New Sciences and Enlightenment of northwestern Europe, there was nevertheless scientific research on tropical diseases, plants, and animals. The extent of this research was long kept secret by the Spanish and Portuguese monarchs from their European competitors.

Furthermore, missionary monks collected and recorded Native American manuscripts and oral traditions, such as the Aztec *Anales de Tula* and the Maya *Popol Vuh*. Others wrote histories and ethnographies of the indigenous peoples.

Jesuit missionaries, from the Church of San Pedro in Lima, Peru, ca. 1700

A number of Native American and mestizo chroniclers, historians, and commentators on the early modern state and society are similarly noteworthy. Felipe Guamán Poma de Ayala (ca. 1535–1616), a native Peruvian, is of particular interest. He accompanied his 800-page manuscript, entitled (in English translation) *The First New Chronicle and Good Government*, with some 400 drawings of daily-life activities in the Peruvian villages. Unfortunately, King Philip II of Spain forbade in 1577 the publication of all manuscripts dealing with what he called idolatry and superstition. Many manuscripts lay hidden in archives until modern times.

illustration from Willem Piso's *Natural History of Brazil* (1637)

Protestantism in New England   Religious diversity was a defining cultural trait of English settlements in North America. The spectrum of Christian denominations ranged from English and continental European versions of Protestantism to Anglicanism and a minority of Catholics. Dissenters frequently split from the existing denominations, moved into new territory, and founded new settlements.

An early example of religious splintering was the rise of an antinomian ("anti-law") group within Puritan-dominated Massachusetts. The preachers and settlers represented in the General Court, as their assembly was called, were committed to the Calvinist balance between "inner" personal grace obtained from God and "outer" works according to the law. The antinomian group, however, advocated an exclusive commitment to inner grace through spiritual perfection.

Their leader was Anne Hutchinson, an early proponent of women's rights and an inspiring preacher. She was accused of arguing that she could recognize those believers in Calvinist Protestantism who were predestined for salvation and that these believers would be saved even if they had sinned. After a power struggle, the General Court prevailed and forced the antinomians to move to Rhode Island in 1638.

The example of Hutchinson is noteworthy because it led to the founding of Harvard College in 1636 by the General Court. Harvard was the first institution of higher learning in North America.

Witch Trial. In the course of the 1600s, in the relatively autonomous English colonies of Northeast America, more persons were accused, tried, and convicted of witchcraft than anywhere else. Of the 140 persons coming to trial between 1620 and 1725, 86 percent were women. Three witch panics are recorded: Bermuda, 1651; Hartford, Connecticut, 1652–1665; and Salem, Massachusetts, 1692–1693. This anonymous American woodcut of the early 1600s shows one method used to try someone for witchcraft: The accused would swim or float, if guilty—or sink, if innocent.

New Sciences Research   As discussed in Chapter 17, the New Sciences had their most hospitable home in northwestern Europe, where the rivalry between Protestantism and Catholicism had left enough of an authority-free space for the New Sciences to flourish. Under similar circumstances—intense rivalry among denominations—English North America also proved hospitable to the New Sciences. An early practitioner was Benjamin Franklin (1706–1790), who began his career as a printer, journalist, and newspaper editor. Franklin founded the University of Pennsylvania (1740), the first secular university in North America, and the American Philosophical Society (1743), the first scientific society. This hospitality for the New Sciences in North America was in contrast to Latin America, where a uniform Catholic Reformation prevented its rise.

Witch Hunts   In the last decade of the seventeenth century, religious intensity was at the root of a witchcraft frenzy that seized New England. Witches, male and female, were believed to be persons exerting a negative influence, or black magic, on their victims. In medieval Europe, the church had kept witchcraft hidden, but in the wake of challenges to church authority, it had become more visible. In the North American colonies, with no overarching religious authority, the visibility of witchcraft was particularly high.

This sensitivity erupted into hysteria in Salem, Massachusetts, in 1692. Tituba, a Native American slave from Barbados, worked in the household of a pastor. She practiced voodoo, the West African–originated, part-African and part-Christian religious practice of influencing others. When young girls in the pastor's household suffered from convulsions, mass hysteria broke out, in which 20 women accused of being witches were executed. (Tituba, ironically, survived.) A new governor finally restored order.

Revivalism   Religious fervor expressed itself also in periodic Protestant renewal movements, such as the "Great Awakening" of the 1730s and 1740s. The main impulse for this revivalist movement came from the brothers John and Charles Wesley, two Methodist preachers in England who toured Georgia in 1735. Preachers from other denominations joined, all exhorting Protestants to literally "start anew" in their relationship with God. Thus, revivalism, recurring with great regularity to the present, became a potent force in Protestant America, at opposing purposes with secular founding-father constitutionalism.

» Putting It All Together

interactive concept map

During the period 1500–1800 the contours of a new pattern in which the Americas formed a resource-rich extension of Europe took shape. During this time, China and India continued to be the most populous and wealthiest agrarian–urban regions of the world. In 1500, Europe was struggling to defend itself against the push of the Ottoman Empire into eastern Europe and the western Mediterranean. But its successful conquest of Iberia from the Muslims led to the discovery of the Americas. Possession of the Americas made Europe similar to China and India in that it now encompassed, in addition to its northerly cold climates, subtropical and tropical regions that produced cash crops as well as precious metals. Over the next 300 years, Europe narrowed the gap between itself and China and India.

However, because of fierce competition both with the Ottoman Empire and internally, much of the wealth Europe gained in the Americas was wasted on warfare. The centralizing state, created in part to support war, ran into insurmountable budgetary barriers. Even mercantilism, a logical extension of the centralizing state, had limited effects. Its centerpiece, state support for the export of manufactures to the American colonies, functioned unevenly. The Spanish and Portuguese governments, with weak urban infrastructures and low manufacturing capabilities, were unable to enforce this state-supported trade until the eighteenth century and even then only in very limited ways. France and England practiced mercantilism more successfully, but were able to do so in the Americas only from the late seventeenth century onward, when their plantation systems began to take shape. Although the American extension of Europe had the potential of making Europe self-sufficient, this potential was realized only partially during the colonial period.

Debate continues over the question of the degree of wealth the Americas added to Europe. On one hand, research has established that the British slave trade for sugar plantations added at best 1 percent to the British gross domestic product (GDP). The profits from the production of sugar on the English island of Jamaica may have added another 4 percent to the British GDP. Without doubt, private slave-trading and sugar-producing enterprises were immensely profitable to individuals and groups. However, these profits were smaller if one takes into account the immense waste of revenues on military ventures—hence, the doubts raised by scholars today about large gains made by Europe through its American colonial acquisitions.

On the other hand, the European extension to the Americas was clearly a momentous event in world history. It might have produced dubious overall profits for Europe, but it definitely encouraged the parting of ways between Europe on one hand and Asia and Africa on the other, once a new scientific–industrial society began to emerge around 1800.

Review and Relate

Thinking Through Patterns

Examine the ways historians approach the big questions of this chapter.

In their role as subtropical and tropical extensions of Europe, the Americas had a considerable impact on Europe's changing position in the world. First, Europe acquired large quantities of precious metals, which its two largest competitors, India and China, lacked. Second, with its new access to warm-weather agricultural products, Europe rose to a position of agrarian autonomy similar to that of India and China. In terms of resources, compared with the principal religious civilizations of India and China, Europe grew between 1550 and 1800 from a position of inferiority to one of near parity.

> What is the significance of western Europeans acquiring the Americas as a warm-weather extension of their northern continent?

Because the numbers of Europeans who emigrated to the Americas was low for most of the colonial period, they never exceeded the numbers of Native Americans or African slaves. The result was a privileged settler society that held superior positions on the top rung of the social hierarchy. In principle, given an initially large indigenous population, labor was cheap and should have become more expensive as diseases reduced the Native Americans. In fact, labor always remained cheap, in part because of forced labor and in part because of racial prejudice.

> What was the main pattern of social development in colonial America during the period 1500–1800?

> ≫ **Why and how did European settlers in South and North America strive for self-government, and how successful were they in achieving their goals?**

Two contrasting patterns characterized the way in which European colonies were governed. The Spanish and Portuguese crowns, interested in extracting minerals and warm-weather products from the colonies, were motivated to exercise centralized control over their possessions in the Americas. In contrast, the British crown granted self-government to the Northeast American colonies from the start, in part because the colonies were far less important economically and in part because of a long tradition of self-rule at home. Nevertheless, even though Latin American settlers achieved only partial self-rule in their towns and cities, they destroyed central rule indirectly through the purchase of offices. After financial reforms, Spain and Portugal reestablished a degree of central rule through the appointment of officers from the home countries.

| Against the Grain

Consider this as a counterpoint to the main patterns examined in this chapter.

Juana Inés de la Cruz

- Why were the Latin American colonies more socially conservative than Europe?

- Was de la Cruz right to stop her correspondence with the Mexican clergy in 1693?

In the wake of the Protestant and Catholic Reformations of the 1500s, it was no longer unusual for European women to pursue higher education. In the more conservative Latin American colonies of Spain, Juana Inés de la Cruz (1651–1695) was less fortunate, even though her fame as the intellectually most brilliant figure of the seventeenth century in the colonies endured.

De la Cruz was the illegitimate child of a Spanish immigrant father and a Creole mother. She grew up on the hacienda of her maternal grandfather, in whose library she secretly studied Latin, Greek, and Nahuatl, and also composed her first poems. Unable, as a woman, to be admitted to the university in Mexico City, de la Cruz was fortunate to receive further education from the wife of the vice regent of New Spain. In order to continue her studies, she entered a convent in 1668. Here, she continued to study and write hundreds of poems, comedies, religious dramas, and theological texts. Her seminars with courtiers and scholarly visitors were a major attraction.

In 1688, however, she lost her protection at court with the departure of her viceregal supporters for Spain. Her superior, the archbishop of Mexico, was an open misogynist. A crisis came in 1690 when the bishop of Puebla published de la Cruz's critique of a famous sermon of 1650 by the Portuguese Jesuit António Vieira on Jesus's act of washing his disciples' feet, together with his own critique of de la Cruz. De la Cruz viewed Vieira's interpretation as more hierarchical/male and her own interpretation as more humble/female.

A year later, in 1691, de la Cruz wrote a spirited riposte to the bishop's apparently well-meaning advice to her in his critique to be more conscious of her status as a woman. Her message was clear: Even though women had to be silent in church, as St. Paul had taught, neither study nor writing was prohibited for women. Before the church could censor her, in 1693 Juana Inés de la Cruz stopped writing. She died two years later.

Key Terms

audio flashcards

Columbian Exchange   419
Creoles   412

Labor assignment
(*repartimiento*)   414

Land-labor grant
(*encomienda*)   408

For additional resources, please go to
www.oup.com/us/vonsivers.
Please see the Further Resources section at the back of the book for additional readings and suggested websites.

Further Resources

Chapter 1

Burroughs, William J. *Climate Change in Prehistory: The End of the Reign of Chaos.* Cambridge: Cambridge University Press, 2005. Very well-researched and up-to-date discussion of climate and human evolution.

Finlayson, Clive. *The Humans Who Went Extinct: Why Neanderthals Died Out and We Survived.* Oxford and New York: Oxford University Press, 2010. A comprehensive history of human evolution in the context of geological and climatic changes, by the excavator of the last Neanderthal traces in Europe.

Flood, Josephine. *Archaeology of the Dreamtime: The Story of Prehistoric Australia and Its People.* New Haven, CT.: Yale University Press, 1989. Overview of the Australian archaeological record; short on discussion of Aboriginal Dreamtime and myths.

Johanson, Donald, and Kate Wong. *Lucy: The Quest for Human Origins.* New York: Three Rivers, 2009.

Lawson, Andrew J. *Painted Caves: Palaeolithic Rock Art in Western Europe.* Oxford and New York: Oxford University Press, 2012. Presents an extensive overview ("gazetteer") of the various sites and analyzes the rock art phenomenon in great detail.

McBrearty, Sally, and Allison S. Brooks. "The Revolution that Wasn't: A New Interpretation of the Origin of Modern Human Behavior." *Journal of Human Evolution* 39 (2000): 453–463. Crucial, pioneering article in which the authors grounded anatomically and intellectually modern *H. sapiens* in Africa.

Pääbo, Svante. *Neanderthal Man: In Search of the Lost Genomes.* New York: Basic Books, 2014. Pääbo is the first palaeogeneticist to sequence the full genome of a Neanderthal fossil as well as that of a new species of hominin, Dinoseva, discovered in Siberia in 2010.

Pauketat, Timothy, ed. *The Oxford North American Handbook of Archaeology.* Oxford and New York: Oxford University Press, 2012. Very detailed coverage of Paleo-Indian migrations and settlements. Needs to be supplemented with the March 2014 article in *Science* by Dennis O'Rourke, John Hoffecker, and Scott Elias on humans being trapped for 10,000 years on the habitable south coast of Beringia.

Tattersall, Ian. *Masters of the Planet: The Search for Human Origins.* New York: Palgrave Macmillan, 2012. A scholarly well-founded overview for the general reader, by one of the leading senior paleoanthropologists.

WEBSITES

Bradshaw Foundation, http://www.bradshawfoundation.com/. The Bradshaw Foundation has a large website on human evolution and rock art, with many images, and a link to Stephen Oppenheimer's website Journey of Mankind: The Peopling of the World, an important overview of *Homo sapiens'* migrations.

Institute of Human Origins, Arizona State University, http://iho.asu.edu/. Arizona State University's Institute of Human Origins runs the popular but scholarly well-founded website Becoming Human (http://www.becominghuman.org/).

Chapter 2

Alcock, Susan E., John Bodel, and Richard J. A. Talbert, eds. *Highways, Byways, and Road Systems in the Pre-Modern World.* Chichester: John Wiley & Sons, 2012. Fascinating global survey of methods of transport and communication.

Assmann, Jan. *The Search for God in Ancient Egypt.* Ithaca, N.Y.: Cornell University Press, 2001. Reflective investigation of the dimensions of Egyptian polytheism by a leading Egyptologist.

Bottéro, Jean. *Mesopotamia: Writing, Reasoning, and the Gods.* Chicago: University of Chicago Press, 1992. Classic intellectual history of ancient Mesopotamia.

Drews, Robert. *The End of the Bronze Age: Changes in Warfare and the Catastrophe ca. 1200 B.C.* Princeton, N.J.: Princeton University Press, 1993. Closely argued essay on the destruction of Mycenaean culture and its consequences for the eastern Mediterranean.

Finkelstein, Israel. *The Archaeology of the Israelite Settlement.* Jerusalem: Israel Exploration Society, 1988. Authoritative presentation of the archaeology of the earliest period of Israelite social formation.

Kramer, Samuel Noah. *The Sumerians: Their History, Culture, and Character.* Chicago: University of Chicago Press, 2010. An expanded version of Kramer's earlier work, *History Begins at Sumer* (1988), this is a fascinating presentation of the many "firsts" originating in the world's earliest urban civilization, written by a leading Sumerologist.

Mithen, Steven. *After the Ice: A Global Human History, 20,000–5000 B.C.* Cambridge, Mass.: Harvard University Press, 2003. Engagingly written story of humans settling, becoming farmers, and founding villages and towns, as seen through the eyes of a modern time traveler.

Podany, Amanda H. *The Ancient Near East: A Very Short Introduction.* Oxford and New York: Oxford University Press, 2014. Readable survey of the origin and development of Near Eastern civilizations.

Van de Mieroop, Marc. *The Ancient Mesopotamian City.* Oxford: Clarendon, 1997. Full examination of Mesopotamian urban institutions, including city assemblies.

WEBSITES

British Museum. Ancient Egypt, http://www.ancientegypt.co.uk/menu.html. Pictorial introduction, with short texts.

Livius.org. "Mesopotamia," http://www.livius.org/babylonia.html. A large collection of translated texts and references to philological articles, with portals on Mesopotamia, Egypt, Anatolia, and Greece.

Oriental Institute, University of Chicago. Ancient Mesopotamia, http://mesopotamia.lib.uchicago.edu/. A user-friendly portal to the world-renowned Mesopotamia collection of the Oriental Institute.

Chapter 3

Bryant, Edwin. *The Quest for the Origins of Vedic Culture: The Indo-Aryan Migration Debate.* Oxford and New York: Oxford University Press, 2001. A scholarly yet readable attempt to address the linguistic and archaeological evidence surrounding the thesis of Aryan migration versus the more recent theory of indigenous Vedic development.

Embree, Ainslee T., ed. *Sources of Indian Tradition*, vol. 1, 2nd ed. New York: Columbia University Press, 1988. Though the language is dated in places, this is still the most comprehensive sourcebook of Indian thought available. Recent additions on women and gender make it even more so. Sophisticated yet readable introductions, glosses, and commentary.

Eraly, Abraham. *Gem in the Lotus: The Seeding of Indian Civilization*. London: Weidenfeld & Nicholson, 2004. Readable, comprehensive survey of recent scholarship from prehistory to the reign of Ashoka during the Mauryan dynasty of the fourth and third centuries BCE. Emphasis on transitional period of sixth-century religious innovations, particularly Buddhism.

Kenoyer, Jonathan Mark. *Ancient Cities of the Indus Valley Civilization*. Oxford and New York: Oxford University Press, 1998. Comprehensive work by team leader of Harappan Research Project. Particularly good on Lothal.

Klostermaier, Klaus. *A Survey of Hinduism*, 3rd ed. Albany, NY: SUNY Press, 2007. Comprehensive thematic treatment of major themes of Hinduism from the Vedas to Hinduism's relationship to modern science.

Possehl, Gregory L., ed. *Harappan Civilization: A Recent Perspective*, 2nd ed. New Delhi: Oxford University Press, 1993. Sound and extensive treatment of recent work and issues in Indus valley archaeology by one of the leading on-site researchers and a former student of Fairservis. Used to best advantage by experienced students.

Singh, Upinder. *A History of Ancient and Early Medieval India: From the Stone Age to the 12th Century*. New Delhi: Pearson, 2008. Sweeping text by a longtime instructor of Indian history at the University of Delhi. Suitable for undergraduates and current on the latest debates on ancient origins.

Trautmann, Thomas. *India: Brief History of a Civilization*. Oxford and New York: Oxford University Press, 2011. A succinct and lucid account of 4,000 years of Indian history, with particular emphasis on early developments.

Wolpert, Stanley. *A New History of India*, 5th ed. Oxford and New York: Oxford University Press, 2004. Another extremely useful, readable, one-volume history from Neolithic times to the present. Excellent first work for serious students.

WEBSITES

Columbia University Libraries. South and Southeast Asian Studies, www.columbia.edu/cu/lweb/indiv/southasia/cuvl/history.html. Run by Columbia University, this site contains links to "WWW.Virtual Library: Indian History"; "Regnal Chronologies"; "Internet Indian History Sourcebook"; and "Medical History of British India."

Harappa, http://www.harappa.com. Contains a wealth of images of artifacts and other archaeological treasures from the Indus Valley.

Chapter 4

Chang, Kwang-chih. *The Archaeology of Ancient China*, 4th ed. New Haven, CT.: Yale University Press, 1986. Sophisticated treatment of archaeology of Shang China. Prime exponent of the view of overlapping periods and territories for the Sandai period. Erudite, yet accessible for experienced students.

Ebrey, Patricia Buckley, ed. *Chinese Civilization: A Sourcebook*, 2nd ed. New York: Free Press, 1993. Wonderful supplement to the preceding volume. Some different classical sources and considerable material on women and social history. Time frame of this work extends to the modern era.

Keightly, David N., ed. *The Origins of Chinese Civilization*. Berkeley and Los Angeles: University of California Press, 1983. Symposium volume on a variety of Sandai topics by leading scholars. Some exposure to early Chinese history and archaeology is necessary in order to best appreciate these essays.

Linduff, Katheryn M., and Yan Sun, eds. *Gender and Chinese Archaeology*. Walnut Creek, CA: Altamira, 2004. Reexamines the role of gender in ancient China in the context of a critique of the general lack of gendered research in archaeology as a whole.

Liu, Xiang. *Exemplary Women of Early China: The Lienu zhuan of Liu Xiang*. Edited and translated by Anne Behnke Kinney. New York: Columbia University Press, 2014. One of the few accounts we have of the lives of women during the Three Dynasties period; covers 120 short biographies of Zhou women.

Lowe, Michael, and Edward L. Shaughnessy, eds. *The Cambridge History of Ancient China: From the Origins of Civilization to 221 B.C.* Cambridge, UK: Cambridge University Press, 1999. The opening volume of the Cambridge History of China series, this is the most complete multiessay collection on all aspects of recent Chinese ancient historical and archaeological work. The place to start for the serious student contemplating in-depth research.

Thorp, Robert L. *China in the Early Bronze Age: Shang Civilization*. Philadelphia: University of Pennsylvania Press, 2006. Comprehensive yet accessible survey of recent archaeological work on the period 2070–1046 BCE, including traditional Xia and Shang periods under the heading of China's "bronze age."

Wang, Aihe. *Cosmology and Political Culture in Early China*. Cambridge: Cambridge University Press, 2000. Part of the Cambridge Studies in Chinese History, Literature, and Institutions series. Wang argues that control of *cosmology*—how the world and universe operate—was a vital key to the wielding of power by the Shang and Zhou rulers. Recommended for serious students.

Wang, Robin. *Images of Women in Chinese Thought and Culture: Writings from the Pre-Qin Period Through the Song Dynasty*. Indianapolis, IN: Hackett Publishing, 2003. Excerpts from classical and more obscure texts on the role and treatment of women in early China. A large and useful section on pre-Confucian texts.

Watson, Burton, trans. *The Tso Chuan: Selections from China's Oldest Narrative History*. New York: Columbia University Press, 1989. Elegant translation by one of the most prolific of scholars working today. Excellent introduction to Zhou period and politics. Appropriate for beginning students, though more useful for those with some prior introduction to the period.

WEBSITES

http://lucian.uchicago.edu/blogs/earlychina/ssec/. This is the site of the journal *Early China*, published by the Society for the Study of Early China.

British Museum. Ancient China, http://www.ancientchina.co.uk. This site provides access to the British Museum's ancient Chinese collections and is highly useful for students seeking illustrations of assorted artifacts in a user-friendly environment.

Chapter 5

The Americas

Bellwood, Peter. *First Migrants: Ancient Migration in Global Perspective*. Chichester, UK: John Wiley & Sons, 2013. An intriguing study of prehistoric migration and its role in shaping the emergence of civilization.

Benson, Sonia, and Deborah J. Baker. *Early Civilizations in the Americas Reference Library*, 3 vols. Farmington Hills, MI: Gale UXL, 2009. Extensive three-volume encyclopedia available as a download or in hard copy. Contains an almanac of historical information and one of biographies and primary sources. Recommended for beginning and experienced students.

Bruhns, Karen Olsen, and Karen E. Stothert. *Women in Ancient America*. Norman: University of Oklahoma Press, 1999. A comprehensive account of women's roles in daily life, religion, politics, and war in foraging and farming as well as urban societies in the Americas.

Fiedel, Stuart J. *Prehistory of the Americas*, 2nd ed. Cambridge, UK: Cambridge University Press, 1992. Accessible, detailed survey of the archaeology of the Americas by a leading American scholar.

Solis, Ruth Shady, Haas, Jonathan, and Creamer, Winifred. "Dating Caral, a Preceramic Site in the Supe Valley on the Central Coast of Peru," *Science* 292:5517(2001): 723-726. Path-breaking early report of early scientific work on Caral Supe and the oldest American cities.

Thomas, David Hurst. *Exploring Native North America*. Oxford and New York: Oxford University Press, 2000. Selected chapters are useful on the major early North American sites, particularly Adena and Hopewell.

Trigger, Bruce G., Wilcomb E. Washburn, Richard E. W. Adams, Murdo J. MacLeod, Frank Salomon, and Stuart B. Schwartz, eds. *Cambridge History of the Native Peoples of the Americas*, 3 vols. Cambridge, UK: Cambridge University Press, 1996–2000. As with all of the Cambridge histories, this is a highly useful set for beginner and accomplished scholar alike. Useful bibliographies with the article entries.

von Hagen, Adriana, and Craig Morris. *The Cities of the Ancient Andes*. New York: Thames & Hudson, 1999. While more geared to later periods, still a useful overview, with illustrations, by specialists on Andean cultures.

Oceania

Carson, Mike T., *First Settlement of Remote Oceania: Earliest Sites in the Mariana Islands*. Heidelberg: Springer-Verlag, 2014. Study based on new archaeological research by a specialist on Pacific research.

Kirch, Patrick V. *The Lapita Peoples: Ancestors of the Oceanic World*. Cambridge, MA: Blackwell, 1997. Basic introduction by one of the pioneers of Polynesian research.

Matsuda, Matt K.. *Pacific Worlds: A History of Seas, Peoples, and Cultures*. Cambridge, UK: Cambridge University Press, 2012. General history of the Pacific with an emphasis on the early modern period.

Vlchek, Andre. *Oceania: Neocolonialism, Nukes and Bones*. Auckland, New Zealand: Atuanui, 2013. Analysis and discussion of the harmful effects of colonialism and neocolonialism on the development of Oceania.

WEBSITES

Foundation for the Advancement of Mesoamerican Studies (FAMSI), http://www.famsi.org/. Home page for the foundation, which has recently begun collaboration with the Los Angeles County Museum of Art and runs a wide range of scholarly, funding, and educational outreach programs aimed at advancing studies of Mesoamerica.

http://www.britannica.com/EBchecked/topic/468832/Polynesian-culture. Good link leading to an 8,000-word essay on leading topics concerning Polynesia and Oceania. In order to access the complete essay the reader must apply for a free trial of the online *Encyclopedia Britannica*.

Chapter 6

Sub-Saharan Africa

Chami, Félix. *The Unity of African Ancient History: 3000 BC to 500 AD*. Dar es Salaam: E&D, 2006. General overview by one of the leading archaeologists of East Africa.

McIntosh, Roderick J. *Ancient Middle Niger: Urbanism and the Self-Organizing Landscape*. Cambridge, UK: Cambridge University Press, 2005. Important revisionist work on the origins of urbanism and kingship in West Africa.

Mitchell, Peter, and Paul Lane. *The Oxford Handbook of African Archaeology*. Oxford: Oxford University Press, 2013. A total of 70 essays by specialists on all aspects of human culture in Africa, with an emphasis on foragers, agriculturalists, and early urbanists.

Vansina, Jan. *Paths in the Rainforests: Toward a History of Political Tradition in Equatorial Africa*. Madison: University of Wisconsin Press, 1990. Magisterial presentation of the Bantu dispersal and village life in the rain forest.

Mesoamerica and the Andes

Aveni, Anthony F. *Skywatchers*, rev. ed. Austin: University of Texas Press, 2001. Classic study on astronomy and calendars of pre-Columbian Americans, including a discussion of the Nazca lines.

Braswell, Geoffrey E., ed. *The Ancient Maya of Mexico: Reinterpreting the Past of the Northern Lowlands*. Milton Park, UK, and New York: Routledge, 2014. Contains articles on the origins of the ballgame and the Mayan "collapse."

Evans, Susan Tobey. *Ancient Mexico and Central America: Archaeology and Culture History*. London: Thames & Hudson, 2004. Densely but clearly written and detailed, with many sidebars on special topics.

Grube, Nikolai, ed. *Maya: Divine Kings of the Rain Forest*. Cologne, Germany: Könemann, 2001. Lavishly illustrated book with short contributions by many hands.

Schele, Linda, and David Freidel. *A Forest of Kings: The Untold Story of the Ancient Maya*. New York: Quill-William Morrow, 1990. Classic study summarizing the results of the decipherment of Maya glyphs, by two pioneers.

Stuart, David. *The Order of Days: Unlocking the Secrets of the Ancient Maya*. New York: Three Rivers Press, 2011. Magisterial summary of our current knowledge of Maya culture.

WEBSITES

Museum of Native American History. http://www.monah.us/precolumbian: Basic but fairly comprehensive website on pre-Columbian peoples and civilizations.

Stanford University Libraries. Africa South of the Sahara, http://www-sul.stanford.edu/depts/ssrg/africa/history.html. A large, resource-filled website based at Stanford University.

Chapter 7

Boatwright, Mary, Daniel J. Gargola, and Richard J. A. Talbert. *The Romans: From Village to Empire*. New York: Oxford University Press, 2004. Clearly written, comprehensive introduction to Roman history.

Boyce, Mary. *A History of Zoroastrianism*. Vol. 1, *The Early Period*, rev. ed. Handbuch der Orientalistik. Leiden, the Netherlands: E. J. Brill, 1989. Standard work by the leading scholar on the subject.

Briant, Pierre. *From Cyrus to Alexander: A History of the Persian Empire*. Winona Lake, IN: Eisenbrauns, 2000. Monumental work; the most detailed and authoritative study of the topic to date.

Cameron, Averil. *The Mediterranean World in Late Antiquity, AD 395–600*. London: Routledge, 1993. New perspective on the strengths and weaknesses of the late Roman empire.

Dignas, Beate, and Engelbert Winter. *Rome and Persia in Late Antiquity: Neighbours and Rivals*. Cambridge, UK: Cambridge University Press, 2007. Detailed historical investigation of the rivalry between Rome and Persia.

Freeman, Phillip. *Alexander the Great*. New York: Simon & Schuster, 2011. Illuminating study of Alexander the Great intended for a general audience.

Hubbard, Thomas K., ed. *A Companion to Greek and Roman Sexualities*. Chichester, UK: John Wiley & Sons, 2014. Far-ranging and informative collection of essays on all aspects of sexuality in ancient Greece and Rome.

Lehoux, Daryn. *What Did the Romans Know? An Inquiry into Science and Worldmaking*. Chicago: University of Chicago Press, 2012. Sophisticated analysis of Roman science in both its derivative and unique aspects.

Mathisen, Ralph. *Ancient Mediterranean Civilizations: From Prehistory to 640 CE*, 2nd ed. Oxford and New York: Oxford University Press, 2014. Revised overview with special emphasis on ethnicity, gender, and slavery.

Shaked, Shaul. *Dualism in Transformation: Varieties of Religion in Sasanian Iran*. London: School of Oriental and African Studies, 1994. Short history of the different religions in Sasanid Persia.

Smith, Mark S. *The Early History of God: Yahweh and the Other Deities in Ancient Israel*. San Francisco: Harper & Row, 1990. Very readable introduction to the problem of early monotheism among Israelites.

WEBSITES

British Museum. Ancient Greece, http://www.ancientgreece.co.uk/menu.html. Open the door to the compelling world of Ancient Greece. The British Museum has compiled a collection of images and information on various aspects of Greek history such as the Acropolis, Athens, daily life, festivals and games, Sparta, war, and gods.

Harvard University. Digital Atlas of Roman and Medieval Civilizations, http://darmc.harvard.edu/icb/icb.do?keyword=k40248&pageid=icb.page188868. Harvard University allows students to tailor searches in order to access specific geopolitical and spatial cartographical representations of the Roman and medieval worlds.

Perseus Digital Library, http://www.perseus.tufts.edu/hopper/. Probably the largest website on Greece and Rome, with immense resources, hosted by Tufts University.

Chapter 8

Auboyer, Jeannine. *Daily Life in Ancient India*. London: Phoenix, 2002. Overview consisting of sections on social structures/religious principles; individual/collective existence; and royal and administrative existence. Multidisciplinary approach appropriate for most undergraduates.

Carter, John Ross, and Mahinda Palihawadana, trans. *The Dhammapada*. Oxford and New York: Oxford University Press, 1987. Erudite but accessible translation of one of the key texts in the Buddhist corpus. Students with some exposure to the introductory ideas of Buddhism will find it very useful in its step-by-step elucidation of a number of central concepts.

Chakravarti, Uma. *The Social Dimensions of Early Buddhism*. New Delhi: Oxford University Press, 1987. Thorough analysis, with extensive glossary, of the influence of the north Indian economic transition to peasant market farming on the social milieu of early Buddhism.

Diem-Lane, Andrea. *Ahimsa: A Brief Guide to Jainism*. Walnut, CA: MSAC Philosophy Group, 2016. Short, student-friendly guide to Jain concepts, history, and Jainism today.

Doniger, Wendy. *The Hindus: An Alternative History*. New York: Penguin, 2009. Vivid but controversial new interpretation of the history of Hinduism by one of the leading scholars of Indian history. The book's portrayals of Hindu history, particularly in the area between myth and history, have prompted a lawsuit in India, which resulted in the withdrawal of the book there by the publisher in early 2014.

Embree, Ainslee T. *Sources of Indian Tradition*, 2 vols, 2nd ed. New York: Columbia University Press, 1988. The latest edition contains a number of new selections useful for the study of social relations in addition to the older religious material. As with all of the works in this series, the level of writing is sophisticated, though accessible; the overviews are masterly; and the works are ably translated.

Keay, John. *India: A History*. New York: Grove, 2000. Lively, highly detailed narrative history, with a number of useful charts and genealogies of ruling houses. Sympathetic treatment of controversial matters.

Knott, Kim. *Hinduism: A Very Short Introduction*. Oxford and New York: Oxford University Press, 1998. Sound, brief discussion of modern Hinduism and its formative influences. Asks provocative questions such as "What is a religion?" and "Is Hinduism something more than the Western conception of religion?"

Nikam, N. A., and Richard McKeon, eds. and trans. *The Edicts of Asoka*. Chicago: University of Chicago Press, 1959. Slim but useful volume for those interested in reading the entire collection of Ashoka's Pillar, Cave, and Rock Edicts. Short, accessible introduction.

Willis, Michael. *The Archaeology of Hindu Ritual*. Cambridge, UK: Cambridge University Press, 2009. Best utilized by experienced students, this book uses site archaeology, Sanskrit documents, and studies of ancient astronomy to plot the development of Hinduism under the Guptas and their use of it in statecraft as they created their vision of a universal empire.

Wolpert, Stanley. *A New History of India*, 6th ed. Oxford and New York: Oxford University Press, 2000. The standard introductory work to the long sweep of Indian history. Evenly divided between the period up to and including the Mughals and the modern era. Good coverage of geography and environment, as well as social and gender issues. Good select bibliography arranged by chapter; highly useful glossary of Indian terms.

WEBSITE

Digital Library of India, http://www.dli.ernet.in. This online resource, hosted by the Indian Institute of Science, Bangalore, contains primary and secondary sources not only for history but also for culture, economics, literature, and a host of other subjects.

Chapter 9

Henricks, Robert C., trans. *Lao-Tzu, Te-Tao Ching. A New Translation Based on the Recently Discovered Ma-wang-tui Texts.* New York: Ballantine Books, 1989. Some of the intitial work done on the earliest extant Daoist texts, reinterpreting our understanding of philosophical Daoism.

Hinsch, Bret. *Women in Early Imperial China.* Lanham, MD: Rowman & Littlefield, 2002. Broad examination of the place of women, and transition of the place of women, during the crucial early Chinese dynasties.

Huang, Ray. *China: A Macro History.* Armonk, NY: M. E. Sharpe, 1997. Readable, entertaining, and highly useful one-volume history. Particularly good on the complex politics of the post-Han and Song–Yuan periods.

Keay, John. *China: A History.* New York: Basic Books, 2009. Adventurous and well-written general history of China from prehistory to the present. Especially good for students with some previous grounding in the essentials of Chinese history.

Lewis, Mark Edward. *The Early Chinese Empires: Qin and Han.* Cambridge, MA: Harvard University Press, 2007. Detailed exploration of the rise and adaptations of China's initial empires. Better for advanced students.

Qian, Sima. *Records of the Grand Historian.* Translated by Burton Watson. 3 vols., rev. ed. New York: Columbia University Press, 1993. Powerful translation of China's supreme historical work by one of its best interpreters. Includes material from the Qin and Han dynasties. Invaluable source for serious students.

Snow, Philip. *The Star Raft: China's Encounter with Africa.* Ithaca, NY: Cornell University Press, 1988. Important, accessible study of the little-known area of China's maritime trade with Africa from Han times to the epic fifteenth-century voyages of Zheng He and beyond.

Yao Xinzhong. *An Introduction to Confucianism.* Cambridge, UK: Cambridge University Press, 2000. Overview of the tradition of the *ru* as it evolved and its status today.

WEBSITES

Asian Topics for Asian Educators. "Defining 'Daoism': A Complex History," http://afe.easia.columbia.edu/cosmos/ort/daoism.htm. Looks at Daoism as a term, its use, and its practice in terms of morality, society, nature, and the self.

http://bulldog2.redlands.edu/Dept/AsianStudiesDept/index.html. *East and Southeast Asia: An Annotated Directory of Internet Resources.* One of the most complete guides to websites dealing with all manner of Chinese and East Asian history and society.

Chapter 10

The Arabian Nights. Translated by Husain Haddawy. New York: Norton, 1990. Translation of the critical edition by Muhsin Mahdi, which reconstitutes the original thirteenth-century text.

Barry, Michael. *Figurative Art in Medieval Islam and the Riddle of Bihazâd of Herât (1465–1535).* Paris: Flammarion, 2004.

Chaudhuri, K. N. *Trade and Civilization in the Indian Ocean.* Cambridge, UK: Cambridge University Press, 1985. Discusses the historical evolution of the trade and its various aspects (sea route, ships, commodities, and capital investments).

Fryde, Edmund. *The Early Palaeologan Renaissance (1261–c. 1360).* Leiden, the Netherlands: E. J. Brill, 2000. Detailed presentation of the main philosophical and scientific figures of Byzantium after the recovery from the Latin interruption.

Herrin, Judith. *Unrivalled Influence: Women and Empire in Byzantium.* Princeton, NJ: Princeton University Press, 2013. Detailed investigation by a leading Byzantine historian and engagegd feminist.

Hoyland, Robert. *In God's Path: The Arab Conquests and the Creation of an Islamic Empire.* Oxford and New York: Oxford University Press, 2014. A new history of Islamic origins, seeking to combine Christian and Islamic sources.

Khalili, Jim al-. *The House of Wisdom: How Arabic Science Saved Ancient Knowledge and Gave Us the Renaissance.* New York: Penguin, 2010. In spite of the somewhat overwrought title, an expertly written introduction to the golden age of Arabic science by a scientist.

Laiou, Angeliki E., and Cécile Morrisson. *The Byzantine Economy.* Cambridge, UK: Cambridge University Press, 2007. Comprehensive and well-researched study of ups and downs in the demography, productive capacity, and long-distance trade of Byzantium.

Lapidus, Ira. *Muslim Cities in the Later Middle Ages.* Cambridge, UK: Cambridge University Press, 1984. Seminal work and still the only study of Muslim urban society, although it should be supplemented by Shlomo D. Goitein's monumental study of Jews, *A Mediterranean Society* (1967–1993).

Rippin, Andrew. *Muslims: Their Religious Beliefs and Practices*, 2nd ed. London: Routledge, 2001. One of the best and most accessible introductions to the basic beliefs and practices of Islam, based on the reevaluation of Islamic origins also presented in this chapter.

Tyerman, Christopher. *God's War: A New History of the Crusades.* Cambridge, MA: Belknap, 2006. Persuasive revisionist history by a leading Crusade historian.

Whittow, Mark. *The Making of Byzantium, 600–1025.* Berkeley and Los Angeles: University of California Press, 1996. Revisionist study of the Byzantine struggle for survival in the early years.

WEBSITES

BBC—Religion: Islam. http://www.bbc.co.uk/religion/religions/islam/. A very basic overview of Islamic Civilization. Most websites on Islam and Islamic civilization are apologetic (pro-Muslim or pro-Christian), and earlier scholarly websites are no longer available.

Islamic Awareness. http://www.islamic-awareness.org/. This website, even though Islam-apologetic, is a fountain of early documents relevant for Islamic history.

Chapter 11

Bartlett, Robert. *The Making of Europe: Conquest, Colonization, and Cultural Change, 950–1350.* Princeton, NJ: Princeton University Press, 1993. Analyzes the expansion of Europe from a cultural perspective.

Berend, Norma, Przemyslaw Urbanczlyk, and Przemyslaw Wiszewski. *Central Europe in the High Middle Ages: Bohemia, Hungary and Poland, ca. 900–ca. 1300.* New York: Cambridge University Press, 2013. Learned and insightful study that explores frequently overlooked aspects of medieval Europe.

Brown, Peter. *The Rise of Western Christendom: Triumph and Diversity, A.D. 200–1000,* 2nd ed. Oxford, UK: Wiley-Blackwell, 2003. Traces the development of Christian Europe from the perspective of the church.

Grant, Edward. *The Foundation of Modern Science in the Middle Ages.* Cambridge, UK: Cambridge University Press, 1996. Seminal study of the contributions of medieval science to the scientific revolution of the seventeenth century.

Lawrence, C. H. *Medieval Monasticism: Forms of Religious Life in Western Europe in the Middle Ages,* 2nd ed. New York: Longman, 1984. Thorough survey of the development of the Western monastic tradition.

McKitterick, Rosamond. *Charlemagne: The Formation of a European Identity.* Cambridge, UK: Cambridge University Press, 2008. An examination of how Charlemagne's policies contributed to the idea of Europe.

Platt, Colin. *King Death: The Black Death and Its Aftermath in Late-Medieval England.* Toronto: University of Toronto Press, 1997. Riveting analysis of the effects of the Black Death on all aspects of society.

Riley-Smith, Jonathan, ed. *The Oxford Illustrated History of the Crusades.* Oxford and New York: Oxford University Press, 1995. A very useful and readable history of the crusading movement.

Turner, Denys. *Thomas Aquinas: A Portrait.* New Haven, CT: Yale University Press, 2013. Up-to-date biography of one of the greatest figures in medieval philosophy.

Wickham, Chris. *Medieval Europe.* New Haven, CT: Yale University Press, 2016. A scintillating and innovative study that presents new interpretations of important turning points in the development of medieval European civilization.

WEBSITES

British Library. Treasures in Full: Magna Carta, http://www. bl.uk/treasures/magnacarta/virtual_curator/vc9.html. An excellent website that makes available a digitized version of Magna Carta. Audio files answer many FAQs about the manuscript and its significance.

Howe, Jeffery. A Digital Archive of Architecture, http://www. bc.edu/bc_org/avp/cas/fnart/arch/gothic_arch.html. Jeffery Howe's Digital Archive of Architecture has a quick index reference guide, which links to images of both early and high Gothic architecture.

Chapter 12

Asif, Manan Ahmed. *A Book of Conquest: The Chachnama and Muslim Origins in South Asia.* Cambridge, MA: Harvard University Press, 2016. Comprehensive study of the pivotal story of deceit and conquest and the contentious legacy surrounding the initial Muslim forays into India.

Bulag, Uradyn Erden. *The Mongols at China's Edge: History and the Politics of National Unity.* Lanham, MD: Rowman & Littlefield, 2002. New historical overview of the Mongols through historical and anthropological lenses that seeks to demythologize their experience and interactions with China and central Asian peoples.

Chiu-Duke, Josephine. *To Rebuild the Empire: Lu Chih's Confucian Pragmatist Approach to the Mid-Tang Predicament.* Albany, NY: SUNY Press, 2000. Political and philosophical study of one of the Tang era's most important prime ministers and his attempts to retrieve Tang fortunes and actions in the beginning of the period's Confucian revival.

De Bary, William T., and Irene Bloom, eds. *Sources of Chinese Tradition,* 2nd ed., vol. 1. New York: Columbia University Press, 1999. Excellent introduction to major Chinese philosophical schools. Extensive coverage of Buddhism and Neo-Confucianism with accessible, highly informative introductions to the documents themselves.

Ebrey, Patricia Buckley, ed. *The Inner Quarters.* Berkeley and Los Angeles: University of California Press, 1993. Perhaps the best scholarly exploration of the roles of women in Song China.

Hansen, Valerie. *The Open Empire: A History of China to 1600.* New York: W. W. Norton, 2000. A fresh and accessible synthesis of pre-modern Chinese history.

Levathes, Louise. *When China Ruled the Seas: The Treasure Fleet of the Dragon Throne 1405–1433.* New York: Simon & Schuster, 1994. Delightful coverage of the voyages of Zheng He from 1405 to 1433. Particularly good on the aftermath of the voyages.

Robinson, Francis. *Islam and Muslim History in South Asia.* Oxford and New York: Oxford University Press, 2004. Compendium of essays and reviews by the author on a variety of subjects concerning the history and status of Islam in the subcontinent. Of particular interest is his response to Samuel Huntington's famous "clash of civilizations" thesis.

Singh, Patwant. *The Sikhs.* London: John Murray, 1999. Readable popular history of the Sikh experience to the present by an adherent. Especially useful on the years from Guru Nanak to the changes of the early eighteenth century and the transition to a more militant faith.

WEBSITES

Asian Topics in World History. "The Mongols in World History," http://afe.easia.columbia.edu/mongols/. With a timeline spanning 1000–1500, "The Mongols in World History" delivers a concise and colorful history of the Mongols' impact on global history.

Fordham University. Internet Indian History Sourcebook, http:// www.fordham.edu/halsall/india/indiasbook.asp. One of the series of online "sourcebooks" by Fordham containing links to important documents, secondary literature, and assorted other web resources.

Fordham University. Internet East Asian History Sourcebook, http://www.fordham.edu/halsall/eastasia/eastasiasbook.asp. As with its counterpart above, this is one in the series of useful online sources and links put together by Fordham, in this case about East Asia, with particular emphasis on the role of China as a center of cultural diffusion.

Chapter 13

General

Holcombe, Charles. *A History of East Asia, From the Origins of Civilization to the Twenty-First Century.* Cambridge, UK: Cambridge University Press, 2011. A top one-volume history of China, Korea, and Japan, with an emphasis on the region's shared past.

Mann, Susan. *East Asia (China, Korea, Japan).* Washington, DC: American Historical Association, 1999. The second volume in the Women's and Gender History in Global Perspective series. Short, informative work with historiographic overviews and cross-cultural comparisons among the three countries named in the title. Critical annotated bibliographies on the use of standard texts in integrating women and gender into Asian studies.

Neuman, W. Lawrence. *East Asian Societies.* Ann Arbor, MI: Association For Asian Studies, 2014. Part of the AAS's "Key Issues in Asian Studies," this provides a short, accessible introduction to the region for beginning students.

Ramusack, Barbara N., and Sharon Sievers. *Women in Asia.* Bloomington: Indiana University Press, 1999. Part of the series Restoring Women to History. Far-ranging book divided into two parts, "Women in South and Southeast Asia" and "Women in East Asia." Coverage of individual countries, extensive chronologies, valuable bibliographies. Most useful for advanced undergraduates.

Korea

De Bary, William T., ed. *Sources of Korean Tradition,* vol. 1. Introduction to Asian Civilizations. New York: Columbia University Press, 1997. Part of the renowned Columbia series on the great traditions of East Asia. Perhaps the most complete body of accessible sources for undergraduates.

Korean Overseas Information Service. *A Handbook of Korea.* Seoul: KOIS, 1993. Wonderfully complete history, geography, guidebook, and sociology text. Excellent source, but students should keep in mind its provenance and treat some of its historical claims to uniqueness accordingly.

Seth, Michael J. *A Concise History of Korea.* 2nd ed. Lanham, MD: Rowman and Littlefield, 2016. Well-researched and comprehensive history of the Korean peninsula from Neolithic times to 2016. Covers both North and South Korea, though the South comes in for the most detailed treatment.

Japan

De Bary, William T., ed. *Sources of Japanese Tradition,* vol. 1. Introduction to Asian Civilizations. 2nd ed. New York: Columbia University Press, 2002. Like the volume above on Korea and the others in this series on India and China, the sources are well selected, the glossaries are sound, and the overviews of the material are masterful. As with the other East Asia volumes, the complexities of the various Buddhist schools are especially well drawn. Students with some

previous experience will derive the most benefit from this excellent volume.

Murasaki Shikibu. *The Diary of Lady Murasaki.* Richard Bowring, trans. New York: Penguin, 1996. Capable translation of the court diary of the author of *The Tale of Genji* and an intimate glimpse into lives of the elite of Heian Japan.

Totman, Conrad. *A History of Japan.* Oxford, UK: Blackwell, 2000. Part of Blackwell's History of the World series. A large, well-balanced, and comprehensive history. More than half of the material is on the pre-1867 period, with extensive coverage of social history and demographics.

Vietnam

Steinberg, Joel David, ed. *In Search of Southeast Asia,* rev. ed. Honolulu: University of Hawaii Press, 1987. Extensive coverage of Vietnam within the context of an area study of Southeast Asia. Though weighted toward the modern period, very good coverage of agricultural and religious life in the opening chapters.

Taylor, Keith W. *The Birth of Vietnam.* Berkeley and Los Angeles: University of California Press, 1983. Comprehensive, magisterial volume on early Vietnamese history and historical identity amid the long Chinese occupation. Best for students with some background in Southeast Asian and Chinese history.

WEBSITES

Department of Prints and Drawings, British Museum, http://www.britishmuseum.org/the_museum/departments/prints_and_drawings.aspx. A comprehensive source for all manner of interests related to Asian studies.

Public Broadcasting Service, Hidden Korea, http://www.pbs.org/hiddenkorea/history.htm. Sound introduction to the geography, people, history and culture of Korea, with links to additional source material.

Cambridge Journals Online, Journal of Southeast Asian Studies, http://journals.cambridge.org/action/displayJournal?jid=SEA. Online version of the scholarly publication of the same name, features articles on the history, sociology, cultural studies, and literature of the region. It aims for scholarly but accessible presentations. Recommended for advanced students.

Chapter 14

Birmingham, David, and Phyllis M. Martin, eds. *History of Central Africa,* vol. 1. London: Longman, 1983. The first chapter, by Birmingham, provides an excellent summary of the history of Luba prior to 1450.

Collins, Robert O., and James M. Burns. *A History of Subsaharan Africa,* 2nd ed. Cambridge: Cambridge University Press, 2014. Authoritative history by two well-known Africanists, updated by James Burns after the death of Robert Collins.

Crummey, David. *Land and Society in the Christian Kingdom of Ethiopia: From the Thirteenth to the Twentieth Century.* Urbana: University of Illinois Press, 2000. The first book in which the rich land records of the church have been used for a reconstruction of agriculture and land tenure.

Horton, Mark, and John Middleton. *The Swahili: The Social Landscape of a Mercantile Society.* Oxford, UK: Blackwell, 2000. A study that gives full attention to the larger context of East Africa in which the Swahilis flourished. Middleton is the author of another important study, *The World of the*

Swahili: An African Mercantile Civilization (Yale University Press, 1992).

Huffman, Thomas N. *Mapungubwe: Ancient African Civilization on the Limpopo.* Johannesburg: Witwatersrand University Press, 2005. Short but illuminating summary of the archaeological record by a leading South African expert, although his interpretation of Zimbabwe in an earlier work (*Snakes and Crocodiles*, Witwatersrand University Press, 1996) is controversial.

Levtzion, Nehemia. *Ancient Ghana and Mali.* New York: Africana, 1980. Originally published London: Methuen, 1973. Standard history of ancient Ghana, Mali, and Songhay based on a thorough knowledge of the Arabic sources; a revision by David Conrad, Paulo Farias, Roderick J. McIntosh, and Susan McIntosh has been announced but has yet to appear.

Robinson, David. *Muslim Societies in African History.* Cambridge, UK: Cambridge University Press, 2004. Advertised as part of a series of new approaches, this book nevertheless presents a conventional view of Islam, albeit in its African context.

Trigger, Bruce. *History and Settlement in Lower Nubia.* Yale University Publications in Anthropology 69. New Haven, CT: Yale University Press, 1965. Chapter 9 is still the best overview of Nubian history, by a scholar with a broad understanding of early civilizations.

WEBSITES

Heilbrunn Timeline of Art History. "Ife (from ca. 350 B.C.)," http://www.metmuseum.org/toah/hd/ife/hd_ife.htm. An excellent introductory website hosted by the Metropolitan Museum of Art. It contains many links and presents clear overviews.

For a website by Patrick Darling, the principal archaeological investigator of the Nigerian earthworks, see http://cohesion.rice.edu/CentersAndInst/SAFA/emplibrary/49_ch09.pdf for a copy of a 1998 article.

Chapter 15

Bruhns, Karen Olsen, and Karen E. Stothert. *Women in Ancient America.* Norman: University of Oklahoma Press, 1999. Comprehensive account of women's role in daily life, religion, politics, and war in forager and agrarian–urban societies.

Brumfield, Elizabeth M., and Gary F. Feinman, eds. *The Aztec World.* New York: Abrams, 2008. Collection of expert short chapters on a variety of topics, richly illustrated.

Carrasco, Davíd. *The Aztecs: A Very Short Introduction.* Oxford and New York: Oxford University Press, 2012. Clear, compressed account by a specialist, containing all essential information.

D'Altroy, Terence. *The Incas.* 2nd ed., Hoboken, NJ: John Wiley and Sons, 2014. Well-organized, comprehensive, and up-to-date overview.

Hassig, Ross. *War and Society in Ancient Mesoamerica.* Berkeley and Los Angeles: University of California Press, 1992. Best study of the rising importance of militarism in Mesoamerican city-states, up to the Aztec Empire.

Julien, Catherine. *Reading Inca History.* Iowa City: University of Iowa Press, 2000. Ambitious "reading" of "genres" of memory in the available, mostly Spanish sources.

Malpass, Michael A. *Daily Life in the Inca Empire,* 2nd ed. Westport, CT: Greenwood, 2009. Clear, straightforward, and readable account of ordinary people's lives by a specialist.

Smith, Michael E., *The Aztecs,* 3rd ed. Hoboken, NJ: Wiley, 2013. Up-to-date, extensive account of all aspects of Inca history and civilization.

WEBSITE

Aztec History, http://www.aztec-history.com/. Introductory website, easily navigable, with links.

Chapter 16

Ágoston, Gábor. *Guns for the Sultan: Military Power and the Weapons Industry in the Ottoman Empire.* Cambridge, UK: Cambridge University Press, 2005. Thorough study, which is based on newly accessible Ottoman archival materials and emphasizes the technological prowess of Ottoman gunsmiths.

Casale, Giancarlo. *The Ottoman Age of Exploration.* Oxford and New York: Oxford University Press, 2010. Detailed correction, based on Ottoman and Portuguese archives, of the traditional characterization of the Ottoman Empire as a land-oriented power.

Casey, James. *Early Modern Spain: A Social History.* London: Routledge, 1999. Detailed, well-documented analysis of rural–urban and king–nobility tensions.

Elliott, John Huxtable. *Spain, Europe, and the Wider World: 1500–1800.* New Haven, CT: Yale University Press, 2009. A comprehensive overview, particularly strong on culture during the 1500s.

Glete, Jan. *War and the State in Early Modern Europe: Spain, the Dutch Republic, and Sweden as Fiscal–Military States, 1500–1660.* London: Routledge, 2002. A complex but persuasive construction of the forerunner to the absolute state. Unfortunately leaves out the Ottoman Empire.

Murphey, Rhoads. *Ottoman Warfare, 1500–1700.* New Brunswick, NJ: Rutgers University Press, 1999. Author presents a vivid picture of the Janissaries, their discipline, organization, campaigns, and voracious demands for salary increases.

Pamuk, Sevket. *A Monetary History of the Ottoman Empire.* Cambridge, UK: Cambridge University Press, 2000. Superb analysis of Ottoman archival resources on the role and function of American silver in the money economy of the Ottomans.

Ruiz, Teofilo R. *Spanish Society, 1400–1600.* London: Longman, 2001. Richly detailed social studies rewarding anyone interested in changing class structures, rural–urban movement, and extension of the money market into the countryside.

Subrahmanyam, Sanjay. *The Career and Legend of Vasco da Gama.* Cambridge, UK: Cambridge University Press, 1997. Focuses on the religious motivations of Vasco da Gama and the commercial impact of his journey to India.

WEBSITES

Frontline, "Apocalypse! The Evolution of Apocalyptic Belief and How It Shaped the Western World," PBS, 1995, http://www.pbs.org/wgbh/pages/frontline/shows/apocalypse/. The contribution by Bernard McGinn, University of Chicago, under the heading of "Apocalypticism Explained: Joachim of Fiore," is of particular relevance for the understanding of Christopher Columbus viewing himself as a precursor of Christ's Second Coming.

Islam: Empire of Faith: Timeline, http://www.pbs.org/empires/islam/timeline.html. Comprehensive and informative, this

PBS website on the Ottoman Empire examines the various facets of this Islamic culture such as scientific innovations, faith and its leaders.

Chapter 17

Biro, Jacquelin. *On Earth as in Heaven: Cosmography and the Shape of the Earth from Copernicus to Descartes.* Saarbrücken, Germany: VDM Verlag Dr. Müller, 2009. Short study establishing the connection between geography and cosmology in Copernicus. Uses the pathbreaking articles by Thomas Goldberg.

Black, Jeremy. *Kings, Nobles, and Commoners: States and Societies in Early Modern Europe—A Revisionist History.* London: I.B. Tauris, 2004. Available also electronically on ebrary; persuasive thesis, largely accepted by scholars, of a continuity of institutional practices in Europe across the sixteenth and seventeenth centuries, casting doubt on absolutism as being more than a theory.

Cañizares-Esguerra, Jorge. *Nature, Empire, and Nation: Explorations of the History of Science in the Iberian World.* Stanford, CA: Stanford University Press, 2006. A collection of essays that provides new perspectives on the history of science in early modern Iberia.

Geanakoplos, Deno John. *Constantinople and the West: Essays on the Late Byzantine (Palaeologan) and Italian Renaissances and the Byzantine and Roman Churches.* Madison: University of Wisconsin Press, 1989. Fundamental discussion of the extensive transfer of texts and scholars during the 1400s.

Jacob, Margaret C. *Scientific Culture and the Making of the Industrial West.* Oxford and New York: Oxford University Press, 1997. Widely cited short book emphasizing the connections among New Science, scientific societies, and the steam engine.

Margolis, Howard. *It Started with Copernicus: How Turning the World Inside Out Led to the Scientific Revolution.* New York: McGraw-Hill, 2002. Important scholarly study of the connection between the discovery of the Americas and Copernicus's formulation of a sun-centered planetary system.

Nexon, Daniel H. *The Struggle for Power in Early Modern Europe: Religious Conflict, Dynastic Empires and International Change.* Princeton, NJ: Princeton University Press, 2009. Charles Tilly–inspired reevaluation of the changes occurring in sixteenth- and seventeenth-century Europe.

Park, Katharine, and Lorraine Daston, eds. *The Cambridge History of Science.* Vol. 3, *Early Modern Science.* Cambridge, UK: Cambridge University Press, 2006. Voluminous coverage of all aspects of science, under the currently paradigmatic thesis that there was no dramatic scientific revolution in Western Christian civilization.

Rublack, Ulinka. *Reformation Europe.* Cambridge, UK: Cambridge University Press, 2006. Cultural history approach to the effects of Luther and Calvin on western Christians.

Schiebinger, Londa. *The Mind Has No Sex? Women in the Origins of Modern Science.* Cambridge, MA: Harvard University Press, 1989. A pioneering study presenting biographies and summaries of scientific contributions made by women. Discusses the importance of Marie Cunitz.

Wiesner-Hanks, Merry E. *Early Modern Europe, 1450-1789.* 2nd ed. Cambridge, UK: Cambridge University Press, 2013. Textbook in the Cambridge History of Europe series with a braod coverage of topics.

WEBSITES

Ames Research Center. "Johannes Kepler: His Life, His Laws and Times," http://kepler.nasa.gov/Mission/JohannesKepler/. This NASA website looks at the life and views of Johannes Kepler. It examines his discoveries, his contemporaries, and the events that shaped modern science.

Howard, Sharon. "Early Modern Resources," http://sharonhoward. org/earlymodern.html. Website with many links on the full range of institutional and cultural change.

Chapter 18

Alchon, Suzanne A. *A Pest in the Land: New World Epidemics in a Global Perspective.* Albuquerque: University of New Mexico Press, 2003. A broad overview, making medical history comprehensible.

Behringer, Wolfgang. *Witches and Witch-Hunts: A Global History.* Cambridge, UK: Polity, 2004. A well-grounded overview of the phenomenon of the fear of witches, summarizing the scholarship of the past decades.

Bulmer-Thomas, Victor, John S. Coatsworth, and Roberto Cortés Conde, eds. *The Cambridge Economic History of Latin America.* Vol. 1, *The Colonial Era and the Short Nineteenth Century.* Cambridge, UK: Cambridge University Press, 2006. Collection of specialized summary articles on aspects of Iberian colonialism.

Burkholder, Mark A., and Lyman L. Johnson. *Colonial Latin America,* 6th ed. Oxford and New York: Oxford University Press, 2008. A well-established text, updated multiple times.

Eastman, Scott, *Preaching Spanish Nationalism across the Hispanic Atlantic, 1759–1823.* Baton Rouge: Louisiana State University Press, 2012. Close look at the national reform debates in the Iberian Atlantic world at the close of colonialism.

Ekberg, Carl J. *French Roots in the Illinois Country: The Mississippi Frontier in Colonial Times.* Urbana: University of Illinois Press, 1998. Detailed, deeply researched historical account.

Peloso, Vincent. *Race and Ethnicity in Latin America.* Milton Park and New York: Routledge, 2014. Excellent presentation of the publicly enshrined, complex racial and ethnic identities during colonialism and since independence.

Socolow, Susan M. *The Women of Latin America.* Cambridge, UK: Cambridge University Press, 2000. Surveys the patriarchal order and the function of women within it.

Stein, Stanley J., and Barbara H. Stein. *Silver, Trade, and War: Spain and America in the Making of Early Modern Europe.* Baltimore: Johns Hopkins University Press, 2000. Covers the significance of American silver reaching as far as China.

Taylor, Alan. *American Colonies.* London: Penguin, 2001. History of the English colonies in New England, written from a broad Atlantic perspective.

Wood, Michael. *Conquistadors.* Berkeley and Los Angeles: University of California Press, 2000. Accessible, richly illustrated history of the conquest period.

WEBSITE

Conquistadors, http://www.pbs.org/conquistadors/. Wonderful interactive website that allows you to track the journeys made by the Conquistadors such as Cortés, Pizarro, Orellana, and Cabeza de Vaca. Learn more about their conquests in the Americas and the legacy they left behind them.

Chapter 19

Berlin, Ira. *Many Thousands Gone: The First Two Centuries of Slavery in North America.* Cambridge, MA: Harvard University Press, 1998. One of the most authoritative studies of antebellum chattel slavery by one of the era's leading historians.

Carney, Judith A. *Black Rice: The African Origins of Rice Cultivation in the Americas.* Cambridge, MA: Harvard University Press, 2001. Study which goes a long way toward correcting the stereotype that black slaves were unskilled laborers, and carefully documents the transfer of rice-growing culture from West Africa to the Americas.

Dubois, Laurent, and Julius S. Scott, eds. *Origins of the Black Atlantic: Rewriting Histories.* New York: Routledge, 2010. Book that focuses on African slaves in the Americas as they had to arrange themselves in their new lives.

Gray, Richard, and David Birmingham, eds. *Pre-Colonial African Trade.* London and New York: Oxford University Press, 1970. Collective work in which contributors emphasize the growth and intensification of trade in the centuries of 1500–1800.

Hall, Gwendolyn Midlo. *Slavery and African Ethnicities in the Americas: Restoring the Links.* Chapel Hill: University of North Carolina Press, 2005. Study that focuses on slaves in the Americas according to their regions of origin in Africa.

Heywood, Linda M., and John K. Thornton. *Central Africans, Atlantic Creoles, and the Foundation of the Americas.* Cambridge, UK: Cambridge University Press, 2007. Pathbreaking investigation of the creation and role of Creole culture in Africa and the Americas.

Iliffe, John. *Africans: The History of a Continent, 2nd ed.* Cambridge, UK: Cambridge University Press, 2007. Standard historical summary by an established African historian.

Kriger, Colleen E. *Cloth in West African History.* Lanham, MD Altamira, 2006. Detailed investigation of the sophisticated indigenous West African cloth industry.

LaGamma, Alisa. *Kongo: Power and Majesty.* New York: Metropolitan Museum of Art, 2015. Superbly illustrated exhibition catalogue, with articles by leading Africanists.

Oliver, Roland, and Anthony Atmore. *Medieval Africa, 1250–1800.* Cambridge, UK: Cambridge University Press, 2001. Revised and updated historical overview, divided into regions and providing detailed regional histories on the emerging kingdoms.

Stapleton, Timothy J. *A Military History of Africa.* Vol. 1, *The Precolonial Period: From Ancient Egypt to the Zulu Kingdom (Earliest Times to ca. 1870).* Santa Barbara, CA: Praeger, 2013. Summary of the historical evolution of West, East, Central, and South Africa.

Thornton, John. *The Kongolese Saint Anthony: Dona Beatriz Kimpa Vita and the Antonian Movement, 1684–1706.* Cambridge, UK: Cambridge University Press, 1998. Detailed biography of Dona Beatriz, from which the vignette at the beginning of the chapter is borrowed; includes a general overview of the history of Kongo during the civil war.

WEBSITES

British Museum. "Benin: An African Kingdom," www.british museum.org/PDF/british_museum_benin_art.pdf. In addition to offering a brief historical backdrop to the art of the Benin kingdom, the British Museum's PDF also depicts various artifacts taken by the British from the Royal Palace.

Voyages: The Atlantic Slave Trade Database, http://www.slave voyages.org/tast/index.faces. A large electronic website based at Emory University and sponsored by a number of American universities, presenting up-to-date demographic tables.

Chapter 20

Bernier, François. *Travels in the Mogul Empire, A.D. 1656–1668.* Translated by Archibald Constable. Delhi: S. Chand, 1968. One of many fascinating travel accounts by European diplomats, merchants, and missionaries.

Eaton, Richard M. *Essays on Islam and Indian History.* Oxford and New York: Oxford University Press, 2002. A compendium of the new scholarly consensus on, among other things, the differences between the clerical view of Islamic observance and its actual impact in rural India. Contains both historiography and material on civilizational and cultural issues.

Gommans, J. J. L. *Mughal Warfare: Indian Frontiers and Highroads to Empire 1500–1700.* New York: Routledge, 2002. Sound examination of the Mughal Empire as a centralizing state increasingly reliant on a strong military for border defense and extending its sway. Examination of the structure of Mughal forces and the organization and weapons of the military.

Hunt, Margaret R., and Philip J. Stern, eds. *The English East India Company at the Height of Mughal Expansion: A Soldier's Diary of the 1689 Siege of Bombay with Related Documents.* Boston and New York: Bedford/St. Martin's, 2016. Illuminating look at the interplay of Mughal and European actors during the reign of Aurangzeb through the eyes of James Hilton, an English East India Company soldier, whose diary had previously been unpublished.

Kearney, Milo. *The Indian Ocean in World History.* New York: Routledge, 2003. Long view of the history of Indian Ocean trade from ancient times. Particularly relevant in examining the vital period in which the Portuguese and later East Indian Companies come to dominate the trade.

Nizami, Khaliq A. *Akbar and Religion.* Delhi: IAD, 1989. Extensive treatment of Akbar's evolving move toward devising his din-i ilahi movement, by a leading scholar of Indian religious and intellectual history.

Richards, John F. *The Mughal Empire.* Cambridge, UK: Cambridge University Press, 1993. Comprehensive volume in the New Cambridge History of India series. Sophisticated treatment; best suited to advanced students. Extensive glossary and useful bibliographic essay.

Schimmel, Annemarie. *The Empire of the Great Mughals: History, Art, and Culture.* London: Reaktion, 2004. Revised edition of a volume published in German in 2000. Lavish illustrations, wonderfully drawn portraits of key individuals, and extensive treatment of social, family, and gender relations at the Mughal court.

Srivastava, M. P. *The Mughal Administration.* Delhi: Chugh, 1995. Solid overview and analysis of the development and workings of the Mughal bureaucracy. Best utilized by advanced students.

WEBSITES

Association for Asian Studies http://www. asian-studies.org/ As with other Asian topics, one of the most reliable websites is sponsored by the Association for Asian Studies, the largest professional organization for scholars of Asia.

BBC: Religions. "Mughal Empire (1500s, 1600s)" http://www
.bbc.co.uk/religion/religions/islam/history/mughal
empire_1.shtml. The Mughal Empire ruled most of India and
Pakistan in the sixteenth and seventeenth centuries. Learn
more about the religious divides and governance of Muslim
Mughals in a country with a majority of Hindu populace.

Chapter 21

China

Crossley, Pamela K. *A Translucent Mirror: History and Identity in
Qing Imperial Ideology.* Los Angeles: University of California
Press, 1999. Pioneering study of the transformation of Qing
self-image to one of leading a universal, multicultural empire.

De Bary, William T., and Irene Bloom, comps. *Sources of Chinese
Tradition,* 2 vols., 2nd ed. New York: Columbia University
Press, 1999. Thoroughgoing update of the classic sourcebook
for Chinese literature and philosophy, with a considerable
amount of social, family, and women's works now included.

Mungello, D. E. *The Great Encounter of China and West.* Lanham,
MD: Rowman & Littlefield, 1999. Sound historical overview
of the period marking the first European maritime expeditions into East Asia and extending to the height of the Canton
trade and the beginnings of the opium era.

Pomeranz, Kenneth. *The Great Divergence: China, Europe, and the
Making of the Modern World Economy.* Princeton, NJ: Princeton University Press, 2001. Pathbreaking work mounting the
strongest argument yet in favor of the balance of economic
power remaining in East Asia until the Industrial Revolution
was well under way.

Shuo Wang. "Manchu Women in Transition: Gender Relations
and Sexuality," in Stephen A. Wadley and Carsten Naeher,
eds. *Proceedings of the First North American Conference on
Manchu Studies.* Wiesbaden, Germany: Otto Harrassowitz
Verlag, 2006: 105–130. Pathbreaking study of the role of
Manchu women in Qing China in resistance to assimilation
and preserving cultural identity.

Spence, Jonathan. *The Memory Palace of Matteo Ricci.* New York:
Penguin, 1984. Highly original treatment of Ricci and the
beginning of the Jesuit interlude in late Ming and early Qing
China. Attempts to penetrate Ricci's world through the missionary's own memory techniques.

Japan

De Bary, William T., ed. *Sources of Japanese Tradition,* 2 vols. New
York: Columbia University Press, 1964. The Tokugawa era
spans volumes 1 and 2, with its inception and political and
philosophical foundations thoroughly covered in volume
1 and the Shinto revival of national learning, the later Mito
school, and various partisans of national unity in the face of
foreign intrusion covered in the beginning of volume 2.

Duus, Peter. *Feudalism in Japan,* 3rd ed. New York: McGraw-Hill,
1993. Updated version of a short, handy volume spanning
all of Japanese history to 1867, with special emphasis on the
shogunates. Good introduction on the uses and limitations
of the term "feudalism" with reference to Japan within a comparative framework.

Gordon, Andrew. *A Modern History of Japan from Tokugawa Times
to the Present.* Oxford and New York: Oxford University Press,
2009. One of the few treatments of Japanese history that spans

both the Tokugawa and the modern eras, rather than making
the usual break in either 1853 or 1867/1868. Both the continuity of the past and the novelty of the new era are therefore
juxtaposed and highlighted. Most useful for students with a
background at least equivalent to that supplied by this text.

WEBSITE

National Geographic. China's Great Armada, http://ngm.national
geographic.com/ngm/0507/feature2/map.html. Track the
voyages made by Zheng He to Southeast Asia, India, Arabia,
and Africa.

Chapter 22

Herb, Guntram H. *Nations and Nationalism: A Global Historical
Overview.* Santa Barbara, CA: ABC-Clio, 2008. Contains a
large number of articles on the varieties of ethnic nationalism
and culture and the proliferation of nationalism in Europe
and Latin America.

Israel, Jonathan I. *A Revolution of the Mind: Radical Enlightenment and the Origins of Modern Democracy.* Princeton, NJ:
Princeton University Press, 2010. Israel is a pioneer of the
contemporary renewal of intellectual history, and his investigations of the Enlightenment tradition are pathbreaking.

Kaiser, Thomas E., and Dale K. Van Kley, eds. *From Deficit to Deluge:
The Origins of the French Revolution.* Stanford, CA: Stanford
University Press, 2011. Thoughtful reevaluation of the schol-
arly field that takes into account the latest interpretations.

Kitchen, Martin. *A History of Modern Germany: 1800 to the Present.* Hoboken, NJ: Wiley-Blackwell, 2011. A broadly conceived
historical overview, ranging from politics and economics to
culture.

Osterhammel, Jürgen. *The Transformation of the World: A Global
History of the Nineteenth Century.* Princeton, NJ: 2015. Celebrated evaluation of the myriads of changes and transformations characterizing the nineteenth century.

Rakove, Jack. *Revolutionaries: A New History of the Invention of
America.* Boston: Houghton Mifflin, 2010. A new narrative
history focusing on the principal figures in the revolution.

Riall, Lucy. *Risorgimento: The History of Italy from Napoleon to
Nation-State.* New York: Palgrave Macmillan, 2009. Historical summary, incorporating the research of the past half-
century, presented in a clear overview.

West, Elliott. *The Last Indian War: The Nez Perce Story.* Oxford
and New York: Oxford University Press, 2009. Vivid story
of the end of the US wars for the subjugation of the Native
Americans.

Wood, Gordon S. *The American Revolution: A History.* New
York: Modern Library, 2002. A short, readable summary
reflective of many decades of revisionism in the discussion of
the American Revolution.

WEBSITES

Liberty, Equality, Fraternity: Exploring the French Revolution, http://chnm.gmu.edu/revolution/. This website boasts
250 images, 350 text documents, 13 songs, 13 maps, and a timeline all focused on the French Revolution.

Nationalism Project, http://www.nationalismproject.org/. A
large website with links to bibliographies, essays, new books,
and book reviews.

Chapter 23

Adelman, Jeremy. *Sovereignty and Revolution in the Iberian Atlantic*, Princeton, NJ: Princeton University Press, 2006. A leading study in a group of recent works on the transatlantic character of colonial and postcolonial Latin America.

Brown, Matthew. *The Struggle for Power in Post-Independence Colombia and Venezuela*. New York: Palgrave Macmillan, 2012. Detailed history of the forces pulling for democracy as well as authoritarianism on the north coast of South America.

Bulmer-Thomas, Victor. *The Economic History of Latin America since Independence*, 2nd ed. Cambridge, UK: Cambridge University Press, 2003. A highly analytical and sympathetic investigation of the Latin American export and self-sufficiency economies, calling into question the long-dominant dependency theories of Latin America.

Burkholder, Mark, and Lyman Johnson. *Colonial Latin America*, 6th ed. New York: Oxford University Press, 2008. Overview, with focus on social and cultural history.

Dawson, Alexander. *Latin America since Independence: A History with Primary Sources*. New York: Routledge, 2011. Selection of topics with documentary base; for the nineteenth century covers the topics of the nation-state, caudillo politics, race, and the policy of growth through commodity exports.

Drake, Paul W. *Between Tyranny and Anarchy: A History of Democracy in Latin America*. Stanford, CA: Stanford University Press, 2009. The author traces the concepts of constitutionalism, autocracy, and voting rights since independence in clear and persuasive strokes.

Girard, Philippe, *The Slaves Who Defeated Napoléon: Toussaint Louverture and the Haitian War of Independence, 1801–1804*. Tuscaloosa: University of Alabama Press, 2011. Thoroughly researched study of the leader of the revolution, with a number of revisionist conclusions.

Hämäläinen, Pekka. *The Comanche Empire*. New Haven, CT: Yale University Press, 2008. A revisionist account that puts the extraordinary importance of the Comanche empire for the history of Mexico and the United States in the 19th century into the proper perspective.

Moya, Jose C., ed. *The Oxford Handbook of Latin American History*. Oxford and New York: Oxford University Press, 2011. Important collection of political, social, economic, and cultural essays by leading specialists on nineteenth-century Latin America.

Popkin, Jeremy D. *The Haitian Revolution and the Abolition of Slavery*. Cambridge, UK: Cambridge University Press, 2010.

Sanders, James E. *Vanguard of the Atlantic World: Creating Modernity, Nation, and Democracy in Nineteenth-Century Latin America*. Durham, NC: Duke University Press, 2014. Ambitious effort to evaluate the Latin American contributions to the creation of the modern state.

Sater, William F. *Andean Tragedy: Fighting the War of the Pacific, 1879–1884*. Lincoln: University of Nebraska Press, 2007. Close examination of this destructive war on the South American west coast.

Skidmore, Thomas. *Brazil: Five Centuries of Change*, 2nd ed. Oxford and New York: Oxford University Press, 2010. Short but magisterial text on the history of Brazil, with a detailed chapter on Brazil's path toward independence in the nineteenth century.

Wasserman, Mark, and Cheryl English Martin. *Latin America and Its People*, 2nd ed. New York: Pearson Longman, 2007. Thematic approach, drawing general conclusions by comparing and contrasting the individual countries of Latin America.

WEBSITE

Casahistoria. "19th Century Latin America," http://www.casahistoria.net/latin_american_history19.html. Website on nineteenth-century Latin America, for students.

Chapter 24

China

Cohen, Paul. *Discovering History in China*. New York: Columbia University Press, 1984. Pivotal work on the historiography of American writers on China. Critiques their collective ethnocentrism in attempting to fit Chinese history into Western perspectives and approaches.

Fairbank, John K., and Su-yu Teng. *China's Response to the West*. Cambridge, MA: Harvard University Press, 1954. Though dated in approach, still a vitally important collection of sources in translation for the period from the late eighteenth century till 1923.

Kang, David C. *East Asia before the West: Five Centuries of Trade and Tribute*. New York: Columbia University Press, 2010. An excellent companion piece to D. E. Mungello's work covering the period from 1500 to 1800. Especially good on the Ming era.

Meyer-Fong, Tobie. *What Remains: Coming to Terms With Civil War in 19th Century China*. Stanford, CA: Stanford University Press, 2013. Extensive treatment of individual experiences during the world's bloodiest civil war, the Taiping movement.

Platt, Stephen R. *Autumn in the Heavenly Kingdom*. New York: Knopf, 2012. Reinterpretation of the Taiping era as global political and economic phenomena involving the curtailing of US cotton exports during its civil war, their effects on the British textile industry, and the loss of Chinese markets during the Taiping Rebellion.

Spence, Jonathan D. *The Search for Modern China*. New York: Norton, 1990. Extensive, far-reaching interpretation of the period from China's nineteenth-century decline in the face of Western imperialism, through its revolutionary era, and finally to its recent bid for global preeminence.

Japan

Keene, Donald. *Emperor of Japan: Meiji and His World, 1852–1912*. New York: Columbia University Press, 2002. Masterly treatment of Japan's modernizing emperor and his vast influence on Japan and Asia, by one of the twentieth century's finest translators and scholars of Japan.

Reischauer, Edwin O., and Albert M. Craig. *Japan: Tradition and Transformation*. Boston: Houghton Mifflin, 1989. Somewhat dated but still highly useful introductory text by two of the twentieth century's leading scholars of Japanese history.

Totman, Conrad. *Politics in the Tokugawa Bakufu, 1600–1843*. Berkeley: University of California Press, 1988. (Paperback edition with new preface and enhanced bibliography). Updated edition of Totman's breakthrough 1967 work. It remains one of the few highly detailed and deeply sourced monographs on the inner workings of the Tokugawa shogunate.

Walthall, Anne, and M. William Steele, *Politics and Society in Japan's Meiji Restoration: A Brief History with Documents*. New York: Bedford/St. Martin's, 2016. As with others in this series, a sound introduction for students with little or no background in the subject, accompanied by well-chosen documents.

WEBSITES

Association for Asian Studies, http://www.asian-studies.org/. This website of the Association for Asian Studies has links to sources more suited to advanced term papers and seminar projects.

Education about Asia, http://www.asian-studies.org/eaa/. This site provides the best online sources for modern Chinese and Japanese history.

Sino-Japanese War 1894–5, http://sinojapanesewar.com/. Packed with maps, photographs and movies depicting the conflict between Japan and China at the end of the nineteenth century, students can learn more about causes and consequences of the Sino–Japanese War.

Chapter 25

Gaudin, Corinne. *Ruling Peasants: Village and State in Later Imperial Russia*. DeKalb: Northern Illinois University Press, 2007. A close and sympathetic analysis of rural Russia.

Inalcik, Halil, and Donald Quataert, eds. *An Economic and Social History of the Ottoman Empire*. Vol. 2, *1600–1914*. Cambridge, UK: Cambridge University Press, 1994. A pioneering work with contributions by leading Ottoman historians on rural structures, monetary developments, and industrialization efforts.

Kasaba, Resat, ed. *The Cambridge History of Turkey*. Vol. 5, *Turkey in the Modern World*. Cambridge, UK: Cambridge University Press, 2008. An ambitious effort to assemble the leading authorities on the Ottoman Empire and provide a comprehensive overview.

Lieven, Dominic. *Empire: The Russian Empire and Its Rivals*. New Haven, CT: Yale University Press, 2002. Broad, comparative history of the Russian Empire, in the context of the Habsburg, Ottoman, and British Empires.

Massie, Robert K. *Catherine the Great: Portrait of a Woman*. New York: Random House, 2012. A comprehensive and insightful biography of one of the most fascinating women in history, whose policies, reforms, and personal life changed the course of Russian history.

Nikitenko, Aleksandr. *Up from Serfdom: My Childhood and Youth in Russia, 1804–1824*. Translated by Helen Saltz Jacobson. New Haven, CT: Yale University Press, 2001. Touching autobiography summarized at the beginning of the chapter.

Poe, Marshall T. *Russia's Moment in World History*. Princeton, NJ: Princeton University Press, 2003. A superb scholarly overview of Russian history, written from a broad perspective and taking into account a good number of Western stereotypes about Russia, especially in the nineteenth century.

Quataert, Donald. *Manufacturing in the Ottoman Empire and Turkey, 1500–1950*. Albany, NY: State University of New York Press, 1994. The author is still the leading American historian on workers and the early industrialization of the Ottoman Empire.

Riasanovsky, Nicholas, and Mark Steinberg. *A History of Russia*, 8th ed., 2 vols. Oxford and New York: Oxford University Press, 2011. A comprehensive, fully revised history, ranging from politics and economics to literature and the arts.

Uyar, Mesut, and Edward J. Erickson. *A Military History of the Ottomans: From Osman to Atatürk*. Santa Barbara, CA: Praeger Security International, 2009. A detailed, well-documented history of the Ottoman Empire from the perspective of its imperial designs and military forces, by two military officers in academic positions.

Zurcher, Erik J. *The Young Turk Legacy and Nation Building: From the Ottoman Empire to Atatürk's Turkey*. London: I. B. Tauris, 2010. Detailed yet readable account of how the Young Turk movement laid the foundation for Kemal Atatürk's Republic of Turkey.

WEBSITE

Russian Legacy. "Russian Empire (1689–1825)," http://www.russianlegacy.com/en/go_to/history/russian_empire.htm. Russian Legacy, a website devoted to the Russian Empire, organized as a timeline with links.

Chapter 26

Allen, Robert C. *The British Industrial Revolution in Global Perspective*. Cambridge, UK: Cambridge University Press, 2009. An in-depth analysis, well supported by economic data, not only of why the Industrial Revolution occurred first in Britain but also of how new British technologies carried industrialism around the world.

Dublin, Thomas, ed. *Farm to Factory: Women's Letters, 1830–1860*. New York: Columbia University Press, 1981. A fascinating collection of correspondence written by women who describe their experiences in moving from rural areas of New England to urban centers in search of work in textile factories.

Griffin, Emma. *Liberty's Dawn: A People's History of the Industrial Revolution*. New Haven, CT: Yale University Press, 2013. Riveting study of the impact of the Industrial Revolution on the lives of working men and women in Britain, as told in autobiographies and memoirs.

Headrick, Daniel R. *The Tools of Empire: Technology and European Imperialism in the Nineteenth Century*. Oxford and New York: Oxford University Press, 1981. A fascinating and clearly written analysis of the connections between the development of new technologies and their role in European imperialism.

Hobsbawm, Eric. *The Age of Revolution: 1789–1848*. London: Vintage, 1996. A sophisticated analysis of the Industrial Revolution (one element of the "twin revolution," the other being the French Revolution) that examines the effects of industrialism on social and cultural developments from a Marxist perspective.

More, Charles. *Understanding the Industrial Revolution*. London: Routledge, 2000. A comprehensive explanation of how theories of economic growth account for the development of the industrial movement in Britain.

Rosen, William. *The Most Powerful Idea in the World: A Story of Steam, Industry, and Innovation*. Chicago: University of Chicago Press, 2012. Absorbing history of the importance of steam technologies in the development of industrialism.

Roudinesco, Elisabeth, and Catherine Porter. *Freud: In His Time and Ours*. Cambridge, MA: Harvard University Press, 2016. A bold, comprehensive, and innovative analysis of one of the most influential—and complex—figures at the turn of the twentieth century.

Sperber, Jonathan. *Karl Marx: A Nineteenth-Century Life*. New York: W. W. Norton, 2013. A carefully researched biography that contextualizes Marx vis-à-vis the age of early industrialism and in comparison with other luminaries in the turbulent nineteenth century.

WEBSITES

Claude Monet: Life and Paintings, http://www.monetpainting .net/. A visually beautiful website which reproduces many of Monet's masterpieces; this site also includes an extensive biographical account of the famous painter's life and works. It also includes information about his wife Camille, his gardens at Giverny, and a chronology.

Darwin Online, http://darwin-online.org.uk/. This website has reproduced, in full, the works of Charles Darwin. In addition to providing digitized facsimiles of his works, private papers, and manuscripts, it has also added a concise biographical account of Darwin and numerous images of Darwin throughout his life.

Einstein Archives Online, http://www.alberteinstein.info/. Fantastic and informative website that houses digitized manuscripts of Einstein's work. Also includes a gallery of images.

ThomasEdison.org, http://www.thomasedison.org/. Remarkable website that explores Thomas Edison's impact on modernity through his innovations and inventions. This site also reproduces all of Edison's scientific sketches, which are available to download as PDF files.

Chapter 27

Belich, James. *Replenishing the Earth: The Settler Revolution and the Rise of the Anglo-World, 1783–1939.* Oxford and New York: Oxford University Press, 2009. Important study by an Australian historian, focusing on the British settler colonies.

Chamberlain, M. E. *The Scramble for Africa.* New York: Routledge, 2013. Insightful account of the European colonization of Africa during the period 1870 to 1914.

Ferguson, Niall. *Empire: The Rise and Demise of the British World Order and the Lessons for Global Power.* New York: Perseus, 2002. Controversial but widely acknowledged analysis of the question of whether imperialism deserves its negative reputation or not.

Hobsbawm, Eric. *The Age of Empire, 1875–1914.* New York: Vintage, 1989. Immensely well-informed investigation of the climactic period of the new imperialism at the end of the nineteenth century.

Hochschild, Adam. *King Leopold's Ghost: A Story of Greed, Terror, and Heroism in Colonial Africa.* New York: Houghton Mifflin, 1998. A gripping exposé of Leopold II's brutal tactics in seizing territory and exploiting African labor in the Congo.

Jefferies, Matthew. *Contesting the German Empire, 1871–1918.* Malden, MA: Blackwell, 2008. Up-to-date summary of the German historical debate on the colonial period.

Münkler, Herfried. *Empires: The Logic of World Domination from Ancient Rome to the United States.* Cambridge, UK: Polity Press, 2007. Short but wide-ranging and historically well-informed analysis of the phenomena of empire and imperial hegemony in world history.

Vickers, Adrian. *A History of Modern Indonesia,* 2nd ed. Cambridge, UK: Cambridge University Press, 2013. Well-written account of Indonesia growing from heteregenous Dutch colonial islands into a modern nation state.

Singer, Barnett, and John Langdon. *Cultured Force: Makers and Defenders of the French Colonial Empire.* Madison: University of Wisconsin Press, 2004. Study of the principal (military) figures who helped create the French nineteenth-century empire.

Streets-Salter, Heather, and Trevor R. Getz, *Empires and Colonies in the World: A Global Perspective.* Oxford and New York: Oxford University Press, 2015. Particularly illuminative chapters on the new imperialism in the nineteenth century.

WEBSITES

The Colonization of Africa, http://exhibitions.nypl.org/africana age/essay-colonization-of-africa.html. An academically based summary with further essays on African topics, as well as multimedia functions.

South Asian History—*Colonial* India, http://www.lib.berkeley .edu/SSEAL/SouthAsia/india_colonial.html. Very detailed website with primary documents and subtopics of nineteenth-century British India.

Chapter 28

Berend, Ivan T. *An Economic History of Twentieth-Century Europe: Economic Regimes from Laissez-Faire to Globalization.* Cambridge, UK: Cambridge University Press, 2006. Includes Europe-wide, comparative chapters on laissez-faire and state-directed economies, including deficit spending.

Bose, Sugata, and Ayesha Jalal. *Modern South Asia: History, Culture, Political Economy.* New York: Routledge, 2004. Well-informed analyses by two of the foremost South Asia specialists.

Clark, Christopher. *The Sleepwalkers: How Europe Went to War in 1914.* New York: HarperPerennial, 2014. One of a slew of new investigations into the origins of the war published to mark its centennial; emphasizes the Austrian–Serbian roots of the war.

Cohen, Adam. *Imbeciles: The Supreme Court, American Eugenics, and the Sterilization of Carrie Buck.* New York: Penguin, 2016.

Fritzsche, Peter. *Life and Death in the Third Reich.* Cambridge, MA: Harvard University Press, 2008. Book that seeks to understand the German nation's choice of arranging itself to Nazi rule.

Gelvin, James L. *The Modern Middle East: A History,* 4th ed. Oxford and New York: Oxford University Press, 2015. Contains chapters on Arab nationalism, British and French colonialism, and Turkey and Iran in the interwar period.

Gordon, Andrew. *A Modern History of Japan: From Tokugawa Times to the Present,* 2nd ed. Oxford and New York: Oxford University Press, 2009. Detailed overview of Japan's interwar period in the middle chapters.

Grasso, June M., J. P. Corrin, and Michael Kort. *Modernization and Revolution in Modern China: From the Opium Wars to the Olympics,* 4th ed. Armonk, NY: M. E. Sharpe, 2009. General overview with a focus on modernization in relation to the strong survival of tradition.

Martel, Gordon, ed. *A Companion to Europe 1900–1945.* Malden, MA: Wiley-Blackwell, 2010. Collective work covering a large variety of cultural, social, and political European topics in the interwar period.

Meade, Teresa A. *A History of Modern Latin America: 1800 to the Present.* Malden, MA: Wiley-Routledge, 2010. Topical discussion of the major issues in Latin American history, with chapters on the first half of the twentieth century.

Neiberg, Michael S. *The Treaty of Versailles: A Concise Study.* Oxford and New York: Oxford University Press, 2017. An assessment of the complexities attending the settlement of World War I, along with the consequences of its many flaws and failures.

Snyder, Timothy. *Bloodlands: Europe between Hitler and Stalin.* New York: Basic Books, 2010. Book that chronicles the horrific destruction left behind by these two dictators.

Wilson, Mark R. *Destructive Creation: American Business and the Winning of World War II*. Philadelphia: University of Pennsylvania Press, 2016. A thoroughly researched revisionist interpretation of the strained relationship between big business and the federal government as America mobilized for, and engaged in, World War II.

WEBSITES

BBC. World War One, http://www.bbc.co.uk/ww1, and World War Two, http://www.bbc.co.uk/history/worldwars/wwtwo/. The BBC's treatment of the causes, course, and consequences of both WWI and WWII from an Allied position.

Marxists Internet Archive. "The Bolsheviks," http://www.marxists.org/subject/bolsheviks/index.htm. A complete review of the Bolshevik party members, including biographies and links to archives which contain their works.

1937 Nanking Massacre, http://www.nanking-massacre.com/Home.html. A disturbing collection of pictures and articles tell the gruesome history of the Rape of Nanjing.

United States Holocaust Memorial Museum. Holocaust Encyclopedia, http://www.ushmm.org/wlc/en/article.php?ModuleId=10005151. The US Holocaust Memorial Museum looks back on one of the darkest times in Western history.

U.S. History, http://www.ushistory.org/us/. Maintained by Independence Hall Association in Philadelphia, this website contains many links to topics discussed in this chapter.

Chapter 29

Baret, Roby Carol. *The Greater Middle East and the Cold War: US Foreign Policy under Eisenhower and Kennedy*. London: I.B. Tauris, 2007. Thoroughly researched analysis of American policies in the Middle East, North Africa, and South Asia.

Birmingham, David. *Kwame Nkrumah: Father of African Nationalism*. Athens: University of Ohio Press, 1998. Short biography by a leading modern African historian.

Conniff, Michael L. *Populism in Latin America*. Tuscaloosa: University of Alabama Press, 1999. The author is a well-published scholar on modern Latin America.

Damrosch, David, David Lawrence Pike, Djelal Kadir, and Ursula K. Heise, eds. *The Longman Anthology of World Literature*. Vol. F, *The Twentieth Century*. New York: Longman/Pearson, 2008. A rich, diverse selection of texts. Alternatively, Norton published a similar, somewhat larger anthology of world literature in 2003.

De Witte, Ludo. *The Assassination of Lumumba*. Translated by Ann Wright and Renée Fenby. London: Verso, 2002. An admirably researched study of the machinations of the Belgian government in protecting its mining interests, with the connivance of CIA director Allen Dulles and President Dwight D. Eisenhower.

Goscha, Christopher E., and Christian F. Ostermann. *Connecting Histories: Decolonization and the Cold War in Southeast Asia, 1945–1962*. Stanford, CA: Stanford University Press, 2009.

Guha, Ramachandra. *India after Gandhi: A History of the World's Largest Democracy*. New York: Harper Collins, 2007. Highly readable, popular history with well-sketched biographical treatments of leading individuals, more obscure cultural figures, and ordinary people. Accessible to even beginning students.

Hasegawa, Tsuyoshi. *The Cold War in East Asia, 1945–1991*. Stanford, CA: Stanford University Press, 2011. A new summary, based on archival research by a leading Japanese historian teaching in the United States. New insights on the Soviet entry into World War II against Japan.

Herman, Arthur. *Joseph McCarthy: Reexamining the Life and Legacy of America's Most Hated Senator*. New York: Free Press, 2000. A fascinating study of the Wisconsin senator whose virulent campaign against communism launched decades of fear and reprisals in America during the Cold War era.

Jansen, Jan C., and Jürgen Osterhammel. *Decolonization: A Short History*. Princeton, NJ: Princeton University Press, 2017. Superb, analytical well-grounded summary of the decolonization process and its aftermath in the second half of the twentieth century.

Meredith, Martin. *The Fate of Africa: A History of the Continent since Independence*. Philadelphia: Perseus, 2011. A revised and up-to-date study of a fundamental analysis of Africa during the modern era.

WEBSITES

Economist. "The Suez Crisis: An Affair to Remember," http://www.economist.com/node/7218678. The *Economist* magazine looks back on the Suez Crisis.

NASA. "Yuri Gagarin: First Man in Space," http://www.nasa.gov/mission_pages/shuttle/sts1/gagarin_anniversary.html. In addition to information and video footage regarding Yuri Gagarin's orbit of the earth, students will also find information on America's space history.

Newseum. The Berlin Wall, http://www.newseum.org/berlinwall/. The Newseum's interactive website looks at what life was like on both sides of the Berlin Wall.

Chapter 30

Ash, Timothy Garton. *The Magic Lantern: The Revolution of '89 Witnessed in Warsaw, Budapest, Berlin, and Prague*. New York: Random House, 1999. A gripping first-hand account of the wave of anticommunist revolutions that rocked Eastern Europe after 1989.

Duara, Prasenjit, ed. *Decolonization: Perspectives from Now and Then*. London: Routledge, 2004. A leading scholar of China and postcolonial studies edits essays in this offering in the Rewriting Histories series on the fall of the colonial empires by scholars such as Michael Adas and John Voll and activists and leaders such as Frantz Fanon and Kwame Nkrumah.

Fanon, Frantz. *The Wretched of the Earth*. New York: Grove, 1961. One of the most provocative and influential treatments of theoretical and practical issues surrounding decolonization. Fanon champions violence as an essential part of the decolonization process and advocates a modified Marxist approach that takes into consideration the nuances of race and the legacies of colonialism.

Frieden, Jeffrey. *Global Capitalism: Its Fall and Rise in the Twentieth Century*. New York: W. W. Norton, 2006. Despite the title, a comprehensive history of global networks from the days of mercantilism to the twenty-first century. Predominant emphasis on twentieth century; highly readable, though the material is best suited for the nonbeginning student.

Gaddis, John Lewis. *The Cold War: A New History*. New York: Penguin, 2005. Though criticized by some scholars for his pro-American positions, America's foremost historian of the Cold War produces here a vivid, at times counterintuitive, view of the Cold War and its global impact. Readable even for beginning students.

Gitlin, Todd. *The Sixties: Years of Hope, Days of Rage*, rev. ed. New York: Bantam, 1993. Lively, provocative account of this pivotal decade by the former radical, now a sociologist. Especially effective at depicting the personalities of the pivotal period 1967–1969.

Goodwin, Doris Kearns. *Lyndon Johnson and the American Dream*. New York: St. Martin's Press, 1991. Insightful and probing study of President Johnson's character and personality, from its formation in his early years through his extensive political career.

Harmer, Tanya. *Allende's Chile and the Inter-American Cold War*. Chapel Hill: University of North Carolina Press, 2014. A reinterpretation of American determination to overturn Allende's leftist government and its subsequent results.

Liang Heng, and Judith Shapiro. *After the Nightmare: A Survivor of the Cultural Revolution Reports on China Today*. New York: Knopf, 1986. Highly readable, poignant, first-person accounts of people's experiences during the trauma of China's Cultural Revolution by a former husband-and-wife team. Especially interesting because China was at the beginning of its Four Modernizations when this was written, and the wounds of the Cultural Revolution were still fresh.

Raleigh, Donald J. *Soviet Baby Boomers: An Oral History of Russia's Cold War Generation*. Oxford and New York: Oxford University Press, 2012. A revealing and entertaining account of new social and cultural trends among Russia's youth, as told in a series of interviews.

Smith, Bonnie, ed. *Global Feminisms since 1945*. London: Routledge, 2000. Part of the Rewriting Histories series, this work brings together under the editorship of Smith a host of essays by writers such as Sara Evans, Mary Ann Tetreault, and Miriam Ching Yoon Louie on feminism in Asia, Africa, and Latin America, as well as Europe and the United States. Sections are thematically arranged under such headings as "Nation-Building," "Sources of Activism," "Women's Liberation," and "New Waves in the 1980s and 1990s." Comprehensive and readable, though some background in women's history is recommended.

WEBSITES

Cold War International History Project, http://www.wilson center.org/program/cold-war-international-history-project. Run by the Woodrow Wilson International Center for Scholars. Rich archival materials including collections on the end of the Cold War, Soviet invasion of Afghanistan, Cuban Missile Crisis, and Chinese foreign policy documents.

College of DuPage Library, http:codlibrary.org. Entering "Research guide to 1960s websites" in the search box yields a wide-ranging set of relevant topics.

Chapter 31

Chau, Adam Yuet, ed. *Religion in Contemporary China*. New York: Routledge, 2011. Collection of fascinating chapters on the revival of Daoist, Confucian, and Buddhist traditions and their adaption to middle-class modernity, with their proponents operating often in a gray zone between official recognition and suppression.

Daniels, Robert V. *The Rise and Fall of Communism in the Soviet Union*. New Haven, CT: Yale University Press, 2010. A magisterial summary of the communist period by a specialist.

Dillon, Michael. *Contemporary China: An Introduction*. New York: Routledge, 2009. Concise yet quite specific overview of the economy, society, and politics of the country.

Eichengreen, Barry. *Exorbitant Privilege: The Rise and Fall of the Dollar and the Future of the Monetary System*. Oxford and New York: Oxford University Press, 2011. The author is an academic specialist on US monetary policies, writing in an accessible style and presenting a fascinating picture of the role of something as prosaic as greenbacks.

Faust, Aaron M. *The Ba'thification of Iraq: Saddam Hussein's Totalitarianism*. Austin: University of Texas Press, 2015. Based on meticulous research among Ba'th Party documents, this study reveals how Saddam Hussein developed a totalitarian regime in Iraq, and why his dictatorship succeeded in gaining the loyalty of millions of Iraqis for nearly 25 years.

Gelvin, James L. *The Arab Uprisings: What Everyone Needs to Know*. Oxford and New York: Oxford University Press, 2012. Concise overview of the Arab Spring events with carefully selected background information.

Houghton, John. *Global Warming: The Complete Briefing*. 5th ed. Cambridge, UK: Cambridge University Press, 2015. One of the most authoritative summaries of all aspects of global warming.

Jacka, Tamara, Andrew Kipnis, and Sally Sargeson. *Contemporary China: Society and Social Change*. Cambridge, UK: Cambridge University Press, 2013. Ambitious sociological–historical study focusing on the many differences within Chinese society and the forces that drive change in contemporary China.

Meade, Teresa A. *A History of Modern Latin America: 1800 to the Present*. 2nd ed. Malden, MA: Wiley-Blackwell, 2016. The book is an excellent, comprehensive analysis and has a strong final chapter on recent Latin America.

Saxonberg, Steven. *The Fall: A Comparative Study of the End of Communism in Czechoslovakia, East Germany, Hungary, and Poland*. Amsterdam, The Netherlands: Harwood Academic, 2001. A well-informed overview of the different trajectories by an academic teaching in Prague.

Swanimathan, Jayshankar M. *Indian Economic Superpower: Fact or Fiction?* Singapore: World Scientific Publishing, 2009. A thoughtful evaluation of the pros and cons of economic growth in India, in concise overviews.

WEBSITES

BBC. Nelson Mandela's Life and Times, http://www.bbc.co.uk/news/world-africa-12305154. The BBC News looks back at the life and career of Nelson Mandela.

Environmental Protection Agency. Climate Change, http://www.epa.gov/climatechange/. The US Environmental Protection Agency's website on climate change reviews the threat to the world's climate and the implications of consistent abuse. The site also looks at various initiatives to help reverse some of the damage already done.

Sierra Club, http://sierraclub.org/. Balanced and informative environmental websites.

Credits

Chapter 15: Granger Historical Picture Archive/Alamy Stock Photo, p. 337; Album/Art Resource, NY, p. 341; DEA/M. Seemuller/Getty Images, p. 342; Bpk/Ibero-Amerikannisches Institut Stiftung Pressischer Kulturbesitz, Berlin, Germany, p. 345; © Gianni Dagli Orti/The Art Archive at Art Resource, NY, p. 347; Joerg Steber/Shutterstock.com; (b) © RICKEY ROGERS/Reuters Inca Roads, p. 349; © Ellisphotos/Alamy Stock Photo, p. 351; Bettmann/Getty Images, p. 352.

Chapter 16: Courtesy of the Library of Congress, p. 358; (a) © DeA Picture Library/Art Resource, NY; (b) ART Collection/Alamy Stock Photo; (c) © John Warburton-Lee Photography/Alamy Stock Photo, p. 364; (a) AP Photo/Thomas Haentzschel; (b) North Wind Picture Archives/Alamy Stock Photo Patterns of Shipbuilding. From top: (d) Baltic cog, and (e) Iberian caravel. These ships illustrate the varieties of shipbuilding traditions that developed over thousands of years, p.365; © The Granger Collection, NEW York, p. 366; Cameraphoto Arte, Venice/Art Resource, NY, p. 371; Topkapi Palace Museum, Istanbul, Turkey/ The Bridgeman Art Library, p. 372; Bridgeman-Giraudon/Art Resource, NY, p. 373; Kerry Whitworth/Alamy Stock Photo, p. 375; Erich Lessing/Art Resource, NY, p. 377.

Chapter 17: Courtesy of the Library of Congress, p. 380; (a) Alinari/Art Resource, NY; (b) Reunion des Musees Nationaux/Art Resource, NY; (c) Image copyright © The Metropolitan Museum of Art. Image source: Art Resource, NY, p. 384; Courtesy of the Library of Congress, p. 385; akg-images/Guericke/Magdeburg Hemispheres, p. 388; Wikimedia Commons, p. 391; Sueddeutsche Seitung Photo/Alamy Stock Photo, p. 399; akg-images, p. 401.

Chapter 18: Courtesy of the Library of Congress, p. 406; Archives Charmet/Bridgeman Images, p. 408; (a) bpk, Berlin/Ethnologisches Museum /Dietrich Graf/Art Resource, NY; (b) INTERFOTO/Alamy Stock Photo, p. 411; Scala/White Images/Art Resource, NY, p. 412; DEA/G. DAGLI ORTI / Getty Images, p. 416; Courtesy of The Hispanic Society of America, New York, p. 422; LINE ART, p. 423; Granger Historical Picture Archive/Alamy Stock Photo, p. 426; © The Stapleton Collection/Bridgeman Images, p. 427.

Chapter 19: (a) akg-images/De Agostini Picture Library/G. Dagli Orti; (b) Werner Forman/Art Resource, NY, p. 438; Werner Forman/Art Resource, NY, p. 439; Image copyright © The Metropolitan Museum of Art. Image source: Art Resource, NY, p. 440; Art Resource/Art Resource, NY, p. 445; © Robert Holmes/CORBIS/VCG/Getty Images, p. 450; Collection of Herbert M. and Shelley Cole. Photo by Don Cole, p. 451; Abby Aldrich Rockefeller Fold Art Museum, The colonial Williamsburg Foundation, Williamsburg, Va, 451.

Chapter 20: © travelib prime/Alamy Stock Photo, p. 456; V&A Images/The Art Archive at Art Resource, NY, p. 460; ©

British Library Board/Robana/Art Resource, NY, p. 461; © The Metropolitan Museum of Art/Art Resource, NY, p. 462; Joana Kruse/Alamy Stock Photo, p. 462; Akbar and the Jesuits, The Book of Akbar (In 03.263), © The Trustees of the Chester Beatty Library, Dublin, p. 464; Digital Image ©2009 Museum Associates/LACMA . Licensed by Art Resource, NY, p. 469; Erich Lessing/Art Resource, NY, p. 473.

Chapter 21: John C. Weber Collection. Photo: John Bigelow Taylor, p. 476; The Metropolitan Museum of Art, p. 480; The Metropolitan Museum of Art/Art Resource, NY, p. 481; Bettmann/Getty Images, p. 484; Roy Miles Fine Paintings/Bridgeman Images, p. 485; © The Granger Collection, NEW York, p. 490; akg-images, p. 494; V&A Images, London/Art Resource, NY, p. 496.

Chapter 22: HIP/Art Resource, NY, p. 502; (a) (top left) © Bettmann/Getty Images; (b) (bottom left) Classic Images/Alamy Stock Photo; (c) (right) Niday Picture Library/Alamy Stock Photo, p. 507; Print Collector/Getty Images, p. 508; © RMN-Grand Palais/Art Resource, NY, p. 509; Wellcome Images/Science Source, p. 513; Culture Club/Getty Images, p. 517; Artokoloro Quint Lox Limited/Alamy Stock Photo, p. 521; Hulton-Deutsch Collection/Getty Images, p. 524.

Chapter 23: Courtesy of the Library of Congress, p. 528; Library of Congress Reproduction Number: LC-USZ62-99485, p. 531; Gianni Dagli Orti/Topkapi Museum Istanbul/The Art Archive/Art Resource, NY, p. 534; Schalkwijk/Art Resource, NY. © 2017 Banco de Mexico Diego Rivera Frida Kahlo Museums Trust, Mexico, D.F./Artists Rights Society (ARS), New York, p. 536; Library of Congress/Getty Image, p. 537; Erich Lessing/Art Resource, NY, p. 539; Library of Congress reproduction number LC-USZ62-73425, p. 541; The Granger Collection, New York, p. 542; Courtesy of the Library of Congress, p. 547.

Chapter 24: Collection of Museum of Fine Arts, Boston via Wikipedia Commons, p. 553; The Art Archive at Art Resource, NY, p. 557; Hirarchivium Press/Alamy Stock Photo, p. 553; (a) akg-images/British Library; (b) Peter NEWark Pictures/Bridgeman Images, p. 561; Heritage Images/Getty Images, p. 563; Courtesy of the Library of Congress, p. 570.

Chapter 25: Bettmann/Getty Images, p. 582; Bettmann/Getty Images, p. 583; SEF/Art Resource, NY, p. 584; Michael Kappler/AP Photo, p. 586; Print Collector/Getty Images, p. 590; North Wind Picture Archives/Alamy Stock Photo, p. 591; RussiaSputnik/Bettman Images, p. 495.

Chapter 26: SSPL/Science Museum/ Art Resource, NY, p. 598; Science & Society Picture Library/Getty Images, p. 605; Robert Hunt Library/Chronicle/Alamy Stock Photo, p. 607; The Print Collector/Alamy Stock Photo, p. 611; The

Subject Index

Page numbers followed by *f* denote a figure, page numbers followed by *m* denote a map, and page numbers in italics denote a picture.